BELGIUM
1994

1994 Fielding Titles

Fielding's Australia 1994

Fielding's Belgium 1994

Fielding's Bermuda/Bahamas 1994

Fielding's Brazil 1994

Fielding's Britain 1994

Fielding's Budget Europe 1994

Fielding's Caribbean 1994

Fielding's Europe 1994

Fielding's Far East 1994

Fielding's France 1994

Fielding's The Great Sights of Europe 1994

Fielding's Hawaii 1994

Fielding's Holland 1994

Fielding's Italy 1994

Fielding's Mexico 1994

Fielding's New Zealand 1994

Fielding's Scandinavia 1994

Fielding's Spain & Portugal 1994

Fielding's Switzerland & the Alpine Region 1994

Fielding's Worldwide Cruises 1994

Fielding's Shopping Guide to Europe 1994

BELGIUM 1994

The Most In-depth and Entertaining Guide to the Charms and Pleasures of Belgium

H. Constance Hill

Fielding Worldwide, Inc.

308 South Catalina Avenue

Redondo Beach, California 90277 U.S.A.

Fielding's Belgium 1994

Published by Fielding Worldwide, Inc.

Text Copyright ©1993 H. Constance Hill

Icons & Illustrations Copyright ©1993 FWI

Photo Copyrights ©1993 to Individual Photographers

FIELDING WORLDWIDE INC.

PUBLISHER AND CEO	Robert Young Pelton
DIRECTOR OF PUBLISHING	Paul T. Snapp
CO-DIR. OF ELECTRONIC PUBLISHING	Tony E. Hulette
CO-DIR. OF ELECTRONIC PUBLISHING	Larry E. Hart
PRODUCTION SUPERVISOR	Michael Rowley
PRODUCTION MANAGEMENT	Beverly Riess
EDITORIAL MANAGER	Wink Dulles
OFFICE MANAGER	Christy Donaldson
CUSTOMER SERVICE MANAGER	Theresa Martin

EDITORS

Linda Charlton	Kathy Knoles
Tina Gentile	Evelyn Lager
Loretta Rooney Hess	Jane M. Martin
Dixie Hulette	Peggy Plendl
Ann Imberman	Jeanne-Marie Swann
Forrest Kerr	Gladis R. Zaimah

PRODUCTION

Norm Imberman	Harold Pierson
Bryan Kring	Kip Riggins
Lyne Lawrence	Munir Shaikh
Chris Medeiros	Chris Snyder
Lillian Tse	

COVER DESIGNED BY	Pelton & Associates, Inc.
COVER PHOTOGRAPHERS — Front Cover	Photo Library Int'l/Westlight
Background Photo, Front Cover	Robert Young Pelton/Westlight
Back Cover	Koji Yamashita/Panoramic Stock Images
INSIDE PHOTOS	Belgian Tourist Office
	Luxembourg Tourist Office
	Netherlands Board of Tourism
	Robert Young Pelton/Westlight
AUTHOR'S PHOTO	Jean O'Neil

Inquiries should be addressed to: Fielding Worldwide, Inc., 308 South Catalina Ave., Redondo Beach, California 90277 U.S.A., Telephone (310) 372-4474, Facsimile (310) 376-8064, 8:30 a.m. - 5:30 p.m. Pacific Standard Time.

ISBN 1-56952-020-8

Printed in the United States of America

Letter from the Publisher

In 1946, Temple Fielding began the first of what would be a remarkable new series of well-written, highly personalized guide books for independent travelers. Temple's opinionated, witty, and oft-imitated books have now guided travelers for almost a half-century. More important to some was Fielding's humorous and direct method of steering travelers away from the dull and the insipid. Today, Fielding Travel Guides are still written by experienced travelers for experienced travelers. Our authors carry on Fielding's reputation for creating travel experiences that deliver insight with a sense of discovery and style.

Like a delicate pastry at the end of a satiating meal, Belgium is often not fully appreciated on many European itineraries. Connie Hill has created the most in-depth guidebook on Belgium, ensuring that experienced travelers never run out of memorable experiences in this small country. Whether your interests are culinary, historic, or just plain touristic, trust Connie to lead you to the finest, the most rewarding and the most intriguing corners of alluring Belgium.

In 1994, the concept of independent travel has never been bigger. Our policy of *brutal honesty* and a highly personal point of view has never changed; it just seems the travel world has caught up with us.

Enjoy your Belgium adventure with Connie Hill and Fielding.

Robert Young Pelton
Publisher and CEO
Fielding Worldwide, Inc.

DEDICATION

For J.H. Daingerfield Perry

So it is in traveling: A man must carry knowledge with him if he would bring home knowledge.

... Samuel Johnson

ACKNOWLEDGMENTS

Words can only begin to convey my appreciation to the many people who counseled and encouraged me during the creation of this book. Those who have helped with arrangements for the substantial personal research involved include Frederique Raeymaekers and Marlene Bervoets at the Belgian Tourist Office in New York; and in Brussels, Elizabeth Puttaert of Tourist Information Brussels (T.I.B.); Jan Wittouck and Cecile Pierard of the Flemish Tourist Office (VCGT); and Annette Beautrix of the Office de Promotion du Tourisme de la Communauté Française de Belgique (OPT). Many provincial and local tourism officials and guides throughout Belgium—and in Holland and Luxembourg—also contributed considerably to my research for this volume, and I thank them for both their aid and interest.

In addition, I am indebted to Helen Goss Thomas for her inspiring example. And to Jean O'Neil for her photograph of the author.

ABOUT THE AUTHOR

H. Constance Hill

H. Constance Hill is a freelance writer whose work has taken her to six continents, of which *the* Continent is a favorite. She has lived in Holland and England and brings experiences from twenty-five years of travel to and through Belgium and Europe to this book. Her articles appear in a variety of newspapers and periodicals in the United States and Canada. When not in Belgium or on another travel beat, she lives in Boston.

Fielding Rating Icons

The Fielding Rating Icons are highly personal and awarded to help the besieged traveler choose from among the dizzying array of activities, attractions, hotels, restaurants and sights. The awarding of an icon denotes unusual or exceptional qualities in the relevant category. We encourage you to create your own icons in the margin to help you find those special places that make each trip unforgettable.

Fielding Selection	Author Selection	Money Saver	Expensive	Quality	Warning
Homey	Luxurious	Rustic	Simple	Scenic	Business
Great Scenery	Picturesque	Beaches & Resorts	Spectacular Cuisine	Romantic	Relaxing
Museum/ Art Gallery	Artistically Important	Architecturally Interesting	History	Book Reference	Musically Interesting
Shopping	Festivals	Nightlife	Wine Tasting	Crafts	etc.
Cycling	Hiking	Golf	Tennis	Strolling	Horseback Riding
Cross-country Skiing	Downhill Skiing	Deep-sea Fishing	Fresh-water Fishing	Snorkeling & Diving	Sailing
Arrival & Departure	By Bus/Local Transportation	By Air	By Road	By Water	By R'

TABLE OF CONTENTS

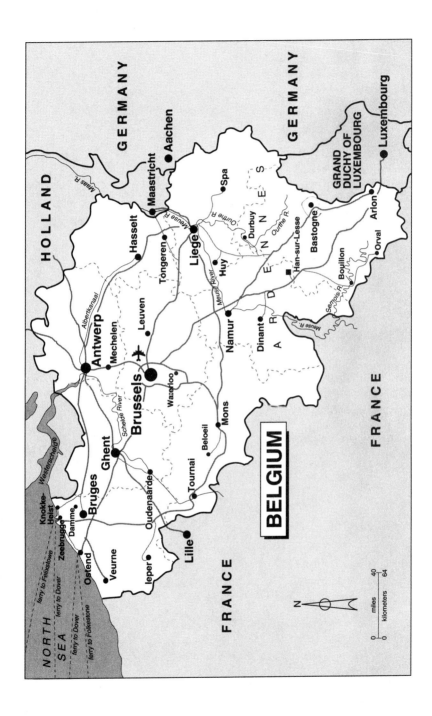

INTRODUCTION

Cafés at Brussel's Galleries Saint Hubert.

One of the Continent's smallest countries, Belgium is, nevertheless, a significant European constitutional kingdom. With a flat barrierless landscape and continental crossroads location that virtually invited vying European empire builders—Spain, France, Austria, and Germany—Belgium, for better and worse, has been at the heart of European history for centuries.

Moreover, its capital, Brussels, is now the *de facto* capital of Europe by virtue of being headquarters of the European Community (EC). But Belgium remains shortchanged in most travel guides. As a result, travelers, inadequately informed, continue to short-shrift sights worthy of a much more lingering look. Hopefully, the information presented here will help correct such shortsighted sightseeing.

Due to outstanding economic development in early Flemish towns, Belgium boasts a remarkable array of art and architectural treasures and other attractions in a compact area. And, as developers of Europe's first railway line (1835), Belgians connected them all by train for the convenience of travelers.

Belgium's pint-size proportions offer the advantage of short travel distances. However, too many travelers use Belgium's small size as a rationale to "do" its destinations on day trips, leaving them little time to appreciate the unexpectedly rich rewards that await. Belgium's trains are terrific, so it's entirely possible to base yourself in Brussels and head out by day to Bruges, Antwerp, and Ghent. However, Belgium's capital is the most expensive overnight place to park yourself, not to mention a car. And, apart from price, if you don't spend a night in a destination that truly warrants being experienced at night as much as by day, you may miss out on what might have been a milestone on your trip. I find much to hold my attention in Brussels and, as much as any other traveler, am glad not to move luggage and change hotels too often. But this book will suggest that you do just that occasionally in order to experience the best of Belgium.

In general, the focus of this guide is on the cultural aspects and attractions that make Belgium delightfully distinctive within Europe. The purpose of the *star rating of sights* is to help you assess travel options, and plan and prioritize a trip according to *your* preferred style, tastes, and interests. For those who are "vacation poor," getting travel *time's worth* is at least as important as getting *money's worth* —and I hope this book will help you do that.

Foremost attention is focused on those Belgian destinations and attractions that have delighted travelers over the decades, since places—like works of literature or music—become "classics" for a reason. Facts are rounded out with flavorful details that put the place or attraction in context. Both first-time and repeat travelers to Belgium should find coverage enough to enrich their exploration. Driving routes in attractive, interesting areas off the tourist track are included in "On The Road" chapters.

This single volume travel companion provides both background essays ("The Belgian Cultural Legacy" under "Art," "Architecture," "Decorative Arts and Traditional Crafts," "Music," and "The Muse") for armchair reading, and comprehensive on-the-road resources for when you're traveling. (See "Transportation" in "Keys to the Belgian Kingdom: Practical Travel Information" for information on getting around Belgium.) Food for thought can lead to the thought of food, which is big business in Belgium. (See "Food and Drink," including "Belgian Beer," and under "Where to Eat" in individual cities.) For ideas as to where to hang your hat, consult "Where to Stay" (star-rated, in several price ranges, under the appropriate city or town). The "Hotel Quick Reference Chart" at the back of the book provides current prices. "Shopping" suggestions are noted under individual destinations, but you might also want to consult "Decorative Arts and Traditional Crafts" for ideas.

During the decade of Europe's passage from the 20th century into the 21st under the initiatives of the European Community's (EC) *Single Europe Act*, Belgium and Brussels increasingly will attract our attention. It's appropriate that Brussels is capital of the EC, since Belgium was a founding member of the forerunner of that organization. In 1948, the BENELUX—an acronym for BElgium, NEtherlands, and LUXembourg—was formed by that small trio of troubled post-Second World War economies to simplify and stimulate trade amongst themselves. Success in its mandate—"bringing about total economic integration by ensuring free circulation of persons, goods, capital, and services, and by following a coordinated policy in the economic, financial, and social fields, and by pursuing a common policy with regard to foreign trade"—inspired the 1967 six-nation *European Economic Community (or Common Market)*, whose members now number 12.

Although the EC, "Euro-culture" and multinationals seem to thrive in Belgium, the country's distinctive features and unique qualities have not disappeared. When you visit Belgium, you'll find charming characteristics of its culture wherever you seek them.

STAR-RATED SIGHTS

For readers who find such guidance helpful, the attractions included herein have been star rated. Travelers, most of whom have limited time, and all of whom face choices as to how to spend the time they do have, may welcome the indication of relative importance consistently applied that this assigning of stars strives to provide, though, naturally, you will organize sightseeing according to your interests. In assigning stars—which has been based on the broad considerations outlined below—I have taken into account such factors as the general consensus about a sight's significance, which would include the fact that a work or collection of art is regularly mentioned in textbooks or catalogs; longstanding popularity with tourists; and my insight into the comparative interest of the attraction in relation to other competing ones in the area. Often, viewpoints and sense-of-place sites, interiors and exteriors, day and night appearances, and events also have been rated. Inevitably, the ratings in this guide cannot help but reflect my interests and tastes. However your opinions and mine may differ, I hope the ratings in this guide enable you to have a more enjoyable trip.

★★★ This indicates a *must-see* sight. It should be a clear-cut First Choice for those on a short visit, one worth planning an itinerary specifically to include.

★★ This indicates a significant sight, one that substantially contributes to a visitor's impression of the destination or sense of place.

★ A sight worth consideration as interest and time dictate.

No stars: Of sufficient interest to warrant mention.

PRICES

The value of the Belgian franc varies against other currencies. And there's inflation to contend with, too. Prices for accommodations are raised periodically: Belgian hotels tend to review/raise prices every January first. Thus, even if you are using this book hot off the press, prices listed in the "Hotel Quick-Reference Table" at the back, and price categories used, may already have changed. As a result, you are cautioned to use the prices quoted as a comparative guide rather than hard fact.

When you wisely select *prix fixe, tourist menu,* or *dagschotel* (day menu) meal choice options, you may lower the price category for a listed restaurant since it is based on *à la carte* courses. The elimination of a course—servings usually are substantial in Belgium—also can make a meal at a given restaurant less expensive than indicated.

HOTEL PRICE CATEGORIES

Prices are based on a room for two, including private bathroom, VAT, and service. Belgian-style continental breakfast is included at most moderate and lower-price hotels, rarely for expensive ones.

Very Expensive	**BF 8000 and up.**
Expensive	**5000–8000.**
Moderate	**3000–5000.**
Inexpensive	**3000 or less.**

RESTAURANT PRICE CATEGORIES

The following price categories are based on a three-course dinner for one, without drinks, but *inclusive* of VAT tax and service.

Very Expensive -------------------------------- **BF 3000 or more.**

Expensive -- **2000–3000.**

Moderate -- **1000–2000.**

Inexpensive -------------------------------------- **1000 or less.**

HOTEL RATINGS

I have used a star (★) system rating to assist you in selecting hotels. The hotel selection in this guide is not meant to be comprehensive, particularly in major cities; rather, it includes properties in a range of prices chosen subjectively for various tangible and intangible factors. Among these are atmosphere, visual appeal and views, furnishings, size of bedrooms and bathrooms, friendliness of the staff, and—as for real estate decisions anywhere—location. An emphasis has been placed on properties which are central or close to districts with sights of interest, convenient to public transportation, and, when available, in scenic settings.

Deluxe Hotel

A hotel with excellent standards of service and cuisine, and outstanding quality in amenities and atmosphere. The property will have special features, location, or view that raises it above the four-star rating, 24-hour room service, a specialty à la carte restaurant as well as a less formal eatery, and often some in-house recreational facilities.

First Class Hotel

One with superior standards of comfort, cuisine, service, and setting. All rooms with private bath and shower, and all accessible by elevator. A wide range of amenities, including restaurant and room service.

Recommended Hotel

A comfortable hotel, with many amenities, including a breakfast room, bar, and sometimes a restaurant with limited choice menu. Most rooms have private toilet, plus shower and/or bathtub; those without private facilities will have an in-room basin. Some rooms may be accessible by elevator.

Reasonable Hotel

A hotel with simple standards but considered above the minimum by virtue of some feature. Lobby or other public room used for breakfast service. Some rooms have private facilities. No elevator.

Budget Hotel   ★

A hotel that meets minimal acceptable standards for plain but decent accommodation. Private facilities unlikely. Breakfast may be available only in one's room due to the lack of a lobby lounge/breakfast room.

UPDATES

Considerable care has been taken to ensure that the information included in this volume is correct, but change is a constant in the world, even the small corner of it covered here. While the facts presented are the most up-to-date possible at press time, changes could occur by the time of your visit. When travel arrangement particulars are important, it's wise to confirm them in order to save yourself inconvenience and expense. Although I cannot be responsible for inaccuracies that result from changes in the travel environment, I will make every effort to keep informed of such developments. Your comments and suggestions for or about the guide are welcome. Write to me c/o Fielding Worldwide, Inc., 308 South Catalina Avenue, Redondo Beach CA 90277.

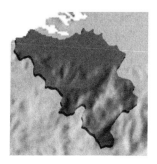

KEYS TO THE BELGIAN KINGDOM

Bruges' medieval beauty

PRACTICAL TRAVEL INFORMATION

Belgium is well organized for travelers, with information offices located throughout the country. The great degree to which English is spoken (and written, in brochures and other travel documentation) will be reassuring. Nevertheless, even though you can rely on almost always finding someone to answer your questions in English, there may be times when you welcome having the information included in this chapter at your fingertips.

PLANNING YOUR TRIP
PLANNING AIDS

Belgian tourist offices both overseas and locally can provide a great selection of free travel literature in English. Contact the nearest office for information before you go.

In the United States:

Belgian Tourist Office, 780 Third Avenue, Suite 1501, New York, NY 10017, ☎ *(212) 758-8130, FAX (212) 355-7675.*

In Canada:

Belgian Tourist Office, P.O. Box 760, Succursale N.D.G., Montreal, Quebec, 44A 352, ☎ *(514) 845-7500.*

In the United Kingdom:

Belgian Tourist Office, Premier House, 2 Gayton Rd., Harrow, Middlesex, HA1 2XU, ☎ *(081) 861-3300, FAX (081) 427-6760.*

LOCAL TOURIST OFFICES

Due to federalism, Belgium now has parallel and autonomous government departments for all functions, including tourism, for both language communities: in Flanders it's the **Vlaams Commissariaat-Generaal for Toerisme**, or VCGT, and in Wallonia the **Office for the Promotion du Tourisme de la Communauté Française**, or OPT. Each publishes its own tourism literature (although, when interests overlap and for national "theme" brochures, castles for instance, information is published jointly); all is available in Brussels off the Grand-Place at *rue Marché aux Herbes 61* (☎ *513.30.30*). Brussels, being distinct from either of the above departments, has its own tourist office, with offices in the magnificent **Hôtel de Ville** on the Grand-Place. The **Tourist Information Brussels** (*T.I.B.*; ☎ *513. 89.40*) handles all materials and matters related to Brussels. At both, you'll be well served with English-language literature, at least for major cities and attractions. Elsewhere in Belgium, local tourist offices, indicated with an "i" for information and usually centrally located in towns or cities at or near the *rail station* or *Grote Markt/Grand-Place* (main square), will provide materials on their area and possibly the greater region, so long as it is part of the same cultural community.

Local tourist offices usually are the best sources for city and regional walking, biking, and driving route maps. Open times for most tourist offices follow local office hours at a minimum, but many are open longer (until 8 p.m. or later weekdays) and on Saturday and Sunday in summer and during other periods of heavy travel, such as

Easter weekend. Local tourist offices are the best source of information and may book accommodations in private homes.

DOCUMENTS

A passport is required to enter Belgium, but visitors from the U.S., Canada, members of the EC, and most of the British Commonwealth countries, do not need a visa for stays up to three months. No immunization certificates are required to enter Belgium, and no certificate of vaccination is required by U.S. or Canadian authorities from returning residents.

U.S. Passports: Major post offices throughout the country now are able to process passport applications; if your local office doesn't have the forms, it can direct you to the nearest one that does. Federal office buildings also have passport offices. For your initial passport, or if your previous one was issued more than 12 years ago, you need to apply in person (not required for children under 13), with a completed application, proof of U.S. citizenship (a certified copy of birth certificate or naturalization papers), a photo ID, and 2 recent identical passport photos (full-face, 2" x 2," plain background), and $65 (exact currency, check made out to Passport Services, or money order). If you have a passport not more than 12 years old, you can mail or take it, together with an application and $40 payment, to the nearest passport office. Passports are good for ten years. In an emergency it's possible to get a passport in short order (you can indicate your departure date on the application), but one normally should allow at least six weeks and try to avoid the spring rush for summer travel. Your passport is returned by mail. If an applicant is under 18, there are some exceptions to the above; check with the Washington Passport Agency, Dept. of State, *1425 K St., Washington, D.C. 20522;* ☎ *(202) 326-6060.*

Canadian Passports: Take a completed passport application form, obtainable from a passport office, travel agency, or post office, to one of the regional passport offices, or mail it (*Passport Office, Dept. of External Affairs, Ottawa, Ont. K1A 0G3*) with proof of Canadian citizenship, two identical passport photos signed by you and co-signed by a professional who has known you at least two years, and $28 Canadian. Application in winter is suggested. The document is valid for five years.

United Kingdom Passports: Passport forms are available at most travel agencies and local post offices. Apply in person at a local passport office, with a certification of birth, two recent identical photos signed and countersigned, 15 pounds sterling, and, if appropriate, a copy of your marriage certificate. Passports are valid for ten years, except for those under 16, and take about a month for processing.

HEALTH TIPS

The standard of health care in Belgium is excellent. Rest assured that if anything untoward should occur during your travels there, you'll be well looked after. Most health care professionals in Belgium have a mastery of English.

Water: You can safely drink the water virtually everywhere in Belgium. On the rare occasion when this is not the case—such as from a sink in the toilet on a train or one in a rural restaurant—there will be international signage and the words *nonpotable* (nondrinkable) clearly posted. Bottled water or other liquids are usually available on a train, from a refreshment car or cart. At restaurants, one normally is expected to buy bottled mineral water, but if you've ordered something else to drink and want water too, ask the waiter for a glass of ordinary tap water. It is unlikely to come with ice. Bottled water is available at all grocery stores and many snack stands. It comes in *gaz* or *sin gaz* (carbonated or noncarbonated) varieties.

Insurance: Travelers covered by medical insurance are entitled to medical treatment, so it behooves you to check your policy about coverage abroad and the special procedures to follow for reimbursement. Carry your insurance I.D. with you while traveling, and keep all medical receipts for your insurance company back home. It's an excellent idea to carry photocopies of your insurance policy so that you can hand one over immediately if you require treatment, thereby possibly preventing the need for direct payment. Your hotel staff should have the names of English-speaking doctors to recommend, and can inform you as to which of the pharmacies/chemists (that open, in rotation, to cover nights and weekends) is on duty.

In Belgium, ☎ *100*, in the case of an accident for which emergency medical help is needed.

SENIOR CITIZENS

Senior citizens who have flexibility of schedule by virtue of being retired are in a position to take advantage of last-minute travel bargain tours and reduced overseas airfares with restrictions they can live with. Some organizations specifically for senior citizens offer discount travel options. The one with the largest membership, and therefore potentially the most negotiating clout, is the **American Association of Retired Persons** (*AARP, 1909 K St. N.W., Washington, D.C. 20049; toll-free in U.S.* ☎ *(800) 227-7737*). It is open to all people 50 years and older willing to pay a small membership fee. The **National Council for Senior Citizens** (*925 15th St. N.W., Washington, D.C. 20005*) makes available travel and discount information. Among tour operators that specialize in travel for senior citizens are **Elderhostel** (*75 Federal St., Boston, MA 02110, ☎ (617) 426-8056*), with interesting cultural and educational tours among its offerings, and **Saga International**, (*222 Berkeley St., Boston, MA 02116, ☎ (617) 262-2262*), which offers a selection of value-conscious tours worldwide for travelers 60 and over.

STUDENTS

The *Student Travel Catalog* available from the **Council for International Education Exchange** (*CIEE, 205 E. 42nd St., New York, NY 10017*) is a basic source for discount and tour travel information and services for people under 26, students, and teachers. If you qualify for one, make sure to get an **International Student Identity Card**, available from CIEE, before you head for Belgium. It opens the door to many discounted rates and fares.

TRAVEL FOR THE DISABLED

Disabled travelers will find certain accommodations to accessibility at tourist attractions, hotels, restaurants, and public transportation in Belgium. For more travel specifics, a book by Louise Weiss, *Access to the World: A Travel Guide for the Handicapped* (published by Facts on File, ☎ *(212) 683-2244*), contains useful advice and hotel listings. **Mobility International** (*Box 3551, Eugene, OR 97403*) and **Whole Person Tours** (*Box 1084, Bayonne, NJ 07002*) both publish newsletters and magazines for members, and organize trips. The **Information Center for Individuals with Disabilities** (*20 Providence St., Boston, MA, ☎ (617) 727-5540*) will, for a small fee, provide a list of specialized travel agencies, tour operators, and publications. And the **Travel Information Center** (*Moss Rehabilitation Hospital, Tabor & 12th, Philadelphia, PA 19141*), will also send, for a small fee, travel information for up to three cities.

WHEN TO TRAVEL

As a sacred celebration of spring, Easter is a four-day holiday weekend in Belgium, and throughout Europe, that results in mass travel movements. Reserve well ahead if your travels are going to span this weekend. Many tourist attractions use Easter as the occasion to open for the tourist season, though some shut again after Easter until early June.

As in much of northern Europe, summer and an eternal hope for sun and warmth keep many Belgian citizens at home to enjoy it. The daylight hours in summer are dramatically longer than many readers—other than those from Great Britain and Ireland—will be used to, due to the northern latitude. Hotels at coastal resorts along the North Sea in Belgium, especially those with a beach view, can be expected to be fully booked if the summer weather is inviting. Camping, caravaning, and rented bungalows or apartments all are common ways for Europeans to have affordable family vacations in the coastal and resort areas of Belgium. Travelers interested in such forms of accommodation should book well ahead, as they would for summer holidays at popular destinations at home. Most North Americans, however, will be seeking hotel rooms in cities and towns. Because business travel is slower in summer, city hotels may offer bargain prices then.

In September, there's competition for beds at the best hotels in Brussels and other business centers due to start-up sessions of the European Community, the post-summer renewal of corporate travel, and a new autumn season of trade and professional congresses (conventions). The busiest business months are September, October May, and June. Away from cities, September can be a lovely and less busy time for travel. In the Belgian Ardennes, lingering midday warmth and misty early mornings in valley villages are a backdrop for all-inclusive gastronomic weekends specializing in game dishes during the fall hunting season.

The word for winter in Belgium is dark. Daylight lasts only from approximately 8 a.m. until 4 p.m. in December and January. But Belgium can be at its coziest in winter, with candlelit restaurants and pubs, gala events on the cultural calendar, and a festive celebration of the holiday season.

SEASONS, CELEBRATIONS, AND CEREMONIES

SPRING

Carnival is celebrated in Belgium in such a big way not only for its fancy dress fun and kicking up of heels before the beginning of Lent, but also to throw off the winter blahs. In **Aalst** on Shrove Sunday (three days before Ash Wednesday), there's a traditional cortege. **Binche** has Belgium's biggest Carnival binge on Shrove Tuesday (Mardi Gras) with the famous **Gilles** in full costume. Other pre-Lenten carnivals take place in **Eupen**, in the Germanic eastern part of the country, and in **Malmedy**, in the Ardennes, where there's a particularly spirited affair that starts on the Saturday before the start of Lent, with the town remaining *en fête* for four days. Unusual compared to other countries are Belgium's colorful processions and fêtes that take place *during* Lent on Sundays (considered feast days). Many attractions and activities in Belgium open on the long **Easter** weekend for the tourist season (until September or October).

The annual **Procession of the Holy Blood** in Bruges on *Ascension Day* (a national holiday) comes replete with costumes and a ceremony that recounts the return from the *Second Crusade* with a relic of the Holy Blood. The month-long **Queen Elizabeth Music Competition** (in violin, piano, or voice) comes each May to Brussels. And the May opening of the fresh **asparagus** ("white gold") **season** gives everyone in Belgium gastronomic cause to celebrate. **Blessing of the Sea** at Blankenberge is Belgium's best-known fishing fleet ceremony.

SUMMER

Belgium's northern latitude brings late-light nights (until 10:30 or 11 p.m. at midsummer) for lingering sightseeing, followed by night-seeing, viewing the marvelously **illuminated building facades**, bridges, towers, and other monuments. Architectural details are tastefully highlighted with spotlights, producing scenic (and romantic) settings. During the June **Shrimp Pageant**, fishermen in **Oostduinkerke**, on the southern Belgian coast, pull their nets from the sea on horseback, in an event that now exists virtually only for tourists. June brings the seasonal start-up of Monday night **carillon concerts** in Mechelen and Antwerp. Music of many kinds fills the stages set for Belgium's **Festival of Flanders** and **Festival of Wallonia**, which last through September. The **Ommegang**, an impressive medieval-costumed procession recalling the era of the Dukes of Burgundy, takes place on Brussels' *Grand-Place* the first Thursday evening each July. Other nights in summer the Grand-Place is the magnificent setting for free music and light shows, best enjoyed with a Belgian beer at one of the square's many outdoor cafes. The **Flower Carpet** on the Grand-Place (every even year in August) is a wondrous work.

FALL

In September the time returns for taking **mussels** from their seabeds (during months ending with an "r"), and mouths begin to water. Weekend **Wieze Beer Festivals** stand as testaments to Belgium's nearly 600 brewed beers, a tradition that produces some unique tastes.

WINTER

Winter in Belgium brings a cultural glut of goodies: opera, ballet, symphony, and dance from fine residential and guest performing arts companies. Christmas season specialties include **Christmas markets** in Brussels and Eupen.

NATIONAL HOLIDAYS

New Year's Day; Easter Monday; Labor Day (May 1); Ascension Day (in May); Whit Monday; National Day (July 21); Assumption Day (in August); All Saints' Day (Nov. 1); Armistice Day (Nov. 11); Christmas Day.

WEATHER

The weather in Belgium, especially in Flanders—with its proximity to the North Sea—can be remarkably changeable. Throughout the country, conditions vary considerably, depending primarily on geography. At times, (more commonly in winter), dreary-drizzily-windy days can linger on, but sustained rain for lengthy periods is not the rule. Despite the high northern latitude of Belgium—on a par with Newfoundland in Canada—the sea keeps coastal Belgium temperate—not unlike the U.K.—with the extremes of cold and hot much less than in many areas of North America. The forested Ardennes in southeast Belgium, with its greater altitude and less influence from the sea, has a greater extreme between daily high and low temperatures. Countrywide, average temperatures in summer vary between 54° to 72° Fahrenheit (12°–23°C.), and from 32° to 43° (0°–6°C.) in winter.

Average daily high and low temperatures by month for Brussels are given below in Fahrenheit, but, locally, temperatures are given exclusively in Centigrade (Celsius). The standard conversion formulas are: to turn Centigrade into Fahrenheit, multiply by 9, divide by 5, and add 32; to convert Fahrenheit to Centigrade, subtract 32, multiply by 5, and divide by 9. (People who travel a lot always figure a way to make the conversion easier. One easy way to figure this in your head is to double the Centigrade reading, subtract 10% and add 32. Example: The local temperature is 23°C. 23 X 2=46. 46-5 [and rounded up 10%] =41. 41+32=73°F. To convert the other direction, subtract 32 from the Fahrenheit reading, add 10% and halve the net. This, in fact, is the same in mathematical terms as the standard conversion method, but it is easier to accomplish. Another method is listed in the next paragraph.)

The chart that follows has done the conversion for you. However, if you don't have it handy and want to quickly compute the outside temperature to dress for, this decidedly unscientific method will provide you with an answer within a degree or so. First, remember that 16 (C) is equal to its inverted number 61 (F); the same holds true for 28 (C) = 82 (F). Using those as baselines, one Celsius degree is roughly equivalent to two Fahrenheit for temperatures in between.

Average high and low temperatures by month in Brussels (in Fahrenheit)

WEATHER IN BRUSSELS Latitude N50° 50' —Altitude 190'											
Jan.	Feb.	Mar.	Apr.	May	June	July	Aug.	Sept.	Oct.	Nov.	Dec.
Lows											
30°	33°	35°	40°	46°	52°	55°	55°	52°	44°	38°	33°
Highs											
39°	43°	49°	57°	64°	70°	73°	72°	67°	56°	48°	42°
Days With No Rain											
16	13	16	14	15	13	15	15	14	14	12	15

CONVERSION CHART: CELSIUS(CENTIGRADE)°C/FAHRENHEIT°F					
°C	°F	°C	°F	°C	°F
34	93.2	19	66.2	4	39.2
33	91.4	18	64.4	3	37.4
32	89.6	17	62.6	2	35.6
31	87.8	16	60.8	1	33.8
30	86.0	15	59.0	0	32.0
29	84.2	14	57.2	-1	30.2
28	82.4	13	55.4	-2	28.4
27	80.6	12	53.6	-3	26.6
26	78.8	11	51.8	-4	24.8
25	77.0	10	50.0	-5	23.0
24	75.2	9	48.2	-6	21.2
23	73.4	8	46.4	-7	19.4
22	71.6	7	44.6	-8	17.6
21	69.8	6	42.8	-9	15.8
20	68.0	5	41.0	-10	14.0

TIME

Belgium is in the Central European time zone, which puts it six hours ahead of North America's Eastern Standard Time (nine hours ahead of the West Coast) and one hour ahead of Great Britain and

Ireland time. Clocks are put ahead one hour on the last Sunday in March, and back an hour on the last Sunday in September. (These dates may differ somewhat from "summer time" changes in the United Kingdom and Ireland). Generally, plane, train, and ferry schedules reflect these time changes, but if you are traveling near the date of a time change, it's worth double checking departure times.

The 24-hour clock: Since the 24-hour clock often is used to indicate times on transportation schedules and opening hours for museums and restaurants, it's a good idea to understand the concept. The hours after 12:00 noon continue in numerical order from 1300 through 2400 hours. To translate a time past noon from or to the 24-hour clock, simply add or subtract 12 from the time shown. For example, for a rendezvous at 2000 hours, *subtract* 12 from 20 and you arrive at a correct arrival time of 8 p.m. If you wish to take a train at 3 p.m., *add* 12 to 3 and then look on the schedule for a 1500 hours departure.

WHAT TO BRING

In addition to prescription medicines, extra prescription eyeglasses, and copies of actual prescriptions, you know best what personal items are essential to your well-being, at home or away: a small pair of scissors, a sewing kit, double-sided Scotch tape to secure a hem you don't have time to sew, and several sizes of safety pins. A light-weight corkscrew is handy if you plan on picnics, either outdoors or in your hotel room. Clip clothespins with hanger-shaped tops that fit on a shower curtain rod or other hooks come in handy for hand laundry, for which you should bring a small plastic bottle filled with liquid detergent. A pocket calculator can be useful if you don't like converting the prices of things in your head.

If sound and light are liable to affect your sleep, it's wise to make earplugs and an eyeshade regular travel companions. With earplugs, you can get your beauty sleep while avoiding the wrenching necessity of having to turn down a front hotel room with a fabulous view because of concern about evening and early morning noise from a nearby tram or on-the-hour and half-hour carillon bells. If you wake with dawn's early light, be aware that it comes as early as 4 a.m. in summer in far-to-the-north Belgium; best pack an eye mask, however unglamorous it may seem. Once you've worked out how to get a good night's sleep, to make sure you wake up, bring a small travel alarm clock, a reassuring backup even if you're staying at hotels with wake-up service.

Then there's the trusty collapsible umbrella. In much of Belgium, especially Flanders, it should be part of your basic wardrobe when you head out each morning, even if there's not a cloud in the sky. Bring one small enough to fit in your purse or carry-all, two if there are two of you traveling. Once you've thus insulated yourself from the threat of a little rain, you can take pleasure if you should see dark clouds doing a furious dance in the high skies above flat Flanders, a sight that often compelled Flemish landscapists to paint.

If you're a shop-till-you-drop sort, pack especially lightly and include in your suitcase an *empty* durable nylon, hand-luggage-size foldable bag for your acquisitions. Should you forget an item, or run into weather that runs contrary to what you've prepared for, never mind: Belgium has well-stocked, sophisticated stores where you will find what you need and may even discover a better-designed version of the item you left at home.

CLOTHES

Experienced wanderers will follow the layered, color-coordinated separates, wrinkle-resistant, wash-and-wear wardrobe ideas that enable one to travel lightly while being prepared for a variety of social situations. In Belgian cities, business dress is best for fine restaurants (and top ones in the countryside) and major cultural events, although you'll see everything from student casual to evening wear. In the touristic summer season, dress, even in cities, is somewhat less formal at night, and can be very casual during the day. A raincoat, or rain and windproof jacket, is a suggested outer covering any time of year.

Don't skimp on packing sturdy shoes. You may even consider bringing more than one pair of walking shoes; a second could come in handy if the weather turns wet or when those charming cobblestone streets exact their toll on your soles. You'll be able to buy shoes in Belgium, but that's hardly the best use of your travel time, and it can be perilous breaking in a new pair during heavy-duty touring. Bring practical evening shoes (low, wide heels and, perhaps, insole cushions); the cobblestones in historic city centers don't disappear with the daylight.

PACKING AND LUGGAGE

When considering what to pack, it's useful to mentally "walk through" your trip, keeping in mind planned activities and possible temperature variations. Anticipating the likely range of weather conditions is vital. In addition to keeping a running list of things you want to take, a good way to remember items that sometimes get overlooked during last-minute packing is to put out an empty suitcase a week or so before departure and, when an item occurs to you, put it in the case *then and there*.

It's not possible to overemphasize the importance of packing lightly. The flexibility afforded when you free yourself from excess baggage is a major physical and mental lift. My personal packing goal is not to lug around a single item I don't use—except an umbrella. If you're using one city as a base but spending some nights in other places, or will be returning to a city for your flight home, you might consider leaving a bag of items you won't need for the next segment of your trip either as checked luggage at the hotel you're leaving—for which there usually is no fee, just a tip to the porter—or leaving unnecessary luggage at a conveniently located (in terms of later travel) train station or airport locker or baggage office. When packing for your trip, try always to keep in mind that there probably will be occasions when you must be able to manage all of your luggage by yourself.

TRAVELING IN BELGIUM
MONEY

Belgian francs (abbreviated BF) come in 1-, 5-, 20-, and 50-franc pieces, and a 50-centime piece (100 centimes = 1 franc). Bank notes exist for 100, 500, 1000, and 5000 francs. At press time, the U.S.$ was equal to approximately BF 35.14.

Exchanging Money: Currency exchange rates change daily, so check the financial pages of a newspaper for the most current before you leave. The newspaper figures will be slightly higher than those posted at the exchange (or bureau de change) desk at banks in Belgium. Travelers' checks usually have a slightly more advantageous exchange rate than currency. No doubt you know the adage: exchange money *only* at banks. Like much advice that's been around for years, it's basically sound. However, bank service charges now often are high enough (several dollars) to warrant thinking about *how often* you undertake exchange transactions, as well as *where*. Unless you get free travelers' checks, as you can from the Automobile Association of America (AAA) if you are a member, you'll be paying coming and going with travelers' checks. But you might as well accept the fact, since, in terms of their replaceability when lost or stolen—*if* you can supply the check numbers—they're worth the fees. No matter how many larger traveler's checks you buy, always take plenty in the useful $20 denomination. You will need your passport to exchange travelers' checks into Belgian franks at banks.

Credit cards are widely accepted in Belgium, although by no means does every hotel, restaurant, and shop do so. Inquire specifically if/which cards are accepted when making reservations at hotels and restaurants. As at home, fewer places take *American Express* than take *Visa* (probably the most widely accepted credit card internationally) and *MasterCard*. When you use a credit card abroad, you are charged the exchange rate in effect the day the sale is processed (*not* the day of purchase). Obviously, a lag in transaction processing (which by no means always happens) can work either to the buyer's or the supplier's advantage, depending upon whether your currency is strengthening against the guilder or franc, or falling, but it's worth remembering that variations in exchange rates from one day to the next rarely amount to a significant percentage. In my experience, foreign charges have been processed fairly, and using a credit card while traveling abroad certainly can be a considerable convenience. With a major credit card, you can get a cash advance at certain banks in Belgium. Check with your card-issuing institution at home for specific details and locations. Just in case, you always should travel with the appropriate local telephone numbers and instructions for reporting lost or stolen credit cards.

LANGUAGE

English is widely spoken in Belgium—especially so in Brussels and Flanders—so you'll find it easy to travel there. And *that's* the overriding fact to keep in focus when the subject of language in Belgium begins to *sound* complicated.

Brussels, capital of the European Communtiy and headquarters of multiple multinational corporations, is officially bilingual in **Flemish** (**Dutch**) and **French**. In this Common Market country, English has long been a common-ground language. In rural areas and among older citizens (and more so in the southern Belgian region of Wallonia), perhaps not everyone will speak English, but there surely will be someone handy who does.

Flemish, a Germanic-rooted tongue, in written form almost identical to Dutch, is the language of the northern part of Belgium known as Flanders. A *language frontier* (see map in "The Belgian People") divides Belgium roughly in half, north and south, along Romance and Teutonic linguistic and cultural lines that have existed, essentially unchanged, since the 5th century (when Romans left the region, and Frankish tribes took over). The southern half of Belgium, Wallonia, is French-speaking. Belgium also has a small German-speaking region in the east, along its shared border with Germany.

The bilingual/bicultural issue has shaped Belgium. As a visitor, however, you needn't make more of it than your natural curiosity leads you to. English is widely spoken in all Belgian tourism areas. Brussels is officially bilingual; all street signs and public facilities must be designated in both French and Dutch. The city's large multinational community (members of the European Community and NATO missions, diplomats, and the staff of international corporations) often meets, linguistically speaking, in English.

Travelers may observe that language can be a sensitive subject *between Belgians*. For visitors to this foreign destination, it almost can be an advantage *not* to know the local languages. The use of English will not offend members of either community, whereas an attempt at French in Flanders or to a Flemish-speaking person in Brussels, or in Dutch to a Walloon, could. You can't rely on a surname to tell whether a Belgian is Flemish or French. The use of English establishes straight away that you are *not* Belgian, a vastly preferable situation to being mistaken for a member of one community who refuses to use the language of the other.

ALTERNATIVE PLACE NAMES

An aspect of travel in Belgium is that the names of places located in one language community often are translated into the other community's version. This means that you may see roadsigns directing you to such heretofore unknown corners of the country as **Doornik** (which is the Flemish version of the Walloon city of **Tournai**) or **Malines** (French for the Flemish city of **Mechelen**). The country Belgium is written either **Belgie** or **La Belgique**, and the officially bilingual city of Brussels (the only place with a real right to two names) is **Bruxelles/Brussel**. Selected place names are listed below alphabetically under the region Flanders (North) or Wallonia (South) in which they actually are located, with the other language-group name (and a third, English version, if such exists) in the second column.

FLEMISH BELGIUM			
Flemish/Dutch	**French/English**	**Flemish/Dutch**	**French/English**
Aalst	Alost	Leuven	Louvain
Antwerpen	Anvers/Antwerp	Lier	Lierre
Brugge	Bruges	Maas	Meuse
De Haan	Le Coq	Mechelen	Malines
De Panne	La Panne	Oostende	Ostende/Ostend
Gent	Gand/Ghent	Oudenaarde	Audenarde

FLEMISH BELGIUM			
Flemish/Dutch	French/English	Flemish/Dutch	French/English
Halle	Hal	Schelde River	Escaut/Scheldt
Ieper	Ypres/Wipers	Tongeren	Tongres
Ijzer	Yser	Veurne	Furnes
Kempen	Campine	Vlaanderen	La Flandre/Flanders
Kortrijk	Courtrai	Zeebrugge	Zeebruges
Leie	Lys		

WALLOON BELGIUM			
French	Flemish/Dutch	French	Flemish/Dutch
Ath	Aat	Mons	Bergen
Bruxelles	Brussel/Brussels	Namur	Namen
Hainaut	Henegouwen	Nivelles	Nijvel
Huy	Hoei	Soignies	Zinnik
Liège	Luik	Tournai	Doornik
Meuse River	Maas	Wallonie	Walloon/Wallonia

Just to prepare you, Belgians also feel free to change the names of places near to, but beyond their borders, at least on their internal signage. See below.

German/English	French	Flemish/Dutch
Aachen	Aix-le-Chapelle	Aken
Trier	Trèves	
Koln	Cologne	Keulen
	Paris	Parijs
The Hague	La Haye	Den Haag
	Bois le Duc	's Hertogenbosch
	Nimegue	Nijmegen
	Lille	Rijsel
Dunkirk	Dunkerque	Duinkerken
Flushing		Vlissingen

WHERE TO STAY

Cleanliness *is* next to godliness in Belgium, in every category of hotel and accommodations. Most hotels in Belgium have far fewer rooms than North American travelers might expect. Since hotels are smaller, atmospheric, well located, reasonably priced properties are liable to be fully booked especially in tourist seasons (see "When to

Travel"); reserve as far ahead as possible, although it's always worth inquiring at the last minute, in case of a cancellation or "no-show." VAT (value-added tax) and service are always included in room rates. Breakfast—some variation on the "continental buffet": breads/rolls, jam, sliced cheese, cold cuts, hard-boiled eggs, fruit, yogurt, cold cereal, and coffee or tea; for an extra charge, you often can order cooked eggs—is usually included in the price at hotels in the three-star and lower category, occasionally at the four-star category. As elsewhere in Europe these days, the more expensive the hotel, the less likely you are to have breakfast included in the price.

HOTEL AND CULTURAL PERFORMANCE RESERVATIONS

Belgium Tourist Reservations (BTR) provides a free booking service for hotels of all categories throughout the country. You can telephone (*from the U.S.* ☎ *011.32.2.230.50.29, from U.K.* ☎ *010.32.2.230.50.29*) or write (*Post Office Box 41, 1000 Brussels 23*) giving your accommodations requirements: dates; town or location; whether you'll be travelling by public transportation or car; amenity and price category preferred; number of people in your party; and number of rooms (twin beds or double/*grand lit*), with or without bath. BTR responds to your requests promptly, usually telephoning you to give you the details, and following up with a mailed written confirmation. The system runs on good faith; no deposit is required, although your major credit card number will be taken if the hotel accepts such. To contact BTR from within Belgium, the telephone number in Brussels is ☎ *230.50.29*. The reservation system is widely used by Europeans and the British, though it is less well known in North America: in 1990, BTR processed 90,000 reservations in Brussels alone.

BALCONOP (an acronym for BAllet, CONcert, and OPera) will make reservations for performances at Brussel's **Monnaie Theater**, the **Société Philharmonique de Bruxelles** and the **Opera Royal de Wallonie**, among other companies. The address of BALCONOP (a division of the Service Artistique of OPT) is rue Marché-aux-Herbes, 61, 1000 Brussels, upstairs from the Belgium tourist information office on the ground floor (☎ *518.14.94, FAX 513.69.50*).

WHERE TO EAT

Travelers should be aware that if you use the word *restaurant* when inquiring about where to eat in Belgium, you may be directed to a more formal, and therefore more expensive, dining establishment than you had in mind, since in the local dining lexicon that's what the word "restaurant" implies. There's a whole range of lower to mid-range-price dining places—designated as *bistro, cafe, restau-rant-cafe, brasserie, petit-restaurant, tearoom, eet cafe, traiteur, snackbar, koffieshop, broodjeswinkel* (sandwich shop), *or pan-nekoekhuisje* (pancake house)—that might fill the bill and suit your tastes, much better.

It may also be useful to know that the term *menu* most often refers to a dining establishment's preselected daily special (a single dish or three-course meal). It's similar to a *prix fixe, table d'hôte, dagschotel,* or *tourist menu.* If you really do want to see the menu (the whole se-lection of food available), ask for the *kaart* (Dutch) or *carte* (French).

NOTE ... In the countryside in Belgium, owners may bring their dogs into restaurants (where they generally sit quietly under the table). This is rarely done in towns or cities, and is nowhere near as common a practice as it is in France.

LIQUOR LICENSING LAWS

Although loosening, Belgium's liquor license laws still limit the sale of alcoholic beverages to wine and beer in a number of establish-ments. Places that do restrict the sale of high alcohol-content spirits usually also offer diverse aperitifs such as vermouth, sherry, and *kir* (white wine with *cassis*).

CITY SIGHT-SEEING TOURS

Introduced within the last few years as an alternative to large motorcoach tours of Belgian cities are the minivans of the **Sightsee-ing Line** company. Beginning several times daily at central sites in Brussels, Bruges, Antwerp, and Ghent, the minivans, which hold about a dozen passengers, are much better suited to the not-made-for-motor-vehicles streets in these old cities. The vans enable the tour to encompass some medieval sections of the cities that would be impossible for larger coaches to traverse. The commentary for the driving route is taped in each of nine languages (tourists select the correct channel on their headsets), which means that everyone gets the full story told at each attraction passed. Also, if you run into an inner-city traffic jam, the tape can be stopped and relaxing classical music substituted until the tour (which, without delays, may run from 60 to 90 minutes) recommences. For details, ask for Sightsee-ing Line brochures at local tourist offices.

NIGHT-SEEING OR ILLUMINATIONS

Some of the most memorable moments during your travels in Bel-gium will be seeing public buildings, churches, castles, and monuments illuminated after dark. After dark can be after 10 p.m. in summer in this northern latitude, but the night sights are well worth staying up for. You'll not soon forget Brussels' Grand-Place glamorously aglow, and Antwerp's Cathedral, Ghent's Castle of the Counts, or Bruges' Belfry artfully floodlit. The summer season, sometimes extended from Easter through September, is when the most monuments are spotlighted, but an increasing number are highlighted year round.

PERSONAL SECURITY

There is considerably less personal violent crime in Belgium than in the United States, but petty pickpockets and car burglars seem part of the worldwide scene these days. Cities have a greater problem with such random occurrences. Use bags or purses that close tightly, and carry them close to your body. Keep them in your lap (and/or with straps looped through the arms of chairs at outdoor cafes) in public or congested places, and on public transportation.

A good rule of thumb is: if you won't be needing an item, don't take it out on the street with you. Leave passports (you'll need yours only when checking into a hotel, or cashing traveler's checks), extra cash, traveler's checks, airline tickets, rail passes, credit cards, and other valuables in a hotel safe deposit box (available at the front desk if there isn't a safe in your room). There's little inconvenience involved in using one, compared to your increased peace of mind. If two of you are traveling together, make it a habit to split your cash, checks, and credit cards between you, thereby minimizing the risk of losing everything in a single incident, whether through forgetfulness or theft. An individual traveling alone should put money and valuables in several places or pockets, never carrying everything in any single purse, wallet, or carry-all.

It's smart to keep important information and photocopies of documents where you can put your hands on them with certainty (perhaps in the bottom of your suitcase in a hotel room, better in a safe). The packet should include photocopies of passports (the page spread with your picture is sufficient), instructions of what to do in case of lost credit cards, health insurance procedures, and an accurate list of the numbers of unused traveler's checks. Taking such measures *ahead of time* can save a lot of self-recrimination in the unlikely event that something happens later.

EMERGENCIES

If you need to report a theft or other loss in Belgium, go to the nearest police station to file a report, a copy of which will be given to you. If you plan to make a claim back home, your insurance company will want to see a copy of this report as proof of loss. Dial ☎ *100* in Belgium in case of an accident for which **medical help** is needed.

EMBASSIES/CONSULATES

U.S. Embassy, Blvd. du Regent 27, 1000 Brussels, ☎ *513.38.30*

U.S. Consulate, Nationalestraat 5, 2000 Antwerp, ☎ *232.18.00*

Canadian Embassy, Ave. de Tervuren 2, 1040 Brussels, ☎ *735.60.40*

U.K. Embassy, Rue Joseph II 28, 1040 Brussels, ☎ *217.90.00*

U.K. Consulate, Lange Klarenstraat 24, 2000 Antwerp, ☎ *232.69.40*

POSTAL/TELEPHONE/TELEGRAM/FAX

Post Offices: In Belgium, postal hours are Mon.–Fri. 9 a.m.–12 noon and 2-4 p.m., except for offices located near railway stations in larger towns, which may remain open continuously from 9 a.m.–5 p.m.

PTT: In Belgium, there are government PTT (*post, telefon*, and *telegraaf*) centers where you can make the lowest cost long-distance and foreign calls. An operator dials the call, and puts it through to you in an assigned booth; when the call is completed, you pay the exact charges. (There's no extra service fee such as hotels add, which can make overseas calls exorbitant.) For direct overseas calls from Belgium, dial ☎ *11.00.10* for an AT&T USA Direct operator.

Pay Telephones: Instructions for using coin-operated telephones are given in several languages, including English. You can make international calls from telephone boxes that display signs with international flags. Calls from Belgian pay telephones take 5 and 20-franc coins. Rates for calls on all telephones change during the day, and are highest until 1 p.m. on business days, lowest in the evening.

ELECTRIC CURRENT

Voltage in Belgium generally is 220 AC, 50 cycles, but in some places it is 110. If you are bringing small electrical appliances, you'll need a transformer and a variety of adapter plugs in order to ensure a match to varying socket shapes. Personally, I'm for *not* taking electrical gadgets on travels, primarily because of luggage weight. If you're planning to stay in First Class properties, you'll often find a hair dryer in the bathroom, frequently a pants-press, perhaps a self-service shoe shine machine in the hall. At many hotels, you can borrow an iron and board or hair dryer by contacting the front desk.

SMOKING

Nonsmoking North Americans may be unprepared for the *lack* of designated nonsmoking areas in Europe. And cigar smoking still is a tradition in Holland. For years, trains have had nonsmoking cars (in second as well as first class), but progress toward nonsmoking sections in restaurants and nonsmoking rooms in hotels (your best bet is at international chain properties) is slow. Statistics do show that more citizens in Belgium have stopped smoking than in some other European countries.

PUBLIC TOILETS

The initials W.C. (for water closet) are the most international indication for public facilities, though the term *toilets* is most common. (Don't ask for the "bathroom" unless you want to take a bath; even in hotel rooms with private facilities, the bathtub and/or shower often is separate from the toilet.) Americans will find public toilets far more available than at home, and almost always clean. Facilities may be free, though it's a good idea to keep a couple of 5-franc pieces handy for coin-operated toilets. Often there are attendants who make change and keep the place clean. Toilets in Flemish Belgium are marked *heren* for men, *dames* for women, and *madames* (woman) and *messieurs* (men) in the rest of the country. International signs, with figures in skirts and in pants, are often used.

TIPPING, VAT

Throughout Belgium, VAT (value-added tax) and service are added to hotel and restaurant bills. Tips are included in metered taxi fares, which are expensive, and there are extra charges for baggage, Sundays, and night trips.

Refund of VAT on Qualifying Purchases: A resident of a non-EC country who buys an item in a Belgian store with a value over the equivalent of $154 is entitled to a refund of the VAT (19%). Inquire within Belgium at the time of purchase about the procedure for VAT refunds.

NEWS AND NEWSPAPERS

Even certified news junkies will be able to keep up on international events in Belgium. In addition to the *International Herald Tribune* (with its American sports scores and standings for the addicted), European-printed editions of *The Wall Street Journal* and *USA Today*, and British dailies such as the *Financial Times, Daily Telegraph*, and *The Times* all are available at major hotels and many news shops in Brussels and other commercial centers. Cable TV channels now available in many hotels will, in the western regions of Belgium nearer to England, pull in the news on the BBC stations from London. CNN International is available at an increasing number of better hotels. Weekly news magazines in English (*The Economist, Time, Newsweek,* Murdoch's *The European*) and plentiful paperbacks are available at airports, major hotels, and in many book stores.

BUSINESS/SHOPPING HOURS

Basic store and business hours are 9 a.m.–6 p.m. Mon.–Sat. Small shops, bakeries, and news/tobacco stands can open as early as 7:30 or 8 a.m. Hours are posted on shop doors. Only outside of cities in Belgium will stores close at noon for an hour or two—in which case they'll remain open until 7 or 8 p.m. In season at holidays resorts on the coast or in the Ardennes, family shops and stores may stay open as late as 9 or 10 p.m. Sundays in Belgium, bakeries, grocery stores, and flower shops are open 8 a.m.–noon; patisseries are open for your pleasure all day. Many Belgian shops are small family-run businesses that keep long hours; to prevent unfair competition, the overnment requires a compulsory closing day—shopowner's choice—once a week. Late night shopping until 8 or 9 p.m. one weeknight (which varies from town to town) is usual throughout Belgium.

METRIC WEIGHTS AND MEASURES

Most of the world, including Belgium, runs by the metric system (though not the U.S., which still steadfastly resists its adoption). Whether you need to decipher the temperature in Celsius (see this section under "Planning Your Trip: Weather") in order to dress for the day, can't wait to buy 250 grams of handmade Belgian chocolate pralines or a 1.5 meter length of Belgian lace, want to know how high that handsome town hall tower (given in meters in the town's tourist pamphlet) really is, need to fill up the tank of your rental car with liters of petrol, or must know how many kilometers it is to your next destination (see under "Transportation: Car"), you have the means below by which to make sense of metrics—with, perhaps, a little help from a hand calculator.

Metric		English
1 ounce	=	28.25 grams
100 grams	=	3.52 ounces
1 U.S. pound	=	0.45 kilogram (kilo)
500 grams	=	a half kilo (or 1.1 U.S. pounds)

Metric		English
1000 grams	=	1 kilo (or 2.2 U.S. pounds)
1 acre	=	0.40 hectare
1 hectare	=	2.47 acres
1 U.S. pint	=	0.47 liter
1 U.S. quart	=	0.94 liter
1 liter	=	2.12 U.S. pints
1 U.S. gallon	=	3.78 liters
1 Imperial gallon	=	4.54 liters
1 centimeter	=	0.39 inch
1 inch	=	2.54 centimeters
1 foot	=	30.4 centimeters
1 yard	=	0.91 meters

CONVERSION CHART: FEET/METERS

Meters	Feet		Meters	Feet	
0.30	1	3.28	13.72	45	147.64
0.61	2	6.56	15.24	50	164.04
0.91	3	9.84	18.29	60	196.85
1.22	4	13.12	21.34	70	229.66
1.52	5	16.40	24.38	80	262.47
1.83	6	19.69	27.43	90	295.28
2.13	7	22.97	30.48	100	328.08
2.44	8	26.25	60.96	200	656.17
2.74	9	29.53	91.44	300	984.25
3.05	10	32.81	121.92	400	1312.34
4.57	15	49.21	152.40	500	1640.42
6.10	20	65.62	182.88	600	1968.51
7.62	25	82.02	213.36	700	2296.59
9.14	30	98.43	243.84	800	2624.67
10.67	35	114.83	274.32	900	2952.76
12.19	40	131.23	304.80	1000	3280.84

If you want to convert from feet to meters, read from the center column to the left (1 foot = 30 meters). When converting meters to feet, read from the center column to the right (1 meter = 3.28 feet).

FILM

Airport X-ray machines will become ever more evident in today's screened-for-security travel world. Professional photographers know that, at any setting, X-ray machines can cloud your processed and unprocessed film—low ASA is less sensitive—from its first time through the machine. Effects are cumulative, as with each transfer and connecting flight your carry-on belongings are required to make additional passages through X-ray. I *politely* ask a member of the security staff (they are *not* employees of any airline) to hand inspect my rolls of film and camera if it has film in it; however, he or she is under no obligation and, with security demands tightened, may not have the time nor temperament to do so. If your request for hand inspection is refused, there is virtually nothing you can do about it, hence the wisdom of using a lead-shield pack for both exposed and unexposed rolls of film (although I have heard it said that the X-ray operator then just pushes the setting higher to see through the shield). Film is more expensive in Belgium than at home, but if you run out there it is readily available at many museum and other shops.

CUSTOMS

U.S. residents are exempt from duty on the first $400 of combined purchases made abroad, as long as they have not made other such claims within 30 days and as long as the items are for personal use, not resale. Family members may pool their exemption by filling out a single customs form. Those over 21 may include one liter of alcohol in their exemption. Purchases of documented (keep the papers to show customs officials) antiques (over 100 years old) and original art works are duty exempt. You may send packages to friends that are clearly marked *Unsolicited Gift of Value Less than $50*, (only one package per address) without paying duty on them. If you're following this procedure to avoid duty—packages sent to your home are not allowed as part of your $400 exemption, and separate duty must be paid on them—consider paying the flat 10% of value charged for the first $1000 in purchases over your exemption for the security of carrying your items rather than risking damage or loss in the mail.

Certain items are restricted by U.S. law from entry into the U.S. These include articles made with any part of an endangered species (The World Wildlife Fund's brochure *Buyer Beware* is available from ☎ *(800) 634-4444* if you're considering designer leathers, furs, etc.). Cuban cigars are not permitted, but the fine Dutch ones are. Food products often cause confusion as to what's allowable into the U.S. Cheeses and vacuum-wrapped smoked fish and other items usually are acceptable, especially coming from such a "clean" agricultural country as Belgium. Sealed, boxed, dry items, such as crackers, cookies, and cakes are fine. Fruit, vegetables, and other plants are never allowed, and most meat is not.

If you take any significant foreign-made articles, such as expensive watches, cameras, binoculars, or designer clothing with you on the trip, it's a good idea to bring the receipts (or other evidence that the items were brought from home) with you for clearing U.S. Customs on return. If you are traveling with prescription drugs, you would be wise to have the prescription with you to avoid possible delays in Customs.

Canadian citizens who remain out of the country for at least seven days may receive an exemption on duty for personal goods up to the value of $300 (Canadian), but only once a year. Allowances of $100 can be claimed once a calendar quarter after being outside the country 48 hours. Families may not pool their exemptions. The first $300 in excess of the exemption is taxed at a flat 20%. Unsolicited gift packages (so marked) with a value of $40 or less can be sent to friends duty free, but you might as well carry all purchases for yourself with you, as they are subject to duty.

TRANSPORTATION

Brussels, with a central situation in Belgium, as well as within Europe, posts the following traveling distances to other cities.

City	Miles	Km
Amsterdam	122	198
Frankfurt	254	409
Koln (Cologne)	125	203
London	201	325
Luxembourg City	127	205
Paris	181	292

AIR

Most North Americans will arrive in Europe by air. The main carrier at Brussels' **Zaventem Airport** is Belgium's **Sabena World Airlines**, which flies nonstop to/from New York, Boston, Chicago, and Montreal in North America. ☎ *(800) 955-2000.* The Sabena route system includes many major cities in Europe and beyond. Although intra-European air service remains an expensive way to travel between European cities, the anticipated increase in competition between European airlines on European routes as a result of the *Single Europe Act* is expected to reduce rates eventually.

RAIL

Belgium—which built the first European rail line, between Brussels and Mechelen, in 1835—today has the most dense rail network in the world. The system is characterized by frequent service, integrated schedules, on-time arrivals, and international connections that provide efficient connections between Brussels and all other major cities on the continent. Trains are clean, comfortable, fast, and affordable, making them a practical and pleasurable way to tour. Tickets are sold for First and Second class; First Class is about 50% more and less crowded, but certainly not essential for comfortable travel. There are smoking and nonsmoking cars in both classes.

Train travel to Belgian cities is highly recommended, especially since, once there, attractions usually are best appreciated on foot. The frequency of trains between Brussels and other towns of reasonable size and importance is two or three times an hour; smaller places usually are served by at least one train an hour from the nearest major town. Here are some sample rail travel times from Brussels to other major towns in Belgium; Mechelen 20 mins.; Antwerp 30 mins.; Ghent 45 mins.; Bruges 55 mins.; Tournai 60 mins.; Liège 65 mins.; and Ostend 75 mins. Belgium has a joint venture with France for a high-speed TGV train that will reduce travel time between Brussels and Paris to 1.5 hrs.

Rail Passes: Several rail passes are available, all representing considerable savings and flexibility, but it's important to analyze your particular travel plans to see if one meets your needs. Belgium is a member of the 23-nation **Eurail Pass** network, but Eurail should be purchased only if you plan to make a long-distance sweep of Europe, since if you "buy" more territory than you need on a rail pass, you cut into your savings. The **Benelux Tourrail Pass** provides unlimited train travel in Holland, Belgium, and Luxembourg for any five days (they needn't be consecutive) in a period of 17 days. A second-class ticket costs BF 3,080; first-class BF 4,620, and both are less for those under 26 years of age (1993 prices).

For travel solely within Belgium, the Tourrail Pass is good for any five days out of 17; prices are BF 1,800 (BF 2700 first-class), with a junior-pass (ages 6–25) for BF 1,350. A Belgian Reduction Card, for sale (550 BF) only within Belgium and good for one month, entitles the holder to purchase at 50% off any Belgian rail tickets priced over 60 BF. Inquire about reduced rate weekend round-trip rail tickets. Brochures and prices are available from the Belgian Tourist Office. For information on all train travel within and beyond Belgium, contact S.N.C.B. (Société Nationale des Chemins de Fer Belges) in Brussels (☎ 219.26.40)

The English Channel Tunnel: From 1994, an engineering wonder, the *English Channel Tunnel* (nicknamed the "Chunnel"), will connect England and France. The beneath-the-channel rail lines will make train travel between London and Brussels considerably shorter and a great "conversation piece."

FERRY

For U.K. citizens and travelers who come to Belgium via England, a number of ferry routes are in service. The quickest (just under five hours) is on the Jetfoil, rail-connected service between London's Victoria Station and Brussels. The same route is served by traditional ferries (nearly nine hours, but minus the Jetfoil supplemental cost). The Belgian ports of Zeebrugge and Ostend offer various crossings of the North Sea and English Channel to and from England's Dover, Hull, and Yarmouth. *Boat trains* to/from London and Brussels, and farther afield, are scheduled to connect with respective ferry terminals in time for crossings.

Ferries are the least expensive, most adventuresome means of crossing the North Sea, but also the most time consuming. North Americans need to assess whether the experience and/or savings are worth it.

BICYCLE

Bikes can be rented at 48 train stations throughout the country as well as many in-town locations. Contact the Belgium Tourist Office for particulars.

BUS

Belgium has a network of national and local buses. There are few places in the country that you cannot reach by bus. If you are traveling solely by public transportation, and want the lowest transportation cost-per-kilometer, you may well find yourself on a bus in Belgium. Local tourist offices will have information and schedules.

CAR

It must be said that Belgian drivers as a group are considered by other citizens on the European continent to be less than adept at driving (and the butt of jokes on that score). More seriously, the driving accident and fatality rates in Belgium are seven times that of the U.S. The situation is undoubtedly contributed to by the fact that until 1967 no demonstration of driving skill was required, since no driving licenses were issued in Belgium. Plans to harmonize driver standards and traffic laws throughout the EC have been greeted with relief by all, but meanwhile the word in Belgium is be wary and understand the rules of the road here as well as you can.

An International Driver's License is *not* necessary. Your current U.S., Canadian, or U.K. operator's license is sufficient. Driving in

Belgium is on the right, the same as in North America and other continental European countries, but not the U.K. Southern Belgium's hillier, curvier roads will slow you down even if the scenery doesn't. The major rental car companies have offices in large cities, but you should book in advance from North America to get the best rates. If you can drive a standard shift (in lieu of an automatic transmission, which is rarer in Europe), you'll save on the cost of the rental car. Rentals of one week or more may qualify for a special rate: try for unlimited mileage, at a minimum. Remember to ask for all charges up front, expecially insurance and VAT (which adds a hefty 19% to your rental bill in Belgium right off the bat). Some companies offer leasing arrangements for a minimum period of three weeks, for which rates are tax-free, and include insurance and unlimited mileage. Gasoline (petrol, benzine) is pricey, at least twice what it is in the U.S., but driving distances are shorter.

When you rent a car, you won't be required to pass any test of Belgium's rules of the road. And while you'll probably do fine by following the example of drivers on the road ahead of you, it's a good idea to know as much as possible about the procedure. Most important is to be aware of the **priorité à droite**: traffic coming from the right *always* has the right of way, even when you're on the main road and a car is entering from an insignificant side street. Generally, Belgium drivers make a point of claiming their priority, so keep the rule very much in mind. Low beams are required when driving between nightfall and dawn, as well as in bad weather. Seat belts must be worn by both driver and front seat passenger. There is usually a minimum speed on motorways of 70 km per hour; maximum speed limit is 120 km (75 mph). Belgium takes a tough stance on drinking and driving.

Road conditions vary considerably throughout the country; the country's motorways are always well maintained, but rural roads, especially in the Ardennes, may not be as well looked after. The **Royal Automobile Club de Belgique** is located in Brussels at rue d'Arlon 53 (☎ *230 08 10*). Belgium's **Touring Secours** (Wegenhulp), which employs distinctive yellow vehicles, is ready, able, and willing to help distressed drivers on principal roads.

Parking: In cities and many towns in Belgium, you will encounter the same problems parking your car as you do at home. Some city hotels offer parking (for a fee), but many can't. This is a major reason to consider planning a trip without a rental car, or getting one only when exploring and staying in the countryside. Public parking lots and garages generally are well indicated by signs showing a "**P**".

Especially in cities, but a good idea everywhere, do not leave valuables in your vehicle, even in a locked trunk or glove compartment. And *never* leave anything in sight inside your car..

CONVERSION CHART: KILOMETERS/MILES

Kilometers		Miles	Kilometers		Miles
1.6	1	0.6	80.4	50	31.0
3.2	2	1.2	88.5	55	34.1
4.8	3	1.8	96.5	60	37.2
6.4	4	2.4	104.6	65	40.3
8.0	5	3.1	112.6	70	43.5
9.6	6	3.7	120.7	75	46.6
11.2	7	4.3	128.7	80	49.7
12.8	8	4.9	136.7	85	52.8
14.4	9	5.5	144.8	90	55.9
16.0	10	6.2	152.8	95	59.0
24.1	15	9.3	160.9	100	62.1
32.1	20	12.4	241.4	150	93.2
40.2	25	15.5	321.8	200	124.2
48.2	30	18.6	482.7	300	186.4
56.3	35	21.7	643.7	400	248.5
64.3	40	24.8	804.6	900	310.6
72.4	45	27.9	1609.3	1000	621.3

If you want to convert from miles to kilometers, read from the center column to the left (1 mile=1.6 kilometers). When converting kilometers to miles, read from the center column to the right (1 kilometer=0.6 mile).

CONVERSION CHART: LITERS/U.S. GALLONS/IMP. GALLONS

Liters	U.S. Gallons	Imp. Gallons	Liters	U.S. Gallons	Imp. Gallons
1	0.26	0.22	25	6.61	5.50
2	0.53	0.44	30	7.93	6.60
3	0.79	0.66	35	9.25	7.70
4	1.06	0.88	40	10.57	8.80
5	1.32	1.10	45	11.89	9.90
10	2.64	2.20	50	13.21	11.00
15	3.96	3.30	60	15.85	13.20

Danger

No entry

**Closed to all
vehicles in both
directions**

**End
Restriction**

**Speed limit
(in kilometers
per hour)**

**End of
speed limit**

**Parking
prohibited or
restricted**

**Standing
and parking
prohibited or
restricted**

**Priority over
oncoming
traffic**

**Oncoming
traffic has
priority**

Yield

**Priority
crossing**

**Traffic on
roundabouts
must give way to
traffic entering
from the right**

Motorway

**Expressway:
main road with dual
carriageway with
two-level
intersections**

**Uneven
Road**

**Compulsory path
for cyclist and
riders of
mopeds**

**Cycle track,
forbidden to
mopeds with motor
switched on**

**Tourist
Information**

**Local Dutch
Tourist
Office**

In the lexicon of international signage, round mean restrictions or prohibitions, square provides information and triangular warnings.

MISCELLANEOUS
THE FLAG(S)

The national flag of Belgium consists of broad vertical bands in black, gold, and red, the historic colors of the Brabant province. Equally (perhaps more) inspiring to Belgians are the honored emblems of the Flemish and Walloon communities. In the north, banners showing the rampant lion symbol from the medieval coat of arms of the Counts of Flanders fly proudly over the land. To the south, the strutting cock, a symbol of courage used steadily in the centuries since Caesarean Gaul, oversees Wallonia.

THE ROYAL FAMILY

Baudouin, fifth king of the Belgians, died unexpectedly on July 31, 1993. He had ascended the throne at the age of 21 in 1951 when his father, Leopold III abdicated. (See "An Historical Perspective" under "Belgium.") Baudouin and his wife, Spanish noblewoman Fabiola Mora y Aragon, to whom he had been married since 1960, were childless.

When it had become clear that the marriage would not produce an heir, Baudouin's three years younger brother **Albert**, who was heir apparent, let it be known that if Baudouin predeceased him, he intended to stand down in favor of his eldest son Philippe, since, expecting that Baudouin would live much longer, Albert himself would be elderly before such a situation arose. Philippe, who was born in 1960, thus was educated as the heir presumed. However, Philippe is still unmarried and has been widely thought to be as yet ill prepared to assume the role of king. Thus, with Baudouin's untimely death, Albert gave in to pressure from Belgian Parliament officials who sought a successor with more experience than youth to guide Belgium through its present economic difficulties and to provide a spirit of continuity for ushering in the country's new federal constitution (which became law in April 1993). A day after Baudouin's death, Belgian Prime Minister Jean-Luc Dehaene made the surprise announcement of succession.

King Albert II was ten years old when the Allies landed in Normandy 50 years ago. At that time, he and the other members of the Belgian royal family were deported from Nazi-occupied Belgium to Germany and then to Austria. Albert later received schooling in Switzerland and returned to Belgium only in 1950, after the *Royal Question* had been decided. In 1959, while representing Belgium at the enthronement of Pope John XXIII in Rome, Albert met his future wife, Italian **Princess Paola** Ruffo di Calabria. Their marriage six months later was highly popular among Belgians. The royal couple has three children: Philippe, b. 1960; Astrid, b. 1962; and Laurent, b. 1963.

One of Albert's major contributions to his country has been 30 years as honorary president of the *Belgian Foreign Trade Agency*, in which capacity he has led more than 100 delegations of Belgian businessmen abroad. Albert, affable and with an unstuffy manner, is a natural diplomat, with a more outgoing personality than his late brother. As Queen, Paola, popular with her people, will now face more pressure about her poor command of Flemish, the language of 57% of her subjects.

The royal family, since it represents the Belgian nation as an entity, is not of surpassing importance to many of the country's Flemings *or* Walloons. Nevertheless, the Belgian monarch, even with his limited constitutional powers, has great symbolic importance in fostering the bond between the Dutch-speaking majority and the French-speaking minority. King Baudouin and Queen Fabiola were scrupulous in their efforts at displaying an even handed attitude toward the two Belgian cultural communities. If King Albert II can be as successful in dealing with the Belgian politicians from the country's two quarrelsome language communities as was his brother, he will be on course toward achieving the near-universal respect which Baudouin had earned by the end of his reign.

The older sister of King Albert II and the late King Baudouin, Josephine-Charlotte, is married to Grand Duke Jean of Luxembourg.

ODDS AND ENDS

For meetings and greetings in Belgium, handshakes are the rule with everyone you meet. There's no separate etiquette for women or men, and it doesn't matter who extends the first hand. A person joining a group already assembled should shake hands with everyone. Handshakes also are repeated all around on departure. If relations with a Belgian acquaintance (man or woman) proceed further, handshakes are replaced with kisses on the cheek. One-time differences in kissing etiquette—one cheek in Holland, both cheeks in France, and three in Belgium—seem to have become standardized into a "European kiss," which takes Belgium's lead (Brussels, after all, is capital of the EC) of three kisses on alternating cheeks.

- If there are no empty tables at a cafe or casual eatery with self seating, it is acceptable to ask those sitting at a table that has room for you if you may sit down. While it's not suggested you infringe on the others at the table, the situation can lead to pleasant exchanges.

- As in most of Europe, the story *above* the ground or lobby level is designated the *first floor* in hotels, offices, and apartment buildings.

- In Europe, calendar dates in events listings, etc., are written *day/month/year:* April 19, 1993, would be indicated 19/04/93. Since mix-ups in days and months could have serious consequences in matters of hotel reservations or appointments, I find it's best to deal with dates by writing out the name of the month, preceded by the numerical day: 19 April 1993.

- *Queuing,* the civilized practice of waiting in line until one's turn that's been refined by the British, is not much observed in Belgium. For buses, trams, and even shops, it can be everyone for one's self. But do look around in banks, bakeries, etc.—which sometimes have them in effect just during busy times—for machines from which to take a numbered ticket that places you in line for service.

THE BELGIAN CULTURAL LEGACY: ART AND ARCHITECTURE, MUSIC AND THE MUSE

Detail from Jan van Eyck's early Flemish masterpiece The Adoration of the Mystical Lamb

ART

Artists from Belgium have contributed substantially to the stores of Western art and architecture and have supplied seminal ideas in many areas of artistic endeavor. In the Netherlands, or Low Countries, of which what today is Belgium was a part, geograpic location—northern europe, in contrast to Italy in the south—and the influence of and reaction to ideas introduced by various occupying foreign regimes, played a hand in Belgium's artistic development.

Architectural monuments, under usual circumstances, are bound to the land on which they take form. Thus, save for fire, warfare, and urban updating, visitors to Belgium in one era and those in the next should be able to see the same visually appealing and artistically significant landmark buildings. Paintings and other smaller fine arts works, on the other hand, are portable, and thus do not remain as dependably on deposit in the countries of their creators.

In Belgium and Holland, numerous foreign occupation forces (as recently as the mid-20th century under the Nazis), greatly affected the native art that remains to be seen there. For example, Dutch painter **Hieronymus Bosch** was a favorite with the Spanish Hapsburg ruler King Philip II of the Netherlands—which then included Flanders, as well as what today is Holland. Philip had much of the mystical artist's work brought to him in Spain, where today it can be seen in Madrid's **Prado Museum**. When the Austrian Hapsburgs oversaw the Netherlands, a large number of early Flemish paintings and a particularly impressive collection by **Pieter Bruegel the Elder** found their way to Vienna, eventually winding up on the walls of that city's **Kunsthistorisches Museum**.

Although many of Belgium's and Holland's artists have long been recognized as masters of such merit that their works hang in galleries around the world, museums in these countries remain rich in major and representative pieces by their own most renowned artists. Some of the most significant and prolific painters, among them **Rubens** and **Rembrandt**, are extremely well represented on their home soil, so much so that certain of the countries' museums are virtual places of pilgrimage for their art.

FLEMISH FOUNDATIONS

The distinctive subjects and styles that we particularly associate with Dutch art from the 15th through the 17th centuries and more recently, first took form in the late 14th century, in the miniature paintings created to adorn the prayer books and diaries of members of the privileged classes. Those small scenes of the seasons and of daily life, early genre works if you will, revealed the realism, however naive, that was to become such a differentiating element in the art created in northern Europe from that of Italy. The outstanding example is the *Très Riches Heures de Duc du Berry*, painted between

1410–1416 by **Pol de Limbourg** (from the region that is today's Belgian and Dutch Limburg provinces) and his two brothers.

The **Master of Flemalle**, today widely thought to be **Robert Campin** (1378/9–1444), the foremost painter of Tournai (Belgium), was the creator of *The Merode Altarpiece* (1425–1428). The center panel of that triptych portrays an annunciation scene and is one of the earliest instances in which viewers can see into a spatial world where everyday reality is represented. The Master of Flemalle did not use an aristocratic or court environment, but a Flemish burgher's house as the setting for the annunciation, an approach that was a significant departure from the Italian Renaissance aim of representing an ideal world. While some medieval religious symbolism survived in Flemish painting, the desire to depict the world of everyday articles and life framed a whole new sense of **realism**. Gradually, the reverential artistic treatment once reserved solely for religious subjects was applied to all aspects of daily life. Ordinary items thus became "sanctified," and Flemish artists were freed from being restricted to religious subjects in order to portray the physical world.

The work of Robert Campin (Master of Flemalle) also marks a divergence between Late Gothic northern European art and Italy's concurrent Early Renaissance in its use of *oil* in the paint. Previously, medieval panel painters had employed *tempera*, in which finely ground pigments were "tempered," or mixed, with diluted egg yolk. With the substitution of oil for the water-and-egg-yolk mixture, thicker layers of paints were possible. This material enhanced artists' ability to render depth, rich velvety hues and a variety of textures from thin to thick—all of which greatly increased the possibilities for portraying reality. Campin and his contemporaries are called the "fathers of modern painting" not only for their fresh visions of reality, but also for their innovative painting medium.

LATE GOTHIC/NORTHERN RENAISSANCE PERIOD

Jan van Eyck (c.1390–1441), long credited with "inventing" oil painting, did indeed add substantial new dimensions to the effects that medium could achieve. He worked in Holland and elsewhere before settling in Bruges in Flanders. Among the signed and dated pieces by Jan van Eyck is the famous Ghent altarpiece, *The Adoration of the Mystical Lamb* (1432), which had been started by Jan's brother Hubert. The recently restored altarpiece, widely considered the greatest monument of early Flemish painting, has been repositioned in Ghent's St. Bavo church, to aid the viewing of all 20 panels on both sides of the work. A fundamental aim pursued by Jan van Eyck in his painting was "atmospheric perspective," which actually is more important to a realistic perception of deep space than linear perspective, upon which the Italians placed such high priority.

A third great master of early Flemish painting was, like Campin, from Tournai: **Rogier van der Weyden** (1399–1464), sometimes referred to by the French version of his name *Rogier de la Pasture*. Whereas Jan van Eyck explored the reality made visible by light, shadow, and color, van der Weyden concerned himself more with human feeling. In his portraits, he "interprets" personality, rather than leaving faces psychologically "neutral." By the time of his death, van der Weyden had had 30 unbroken years of artistic activity in Brussels (where he was the official town painter), and was considered the most influential European painter north of the Alps.

The technically superb works of **Hans Memling** (1435–1494) —many of which are in historic St. Jan's Hospital in Bruges, his adopted home—produced a generation later, are more idealized than van der Weyden's. Those of **Hugo van der Goes** (1445–1482), who also painted primarily in Bruges, evoke a more emotionally intense response from the viewer.

In the 16th century, the Netherlands (or Low Countries) experienced the most turbulent events of any European country north of the Alps. When the **Reformation** began, the Netherlands was a part of the far-flung empire of the Hapsburgs under Charles V, who was also king of Spain and had been born in the Netherlands' city of Ghent. Protestantism quickly became powerful in the northern Netherlands (today's Holland), and attempts by the Roman Catholic rulers to suppress it led to open revolt. After a bloody struggle, Holland emerged independent and widely Protestant, and the southern Netherlands (roughly corresponding to modern-day Belgium) remained in Catholic-Spanish hands. Amazingly, the political and religious strife of the Reformation, which was particularly intense in the northern and southern Netherlands from 1550 to 1600, did not have a devastating effect on art in Flanders and Holland.

The Reformation, which began in earnest about 1520, did place northern Europe painting in crisis. The question arose as to whether painting could, or should, continue at all, since many Protestants objected to images of saints in churches, regarding them as signs of popish idolatry. As early as 1526, Humanist **Erasmus** of Rotterdam wrote from Switzerland of northern Europe's artistically troubled situation. In a letter commending the German painter Hans Holbein to friends in England, Erasmus wrote: "The arts here are freezing." In fact, only one Protestant region in Europe fully survived the crisis of the Reformation in the art arena: the Netherlands.

During the 16th century, Netherlands' painters struggled—successfully—with two main issues. Even prior to the Reformation, the first had presented itself: how to assimilate the influence of Italian Renaissance art. The second issue, a direct consequence of the Reformation, was the loss in Protestant regions of painters' single best source of income: altar panels (for Roman Catholic churches). The loss of such traditional commissions led artists to create a repertory of specialized nonreligious subject matter to which the Protestant clergy could raise no objections. All the secular themes that feature so prominently in Dutch and Flemish painting of the baroque era— *portrait, still life, landscape,* and *genre* (scenes of everyday life)—had actually been present earlier, as ancillary elements in the works of the brothers Limbourg and van Eyck, but gradually became better defined between 1500 and 1600. Many artists began to specialize in one particular area.

The idea of specialization in art was not a new one in the Netherlands. **Hieronymus Bosch** (1474–1516), a Dutch artist who was born and worked most of his life in the North Brabant provincial town of 's Hertogenbosch (Den Bosch), filled paintings such as *The Garden of Delights* with fantastic figures and imagery. Clearly, some symbols are suggestive, some in remarkably Freudian form. Original Sin seems to loom large, but Bosch's own meanings for his images are mostly unknown to us today. His strange human figures may seem almost otherworldly, but there's no question of their connection with the genre tradition that reached rare heights under the genius of **Pieter Bruegel the Elder** (1525?–1569). Though Bruegel had traveled to Italy, his paintings of peasant life executed in Antwerp and Brussels were thoroughly Flemish in form and content. Well- educated, a humanist, and patronized by the Hapsburg court, Bruegel chose to paint peasants, with a wealth of wit and anecdote that revealed a degree of observation that was far from simple, and he served as an example for genre painters in the Netherlands for generations. Though best known for his specialized attention to peasant scenes, Bruegel's *Return of the Hunters* is one of the first in which landscape is the main subject of a painting.

BELGIUM'S BAROQUE "GOLDEN AGE"

In Roman Catholic southern Netherlands, setting of the *Counter Reformation*, **Pieter Paul Rubens** (1577–1640) was the most widely collected painter of his time, and the dominant figure in Flemish art during his life and well after. As a trained master painter, Rubens went in 1600 to Rome, birthplace of the baroque style, spending some seven years there. With keen interest, Rubens listened and learned in Italy, but did not join any of the artistic "movements" there—though he was certainly influenced by the lighting of Caravaggio's work. Rubens remained an artist in the Flemish tradition. By absorbing the Italian tradition far more thoroughly than had any previous northern painter, he played a role of unique importance in helping to make the baroque style international. His influence helped to break down the artistic barriers between southern and northern Europe.

Rubens' exuberant, optimistic style and his skill in making his works seem intensely alive counteracted the spiritual crisis caused by the explosion of new knowledge of the world. (Copernicus' early 16th-century discovery that the earth was *not* the center of the solar system had been an unsettling one for many people.) The immediacy and dazzling use of color in Rubens' paintings instilled faith and emotionally lifted people out of their ordinary lives. Particularly in the 1620s, Rubens used his dynamic style in the design of decorative schemes for churches and palaces. Rubens maintained a robust studio with many pupils and guild-member artists who were well trained in his style, and who would complete paintings after the master had finished making his mark. The differences in talent between Rubens' work and that of pupils who finished his pieces is most noticeable in paintings originally made to serve as altar panels—several remain *in situ* in Antwerp—that have been removed to museums.

Anthonie van Dyck (1599-1641) (a.k.a. Sir Anthony van Dyck), a child prodigy who had become Ruben's most valued assistant before he was 20, was the only other Flemish baroque artist to achieve international renown. His mature work consists mainly of portraits, especially those executed while he served as court painter to England's Charles I. The aristocrat portrait tradition that van Dyck created had considerable continental influence until late in the 18th century.

HOLLAND'S 17th-CENTURY "GOLDEN AGE"

Antwerp's 16th century Golden Age in the southern Netherlands was a foundation upon which the northern Netherlands built its illustrious 17th century golden era.

Having achieved *de facto* independence from Spain in 1579, Holland—the seven Protestant northern provinces of the Netherlands—was ready to make the most of a century that promised unprecedented prosperity and growth. Dutch 17th-century art is unique not only for its quantity of artists who demonstrated superb craftsmanship—besides the acknowledged geniuses, there were many "little masters," a non-pejorative term used only to indicate that these painters are less widely known—but also for the realism with which it recorded the face of Holland and its people.

Never before 17th-century Holland had a group of artists looked at the physical world around them with such clarity and set down their observations with such fidelity. Turning away from the religious, mythological, and allegorical subjects that had been the themes of the Renaissance (and remained so, to some extent, in Rubens' Flanders), the Dutch portrayed what they saw around them with great artistry but without affectation. It was no coincidence that this new emphasis on realism in art came when and where it did. The age that produced Rembrandt had reason as a guiding principle for its philosophers. One of the foremost was rationalist René Descartes ("I think, therefore I am"), who chose to live most of his adult life in Holland.

The development of certain areas of science paralleled the development of art in Holland. The first important portrait commission that **Rembrandt van Rijn** (1606–1669) received as a trained painter was for the 1632 *Anatomy Lesson of Dr. Tulp* (in the **Mauritshuis** in The Hague). It is an unusual group portrait featuring realistic treatment of a potentially distasteful subject (a human dissection), but its success seems to show that the Dutch were ready to look at the world with realist eyes.

A scientific subject of considerable contemporary interest was optics, and the Dutch were preeminent in the field. The telescope that Galileo adapted for his research had been invented by lens grinders in the Netherlands. Light was of interest to the Dutch artistically as well as scientifically. The light reflected from their flat, waterlogged, land lent a special atmosphere to the increasingly popular landscape paintings. Vermeer flooded his subjects with light, while Rembrandt turned the lamps low for dramatic effect. One of Rembrandt's teachers, Pieter Lastman, who had traveled to Italy and seen what Caravaggio's work conveyed through *chiaroscuro* (the interplay of light and shadow), passed his impressions on to his pupil, who began to use the device with a skill no other artist has since surpassed.

In the 17th century many Dutch towns, such as Haarlem, Leiden, and Delft, had artists' guilds that sought to solicit business for members while controlling competition from outsiders. Amsterdam, however, was an open art market in which, for the first time in the history of Western art, traditional patronage and guild support were replaced by the interests and tastes of a buying public. The city's expanding prosperous merchant class was the most common source of commissions, but there also was brisk business at artists' own shops, art dealers, and at annual fairs and markets where ordinary citizens could afford to buy paintings. Prices varied, with artists of repute naturally fetching higher prices for their work than more obscure colleagues. The average price for an unsigned picture of a high standard cost about the equivalent of a fisherman's weekly wage. Thus, while art was comparatively expensive, it remained within reach of a large cross section of the public.

It was a remarkably compact period during which so many outstanding Dutch artists were born—beginning with Frans Hals in 1580. For the following 75 years, the world was nearly overwhelmed with the output of artistic works of genius and high talent in Holland. Sales of paintings were supported by a broad segment of society, with members of the general public—whether or not they could afford to—developing a nearly insatiable appetite for investing in pictures. Supply kept up with demand, with sales of literally tens of thousands of paintings of a consistent, astonishingly high standard. A Frenchman who taught at the University of Leiden in the 17th century wrote, "There can surely be no other country in the world where there are so many, and such excellent, paintings."

18th AND 19th CENTURIES

Quite suddenly, Holland's 17th-century artistic fire burned itself out. With French King Louis XIV's invasion of both the southern and northern Netherlands in 1672–78, the entire regional atmosphere changed. Mostly lackluster artistic efforts ensued until the middle of the 19th century.

The giant among 19th-century Dutch painters was **Vincent van Gogh** (1853–1890), a self-taught post-Impressionist painter whose monumental talent was just on the brink of being widely recognized when he died at the age of 37 from a self-inflicted wound in 1890. Van Gogh, who decided to become an artist at the age of 27, did so while he was living in Belgium. Originally, he had gone to Wallonia's *Borinage* as a pastor-on-probation working among the miners in that coal-producing region. Having failed at that job, he remained in Belgium during a self-described "molting time," from which he emerged determined to become an artist. His beginning sketches were of Belgian coal miners and their surroundings, and his first studio was in the cottage of a Borinage coal miner. (See also "Wallonia: An Introduction.") Van Gogh left Wallonia in the fall of 1880 for Brussels, where he spent the winter working at drawing.

20th CENTURY

Belgian art in the 20th century brought several respected names. In the paintings of **James Ensor** (1860–1949), the pessimistic view of the human condition, presented centuries earlier by Hieronymous Bosch, reappears. Nightmarish images of demons and masks fill the works of the reclusive Ensor, *Impressionist* turned *Father of Surrealism*, who lived most of his life inside his house in Ostend. One of the most important Surrealist painters is Belgian **Rene Magritte** (1898–1967), whose juxtaposed motifs have been highly influential. **Paul Delvaux** (b. 1897) played an important role early in the movement of Surrealism. Delvaux's paintings, a significant and well-displayed selection of which are on view in a museum in his house near de Panne on the Belgian coast, show strong obsessional images of sexuality, travel, and death. Among the Belgian group broadly called the *Brabant Fauvists* because of their use of bold outlines and bright blocks of color are the painters **Jean Brusselmans** (1884–1953), **Rik Wouters** (1882–1916), and **Henri Wolvens** (1896–1977), all represented at Brussels' **Museum of Modern Art**.

Also at the museum are works by members of the **COBRA** group (an acronym for **CO**penhagen, **BR**ussels, and **A**msterdam), founded in 1948, three years after the end of World War II. The group's works are characterized by spontaneity; vivid warm color, and a form and content reminiscent of children's drawing. As founding member **Constant** claimed: "We have been stripped of every certainty; no faith remains but this, that we are alive and that it is part of the essence of life to manifest oneself."

Visitors to Brussels interested in contemporary Belgian art can encounter it in the **Metro**. (See under "What to See and Do", in Brussels.) Most stations throughout the system have works which range from tapestries and tiles to the largest photograph in the world, fantasy landscapes to flights of angels on the ceiling, and sculpture to murals. (One mural by Paul Delvaux is at *Bourse Station*.) One station, *Vandervelde*, has the world's largest ceiling fresco after the Sistine Chapel; another, *Alma*, has been given a complete look of Nature: the pillars are tree stumps, the ceiling is a painted sky with clouds; the walls of *Station Stockel* are completely lined in the cartoon figures of **de Herge**.

ARCHITECTURE

Dolmens found in the Ourthe Valley (near Liège, Belgium) attest to Celtic community life in the region prior to and until about the 5th century B.C. One of the Celtic tribes was known as the *Belgae*. Julius Caesar came, saw, and conquered the area circa 50 B.C. He founded Tongeren—Belgium's oldest town—in 57 B.C., and in 15 B.C. *Gallia Belgica* was established as a northern imperial province of the Roman Empire. Tongeren has a provincial museum with Gallo-Roman remains and artifacts (as does nearby Maastricht, just north over the border in Holland). The Romans remained until the 5th century, after which the region was subjected periodically to vigorous Viking attacks into the 10th century.

As the Roman hold weakened during the 3rd century, Germanic Frankish tribes began to penetrate; once the Romans departed, individualistic artistic influences of the Franks (*Rhineland* or *Rhenish*) began to have an impact on the bordering Maas (Meuse) river region. When the Frankish King Charlemagne—whom the Pope had declared emperor of the West (from Denmark to Italy, and from Spain to the Oder)—established his court at Aachen, Germany, the move conferred increased importance on its neighbors, particularly Liège, which had received an important Bishopric in 721, and Maastricht, which dated from Roman days. In the division of the Carolingian Empire (Charlemagne died in 814), the *Treaty of Verdun* (843) separated what is present-day Belgium both culturally and politically, and led to the development of two distinct *Romanesque* styles. The territory west of the Scheldt River fell to France and became associated with the *Scaldian* style, while from the Meuse River to the east, the *Mosan* style of **Romanesque** architecture developed.

Mosan architecture in the 11th century was in both construction and decoration simple, strong, and austere. An impressive example of the style's fortresslike west wall (*westwerk*) can be seen at the **Onze Lieve Vrouwekerk** in Maastricht. The legacy of the Rhine-Meuse style includes two fine arts masterpieces that remain in Belgium: goldsmith **Nicholas of Verdun's** *Shrine of the Virgin* (1205) at Tournai Cathedral and the cast bronze font with 12 oxen at the **Church of St. Barthelemy** in Liège by **Renier de Huy** (c. 1113).

The *Scaldian* style, more elaborate than Mosan and influenced by the French who controlled the valley of the Scheldt, came into its own in the 12th century before eventually evolving into the Gothic style. Belgium's unusual five-towered **Tournai Cathedral**, whose multistoried nave dates from 1171, has been called "the cradle of

Scaldian-Gothic Art"; two developments of the style visible at Tournai are the cathedral's exterior decoration, which grows more ornate towards the top, and the addition of an entrance to the *westwerk*.

A major feature of early Belgian architectural history were the **Flemish burgher** (town aldermen) **houses** of the late Middle Ages. What are perhaps the earliest (1175–1200) remaining examples in western Europe are in Tournai, and served as the prototypes of lay architecture in the Scheldt valley. The finest extant examples of early medieval feudal fortresses are Ghent's **Gravensteen** (Castle of the Counts), begun in 1180 although parts visible in the cellar date from the 9th century, and the **Steen** c. 1250 (now the Maritime Museum) in Antwerp, Ghent's **Koonstapelhuis**, c. 1200, on the *Graslei* is an exceptional example of a Romanesque public grain warehouse.

The *Gothic* era started more slowly and lingered longer in the southern (roughly what today is Belgium) and northern Netherlands (today's Holland) than elsewhere in Europe. Once embraced, Early Gothic (13th century) progressed to the more richly detailed High Gothic (14th century) and on to Flamboyant Gothic (15th and 16th centuries). In Belgium, there were further variations on the theme: Scheldt Gothic, Limburg Gothic, and Brabant Gothic. Many of the region's finest cathedrals took their present shape during Gothic times, including **St. Rombout's** in Mechelen (early 14th–early 16th century), and the similarly aged **Onze Lieve Vrowe Cathedral** in Antwerp. It is the largest Gothic church in Belgium; 12th-century Romanesque sections were revealed during recent extensive restoration.

Secular architecture in the form of magnificently ornate municipal buildings may have been the most splendid achievements of the Gothic era in Belgium. The sense of independence that came with town charters and an increasing commercial confidence (due especially to the Flemish cloth industry) led burghers in Belgian Flanders to build great Gothic flights of fancy—belfries, cloth halls, guild houses, and town halls—to illustrate their successes. Some of the richest examples are the **Ypres Cloth Hall** (a faithful reconstruction of the 13th-century original that was destroyed in World War I); the **Bruges stadhuis** (town hall—late 14th century); and **Brussels' Town Hall** (early 15th century), the only building on the Grand Place to survive the 1695 bombardment ordered by French King Louis XIV. Others include the **stadhuizen** (town halls) in **Louvain** (1450), **Ghent** (1518–35), and **Oudenaarde** (1526–36).

Pride and pleasure in such architectural achievements resulted in a stick-with-tradition spirit that postponed acceptance of the Italian Renaissance influence in the area. **Cornelis Floris** (1514–1575) was the first Flemish architect to represent the Renaissance—albeit reinterpreted by local tastes—in **Antwerp's stadhuis** (1561–1565). Though built along Italian lines, it retained traditional, late Gothic Flemish design overlaid with "copybook" Renaissance details. That combination added eccentricity to the splendor of guild houses and other buildings on many a Belgian Grote Markt (main square). A fine Renaissance house (c. 1576), also in Antwerp, is the mansion built for printer Plantin (today the **Plantin-Moretus Museum**), which made a successful marriage of local building methods and Renaissance forms. The pure Italian Renaissance concept of proportion was not employed in Belgium until the 17th century, and then sparingly.

Religious upheavals in the 16th century set in motion circumstances that shaped the long-term development of both architecture and art in Belgium (and Holland). The **Reformation**, which began about 1520, left men's lives and their families' fortunes in shambles if they couldn't be politic in their ecclesiastical politics. The times took a terrible toll on the artistic past. By 1579, the Netherlands had split into the Dutch Protestant northern provinces, with Belgium (the southern Netherlands) remaining under the rule of Roman Catholic Spain. Following the separation of the southern Netherlands from the seven united northern provinces of the new Dutch Republic, architecture and art developed differently in the two countries.

In Holland, the 17th century took shape in buildings that showed a restrained form of *classicism*. In Belgium, the *baroque* style that had begun in Italy and was favored by the Roman Catholic church (at least partially because of its complete contrast to sober Protestant puritanism) became popular. It found exuberant expression by Pieter Paul Rubens in Antwerp. Rubens' house in Antwerp (designed by the artist 1613–1617), although restored, remains full of fine baroque architectural ornamentation, applied to traditional form. Rubens designed the impressive facade of Antwerp's **St. Carolus Borromeus** (1615–1621). Probably Belgium's most important baroque church is **St. Pieter's** in Ghent, in which the unknown architect made interesting use of space and light.

With the occupation of Antwerp by the Spanish in 1585, many architects and artists—and rich burghers who might eventually have patronized their creative efforts—fled north to Holland to free themselves from the Spanish yoke. **Lieven de Key** of Ghent, for instance, became the municipal architect for Haarlem, building that town's **Vleeshuis** (meat hall, 1602–03) and Leiden's magnificent **Stadhuis** (1597), a last flowering of the florid 16th-century gable style. Afterwards, the area settled down for what proved to be a couple of relatively quiet centuries, architecturally.

Early in the 19th century, Belgium witnessed an epic European event: the final defeat of Napoleon at Waterloo, just outside Brussels, in 1815. Belgium's own independence in 1830 brought thoughts of a new look for its capital, and several neoclassical plans resulted in Brussels' upper town, including the reconstruction along Louis XVI lines of the **Place Royale**. The monumental (some say monstrous) **Palais de Justice** was built between 1866 and 1883 to the design of **Joseph Poelaert**. Its plateau site is appropriate (the medieval city's gallows stood there), but the 300-foot-high domed building (in overall area larger than St. Peter's in the Vatican) can only have meant much displacement in the still typically working class Brussels' lower town *Quartier des Marolles*. Much more elegant are the arcades of Brussels' **Galeries St. Hubert** by **J.P. Cluysenaer** in 1846.

The advent of **art nouveau** in Belgium—most plentifully in Brussels—came in the 1890s and was very much an artistic accompaniment to the socialist movement. Free thinkers, liberals, and socialists of the period favored art nouveau architecture and ornamentation, while the more conservative Catholics favored Gothic and Flemish Renaissance. Certain Brussels neighborhoods and boroughs—Ixelles, Uccle, and on and around Avenue Louise—became steeped in the new style.

Art nouveau's reign was brief and beauteous, and its stylish, sinuous curves were abandoned shortly after 1905. The first two houses in the revolutionary style were built in 1893 by **Victor Horta** and **Paul Hankar** who, together with **Henry van de Velde**, were the movement's main proponents in Belgium. In keeping true to the concept, the woodwork, furniture, and all the curvilinear *fin-dè-siecle* fittings were included in a specific project's design. **Victor Horta's House** and studio (so-called even though he did not live there long and sold it before paying off all who worked on it) was finished in 1898, and became a museum in 1969. It reflects loving attention to art nouveau detail; there's hardly a right angle in the house—Horta hated them. Victor Horta also designed the **Musée des Beaux Arts** in Brussels, **Brussels Centrale Station**, as well as the **Musée des Beaux Arts** in Tournai (1928), which shows spatial originality in its concept of exhibit rooms set around a central polygonal entrance hall. Only one of the six Brussels' department stores Horta designed still stands, having been restored to become the **Museum of the Comic**. Little of van de Velde's work remains in Belgium, but one of his most famous buildings is the **Kroller-Muller Museum** in Otterlo, Holland, a 1934 work that reflects the austerity and refinement found in the best early 20th-century Belgian architecture.

Sadly, many of Brussels most significant buildings in the art nouveau style, including Horta's Maison de Peuple, headquarters for the socialists, have been razed. (For more information on art nouveau sites that still exist, see "Brussels," "What To See and Do," "Victor Horta House.")

Brussels continues to practice controversial urban expansion. As recently as the late 1980s, whole residential blocks in the city were leveled to make room for a large European Community building that can seat the entire European Parliament, which over the years has greatly expanded with the addition of new members in the EC.

DECORATIVE ARTS AND TRADITIONAL CRAFTS

LACE

Lacework (*kantwerk* in Dutch, *dentelles* in French) originated in Belgium as a result of the 15th-century fashion for trimming garments with it. Flemish lace was much sought after; both male and female figures wear it prominently in portraits by Netherlands painters of that and later periods. Bruges lace was the most prized of all, since that town's local lacemakers specialized in the popular rose-lace flower pattern and the extremely fine "Fairy Queen" stitch. Bruges has always been home to bobbin lace, which is executed on a large lap pillow. Mechelen became well known for lace in the 17th and 18th centuries, and Brussels also was a center for the craft. Since the 1970s, Bruges has seen a revival of lacemaking by hand, which has both revitalized the traditional craft and made it competitive as a contemporary art form.

The **Bruges Lace Center** (*Kantcentrum*) has its roots in a lace school founded in 1717, when the Bishop of Bruges decided that lacemaking would ensure a certain income for families in the then poverty-stricken town. The school served its immediate purpose and proved an ongoing success: in 1860 it had 400 pupils. But, by the beginning of the 20th century, there had been a sharp drop in attendance and interest. From 1930 onward, there was a general decline in the lace industry, partly because it had gone out of fashion and partly because what lace was needed could be mechanically produced abroad and imported for less. By 1960, only an evening division of the 250-year-old school remained open. But because lacemaking was such a traditional handicraft in Bruges that no one wanted to see it disappear entirely, the mayor and the municipality of Bruges arranged for the buildings in Balstraat to be donated for the cause, and the Lace Center was opened in 1972.

The number of women interested in the purely personal enjoyment of lacemaking encouraged the Lace Center to institute a daily group for those already familiar with the craft who could come to the Center when they wanted advice or wished to try their hand at a new pattern in a group setting. Visitors to the center see participants in such groups. Many of the local lace makers have learned to design their own lace creations, and some of their works are also on display. The Center, which gives many courses, annually offers one in designing and making contemporary laces. Also at the center is a museum with many different styles and samples of lace on display; on the walls are copies of 15th– to 17th-century paintings that show clothing richly decorated with similar lace. Bruges' **Gruuthuse Museum** has a wonderful collection of modern and ancient lace, and Brussels' **Royal Museum of Art and History** has its important exhibit of lace on public view.

A number of shops in Bruges and Brussels sell lace. Would-be buyers are cautioned that some items advertised as "real lace" may indeed be handmade, but in the Far East, not Belgium. Machine-made pieces may better suit your pocketbook, so ask questions of shopkeepers and compare prices. One way to be sure of what you're buying is to stick to the several official *Quality Control* lace shops in Bruges which guarantee, by government certificate, that the lace is original local work. The Bruges Tourist Office can supply names. (Also see "Shopping" under "Bruges.")

DIAMOND CUTTING

Today, 47% of the world's consumption of polished diamonds takes place in Antwerp, where the diamond industry has existed since the second half of the 15th century. By late in the 16th century, a diamond cutters' guild flourished in Antwerp. Sea routes to India introduced the western world to its first major supply of raw diamonds and produced a highly successful 17th-century trade. But by the 18th century, those fields had been exhausted, and the diamond industry was in decline worldwide. Nevertheless, such was Antwerp's residual reputation in diamonds that in 1787 France's Louis XVI had his crown jewels repolished there. Antwerp's affair with the ancient pure carbon objects—an untempting but accurate description—was rekindled by the South African diamond rush which began in 1869. With a steady supply of top quality goods again assured, Antwerp sparkled anew in the business, and diamond workshops sprang up everywhere. It was Englishman Cecil Rhodes, later prime minister of the Cape Colony, who founded the De Beers Mining Company in 1881. (Today, De Beers Consolidated Mining handles 80% of the world's mined diamonds.) Beginning in 1913, mines from the Belgian Congo (now Zaire) also began sending diamonds to Antwerp. The hardest substance on earth, diamonds can be used to cut anything. In the 19th century they began to be used industrially; in 1879, the St. Gotthard Tunnel through the Alps was built with the help of diamond-tipped tools. More than 50% of the diamonds mined today are for industrial use.

Of the 20 diamond bourses worldwide, Antwerp has four, including the largest. (Amsterdam has the second largest.) All told, Antwerp's inner-city diamond industry compound of buyers, bankers, brokers, dealers, and craftsmen employs 35,000 people. In Amsterdam you can visit one of several diamond houses for a view of the diamond cutting process, but for background on all the fascinating facets of the diamond business, a trip to Antwerp's **Diamantmuseum (Diamond Museum)** (opened in 1988 in Antwerp's diamond district near the Centraal Station) is a brilliant idea. As the museum shows, there's much more to the story of diamonds than carat-color-clarity-cut. Exhibits run the gamut from mining to the materialization of a splendidly polished stone; the "Antwerp cut," which makes stones sparkle more than any other, is universally recognized as the best, and it proves that all that glitters is *not* gold. Diamonds get their dazzle from being cut in a way that forms multiple facets—57 create "perfect fire"—at carefully calculated angles. *Rose* cuts (the *Antwerp* or *fashion rose*, and the *Amsterdam* or *full rose*) date from about 1600, and the *brilliant* cut has been known since 1680, but not until this century were the ideal proportions of diamond cuts scientifically determined. After the First World War, new cuts such as the *baguette* and the *emerald* were created.

The museum has a treasure room where some of the precious gems themselves illustrate the history of fashion's delight with the diamond. Examples from many styles of jewelry are shown, including art nouveau and recent winners of the annual *Antwerp Diamond High Council* competition. A video (in an English version) on Antwerp's historic diamond trade can be viewed. (See also "Diamantmuseum" under "What To See and Do in Antwerp.")

TAPESTRIES

No one claims it's the oldest, but the 1402 tapestry at Tournai Cathedral is the only one of its period that can be certified as an authentic *Arras*. Belgium's **Flanders**, which once included Tournai (today in Belgium's Wallonia), was the center of Europe's tapestry making for centuries. Tapestry was in great demand during the Middle Ages, when the great ornamental pieces carpeted the walls of palaces and churches with not only beauty, but warmth as well. **Brussels, Bruges, Tournai, Oudennaarde, Antwerp, Grardsbergen**, and **Edingen** were the sources of the finest Flemish tapestries. Much later, when tapestry workshops began in Paris (*Gobelin* and *Aubusson*), they were set up and initially manned by the Flemish.

The Cathedral of Tournai received its Arras (by Pierrot Fere, the Arras master weaver), which illustrates the lives of St. Piat and St. Eleutherus, as a gift in 1402. Though tapestries from this early period typically lack "depth" in their design and have a limited palette, lively reds and blues highlight the vast area of the Tournai tapestry—Flemish tapestries left hardly any empty spaces—that is filled with figures and buildings revealing some of the history of Tournai and its renowned church, and shows scenes of the city's second plague. In Tournai's **Museum of History and Archaeology** are two large, still remarkably brightly colored, 15th-century Tournai-made tapestries.

Bruges was one of the Flemish strongholds of tapestry weaving. Works from Bruges often were smaller than those from other tapestry centers, and distinctive for their pastoral scenes. The **Gruuthuse Museum** has some on display. Many Flemish tapestries incorporated the same subject matter as the master painters of the day; Rembrandt, Teniers, and others often drew "cartoons" (designs) for tapestries. Thus, tapestries reflected *genre* (everyday life), *verdures*, (landscapes or nature), and religious, historical, and allegorical scenes. In many cases, Flemish tapestries were made in sets.

Masterpieces among the many tapestries in Brussels' **Royal Museum of Art and History** (it owns 150, of which one-third hang on view) are eight of the original ten *History of Jacob* tapestries, considered to be one of the finest tapestry sets from the Flemish Renaissance. Woven in wool and silk in 1534 from cartoons made by Brussels artist **Bernard van Orley**, the massive set was sold to an Italian cardinal in the 1530s and remained in the same family in Bologna until the end of the 19th century. The Belgian government purchased them in 1950 and had them restored by the **Royal Manufacturers of Tapestry Gaspard de Wit Ltd.** in Mechelen.

Guy Delmarcel, head of the tapestry department of the Royal Museum of Art and History, observes, "Tapestry was the movable fresco of the North, and the first art industry." Other historians have referred to tapestries as "mirrors of civilization," noting that one "can read them like books." In fact, nobles are known to have ordered tapestries that illustrated their favorite books. Following the fate of other decorative art forms, tapestries, too, passed out of fashion for a phase. For decades during the 19th century people simply discarded them. But a big exhibition in France late in the century led to their rediscovery as a rich art form.

The De Wit weaving establishment in Mechelen is housed in the former refugee house of the Tongerlo Abbeye, which dates from 1483. De Wit (which celebrated its centenary in 1989) is a family tradition: Present owner Yvan Maes is the great-grandson of the founder. The Mechelen tapestry firm, now an institution in the tapestry world, has survived by being one of the first to expand upon a newly specialized skill, *tapestry conservation*, which is fundamentally different and more affordable than tapestry restoration. Conservation aims to preserve and stabilize the existing fabric of a tapestry rather than attempting to weave in new patches. Maes feels conservation is a "more respectful treatment for a tapestry, more honest to its history."

It is the Gaspard de Wit firm's aim not only to preserve the artistic heritage of tapestry weaving by conserving antique pieces for private customers and museums all over the world, but also to keep alive the traditional art form. Nearly half the current tapestry orders are for modern pieces, so the Flemish craft continues in contemporary times. One of De Wit's modern creations, a tapestry of the space shuttle, hangs in the U.S. headquarters of the Northrop Corporation. Another, a work woven from a design produced by Belgian artist Edmond Debrunfaut (and specially treated to repel dust and grime), decorates a Brussels Metro station.

De Wit offers visitors a unique setting of workshops and exhibition halls in which to see an exclusive collection of antique and modern tapestries in a historic building. Tours in English take place Saturday at 10:30 a.m. Contact the Mechelen Tourist Office about the possibility of visits at other times. Although De Wit is the only tapestry business in Belgium today, there are a number of active self-employed weavers in the country.

MUSIC

THE BELL EPOCH:
CENTURIES OF CARILLONS

You may not immediately think of music when Belgium comes to mind, but it's in the air here. Flemish Belgium especially, is carillon country, with bells in church towers and town belfries that ring out the hours with song. More special still, these so-called "singing towers" provide concerts on market days, summer evenings, and other preset times, and there's nothing more delightful or more typically Belgian than settling in with a drink at a sidewalk cafe for a free concert.

Suddenly, a surge of unexpected music spills from a spire, cascades to cobbled streets and squares, and rebounds from fanciful old facades—resounding everywhere at once. Joyful bursts from carillon bells astonish and then delight unsuspecting pedestrians before dispersing in the breezes above Belgium.

It was the small country of Belgium, together with Holland, that gave the world its largest musical instrument. Fittingly, of the nearly 600 carillons worldwide, fully half are found in Belgium and Holland, where the instrument was developed and refined, and has since flourished. Their bells hung high in historic tall towers, carillons send their endearing, unavoidable voices across the Low Countries.

Carillons carry the fond, flowery epithet of "singing towers," and there's a long-standing local saying: "If you can see the tower, you can hear the carillon." Although it's the world's loudest musical instrument, rush-hour traffic in the heart of cities, where the centuries-old carillon towers often are located, can make that statement less than true today. But even when I have to strain to hear them, the short carillon pieces that mark the hour invariably make me smile.

True carillon music doesn't come from the automatic mechanism that's programmed to send forth song on the hour, however. The instrument's real voice is released when a *beiaardier* or *carillonneur* personally claims the keyboard, and the tons of bronze bells in the tower respond to a hands-on touch. When a master carillonneur takes command, even the uninitiated can hear the increased character in the chorus of the bells. Carillons in the playing care of professionals can deliver a surprising delicacy of sound. And the range in variations of pace, power, and style in manual performances provides plenty of challenge. As well as massive chords that crash like stormy surf, a carillonneur can coax notes as light as a length of Belgian lace from the instrument, by skillfully balancing the voices of bells weighing as few as 16 or as many as 16,000 pounds. And the sounds created by these mighty metallic choirs encased in carved-stone towers can be as complex as they are compelling.

An important player in Belgian bell lore is the official *stadbeiaardier*, or town carillonneur, who is paid a salary to serve as keeper of the carillon. Job responsibilities, depending upon the size of the town and status of its carillon, include giving public concerts at set times, such as on market days and Saturdays. (Concerts often are offered more frequently in summer.) The lofty playing position high in a tower can make a stadbeiaardier something of a local celebrity. Included in the job description are upkeep of the instrument, programming the automated carillon for the tower clock whose tunes are changed periodically, and generally creating good vibrations as ambassador of the town bells.

Carillon players need strength to make music, for their art form is more physical than many others. Few carillonneurs have elevators in their high towers: hundreds of spiralling steps, up and down, must be negotiated for each practice and performance. (A number of towers are open to visitors who are up to the ascent.) For the able and interested, there's nothing like a close-up inspection of a bevy of bells, the automated mechanism, and the carillonneur's "cabin" with its keyboard. From it, there's usually a terrific view over the town and out across the flat land of Flanders to the far, low horizon.

To play, a carillonneur sits on a bench before a double row of polished wooden pegs which serve as the "keys." These console pegs tug on a web of rods and wires (the transmission) which, in turn, operates metal clappers attached to each fixed-position bell. Weather conditions, particularly wet and cold, affect the metal of the bells and require the carillonneur to tinker, tune, and tighten the wires that connect the keyboard to the bells. Similar in operation to an organ, the carillon uses a row of foot pedals to play lower notes, the heavy metal sound of the big bass bells.

The carillonneur plays by striking down on the pegs with the side of his closed fist; protective leather pads are worn on the little fingers of each hand. The force of the blow is adjusted for the weight of the bell—the higher the musical note, the lighter and smaller the bell —and the intensity of sound required. Using both fists and feet, carillon players can work up a sweat. In warm weather, they may strip down to shorts for the workout of an hour-long concert. Nevertheless, playing the carillon shouldn't be too taxing an effort if the bells are properly balanced.

The fact that you can't ignore the bold sound of bells is, historically, the very point of their existence. In the Middle Ages, bells were central to the life of communities. Their use became widespread within the monastic system, in which they were rung to announce the offices, a series of services at set times of the day and night.

The use of bells in secular context developed with the rise of towns, which began in northern Europe in the Low Countries (today's Belgium and Holland). Belfries were built to contain the bells that signalled the start and end of the working day, the curfew hour when the town gates were shut and bolted for the night, and warned of the approach of important visitors or hostile troops. There were separate bells for the different alerting functions, with varying pitches so people could tell the rings apart.

Bruges, in Belgium, built one of the earliest town belfries (1299), to house its community bell **Magna Campana**. St. Rombout's church clock tower in Mechelen dates from 1372, and Ghent got its belfry in 1376. Further functions and additional bells were added as urban development proceeded; bells began to be used for summoning officials to public executions, publicizing a market or fish auction, raising the alarm in case of fire or a storm, and announcing the banishment of felons or the death of a citizen.

Eventually, time in towns needed to be measured more precisely, and bells began to mark the hours. The watchman, whose all important job it was to ring the bell at the correct times, used a sundial as an aid and, later, a small, simple clockwork alarm. This gadget eventually led to the development of mechanisms that could chime the hours automatically, giving rise to tower clocks with bells.

Because the tolling of the hour in the tower tended to come unexpectedly, the idea arose of ringing a few notes of warning a few minutes in advance. Originally, this warning was always done on four small bells, struck with wooden mallets. From the name for that four-bell instrument, the **quadrillon**, came the name carillon. From four bells, the number increased to a diatonic series of six or eight tuned bells by the beginning of the 16th century. A simple automatic chime mechanism—the first is thought to have been in **Mons, Belgium**—came into fairly general use soon thereafter.

The development that marked the true beginning of the carillon as an instrument, according to music historians, was replacing the procedure of striking the bells with a hand-held hammer by a rudimentary **clavier**, or keyboard, which enabled the manual playing of the bells. Once the keyboard had been developed, the warning flourishes sounded in advance of the striking of the hour were elaborated into actual music.

According to records, the town of **Oudenaard**, a thriving medieval textile trading center, put the first carillon keyboard into use in the year 1510, thereby establishing Belgium as the birthplace of the carillon. Oudenaard is in Belgium's Dutch-speaking northern Flemish region where, even today, most of the country's nearly 100 carillons are located. By 1541, Antwerp's Onze Lieve Vrouwekerk (Cathedral of Our Dear Lady) possessed a keyboard for its bells; Ghent acquired one in 1553.

Mechelen's St. Rombout's got its first keyboard by 1556, but the church made carillon history in 1583 when it showed off the first instrument fitted out with **foot pedals**. Since that advancement, substantially little change has taken place in the mechanics of the carillon.

The 15th and 16th centuries were periods of prosperity for Flanders. Successful merchants and shipowners in Antwerp and elsewhere watched their treasure pile up, and wanted something to spend it on that would reflect well on their wealth. Cities and towns, too, became richer and competed to proclaim their prosperity and prestige. An investment in carillons, the sweet singing bells that had already become closely connected with the character of the southern/northern Netherlands, became a wonderful way to ring out rank.

The number of carillons increased, and bell foundries multiplied as each prosperous town mounted a campaign to have more bells than its neighbors. It was in the 17th century that the talented François Hemony (born in 1609 in Lorraine, France) and his brother Pierre discovered the secret of perfectly tuning carillon bells.

In this musical metier, François made the name **Hemony** synonymous with the finest sounding carillons ever cast. François and his brother came to Holland at the request of the city fathers of Amsterdam to build a carillon for the town hall on Dam Square (the present Royal Palace). Thereafter, they mainly remained in Amsterdam, setting up a casting foundry there and creating bells with the carefully shaped insides that François Hemony—who took more individual care in the casting, while his brother Pierre was more inclined to cast ready-made carillons assembly-line style—knew to be the secret of their musicality. The shape or "profile" of bells, both inside and out, affects their sound. For example, today's English-cast bells (such as those of *John Taylor & Co.*) have a longer "ringing time," or resonance, than Belgian or Dutch-made bells; this difference is because the inside lips of the latter are squared off, while English bells are cast absolutely rounded.

During the period 1646–1667, the Hemonys achieved great fame by producing approximately 50 exceptional carillons, each containing up to three octaves. Three octaves was a state-of-the-art standard in the Hemonys' day, though serious carillons today should have at least four octaves, 47 bells. (Contemporary instruments with fewer than 23 bells/two octaves are called "chimes.")

Some 30 Hemony instruments can still be heard today, almost all in Belgium or Holland. And every town that has one, including Huy and Antwerp, proclaims the fact loud and clear. Sadly, none of the Hemonys' immediate successors turned out to be capable of producing such high quality bells.

A century later, between 1751–1786, **Andreas Josef Van den Gheyn** of Louvain, near Brussels, rediscovered the tuning method, and the brilliance of his treble bells bested even the sound of the Hemonys. Unfortunately, few of the 23 instruments he made have survived and, with van den Gheyn's death, history repeated itself and the art of tuning bells again disappeared for more than a century. This, and other factors, led to a decline in interest in carillons.

By the end of the 19th century, many an old singing tower had fallen silent because its bells were gone, the instrument was in disrepair, or there was no one left who could play. At the turn of this century, after some 400 years of musical history, even in the Belgian heartland of carillon culture, the elephantine instrument had become an endangered species.

Fortunately, the pre-First World War *Belle Époque* period also became a bell epoch, during which fortuitous forces combined to resurrect interest in and restoration of the carillon. Enthusiasm for its native instrument reemerged, thanks to Belgian **Jef Denijn**. The son of the then Mechelen carillonneur, Jef, although himself more than proficient on the bells, already had begun a career in engineering when the senior Denijn lost his sight. Fate seems to have stepped in, for at the age of 19, the son was allowed to fill his father's shoes at the keyboard in St. Rombout's. Jef Denijn quickly demonstrated such skills as a carillonneur that he became a star. The series of Monday summer evening carillon concerts he initiated in the early years of this century became so popular that special trains had to be put on to transport audiences numbering as many as 20,000, who came from Brussels and Antwerp to hear him.

Not only did Denijn have dazzling keyboard skills, but he introduced a new, distinctively Flemish style of playing the carillon called the *tremolo*, which is still popular today. The *tremolo*, which adds more notes and volume, is produced by the rapid alternation of two notes, a technique meant to simulate resonance. This was a particularly welcome playing aid, since old carillon bells tend to lose resonance, especially in their upper registers.

Carillon music, as an integral aspect of local culture, reflects national tastes. Carillonneurs may compose original music for the bells, or transpose or otherwise adapt other keyboard pieces. The Belgian repetoire is romantic, with more trills and ornamental embellishments on the higher bells. Also, as **Aimé Lombaert**, stadbeiaardier of Bruges, explains, "Because our carillons in Belgium are so high, we need more sound." Hence, bigger bells, played more flamboyantly. North American carillon players tend to favor a less "notey," starker style on their home keyboards.

Under Denijn's direction in Mechelen, the carillon became a more popular instrument with the public than it ever had been. He adapted music from folk songs to classics to current hits to suit the instrument, as well as composing an array of original works. He also made some structural refinements, standardizing the keyboard and improving the clapper system. During World War I, Denijn was a refugee in England, where he used his influence to awaken interest in carillons there. About this time in England, a clergyman from Sussex, **Arthur Simpson**, rediscovered the necessary knowledge to tune bells successfully, which resulted in the opening of two foundries in England which produced superb new instruments. Many of these carillons found their way on board ship to the U.S. and Canada, where the taste for bells was on a rapid rise.

By the early 1920s, Jef Denijn already had been lifted to legendary status for his keyboard brillance, but he made a further contribution to the carillon culture of his country that has long outlasted his personal playing prowess. One of his greatest admirers was the U.S. ambassador to Belgium, William Gorham Rice, whose personal dream was to cover his own country with carillons and populate it with well-trained carillonneurs. Rice wrote books to kindle Americans' interest in bell music, and raised money from the Rockefeller Foundation, augmented by funds from the Belgian government and city officials, which enabled Denijn, in his 25th anniversary year as Mechelen's *stadsbeiaardier*, to open the world's first carillon school in 1922. **Mechelen's Royal Carillon School**, flourishing today in its business of educating new generations of players of the bells, has about 40 international students in attendance each year. One among several U.S. graduates of Mechelen is Massachusetts resident Sally Slade Warner, who is especially glad for Ambassador Rice's dream of more carillons for America. The number of carillons in the U.S. today is approaching 200. A carillonneur for the Phillips Academy, Andover school and St. Stephen's church at Cohasset, Warner benefits professionally from living in the Massachusetts/Connecticut area, where there's a "clump" of nine carillons.

The state of Texas, too, has gathered a congregation of carillons, reaching a baker's dozen in number with the 1988 installation of a new instrument at Baylor University. Many of North America's carillons can be found at colleges, where they add notes of distinction to campuses. In Canada, the province of Ontario has the greatest concentration of carillons, with the 53-bell instrument in the Peace Tower in Ottawa considered by many musicians to be the country's best.

Although its carillon school certainly solidified Mechelen's position as the mecca of bell music, the city's carillon reputation is long standing, as attested to by the fact that the words in the Russian language for carillon are *Mechelen bells*. It's not surprising that back in 1583, Mechelen produced the first carillon with pedals. A town guide told me that, since the 15th century, Mechelen has always sought the newest systems for its bells and was the first town in Flanders to have a Hemony-cast carillon.

So it was simply a continuation of a long history when Mechelen lowered a new state-of-the-art carillon of 49 bells into St. Rombout's tower in June 1981. Though the old Hemony bells were sentimental favorites, the Mechelen city council voted to replace rather than repair the carillon of which they formed a part. Mechelen's old 49-bell carillon was typical of many, in that its bells had accumulated from several foundries, in this case 12, over nearly five centuries (1460–1947). The old carillon remains housed just beneath the new one in St. Rombout's tower, a delicate masterpiece of Gothic Brabant architecture that now holds 80 tons of bells. Famed bell founder and restorer **Eijsbouts** of Asten, Holland, created for Mechelen a new carillon whose brilliance of sound is breathtaking; many experts consider it the best in the world—for the moment.

Despite superb technology of casting and tuning, over the years, certainly over centuries, bells do wear down and begin to ring false. Sally Slade Warner shows a carillonneur's soul when saying, "You learn to love the old carillons despite the jarring jangle of their

worn-out sound." When the sound does go off a bit, the care of carillons can include grinding out some of the insides of a bell, which,
to a limit, can get it to ring true again, though the procedure raises
the pitch.

Appropriate to its position as home of the world's *first* carillon
school—since 1953 there has been a highly-respected *second* one, **De
Nederlandse Beiaardschool**, in Holland, in Amersfoort, near
Utrecht—Mechelen has more (four) carillons than any other city in
the world. In centuries past, however, several Belgium cities had
many more than that number. Before the revolution in 1793, for instance, Liège in Belgium's Wallonia boasted 19; Brussels claimed
nine carillons in the 17th century, but today has only one (in St.
Michel Cathedral, the national church at Belgium), under the care of
Paula van de Wiele, one of Belgium's half dozen women carillonneurs and a graduate of Mechelen's Royal Carillon School.

When Mechelen's music students are in residence (October to
July) and need to practice, there can't be too many carillons in the
city. As it is, visitors to Mechelen may hear carillon music by students
at any time—except, that is, for Silent Week, prior to Easter. Easter
Day brings a resounding resurrection.

In summer, when students are away, there's never a lack of talented
takers at Mechelen's carillon keyboards. The public can enjoy several
regularly scheduled concerts weekly, including Monday nights from
8:30-9:30 p.m., preceeded by an invigorating tour up the 514-step
tower for those who haven't worn out their feet during the day. The
climb is easier in St. Rombout's than in many another carillon tower
because of broad, low steps, a result of the entire tower being restored in the early 1980s to be sure it could shoulder its burden of
bells.

There are several stop-off sights as one travels up the tower to the
carillonneur's "cabin." One room, 160 steps up, reveals a 17th-cen-
tury crane, actually a large wooden wheel, in which two men
"walked around," using solely foot power to lift bells as heavy as
Mechelen's beloved 20,000-pound **Salvator**, Belgium's biggest bell,
which dates from the year 1480, to the top of St. Rombout's
300-foot tower.

Although bells can lose their song through a crack or simply wear
out with use, as the old carillon of Mechelen did, the material of the
bells—metal: 80% brass, 20% tin—historically has made them more
vulnerable to war than to wear and weather. Over the centuries,
many a commander of foreign troops occupying the resistanceless

lands of Belgium and Holland has literally taken a town's toll, by confiscating its carillon bells and sending them home to be melted into mortar. Carillons sometimes survived such ignominious ends through the extraordinary efforts of citizens who somehow managed to lower to the ground, and bury, their bells.

Nazis who occupied Holland and Belgium during World War II followed suit, shipping the insides of many singing towers back to munitions factories in Germany to keep their war machine going against those who had supplied the materials. Most presumably disappeared into the furnaces of Nazi armament factories. While the war took a heavy toll on big bells in Belgium, replacement orders came quickly at its conclusion.

Many who really know bells would argue that the finest carillon in Belgium—some say the world—today is **St. Rombout's** in Mechelen. But despite Mechelen's many merits, it is Bruges that probably can claim to have the most famous of the Flemish instruments, since the bells are heard by the many visitors to the lovely town. One, **Henry Wordsworth Longfellow**, wrote of that carillon in his 1845 *The Belfry of Bruges*: "I heard a heart of iron beating in that ancient tower." The 47 bells, under the able hands of **Aimé Lombaert** and occasional guest carillonneurs, ring out four concerts a week in summer. Nearly 1000 people a day climb the 366 steps to see the 245-year-old instrument and, along the way, get to view the equally aged, world's largest automatic mechanism, a nine-ton brass drum with 30,500 holes set—and reset by hand in new tunes periodically by Lombaert —in careful patterns of pegs, which pull wires to produce the four different melodies that strike the quarter hours on the clock of Bruges' elegant octagonal Belfort.

Not only the people who make and play them, but carillon bells themselves can have personalities and documented histories. Some bells have both names and epitaphs cast around their broad rims. Ghent has such a one, six-ton **Roeland**, the largest in the 53-voice carillon. Around its rim reads an inscription that refers to the historical role of bells in announcing urgent news: "My name is Roeland. When I clap there is fire. When I toll there is a storm in Flanders." Ghent's carillon, the only one remaining of seven that once rang in the city, was restored in the early 1980s. It has a marvelous sound, according to Sally Slade Warner, who has played it and many other carillons in Belgium but, she notes sadly, can't be heard well because of the poor openings in its tower and noise from vehicular traffic around its base.

There's now a 63-bell, five-octave carillon in Belgium, unique in Europe, in the university city of Louvain, near Brussels. After World War I, a carillon—with one bell for each of the 48 states which then constituted the Union—had been presented to Louvain by American engineering societies to commemorate their colleagues who died in that conflict in Belgium. When that carillon fell into disrepair in recent years, Americans again pledged funds, which were added to by Belgians, and now Louvain has an exciting new instrument. The carillon is used by Louvain University students under instruction from visiting carillon players from nearby Mechelen.

Another notable Belgium carillon can be heard in Antwerp at the cathedral. Concerts from its singing tower offer superb occasions to sit, sip a drink, and savor the surroundings of the charming old historic center of town.

Sounds as much as sights impress memories on the mind. The joyful jangle of notes tumbling from a carillon tower could be among the most lasting of your recollections of travels in Belgium. As Aimé Lombaert notes about playing in the Belfort at Bruges: "Music makes people happy, and a carillon is the instrument which can give this feeling more than any other."

ORGANS

Another musical instrument tuned in to Belgian culture is the organ. As **James David Christie**, member of the *American Guild of Organists* and organ player with the *Boston Symphony Orchestra*, notes, Belgium has a number of organs that date from the 17th, 18th, and 19th centuries.

Christie has the credentials to comment on organs in Belgium. In 1979, he won **The International Organ Competition** held in Bruges, the first American ever to do so, and has returned since to serve on the jury for the competition. In 1990, Christie was invited to Brussels to play the dedication concert for the newly reconstructed organ of the **Eglise du Sablon** on the Grand Sablon. It's indicative of the high honor in which organs are held in Belgium that when the American bank J.P. Morgan Inc. wanted to present the city of Brussels with a special gift, the project settled upon was the restoration of this instrument. The Sablon organ is in the Franco-Flemish tradition—a certain style of stop specifications and voicing techniques that affects how the organ "speaks". (It was rebuilt by Georg Westenfelder, a German who now lives and works in Luxembourg, and who Christie considers preeminent among organ builders in the world today.)

In addition to the organ at **St. Gilles**, on which the Bruges International Organ Contest was held, the one in Bruges' **St. Salvator Cathedral**, housed in a beautiful case, has been restored as an electric instrument, designed for an ecclectic range of music. The organ at **St. Annakerk** (near Bruges' Lace School), while not a great musical instrument, is well worth visiting for its lovely case.

Lengthy major restoration—begun in 1965—of **Onze Lieve Vrouwekerk** (the Cathedral) **of Antwerp**, the largest Gothic church in Belgium, was finished in the spring of 1993. (It was a centerpiece for Antwerp's activities in celebration of its selection as Culture Capital of Europe for 1993.) The Cathedral's organ also has been redone, and the combination of music and Rubens' masterpieces specifically painted for the setting provides an experience worth traveling to enjoy.

MUSICIANS

Perhaps Belgium's best known composer is **Cesar Franck** (1822-1890), born and raised in Liège, where he attended that city's *Conservatoire de Musique*—which has erected a monument to its most famous former student. Franck studied piano, making a concert tour when only 11, and received the Liège Conservatoire's first prize for piano at age 13. With his father's encouragement and later, perhaps, exploitation of his talent, at 14 he entered the Paris Conservatory, where he was a brilliant student, winning prizes for piano and also for organ, the instrument upon which he eventually concentrated for both composition and performance. Many authorities find Franck's works for the organ the finest since Bach, and his association with that instrument may well have begun during his formative Belgian days of musical training and development. He was principal organist of Sainte Clotilde in Paris for the last 32 years of his life, when, contemporaries reported, much of his greatest music composition was lost simply because it was improvised during organ concerts and never written down. He was appointed professor of organ at the Paris Conservatory in 1872. Cesar Franck is widely played in his native country of Belgium, where his music received a particularly wide hearing in 1990, in observation of the 100th anniversary of his death.

Born in Dinant, Belgium, in 1814, **Adolphe Sax** presented the world with the *saxophone* shortly after 1840. The keyed instrument with a conical tube and single reed made its first appearance in an orchestra in France in 1845. Although the saxophone and its family members achieved vogue in America in popular orchestras, jazz bands, and symphonic jazz compositions, it also has been employed in serious music without jazz content, in works by Debussy, Ravel, Prokofiev, Shostakovich, Richard Strauss, and Vaughan Williams. Sax died in Paris in 1894.

For the occasion of the centennial of the death of Adolphe Sax, inventor of the saxophone, the Belgian town of Dinant has scheduled events to celebrate its most famous son. **Sax Year** will open with a weekend music festival June 18 and 19. From October 30 through November 5, 1994, Dinant will host an international saxophone competition. The finale of that festival event will be a procession on November 5 of 1,000 saxophonists and the unveiling of the official Adolphe Sax Memorial.

Though Belgium's **Maurice Maeterlink's** tragic masterpiece *Pelleas and Melisande* (1893) was a prose play (see under *The Muse,* following), it inspired many of the period's finest composers to create well-known works. Gabriel Fauré adapted the incidental music he composed for the London stage debut (1898) of Maeterlink's play into an orchestra suite that remains one of his most performed works. Debussy's opera (1902) is also based on the Belgian's play, as is Schoenberg's tone poem (1903). Sibelius' similarly named suite for orchestra is derived from incidental music that the composer wrote for the drama's first presentation in Finland in 1905.

The work of another French-speaking Belgian writer, **Charles de Coster** (1827-1879), best recalled for his *Legend and Adventures of Til Ulenspiegel,* the fateful tale of a Flemish rogue, inspired German composer Richard Strauss's 1895 orchestral tone poem *Till Eulenspiegel's Merry Pranks.*

A more popular and recent composer, **Jacques Brel**, needs no introduction for his songs, which evoke many moods concerning the Belgian people and *le pays plat,* Belgium's flat polder land along the North Sea. There is a Jacques Brel institute in Brussels.

MUSIC FESTIVALS

The **Festival of Flanders** (*Festival van Vlaanderen*) is a multi-month musical affair held throughout the Flemish-speaking northern region of Belgium. Focused in Kortrijk (reputed for its choral music) in April; Tongeren in May; Bruges in August; Ghent, Brussels, and Leuven in September; and Mechelen and Antwerp in October, the Festival of Flanders brings together leading musicians for events in magnificent historic settings. For information, call Brussels ☎ *(02) 648 14 84.*

Naturally, a sister music festival, the **Festival of Wallonia**, takes place annually in Belgium's French-speaking southern provinces of Wallonia, in various cities, including Tournai and Liège, during the summer and fall. Resident companies, international orchestras, and guest soloists perform in varied venues: opera houses, cathedrals, abbeys, and castles. For information, call Liège ☎ (041) 22 32 48.

CELEBRATED COMPETITION

Belgium's **Queen Elizabeth International Music Competition**, one of the world's most exacting and exciting, has existed for more than 30 years. It was founded by the country's former Queen Elizabeth, herself a violinist, and rotates in the three categories of violin, piano, and voice. The elimination rounds and finals (ticketed public events) are held in Brussels in May at the *Conservatoire* and *Palais des Beaux-Arts*, respectively, with the top prizewinners accompanied by the **Orchestre National de Belgique**. Winners also perform in concerts throughout Belgium in May and June.

THE MUSE

The Netherlands (Low Countries) produced its share of scholars, philosophers, and authors over the centuries. Some of the finest early writing to come from the region appeared in times when the *lingua franca* of intellectuals was Latin, but literature in the language of the people became more common after the signing of the *Treaty of Utrecht* (1579), which began the political process that eventually led to the establishment of the separate countries of Belgium and Holland.

In Belgium, no writers of distinction appeared after Flemish Antwerp's 16th-century *Golden Age* until a literary revival began with the country's complete independence from Holland in 1830. Thereafter, a Flemish language movement began, under the influence of **Jan Frans Willems**, a poet who generated interest in Flemish folk songs and literature, and **Hendrik Conscience**. (See *Flanders: An Introduction*.)

More recently, with the few exceptions suitably noted further on, literary critics have paid little attention to Belgian writers beyond their borders. A good deal of the international ignorance about contemporary Belgian literature can be attributed to the ongoing problem of language. Writers from Belgium's French-speaking Wallonia often are considered to *be* French, an understandable impression since many move to Paris to achieve success in the larger French-language marketplace of France. Those in Belgium's Flanders who write in Dutch rarely are translated, the cost being too considerable for any but the most successful books.

BELGIAN AUTHORS

Hendrik Conscience (1812–1883), born in Antwerp to a French-speaking father and Flemish mother, began to write soon after Belgium had become a nation in 1830. He is regarded as the father of modern Flemish literature, since he was the first to write fiction in Flemish, which had been a dying literary language. Conscience is best known for the historical romance *The Lion of Flanders* (published in 1838), which, set in the period 1298-1305 in the Bruges of medieval guilds and clothworkers, in the era of Philip the Fair and the Battle of the Golden Spurs (still colorfully reenacted), remains a good romantic read. Conscience presents highly accurate and ample period detail and pageant-like descriptions of Flemish history.

Maurice Maeterlinck (1862-1949) was born of old Flemish stock, though both parents were French-speaking, into a conservative, wealthy Roman Catholic family in Ghent. In 1911, he won the *Nobel Prize for Literature*, the only Benelux writer ever to have earned that honor. Maeterlinck's best work was produced in the first half of his life. His *Onirologie*, with a U.S.-born principal character who has strange dreams about his unknown Dutch origin, shows the influence of American authors Poe and Hawthorne. His play *The Blind* caused him to be called the creator of static theater, which Samuel Beckett developed some 60 years later. Maeterlinck's masterpiece, *Pelleas and Melisande*, was first published in 1893. His last book, *Bulles Bleues* (1948), which recaptured happy memories of his youth and young manhood in Flanders, was widely read, as were his essays on Ralph Waldo Emerson.

Ironically, though a writer whose poems, plays, and lyric prose inspired many major composers (see under "Musicians" in previous "Music" section), Maeterlinck himself neither understood nor liked music. He lived more than 50 years of his long life in France, but never renounced his Belgian citizenship. Though in midlife a figure of international repute, better appreciated in England and the U.S. than at home, Maeterlinck had fallen into obscurity by the time of his death, and he is now best recognized in his native Belgium.

Georges Simenon (1903–1989) is undoubtedly the best-known of all Belgian authors, although he is often thought to be French, since that is the language in which he wrote and it was to Paris he headed in his early 20s, leaving his native Liège to seek a wider market for his works. Simenon is credited with revising the entire approach to the detective story, the literary form for which he is best known. He created the character *Inspector Maigret* in 1934. Many of the 80-odd Maigret stories seem sordid in setting, but at closer glance can be seen as intense psychological studies that deal less with crime than with uneasy, unfulfilled lives. In later years, Simenon produced more ambitious psychological analyses of modern man. The prodigiously prolific Simenon—he wrote more than 200 novels under his own name and another 300 or so under 17 pseudonyms, with total sales well over half a billion—is one of the most widely translated authors in history, with works appearing in more than 50 languages; perhaps a third of his output has been translated into English.

BELGIAN LITERARY LEGEND

Not an author but a prominent Belgian literary figure nonetheless, created by English mystery writer Agatha Christie, is detective **Hercule Poirot**, who drops information about Belgium as he winds his way through the considerable Christie *oeuvre* in which he is centrally cast. The brilliant, benevolent-despot bachelor character, which Christie created in 1916 for her first detective novel, received his Brussels-born Belgian identity because Christie, like many English in the World War I era, had opened her heart to the World War I sufferings of refugees from German-occupied Belgium, some of whom were being sheltered in a parish near her home. Among the many Belgian characteristics displayed by Poirot is his passionate interest in fine food.

So real had Belgian Hercule Poirot become to readers through the pen of Christie, that when he "died" at her hands in 1975, among his many obituaries was a front-pager in *The New York Times* (8/6/75).

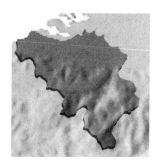

FOOD AND DRINK

White asparagus: Belgium's "white gold."

FOOD

You'll enjoy superior food in Belgium, whether it's a gourmet re-past in a superb setting at one of Brussels' stellar-rated restaurants (many an epicurean European considers Brussels second to none as a culinary capital) or sampling street stand specialties such as *frites* (called French fries, but actually created, and perfected, by *Belgians*) and *gaufres* (waffles) that will redefine your ideas about "fast food." Throughout Belgium, wherever and whenever food is concerned, high standards in ingredients, preparation, and presentation prevail.

Apart from Brussels' most famous and fashionable restaurants, where costs have taken to the stratosphere—Eurocrat and multinational corporate expense accounts help support high prices—travelers will discover that eateries in Belgium in every category deliver value for money. The reason this appetizing situation exists has little to do with tourists and everything to do with the fact that Belgians themselves like to eat well.

The Belgian kitchen is influenced by the French in the use of sauces, but is generally more substantial, with servings less skimpy in size. A statement that's almost a cliché could characterize Belgian cuisine: food having the *quality* of the French and the *quantity* of the German.

Considerable use is made of fresh local seasonal fare. Many kitchens pride themselves on regional dishes, some of which have become known far beyond regional boundaries. In the coastal areas of Belgium there's a focus on seafood, while rivers provide plentiful fresh- water fish. Chefs in the Belgium Ardennes pay particular attention to *paté*, the renowned *jambon d'Ardennes* and, in season, concentrate on game.

The Belgian culinary calendar contains several other select seasons. A six-week period in May and June is much anticipated for the white asparagus that's known locally as "white gold," not because of export profits—supply can scarcely meet local demand—but for its delicate taste. The traditional style of serving asparagus is with a sauce of melted butter, chopped hard-boiled egg, and bits of cooked ham. During approximately the same spring period, the much-savored first tender shoots of the hops plants (grown for use in Belgium's intensive beer production) also are served up.

Mussels (*moules/mosselen*) are such favored fare in Belgium that the coming of a new season—in the months with a letter "R," in the name, beginning with September—is eagerly anticipated. Restaurants may post signs proclaiming *Les moules sont arrivées* ("Mussels have arrived!"). You'll look like a local feasting on mussels—waiters will keep bringing bowls full, until you beg off—if you hold a full shell in your left hand (if you're right-handed), and use an empty hinged- shell in your right hand as an eating utensil. One of the most popular methods of preparation is *Moules à la Bruxelloise*: steamed in dry white wine and chopped onions.

Despite the importance of seasons for some foods, the rich flat polderlands of Belgium boast an incredible acreage of greenhouses, and the intensive agriculture undertaken in them now makes a

healthy variety of hothouse vegetables available year-round. They
supply not only shops and family tables in Belgium and the rest of
the EC, but supermarkets across the U.S. and Canada. Thanks to
tender packing and air transport from Brussels' Zaventem—located
not far from the vegetable auctions held at Mechelen, a town so
proud of its produce that it puts it on parade each September in the
amusing *Vegetable Corso*—an appealing array finds its way to kitchens
worldwide.

Appetizing appetizers to a Belgian meal include small North Sea
"grey" shrimp, which Belgians eat on buttered bread, or *tomates aux
crevettes* (tomatoes stuffed with the tiny shrimp). Ostend oysters are
considered superior in these parts. Belgian chicory, or *witloof*
("white leaf" endive), and Brussels sprouts duly make their welcome
appearance (though sprouts are not offered as often in Brussels as
they are in the U.K.).

In cosmopolitan centers like Brussels, continental/French cuisine
is the rule at many restaurants. But typical Belgian dishes are found
on many a menu. *Carbonnades Flamandes*, a beer-simmered beef
stew is a popular Belgian dish. An order for *filet américain* could
come as a surprise: it's not Chicago steak, but *steak tartare* (raw
chopped beef mixed with many herbs). Ghent's famous *waterzooi* is
a satisfying creamy fish—sometimes chicken—stew.

Rabbit is a mainstay on menus in Belgium. Two of the best-known
dishes are *lapin aux pruneaux* (marinated rabbit fried with prunes)
and *lapin de garenne aux griottes* (wild rabbit cooked with vegetables, white wine, and sour cherries). Pork is popular in the Belgian
Ardennes. Also a delicacy from the Ardennes in hunting season is
marcassin (young wild boar). *Boudin de Liège* is a savory, herb-fla-
vored sausage.

Apart from the region's more formally prepared dishes, informal
fare can be fun. First, there are the famed *frites*, potatoes double-
fried to what many feel is perfection, served at stands throughout
Belgium in sturdy paper cones with a dollop of mayonnaise—which
you may discover to be a more compatible condiment than catsup.

Belgium waffles (*gaufres*), cooked on the spot in sidewalk shops in
cast-iron molds and handed to you warm, come in two kinds: pre-
sweetened dough (Liège-style), and unsweetened dough sprinkled
with confectioners' sugar (Brussels-style). Both have a wonderful vanilla flavoring. *Speculoos* are mixed spice and ginger cookies that may
be baked in oversize figure molds or come packaged in more portable sizes.

Although mention of the fresh, rich, Belgian handmade filled chocolates called *pralines* have been left to the end, you'll probably be
tempted by them early on if you have anything of a sweet tooth—
and heaven help you if you're a chocoholic! *Godiva* is a home-brand
in Brussels, but it's still very pricey there. Buy your chocolates at one
of the several lower-overhead *Leonidas* street-front shops where the
Bruxelloise know the quality is the same and the price much better.

DRINK

Belgian food can be made more pleasurable by indulging in the indigenous drink that rounds out the regional experience. Although
Belgium once produced wine from vineyards located along the
Meuse River, the grape stocks were lost as a result of battles that
raged in the region during World War I. Now beer and a long-
standing brewing tradition make Belgium outstanding—and
unique—in the drink department.

BELGIAN BEER

Belgians themselves support their multiple local breweries by par-
taking in substantial intake. In a recent Brewers Association of Canada poll of the world's top countries ranked for annual beer
consumption *per capita*, Belgians ranked fourth. (Germans placed
first, the U.S. 12th, Canada 14th.) Whether production is the horse
and consumption the cart, or *vice versa*, Belgium is beer territory.

In Belgium, beer is treated with the respect and good form that
elsewhere are reserved for wine. Long a source of pleasure for peasants and working-class people—as can be seen in scenes from 16th-
and 17th-century Flemish paintings by Pieter Bruegel the Elder,
David Teniers, and others—in the late 20th century traditional Belgian beers have found acceptance in the gastronomic world as well.
Although the *hoi polloi* might not care to create a beer list instead of
a wine carte to accompany a six-course repast, serious interest in beer
"culture" certainly is not limited to Belgium's *haut monde*.

While language can't unite Belgium, devotion to beer does. Even
when wine is served with the meal, beer frequently is the Belgian
aperitif of choice. (One aficionado speaks of Brussels' *gueuze* as having the taste of *fino* sherry and the sparkle of champagne.) Small Belgian specialty brewers pride themselves on giving their product
"bouquet," "palate," and "finish" (aftertaste); tasters speak of the
"nose" of the brew. Beer isn't served just to accompany a dish; it
may be used *in* it, in which case regional dishes enter the realm of
cuisine de la bière.

Beers in Belgium may be blended like wines, aged like wines (in wooden casks for two or three years), bottled and corked like wines, presented like wines (in different kinds of stemware: flutes, goblets, snifters), served chilled like white wines or closer to room temperatures like reds, and may even *taste* remarkably like wines, sometimes being referred to as the "Burgundies of Belgium." Of the more than 600 kinds of beer brewed in Belgium, the differences in taste among them can be as substantial as those between a Cabernet and a Chablis.

The alcoholic content of Belgian beer varies considerably from one kind to another. In North America most beers are 3% to 4%, while in Belgium the evocatively named *Duvel* ("devil" in Flemish) isn't the most potent at 8.2%, nor are "Lucifer" or "Forbidden Fruit," both at 9%. Beers in Belgium can be as high as 12% alcohol: those setting out on a "pub crawl" there stand forewarned!

On the large scale, Belgium's modern brewing plants have kept pace with technology, producing classical beers of a high degree of purity for a worldwide population that shows increasing demand. *Stella*, a premium pils from the Artois Brewery, founded in 1366, is the country's best known internationally. At the same time, Belgium maintains tradition with an amazing range of beers from small producers that make its brewing industry unique in the world.

There are three schools of beer brewing in Belgium: low (bottom) fermentation; high (top) fermentation; and spontaneous fermentation. The high and low distinction refers to fermentation temperatures, and has nothing to do with the percentage of alcohol in the beer. Low fermentation beers are brewed from light malt and ferment for ten days at a temperature between 43°–50° F (6°–10°C). During the process, a yeast sediment is formed on the bottom of the vat. All light beers of the *pilsener* type—a method developed in the Czechoslovakian town of Pilzen—are bottom fermented. These beers should be served cold, in clear, tall glasses. Nearly 80% of Belgium's considerable annual beer production is *pils*, primarily produced in large commercial breweries.

High fermentation beers are brewed by infusion from dark malt. The fermentation period lasts a maximum of five days and takes place at the relatively high temperature of 60°–70° F (15°–21°C). At the end of fermentation, the yeast forms a thick scum on the surface of the beer that must be skimmed off. Top fermented beers can be recognized by their dark color, and they include most "special" Belgian beers. These beers should be served warmer than pils, in short-stemmed rounded goblets. Somewhat more than 10% of Belgian beer production is in the wide-ranging number of specialty beers produced at relatively small to very small regional breweries throughout the country.

Apart from their specific brewing processes, color is one of the distinguishing features of Belgian "specials." **Rodenbach**, a slightly bitter beer matured in wooden barrels by the Roulers Brewery, is red. **Hoegaarden**, a village east of Louvain, is among the few remaining breweries producing "white" (a bittersweet wheat) beer. **Oudenaarde**, in the south of East Flanders province, is known for its dark brown beers, which owe their color partly to an addition of caramel. Even deeper in color is the authentic **Trappist beer**, today still produced only by five abbeys in Belgium (and one in Holland).

The final, roughly 10% of Belgium production, is in so-called *spontaneous fermentation* beers, which result, literally, from something "in the air" in Brussels. This category, with curious old names such as *lambic, gueuze, kriek, framboise*, and *faro*, covers beers brewed solely in the Senne River Valley in and around Brussels. A striking detail of these 70% malt/30% wheat beers is that no yeast is added. Whereas air is the worst enemy of brewers of low and high fermentation beers, it is an indispensable ally to creators of spontaneous fermentation beers. Their fermentation results from a natural microflora, existent only in the Senne Valley air, that reacts with the boiled malt/wheat/hops mixture while it cools in large *open* vats. The beer thus produced, *lambic*, must be stored for between one and two years, after which it is bottled, to undergo a secondary fermentation in the bottle. A mix of young and older lambic produces *gueuze*. Still later, cherries may be added to form *kriek*, raspberries to produce *framboise*, or sugar candy to form *faro* beer.

The Belgian Brewers Association has its headquarters on Brussels' Grand Place in the gilt-highlighted **Brewers Guildhall**, which dates from 1696. Appropriately, it also serves as a small beer museum. Of the dozens of breweries that have existed in Brussels over the centuries, only one survives as a traditional *brasserie*: century-old **Cantillon**. It opens as a gueuze "museum" during the brewing season (mid-October through April). It's on the roof of Cantillon that the secret to its success is seen: an enormous vat topped with tiles tilted to let in the air, Brussels' atmospheric "yeast," which creates the city's unique brew.

It is said that there are some 200 different tastes of beer in Belgium, and about 600 labels. (The number changes somewhat, as new or seasonal beers from small breweries come on the market, and others disappear.) That number requires a lot of learning on the part of bartenders-to-be. Not only do they need to know the *kinds* of beers (and the different labels for each), but *which* goes in *what* glass and the proper pouring procedure for each. Imagine having to memorize where as many as 300 kinds of beer are stored—that's the approximate number on sale at *De Bruyne* pub in Bruges, where the owner also runs a Beer Academy—so you can put your hand on any given one when a customer orders it. Plenty of intriguing conversations with waiters await travelers to Belgian beer pubs.

BELGIUM

Belgium's flat Flemish countryside.

THE BELGIAN LANDSCAPE

For its size—30,500 sq. kilometers/11,775 sq. miles—Belgium has a remarkable variety of scenery, with countryside that can change character in two dozen miles. Clockwise from the northwest, where the North Sea fronts Belgium's sand dune and broad beach shore, the country is bordered by Holland to the north, Germany to the east, Luxembourg to the southeast, and France to the southwest.

The north (**Flanders**) and south (**Wallonia**) of Belgium are not only different from each other linguistically and culturally (see "The

Belgian People"), but topographically. In general, the north is much flatter, with some areas, especially in the province of *West Flanders*, lying below sea level. There, the land had to be reclaimed from the sea. Between the 8th and 13th centuries, a 12-by-30-mile-wide strip of low-lying coastal land was, through the use of sluices, transformed from salty swamp into fine polder farmland that remains among Belgium's richest. Rows of sentinel-like trees that form wind-breakers along cross-country canals are one of the distinctive sights in this part of Flanders.

The **Kempen**, in northern Belgium, is a large section of land between the *Schelde* and the *Maas* rivers that reaches through the provinces of Antwerp and Limburg. Its terrain changes from moorland, heath, and lakes to extensive pine forests and orchards as one moves from west to east. West Flanders' **Heuvelland**, a presently peaceful district of lakes and walking trails south of Ieper, was the heart of Belgium's battlefield in World War I.

Wallonia, roughly the southern half of Belgium, also is varied but overall more wooded and hilly than Flanders. This section of the country has an industrial sash stretched across it from Liège to Tournai, and in the past was prominent for coal production.

A large area of Wallonia is covered by the forests of the **Ardennes**. The most elevated area (600 meters/1600 feet, with winter skiing) is the **Hautes Fagnes**, located in the mostly German-speaking **Cantons de l'Est** in the far east of Belgium near the German border. The Ardennes is bounded and intersected by the castle-fortified cliffs of the **Meuse Valley** and the smaller but equally picturesque river valleys of the **Sambre, Ourthe** and **Semois**. Belgium's annual rainfall is lowest on the Belgian coast and highest in the Ardennes, where it feeds the rushing rivers that have carved the countryside. The region is famous for its **caves** (see Han–Sur–Lesse under "The Meuse Valley"). Because of its natural beauty, the Ardennes has been one of Belgium's major tourist areas for several centuries, with towns such as *Spa* and *Dinant* appearing on many a "Grand European Tour" itinerary.

There are few places where rivers or mountains distinctly separate Belgium from Holland, France, Germany, or Luxembourg. This circumstance has left the country open to invasion by foreign armies for virtually all of its recorded history. Yet, internally, Belgium has a very clearly defined border: one of language. Its **language frontier**, running roughly east to west through the country's center, makes the single geopolitical entity of Belgium a nation *divisible* culturally.

THE BELGIAN PEOPLE

While "England and America are two countries separated by the same language" (according to Irishman George Bernard Shaw), Belgium inherited the decidedly stickier situation of being *one country separated by two languages*. Stickier still, Belgium could be said not to be inhabited by Belgians. As people there say, the situation "is not so simple."

Belgium is home to both the **Flemish** in the north and the **Walloons** in the south; the former speak *Dutch*, the latter *French*. The second language of either is as likely to be English as the other of Belgium's two official tongues. Only in such crucial areas as supporting the country's team in *European Cup* football (soccer) or speaking up on behalf of its renowned cuisine, do most Belgians overcome regional identities for a national one.

While the Flemish and the Walloons can be tentative about being Belgian, the 85,000 people who live in the mostly rural Eastern Cantons (125 miles southeast of Brussels) and speak *German* (Belgium's truly "minority language") are ardent believers in Belgium. Though they live near the German border, watch German TV, and buy German products in Germany (where taxes on many items are lower), these Belgians aren't at all ambiguous about what country they are citizens of.

Belgium's internal **"language frontier"** dates back to the fifth century, quite faithfully following the line along which local tribes split into those influenced by the region's *Roman* or *Germanic* heritage. The Celtic **Belgae**, whom Julius Caesar noted as the most courageous, as well as the most troublesome tribe he had had to deal with in his conquests, adopted the Latin-based *French* language. The **Franks** remained true to their Germanic origins in the development of *Dutch/Flemish*, which are essentially identical with *Flemish* in written form.

Residents of the land that today is now Belgium were forced by history to follow a constantly changing course of leadership. The region gradually developed identity through **duchies** (such as that of the *Duke of Brabant*) and **counties** (as under the *Counts of Flanders*).

By the time northern Europe was evolving out of the Middle Ages in the mid-15th century, the people from both cultural areas had come under *French Burgundian* rule. French became not only the favored language of the upper class, but also a fashion copied by the educated *bourgeoisie* (a term derived from *burghers* or town citizens);

a social class that virtually began in Belgium's early-to-flourish Flemish towns. (Though today "bourgeoisie" means "middle class" and often carries overtones of the ordinary, at the end of the Middle Ages being a self-supporting citizen of a town was an accomplishment in a Europe where the serf-driven feudal system still held wide sway.) Thus, at that time, it was only the uneducated peasant population in the rural countryside who used the Flemish tongue. Today, despite a plethora of sociopolitical permutations in the centuries since, Belgians still are basically bourgeois in their life style and values, and the French language still retains something of an upper hand in the country's culture.

Belgian culture developed during 2000 years of often all-too-intimate exposure to that of other—occupying—European countries. As a captive audience for its foreign leaders, Belgians absorbed certain outside fashions, but maintained their own deeply rooted qualities over the centuries, up to the relatively recent establishment of an independent Belgium in 1830.

Over centuries under foreign rule, Belgians of both cultures developed a certain indifference to government, a habit of doing their own thing. As a friend in Bruges describes it: "Even today, Belgians look for an escape clause from government because for generations of occupation foreigners made all the rules for them. Belgians are inclined to see all government, even their own, as 'foreign.' Coming from that attitude, many see our 'black money' system—under-the-table arrangements to avoid government taxes—as a kind of national sport."

Though conservative in many ways, Belgians openly admit to not liking regimentation. They may appear undisciplined because of their aversion to rules. Again, my Bruges friend traces this to Belgium's past: "Historically, since Belgians were not ruled by Belgians, they got used to ignoring leaders, and that has carried over to an avoidance of regulation. Belgians don't like following building codes or traffic signs." He's the first to admit that this "leads to disorganization," but returns to the point that it's a trait that "comes out of history."

Belgium has a population of approximately 10 million: 5.7 million are Dutch-speaking Flemish; 3.1 million are French-speaking Walloons; another 1 million are residents of Brussels (where a large majority is French-speaking). An additional half million are foreigners: Eurocrats and diplomats (many countries post diplomatic missions in *triplicate* to Brussels, one each to the European Community,

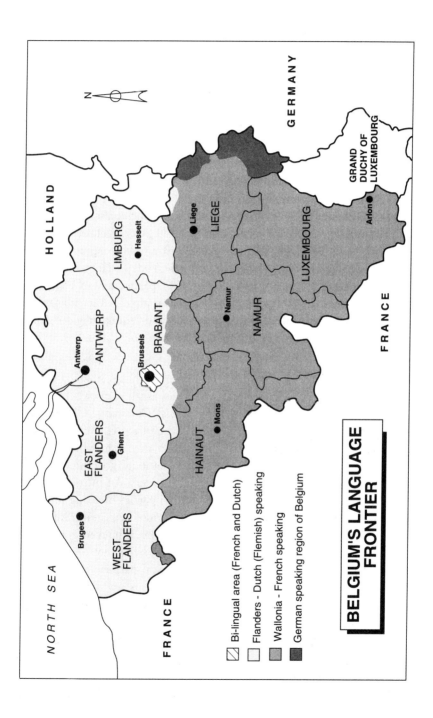

N

HOLLAND

GERMANY

GRAND DUCHY OF LUXEMBOURG

LIMBURG

● Hasselt

● Liege LIEGE

LUXEMBOURG

● Arlon

ANTWERP

● Antwerp

BRABANT

Brussels

● Namur NAMUR

FRANCE

EAST FLANDERS

● Ghent

HAINAUT

● Mons

WEST FLANDERS

● Bruges

NORTH SEA

FRANCE

FRANCE

Bi-lingual area (French and Dutch)

Flanders - Dutch (Flemish) speaking

Wallonia - French speaking

German speaking region of Belgium

BELGIUM'S LANGUAGE FRONTIER

NATO, and the Belgian royal court), as well as immigrant workers (many from Africa, especially Zaire, formerly the Belgian Congo).

As the above figures show, today Belgium's Dutch-speaking Flemish population is decidedly in the majority. Until the last decade or so, however, French speakers more than overcame their numerical inferiority through their domination of the country's culture. While recent legislation on various language issues and the implementation of federalism have worked towards equalizing Belgium's two cultural communities, their "balance" remains part of the Belgian "problem."

During the Reformation in the 16th century, most of Belgium's Protestants eventually headed north to Holland to escape the harsh intolerance of the region's Roman Catholic ruler, Philip II of Spain. With nearly all the population remaining Catholic, religion served as a bridge linking Belgium's two cultures. Today a large number of Belgians still are self-professed Catholics (particularly in Flanders), but during the 20th century, anticlericalism increased so substantially (especially in Wallonia) that eventually the various religious/antireligious movements each wanted their own political parties.

Religion and *politics* affect every Belgian's life, whether or not they choose to participate in either actively. Belgium's political parties represent the same ideological tendencies as those elsewhere in Europe: *Christian Democratic* (called Social Christian), *Conservative* (called Liberal), *Socialist,* and *Green.* When their community's economic situation strengthened in the 1960s, the Flemish began insisting on a stronger voice in the Belgian national government. (For more on the Flemish Movement, see "Flanders: An Introduction.") This resulted in each of the main political parties breaking into two sections, duplicating themselves along linguistic cultural community lines. Since then, *compromis à la Belge* has been an even greater fact of Belgian political life. Despite coalition governments—all but unavoidable due to the splintering of political parties—the language issue often comes ahead of other considerations, and often has led to a falling out, and subsequent "fall" of the current coalition.

Whatever cause for cursing the Flemish and Walloons have between themselves, they stand in similarly estranged circumstances with respect to their contiguous, supposedly culturally related, neighbor countries. In France, for instance, there's little acceptance of French-speaking Walloons as French (in large measure due to their perceived inelegant pronunciation of the language). In Holland the Dutch are inclined to think of the Flemish as rather embarrassing country cousins who speak a dialect. Uncomplimentary Belgian jokes, often taking as their subject a perceived inability to properly use the French or Dutch languages, are told over the borders in both France and Holland. Thus, in the end, Belgium's internal "situation" is so peculiarly its own that it almost creates a national consciousness. Belgians, well aware of the jokes told at their expense, take them pretty well. Some Belgians even manage a smile at the irony that, for all the energy expended on gaining the right to speak their respective languages *inside* their country, *beyond* their borders, Belgians' ability to speak those languages may be regarded as laughable. In any case, only the few extremists in either community ever have thoughts of actually merging with France or Holland—though the issue was the subject of *The Times* of London's annual front-page *April Fools Day* article in 1992.

Other ironic aspects of Belgium's internal language situation can present themselves. In 1986, for example, a small farming village in Flanders, *Fourons*, that lay near the Walloon language boundary (and thus, though officially Flemish-speaking, had a large number of French-speaking residents and was a "protected French-language minority" locale), made headlines. Its French-speaking mayor, Jose Happart, regularly refused to take a required examination that would have revealed his poor knowledge of Flemish. (Fluency in both Belgian languages is legally required in order to hold any government job in Belgium.) Happart expressed his feelings with the logic: "Why should I conduct all official acts in Flemish if most people here speak French?" Flemish officials responded "because Fourons is in Flanders," a not unreasonable insistence, given their hard won right to administer affairs on *their* soil in *their* language. Through media coverage, Happart became a hero in Wallonia, a fiend in Flanders. Today Happart, an elected member of the *European Parliament*, still speaks up on Belgian issues of respective languages and region. However, after a recent lively television debate with a leading Flemish politician, Happart posed a new perspective on the subject by saying: "After all, everybody will speak English in 20 years."

With their complicated sociopolitics, it's no wonder that Belgians take fun in their folklore. Folkloric celebrations in Belgium are loosely referred to as "carnivals." *The* carnival, **Mardi Gras**, is, of course, one of the year's highlights, especially in **Binche**, 30 miles south of Brussels. Then the Walloon town teems with the prancing figures of the *Gilles*, members of a male society who break out annually in dazzling costumes, complete with elaborate eight-pound ostrich-plumed headgear. Although some of Belgium's carnivals are seriously religious—among them Bruges' **Procession of the Holy Blood** and Veurne's brown-cowled, cross-carrying participatory **Process of the Penitents**—many more are only slightly so (as in a David and Goliath-type encounter annually played out by **"giants"** at Ath). Such pagents may also be permeated with pagan traditions, reflect bygone 15th-century Burgundian days, or suggest the 16th--century influence of the Spanish empire.

Historians believe that Belgium's folkloric festivals originated in pre-Christian spring fertility rites (or sun worship—still practiced by many northern Europeans, though in costumes more appropriate for the beach). The introduction of the pageantry element into Belgian folk history can be pinpointed precisely. In response to the **Reformation**, Ghent-born Emperor Charles V, who ruled over much of continental Europe, is credited with creating festivals beginning in 1549 to show the "romance" of Roman Catholicism—in contrast to the puritanism of the Protestant approach to life. Brussels' annual July **Ommegang**, a florid Flemish historical "walkabout" in the Grand Place, is Belgium's grandest show of this kind of carnival. Ostend's **Blessing of the Sea** is a straightforward celebration of that town's fishing industry and longtime maritime flavor. Most Belgian carnival celebrations are fanciful and cheerful, but some meander into the macabre, their enactment giving a glimpse of the *grotesque*, a quality that has been reflected in the area's art over the centuries, from Bosch and Bruegel to 20th-century surrealists Ensor, Magritte, and Delvaux.

Belgians' relationships with their country can be complex, but individual passions are clear. To a person, they appreciate the good things in life, including food and drink. It's a trait said to have held since the country's Burgundian days five centuries ago. Along with a *de rigueur* fervor for football (soccer), cycle-racing stirs the souls of Belgian participants and spectators alike. The annual Flemish **Ronde van Vlaanderen** cycle race is one of the runners-up in excitement to the **Tour de France**.

Many Belgians find pleasure in specialty interests, such as radical adult puppet theater. The **Toone Puppet Theater**, tucked into Brussels' ancient *l'Ilot Sacre* district is the best known of the "establishment" puppet theaters, which dole out strong satire (though usually not in English). See under "Brussels, Entertainment and Events." Comic strip art is so popular that there's a museum, the **Belgian Comic Strip Center**, in Brussels (see also under "What To See and Do") devoted to it. (The late Pierre Culliford, a Belgian artist better known under the professional name of "**Peyo**," was the creator of the *Smurfs*, the internationally popular little blue characters that reflect the local fondness for cartoon and comics art.)

Most unusual of all may be the near mania in certain circles for **pigeon racing**. Before becoming aware of that sport I had, most mistakenly, assumed that the caged pigeons I saw at the Sunday morning *Bird Market* on Brussels' Grand place were destined for dinner tables. The much more interesting story behind the contents of those cages is that Belgium is home to the world's largest number (some 120,000) of *colombophiles* (pigeon fanciers), who get passionate about the roughly 25,000 pigeon races held there each year. Betting on the birds can involve substantial sums.

Unlike their Dutch neighbors to the north, Belgians were not shaped by the sea. While Dutch merchants spent the 17th century garnering wealth by sailing the world, Belgians made their money as at-home industrialists. As a result the Belgian character is clothed in a bourgeois life-style and fed by conservative capitalist ideology. Belgium's prudent and productive market economy runs by methodical, nonspontaneous means. An historically strong belief in free trade results in the basically hardworking labor unions occasionally calling strikes to keep the populace aware of their contribution.

Beyond doubt, Belgians and Belgium defy easy definition But while the country's internal situation can be frustrating and fraught with overtones for residents, visitors with a little insight into the complex nature of the country's bicultural society can enjoy observing the whole intriguing situation.

AN HISTORICAL PERSPECTIVE

Between 57 and 50 B.C., Julius Caesar conquered the northern sector of tri-parted *Gaul*, the land lying in the basins of the *Scheldt* and the *Meuse* rivers. At the time, it was inhabited by Gallo-Celtic tribes, including the *Belgae*. The *Romans* named the region **Gallia Belgica** and occupied it until the 5th century. From the 3rd century, however, Rome's hold began to weaken, and the *Franks*, a loose federation of German tribes, began to penetrate the area. Eventually, the Franks colonized the lower Scheldt, which left only a thin forested stretch from the Scheldt to the Ardennes separating them from the *Wala* (Walloons, or romanized Celts). Thus was set what virtually is the same ethnic and linguistic frontier that runs through the center of Belgium today.

Once the Romans departed, **Clovis**, who was born in 465 in Tournai—then the capital of the Frankish Merovingian kings—conquered all of Gaul (except Burgundy and Provence). He then declared himself Christian, thereby gaining the support of the Roman Catholic Church. After his death in 511, the Gallic territory became splintered, with what today is Belgium becoming merely a remote corner. In 751 **Pepin the Short** ousted the last weak Merovingian ruler and founded the Carolingian dynasty. His son, **Charlemagne**, who reigned from 768 to 814, was declared Emperor of the West by the Pope in 800; his lands reached from Denmark to southern Italy and from northern Spain to the Oder. Under Charlemagne, Belgium had an important position in the empire.

Upon Charlemagne's death, however, fierce fighting broke out between his grandsons, and what had been achieved during his reign was lost in the partitioning of the region. As a result of the warring, the 843 **Treaty of Verdun** divided the "Belgian" area between Charles the Bald and Lothair. Charles, king of West Francia—France, as we more or less know it—received the territory west of the Scheldt (which would become Flanders, and included a part of what is Walloon territory today).

The dissolution of the Carolingian Empire led to the founding of numerous principalities—many of them having kept their names as modern provinces—whose powers were determined by frequently changing alliances. In 864 the **Flanders countship** came into being and, through marriage between dynasties, became strong and unified.

While much of Europe still slept in the Dark Ages—also known as the Middle Ages, lasting until about 1450—Belgium's Flanders began awaking. The **rise of towns** there led to new structures for society by redistributing the population from the countryside where the feudal system still flourished. By 1100 Flanders was firmly established, with Bruges, Ghent, and Ypres rapidly becoming city-states through the power of the privileges bestowed upon them by the Flemish counts. A mastery of mercantilism resulted in wealth that encouraged and supported an active artistic environment. In the 1200s, Ghent and Bruges had become so independent-minded that they hardly recognized the Counts of Flanders' authority, much less that of the French King, to whom Flanders was allegiance-bound.

In 1302 French King-to-be Philip the Fair decided to do away with Flanders (by invading it and overpowering the Count) in order to annex the region's riches to France. Flemish citizens quickly showed how fiercely they were willing to fight for their freedom. Led by weaver Jan Breydel and butcher Pieter de Coninck, a rough-and-ready crowd of tradesmen and craftsmen met at **Kortrijk** to confront an army of France's finest mail-clad knights. The Flemings were armed primarily with devices called *goedendags* ("how do you do's"), small spiked balls of iron that were swung on four-foot chains in circles over their heads and let loose to slash the enemy. Though the French were contemptuous of their low-born opponents, they couldn't defeat the brave Flemish citizens. At battle's end, the French dead numbered 63 nobles, including commander Robert d'Artois and 700 knights, from each of whom was removed a pair of golden spurs, ornaments which gave the battle its name. Still regularly reenacted as one of Belgium's most colorful folkloric events on the actual site in Kortrijk is the **Battle of the Golden Spurs**. It is significant for being the first occasion on which common citizens defeated well-armed and protected knights. In addition to making medieval military and social history, the battle marked the beginning of the end of the era of chivalry.

During the 14th century, various developments combined to bring about instability in Flanders. There were local guild rivalries and tyranny by the urban oligarchy over the rural peasantry. Changing trade patterns affected Flanders' all-important cloth industry and led to the emigration of many weavers to England. The marriage of Margaret (heir of Count of Flanders Louis de Male) to Philip the Bold of Burgundy resulted in the end of Flanders as a separate state and the beginning of **the Burgundian period** in 1384. The **Dukes of Burgundy**, who ruled the region until 1473, united almost the whole of the Netherlands.

Under the tenure of **Philip the Good** (1419–1467), there was an increase in trade and luxury, and the first flowering of Flemish painting occurred, (**Jan van Eyck** was court painter to Philip.) Philip was set on having monarchical status: in 1421 he bought Namur; in 1430 he inherited Brabant, Limburg, and Antwerp; in 1433, after deposing the previous ruler, he took over Hainaut, Holland, and Zeeland; and, in 1443, he bought Luxembourg. For an extra measure of authority, in 1456 Philip had his nephew Louis de Bourbon elected Bishop of Liège and made his bastard son Bishop of Utrecht. In the meantime, he forced Bruges and Ghent (which had mounted an unsuccessful revolt in response) to surrender many of their privileges. *That*, after having honored their superior wool-weaving by establishing the *Order of the Golden Fleece* in Bruges in 1430.

Philip was succeeded by his son **Charles the Bold**, the richest and most ambitious prince of his day. He, too, held the nobles and cities in check, and in his desire to be a king, married Margaret of York, sister of Edward IV of England. Overextending himself in a military campaign in Lorraine, Charles was killed at *Nancy* in 1477. He left extensive lands in turmoil to his daughter **Mary**, whom the Flemish held virtual hostage until she signed *The Great Privilege* charter that granted far-reaching rights back to the towns. In the same tempestuous year that her father died, Mary (in response to demands from the French king to marry his son) arranged to marry **Maximilian of Austria**, whereby the Netherlands passed from the Burgundians to the **Hapsburgs** of Vienna.

Mary and Maximilian had a son, **Philip the Fair**, to whom Maximilian, upon his election as *Holy Roman Emperor* in 1494, handed over the Netherlands and other lands, including Spain. Philip died young, and in 1506 the Burgundian land inheritance passed to his six-year-old son Charles, who had been born in Ghent.

Charles, who was to become one of the dominant figures of European history, spent his childhood under the governorship of his aunt, **Margaret of Austria**, who established herself and Charles in Mechelen. In 1515, the *Netherlands' States General* declared Charles (then 15) of age to lead their lands. In 1516 Charles also became King of Spain and, in 1519, Emperor of the Hapsburg empire, having inherited the title from his grandfather.

As Charles V (Charles Quint) and later *Holy Roman Emperor*, he ruled over greater European domains—from Spain to Hungary, and from Sicily to the Netherlands—than any single person before or since. In 1530, Charles V appointed his sister, Mary of Hungary, as regent of the Netherlands. She exacted heavy taxes in order to support the wars that Charles waged elsewhere (particularly in France) to keep his empire intact. In 1540, Ghent rebelled against paying for such wars. Charles personally suppressed the uprising and, in keeping with his aim to diminish the ancient privileges of towns that impaired the power of his crown, he rescinded many of Ghent's rights.

But the business of managing his empire militarily increasingly became overshadowed for the Roman Catholic Charles by concern about the Protestant **Reformation**. First Martin Luther in Germany (beginning in 1520), and then John Calvin in Switzerland, attacked the corruption of the Catholic Church, particularly the selling of indulgences and the self-indulgent lives of priests and the Pope. From Switzerland, the austere fundamentalist beliefs of *Calvinism* spread to Belgium (and on to Holland where, after 1550, Calvinism was the prevailing religion). In Belgium, Calvinist orators attracted and converted thousands in the forests outside towns from Bruges to Liège and Antwerp to Tournai. The number of Protestant converts increased continually. Charles tried to hold back the tide, first by prosecuting individual "heretics," and then moving to more wholesale action under the **Edict of Blood**, which decreed death for those convicted.

In 1555, an exhausted (perhaps ill—he died in 1558) Charles abdicated in favor of his son **Philip II of Spain**. A contemporary painting of the actual transfer of power ceremonial event depicts some of the main characters (**Charles** entering on the arm of **Willem the Silent** of Orange, **Philip II**, **Duke of Alva**, and the **Counts of Egmont** and **Hoorn**) for the upcoming **Eighty Years' War**. It is said that at the end of his father's abdication address in the throne room of Brussels' Coudenberg Palace, Philip, who could speak neither Dutch nor French, had his acceptance speech read by another. Philip never learned either language and wound up loathing the "Lowlanders," never setting foot in the Netherlands again after 1559, though he lived until 1598. Philip did, however, favor Flemish art. He had many works by **Hieronymus Bosch** (1474–1516) sent to him in Madrid; Utrecht-born and Belgium-educated painter **Antonio Moro** (c.1519–1576) was frequently called upon to paint Spanish court portraits.

The year prior to assuming power in the Netherlands, Philip II had married Queen **Mary Tudor of England** (1516–1558, herself a Catholic with a passion against Protestants—the treatment of whom earned her the epithet "Bloody Mary"). Philip's narrow-minded religious views fanned smouldering controversies into flames, spreading Protestantism further. He countered the Reformation in every way he could, ordering the ruthless persecution of all Protestants (and many others he accused of heresy).

For their part, Protestants participated in events such as the **Iconoclastic Fury** of 1566, a month-long spree during which hundreds of Catholic churches throughout the Netherlands were broken into, statues smashed, religious images burned, and tombs opened. Antwerp was particularly hard hit by damage from extreme Calvinists; to this day one sees churches there with empty niches and disfigured statues. It resulted in the loss of much of the Netherlands' early artistic legacy.

One extremist action provoked another. Within a year (1567), Philip sent the fanatical **Duke of Alva** (a.k.a. **Alba**) to the Netherlands with an army of 10,000 Spanish troops. He outlawed Willem of Orange, garrisoned towns with his troops, and set up the so-called **Council of Blood**, which he used as a means to execute many of the nobles, including **Counts Egmont** and **Hoorn**, who had become Protestants.

Dutch Prince **Willem (the Silent) of Orange**, who had lived in Brussels (having been brought up there at the court of Charles V), was unable to convince Philip II of Spain to follow a moderate course in the Reformation rather than persecuting Protestants. Willem left Brussels in 1568, collected troops, and headed north to Holland to lead an armed resistance from there. Protestant rebels under Willem began to see some success beginning in 1572 with the capture of Vlissingen (Flushing) in Zeeland. By the end of the year, they controlled most of the province of Holland and Willem had been declared Stadholder. The Duke of Alva concentrated on stamping out the simultaneous uprisings in the southern Netherlands (today's Belgium). In 1573, just before his return to Spain, Alva's soldiers, unpaid and mutinous, unleashed their anger in the brutal sacking of Antwerp known as the **Spanish Fury**. Alva's Spanish replacement, Luis de Requesens (who died in 1576 and was in turn replaced by the Duke of Parma), continued the fighting in the Netherlands, mostly against Willem's forces in the now Protestant-controlled north (Holland), since the south seemed ready for compromise.

In 1579, the signing of the **Union of Arras**—which declared faith in Roman Catholicism and loyalty to Philip II—by the deputies of certain southern regions ended the last hope for unity between the northern and southern Netherlands. It was followed shortly by the **Utrecht Union of the Seven United Provinces**, which established the Protestant northern Netherlands (roughly, today's Holland) as separate from the southern Netherlands (roughly, today's Belgium). Most Protestants had fled either to Holland, or England by the time the Duke of Alva had finished his reign of religious persecution. (Amsterdam had to tear down its walls and expand the city to accommodate all the immigrants).

Before his death in 1598, Philip II ceded the southern Netherlands to his daughter Isabella who, married to **Archduke Albert of Austria**, was made an archduke in her own right. The *Reign of the Archdukes* (which lasted until 1621) was a period of economic recovery and great intellectual and artistic brilliance led by Antwerp-based baroque age genius **Pieter Paul Rubens**.

The southern Netherlands was returned to Spanish rule in 1621 and became contested territory between the Hapsburgs and the Bourbons during the **Thirty Years' War** (1618–1648). The war ended with the *Treaty of Munster*, which gave official acknowledgment of the United Provinces' (Holland) complete independence, and secured Spanish agreement to the Dutch-imposed condition that the Scheldt River estuary be closed. Antwerp, predictably, went into decline, and its trade and prosperity shifted northward to Holland's North Sea ports.

During the late 17th century, it became increasingly important to France's **Louis XIV** (who had married the **Spanish Infanta**) to have the Spanish southern Netherlands subject to him. To achieve that he went so far as to invade Holland but was unsuccessful there, due to England's help in opposing the French Louis' plan. All parties wound up one way or another in the **War of the Spanish Succession** (1702–1713). In the *Treaty of Utrecht* signed in 1713, France finally abandoned all claim to the Spanish southern Netherlands, which passed to the Austrian Hapsburgs.

The Southern Netherlands remained essentially independent as the **Austrian Netherlands**, undergoing little more change than the name of the sovereign, which for much of the period was **Maria Theresa**. Her popular and enlightened Brussels representative, **Charles of Lorraine**, ushered in a period of prosperity and renewed interest in culture. Transportation networks were constructed, agriculture was modernized, and industry (especially coal) was encouraged. Maria Theresa's successor, Joseph II, was (for reasons of personality more than policy) unsuccessful in his dealings with the Austrian Netherlands. In 1792, war broke out between Austria and revolutionary France; by 1794, Austria had been defeated and the southern Netherlands once again came under French occupation.

It was with a measure of acceptance (as opposed to protest) that the southern Netherlands became a dependency of France in 1795. However, the French lost favor with the dependent nation when Napoleon introduced conscription, centralized its government, and French anti-religious revolutionaries (survivors of the French Revolution) persecuted the Roman Catholic Church. Under **Napoleon's** rule from 1799 to 1814, a few positive elements were added under his *code of civilization* (among them the metric system and the first plan for numbering buildings for street addresses). However, after the Corsican Emperor suffered final defeat in 1815 on his own soil at **Waterloo**, the idea of independence loomed large for Belgians.

But Britain had other ideas, fearing that Belgium was too weak to resist if the French made new attempts to control the region's ever-important North Sea ports. The European powers meeting at the *Congress of Vienna* ordered Belgium incorporated into the **Kingdom of the Netherlands**. The plans—described even by the diplomats of the day as being solely for "the convenience of Europe," rather than the welfare of Belgians—proved, unsurprisingly, unpopular. Two points in particular doomed it from day one. The Belgian Roman Catholic Church, especially strong in Flanders, could not tolerate the Dutch Protestant approach to religion. Secondly, Belgians refused to accept mere equal representation in the *Netherlands States General* since they had twice the population of Holland. In addition, King Willem, though Dutch, following the social form of the day, spoke French, which offended the Flemish. Also, Willem paid particular attention to the industrial development of the rich coal fields in Wallonia while virtually ignoring Flanders's economic well-being. Only the port of Antwerp, recovering rapidly after being reopened by Napoleon, benefitted by being part of the Kingdom of the Netherlands.

In 1828, the two Belgian communities, and opposing political parties, put aside their differences in common hostility to Dutch rule. Within weeks of the Revolution of 1830 in France, the Belgians held a brief one of their own, demanding from the European powers —this time successfully—that their independence and "perpetual neutrality" be recognized. The crown of the new **constitutional monarchy** was offered to and accepted by German Prince **Leopold of Saxe-Coburg**, an uncle of and strong influence over England's Queen Victoria. Holland's Willem did not give in to the arrangement willingly and, ironically, the new King Leopold I was forced to call upon France for military reinforcement to flush the Dutch out of Belgium.

No sooner had the Belgians achieved the right to be their own political leaders than they became leaders in the **Industrial Revolution**. The European continent's first steam-operated locomotive and rail line, running between Brussels and Mechelen, began in 1835. Belgians also invented the tram, and in the 19th century built tram networks all over the world.

Leopold II, who did much to foster Belgium's growth and transport systems, came to the throne in 1865. A colonialist to the core, he tried to get the Belgian government interested in acquiring a piece of Africa. When he couldn't, he decided to do so himself. In 1879 Leopold had H. M. Stanley (of "Dr. Livingstone, I presume" association) make agreements with some African chiefs to open up trading stations in an area he called the **Congo Free State**. Using his own resources, Leopold established what amounted to a personal fief—eight times the size of Belgium, with three times the population. The resources he realized in return—copper, cobalt, timber, diamonds, and uranium, among others—made Leopold one of the richest men in the world. Eventually, however, even his own countrymen charged him with exploitation, and, in 1908, the African territory became the **Belgian Congo** colony under a largely reluctant Belgian government rule.

In 1960, the Belgian government granted independence to the Congo. The manner in which it did so reinforced its relative uninvolvement from the start: Belgium simply walked away, leaving only a few indigenous university graduates, doctors, and trained administrators to cope with the change. Renamed **Zaire**, with the capital *Kinshasa* (it had been *Leopoldville* under the Belgians), the newly independent country began life largely in a state of political and social disarray; the internal violence that has dogged it since has been attributed by some to the unprecedented speed with which Belgium cut its colonial connection. In any case, most Belgians agreed with the independence decision at the time, despite the resulting loss of 4% of national income. Today, Zaire continues to be burdened with backwardness and political corruption, but businessmen who seek its still-considerable natural resources keep themselves largely unconcerned about the social conditions of the country.

In Belgium, the 19th century proved relatively calm and stable. A rising demand for social rights and equal education was evident in the demands of the **Flemish Movement** (see "Flanders: An Introduction"). After the *Workers' Congress* at Brussels in 1886, socialism gained a new following. Even art got into the act, as the *art nouveau* style was specifically adopted by those sympathetic to socialism. Art nouveau architect Victor Horta created a marvelous headquarters for the *Workers' Congress* in the **Maison du Peuple** (built 1895, demolished 1966).

Most other issues fell away when Belgium, whose neutrality had been guaranteed by the Great Powers in 1839, was nevertheless invaded and occupied by the Germans at the beginning of the **Great War** (World War I, 1914–1918). Belgium's "language situation" surfaced on the **Ypres Salient** in the form of the *Flemish Front Move-*

ment. At issue was the fact that although an estimated 80% of Belgium's trench- confined conscripts were Dutch-speaking, few of the country's disproportionately large number of French-speaking officers knew the language of their soldiers, punishing some for failing to obey commands they could not understand.

The German occupiers found that the conflict between Belgium's two language communities played into their hands. But working to keep Belgians together in battle was the brave leadership of the beloved **King Albert** and **Queen Elizabeth**, who based themselves at De Panne on the small southwest strip of Belgian soil which—with the help of hundreds of thousands of Allied troops in the trenches around Ypres—remained free for the duration.World War I devastation in Belgium included the loss of much magnificent medieval architecture (though the people eventually rebuilt many of the monuments in their original exterior splendor).

Reconstruction from World War I had not been fully completed when **World War II** began, with the Nazis invading Belgium (and Holland) on May 10, 1940. But for his death in a tragic climbing accident in 1934, King Albert I might have seen his country through another war. Instead, his son **Leopold III** was seated on the throne. Leopold had married the extremely popular Princess Astrid of Sweden in 1926, but, a year after the royal couple was crowned, Astrid died in a motor accident in a car driven by her husband. Misfortune was to rule Leopold's reign.

During World War II, many Belgians were deeply troubled by the feeling that their king was not behaving in the best interests of the nation. Leopold III, stiff and inclined to ignore his ministers' advice, probably never would have won the affection felt by the Belgians for his father, King Albert, who symbolized Belgium's strength under prolonged fire in World War I. Leopold, in contrast, surrendered his armies and permitted himself to be taken prisoner only 18 days after the Nazis invaded Belgium. His initial "wait and see" stand, probably more passive than pro-Nazi, and based on a belief that he could do more for his people from within Belgium than in exile, nevertheless proved wrong on all counts. Staunch Leopold supporters point out that, once a prisoner, he successfully pleaded with Hitler for a less restrictive occupation. (No *Gestapo* were stationed in Belgium, and conditions there were much easier than ones the Dutch had to endure.) But the bottom line was that, once a prisoner in his palace at Laeken (outside Brussles) and seen receiving mild treatment himself from the Nazis, Leopold was forever compromised in the eyes of his Belgian people. (Particularly, they contrasted his actions with those of Holland's **Queen Wilhelmina**, who escaped to England with her government after the Nazi invasion. Once the Dutch got over the shock of her fleeing, Wilhelmina was able to serve as a stirring symbol of resistance for her country.) Leopold spent the war being shifted by the Nazis from one place of imprisonment to another, eventually to Germany in 1944 for safekeeping after the Allied Normandy invasion, and finally to Salzburg, Austria, where he was found in 1945 with his 15 year-old son **Prince Baudouin**.

In exile in Switzerland, Leopold—whose brother Prince Charles had been asked to take over as regent for Belgium—knew he could not wear the Belgian crown again without the issue being resolved. Just short of ten years after the Nazis had invaded Belgium in May 1940, the **Royal Question** was posed to the people: *Should Leopold return to the Belgian throne?* He won the plebiscite, but by a 57 percent of the population that so closely followed the bicultural lines of the country—in general, he was favored by Flemish Catholics and rejected by Walloon anticlerics—that, had Leopold insisted upon reclaiming the crown, Belgium might have seen civil war. Leopold's son **Baudouin** was quietly given constitutional powers and acceded as king in 1951 when he turned 21. More than one Belgian murmured under his breath: "The crisis is dead. Long live the king."

Well before the end of the war, in 1944, from their headquarters in exile in London, the governments of Belgium, Holland, and Luxembourg began talks about a post-war border-free economic union among the three. The name coined was **BENELUX** (BElgium, NEtherlands, LUXembourg), and it marked the beginning of a new era for Europe. The promise of the Benelux association led to the six-membered **European Coal and Steel Community**, which was established to pool coal and steel production within the three Benelux countries plus France, Germany, and Italy. The 1951 plan was called by Walter Lippmann "the most audacious and constructive initiative since the end of the war."

By 1957, yet another new stage in European integration had been reached, with the signing of the *Treaty of Rome* that established the **European Economic Community** (or *Common Market*). The new international body eventually designated **Brussels** as its **capital**. (Belgium, it seems, was small enough so that the privilege conferred upon its capital did not unleash jealousies among the other larger members.) Today, the broader-based **European Community** (EC) has doubled its membership since the Coal and Steel Community days to a full dozen, and new heights of European economic cooperation are being scaled with the *Single Europe Act*.

The anniversary of the founding of the European Economic Community in 1950 is observed in Brussels each May 9th—Eurocrats have dubbed it "St. Schuman's Day," after Common Market co-architect Luxembourg-born Robert Schuman. As far as Belgium is concerned, it's certainly a day worth celebrating, since the EC has changed the course of the country, particularly its capital. After centuries of being a pawn of Europe's empire builders, Belgium has the satisfaction of knowing that its voice is heard as an equal in the European Community. And Belgium's crossroads capital has become virtually the capital of Europe.

Belgium is unique among the bilingual countries of the world in that its two main language groups are so nearly equal in numbers and area. Even more unusual is the extent to which bilingualism has, in the second half of the 20th century, been regulated by legislation. This process has continued under **federalism**. The introduction to Belgium of federalism, in 1988, gave important decision-making powers and regional autonomy to *Flanders, Wallonia* and *Brussels.* In April 1993, both chambers of the Belgian National Parliament voted final approval for a 35-amendment revision to the constitution to turn Belgium into a federal state, which was made official with a nod from the late King Baudouin. Federalism has helped both to stabilize Belgium's political situation and to overcome the lingering linguistic divisions. In the past, when Belgium's internal petty rivalries and hostilities have periodically ignited, it sometimes has seemed that the country would split. Though often predicted, however, that split hasn't happened and now is even less likely to under federalism.

Due to the complexity of Belgium's circumstances, a correctly calibrated federal formula is still evolving for the separate but equal regional governments of Flanders, Wallonia, and Brussels. The national parliament and central government retain responsibility for international affairs, security, defense, consumer protection, labor, social security, and overall economic and monetary policy, which must deal with Belgium's large chronic national budget deficit.

Despite an often wasteful, excessively expensive overlapping of resources, the change to federalism has been deemed largely successful. Nevertheless, a lot of energy that could go into more far-reaching endeavors is expended to maintain Belgium's bicultural balancing act. For example, bilingual switchboard operators for the Belgian Senate must say "Le Senat/De Senaat" when answering the phone on Mondays, Wednesdays, and Fridays, and "De Senaat/Le Senat" on Tuesdays, Thursdays, and Saturdays. Sundays, they rest.

The recovery of the Belgian economy in the 1980s was one of the world's success stories. Despite an unemployment rate above the EC average, small 10-million-people-strong Belgium is surprisingly well poised economically for the 1990s. Eleven of the country's corporations—a mix of metals, merchandising, banking, and utilities—make it onto Forbes magazine's list of the 500 largest companies outside the U.S. Belgium is the highest *per capita* exporter in the world: fully 70% of the GNP leaves the country as exports. The only worry with that is, as *Forbes* points out, "If its trading partners catch colds, Belgium gets pneumonia." Belgium recently found out that, even as the seventh most active financial center in the world and the fourth largest in Europe, it isn't invulnerable to international corporate raiding. Several once proud family-run operations are now in the hands of foreigners.

Many of the internally traumatic turns of Belgium's 20th-century history have barely been noticed beyond its borders. In any case, on the world stage, they pale beside the significance that Belgium has assumed in the latter part of this century as a small but equal state in the European Community. With Brussels moving from the *de facto* to the *de jure* capital of Europe as capital of the European Community, the country has high visibility. Today, Belgium—which perhaps more than any other EC country has loosened the ties of its own nationalism—eagerly awaits Europe's economic integration. This will, among other things, further ease the exit of its exports. Belgians are the first to characterize Europe's adventure in *deregulation* an evolutionary, not revolutionary, process. The distinction suits their essentially conservative character just fine.

BRUSSELS

Brussels' Grand Place at night

GUIDELINES FOR BRUSSELS

SIGHTS

Brussels's **Grand-Place**, with its inspiring 15th-century **Hotel De Ville** (Town Hall, with **Tourist Information Brussels—T.I.B.**) and gilt-highlighted guild houses (late 17th century), is Europe's most magnificent square—and car-free at long last. It's the starting point for all city sightseeing, to be followed by the small surrounding medieval market streets of the Ilot Sacre, including the restaurant-clogged Petit rue des Bouchers. Belgium's finest collection of

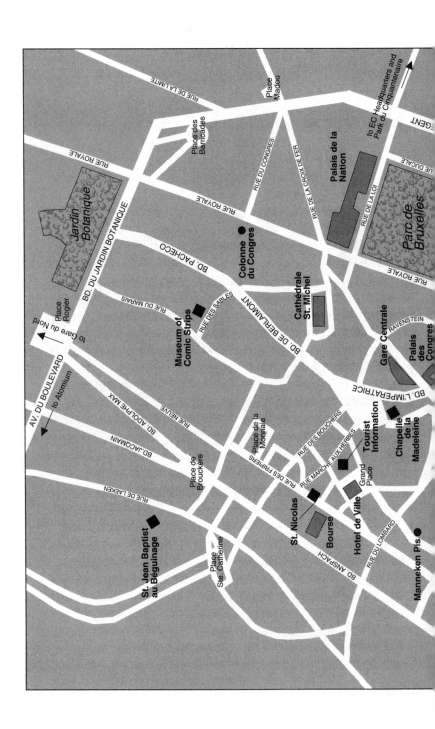

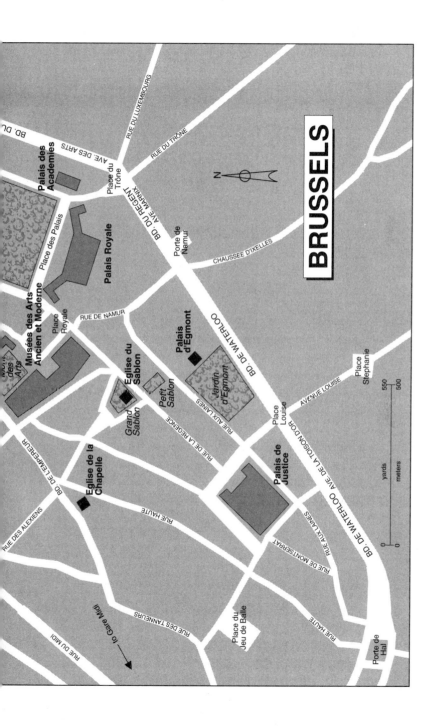

BRUSSELS

Flemish "primitives" paintings, as well as wonderful works from the *Netherlands' 16th and 17th centuries*, and the *Belgian Surrealists*, are at the **Musées de l'Art Ancien et Moderne** on **place Royale**. The sights around the Grand Sablon include its antique shops and weekend outdoor market, art galleries, church, and the **Petit Sablon**, with its restful statue-ornamented garden. Among Brussels' varied architecture are fascinating samples of the turn-of-the-century **art nouveau** style, especially the former house of Belgium's most famous exponent, Victor Horta. City attractions are varied and sometimes surprising. The **after-dark illumination** of monuments creates lasting impressions; the Grand-Place aglow will leave you spellbound.

GETTING AROUND

Belgium's capital city is well equipped for conveying people from one to another of its 19 *communes*. The **Metro** is the fastest, most decorative means. (See "Bourse Station/Metro Art" under "What To See and Do" below); **buses** are next best; then **trams** (colorful but slow, they're gradually being done away with since street cars interfere excessively with Brussels's notorious traffic). Metro and transportation system maps are available from the T.I.B., as are **24-hour tickets** (BF 180) for unlimited use of city Metro, buses, and trams. (The recently instituted *Tourist Passport* includes a 24-hour pass combined with entry reduction vouchers for selected attractions for BF 200, available from T.I.B.) Fares shown on taxi meters include tip. Parking in Brussels is as eventful as in any too-traffic-congested old European city; metered spaces (have BF 5 and 20 pieces handy) have varying rules. Paid car parks (indicated by blue "**P**" signs) can be found at **blvd. de Waterloo**, **place de la Monnaie**, and **place Rogier**.

SHOPPING

Brussels isn't London, Paris, or Rome, but the best designer names from each can be found in the luxury specialty shops and designer boutiques in the **Haut de la Ville** (Upper Town) along the chic **blvd. de Waterloo** and **avenue de la Toison D'Or**. Big-name chain and department stores are clustered primarily in **blvd. Aldolphe Max** and the pedestrianized **rue Neuve**. Late-night shopping is Friday until 8 p.m., though smaller shops and grocery stores that close at lunchtime may remain open until 7 or 8 p.m. other nights, too. Travelers should inquire of shopkeepers about the conditions for duty-free purchases.

ENTERTAINMENT AND EVENTS

The Tourist Information Brussels' publication, *BBB Agenda* (for sale), has a calendar of events in the city, including opera, ballet, and concerts; T.I.B. also can arrange bookings. See, too, events listings in *The Bulletin*, Brussels' English-language weekly newspaper. Cafes, nightclubs, and cinemas (some 35, showing a varied range of films in their original language) are clustered in the upper town between porte Namur and place Louise, and in the lower town between the place de la Bourse and place Rogier.

WHERE TO STAY

Brussels offers plentiful hotel choices in all prices—which have risen across the board in the last several years in this European capital. Because of the start-up each September of European Community meetings, as well as annual fall trade congresses and corporate conventions, hotel rooms then and in October can be scarce.

WHERE TO EAT

If gourmets worldwide consider Brussels one of the top cities for food—restaurants number more than 1,500—you'll hardly want to leave without assessing the celebrated cuisine for yourself. Whether you want *frites* (french fries) from stands, *alfresco* meals of *moules* (mussels) at tables set out along ancient alleys, *vlaams carbonada* (Belgium's beef stew in beer specialty) in an atmospheric cafe, or an extraordinary repast at an elegant dining "institution," it will be hard to find less-than-fine food in Brussels.

ARRIVING

Those arriving by air fly into Brussels' **Zaventem Airport**, 9 mi/14 km northeast of the city. **Sabena World Airlines** is the major Belgian carrier, with both transatlantic routes and air connections onward to many European cities. There's thrice-hourly rail service from the airport into the city (20 minutes, fare BF 70), with the first stop at Brussels' **Gare du Nord** (North Station), then **Gare Centrale**; one train an hour continues on to the **Gare du Midi** (South Station), the city's third main station. If you are arriving in Brussels by train, and already have reservations at a hotel, you'll find it helpful to know *before arrival* which train station is closest to your hotel, although the Metro links all stations, and all have taxi stands. Gare Centrale is closest to the Grand-Place, the heart of old Brussels, and to both the Brussels and the all-Belgium tourist information (*rue Marché aux Herbes 61*) offices. As the de facto capital of Europe, Brussels is well-linked with the continent's major motorways. Ferries arriving from England at Ostend and Zeebrugge are met by Brussels-bound trains.

IN THE AREA

Located in a magnificent building on the eastern outskirts of Brussels at Tervuren is the **Musée Royal de l'Afrique Centrale** which, formerly focused on the former *Belgian Congo* colony, now has exhibits on the whole of Africa. South of Brussels is the rural battleground at **Waterloo** where the Emperor Napoleon—much to the relief of the early 19th-century European heads of state—came but did not conquer.

TRAVEL TIPS

Brussels' museums, offices, and other attractions often close at noon for up to two hours, so plan your midday touring accordingly. The **Art l'Ancien** and **Art Moderne** museums have coordinated their one-hour lunch closures so that one or the other of the underground-connected sections remains open.

BRUSSELS IN CONTEXT

Imagine the scene, seen by an American acquaintance in Brussels, visiting his Belgian in-laws: two Bruxellois conversing, a French-speaker forming questions in his language to a Fleming, who was replying in Dutch—both continuing in that manner without missing a meaning. That's not the way the city's *official bilingualism* is meant to work, of course.

Geographically, Brussels lies well within Dutch/Flemish-speaking Flanders, but, culturally, it remains decidedly French in its orientation. According to William Z. Shetter, author of *The Netherlands in Perspective*, "The power of Brussels to radiate and extend French influence is a source of constant anxiety to the Flemish." By law, no count is made, but it's known that Brussels' French-speaking Belgian-nationality residents outnumber the city's Flemish speakers by an estimated 4 to 1. The 1962 guarantee of equal language rights for the Flemish did not erase French-outlook favoritism in Brussels, though recently Flemish has become a more accepted route to advancement in business and government there. If one could put language aside, the *Bruxellois* are more of an amalgam: while a majority may *speak* French, most *think* like the Dutch, the result being a cultured business acumen.

In addition to having to absorb the complexities of its indigenous inhabitants' bicultural concerns, Brussels, with a population of just under one million, is nearly 25 percent foreign, with many MEPs (*Members* of the *European Parliament*), diplomats, multinational corporate executives, and their families. It may sound like the making of a melting pot, but, according to Brussels-based *Financial Times* reporter Lucy Kellaway, it's not so simple. In an article in that British newspaper, Kellaway explains: "Each nationality keeps to itself, remaining true to all its prejudices, persuasions, and preferences ...Outside work they stick to themselves. They live in little pockets, send their children to national schools, and, distance permitting, go home to their own countries on weekends...While (citizens of EC) member states mix little with each other, they do not mix with the Belgians at all...Language is only partly to blame for this isolationist behaviour. After all, anyone who works in the Commission must be able to speak French, and most people can muster decent English and probably another language too."

While this picture of human nature, almost reminiscent of a colonial lifestyle, may be discouraging to those in the EC who seek to drop their narrow nationalist identities for a "big picture" of Europe, it perhaps proves reassuring to citizens of individual countries in Europe—and travelers from abroad—who have worried that the European Community's *Single Europe Act* might mean the end of an individual country's cultural idiosyncrasies.

Brussels, today one of Belgium's three federalist regions (with Flanders and Wallonia), celebrated its millenium in 1979. That puts its founding back in A.D. 979, when Charles of France, Duke of Lower Lotharingia, built a fortified structure on the island of Saint Gery on marshy land called **Bruoscella**. In 1041, ducal successors built a new castle on the highest land, becoming early residents of the **Haut de la Ville** (Upper Town) at **Coudenberg**, site of the present Royal Palace. Brussels first had fortified walls in the year 1100, and the first version of its Cathédrale Saint Michel appeared in 1225. To embrace the continuing growth, a second series of city walls—where the *inner boulevard* ring road now runs—was finished in time for Brussels' quadricentennial in 1379.

Entering the 15th century, Brussels gained in stature as a residence of the ambitious **House of Burgundy**, which became the most powerful state between France and Germany, acquiring nearly all the secular lordships of the Netherlands. The first stone of the *Hôtel de Ville* (town hall) was laid on the *Grand-Place* in 1402, in response to the need for Brussels to have grander buildings for use by the Burgundian dukes. Their court attracted large numbers of French knights to

Brussels, and the French language became fashionable among the Netherlands nobles.

In 1430, Burgundian duke **Philip the Good**, called "the equal of kings and emperors," took possession of Brabant, thereafter moving his capital from Dijon to Brussels. The city achieved remarkable economic growth by turning to the production of luxury goods: lace, paintings, tapestries, jewelry, and church furnishings. Artists and craftsmen of great renown flocked to Brussels' increasingly ostentatious court. Under Philip, **Jan van Eyck** became court painter, and **Rogier van der Weyden** (*Rogier de la Pasture*) was appointed Brussels' town painter.

Charles V (**Quint**) confirmed the political and administrative preeminence of Brussels by himself settling in the city at the palace of Coudenberg in 1515 and, in 1530, officially moving the Netherlands' court there from Mechelen. As capital of the Netherlands' 17 provinces—land that today includes much of both Belgium and Holland—and with a central location within the immense Hapsburg empire which then ruled the Netherlands, Brussels received great benefits. The original **Ommegang** (still annually reenacted on the Grand-Place) was a brilliant pageant marking the grand entry procession of Charles V, by then *Holy Roman Emperor*, and his son Philip II, King of Spain, into Brussels in 1549. But Brussels also had the unenviable inevitability of being at the center of the **Reformation**.

The stage was set for the **Eighty Years' War** by the 1555 abdication of Charles V at Brussels' Coudenberg Palace. Power over the 17 Netherlands' provinces passed to his son Philip, a fanatic Roman Catholic. In Brussels to receive rule from his father, Philip thereafter oversaw the Netherlands long distance from Spain, dispatching orders and officials to collect unpopular taxes and tributes, suppressing Protestants, and installing his half-sister Margaret, duchess of Parma, as regent in Brussels. Philip's harsh policies inflamed newly converted Protestants, who were filled with anti-papist preaching from Calvinists and Lutherans. A wave of religious rebellion swept the Netherlands. The first action of the Eighty Years' War came April 5, 1566, when hundreds of Netherlands nobles marched through the streets of Brussels to the home of Margaret of Parma to protest religious persecution. Many carried the beggars' bowls that once had signified that their support for the king would last until they were reduced to beggars. Taunted as *geuzen* (beggars) as they walked past regime loyalists, the nobles and their followers adopted the term as a rallying nickname. The year 1566 also produced extremist Protestant crowds that attacked Catholic churches and their contents.

Brussels' **Cathedrale St. Michel** suffered severe damage, and relics in the **Eglise Notre-Dame du Sablon** were destroyed.

Spanish response to the widespread destruction was brutal. In 1567, Philip II sent the **Duke of Alva** (or Alba) and 10,000 troops to the Netherlands to replace the Duchess of Parma. In Brussels, Alva established the *Council of Troubles* for trials of sedition charges against Netherlanders (who called the court the **Council of Blood**). By 1568, groups of 30 to 50 people at a time were being condemned to death, their property confiscated by the Spanish Crown. In only a short time, the tally of the dead reached 8,000.

Perhaps because the earliest resistance to Spanish religious oppression had come from the Netherlands nobility, when the Dutch **Counts Egmont** and **Hoorn**—both of whom had previously served with honor in the armies of Charles V and Philip II—went to Brussels to seek relief for Holland from the persecution of the Protestants there by the Spanish king's representative, Alva wouldn't listen. At 10 a.m. on June 5, 1568, on Brussels' Grand-Place in front of the *Maison du Roi* (which never housed a king, only the Spanish law court), a silent, shocked crowd saw Egmont and Hoorn beheaded. It is said that afterward, many people pushed past the Spanish guards to dip their Belgian lace-trimmed handkerchiefs in the blood of the first martyrs of the war. (Some time later, a memorial commemorating the infamous execution was erected on the spot in front of the steps where it took place; the statues of Egmont and Hoorn and fountain from it were moved to the peaceful *place du Petit Sablon* when the garden there was laid out in 1890). The tide turned in 1576 when **Dutch Prince Willem of Orange** was able to drive the Spanish out of Brussels, and the city enacted anti-Catholic laws that virtually abolished all outward signs of the religion.

From 1585, however, by which time the religious struggles between the Spanish and the Dutch had caused a split between the northern and southern Netherlands provinces, Brussels was reoccupied by Spanish forces and named as the capital of the southern Spanish Netherlands. Thereafter, the city, and most of the rest of what is Belgium today, remained basically loyal to Spain and Roman Catholicism. The pro-Catholic **Counter-Reformation** brought a wave of Jesuits, priests, and nuns to Brussels, and the arrival of Philip II's daughter Archduchess Isabella, who, jointly with her husband Archduke Albert of Austria, was appointed ruler of the Spanish Netherlands in 1598. Life in Brussels again flowed around a fashionable court, and the city became a haven for political exiles, such as the sons of beheaded Roman Catholic English King Charles I.

As Spanish influence flagged at the end of the 17th century, French **King Louis XIV** embarked on an imperialist adventure through the Netherlands. In 1695, he ordered his 70,000-man army to fire cannon and mortars from the heights of Anderlecht on central Brussels. Forty-six hours later, Brussels had lost nearly 4,000 houses, 16 churches, and many major buildings, including all those surrounding the *Grand-Place*, with the exception of the Hôtel de Ville which, miraculously, withstood the onslaught. The Bruxellois response was to build an even more magnificent main square, a goal they accomplished in four short years. French efforts to gain the southern Netherlands, in the **War of the Spanish Succession** (1701–1714), finally went down in defeat due to England's Duke of Marlborough, John Churchill (Winston's ancestor), and Austria's Prince Eugene. This brought the region under Austrian Hapsburg rule.

The Austrian era began oppressively, and social confrontations culminated in the beheading of Brussels' guild leader **Francois Anneessens** in 1719. But **Charles of Lorraine**, a genial Austrian ruler (dispatched from Vienna's Hapsburg household by then Empress Maria Theresa), oversaw the era after the 1745–1748 **War of the Austrian Succession** (during which France reconquered nearly the whole of the country before losing it *again* to Austria). Under Charles, the physical face of Brussels around the **Place Royale** changed to *neoclassical*, as the *Royal Palace, Palais de la Nation*, and *Parc de Bruxelles* took shape. Maria Theresa's son, Joseph II, who ruled from 1765–1790, had a well-intentioned plan for reform, but his overhasty and insensitive implementation aroused a spirit of revolt.

Under the influence of the French Revolution and the leadership of **Henri van der Noot**, the people of Brussels took arms, and in a national uprising, declared the **United Belgian States** (the first use of the "Belgian" name in modern times) in January 1790. The life of the independent republic was short-lived; by agreeing to restore some civil rights that had been rescinded by Joseph II, Austrian Emperor Leopold II was able to reoccupy the country. Between 1792-94, in yet another turnaround of rulership, the *French Revolutionary Army* under **Napoleon Bonaparte** beat the Austrians for Belgium and defeated Holland. Both the southern and northern Netherlands became dependences of France (and were united as the **Batavian Republic** from 1795 to 1808). With the exile of Napoleon to Elba in 1814, the *Congress of Vienna* was poised to bind Belgium to Holland again when its plan had to be postponed because of the reappearance of the French emperor.

Cannon fire from the fields of **Waterloo**—a dozen miles away—could be heard in Brussels during the day of the battle there, June 18, 1815. Many who had gathered lightheartedly at the Duchess of Richmond's "Waterloo" Brussels ball for guest-of-honor the English **Duke of Wellington**—who danced until dawn on June 16—were, on the 18th, sure that Napoleon would bring bloodshed all the way to Brussels. Those fortunate enough to find passage fled to Antwerp on barges.

Shortly after the Battle of Waterloo in 1815 (see "Waterloo" under "In the Area" below), despite Belgian protestations, Holland's Prince Willem became ruler of Belgium as head of the **Kingdom of the Netherlands**, since the European powers, still meeting at the *Congress of Vienna*, were anxious to keep a strong, established, buffer state between themselves and France. Brussels became co-capital (with The Hague) of the new kingdom. But, beneath the surface, Belgians breathed **revolution**, which came in 1830 in Brussels. An opera performance of Auber's *The Mute of Portici*, which carries a strongly suggestive patriotic message, inspired Belgians to take to the streets of Brussels after an August 25, 1830, performance. Some raised the Brabant flag—the same tricolor of black, gold, and red that the new country adopted soon after—over the Hôtel de Ville. Young intellectuals and others rioted, sacking the homes of government ministers, raiding bakeries for bread and bars for alcohol, and destroying machinery in factories. Brussels' Burgomaster Vanderlin den d'Hooghvorst formed an 8,000-man militia that quelled the riot but couldn't stop the movement. Joined by volunteers from the provinces, the Bruxellois rebelled against 14,000 Dutch soldiers who arrived in September. The **Parc de Bruxelles**, in front of the *Palais de la Nation* where the Dutch government had its Brussels headquarters, was the scene of some of the fiercest fighting. On September 27, 1830, a free **Kingdom of Belgium** was finally declared, with Brussels named the capital. In July of 1831, the keys to the city were handed over to the new country's first King **Leopold of Saxe-Coburg**, who swore allegiance to the Belgian people on the steps of *St. Jacques sur Coudenberg* church on **place Royale**.

The energy released with the achievement of Belgian independence produced plentiful signs of progress and prosperity in the capital of the new kingdom. The **Free University of Brussels** was founded in 1834; in 1835, continental Europe's first passenger steam locomotive chugged out of Brussels (to Mechelen); and the Royal Library opened in 1837. Later in the 19th century, the covering of the Senne River took place, largely for sanitary reasons, but it made possible the construction of Brussels' central boulevards (today's **Anspach, Adolphe Max**, etc.). The **Palais du Justice** (built between 1866-1883 by Joseph Poelaert), a Greco-Roman domed domain larger than St. Peter's in Rome, if nothing else showed civic confidence. The 1880 exhibition at the **parc du Cinquantenaire** was held in celebration of the free country's 50th birthday.

In World War I the Nazis violated Belgium's declared neutrality, and used the senate chamber of Brussels' *Palais de la Nation* (Parliament Building) for its wartime tribunal. In that chamber in 1915 the *Nazi Tribunal* condemned courageous English nurse **Edith Cavell** to death by firing squad. She had been running a training school for nurses in Brussels and, uncowed by threats, had willingly harbored and further helped Belgians and Allies seeking to escape across the border to neutral Holland. (She is credited with helping 130 prisoners escape.) Brussels again was occupied in World War II (from May 1940–September 1944).

During 1944, government ministers who had fled from Belgium, Holland, and Luxembourg, and were all operating in exile from London, settled on the idea of the **BENELUX**, a mutually beneficial, barrier-free customs and trade, which, when officially instituted in 1948, helped put the devasted economies of the three countries on the fastest possible post-war recovery track. The BENELUX proved a harbinger of European evolution, and, in 1959, Brussels was selected as capital of the six-nation **European Economic Community** (Common Market). Brussels also blossomed from hosting the extremely successful **World's Fair in 1958**, with *Atomium* being the symbol of its nuclear energy theme. In 1967, Brussels was chosen capital of **NATO** (North Atlantic Treaty Organization). Those developments forever changed the face and mentality of the city. On the domestic front, in 1980, under a new Belgian form of government, Brussels found itself one of the country's three federal regions (together with Flanders and Wallonia).

While the internationalism of Brussels is intriguing to travelers—it's the "company town" for European government, and TV news anchors in countries throughout Europe begin their coverage with "Today in Brussels ..."—it also can create a certain dissatisfaction due to the resulting lack of a well-defined foreign identity. Even its own Belgian population doesn't permit Brussels to present a single cultural face to visitors—though two foreign flavors for one destination could be considered a bonus. The simple fact is that Brussels is complex.

More than with most places, Brussels is the result of its history, which includes major changes in this last decade of the 20th century. They are all revealed on the physical face of the city, nowhere as clearly as in the mixed architectural course the city has followed during the second half of this century. What some call a carelessly conserved architectural heritage, others explain by saying that Brussels wants to be more in the present, not just a pretty face from the past. That shouldn't be a worry, since Brussels, as **capital of the European Community (EC)**, heads the world's largest economic block: the 340 million citizens of an evolving *single-market Europe.*

Brussels' long-standing city symbols, the surprisingly smaller-than-life boy statue mascot **Manneken-Pis** and the **Atomium** molecule multiplied many billion times its size, both seem to have had to step slightly aside for the **EC flag** (a circle of 12 gold stars, representing the 12 European Community member nations, on a field of blue), the city emblem one sees everywhere. But, ever interested in being innovative as well as true to its history, Brussels has adapted: Manneken-Pis' wardrobe has been updated with an official EC outfit.

GUIDEPOSTS

Telephone Code 02

Tourist Office Tourist Information Brussels (T.I.B.) • Hôtel de Ville, Grand-Place, B-1000 Brussels; ☎ *513.89.40*; daily 9 a.m.–6 p.m. (from Oct. 1–March 30 closed Sun.), closed Christmas, New Year's.

Emergencies • Accident ☎ *100*; police ☎ *101*; doctors on duty: ☎ *479.18.18*, ☎ *648.80.00*; dentists on duty: ☎ *426.10.26, 428.58.88.*

Airport • General info. ☎ *02.722.30.00*; SABENA World Airlines: reservations ☎ *511.90.30*, information ☎ *720.71.67.*

Trains • Information for all trains in Belgium and in Europe: ☎ *219.26.40.*

Metro, Tram, Bus • Information day and night: ☎ *515.21.11.*

Lost Property • Lost property office for metro, buses, trams: ☎ *515.23.94*, ave. de la Toison d'Or 15, 9:30 a.m.–12:30 p.m.; for property lost in a taxi, apply to police station nearest point of departure or call ☎ *721.31.11.*

Tours • **ARAU City Tours** in English on such themes as **Brussels 1900, Brussels in the 1930s, Surprising parks and squares**, ☎ *513.47.61* or *512.56.90*. **Sightseeing Line**: 14-seat minibus tours in English (headset) through Brussels' smaller streets, schedule, information ☎ *513.89.40* (T.I.B.).

Taxis • Available at taxi ranks, or by telephone order: **Taxis Oranges** ☎ *513.62.00;* **Taxis Verts** ☎ *511.22.44;* tip is included in meter price.

Post Office • Main office: **Centre Monnaie**, Mon.-Fri. 9 a.m.–5 p.m.; money orders, 8 a.m.–8 p.m.; stamps Sat. 9 a.m.–noon. (Sat. in July & Aug. 9 a.m.–8 p.m. for stamps only.)

Telephone/Telex • Main city office: blvd. de l'Imperatrice 17, daily 7 a.m.-10 p.m.; ☎ *513.44.90.*

Local Newspaper • *The Bulletin*, a Brussels weekly in English; events information.

English Books • *W. H. Smith*, blvd. Adolphe Max 71; ☎ *771.92.00.*

WHAT TO SEE AND DO

By law, the names of Brussels' streets, buildings, etc. must appear in both of the city's official languages (as you'll see on the T.I.B. map). But here, solely for simplicity's sake—and with, I hope, the forgiveness of the Flemish—I often have used only the French. Except for scattered attractions (included at the end), major sights are grouped under three main centers: the **Grand-Place**; the **Place Royale**; and the **Grand Sablon**.

GRAND-PLACE AND SURROUNDING AREA

Grand-Place   ★★★

Grote Markt, main square. It's difficult to overstate the impact the Grand-Place makes as you enter it on foot from any of the confined cobbled streets that lead there. Suddenly, you are assaulted with splendor on a staggering scale, an impression strengthened not only by the great size of the square, but by the architecturally harmonious appearance of the whole. In the disaster-turned-triumph of the 1695 French bombardment, enemy cannons leveled everything around the Grand-Place except what they sought most: the soaring spire of the Hôtel de Ville. Immediately, plans were made to build even grander guild houses and, between 1696 and 1699, many were completed. Baroque and beautifully embellished, with statue-studded gables, pilasters, and balustrades, the gold-leaf detail of the decor glowing in the sun or gleaming under night spotlights, the guild houses surround Brussels' immense (120 by 75 yards, 110 by 70 meters) main square. Most of the buildings served as headquarters for the business and social meetings of Brussels' guilds, identified by the appropriate patron saint or insignia on the facade; all have stories (inquire at the T.I.B. about its audio-tours of the Grand-Place) though none has a

more varied history than the **Maison du Cygne** (swan) at No. 9. Rebuilt in 1698 as a house for Peter Fariseau (a founder of the Brussels opera), it became in 1720 the butchers' guild house. In exile from Germany, **Karl Marx** (1818–1883) moved with his family into the building in about 1846 and, having met Friedrich Engels in Brussels, undoubtedly wrote some of their jointly published (1848 in Belgium) *Communist Manifesto* under its roof. So perhaps it's appropriate that the *Belgian Labor Party* was founded in the Maison du Cygne in 1885. Today, it houses an elegant restaurant of the same name whose prices are most certainly capitalist, not communist.

Hôtel de Ville/ Stadhuis/Town Hall

(multilingual guided tours only, April–Sept., Tues.– Fri., 9:30 a.m.–12:15 p.m., 1:45–5 p.m., (from Oct.–Mar. closes at 4 p.m.), Sun. 10 a.m.–noon, 2–4 p.m.; tours cancelled in case of City Council sessions or receptions; last tour a half hour before closing time, closed Mon., Sat., some holidays; ☎ *512.75.54).* This centerpiece of the Grand-Place is one of the largest (197-foot/60-meter facade) and finest Gothic buildings in the Benelux. With a 295-foot/90-meter openwork spire by Jan van Ruisbroek, topped with a figure of Archangel Michael, patron saint of the city, it was completed in 1454. Included in the guided tour of the interior are reception halls laden with decorative treasures: 15th-, 17th-, and 18th-century Brussels' tapestries, Gothic wood carvings, and fascinating full-length portraits of the likes of Charles V and Philip II.

Museum of the City of Brussels

Maison du Roi, Grand-Place, directly opposite the Hôtel de Ville; Mon–Fri. 10 a.m.–12:30 p.m., 1:30–5 p.m. except 4 p.m. Oct. 1–Mar. 31; Sat., Sun., holidays. 10 a.m.–1 p.m.; ☎ *511.27.42.* Despite a lack of English explanation, much here will capture your attention, including the building itself (though, singly among those on the Grand-Place, it is not as old as it looks). Destroyed in the 1695 bombing, it remained a shattered shell (and eyesore) until rebuilt in 1763, but it was reconstructed in such an ordinary and unharmonizing style that it became neglected and had to be virtually demolished and rebuilt again in 1873, under the patient efforts (22 years worth) of City Architect Victor Jamaer. He used old engravings as his guide, but added the galleries and the tower. The ground floor displays 16th- and 17th-century Brussels' tapestries, including one made from a cartoon by Rubens, 15th-century carved-wood retables, 14th- and 15th-century stonework saved from Brussels' buildings, and 18th- and 19th-century Brussels faience, all highlighted by **Pieter Breugel the Elder's** *Marriage Procession*. The first floor also presents a history of Brussels's city design and development, shown through items such as a model of the 17th-century town, and paintings and prints showing the Senne river harbor before it was filled/covered in the 19th century. The main attraction of the second floor is the display of several dozen of the 400-odd outfits in the ★ ★ wardrobe of Brussels's mascot **Manneken-Pis**. The costumes periodically donned by the two-foot- tall statue range from Roman centurian to American cowboy. Maurice Chevalier penned and published a song to Manneken-Pis in 1949 and gave him an outfit complete with a straw hat of the type the French songster was famous for. On some dates Manneken-Pis is dressed ceremonially: each Sept. 3, in thanks for their liberation of Brussels on that date in 1944, he wears the uniform of the Welsh Guards.

L'Ilot Sacré   ★★

The Sacred Isle. This old section of the lower town, a network of narrow cobbled streets built on the once-marshy land where Brussels was born more than one thousand years ago, covers the area immediately north of the Grand-Place. Its pedestrian back streets carry the names of the businesses conducted here since medieval days: *Marché aux Herbes* (herb market), *rue des Bouchers* (butchers' street), *rue de Beurre* (butter street), *rue de Poivre* (pepper street). Today, L'Ilot Sacre is indeed considered to be sacred, and protected from the demolition and development that have wreaked more havoc on Brussels' buildings than the cannonballs and bombs of any war since the 17th century. One of Brussels' most appetizing tourist sights is the restaurant region of rue des Bouchers and Petit rue des Bouchers: it's often said that if visitors haven't eaten here at least once, they can barely say they've been to Brussels.

Eglise St. Nicolas   ★

rue de Beurre 1; daily 8 a.m.–6 p.m., except Sat. 9 a.m.–6:30 p.m., opens holidays at noon; *511.17.75,* whose origins (the choir is 14th century) go back as far as the activities of the area's merchants to whose patron saint the church is dedicated. It lies at the edge of L'Ilot Sacre. Small shops still abut its sides in the medieval manner. Extensively restored in 1955, St. Nicolas is rich in art works: the *Vladimir Icon* of 1131, paintings by Bernard Van Orley, and one attributed to Rubens.

Art in the Metro/Bourse Station   ★★

blvd. Anspach; Art in the Metro brochure in Dutch and French only. From 1976, when the first stations of the Brussels Metro opened, until 1984, when the city's Museum of Modern Art opened on place Royale, the only real museum of contemporary art in the Belgian capital was underground in the system's shiny new stations. When Metro construction began in 1969, an art-loving politician helped direct its decoration, moving city planners to a totally innovative approach because, as one spokesman said, "we did not want to have a stereotype Metro with kitchen or bathroom-type tiles and every station the same." The Ministry of Transport not only solved much of Brussels' enormous urban traffic problem, which had come to impact the quality of life in the city, but also improved the quality-of-life dimension of the Metro stations (elsewhere so often anonymous, monotonous, user-unfriendly underground spaces). About 1% of the Metro budget was set aside for commissioned works from jury-invited contemporary Belgian artists who, once asked, were given freedom to express themselves in the station space and often were involved right along with the construction. Artists were asked to use materials that would stand up to the underground environment.

Bourse is only one of some three-dozen Metro stations that display some of the 50 works of original art, but since it's central, we'll begin a Metro art inventory there. A large oil painting of old Brussels trams,

painted by Belgium's grandfather of Surrealism **Paul Delvaux**, is quite
in character for the artist who has used train stations as symbols for
years. As with several stations, Bourse has more than one art work; **Pol
Bury** created a *Moving Ceiling* out of 75 welded stainless steel cylinders. At the *Comte de Flandre* station, **Paul van Hoeydonck's** *16 x
Icarus* group of figures "fly" from the ceiling. (Van Hoeydonck, who
lived in the U.S., has the distinction of being the world's only artist to
have a work on the moon: his small statue *Fallen Astronaut* was placed
on the moon's surface by *Apollo 15*'s Armstrong in 1971.) Since the
opening of the new **Stockel** station in 1988, riders have been
delighted by artist **Van Herge's** colorful comic strip figures lining both
long walls. The entire **Alma** station reflects nature: pillars are painted
as tree stumps and the ceiling is a puffy cloud-filled sky. **Vandervelde**
is a fantasy landscape, with the second-largest ceiling fresco in the
world (following, of course, the Sistine Chapel). **Aumale** features the
world's largest photographic work of art. It depicts scenes showing
the Anderlecht neighborhood as it was before and after demolition to
make way for the station. **Hankar** station has Roger Somville's
500-square-yard acrylic wall and ceiling painting called *Notre Temps*,
showing the contradictions of "our times" in vividly colored scenes:
an all-night cafe where people discuss the future of the world, motor-
cyclists refusing to take part in the everyday battle of life. At **Merode**,
Roger Raveel's large oil panel painting *Ensor: Vive La Sociale*, with its
faceless people (in the style of painter Ensor), bright colors, and mirrors, is meant to raise questions. Many of the stations feature sculptures; at **Stuyvenbergh**, **Yves Bosquet** has mounted statues of the
Royal Family against one wall. With the variety of materials used (Station **Louise** has a tapestry), there are stations that do have tiles, but
there's nothing of the bathroom about them: **Tomberg's** are yellow
ceramics with a blue line design; **Merode** has a wonderful wall of blue,
red, yellow, and brown tiles; and **Roodebeek's** tiles mix with marble in
striking black and shades of gray vertical stripes.

It's nice to know that in this city, which has commissioned works from
celebrated artists for more than 500 years, the Ministry of Transport
is continuing the tradition today and has enabled many of Belgium's
best artists to carry out work which many of the artists themselves
consider of decisive importance in their careers. In addition to its aesthetic appeal, the Brussels Metro has statistics that show it has greater
passenger security, less graffiti and vandalism, and fewer suicides than
the underground transportation systems of comparably sized cities.

Théâtre de la Monnaie
place de la Monnaie. So named because, until bombed by Louis XIV's
army in 1695, the **Munt** (Mint) had stood here, and the Theatre de la
Monnaie that replaced it played a role in Belgian independence. In
February 1829, the opera *La Muette de Portici* by French composer
Daniel Francois Auber premiered at the theater at a gala attended by
the Dutch royalty of the Kingdom of the Netherlands. The opera's

libretto told of Neapolitans' struggles against oppressors, and the climactic aria *Amour Sacre de la Patrie* (Sacred Love of the Fatherland) was vigorously applauded by the Belgians, whose emotions obviously had been stirred because of their own unhappy enforced union with Holland since 1815. The audience's reaction caused the opera to be withdrawn from the repertoire for 18 months. When it was staged again on August 25, 1830—only a month after Parisiens had overthrown the French monarch—following the provocative line *Rendsnous l'audace et la fierté* ("give us back boldness and pride"), intellectuals were inspired to join workers outside on the place de la Monnaie in demonstrating against underpayment and unemployment. Those who fell in the ensuing month-long revolution (see *"History"*) are buried beneath a monument at the **Place des Martyrs**, a quiet square two blocks north of the theater off rue d'Argent. The Theatre de la Monnaie standing today was designed by Joseph Poelaert following a fire in 1855; it has recently been lavishly restored.

Sainte Catherine/Saint Géry district   ★

Just across boulevard Anspach from the Bourse is a less explored area of old Brussels, an extension of the narrow market streets found in the Ilot Sacre. A landmark is the large **Eglise Sainte Catherine** *(place Saint-Catherine; 7:30 a.m.–7 p.m., 5 p.m. in winter;* ☎ *513.34.81)*, built in 1854 by Joseph Poelaert in a mixture of styles. A 17th-century belfry from a former church stands nearby, as does the **Tour Noire**, a survivor from the city's 12th-century walls. Running parallel to each other north from the church are **quai au Bois à Brûler** and **quai aux Briques**, once quays on either side of the subsequently covered Senne River, an area known as the ★★**Marché aux Poissons** (Fish Market) and noted for its seafood restaurants. (See *Where to Eat.*) The area's open space and fountains provide a pleasant surprise. Nearby is the **Eglise Saint Jean Baptiste au Béguinage**:*(place de Béguinage; Tues., Thurs., Fri., Sat. 9 a.m.–5 p.m., Sun. 10 a.m.–5 p.m.)*, built from 1657–1676 by Luc Fayd'herbe; its three-gabled Flemish-Italian baroque facade is one of the finest in Belgium. (It and that of Sainte Catherine are both beautifully floodlit at night.)

Adjoining the Sainte-Catherine district to the south is Saint-Géry, within which is **Les Halles**, an 1881 neo-Flemish renaissance marketplace used as a wholesale meat market as recently as 1977 and subsequently saved from demolition by ARAU. (See *Tours* under *Guideposts*) Today Les Halles (which renovating architect Jacques Zajtman admits was influenced by London's Covent Garden), is an upmarket assemblage of clothing, craft, and chocolate shops, and gathering place for the gregarious and street performers. The 32 boutiques and interior stalls are bathed in a special glow by the natural light that pours in through the glass/wrought-iron roof. A mezzanine-level bar runs the length of the building, providing a viewing and drinking stand overlooking shoppers on the floor below; in the low-arched cellars is a restaurant.

Manneken-Pis ★★

rue de l'Etuve at the corner of rue du Chene, some 100 yards/90 meters southwest of the Grand-Place. Manneken-Pis, an unexpectedly small, scarcely two-foot-tall/just over a half-meter-high statue of a naked young boy urinating into a fountain struck such a strong chord with Bruxellois that city fathers in 1619 commissioned a bronze replacement from Jerome Duquesnoy the Elder to replace a similar 15th-century stone statue. Many legends exist concerning the origins of Manneken-Pis, but, even leaving such speculations aside, the story of the statue-turned-city-symbol is absorbing.

His singular popularity and position as city mascot have made Manneken-Pis the subject of a series of kidnappings over the centuries. The first, intercepted, attempt was made by British soldiers in 1745. That effort seems to have inspired French soldiers in 1747, but their plot, too, was uncovered before it played out. However, to recompense Brussels for his soldiers' seizing of the statue, King Louis XV bestowed upon Manneken-Pis a title and gold-embroidered brocade court costume, complete with sword and feathered hat, to wear on festival days. Before long, other groups, both Belgian and foreign, were following suit, gifting Manneken-Pis with sufficient garb to make him the city's best-dressed citizen, one necessitating a wardrobe keeper. (See "Grand-Place, Maison du Roi,"). The most damaging kidnapping incident occurred in 1817 when a supposed ex-convict pulled the statue from his street-corner niche and broke it into pieces. Fortunately, the fragments were found and reassembled to form a mould from which the present statue was cast. In 1956, after yet another attempt, Manneken-Pis was bolted in place and equipped with a burglar alarm. During a snowstorm a few years later, however, the alarm bells froze, and prank-minded students from Antwerp were able to make off with him, though he was returned unharmed the next day.

Galléries Saint Hubert ★★

entrances off rue du Marché aux Herbes, rue des Bouchers, and rue d'Arenberg; always open. At the end of rue des Bouchers, one enters a different era. The Industrial Age made possible the art of glass and metal that found one of its earliest and finest expressions in the skylighted Galleries Saint Hubert, Europe's first covered shopping walkway, built in 1847 by J. P. Cluysenaer. Not only was the arcade an early all-weather environment, but it also provided pedestrians with through passage in an alley area that over the centuries had become choked with impasses. The airy and attractive glass-vaulted arcade splits into the flag-festooned yet elegant **Galerie de la Reine** and **Galerie du Roi**, housing boutiques, cafes, and a theater.

Brussels has other 19th-century arcades: **Bortier Arcade**, browsed for its bookshops, connects rue de l Madeleine to rue Saint-Jean; **North Arcade**, with a broad selection of shops, connects the pedestrian rue

Neuve and the busy boulevard Adolphe Max at the northern end of the place de Brouckère; and **Hirsch Arcade**, though not flourishing, still supports a secondhand bookshop and print and etching shop that have been there since the second World War, and it runs at right angles to place des Martyrs and rue d'Argent.

Belgian Center of the Comic Strip   ★★

rue des Sables 20; daily 10 a.m.–6 p.m., closed Mon. and Jan. 1, Nov. 1, Dec. 25; ☎ *219.19.80.* Opened in 1989, this museum links two distinctively Belgian forms of creative expression. The setting is a 1903 former textile warehouse that was designed by Brussels's leading art nouveau exponent, architect Victor Horta; the contents are what Belgians call the Ninth Art, the social phenomenon and genuine art form of the comic strip. The museum was once the Waucquez Warehouse, the only one remaining of six art nouveau department stores that Horta built in Brussels. It, too, was very nearly lost to the wrecker's ball when the store went out of business in 1965 and buyers couldn't be found for the building, leaving it abandoned to weather and vandals until the middle of the 1980s. Fortunately, visionaries in the '80s seeking a place to gather the fantastic examples of their unusual art form saw the possibility of doing so under the historic Waucquez roof, which was subsequently restored. The displayed comic strips and audiovisual exhibits (more than 60 years of creativity are documented) usually are in French and/or Flemish only, but their visual appeal and that of the wonderful building with its magnificent lobby, ornamental grand staircase, art nouveau details, and space and light on all three floors, make the museum thoroughly worthwhile. There's also a shop with curios and posters, and an attractively ornamented brasserie (omelets, pasta, salads, chicken and seafood dishes, beverages including wine and beer, kitchen open until 3:30 p.m.). The museum's location, rue des Sables, in an area of central Brussels now in transition back to respectability, once teemed with pedestrian traffic because of the public stairs at the end of the street which still lead to the upper town.

PLACE ROYALE AND SURROUNDING AREA

Cathédrale Saint-Michel   ★★

place Sainte-Gudule; Easter to Oct. 31, 7 a.m.–7 p.m.; Nov. to Easter, 7 a.m.–6 p.m.; ☎ *217.83.45.* The cathedral, whose triforium is especially lovely when illuminated, has stood on its sloping site between Brussels's lower and upper town since the mid-13th century; the twin truncated towers, a rarity in Belgium, give it a strong French appearance. Overall, the massive building has a simple Brabant-Gothic style, with the nave and transept dating from the 14th and 15th centuries. Though elevated in rank to cathedral only in 1961 (when it became the seat of the Archbishop of Brussels-Mechelen), St.-Michel, long known as Belgium's national church, has been the setting for all the country's great religious occasions since the time of Duke Philip the

Good of Burgundy. An extensive and extended restoration-in-progress makes uncertain what will be on view to visitors, but the 16th-century stained glass windows in the south and north transepts, created from cartoons by **Bernard van Orley**, are a treasure to search out, as are those of the same period in the **Chapel of the Blessed Sacrament** donated by Charles V and his family, whose granddaughter Archduchess Isabella and her husband are among those buried in the crypt. Also buried in the cathedral is one-time Brussels's city painter **Rogier van der Weyden** (1400–61) and Margaret of York (d. 1322), daughter of England's Edward I. A superb carved-wood baroque pulpit by Hendrik Verbruggen (1669) shows Adam and Eve being expelled from Eden, and six splendid 17th-century tapestries by Van der Borght sometimes are hung in the choir, often in summer when chamber concerts may be given in the chapel.

Rue Ravenstein

Exiting the Victor Horta-designed Gare Centrale (Central Station) through **Galerie Ravenstein**, with its arcade and rotunda, leads to rue Ravenstein. Across it just to the left of Horta's **Palais des Beaux-Arts** is **rue Baron Horta**, formerly the **Escallier Belliard**, on which was located **Pensionnat Heger** to which **Charlotte Brontë** (1816–1855) came in 1842–43, first as a student, then remaining as a teacher, after having fallen in unrequited love with Monsieur Heger. Brontë's Brussels experiences appear as background in her novels *Villete* and *The Professor*, in which rue Ravenstein is called rue Fossette. At the top of rue Ravenstein is the 15th-century **Hotel Ravenstein** (now a restaurant, see *Where to Eat*), Brussel's last surviving mansion from the Burgundian period with a picturesque interior that's been carefully restored. In it was born **Anne of Cleves**, the "Flemish Mare," fourth wife of Henry VIII. Further up is the top of the Mont des Arts.

Mont des Arts

Erected between 1954 and 1965 Mont des Arts is another route from the lower town to the upper with stairs and garden through its center, convention center to the left and Royal Library to the right, with the ★★ **Place du Musée** with the impressive Louis XVI-style palace of Charles of Lorraine at the summit. Its lavish exterior decoration features statues and bas-reliefs celebrating the arts and sciences.

Museum of Ancient Art/Art Ancien;
Museum of Modern Art/Art Moderne ★★★

rue de la Régence 3 for access to both museums; daily 10 a.m.–5 p.m.; lunch closings are coordinated so that when one closes for an hour the other remains open; closed Mon., Jan. 1, May 1, Nov. 1, Nov. 11, Dec. 25, and election days; *508.32.11; catalogues in English.* Simply stated, these museums house the most important collections in Belgium, a country noted for its art. The Museum of Ancient Art, whose focus is on the **Flemish "Primitives"** rather than classical ancients, concentrates on the art of the 15th-17th centuries in the Netherlands. There are some contemporary paintings from Italy and elsewhere included for comparison. Highlights from the rich collection, in which virtually all major Netherlands artists are represented, include *The Annunciation* by the **Master of Flemalle**, *Portrait of Anthony of Burgundy* and *The Lamentation* by Brussels' mid-15th-century city painter **Rogier van der Weyden**. A room is devoted solely to five major works and a fragment by **Pieter Breughel the Elder** (the most important grouping of his works outside of Vienna). In an adjoining room are copies and adaptations of his work done by his son, **Pieter Breugel the Younger**, who was born just a short distance from the museum in 1564. Often called "Hell Breugel" for his own painted visions of life after death, he is responsible through his carefully copied versions of having preserved now-lost original works by his father (who died when his son was only five). Among the copies here are the *Massacre of the Innocents* and *Festival of Flanders* which, though not of the genius of the father's originals, are masterpieces in their own right. The great works in the 17th-century Dutch gallery are displayed in a lovely carpeted and skylighted setting.

The Museum of Modern Art, opened in 1984 and connected—compliments of **Alphonse Balat** (1875–1885)—to the older, neoclassical museum building by passageways and escalator, is a stunningly successful creation of ★★ multilevel exhibit space in the form of a glass half-bowl curved to catch the natural light, and set some eight levels in and beneath the courtyard of Charles of Lorraine's palace. Belgium's entire cast of 19th- and 20th-century painters and sculptors is included, along with a collection of 26 major works by **René Magritte** (*Empire of Lights* and *The Domain of Arnheim* kept by his widow until her death in 1986). A well-marked, color-coded museum plan (comprehensible even in its French/Flemish form) helps make the most of your time. There's a good shop and cafeteria.

Place Royale   ★

This area of the upper town took its shape and neoclassical appearance in the 18th century as Hapsburg rulers instituted a grand Paris-influenced plan meant to make Brussels look a little less like Vienna's country cousin. At the center of the square is an equestrian statue of **Godfrey de Bouillon**, leader of the First Crusade in 1096. (See *Bouillon* under *Wallonia, The Meuse Valley.*) Close by is the ★**Royal Palace** (open to visitors for a period each Aug./Sept., check with T.I.B. for dates, times), currently used for state receptions, royal audiences, and as the king's office. (The royal residence is in suburban Laeken.) The palace was built in the 1730s, more or less on the site of the former **Palace of Coudenberg** (which burned in 1731) that had been used by the dukes of Brabant from the end of the 11th century and by their descendants including Emperor Charles V. The present Royal Palace was expanded and renovated by Leopold II at the beginning of this century.

The marriage of the late King Baudouin and Queen Fabiola took place in 1960 in the ★★regal 500-foot Throne Room, certainly a setting worthy of the royal affair, with its exquisite mosaic parquet floors, gleam of a dozen Val-Saint-Lambert Belgian crystal chandeliers (which in turn glow in the gold-edged mirrors), plasterwork friezes, and wall-and-ceiling ornamentation. The Goya Room is decorated with antique Brussels tapestries based on cartoons by the 18th-century Spanish painter.

Facing the Royal Palace is the ★ **Parc de Bruxelles** *(open daily 6 a.m.–9 p.m.)*. Laid out in its present French park form in 1835, it was previously the park for the dukes of Brabant and was famed throughout Europe as a hunting wood and warren with ponds, fountains, and grottos. During the Belgium "revolution" of 1830, the park was the scene of armed exchanges between Belgians and Dutch King Willem's forces. Today, the espaliered Linden trees, their leafy limbs linked Brabant-style to form a green trellis, shady strolling promenades, and fountains, provide a peaceful, pleasant separation of monarch and state (the **Palais de la Nation/Parliament** being at the opposite side of the park from the palace). **The Belgian Parliament** *(public entrance at rear, rue de Louvain 7; guided visits can be arranged on weekdays between 10 a.m. and 4 p.m. when there are no sessions; call the Senate ☎ 515.82.11 or the House ☎ 519.81.11; English language literature available)*. As a guide pointed out, "The country of Belgium doesn't exist by the grace of God as does the United Kingdom; we Belgians exist by the grace of the Great Powers." Included on a tour of the impressively furnished building, built between 1779 and 1783, is the rich red Senate Chamber and the green-toned House of Representatives, both of which conduct all business with simultaneous translations of Dutch into French and vice versa.

The nearby **Congress Column** *(place du Congres, rue Royale)* commemorates the National Congress of 1831, which proclaimed the Belgian Constitution. The large bronze figures represent freedom of the press, education, religion, and association. An eternal flame at the base pays homage to unknown soldiers from the first and the second World Wars, both represented by a Fleming and a Walloon.

THE SABLON AND MAROLLES DISTRICTS

Place du Grand-Sablon/Grote Zavel

rue de la Regence, a short distance southwest of Place Royale. Far more refined than its name in French ("sandy wasteland") suggests, the Sablon is an elegant, elongated square, encircled by smart antique and art shops, trendy bars and restaurants. It first became fashionable in the 16th century. It's at its most colorful on weekends, when the red-and-green-awninged stalls of the antiques market are set at the top of the square.

Eglise Notre-Dame du Grand Sablon ★★

rue de Regence 3B; Mon.–Fri. 7 a.m.–6:30 p.m., Sat., Sun., holidays 9 a.m.–7 p.m., guided tour Sun. 4 p.m.; ☎ *511.57.41.* A lovely example of late flamboyant Gothic style, the church developed from a 1304 chapel built by the Guild of Crossbowmen. In 1615, Archduchess Isabella, using a crossbow, shot down the guild's target bird atop the church, which garnered her much admiration. The interior has some fine detail, including Gothic carvings on the cornerstones, but the church also is much admired simply for its overall harmony with the setting. The fine stained glass windows are illuminated wonderfully from ★★within at night. Rededicated (by American organist James David Christie) in 1990 after its rebuilding, the organ is often used for concerts.

Place du Petit-Sablon ★★

across rue de Regence from Notre-Dame is a tranquil Renaissance-style garden with benches well used by area residents. Elegant effigies of counts Egmont and Hoorn (who met their death by beheading on the Grand-Place in 1568) have been given a place of honor; the Egmonts were one of the noble families who settled on the Sablon in the 16th century. The pretty park is surrounded by a wrought iron fence, with each of its 48 supporting columns topped with a small bronze statue representing one of Brussels' 16th-century guilds.

Among the greenery of the **Jardin Du Palais d'Egmont** (*access from rue du Grand-Cerf, off rue aux Laines/Wolstraat at the southeast corner of Petit-Sablon*), seek out the statue of ★ **Peter Pan**, a twin casting by Frampton of the whimsical figure with animal friends that's tucked among trees in London's Kensington Gardens. At **Palais d'Egmont** *(not open to the public)*, now the property of the Belgian Ministry of Foreign Affairs and used for major conferences, in 1973, the United Kingdom, Ireland, and Denmark signed the documents that made them full members of the European Community. (Greece followed suit in 1981, Spain and Portugal in 1986.)

At the end of rue aux Laines, past graceful 19th-century houses, sits the enormous bulk of the ★ **Palais du Justice** *(Law Courts; place Poelaert)*, 17 years in the making to the mid-19th-century design of **Joseph Poelaert**. He obviously was moved to create a monumental work, since the 2.5 acre-structure is larger by half again than that of St. Peter's in Rome. Perhaps appropriately, the Palais du Justice sits on the former site of Brussels' gallows; it was the hoi polloi (not those worth bringing to the Grand-Place to be executed publicly) who were hanged here. The Nazis set the buildings on fire on Sept. 3, 1944, and the huge 345-foot-high dome caved in. It's long since been reconstructed and dominates the skyline and the ★ **Marolles** district, located at the base of its plateau.

The **Marolles**, famous for its ancient Brussels dialect and flea market, is well stocked with faces familiar from Flemish paintings created four centuries ago. So it may not be surprising to learn that **Pieter Breugel the Elder** lived here in the **Breugel House** *(rue Haute 132; plans to open the authentically restored house as a museum remain uncertain, inquire at the T.I.B.).* Pieter Breugel the Elder (1525–1569) was born in the North Brabant province in Holland and lived there for the last six years of his life. Most likely apprenticed to master painter Peter Coeck in Antwerp from about 1545 to 1550, he was created a Freemaster in the Guild of St. Luke there in 1551. Breugel traveled in Italy in the early 1550s, and from 1559 began producing signed and dated paintings with regularity. In 1563 he married the daughter of his former master and settled in Brussels. Two sons (Pieter "Hellfire," the Younger and Jan "Velvet") were born in the house in 1564 and 1568, but sadly Pieter the Elder died here in September 1569. He was buried in the partly 13th-century **Eglise Notre Dame de la Chapelle** *(at the end of the road, corner of rue Haute and rue Blaes),* where he had been married only six years earlier. Breugel's memorial, in the third chapel off the south aisle, was erected by his son Pieter and once was adorned with a painting (now in a private collection) by Pieter Paul Rubens, with whom son Jan Breugel later studied and worked. Undoubtedly, the elder artist strolled these working-class streets searching for faces and figures to put into his well-peopled paintings and, today, Breugelian characters still serve or sit over steins of beer in the cafes.

ATTRACTIONS ELSEWHERE IN BRUSSELS

Palais du Berlaymont

rue de la Loi, Rond-point Robert Schuman; no public visits; Metro station Schuman. The rather too grandly named building, never noted other than for its shape (the best description of which I've heard is a four-armed starfish), has, since its opening in 1969, been Brussels' symbol of the European Community, serving as office space for some 5,000 Eurocrats. Now the building's been found to be full of asbestos and may, in fact, have come down by the time you read this. Construction on other EC complexes already has brought most other activity in the district to a halt; the next building to come on-line will be large enough to house the whole European Parliament (much expanded with 13 member countries, compared with the original six).

Musées Royaux d'Art et d'Histoire   ★

Royal Art and History Museums; *Parc du Cinquantenaire; year-round Tues.–Fri. 9:30 a.m.–5 p.m.; Sat., Sun. 10 a.m.–5 p.m., closed Mon.; however, some sections of this enormous institution are staffed only on certain days, with some collections open solely on odd or even days; it's best to call ahead if you are interested in a particular exhibit;* ☎ *741.72.11; Metro station Schuman; color-coded museum plan, exhibit notes in French/Flemish only.* The monumental museum wings, surrounded by the 90-acre/ 36-hectare **Parc du Cinquantenaire**, were built for a national exhibition held in 1880 to celebrate 50 years of Belgian independence; the triple triumphal arch that connects the two colonnaded buildings was built in 1904–05 by architect Charles Girault. The *Museums of Art and History* are in the wing on the right. Among the extensive collections that cross all eras and areas (a fine model/maquette of ancient Rome, for example) are a number of excellent Belgium-related exhibits: the remarkable Flemish Renaissance *Story of Jacob* ★★ tapestry set (see "Tapestries" under "Decorative Arts and Traditional Crafts"); ★★ art nouveau and art deco vases, stained glass, and jewelry; ★★ Belgian lace and furniture; and porcelain from Tournai.

The wing to the left houses the Museums of the Army and Military History, which provide a general impression of the major military and historical events that have taken place on Belgian soil since 1789. Of perhaps more interest to non-Belgians, and not as dependent on non-existent English exhibit notes, are the *armored car* and *aviation* sections that focus mostly on the first and second World Wars. One huge room offers an exceptional collection of World War I fighter planes and *Battle of Britain* (1940) spitfires; gondolas from balloons and airships also are on display.

Atomium ★

blvd. du Centenaire, Laeken; daily year-round 9:45 a.m.–6 p.m.; April to mid-Sept. until 6:30 p.m., and panorama only until 10 p.m.; ☎ *477.09.77; Heysel Metro station.* This imaginatively conceived, skillfully constructed symbol of the **1958 Brussels' World's Fair** (and, since then, of the city) has just received a long-overdue overhaul. The aluminium-covered steel model of an iron crystal molecule, magnified some 200 billion times, represented the Atomic Age at the World's Fair and later offered exhibits on the peaceful uses of nuclear power. Atomium has nine "electrons," large (60 ft./18 m. in diameter), shiny exhibition-space spheres that are connected by elevators and escalators running up inside 10-foot/3 meter-wide supporting pylons. Since renovation, during which the structural integrity was examined and the interior escalator (the longest in Europe) replaced, a new exhibit devoted to the evolution and recent developments of medical research has been installed. Atomium's top sphere, at 335 feet/102 meters much higher than Brussels' Hotel de Ville's spire, has a panoramic observation area and restaurant.

Mini-Europe

Adjacent to Atomium in Bruparck Center; daily April 1–Jan. 6, 9 a.m.–6 p.m., except in July & Aug. until 8 p.m., weekends 9 p.m.; ☎ *477.03.77. Heysel Metro station* features a landscaped layout of approximately 70 major 1:25 scale models of landmark buildings in the 12 EC member states. The detail on some (the Louvain Hotel de Ville, London's Parliament Buildings, Paris's Pompidou Center and Sacre-Coeur, Athens' Acropolis) is remarkable. Pricey (combined ticket with Atomium: BF 480) but worth consideration if you enjoy this sort of attraction.

At nearby **Laeken**, you can tell if King Albert and Queen Paola are home by whether or not Belgium's black, gold, and red standard is sighted over the Royal Palace. The royal residence is never open to the public, but the ★ ★ **Royal Greenhouses** are, for about ten days during April and May. (Exact dates and times, including evenings when greenhouses are illuminated, are available after Jan. 1 from the Tourist Office.) Located in the 460-acre/185 hectare Royal Park, the greenhouses, themselves six acres under neoclassical glass-domed rotundas and galleries, were ordered built for the royal blooms, including tropical species brought back from the Belgian Congo (now Zaire), by King Leopold II in the 1870s. It's nearly a one-mile/1.5 kms. round trip through the greenhouses, highlighted by the azalea house. There are connecting walks filled with climbing geraniums and fuchsias, whose bell-like blossoms form a colorful overhead canopy, and ferns, songbirds, glades, and grottos. The architectural treasure, 323,000 square feet of glass set in elaborate ironwork, is a translation of royal vision into reality by architect **Alphonse Balat**. That the structure greatly influenced the development of art nouveau in Belgium and elsewhere was credited by **Victor Horta**, Balat's most famous student, who always counted the Royal Greenhouses as a major source of inspiration for his own art nouveau efforts.

Victor Horta House

rue Américaine 25, 1060 Saint-Gilles; year-round Tues.–Sat. 2–5:30 p.m., closed Sun., Mon., holidays; ☎ *537.16.92; tram 81, 92, bus, 54, 60.* From the moment you reach for the door handle, your fun has begun. Art nouveau, a style determined to do away with straight lines, puts arabesques in iron, curls in wood, and whirls and whiplashes in many materials that normally defy such shapes; its inventive practicality delights. Victor Horta (1861–1947), Belgium's leading exponent of art nouveau, trained under Alphonse Balat and, receiving commissions for houses by 1890—the earliest days of the style—in 1898 bought two plots of land on rue Americaine and began designing his house and studio. One of the few art nouveau interiors on view to the public, the whole house exudes Horta's sense of creative exhilaration and reflects the purest realization of his mature artistic concepts. Applied arts flourished in the art nouveau period and Horta, who always aspired to full unity between architecture and interior design, wrote—"in every house, I designed and created the models for each piece of furniture, for every single hinge and door handle, the carpets, and the wall decorations." Horta's art nouveau elements are organic and use a proliferation of vegetable forms, such as flower petal and leaf shapes; a ceiling may be shaped like a calla lily. Throughout the house, banisters curl up staircases like ribbons; cabinets seem to grow out of corners.

Horta based his art nouveau designs on the concept that structural elements could become artistic ones. He showed that iron and stone and bricks and wood could work together in a "human" architecture, and materials formerly used only for industrial buildings could make extra height and light possible in homes. Art nouveau sought to bring light and air into the dark and stuffy decor of the Victorian era. For light, Horta created revolutionary winter gardens by putting open stairwells in the core of a building, topped by a skylight. He often made use of the contoured opalescent glass developed by Americans **La Farge** and **Tiffany** in the 1870s for its soft effect. The pale-colored walls we take for granted are a legacy from the progressive properties of art nouveau.

Horta houses that have survived and can be viewed from the exterior include: the **Tassel House** *(rue Paul Emile Janson 6; 1893)*; the **Solvay Mansion** *(avenue Louise 224; 1894)*; and the **Van Eetvelde Mansion** *(avenue Palmerston 4; 1895)*. Tours through **ARAU** (see "Tours" under "Guideposts"), may get you inside the astonishing, delightful, art nouveau-detailed ★ ★ Van Eetvelde mansion (originally ordered and owned by a baron who was Secretary General of the Belgian Congo in Brussels), which now serves as the offices of the **Federation de l'Industrie du Gaz.** It's located not far from EC headquarters at Rond-Point Schuman, an area worth exploring on foot for the art nouveau exteriors.

In 1916 Horta went to America, where he lectured in architecture and remained until 1919. When he returned to Brussels he began to work in **art deco**. (One of the reasons art nouveau died out as quickly as it did was that it had become so expensive.) Horta drew up the first plans for the Palais des Beaux-Arts in 1919 (undertaken in 1928) and finished final plans for Brussels *Gare Centrale* (Central Station) in 1937.

David and Alice Van Buuren House   ★ ★

avenue Leo Errera 41, 1180 Uccle; guided tour, open only on Mon. 2–4 p.m., groups of 10 or more at other times by appointment; ☎ *343.48.51, 344.28.30; from Montgomery Metro station take tram 23, 90 to Churchill stop; booklet in English.* Though its location (a time-consuming, confusing trip on public transportation; you may want to consider a cab) and restrictive opening hours will limit those able to include it in their itinerary, even those relatively uninitiated (as was I) in the linear (particularly when compared with art nouveau) *art deco* style will be intrigued by this highly original house of the 1930s. In fact, the art deco decor occasionally strays from the 1930s, with an original version of "The Fall of Icarus" by Pieter Breugel the Elder and a regal collection of 18th-century blue Delftware.

The house was built in 1929 by Dutchman David van Buuren, who became a private financier and was an experienced collector with reliable, eclectic taste, and his wife Alice, who, after her husband died in 1955, conceived the idea of turning the house (whose every detail had been specially created) into a museum. The house was built and decorated during the "high" art deco period (1925–1939), and the exotic materials typical of the style are much in evidence: black marble from Labrador, furniture made of rosewood from Brazil, brown horsehair upholstery and black horsehair wall covering, white sycamore wood, and black wax polish on oak floors. The talents of **Rene Lalique**, the best glass designer of the times, were used for chandeliers, and **Raoul Dufy** designed bold, brightly colored carpets for the dining room and Van Buuren's office; the favored Oriental and linear influences are felt throughout.

A substantial part of the pleasure of a visit to the Van Buuren house comes from the garden, divided into several distinct parts. Created from irregularly shaped and uneven landscape are the 1/2 mi. *labyrinth* in yew with a cedar tree at its center, the *garden of the heart* planted in pink and red dwarf and old fashioned roses, and the *picturesque garden*, sloped and with an open pavilion.

Erasmus House ★★

rue du Chapitre 31, 1070 Anderlecht; 10 a.m.–noon, 2–5 p.m., closed Tues. & Fri.; ☎ 521.13.83; Metro Saint-Guidon, tram 103, bus 47, 49; booklet in English. The great Netherlands humanist **Desiderius Erasmus** lived here only five months in the year 1521, invited as a guest by Canon Wychman to get away from the stench of Brussels to the clean air of the country (the setting was then rural). Erasmus wrote of the comfort, relaxation, and renewed health he enjoyed during his stay in this charming, mid-15th-century, Burgundian-style brick house, during which he worked on translations of his works. Knowing his feelings for this environment, visitors can get a feel for the life of the remarkable author, and see the ★★ exceptional collection of documents, manuscripts, and mementos contained here. The house was authentically restored and opened to the public in 1932. It has been decorated with a harmonious blend of period furnishings and art, and copies of his own work that bring Erasmus to life. We can see Erasmus in portraits by Quinten Metsys, Albert Durer, and Hans Holbein, as well as in a self-portrait cartoon. And almost sense him sitting—quill pen at the ready—at the desk looking out to the garden through windows of old glass that "wobble" views through it. In the display cases in the library are ancient and modern editions of the scholar's works; of particular impact are those that, in his troubled times, were censored— here seen with great hand-inked Xs across many of the words. When Erasmus left this house, he went to Basel, Switzerland, because the Reformation was making it too dangerous to stay. While Erasmus supported reformation of the Catholic Church, he came to oppose Martin Luther's violent Reformation methods (as he wrote in *Discourse on Freewill*, 1524).

Eglise Saint Pierre et Saint Guidon

place de la Vaillance; 9 a.m.–noon, 2:30–7 p.m., Sun. 9 a.m.–noon, 4–7 p.m., closed holidays, during services; ☎ 521.84.15. Located in the center of this Brussels commune of Anderlecht is a superb 14th- and 15th-century Gothic church with wall paintings. The 11th-century Romanesque crypt, one of the most interesting in Belgium, contains the 12th-century tomb of St. Guidon. Just north of the church is a small, recently restored, **Beguinage** *(rue du Chapelain 8; 10 a.m.–noon, 2–5 p.m., closed Tues. & Fri., New Year's;* ☎ *521.20.87),* dating from 1252. Though the nuns left 200 years ago, their presence is still felt.

SHOPPING

Belgium's Val Saint Lambert hand-cut crystal is on display at **Art & Selection** (*rue Marché-aux-Herbes 83*). Belgian lace (covered with a focus on Bruges in the *Decorative Arts and Traditional Crafts* section at the front of this book) is also a Brussels business of long-standing. Lace shops (with machine- as well as handmade items) are concentrated in the small streets off the Grand-Place, particularly **rue de l'Etuve** in the direction of **Manneken-Pis**; you'll also see shops selling machine-made tapestries. At rue de l'Etuve 26 and 43 are *Semal* shops, which, despite being located on Brussels' most touristic street, actually sell some good quality Belgian souvenirs. If you're looking for EC flag-bearing gear (T-shirts, carry-alls, umbrellas, and smaller items), shops here are worth checking out. Nearby **Picard** (*rue de Lombard 71*), which deals in carnival masks and other party paraphernalia, makes an amusing stop.

Its open-air markets are among Brussels' most mentioned attractions. The daily **flower market** carries on a tradition in the **Grand-Place**, which for centuries was the center of market activity in the town. The square's Sunday **bird market** (*7 a.m.–2 p.m.*) has its roots in the exploration of the 15th and 16th centuries, when previously unknown exotic and tropical species were brought to the old world from the far corners of the new. They are displayed here to the amazement of all. More diverse items tempt at the **antique and book market** held on the **Grand Sablon** Saturdays from 9 a.m.-6 p.m. and Sundays from 9 a.m.–2 p.m. Casual and avid collectors will find much to catch their attention on the canvas-awninged tables covered with antiques and almost-antiques. The genteel Sablon square, surrounded by well-kept townhouses, is a chic showplace of antique shops and art galleries with an elegant air, unbroken since the 16th century when it became a residential neighborhood for nobility.

Less pretentious but as much a microcosm of its milieu, the **Marolles** quarter, which it has operated since the 17th century, is the **Vieux Marché** (old market). The flea market takes place on the **place du Jeu de Balle** daily 7 a.m.-2 p.m., though Saturdays and Sundays are the best days; there's direct access on buses 20, 21, 48, within walking distance of tram stops at **Porte de Hal**. It's situated just off **rue Blaes**, which parallels **rue Haute** running through the center of the Marollies. For those seeking a "find," who like to bargain, and are as interested in people-watching as picking through the *brol* (acknowledged junk) and *brocante* (a better class of junk), this is the place. Many of the 200 stall-holders come from the working-class and immigrant-occupied Marolles surroundings, which gives the Vieux Marché the feeling of a neighborhood affair, even though dealers from as far away as Britain and Germany may be among the early-bird buyers doing business off the backs of trucks at 7 a.m.

WHERE TO STAY

Because the city is dominated by the EC, NATO, trade congresses, and multinationals, Brussels' hotels in all price categories have a large business traveler clientele. With the Monday-to-Friday corporate crowd providing their bread and butter, many hotels, particularly the more expensive ones, may offer substantially reduced rates on weekends year-round, and daily during the summer business holiday months of July and August. Always ask about special rates.

VERY EXPENSIVE

Brussels Hilton

blvd. de Waterloo 38; ☎ *504.11.11, in U.S.* ☎ *1-800-HILTONS, Canada* ☎ *1-800-268-9275, U.K.* ☎ *0800-289-303, FAX 513.72.33.* Located in the exclusive Upper Town, the 24-story, 454-room Hilton, opened in 1967, overlooks the Jardin d'Egmont and the mammoth domed Palais du Justice (floodlit at night). With an elegant international atmosphere, the recently renovated leather-upholstered, flower- and art-adorned lobby is a gathering spot for the Bruxellois as well as hotel guests for light meals, tea, and drinks. Tasteful, quiet-colored standard guest rooms have minibar, cable TV with CNN, hair dryers, overnight shoeshine; executive floors offer private lounge, breakfast. The Hilton has three fine restaurants: lighthearted **Café d'Egmont** overlooks that garden's greenery; the formal gourmet **Maison du Boeuf**; and the fashionable **En Plein Ciel** (also a supper club with live music and dancing) on the 27th floor with panoramic view. Health club with sauna, solarium, weights.

Conrad Brussels

avenue Louise, 51; 1050 Brussels; ☎ *542.42.42, in U.S.* ☎ *1-800-HILTONS, in Canada* ☎ *1-800-268-9275; FAX 542.4342.* This 269-guestroom property, which opened in 1993 in a magnificently restored 119-year-old building with original period loggias, balconies, and terraces in one of Brussels' most fashionable neighborhoods, is the Belgian capital city's most luxurious hotel. All rooms in the stylish designed, richly furnished Conrad feature materials specially commissioned by Belgian artists. Bedrooms are the most generously sized in the city; bathrooms feature separate glass-walled stall showers, marble floors, and crystal light fittings. All rooms have color satellite TV, voice mail with remote message recall, three telephones with two-line capacity. As well as having a restaurant with a Michelin-starred chef, the Conrad has elegant meeting facilities and a 24-hour business center; a fully equipped fitness center is set to open in 1994.

Jolly Hotel du Grand Sablon

place du Grand-Sablon; ☎ *512.88.00, FAX 512.67.66, in U.S.* ☎ *1-800-221-2626, in Canada* ☎ *1-800-237-0319.* Opened in July 1991, in a uniquely interesting location on the Grand Sablon (at the "top," by the weekend antique market and Eglise Notre Dame du

Grand Sablon), the 197-room Italian-operated hotel includes a buffet breakfast in its price. The tasteful period-decorated guestrooms in the highest of the three price categories have Jacuzzis. Restaurant, piano bar, hotel garage; 24-hour room service; shuttle service to/from airport.

Metropole   ★★★★★

place de Brouckere 31; ☎ *217.23.00, in U.S.* ☎ *1-800-THE OMNI, FAX 218.02.20.* Brussels' only remaining grand 19th-century hotel, the 410-room Metropole, opened in 1895, still is situated near the center of things, a block from the Monnaie Opera House, and an easy walk to the Grand-Place. The public rooms, worth a look even if you're not staying, are wonderful: a French Renaissance entrance hall, a reception hall with chandeliers, decorated ceilings, gilted molding details, stained glass, and polished wood; lounge/bar in the style of a gentlemen's club with deep leather sofas, marble columns, mirrors, piano and potted palms. The ground floor restaurant and cafe (whose sidewalk section is one of Brussels' premier people-watching places) offer more amazement. Rooms on five floors, served by three elevators and located along sprawling corridors (bellhop service) come in many shapes, sizes, and degrees of modernity. (Older rooms may have more atmospheric appeal.) All have minibar, private bath, color TV, 24-hour room service, 24-hour drycleaning, turn-down service. The setting is lovely, but I did find front-desk service lackadaisical on a recent visit.

SAS Royal   ★★★★★

rue du Fosse-aux-Loups ☎ *47; 219.28.28, FAX 219.62.62.* Opened in 1990 behind the place de la Monnaie, the SAS features a dramatic, seven-floor, glass elevator-served, atrium lobby that is decorated with black-and-white marble, bamboo furniture, greenery, and a waterfall, all set against the backdrop of an original 12th-century city wall. The 281 rooms follow SAS's choose-your-own-decor concept: Scandinavian, Italian, Japanese, or Royal Club executive. All rooms have personal answering machines, telephone in bath, minibar, massage showerhead, with a shoeshine machine on each floor. There are some nonsmoking and handicap-accessible rooms. In-house eateries include a gourmet fish restaurant, an American 1950s-theme casual bar & grill, an 8th-floor restaurant which serves *smorrebrod* and Belgian specialties, and a lobby bar. Covered parking; fitness center (weights, treadmill, cycles, whirlpool and sauna).

Brussels Sheraton Hotel & Towers   ★★★★★

place Rogier 3, 1210 Brussels; ☎ *224.31.11, U.S. & Canada.* ☎ *1-800-325-3535, UK* ☎ *0800-353535, FAX 218.66.18.* Anchoring place Rogier (Metro stop), not far from the North Station (*Gare Nord*), and at the end of boulevard Adolphe Max with its department stores and entertainment, the 600-room, 39-story Brussels Sheraton is a modern, self-contained living complex. In addition to superior category rooms (on the smallish side), the Sheraton Towers ("a small VIP hotel within a hotel") has larger rooms, separate sit-down check-in, breakfast (included) in its lounge, turn-down service, and special amenities. For all guests, there's a top floor fitness club, with sauna, solarium, gym, and the city's only hotel indoor swimming pool. In the lobby is the gourmet **Les Comtes de Flandre** restaurant and a popular bar. Lobby shops; 24-hour room service; underground parking. Note: There's a small "red light" district beyond the Sheraton in the direction of North Station.

Royal Windsor

rue Duquesnoy 5; ☎ *511.42.15, FAX 511.60.04; in U.S. and Canada* ☎ *1-800-223-6800.* This modern 300-room hotel with smart marble lobby is several blocks from the Grand-Place and an equal distance from the Central Station (Gare Centrale). The attractive, wood-accented guestrooms are small, as are the marble baths. The hotel's gourmet restaurant **Les 4 Saisons** offers fine French cuisine; the Edwardian-style **Duke of Wellington** pub, with polished mahogany, leather upholstery, and etched glass, is a popular local rendezvous; the **Crocodile Club** has late-night live music. Continental breakfast included; 24-hour room service; underground parking at hotel.

Stanhope

rue du Commerce 9; ☎ *506.91.11, FAX 512.17.08.* Six years of recent renovation of three adjoining 18th-century houses have produced this deluxe 50-room (25 are suites) hotel, located near the European Community center and the luxury shopping street *La Toison d'Or.* Rooms, each individually and tastefully decorated with English furniture and featuring a full range of amenities, have twice daily service, fax availability, and personal V.I.P. attention. Library-like bar; health club with sauna and exercise machines; book-lined elevators. The elegant hotel restaurant, decorated by the same craftsmen who restored the Royal Pavilion in Brighton, England, opens onto brick-walled garden. Rates (inclusive of buffet breakfast) reduced on weekends.

EXPENSIVE

Amigo

rue de l'Amigo 1; ☎ *547.47.47, FAX 513.52.77.* A block from the Grote Markt, the Amigo offers Brussels' most central accommodations. The oldest part of the six-floor Spanish Renaissance-style hotel building was formerly a prison: a popular contemporary saying was that a one-night stay here made one a true citizen of Brussels. Although the most visible half of the well-blended building dates only from 1956, the Amigo feels as much like an old country home as a well-serviced hotel. The flagstone-floor lobby has been newly redone, although it still features antiques and a clubby bar. Most of the recently updated 200 traditionally furnished rooms have hair dryers, heated towel racks, alarm cords in bathrooms, and air conditioning. Continental breakfast included; restaurant; 24-hour room service;

under-hotel parking. When the present-day Duke of Wellington returns to the victory scene of his ancestor, he uses the Amigo's Spanish-style suite.

Pullman Astoria

rue Royale 103; ☎ *217.62.90, in U.S.* ☎ *1-800-223-9862, FAX 217.11.50.* Built in 1908, during the Belle Époque, and completely redone in 1987, the Astoria once was the hotel of Brussels with its art nouveau decor. The spacious lobby with Louis XV furnishings, marble pillars with gold leaf Corinthian capitals, mirrors, sconces, standing chandeliers, palms, grand stairway up to the stained glass ceiling mezzanine, and plush lobby bar (with live music nightly except Sun.) remain most impressive, and popular with the Bruxellois. All guest rooms (standard and larger) have minibar, hair dryer, color cable TV, room service until 10 p.m., modern tile bath, coffee/tea maker; larger rooms add a trouser press, double basins and piped-in music in the bath. Restaurant; no parking; on bus route, within walking distance of Metro.

Sofitel Brussels

ave. de la Toison d'Or, 1060 Brussels; ☎ *514.22.00, FAX 514.57.44.* Thoroughly modern, the Sofitel is imaginatively tucked into a shopping complex of 80 elegant shops in the upper town; the sleek hotel lobby is up a long escalator from street-level (where there is a bellhop). The 171 well-upholstered, light wood-furnished rooms have twin or king beds, marble baths with glass-stall showers and tubs, minibars, three telephones, and double-glazing on front windows to reduce traffic noise. (Quieter rooms in back overlook the garden.) The off-lobby restaurant with back garden terrace and bar has a very agreeable atmosphere. Nonsmoking rooms available; 24-hour room service; same-day dry cleaning, pressing.

Le Dome

blvd. du Jardin Botanique 12; ☎ *218.06.80, FAX 218.41.12.* Reopened in 1989 after a complete renovation, the hospitable 77-room Le Dome was built in 1902 and has details of the art nouveau style in vogue then, particularly in the **Bar 1902**. The comfortably upholstered lobby and off-lobby restaurant, **Cafe du Dome**, feature **Gustav Klimt** prints, greenery, smoked-glass mirrors, and a pleasing light turquoise trim/pink wall color scheme. All guest rooms have minibar, coffee maker, trouser press, remote control color TV, hair dryer. A breakfast buffet is included. Located on the in-town side of Place Rogier (Metro), a 15-minute walk along the shop-lined boulevard Adolphe Max to the edge of the **Ilot Sacre.**

Archimede

rue Archimede 22; ☎ *231.09.09, FAX 230.33.71.* The hotel is situated on a tree and restaurant-lined residential street a block from the European Community's Berlaymont building, and is popular with visiting EC staffers. The fully renovated modern interior is eclectically decorated with faux marble in the elevators and hallways, fine wood-work and formally dressed mannequins that greet guests in the lobby. The basement breakfast room (extensive buffet included) is decorated as an ocean liner, with deck chairs, ship railings, and portholes with views on to a garden. All 56 rooms have remote cable TV, radio, tele-phone with message system, hair dryer, trouser press.

MODERATE

Manos

chaussée de Charleroi 100, 1060 Brussels; ☎ *537.96.82, FAX 539.36.55.* Built in the 1930s, this hotel features high ceilings and plaster mold-ing details in many rooms. Off the small elegant marble reception area is a lounge decorated with bamboo furniture, paintings, wall panels, marble fireplace, and chandelier; there's also a small library with leather chairs, a pleasant ground floor bar, breakfast (only) room, and walled patio with white iron furniture, and resident white rabbit. All 38 guest rooms have tasteful contemporary furnishings, cable TV, small fridge, modern tile bath, hair dryer. Located on a busy street (tram to Place Royale) off fashionable avenue Louise, three blocks from the Victor Horta Museum.

Chambord

rue de Namur 82; ☎ *513.41.19, FAX 514.08.47.* Located at the edge of the fashionable upper town at Porte Namur (Metro stop), the 64-room Chambord also is just a walk down the hill to the Place Roy-ale. There's light-hearted, light-colored decor in the reasonably sized rooms, which have small marble baths, minibar, color cable TV; front rooms have small balconies. The pleasant, partially skylighted piano bar (light food service) also serves for breakfast (continental only, included). Clientele is a mix of business and leisure travelers from sev-eral nations. Safe-deposit boxes at hospitable, helpful front desk.

Arcade Saint-Catherine

rue Joseph Plateau 2; ☎ *513.76.20, FAX 514.22.14.* A modern 234-room hotel in an interesting, old section of central Brussels worth exploring; well-situated for the Metro, within walking distance of the Grand-Place. Rooms, in cheerful soft colors, all have compact stall/shower, toilet, remote control TV, telephone, individual heat control. Open closet rack, with built-in bench below for suitcase. Inside courtyard rooms are quieter. Buffet breakfast (only, included) served in lobby lounge/bar with nonsmoking section. Credit cards; elevator.

Atlas

rue du Vieux Marché aux Grains, 30; ☎ *502.60.06, FAX 502.69.35.* Located just off Brussels' fashion house row, and a half-block from a tree-lined stretch of Vieux Graan Markt, the 88-room Atlas is a recently converted property behind a restored old facade on a conve-nient cobbled residential street near the historic center. Service is personable and the property's public rooms very pleasing, with original art, plants, and a cheerful color scheme. All rooms in the 4-floor hotel have baths, TV, minibar; 8 rooms under the eaves have skylights, 6 others have kitchenettes, 5 rooms take 4 persons.

Ibis Brussels Center

rue du Marche aux Herbes 100; ☎ *514.40.40, FAX 514.50.667.* New in 1989, in the Ilot Sacre between the Grand-Place and Central Station (Metro), the Ibis is a cheerful, convenient, value-priced basic property. The 170 average-size rooms include bath/shower, color cable TV, telephone, carpeting (thin). There are luggage carts in lobby for self-porterage in the elevators. The large light lobby with greenery and upholstered furniture includes a restaurant (also used for breakfast, included), and bar. Four accessible rooms; public parking nearby.

Hotel Vendome

boulevard Adolphe Max 98; ☎ *218.00.70, FAX 218.06.83.* This remodeled 19th-century townhouse-turned-hotel is located on a main boulevard near good shopping and transportation, a slightly lengthy but reasonable walk from the Grand-Place. The 100 rooms are basic but cheerful and comfy, with minibars and color cable TV. Breakfast (only, included) is served in the skylighted, greenery filled winter garden; there's also a hotel bar, and front desk service is helpful and friendly.

New Hotel Siru ★★★

place Rogier, 1210 Brussels; ☎ *217.75.80, FAX 218.33.03.* If, among other things, you are coming to Brussels to enjoy its contemporary art, you could do no better than to bed down here where many (eventually all) of the 101 rooms have been individually decorated by Belgian artists or sculptors. The contemporary furniture often fits into the scheme of the whole design: in Room 704, for example, a 3-dimensional sculptured couple is stretched over the headboard reading travel brochures and maps. The owners never asked for changes in an artist's concept, though they did reject an entire design if they believed that the resulting room might produce bad dreams. That certainly wouldn't be the case with Room 108: the ceiling fresco by painter Roger Raveel above the bed is entitled "Valium" and is a field of sheep made easy to count. Back to basics. The hotel is located at the corner of place Rogier (Metro, near North Station), and was remodeled in 1988. There's friendly desk service, breakfast (continental included) served in the attached corner cafe (continue beyond the breakfast room); elevators.

INEXPENSIVE

Arlequin

rue de la Fourche 17; ☎ *514.16.15, FAX 514.18.25.* New in the late '80s, this 60-room hotel has an extraordinarily central location near the Grand-Place, tucked away in a commercial center in the **Ilot Sacre.**

All rooms with a tidy modern decor have tiled bath (tub and hand shower), remote cable TV, decent mattresses, and built-in desk which can double as a suitcase rack. Several business suites are available, and some of the more quiet rooms at the back have views of the **Hôtel de Ville's** handsome tower. There's a small lobby with chairs by reception (friendly), a bar, and breakfast (only) room. Major credit cards; elevator.

La Madeleine ★ ★ ★

rue de la Montagne 22; ☎ *513.29.73, FAX 502.13.50.* Steps from the Grand-Place, Galleries Saint Hubert, and Gare Centrale, there's a real local feeling behind the 15th-century facade of this hotel for budget-conscious guests. All 55 clean and basic bedrooms should have been upgraded by the end of 1991: rooms have folding doors to private baths, hand-held shower heads in tubs, and overhead and beside bed lights; some larger rooms available for a supplement. There's no lobby to speak of and no room service, but you're welcome to bring in your own treats to the ground-floor lounge; the breakfast (only, continental, included) room is decorated in a pleasant garden-style. Central heating; major credit cards; elevator; helpful manager.

Opera ★ ★

rue Grétry 53; ☎ *219.43.43.* Located in the heart of Brussels' ancient **L'Ilot Sacre,** this medium-size (52 rooms) clean and utilitarian property has the feel of—and is—a thoroughly European budget hotel. But it's tasteful in its way: restful tones in the decor; halls carpeted and walls papered; functional front desk with youthful English-speakers. Windows of front rooms open onto pedestrian street scenes; back rooms are quieter. Rooms include small built-in desk (can be used as luggage rack), two chairs, wardrobe closet, small curtain-enclosed shower stall. There's a button by each bedroom door to turn on hall lights. Elevator, major credit cards.

Welcome ★ ★

rue du Reuplier 5; ☎ *219.95.46, FAX 217.18.87.* Located just off the-Marché aux Poissons (Fish Market with its fish restaurant row), this small hotel has just six rooms; 2 small, 2 medium, 2 large; prices vary, but all in inexpensive category. All have bath, tiled stall shower, TV, telephone, alarm/radio, and heat; larger ones have hair dryers, the largest a minibar. Friendly owner. No elevator. Continental/cooked breakfast extra: BF 250/BF350.

WHERE TO EAT

Culinary connoisseurs frequently rate Brussels as one of the top three restaurant cities—along with Paris and Hong Kong—in the world. The chapter on *Food and Drink* at the front of this book describes traditional Belgian dishes, which are as much a part of the Brussels food scene as classic French *haute cuisine.* The background on *Belgian Beer* may prove helpful as you sample it in Brussels' cafes. Except at name restaurants, where high prices are sustained by the plethora of expense-account business travelers, restaurant costs in Brussels should not seem steep to those familiar with major cities in northeast North America, and should seem reasonable to visitors from London. Virtually all Brussels (and Belgian) restaurants pride themselves on providing value for money, and tax and service are always included in the price. Remember that selecting a *menu* (several courses for one fixed price; be sure to inquire if you don't see it listed) will always save over multicourse *à la carte* ordering. Many Brussels restaurants that are priced in the *expensive* category in the evening can be brought down to *moderate* by going there at lunch and/or ordering the *plat du jour* (daily special). Many eateries in central Brussels cater to workers at midday with three-course *menus* in the BF250–400 range.

Hotel restaurants (some of which are among Brussels' best) have not been included below, but have been mentioned under the hotel's listing. They will be open on Sundays when many independent restaurants close. For any but the most casual establishments, it's wise to at least inquire about reservations if you hope to dine at a particular place. Reservations (as far ahead as possible) are *essential* for any of the top restaurants.

Many opinions (almost as many as there are diners) exist as to which is the city's best restaurant. The Bruxellois discuss the topic among themselves as heatedly as they do sports or bicultural politics. You can count on the following selection, presented in no particular order, to include the restaurants that most experts variously purport to be the best. Unless otherwise indicated, all serve classic French cuisine in an elegant atmosphere; some are located outside the metropolitan city. To begin with a flourish:

Comme Chez Soi

> *place Rouppe 23; closed Sun. and Mon., and July;* ☎ *512.29.21, FAX 511.80.52; expensive/very expensive*, whose proprieter and **Chef Pierre Wynants** is nothing short of a celebrity (both in his 14-table home territory and in culinary circles around the world) remains an institution in the rarified Brussels culinary realm where dining is an *event*. To dine amid the renovated Victor Horta-style art nouveau decor, however, visitors need to be farsighted and/or favored by the gods: friends in the know tell me that reservations should be made a *minimum* of two months ahead.

It's also wise to plan as far ahead as possible for the following: **Bruneau** *(avenue Broustin 73; closed Tues. for dinner, Wed., holidays, mid-June–mid-July;* ☎ *427.69.78; very expensive)* serves seasonal fare with a flair in the Uccle area; **Romeyer** *(chaussee de Groenendaal 109; closed Sun. evening, Mon., Feb., first half of Aug.;* ☎ *657.05.81; very expensive)* offers innovative culinary creations in an old country house in the *Forêt de Soignes*; **Villa Lorraine** *(avenue du Vivier d'Oie 75; closed Sun., and August;* ☎ *374.31.63; expensive)* delights diners with its garden-like indoor and outdoor setting in a renovated chateau on the fringe of *Bois de la Cambre* forest; **Ecailler du Palais Royal** *(rue Bodenbroek 18; closed Sun., holidays and August;* ☎ *512.87.51; expensive, plat du jour moderate)*, where seafood is the speciality, is located at the top of the Grand Sablon; and **La Maison du Cygne** *(rue Charles Buls 2, off Grand-Place; closed Sat. lunch, Sun., and August, between Christmas and New Years;* ☎ *511.82.44; expensive)* has a dream location fronting the Grand-Place.

While the above "best" restaurants are all on the expensive side, I repeat the point that it is *not* necessary to pay dearly to dine divinely in Brussels. And apart from money, for many, the reservation requirements of Brussels' stellar establishments don't leave sufficient room for spontaneous dining decisions. The ordinary mortals among us who are seeking memorable morsels *can* be more spur-of-the-moment about our meals: Brussels surely is one place where if the *carte* posted in the window and the view from the door both strike your fancy, you should feel free to follow your instincts, since almost certainly good, and perhaps great, food awaits.

Traditional Belgian fare first. In a restored, former 16th-century nobleman's world with lots of Flemish details such as the copper-hooded fireplaces, wood-paneling, and tiles is **Ravenstein** *(rue Ravenstein 1; closed Sat. lunch, Sun., and August;* ☎ *512.77.68; inexpensive/moderate)*, which, in addition to local fare, specializes in seafood and continental cuisine. **Au Duc d'Arenberg** *(petit Sablon 9; daily noon–2:30 p.m., 7–10:30 p.m., closed Sun., holidays, last week of Dec.;* ☎ *511.14.75; moderate)* offers rustic decor and traditional food in its tavern/restaurant. Although eateries serving *moules* (mussels) abound in the **Ilot Sacre, Au Vieux Bruxelles** *(rue Saint-Boniface 35; closed Sun., Mon., holidays, June and July;* ☎ *513.01.81; inexpensive)*, near avenue Louise, is *the* place for them as far as the Bruxellois are concerned. **Aux Armes de Bruxelles** *(rue des Bouchers 13; noon to 11:15 p.m., closed Mon., month of June;* ☎ *511.55.98; moderate, plat du jour inexpensive)*, located on Brussels' "street of restaurants," is an excellent introduction to Belgian specialities, and *moules* prepared in many ways, *waterzooi de homard* (lobster stew), and *croquettes aux crevettes* (North Sea shrimp croquettes) to *carbonnades flamandes a la biere* (beef stewed in beer), in a pleasant setting. At **'t Kelderke** *(Grand-Place 15; daily noon–2 a.m.;* ☎ *513.73.44; inexpensive)* typical Belgian dishes such as *lapin* (rabbit) cooked with Brussels' *queuze* beer are offered—as well as helpful counsel about the dishes and drink—in an atmospheric 16th-century cellar. **La Roue D'Or** *(rue des Chaplies 26; until 12:30 a.m., closed mid-July–mid-Aug.;* ☎ *514.25.54; inexpensive)* is a brasserie near the Grand-Place with a varied menu of traditional fare and daily specials.

A search for seafood in Brussels will take you to the Sainte-Catherine district to what used to be the banks of the river Senne, still referred to as the *March aux Poisson* (Fish Market). Virtually all the restaurants in the region feature fish, but special among them is **La Sirene d'Or** *(place Sainte-Catherine 1A; open lunch and dinner, closed Sun., Mon., mid-July to mid-Aug.;* ☎ *513.51.98, FAX 502.13.05; plat du jour inexpensive, menu moderate)*, small, and quite elegant with touches of velvet, lace, and old beams in the decor, and serving dishes such as *bouillabaisse Grand-Marius, fricassee de homard aux asperges.* Thoroughly atmospheric is the **La Truite d'Argent** *(quai au Bois à Brûler 23; noon–2:30 p.m., 7–11:30 p.m., closed Sat. lunch,*

Sun., late July–mid- Aug.; ☎ *218.95.46; moderate),* whose specialty is lobster and scallops with wild mushrooms. **Jacques** *(quai aux Briques;* ☎ *513.27.62; inexpensive)* is small, quite plain, and apparently the perfect choice for the many Bruxellois who call it their favorite bargain fish brasserie in the Marché aux Poissons district. **Scheltema** *(rue des Dominicains 7; 11:30 a.m.–3 p.m., 6:30 p.m.–12:30 a.m., closed Sun.* ☎ *512.20.84; moderate, lunch inexpensive),* with specialties like *saumon grillé à l'orange* and *jardiniere de sole,* is where locals come for seafood (although the menu has other offerings), and to seriously eat, not chat.

When your tastebuds want to travel beyond Belgian borders, the enormous variety of cuisines available in Brussels will be obvious. Among the most numerous are Italian, Spanish and Chinese. And with some of the other ethnic choices (Turkish, North African, Central African—Zaire) available, it can sometimes seem as if the Third World is feeding the First in Brussels. Belgium's lingering occupation by the Spanish may be one of the reasons for the interest in that country's cuisine. In any case, Brussels' seems to have a thriving taste for *paella valenciane,* the specialty at **Casa Manuel** *(Grand-Place 34; daily noon until 1 a.m.;* ☎ *511.47.47; inexpensive; musicians).* Also highly popular among the many Spanish restaurants in the Marolles neighborhood is **Alicante** *(rue Haute 411; daily 11 a.m.–5 p.m., 6 p.m.–midnight;* ☎ *538.25.54; inexpensive).* A popular choice for Italian is **Al Piccolo Mondo** *(rue Jourdan 19; daily until midnight;* ☎ *538.87.94; inexpensive),* just off trendy avenue Louise near Waterloo boulevard. It has a cozy, if non-Italian, environment of brick walls and arches, wood-burning fireplaces, and oil paintings. Dishes such as *saltimbocca alla romana, veal cutlets Milanaise,* and *pastas* are served.

You'll come across pleasant places to pause for liquid refreshment or light cafe fare at every stop of your way around Brussels. On the Grand Sablon, try **Au Vieux Saint Martin** *(Grand Sablon 38; daily 10 a.m.–midnight;* ☎ *512.64.76; inexpensive)* for sandwiches, omelets, salads, and some heartier fare on the square, and **Les Jardins du Sablon** *(Grand Sablon 30; moderate)* inside the skylighted upmarket complex of art galleries, book shops, and antique shops. On the Grand-Place, a favorite with the Bruxellois is **La Brouette** *(Grand-Place 2; lunch to late evening;* ☎ *511.54.94; inexpensive)* for sandwiches and salads, and special plates served inside or on the cafe's terrace in the shadow of the Hôtel de Ville and full view of the glorious square.

When dining out becomes a drag, as it sometimes does—*temporarily*—during travels, head to Brussels' huge supermarket in the basement of the **City 2** on *rue Neuve* near *place Rogier,* for ingredients for an exceptional picnic. To satisfy your sweet tooth in traditional Belgian style, you can start simply, following the smell of vanilla in the air to any of the street-front waffle *(gaufre)* shops on and off the appropriately-named **rue au Beurre** (Butter Street) off Grand-Place. While on the street, at least visit **Biscuiterie Dandoy** *(rue au Beurre 31, daily 8:30 a.m.–6:30 p.m., Sun. 10:30 a.m.–6:30 p.m.)* to see its large wooden *speculoos* (spiced cookie) molds, and sample the marvelous (smaller) cookies available by 100-gram servings. **Le pain à** la Grecque (despite its name, a Belgian specialty) is another famed sweet treat at this 1829 institution. There's a second **Dandoy** *(rue Charles Buls)*, off the Grand-Place in the direction of *Manneken-Pis*. For the height of self-indulgence, head to fashionable **Wittamer** *(place du Grand Sablon 12; daily 8 a.m.–7 p.m., Sun. 7:30 a.m.–6 p.m., closed Monday)* for Brussels' most outrageous *pralines* (handmade, filled chocolates), *manons* (fresh cream-filled chocolates), Viennoise and French pastries, and caramelized fruits.

Although they usually also serve traditional, informal Belgian dishes (and great *frites* with almost anything), **cafes** offer the opportunity to sample Belgium's amazing beers, especially Brussels' own *queuze, kriek*, and 1. There could be no better place to begin than at **Falstaff** *(rue Henri Maus 25;* ☎ *511.87.89; daily 7 a.m. til 4 a.m.)*, with its art nouveau interior, and large open, overhead-heated outdoor terrace facing the Bourse. Close to the Grand-Place in the opposite direction is **La Mort Subite** *(rue Montagne-aux-Herbes-Potageres 7;* ☎ *513.13.18)*; its name means *sudden death*, but the place is life to many regulars for the large selection of Belgian beers. Featuring another memorable name is **De Ultieme Hallucinatie** *(Koningsstraat/rue Royale 316;* ☎ *217.06.14; open until 3 a.m.)*, a former house, with three rooms front to back, each with a different character, each a treasure trove of rational-style *art nouveau* detail, each serving cafe or restaurant fare. And, under another great name, **Le Jugement Dernier** *(The Last Judgment; chaussee de Haecht 165)* is said to serve the city's largest selection of beers, up to 300, including "seasonal" specials. **La Becasse** *(rue Tabora 11;* ☎ *511.00.06)*, down an alley near the Bourse, is known for its jugs of beer served by stiff-aproned waiters. **La Fleur En Papier Dore** *(rue des Alexiens 53;* ☎ *511.16.59)* has been called a temple of surrealism, though it's also a favorite quiet tavern. Offering a typical Brussels evening of cafe theater and music (mostly jazz) is **Chez LaGaffe** *(rue de l'Epee 4;* ☎ *511.76.39; music from 9 p.m.)*, located in the Marolles neighborhood.

Note: To insure that your cafe hopping is entirely pleasant, here's a reminder—valid for cities everywhere—**not** to hang your purse or camera on the back of your chair or put them on the ground, especially when outside on a terrace.

ENTERTAINMENT AND EVENTS

The **Palais des Beaux-Arts** *(rue Ravenstein 23 and rue Royale 10; Mon.– Sat. 10 a.m.–10 p.m., Sun. 10 a.m.–6 p.m.; program information* ☎ *507.82.00)*, built between 1922 and 1929 to the design of art nouveau architect Victor Horta, is one of Brussels' most important cultural complexes, with concerts halls, art galleries, cinema, and cafes. It is highly regarded for the organ and acoustics in the 2,200-seat main hall. Both it and the **Brussels Conservatory of Music** are settings for the prestigious **Queen Elizabeth of Belgium International Music Competition**. Organized by the late monarch in 1951 for violinists (Queen Elizabeth herself was an accomplished one), the competition was later expanded to include piano, composition, and, in 1988, voice. All concerts of the competition, which welcomes contestants from around the world and takes place before an international jury of musicians, are open to the public (from elimination rounds to finals, and special Laureate performances). The competition begins in early May and lasts until mid-June. It is held three out of four years. The cycle, which repeats itself, is as follows: first year—violin; second year—nothing; third year—piano; fourth year—composition and voice. The year 1994 is mid-cycle and falls into the second year of the cycle.

Note: Near the beginning of the 1980 American film *The Competition*, about competing pianists in a fictional, San-Francisco-based situation not unlike the Queen Elizabeth Competition, the character Heidi (Amy Irving) asks Paul (Richard Dreyfuss) if he had gone to compete at Brussels as planned.

The **Palais des Beaux-Arts**, the **Conservatory**, and the **Cathédrale Saint-Michel** are all used as venues for Brussels' performances in the annual September–October **Festival of Flanders** concerts. The Cathédrale has *Musical Sundays* from late June through September, with special music (Gregorian Chant, Scarlatti, Haydn, Mozart, Palestrina, Britten, Fauré) at the 10 a.m. Mass (information: ☎ 217.83.45). Check with the Tourist Office about scheduled concerts on the superb and newly restored organ of the **Eglise Notre-Dame du Sablon** (see *Organs* under "Music" section of "Belgian Cultural Legacy" chapter).

The **Theatre Royal de la Monnaie** (*place de la Monnaie;* ☎ *218.12.02*) is notable for its acoustics and recent lavish renovation. Designated the National Opera House in 1963, it is home to the opera company that bears its name; during the late September-April season, artistic director Anne-Theresa Dekeersmaeker stages widely acclaimed, original language productions with international casts.

One of Brussels's entertainment institutions is **Toone VII Puppet Theater** (*impasse Schuddeveld 6, off Petite rue des Bouchers 21; performances at 8:30 p.m., puppet museum open free during intervals between sketches, closed Sun., cafe on premises open noon-midnight; reservations recommended:* ☎ *511.71.37, 513.54.86*). It began with Toone I who, from 1835 to 1880, performed with puppets in a cellar in the Marolles district, and introduced the character **Woltje**, a Brussels street urchin in a checked jacket and jaunty angled cap who speaks the Marolle-Brussels dialect. Toone, the VIIth of the tradition, opened in the present theater in 1966, and continues the use of the Brussels dialect, which makes it unlikely you'll understand much of the dialogue (and piquant asides) in the *Cyrano, Faust, The Three Musketeers, Nativity,* or *Massacre of the Innocents* fare on the program—though that may not matter if you want to see something true to Brussels. The tradition of puppet plays here actually goes back long before Toone—to Spanish times. When the occupying Spanish had heard all they cared to of the criticism and insults hurled at them from the legitimate stage, they closed the theaters. But imaginative minds came up with the idea of using highly portable (and easily hidden) puppets as a means of reaching the population with revilements for the foreign forces. Puppet theater in Brussels is still a place for provocative political and social commentary.

Events from Brussels' annual calendar include the late-April, early May openings of the **Royal Greenhouses** at Laeken. The twice-in-early-July **Ommegang** (which comes from a Flemish word meaning "walkabout") is a splendidly costumed reenactment of the festivities staged in 1549 for the entrance into Brussels of Charles V, his son Philip II (then Duke of Brabant), and his sisters—performed on the floodlit Grand-Place, which is a source of wonderment even for those blasé bureaucrats inclined to call Brussels boring. From June–Sept. there are free nightly **music and light** shows after dark on the Grand-Place. Laid out on the Grand-Place in August in even years is a fabulous **Flower Carpet** (dates for 1994 are Fri–Sun, Aug. 13–15). From late July to late August the annual **Brussels Fair** is held in the Midi, and September brings **Bruegel festivities**. In December, there's a traditional **Christmas market** on the Sablon (always the second weekend of the month). In addition to the longstanding traditional nativity scene and Christmas tree on the Grand-Place, there's a new, free holiday offering on that grand square: **Music and Light** shows of carols from EC countries nightly at 7:30–8 p.m.

IN THE AREA

Musée Royal de l'Afrique Centrale ★

Royal Museum of Central Africa; Leuvensesteenweg 13; Tervuren; daily mid-Mar.–mid-Oct. 9 a.m.–5:30 p.m., mid-Oct.-mid-Mar. 10 a.m.–4:30 p.m.; ☎ 769.52.11; Brussels' metro to **Montgomery**, *then Tram 44 through the lovely 10,000-acre ancient beech tree* **Forest de Soignes***; museum plan but no exhibit descriptions in English.* Begun in 1898 as the **Musée du Congo**, this museum was an important scientific institute where the information of the Congo could be collected and synthesized. In 1960, the year of the Belgian Congo's independence, its scope was extended to cover all of Africa. Exhibits are arranged in sections covering anthropology, history, and economy. There are zoological dioramas, ethnic sculpture, and souvenirs of the great explorers; of particular interest are those on mineralogy and art, including jewelry and tribal ornaments. The museum—housed in a Charles Girault-designed Louis XVI-style palace built for Leopold II and surrounded by exceptional French gardens—is located in **Tervuren Park**, which also features scenic lakes, the picturesque **Moulin de Gordeal** (windmill), an Arboretum, a Renaissance chapel to Saint Hubert (patron saint of hunters), and stables remaining from the 17th-century castle of Austrian-Hapsburg ruler Charles of Lorraine.

Waterloo

town of 25,000, 12 mi./20 km. south of Brussels on Charleroi Road; public bus W from Brussels' **place Rouppe** *twice hourly, takes about an hour.* Today a pleasant Brussels suburb where many resident-alien Americans live, *Waterloo* is also a household word for *defeat* that joined our vocabulary after the retreat of **Napoleon Bonaparte** from the 1815 battle fought there that determined the future of Europe. No one who has seen the magnificent gifts (on display at **Apsley House** in London)

presented to Englishman Arthur Wellesley, **Duke of Wellington**, by European leaders after he defeated Napoleon's armies, can doubt their relief at the fall of the charismatic Corsican.

To set the stage: After taking over the leadership of the French forces that had occupied the Netherlands, north and south, in the late 18th century (and showing himself to be a well-rounded genius by introducing such modern measures as the metric system and house numbers for addresses), Napoleon arranged to have himself pronounced Emperor of France in the presence of the Pope in 1804. He continued to turn Europe inside-out with a series of successful military campaigns, before overextending himself in 1812. From the Royal Palace at Laeken outside Brussels, Napoleon signed the order for the advance of his 600,000-strong army into Russia, where climate, unorthodox opponents, and sheer distance defeated him. Back in Central Europe in 1814, Napoleon again met more than his match, and was exiled to the island of Elba off Italy by the allied powers of Austria, Prussia, Russia, and England, who then convened the **Congress of Vienna** to restructure the political entities of Europe. It was settled that the Belgian territory would be bonded to Holland, but before the details had been dealt with, word came to the diplomats in Vienna that Napoleon had escaped from Elba. Bonaparte made his way to Paris without a shot being fired, easily and quickly rallying the French forces still faithful to him. Newly installed King Louis XVIII fled to Belgium's Ghent. Of the European armies, which quickly regrouped to confront the Corsican, it was the troops of England's **Duke of Wellington**, Prussia's 73-year-old **General Marshal Blucher**, and Holland's **Prince Willem of Orange**, gathered in central Belgium, who would fight the inevitable battle.

Ironically, only a year before, the Duke of Wellington had passed through Waterloo and made the statement that if he were ever to fight in the Netherlands, he would choose the fields at Waterloo for the battle. Yet, it was Napoleon, beating a path to Brussels, which he hoped to recapture (believing, as, indeed, even many of his political opponents did, that Belgium rightfully belonged to France), whose actions largely established the farming village of Waterloo as the site where scores of thousands of soldiers would meet history head-on.

The opposing forces that squared off at Waterloo on Sunday, June 18, were headed by two men of great stature but slight height: Napoleon stood 5 feet 3 inches tall; Wellington measured in at 5 feet. Napoleon commanded 72,000 men and had more heavy hardware than Wellington, who as supreme commander for the British, Dutch, Belgian, and German forces, had 60,000 (though the Prussian reinforcements who arrived progressively during the day numbered nearly another 45,000). But, as in many battles, Waterloo's outcome was as much the result of weather and the health of its leaders as it was other elements. Through the night before the battle it rained heavily, and Napoleon postponed the beginning of battle until late the following morning to give the ground some time to dry (maneuvering heavy artillery through mud was unwieldy). But those elapsed morning hours later in the battle day added enough time for Marshal Blucher to get to the battlefront with fresh Prussian troops for Wellington. Although the two generals were the same age (45) at Waterloo, Wellington was well and Napoleon was not (suffering so badly from hemorrhoids that he spent most of the battle day outside the house, **Caillou**, he used as headquarters, in a chair from which the seat had been removed for his comfort). Wellington spent it on his horse, Copenhagen, constantly traversing the undulating terrain that hid battlefield hollows and allowed no single good vantage point for the action, and encouraging his troops. (So close to the action did Wellington stay that day that many of his soldiers were amazed that he survived.)

An account from the diary of a Waterloo resident that cloudy Sunday of June 18, 1815, reads: "The whole morning, soldiers pass in mass formation. Towards 10 o'clock a heavy silence reigns around us. Everyone is struck dumb with the approach of the events which are due to take place." At about 11:30 a.m., Napoleon's forces opened battle against the more securely positioned Wellington forces. (Napoleon later said of Wellington, "In the management of an army he is full equal to myself with the advantage of possessing more prudence.") Napoleon, uncharacteristically, tried to apply head-to-head brute force while waiting for reinforcements from a division he had previously sent after the Prussian Blucher. Wellington, having to endure the full force of the French attack alone for far longer than expected, was waiting for Blucher himself, who had met with him at 2 that morning and promised troops. Movement on the distant horizon at about 1 p.m. raised hopes on both sides, but it turned out to be Blucher progressing very slowly because of the mud.

From that time on, Napoleon (who hadn't expected Blucher to be a factor in the fight) was in a race against time. At 4 p.m., he launched a massive cavalry charge, but Wellington's "squares" held. Later, however, a breakthrough for the French seemed possible, and the Duke of Wellington worried, "Night or the Prussians must come." Afterwards, an officer said, "I never heard yet of a battle in which every one was killed, but this seemed likely to be an exception." The French marshal who was trying to effect the turnaround requested reinforcements, but Napoleon, thinking of the Prussians marching ever closer, delayed an hour before finally sending the marshal his final reserve, the impressive Imperial Guard. By then, however, they were tactically too late; Wellington had had a chance to regroup and, after the Prussians arrived about 7:30 p.m., what was considered Napoleon's finest force was routed during the general charge mounted against it at 8:15 p.m.

Taking less than 10 hours, Waterloo was a short battle that was long and decisive enough to produce something like peace—at a great cost, however, and only for a short time. The toll for both sides was more than 50,000 casualties. Some 7,000 in Wellington's army were killed or wounded, and the Prussians lost nearly the same number. An accurate count of French army losses was impossible to come by after the final rout, during which many of the men simply slipped away. But a minimum of 30,000 were killed, wounded, or captured. Ten days after the battle, the wounded were still being brought into Brussels.

Tourists sought out Waterloo from the start. That very year, the king of England came to view the battlefield, and on the first anniversary a crowd from many countries gathered in commemoration. **Lord Byron** wrote of Waterloo in his poem *Childe Harold*, and **Victor Hugo** walked the battleground 40 years later seeking inspiration for the Waterloo scenes in *Les Miserables*. Today, from atop the ★ **Butte du Lion** *(Lion Mound; 3 miles south of Waterloo center; 226 steps; daily, same hours as Waterloo Visitor's Center, below)*, visitors have a panoramic view of the Waterloo terrain that neither commander nor any combatant on the battle day had. The vast circular Lion Mound was built as a Dutch memorial between 1823–1826 on the site along Wellington's line where the Dutch **Willem of Orange** (who would be crowned king of the less-than-pleased Belgians only three months after Waterloo) was wounded in the shoulder. At the base of Lion Mound is the ★★**Waterloo Visitor's Center** *(route du Lion 252; daily April 1–Oct. 31, 9:30 a.m.–6:30 p.m.; Nov.1–March 31, 10:30 p.m.–4 p.m.; ☎ 02/385.19.12; English-language materials and exhibits)*, a well-executed and welcome addition to the site. The 40-minute program includes a sound and light model that retraces the main phases of the fighting, and a 200-slide show that—with its imaginative script and extracts from Columbia's Bondartchouk-directed film *Waterloo*—involves viewers in the experience of the battle. The center has maps and illustrations that give visitors a better grasp of where and how the fighting took place. Interactive computerized information terminals have a data base that enables you to ask questions (in English) about the battle. Items in the gift/book shop featuring the losing leader vastly outnumber those concerned with the winner at Waterloo.

Next door is the hard-to-miss round building that houses the ★**Panorama**, which dates back to 1912. Definitely old-fashioned (though restored), this nostalgic in-the-round art work is a 360-degree, 360-foot/110-meter, 40-foot/12-meter painting by Frenchman Louis Dumoulin, his art assistants, and military consultant that places you literally in the center of Waterloo's French calvary charge. Standing on the viewing platform at the center, you can't help but be involved, from the cloudy sky from the recent rain, clouds of smoke from the cannon, and foreground of three-dimensional figures (a wounded horse, soldiers, fences, dirt) that all lend verisimilitude to the scene. Unless you're addicted to such attractions, the **Wax Museum** across the road isn't a necessary stop, though the cafe **Bivodac de L'Empereur** next to it might be.

An alternative site at which to begin your visit to Waterloo is in the town at the ★**Wellington Museum** *(chaussée de Bruxelles 147; daily April 1–Nov. 15 9:30 a.m.–6:30 p.m., Nov. 16–Mar. 31 10:10 a.m.–5 p.m., closed Christmas and New Years;* ☎ *354.59.54; booklet, exhibit notes, and other items in English)*. Of the many items of interest in the several rooms of this old coaching inn (at which Wellington spent the night before and the night after the battle), none is more meaningful than the duke's own bedroom. In it, in the pre-dawn hours of the 18th, he received confirmation that the Prussians would join him in battle against Napoleon later that day, at which point he definitely decided on undertaking the task at Waterloo. And it was to this room that he returned after battle to write the report that was published in *The Times* in London on June 22. In the wing to the rear of the museum are illuminated battle-phase maps that show the relative positions of units at each stage of the struggle.

Next door is the **Tourist Information** office for Waterloo *(chaussée de Bruxelles 149;* ☎ *354.99.10)*, which can provide specific information about rental bicycles, the sightseeing train which during July and August links up with Waterloo train station, and hours/details about other Waterloo sights. Across the street is the domed 17th-century **Royal Chapel/St. Joseph's Church** (restored). The only object in its large rotunda is a white marble bust of the duke of Wellington; many burial plaques and other memorials are exhibited on the side walls of the church.

If you are traveling by car to Waterloo and want to see every sight, there's **Caillou**, a farm where Napoleon spent the night before the battle. **La Belle Alliance** is where Napoleon spent much of the day of the battle, and Wellington and Blucher met in happy victory at the end of the battle. From it you can realize how little Napoleon can have known of what was happening on the actual battle front. Various division monuments are located along the sides of roads in the region.

WHERE TO STAY AND EAT IN THE AREA

Chateau du Lac

ave. du Lac 87, Genval; ☎ *654.11.22, FAX 653.62.00; very expensive.* This is a lakeside castle hotel 20 minutes south of Brussels, not far cross-country from Waterloo. Fine contemporary decor in an elegant setting, with a good selection of recreational facilities (tennis, golf, riding, watersports). The hotel's restaurant **Le Trefle** *(closed Mon., Tues., early Jan.–early Feb.; expensive)* is considered one of nearby Brussels' best.

FLANDERS: AN INTRODUCTION

Belgium's 5.7 million Flemish (*de Vlamingen* to themselves, *les Flamands* to the French-speaking Walloons) constitute nearly 60 percent of the country's total population, who live in the northern provinces of **West** and **East Flanders, Antwerp, Limburg**, and the northern section of **Brabant**. With the exception of Brabant, each province borders on Holland, with whom Flanders shares the Dutch language.

Despite an attractive beach-bound North Sea coastline—all of Belgium's seashore is located in the province of West Flanders— Flanders' main appeal to overseas visitors is its medieval mercantile towns. Flanders' **Ghent, Bruges, Antwerp**, and **Brussels**—all cloth manufacturing and trading centers with a prosperous burgher class—formed the early core of the Low Countries' (Netherlands') culture. Noted for their prosperity, Flemish towns attracted artisans and became treasure-troves of 14th-, 15th-, and 16th-century architecture and painting. If you've provided yourself generously with time for touring Belgium, you'll find additional examples of sacred and secular structures in Flanders' fascinating flamboyant Gothic style—exuberant evidence of an opulent past—in **Ypres, Louvain, Mechelen**, and **Oudenaarde**.

While Flanders' early urbanized areas virtually *demand* the attention of travelers, the region also has a variety of rural landscape: moor and heath in the *Kempen*, modest height in the *Flemish Ardennes*, and rich flat *polderland* just behind the *coastal dunes*.

151

Farming has long been a prime livelihood in Flanders, on both its rich and poor soil. The open-air museum of **Bokrijk** *(in Bokrijk, northeast of Hasselt; open daily Easter–Oct. 10 a.m.–6 p.m.;* ☎ *(011) 22.27.11)* pays homage to Flanders' farming heritage.

Urban Flanders can trace its beginnings to a gradual shift following the Frankish period in the region's transportation routes. Inland highways that had crossed the Roman Empire increasingly were supplanted in importance by continental waterways and their outlets at the sea. Medieval Flemish settlements located on rivers developed as trading sites, eventually evolving into powerful commercial urban entities.

During the **Crusade era**, the **counts of Flanders**—the countship had come into being in A.D. 864—became the "Latin" emperors of Constantinople from 1204–1261. The opening up of sea trade routes to the **East** during earlier crusades (the **First Crusade** was in 1099) brought new commercial development to Flanders. The region as a whole flourished over several centuries, particularly in the **cloth and wool trades** with England, in which Flanders had a virtual monopoly.

All of Flanders was affected by the **Reformation**, which began in the early 16th century. The earliest confrontations resulting from the introduction of **Protestantism** into the Netherlands were in Flanders. In the southern Netherlands (today's Belgium), Spanish-Roman Catholic King Philip II embarked on a punishing course of action. When his Spanish inquisition forces became completely unrestrained, many Protestants fled from what had been a flourishing Flanders north to Holland. Such were the numbers of the multitalented Flemish Protestants who left that their departure constituted a "brain drain." The flight of talent from Flanders to Holland in the late 16th century (Flemish Antwerp's *Golden Age*) was so great that there's no doubt it nourished Holland's 17th-century *Golden Age*. By the early 17th century, the population of Middelburg in Zeeland (southern Holland) was 60 percent Flemish. The decrease in Flanders' population during the period was so dramatic that not until after the turn of the 19th century did Flemings once again equal, and then overtake, the Walloon population of southern Belgium. (See also "Wallonia: An Introduction.")

Flanders' decline in population was accompanied by a falling off of prosperity. Under the 1648 *Treaty of Munster*, which ended Holland's *Eighty Years' War* with Spain, the southern Netherlands remained under the Spanish, who agreed to the anticompetitive

Dutch demand to close the Scheldt. (The Dutch controlled the land on both banks of the river estuary.) This action effectively closed the port of Antwerp, leading to a prolonged period of economic ruin for the city and adversely affecting the economy of all Flanders. Not until the end of the 18th century, under the rule of Napoleon, were the Scheldt and the port of Antwerp reopened and revitalized.

With their population once again a majority in Belgium by the early 19th century, the Flemings had an impetus to push for the equality of the Flemish language with the French. But numbers alone wouldn't achieve that goal.

The use of the French language in the Walloon (southern) section of Belgium has been traced back almost to the end of Roman rule in the area. And for centuries its use had been deeply ensconced in Europe. The business, and pleasure, of most royal courts were conducted in French, and the language was the standard for European statecraft. So widespread was the fashion that even the English court effused in French during various reigns, though England itself often had a less-than-fond relationship with France. The international fashion for French remained strong for a long period, and still has vestiges. To this day French has something of a cultural advantage in the Belgian capital of Brussels.

The situation has made it hard for the Flemish to get their language claims across. Even before the Burgundian days in the late 14th century, Flemings were forced to conduct their schooling, government, and legal affairs in French. Those who couldn't comprehend French couldn't make sense of the sociopolitical system. Only peasants used Flemish, which was considered a countrified tongue. Once the Dutch in Holland established an "authorized" version of their language, Flemish—identical to it in writing—was considered by many to be a mere dialect of Dutch.

When the independent Belgian state came into being in 1830, though the Flemish by then again outnumbered the Walloons, a favoritism for French in all administrative matters was firmly established from the onset. This was the result not only of tradition, but also of a not entirely unpopular period of **French Napoleonic** rule from 1799 to 1814, followed—after the fall of Napoleon at Waterloo—by the rule of Dutch King Willem I (from 1815–1830), which was unpopular with all Belgians. Although he faced a near-impossible situation from the start, Willem's autocratic manner managed to offend both of Belgium's communities even more. Finally, in 1830, the European powers gave recognition to Belgium's insistence on independence. But, while the constitution adopted by the temporary Belgium congress was the most liberal charter to date on the continent, the "new" Belgium clung to old ways: French was set as the sole language for conducting the business of education, law, and government.

A **Flemish Movement** wasn't long in coming. Under Dutch rule, the Flemish language had come into much wider use. After Belgian independence and the reestablishment of the French standard, Flemish writer **Hendrik Conscience** (see "The Muse" under "The Belgian Cultural Legacy") spoke to fellow Flemings through his book *The Lion of Flanders* (1838). The romantic novel was meant to incite a national awakening of pride in the Flemish culture and language by linking the 14th-century struggle of Flanders against France (in the 1302 **Battle of the Golden Spurs**; see "An Historical Perspective" under "Belgium") to the need for 19th-century Flemish Belgians to stand up to their French-speaking countrymen. Conscience was explicit in his aims when he wrote in 1839: "There are twice as many Flemings as there are Walloons. We pay twice as much in taxes as they do. And they want to make Walloons out of us, to sacrifice us, our old race, our language, our splendid history, and all that we have inherited." Some Flemings would find that statement still speaking to their situation today.

Conscience's monument is marked with the words: "He taught his people to read." His works raised the consciousness of some officials, who convened an investigation into the complaints of the Flemish in 1856. The commission found many of the grievances to have merit and recommended equal language rights for the Flemish. But there were few practical results; political power in the hands of unempathic Liberals prevented implementation of any measures. Only in the periods when the Catholic party predominated (1871–1879 and 1884–1914) was progress made on the issue of Flemish equal-language rights.

In the last decades of the 19th century, Flemish nationalism rose alongside the **workers' movement**, a natural alignment since Belgium's propertied class was French-speaking, and social mobility depended largely on use of that language. Flemish demands focused on gaining an administration and judiciary in Dutch and having a Flemish-speaking university, so that a knowledge of French wouldn't be the only means of entry into the professions. In 1890, it finally became possible to submit doctoral theses in Dutch to the University of Ghent, and by the beginning of World War I, a number of courses at Ghent (which is, after all, in Flanders) were being offered in Flemish.

During World War I, extreme Flemish nationalists were encouraged by the occupying Germans, who had more concern for the Germanic-rooted, Dutch-speaking Flemish than the French Walloons and were not unaware of the benefits of keeping the level of tension high between Belgium's two competing cultural communities. Extremist Flemings formed the *Activist Party,* which more or less collaborated with the Germans, who, in turn, rewarded them by making the University of Ghent an all Dutch-language institution. The Germans also enforced Flemish language laws, which had been passed but largely ignored by Belgian politicians. Flemish nationalists who supported the activists' aims but could not bring themselves to work with the Germans were called *passivists.*

After the war, the language reforms granted by the Germans to the Flemish were revoked. Forty-five of the most flagrant activists were condemned to death in trials for "collaboration" (though none of the sentences was carried out). Flemish nationalists as a group were publicly judged "traitors to the Belgian motherland," which made the mainstream Flemish Movement ineffective. However, some war-era Flemish passivists surfaced as *maximalists,* wanting to work toward their aims within the existing political structure. They had the support of King Albert I, who addressed the Belgian Parliament directly after the armistice and promised: "In the domain of languages the strictest equality and the most absolute justice will characterize bills which the government will submit."

The Flemish Movement revived in the 1930s under the economic pressures produced by the *Great Depression,* and some results were finally forthcoming. Laws were passed that permitted the use of Flemish in administration, education, the courts, and the military, in the regions where it was the mother tongue. In 1930, the University of Ghent was officially declared Flemish-speaking. Nevertheless, French speakers still retained the economic base of power in Belgium.

With the invasion and occupation of Belgium by the German Nazis in World War II, extreme Flemish nationalists, still smarting from a perceived continued political subjugation by French speakers during the period between the wars, again found certain favor from the Germans; Hitler was said to have found the Flemings "sympathetic" since their language was closer to German, and ordered less harsh treatment for them. Some extremists, convinced that the Nazis would win the war and advance the Flemish cause after it was over, collaborated with the occupiers.

Following World War II, retribution for such behavior was demanded. In the many trials held in Belgium, more than three times the number of Flemings as Walloons were sentenced. Since then, the most despicable name a Walloon can call a Fleming has been "collaborator"—although enough Walloons had faced similar charges to make the name-calling hypocritical.

Belgium's **King Leopold III**—who had come to the throne between the wars following his popular father, Albert's, tragic death in a climbing accident in 1934—himself was suspected of collaboration. Many of his subjects believed that he should not have remained in Belgium after the Nazi invasion, thereby creating the appearance of cooperation with the occupiers. After the war, this issue boiled over into demonstrations and riots, which eventually found resolution in the so-called **Royal Question** referendum. Leopold won by 57 percent the March 1950 plebiscite as to whether he should resume the throne. But the vote was split along lines that directly reflected the country's cultural communities. He was supported by the Roman Catholics, mostly Flemish, and opposed by the anticlerics, who were largely Walloon. Knowing the Walloons would have considered him only "King of the Flemings," Leopold decided to hand the crown to his son **Baudouin**.

The intense emotions stirred by events during and following World War II hardly helped the Flemish cause. It took a mid-century economic evolution to even partially unparalyze Belgium's polarized politics.

In the 1960s, with its industrious but comparatively unprosperous agricultural business largely ignored and neglected, Flanders finally found its way to the economic forefront. As Wallonia's coal mines were being closed during that decade, Flanders' economy finally was addressed, with a conscious effort at encouraging light industry: chemicals, pharmaceuticals, and electrical goods. Flanders forged ahead, and its increasingly energetic economy added to its importance politically. It became Flanders' turn at favored financial region status. Today, its agricultural production benefits from generous Common Market subsidies. Port expansion in Zeebrugge, Ostend, and Antwerp (now the world's 5th largest), has made Flanders the most active stretch of shipping anywhere on the North Sea.

Financial success made it easier for Flemings to insist on exercising greater political power in the Flemish mother tongue, to insist on proving that Flemish could be just as competent a voice of government as French. The changes in relative economic strength challenged the political relationship between Belgium's two communities. In 1962, a "language boundary" (see map in "The Belgian People") was officially fixed, and reciprocal rights on both sides of the "border" were spelled out.

During the 1960s, all the traditional nationwide political parties—Socialists, Catholics, and Conservatives—separated into two sections, one for the Flemish and one for Walloons. This increased the number of component parts needed to make political compromises. With language concerns coming ahead of all others, it was ever more difficult to deal with Belgium's national issues. On lesser questions, language matters in Belgium run the gamut from the serious to the stupefying. One widely reported situation had Flemish- and French-speaking farmers at a standoff over the question as to whether or not artificial insemination of their cows should be limited to bulls from the same language area.

After a period of increasingly strident bilingual battle cries, during which it was presumed that a strong central government was necessary to keep the Dutch-speaking Flemish and the French-speaking Walloons away from each other's throats, a new concept emerged that allowed the two communities to function while keeping at a comfortable arm's length from each other. In 1980, the *federalization* of Belgium began. Gradually throughout the 1980s, **Flanders** and **Wallonia** (and **Brussels**, which forms a third autonomous federal region) assumed strong separate-but-equal grips on their own matters. Since 1988, each community has had full decision-making powers in such fields as economy, education, energy, environment, housing, health, cultural affairs, public works, and tourism, and the national budget has been regionalized. In April 1993, the Belgian National Parliament voted final approval for the revision to the constitution officially making Belgium a federal state.

It's unlikely that federalism is the last word on Belgium's language issue. Many Flemish still feel they make more concessions on their side of bilingualism, finding themselves in the uniquely uncomfortable posture of a majority unable to escape from the mentality of the minority.

The losses incurred when a country allows itself to be divided in the name of bilingualism are illustrated in the history of **Louvain University**. Located in Flanders (not far northeast of Brussels), Louvain was founded in 1425 by Pope Martin V and Duke John IV of Brabant.

Within a century it had become one of the leading universities in Europe, with 6,000 students and 52 colleges, one of which was founded in 1517 by Rotterdam-born **Desiderius Erasmus**. (Erasmus had a dream of offering liberal Roman Catholic education at Louvain, but was caught up in the times of Luther and the Protestant Reformation, in response to which strict Catholic orthodoxy was enforced under an official inquisition.) Renowned cartographer Gerhard Mercator (1512–1594) learned his geography at Louvain, where he later founded and ran an institute of cartography (until he was chased from the Spanish Netherlands in 1544 for his heretical views of the world). Ghent-born Charles V was tutored by some of Louvain's leading lecturers.

In many ways, Louvain University's history reflects Flanders'. Once the *lingua franca* for European university instruction was no longer *Latin*, Louvain adopted the culturally correct French language (hence our easier recognition of the historic institution under its French name Louvain, despite its location in Dutch-speaking Flanders and correct Flemish name **Leuven**).

Flanders made a breakthrough in 1930 when the University at Ghent finally was authorized to give its classes in Flemish. At Louvain, eventually the Flemish Movement made enough show of force to make it mandatory that every course offered to the university's more than 15,000 students be available in Flemish as well as French. In 1962, the policy of duplication of curriculum in both languages was reaffirmed although it placed great stress on the university's financial and other resources. That resulted in violent disputes on the issue, however, and led to the expulsion of the French section in 1968, with Flemings insisting that classes conducted in French on Flemish soil were no longer acceptable. Historic Louvain officially became Flemish-speaking **Leuven University** and, in 1970, the decision was made to establish a new, French-speaking university, at **Louvain-la-Neuve** (New Louvain), 28 km/17 mi. south in the Walloon area of Brabant province.

For centuries Louvain University's **library** had been famous in Europe for its many fine manuscripts. Among these were a collection of *Irish literature*, 500 *illuminated manuscripts*, and 1,000 *incunabula* (books printed before A.D. 1500 in the earliest years of moveable type—many at Louvain itself). In 1914, at the beginning of World War I, the central section of the town of Leuven was badly burned by the German army; the Cloth Hall, which the university had occupied since 1432, was demolished and the University Library virtually so. At the end of the war, the *Treaty of Versailles* decreed that Germany must furnish to Louvain library materials of equal value to those destroyed. Other generous contributions of books to restock the Louvain library were made by many institutions, especially in Great Britain and the United States, all of whose donors' names are inscribed on the rebuilt library's walls. The library, reconstructed in Flemish Renaissance style by architect Whitney Warren, reopened in 1928. It again suffered damage, though not as extensive, from Nazi bombs in World War II.

While acknowledging the library's tragic losses due to war, a case can be made that the greatest devastation to the Louvain University library came at the hands of Belgians themselves. No one can fail to be saddened by the disposition of the books in this historic library that resulted from the opening of the French-speaking Louvain-la-Neuve University. In a solution that speaks volumes about Belgium's bicultural struggle, the contents of the original Louvain University library were split between the old and the new, the Flemish and the French-speaking universities, strictly by the number. Books whose call number ended in an even digit went to one institution, those ending in odd went to the other.

Antwerp's cathedral illuminated at night.

ANTWERP

Room in Ruben's house.

GUIDELINES FOR ANTWERP

SIGHTS

Three "must-see" sights in Antwerp (Antwerpen, Anvers) are baroque painter **Pieter Paul Rubens' house**, the **Plantin-Moretus house** and the **Gothic cathedral** (Belgium's largest). Other major attractions include the **Royal Museum of Fine Arts**, the **Diamond Museum**, and the **port**.

One of the remarkable aspects about art in Antwerp is that so much of it remains in the specific spaces for which it originally was created:

city churches and **patrician townhouses** (several now furnished museums) of contemporaries of Rubens. Old Antwerp, around the grand **Grote Markt**, is linked by appealing streets (many pedestrian-only), quaint cobbled alleys, and quiet old squares. Belgium's proud port city is inextricably tied to the **river Scheldt**, the riverfront of interest for its ancient fortress/prison **Steen** (now the **Maritime Museum**), the **Flandria** cruise boat pier, riverbank promenades, and a pedestrian tunnel under the water that leads to a fine view of Antwerp from the far bank. There's striking **after-dark illumination** of the cathedral, the Stadhuis on the Grote Markt, and other buildings and monuments.

GETTING AROUND

Antwerp (with a core city population of 250,000, greater city 500,000) sprawls, but several important sights are within a few blocks of the centrally located **Grote Markt**, on which is located the main **city tourist office**. Most others are within walking distance either north or south of **Meir** (pronounced *mare*, as in horse), Antwerp's confusingly multiple-named, but essentially straight, main midcity street, running from **Centraal Station** to the river **Scheldt**. Some 20 percent of the old city center is now pedestrianized. The city's public transport network includes trams, metro, and buses (system map at tourist office); tickets are sold by 8-ride strip, 24-hour day pass, or single ride. Near the cathedral and Grote Markt, several tram and bus lines converge at **Groenplaats** (identifiable by its statue of Rubens), beneath which is a stop on the metro line which runs under Meir to the Centraal Station. Groenplaats, and **Koning Astridplein** in front of Centraal Station, have taxi stands. Antwerp has a reasonable number of paid parking lots; those in cars should avoid the area around the Grote Markt, which has the most pedestrian-only and congested streets.

SHOPPING

Antwerp provides sophisticated shopping, with all the expected Belgian and European department, clothing, and specialty stores, most located along **Meir** (Fridays until 9 p.m., other nights until 6 p.m.). The city is noted as an innovative international fashion design center thanks to the styles of the so-called **Antwerp Six**. Antique and secondhand shops are scattered throughout the city, and with Antwerp's history as an international trading hub, one never knows what objects might turn up. The 16th-century cobbled **Vlaeykensgang alleyway** off Oude Koornmarkt is as much worth seeking out for its picturesqueness as its antiques. Art galleries continue to open in

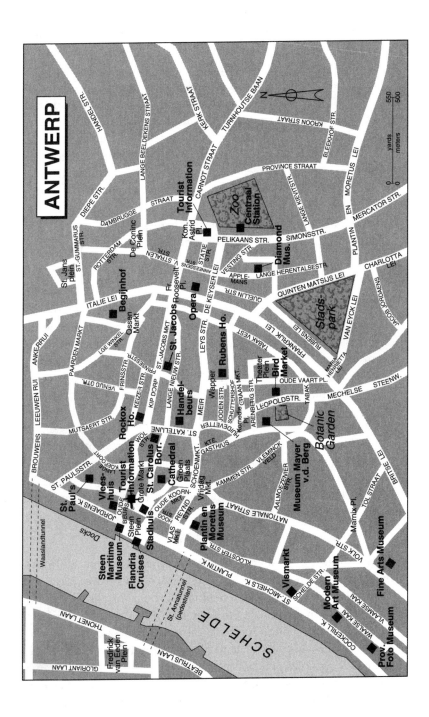

Antwerp, many branches of Brussels' establishments. Antwerp's brilliantly cut diamonds are sold wholesale and retail in nondescript shops along the side of **Centraal Station**; prices for unset stones are some 40 percent off those in the U.S. If you're looking for a gem, though not necessarily a jewel, save Sunday mornings (8:30 a.m.-1 p.m.) for the **Vogelmarkt** or bird market, a 600-year tradition on the site (near the City Theater). Originally solely geese and chickens were sold, hence its name, but today it's also a flea market. Saturdays (10 a.m.-6 p.m.) from Easter through Sept. there's an antiques market on *Lijnwaadmarkt*, north of the cathedral. During the same season, also on Saturdays, artists display their work in the open air on the *Wapper* outside Rubens' house. Wednesday and Friday mornings at the **Vrijdaymarkt** there are public auctions of secondhand furniture and household goods.

ENTERTAINMENT AND EVENTS

A remarkably cosmopolitan and cultured city, Antwerp offers its citizens and visitors a wide variety of regularly scheduled and special events. The monthly *Kalender Antwerpen* (available from the tourist office) lists programs for the city's concert, opera, ballet, and theater companies, as well as the 50-odd cinemas (where films are shown in the original language—many in English—with Dutch subtitles), cabaret, exhibitions, and other events.

WHERE TO STAY

In addition to modern international chain business hotels outside the city center, Antwerp offers a limited but interesting selection of pleasant in-town properties. Since central Antwerp is spread out, no hotel will be convenient to all attractions, though most are near public transport.

WHERE TO EAT

Antwerpians like to dine with wine. With an estimated 800 cafes and restaurants and perhaps 2,000 pubs, there's no lack of places for visitors to fit in with local food fashion. Tasters' choices range from a traditional Flemish stew pot to a melting pot of ethnic eateries to meet the culinary preferences of Antwerp's cosmopolitan population. You can satisfy a sweet tooth for Antwerp's *pralines* (filled, handmade chocolates) least expensively at small sidewalk shops, and most imaginatively at **H. Burie** (where white chocolate is molded in *stalks* resembling Belgium's famed white asparagus ☎ *32.36.88*). Antwerpse *handjes* ("little hands") are rich butter and almond cookies that honor the city's *Brabo* legend. (See "Antwerp in Context.")

ARRIVING

There is frequent half-hour train service between Antwerp's **Centraal Station** (the so-called "railway cathedral") and all three Brussels' stations. Belgium's dense rail network also makes Antwerp easily accessible from elsewhere in the country and from most anywhere in Europe (connections through Brussels). Antwerp is less than three hours from Amsterdam on numerous direct trains. Belgium's **SABENA World Airlines** runs regularly scheduled buses between Antwerp (from near SABENA's office on *de Keyserlei*, across from Centraal Station) and Brussels' **Zaventem Airport**. Those arriving from England by North Sea ferry at Ostend or Zeebrugge can reach Antwerp by rail with a transfer either at Ghent or Brussels (Gare du Nord). Antwerp is well served on the Belgium/European motorway system.

IN THE AREA

A short bus ride from Centraal Station to a southern Antwerp neighborhood brings you to the **Middelheim Open-Air Museum**, one of the world's finest sculpture gardens. Also accessible by bus, the streets **Cogels-Osylei** in the city's southeast district of Berchem offer a turn-of-the-century architectural free-for-all, with plenty of fanciful *jugendstil* ("art nouveau"). Less than 15 minutes by frequent train from Antwerp is attractive **Mechelen**, city of carillon concerts, tapestry tradition, and once a historic Hapsburg Court.

TRAVEL TRIPS

In 1993 Antwerp was spotlighted as the European Community's Cultural Capital. For the occasion, Antwerp polished itself citywide as carefully as it would one of its own fine diamonds. Visitors in 1994 will reap the results—completed restorations of the *Cathedral, Bourla Theatre* and *Centraal Station* are among the permanent improvements to the city—without the extra crowds.

ANTWERP IN CONTEXT

Antwerp's most famous son, artist Pieter Paul Rubens, once observed: "It is not a question of living long, but of living well." Rubens may not have been referring to cities, but his historic and handsome home town has nevertheless seen fit to follow the suggestion. Antwerp, which dates from Roman days, not only lives graciously with its long and prestigious past, but enjoys an enviably lively and prosperous present.

Although it is by Belgian standards a populous city, with a half million inhabitants, Antwerp retains the feeling and friendliness of a small town. And though Antwerp is one of the world's premier ports and the diamond capital of the world, its ambiance is akin to a cosmopolitan village. Antwerpians have devised a life-style of their own, and seem to identify more with their city than with the rest of Flanders, let alone Belgium. Some residents claim that a lingering influence from the days of Spanish occupation accounts for Antwerpians' being more intuitive and emotional than most northern Europeans. One told me, "In Antwerp we have our own way of life, but we are xenophiles, not xenophobes." Antwerp's agreeably integrated population proves it: some 117 nationalities make up the mix.

The inevitable influence of its port (the fifth largest in the world, and a regular port of call or home port for approximately 300 shipping lines from more than 100 countries) adds more foreign flavor. Some who first came to Antwerp to discuss international trade found the city so well suited to living well that they returned to stay. Those fortunate enough to be native Antwerpians, though healthily chauvinistic, also are an outlooking lot, having grown up with the tradition of the seven seas on their doorstep. But of the many who leave to see something else of the world, most return to Antwerp's exceptional environment.

Antwerp calls the 16th century its **Golden Age**. The period was the most prosperous of any in Antwerp's history—though the present could come to rival it: currently, the city of Antwerp provides the country of Belgium with close to half the Gross National Product (GNP).

Antwerp's prosperity has always been linked to its port on the Scheldt. More than one Antwerpian may quote the old saying: "The town owes its river to God, but everything else it owes to its river." The Scheldt features in a favorite fable about the city's Roman days. The river at Antwerp, so it is told, was ruled by a giant who demanded tolls from passing ships. Sailors who didn't pay had their hands cut off. Finally, a Roman soldier named **Brabo** decided to defy the giant. In a struggle reminiscent of David and Goliath's, Brabo defeated the giant, whose huge hand he cut off and threw into the river (the very action captured in the *Brabo Fountain* sculpture on the Grote Markt). From this tale, the source of the name Antwerp, from the Flemish *handwerpen* ("throwing the hand") has been suggested. But the more prosaic, and probable, derivation is *aanwerp* ("a promontory in the river"), which describes the present site of **the Steen**, where Antwerp's earliest settlement was founded.

Battered even earlier by Norsemen and Normans, Antwerp was noted as a port by A.D. 1031. In the 12th century, the city gained municipal rights from the dukes of Brabant. The **Hanseatic League** set up an establishment here in 1313 and Antwerp also acquired the important right of staple for English wool. Both events brought foreign merchants to the town on the Scheldt in increasing numbers. Residence in Antwerp by the *counts of Flanders* (who became unified with Brabant under the Burgundians in 1406) marked the beginning of a period of even greater commercial recognition. While benefitting from association with Brabant's economic progress, Antwerp also gained at the expense of the once flourishing Flemish city of Bruges. That town lost its access to the North Sea as the river Zwin silted up, while Antwerp's access increased as the mouth of the Scheldt was considerably widened by flooding in Zeeland.

By the end of the 15th century Antwerp had become the chief port in all the Netherlands. Major sources of trade were sugar, soap, beer, diamonds, and textiles. (The city had gained control of *alum*, a substance indispensable to the cloth industry, by imposing a stage tax for it on the Scheldt.) In 1454, Philip the Good established the Antwerp **Guild of St. Luke** for the encouragement of painting, an act which served as a foundation for the *Flemish School*. The guild played host to Albrecht Dürer during his stay in Antwerp in 1520–1521.

In the 16th century, Antwerp continued to grow as an important trading center for spices and staples, and by then, Antwerp's diamond industry had been in business for a century. Merchants from many cultures—English, German, Italian, Spanish, and Portuguese—met and mingled in the port city. The city's financial establishments lent money to kings and emperors dealing at Europe's first international exchange building, which opened in Antwerp in 1460 (and served as a model for subsequent exchanges in London and elsewhere in Europe). Antwerp became the continent's foremost center of commerce, navigation, finance, and art. Up to 300 vessels put in and out of Antwerp's port daily, and more than 1,000 foreign trading concerns had offices here. Even a Venetian ambassador to the city called Antwerp "the first trading center of the world." Another dubbed the port "the most noble warehouse of the whole world."

Finally there was enough money to finish Antwerp's cathedral, whose construction, begun in 1352, had frequently floundered thereafter for lack of funds. Its magnificent tower (400 feet/123 meters), added in 1518, marked the completion of the largest Gothic church in the Netherlands. In 1514, Antwerp had a population of

40,000 (which, even then, made it as large as London, and three times the size of any town in Holland). By 1560, the city had exploded to 100,000. Truly, it was a Golden Age.

But Emperor Charles V, who had ruled the Netherlands through the opening phases of the rapidly spreading **Reformation**, abdicated in 1555 to his son Philip II of Spain. Philip's response to the Protestants practically decreed that prosperous times in Antwerp, by then rent with religious dissent, would not survive his reign. Antwerp's cathedral and other churches were pillaged by Protestant Calvinists in the 1566 *Iconoclast*, which took a great toll on the city's artistic achievements. The 1576 *Spanish Fury's* toll was in lives, when the city was sacked, and 7,000 citizens were killed in an attack by angry Spanish soldiers, mutinous from not having received their pay from the **duke of Alva**. (The Spanish Fury caused many Protestants to flee for their lives, including one **Jan Rubens**, a Lutheran lawyer whose son **Pieter Paul** was born the next year in exile in Westphalia, Germany.) In 1577, with help from Holland's **Prince Willem (the Silent) of Orange**, whose rebel forces were for a while headquartered in Flanders, Antwerp, stood up to the Spanish so successfully that for the next eight years the open practice of Roman Catholicism in the city was forbidden. (The Rubens' family wasn't yet able to return from Germany because Pieter Paul's mother was Catholic.)

In 1585, after a two-year siege, the duke of Parma recaptured Antwerp for Spain. This turn of fortune established that Antwerp's future would be with the Spanish or southern Netherlands (the future Belgium) rather than the northern Netherlands (Holland). The firm establishment of Antwerp as a Roman Catholic city under Spanish rule drove thousands more Protestants to Holland: diamond cutters went to Amsterdam, tile workers found employment in Delft, and the family of five-year-old **Frans Hals** left for Haarlem. (Finally, his Protestant father having died, Pieter Paul Rubens and his mother returned to Antwerp.) The many Antwerp artisans and artists who emigrated north to Holland can truly be said to have had a hand in that country's upcoming golden 17th century.

The relatively peaceful reign of the equally-entitled **archdukes** (Isabella, daughter of Philip II, and her husband Albert) from 1598–1621 was a period of economic recovery for Antwerp and its port. Baroque art blossomed under **Pieter Paul Rubens,** whose students, studio helpers, and collaborators included **Jacob Jordaens, Anthony Van Dyck, Adriaen Brouwer**, and **David Teniers Elder** and **Younger**. At the same time an intellectual coterie, which included Rubens, arose around the brilliant **Balthasar Moretus** of the printing house *Plantin-Moretus.* The period left a physical imprint upon Antwerp that visitors can see today. In 1620, using almost touristic terms, Jan Woverius, humanist, town-clerk, and one-time learned counsellor to the archdukes, wrote: "Our City of Antwerp is happy to possess two such great citizens as Rubens and Moretus...their houses will evoke the astonishment and admiration of visitors."

No end to an era could be more definitive than that which came to Antwerp with the signing of the 1648 *Peace of Westphalia.* In the agreement that officially ended the 80-year Spanish/Netherlands war, the Spanish accepted the Dutch terms that demanded the **closing of the Scheldt** to ships. (The banks on both sides of the river estuary are in Dutch territory.) The Dutch move to do away with competition for the port of Amsterdam by closing the Scheldt effectively closed the port at Antwerp. As it happened, the port would not be reopened for a century and a half. Cut off from sea trade, Antwerp foundered. Its population plummeted: by 1790, it was back to the size it had been in 1514: 40,000.

The port of Antwerp owes its revival to **Napoleon,** who in 1799 took over the reins of the *French Revolutionary Army,* which earlier in the 1790s had conquered both the southern and northern Netherlands. The French Napoleon reopened the Scheldt with an ulterior motive: to have a naval "pistol pointed at the heart of England." Between 1800 and 1803, dock basins and river quays were built; the Bonaparte Lock was inaugurated in 1811 (and still is in operation). With its port once again open to commerce, Antwerp experienced an astonishing revival.

When Napoleon was defeated at **Waterloo** in 1815, Antwerp came under Dutch rule in the *United Kingdom of the Netherlands* partnership enforced upon Belgium by outside European powers. With Antwerp then doing business under the same flag as the Dutch, its port's revitalization was encouraged. With the improvements, Antwerp developed into the largest port in the Netherlands. Dutch trade with its colonies in Indonesia and the Caribbean provided steady traffic in and out of all Netherlands ports, but Antwerp's share of the shipping stopped with Belgium's revolt against Dutch rule in 1830. Whatever Dutch King Willem I felt about being thus "divested" of Belgium, he had no intention of giving up Antwerp's preeminent port without a fight. The Dutch dug in, and great damage was done to the port by bombardment and sieges in 1830 and 1832 before they were dislodged. (The new Belgian King **Leopold I** eventually called in the French for help.)

In the 1839 peace that finally established the present national borders, Holland was granted the the right of levying navigation dues on shipping in the Scheldt. In 1863, Antwerp, with the help of the Belgian government, bought out Holland's right to the levies for a considerable compensation. At the turn of the century, Antwerp became important as the port for the *Kongobootes* that sailed the seas to and from **Belgium's Congo colony** (now **Zaire**). When the big ships steamed into Antwerp from Africa, they always caused a stir and raised a crowd, and often attracted brass bands on the piers.

Antwerp's World War II destruction was heaviest toward the end; when retaken by the Allies, the port suffered Nazi V-1 and V-2 attacks in late 1944 and early 1945. Antwerp was the goal of Hitler's last-gasp across-Belgium campaign in the winter of 1944–45, but what became known as the *Battle of the Bulge* became bogged down where it began: in the Ardennes. That Hitler had even thought of attempting to regain Antwerp so late in the war was a testament to the port's strategic value. Its location remained important when peace came, and the two world wars proved to be only interruptions in the port's 20th-century progress.

Today, Antwerp on the Scheldt, situated some 50 mi./85 km. from the North Sea, is becoming ever more significant as an international crossroads for maritime and continental shipping and distribution. In tonnage and traffic, the city has the world's fifth largest port and, by many accounts, Europe's most efficient in turnaround time. Port pilots are taken aboard incoming ships at Holland's Vlissengen (Flushing), and in Antwerp proper, on out-sailing vessels, their knowledge is vital because of the Scheldt's shifting sandbars and waters—tidal water well above Antwerp—which rise and fall about 13 feet between tides. The 37,000-acre/15,000-hectare, state-of-the-art port, has a control tower with a computerized system to plan and control shipping, and as of 1991 the world's longest radar chain (78 mi./130 km.), stretching down the Scheldt to the North Sea.

The relative quiet along the waterfront in the center of Antwerp, where old warehouses with stylish iron pediments lie abandoned except for scenery-seeking, riverbank pedestrians, belies the port's actual activity. Increasingly after World War II, Antwerp's port spread downstream (nearer to the North Sea) to accommodate larger ocean-going vessels; it now has some 100 kilometers of wet and dry docks, extending north to the Dutch border. Along the Scheldt are five sea-locks, of which the newest, **Berendrecht Lock** (opened in 1989) is the largest in the world. Major port industries at Antwerp include oil refineries, petrochemical and automobile assembly plants, grain companies, trans-shipment yards, and multinational firms such as *Bayer* and *Montsanto*. Even segments of Antwerp's old sailors' quarter have moved on down the river, and some of the brothels and rooming houses in the city's waterfront district have been converted into apartments and artists' lofts.

Dockers' pride in their port has helped make Antwerp a highly efficient installation. Four shifts are needed to keep the river-borne, business moving during the port's 24-hour day. Antwerp's dock workers' ways are traditional, but unions, management, supervisors, and stevedores in the hiring hall haven't come up with anything they like better, and there hasn't been a strike since 1963. Being strike-free has played a big part in Antwerp's having won business away from the ports of Rotterdam and London.

There are two possibilities for visitors to see something of Antwerp's port. The boats of **Flandri** (berthed on the Scheldt near the *Steenplein* in central Antwerp), whose 50-minute cruises don't get far enough downstream to show much of the port, also offer day or evening 3-hour port excursions. For those traveling by car, the 40-mi./65-km., self-guiding *Havenroute* (map available from the tourist office), best undertaken when there's a passenger who can serve as navigator, provides insight into the workings of the port.

As visitors discover, Antwerp is a destination with many dimensions, one that integrates new ideas with older ones. The intellectual environment that blossomed as an accompaniment to the baroque art of Antwerp's Golden Age at the end of the 16th century had its birth at the beginning of that century. At that time **Thomas More** (1477–1535), an English humanist and a *Man for All Seasons*, used Antwerp as a setting for his book *Utopia*. Considered one of the most influential books in Western philosophy, *Utopia* described a mythical island off South America where wealth was divided equally and all lived in happy cooperation free of war and want.

Book One of *Utopia* opens with More recounting: "The most invincible king of England, Henry the Eighth of that name, sent me into Flanders as his spokesman (and) since my business required it, I went to Antwerp." More lived in Antwerp from May to October in 1515, and in *Utopia* speaks of his Antwerpian friend Peter Giles, whose house until recently stood just behind the *Grote Markt* at *16 Oude Beurs*. He visited it many times, since it was a prominent meeting place for fellow **humanists**, including Erasmus. Thomas More was an intimate of Rotterdam-born humanist Erasmus (with whom he founded a college at Louvain University—see "Flanders: An

Introduction"—where *Utopia* was first published in 1516). Humanism was an intellectual and cultural movement concerned with the interest and ideals of people rather than religion. In the pages of *Utopia*, Peter Giles introduces Thomas More to Raphael, who tells them both of the wonders of the world that he—Raphael—had heard recounted by explorer Amerigo Vespucci (1451–1512). At this time, in accordance with their individual beliefs, most Europeans were either entranced or alarmed by tales about overseas expeditions, but the philosophers of the day saw in the broadened horizons a fresh chance for men to create a better way of life. Hence, More, inspired by Vespucci's voyages, conceived in *Utopia* how an idealistic society might be set up in an unspoiled new world.

During his stay in Antwerp, early on in the city's Golden Age, Thomas More would have observed a metropolis that mixed material success with humanism. More than 450 years later, an antiques dealer has this to say about his city: "We are at a very similar point in history: the humanism of the Renaissance is a philosophy that suits our present." He believes that Antwerpians are open, seeking, and creative, and may well be in the midst of a renaissance that will rival the city's 16th-century glory.

GUIDEPOSTS

Telephone Code 03

Tourist Information • City Tourist Office: Head Office: Grote Markt 15; B-2000 Antwerp; Mon.–Fri., 8:30 a.m.–6:00 p.m., Sat., Sun., holidays, 9 a.m.–5 p.m.; ☎ *232.01.03.* Information pavilion: Koningin Astridplein in front of Centraal Station: same hours as head office except Mon.-Fri., until 8 p.m., Sat. to 7 p.m; ☎ *232.05.70.*; both offices closed Christmas and New Year's Day. Accommodations booking assistance.

City Transport • M.I.V.A. Head Office: Grotehondstraat 58; Mon.–Fri., 8:30 a.m.–4:00 p.m.; ☎ *218.14.20.*

Trains • Centraal Station inquiries: Mon.–Sat. 8 a.m.–10 p.m., Sun. and holidays, 9 a.m.–5 p.m.

Airport Bus Service • SABENA office: De Keyserlei 74; ☎ *231.68.25.* Regularly scheduled coaches to Brussels Zaventem Airport.

Port Cruises • *Flandria*: Steenplein, ☎ *233.74.22.*

City Tours • Sightseeing Line: 13-passenger 50-minute narrated (head sets, 7 languages) mini-van tours from Grote Markt: schedule and reservations at Tourist Office.

Consulates • U.S.A.: Nationalestraat 5; ☎ *225.00.71.* Great Britain: Korte Klarenstraat 7; ☎ *232.69.40.* Ireland: Rudolfstraat 16; ☎ *237.69.94.*

Emergencies • Police: ☎ *101*; accident: ☎ *100*; a list of doctors and pharmacists/chemists on night and weekend duty is published in the weekend editions of local newspapers, and available from the Tourist Office or at hotel.

Automobile Aid • Royal Automobile Club of Belgium: ☎ *232.16.93.*

Lost Property • Police headquarters: ☎ *231.68.80*; Centraal Railway Station: ☎ *231.76.90*; city tram/bus office: ☎ *218.14.11.*

Post Office • Main Post Office: Groenplaats 42; Mon.–Fri., 9 a.m.–6 p.m., Sat. 9 a.m.–noon; ☎ *231.06.70.*

Telephone/Telegraph • Head Office: Jezusstraat 1; daily 8 a.m.–8 p.m.; ☎ *232.58.10.*

WHAT TO SEE AND DO

Central Antwerp's attractions are grouped below in three general areas, each of which can be covered fairly easily on foot. The most distant site is the Fine Arts Museum (more than a mile from the **Grote Markt**), to which most visitors take a tram or taxi. Sights start with those within walking distance of the Grote Markt (the tourist office there has maps and printed English commentary on eight suggested walking tours), and riverfront, following which are descriptions of sites south and then north of **Meir**. Local custom calls for time out at cafes along the way. Many museums in Antwerp are open on Monday; holidays on which they are commonly closed are Jan. 1 and 2, May 1, Ascension Day, Nov. 1 and 2, Dec. 25 and 26.

AROUND THE GROTE MARKT AND RIVERFRONT

Grote Markt ★★

This is the heart of Antwerp and at the great square's center; replacing the former tree of liberty is the **Brabo Fountain** (1887, sculpted by **Jef Lambeaux**). Rimming it are dignified 16th-century guild houses, each topped with a gilt-adorned patron saint appropriate to the particular craft or trade (drapers, haberdashers, coopers, and crossbows) once headquartered therein. The guild houses (some original, such as numbers 38 and 40, others reconstructions of those that once stood elsewhere, such as 15 and 25) are in Renaissance style, which gives Antwerp's Grote Markt a less ornate appearance than Brussels' baroque-era main square. Though not used for weekly general markets, Antwerp's Grote Markt is the setting for special festival markets.

Southwest off the Grote Markt is the statue of the **Dock Worker** (by **Constantin Meunier**). Out the northeast corner across Oude Beurs, at 15 Hofstraat, is Antwerp's old **stock exchange**, a beautiful Gothic building from 1515 that now serves as the city's education office (the lovely inner courtyard can be viewed during office hours). Behind Grote Markt to the right of the **Stadhuis**, and between it and the not-distant **Vleehuis**, one finds exemplary urban renewal in one of the city's most historic sections. An extensive housing project (following the clearance deemed necessary due to ancient buildings that had become slum like) has been built to blend in scale and materials with original old city buildings.

Stadhuis   ★★

Grote Markt; Mon.–Sat. 9 a.m.–3 p.m., except Mon. 9 a.m.–noon, Fri. noon–3 p.m., Sat. til 4 p.m., closed Sun. and holidays; ☎ *220.82.11.* The Grote Markt is dominated by the *Stadhuis* ("town hall"), whose 247-foot facade has a coat of many colors of marble. Built from 1561–1565 by Antwerp architect Cornelis Floris, it is one of Flanders' earliest and finest buildings in the Renaissance style. During summer months the Stadhuis festively flaunts some of the flags of the more than 100 countries whose ships put into Antwerp's port. The impressive interior decoration dates mostly from the city's prosperous 19th century, many earlier works of art having been destroyed or stolen during the French occupation at the end of the 18th century. The former Lords' Chamber, now the **Leys Room**, is decorated with four historical paintings by Henri Leys representing the main privileges of Antwerp. Murals on the staircase walls and in the marriage chamber are also notable.

The statue in the center niche in the front of the Stadhuis is of the Virgin Mary, patron saint of the city, and it recalls the other Madonnas you'll see by the dozen in street corner niches. Two reasons account for their great number. During the days of the St. Luke's Guild, in order to become a *master* member, an artist had to create a *masterpiece*; often, Antwerp sculptors selected the Madonna as their subject, and later presented the completed work to the district in which they lived. Secondly, when these statuettes of the Virgin, displayed on street corners, were lighted by votives, the districts avoided the taxes that otherwise were levied on private street lights.

Onze Lieve Vrouw/Notre Dame cathedral   ★★★

Groenplaats 21; Mon.– Fri. 10 a.m.–5 p.m., Sat. 10 a.m.–3 p.m., Sun. and church festivals 1–4 p.m., not accessible during church services; ☎ *231.30.33.* Because of its position on the ground and the prominence of its steeple in the sky, Antwerp's cathedral is *the* landmark of the city. Hemmed in by buildings, the cathedral body cannot be seen as a whole, but the structure nevertheless is an omnipresence in the old center. The largest Gothic church in Belgium, the cathedral was begun in 1352 under a general design by Jan Appelmans. (See the imaginative **Appelmans Monument** by **Jef Lambeaux**, 1935, to the right of the cathedral's main door on **Handschotenmarkt**.) With construction spread out until 1521 due to erratic funding, the nave, originally Romanesque, was demolished in about 1425 and begun again in Gothic. The seven-aisle interior is of startling size, only recently (1993) revealed following a long-term $70 million-plus fundamental restoration. (Belgium's king and queen attended the rededication ceremonies in April 1993.) At 400 feet/122 meters, the cathedral's soaring spire, completed in 1521, is the highest in the Netherlands, resembling Belgian lace in its delicacy. Unwrapped in 1990 from scaffolding that had contained it since 1965, it brings fresh meaning to the word *inspiring*. The view from its inside out, if you aspire to climb the tower, is pure panorama.

Cathedral treasures include three of Rubens' most famous paintings: *Raising of the Cross* (triptych, 1610), *Descent from the Cross* (triptych, 1611–1614), and *Assumption* (1626). The central panel of *Descent from the Cross*, with its strong diagonal line that draws viewers into the action and emotion of the moment, is the essence of Rubens' best baroque work. Concerts occasionally are performed on the 5625-pipe organ. Many flat tombstones can be seen in the cathedral floor; people paid a lot to be buried here because of the one-time belief that if on Judgment Day they were raised to their feet inside a church, they would fare better than if in a cemetery.

Handschoenmarkt   ★★

This lovely square in front of the cathedral's main door has retained its historic Frankish triangle shape, which facilitated the protective containment of cattle. At No. 13 is the house (with plaque) in which the artist **David Teniers the Younger** was born in 1610. The cafe-rimmed, square is a delightful locale for listening to concerts on the cathedral's 47-bell carillon (*Fridays from 11:30 a.m.–12:30 p.m. year-round, and Mondays from 9–10 p.m. from mid-June to mid-September*).

In the square is a stone well with a lovely ironwork canopy (c. 1495). The canopy is ascribed to **Quinten Metsys** (or *Matsys* and *Massys*, c. 1460–1530), a favorite adopted son of Antwerp, who arrived from Louvain trained as a blacksmith and with a talent for intricate ironwork. But an *artisan* wasn't good enough for the *artist* whose daughter Metsys fell in love with in his new city. As the story of the courtship is recounted, Metsys continued to visit the young lady at her home, and one day, speaking with her in her father's studio, he picked up a brush and painted a fly on a canvas that her father had left to dry. A few days later when the father had occasion to look at the painting again, he tried to brush off the fly. When he realized that it was painted and inquired of his daughter who the artist was, he was persuaded to give permission for her to marry Metsys. The Latin phrase inscribed on a tablet to Quinten Metsys on the facade of the cathedral (to the left of the door near the well) translates: "Twas love connubial taught the smith to paint." Metsys, who today is considered the first major artist of the Antwerp School, is represented by *The Lamentation of Christ Triptych*, and five other paintings in Antwerp's **Royal Fine Arts Museum** (which has none by his "artist" father-in-law).

Steenplein and Riverfront   ★

The Scheldt is nearly a third of a mile (500 meters) wide in front of the Steenplein, where a statue of **Minerva**, the Roman goddess of wisdom and industry, reflects upon the river. Though much of the shipping that makes the *Port of Antwerp's* statistics so impressive must now be accommodated downstream by facilities fit to handle it, you'll still find the flavor of river traffic in the center of the city, from the barges heading upstream on the waterway into the heart of the European continent. The entrance to the under-river pedestrian **St. Annatunnel** (built in 1933, about 1/3 mile long) is located west of the *Vrijdaymarkt* at *St. Jansvliet.*

The Steen (National Maritime Museum)   ★★

Steenplein 1; daily 10 a.m.–5 p.m.; ☎ *232.08.50; exhibits with English explanation.* On the waterfront is Antwerp's oldest (12th century) edifice, the Steen, situated on the site of the city's earliest development. Built as a fortress, and for centuries used as a prison, the Steen was restored (by architects De Waghemakere and Keldermans, who had just completed work on the cathedral) about 1520 by order of Charles V, whose coat of arms can still be seen on the lovely loggia over the entrance gate. Under Charles' son Spanish King Philip II and the dread duke of Alva, however, the Steen deteriorated into a torture chamber. Today, no longer fusty or frightening, it is the fascinating setting for the National Maritime Museum. Within the wonderful building are nautical exhibits that include a copy of the state barge built in Antwerp for the Emperor Napoleon on his visit in 1810, sailors' old tatoo paraphernalia, an elaborate tile panel showing a 17th-century sea battle between the Dutch and the English, and a model of Antwerp harbor c. 1515. The widely varied exhibits are shown in 12 sections in a series of mostly small rooms separated by narrow passageways and some steep stairs. There's a cafe in the basement.

Beyond the Steen on the ★★ promenade along the Scheldt are ships and sailors from around the world, and waterfront cafes at *Noorderterras* and *Ziderterras* ("North and South terrace") are great places from which to watch them.

Vleeshuis (Butchers' Hall Museum)   ★

Vleeshouwersstraat 38-40; daily 10a.m.-5 p.m., closed Mondays except Easter Monday, Whit Monday, and the Monday after the 2nd Sunday in August; ☎ *233.64.04.* This large and impressive building was commissioned by De Waghemakere, one of Antwerp Cathedral's architects, for the Butchers' Guild for use as its market and meeting hall. Perhaps Antwerp's finest secular Gothic style building, the Vleeshuis is, appropriately for butchers, an excellent example of so-called "bacon" construction: horizontal layers of red brick are interspersed with white limestone, which gives the impression of pink meat layered with lard. The exterior view is particularly recommended, but if you have plenty of time in Antwerp, the museum within offers exhibits of local history and crafts, furniture, old musical instruments, and the room on the top floor has a unique wooden ceiling.

SOUTH OF MEIR

Rubenshuis   ★★★

Wapper 9; daily 10 a.m.–5 p.m., closed major holidays.; *232.47.47;*
English language guidebook available. The best place to appreciate
Pieter Paul Rubens' personality, if not his works, is the house he
began building in 1610 and lived in from 1616 until his death there
in 1640. The mansion, with its restrained Flemish Renaissance street-
front facade, makes way for the family living quarters and the artist's
exuberant statue-studded studio, linked together by an imposing portico topped with figures of the Roman gods *Mercury* and *Minerva* that
appear in several of his paintings. With stature as "the prince of painters, and the painter of princes," Rubens dominated the baroque age in
Antwerp.

Rubens was the son of a Lutheran lawyer who had to flee Antwerp for
religious reasons. Thus Rubens was born in Westphalia, Germany in
1577, returning to Antwerp about 1585 with his Catholic mother
(who converted her son to her religion). He was apprenticed succes-
sively to three Flemish artists, and in 1598 became a master in Antwerp's artists **Guild of St. Luke**, of which he later was dean. In the corner bedroom of his house is the actual chair (with the gilt lettering
"PET. PAUL. RUBENS 1633" on the back) that was reserved for him
in the painters' room of the guild's headquarters.

In 1600, Rubens went to Italy, staying in Rome, Venice, and Genoa,
and studying with masters there. During his eight years in Italy, he
also went to Spain on diplomatic business for Vincenzo Gonzaga of
Mantua, a patron in whose service he worked. Rubens returned to
Antwerp in 1608 because of the ill health of his mother (she died
while he was enroute home). The next year, 1609, he became court
painter to the Archdukes Isabella and Albert and married Isabella
Brant. In 1610, he made an immense investment in land on what is
now the Wapper and began designing and building a house and studio
(into which he moved five years later, though the buildings were not
yet finished). By 1611 he was at work on two monumental works for
Antwerp cathedral where they can be seen today: the triptychs *Raising
of the Cross* and *Descent from the Cross.*

The fleshy flamboyance of Rubens' figures may not be fashionable
today, but the flourishing of the baroque period when and where it
did is thoroughly comprehensible in the context of the times. The
baroque style, with its massive forms and nearly excessive ornamentation, was embraced by the Roman Catholic Church in Europe during
the Counter-Reformation, undoubtedly the more so for its being in
such complete contrast to the unadorned style decreed by Calvinist
Protestantism.

But though he breathed baroque with every brush stroke, Rubens
himself was something of a Renaissance man. Having studied the clas-

sics until the age of 12, and having used his eight years in Italy to study archaelogy and to begin a collection of classical statuary, Rubens revealed his close identification with the ancients in the statesmen and gods whose likenesses grace his home, inside and out. Within the house, off the painting gallery where he displayed the favorites of his excellent and extensive personal collection, a marble half-pantheon or apsidal gallery served as a display case for his treasured antique busts and statues. In 1618 Rubens exchanged some of his paintings for Greek and Roman statues and other antiquities from the collection of Antwerp's English ambassador Sir Dudley Carlton. "Art above gold for investment," he believed.

Rubens' carefully acquired collection of classical art was admired by all who saw it, and he was praised as an archaeologist by learned men of his time. One wrote, "Especially with regard to antiquities, Rubens has the most universal and remarkable knowledge I ever met with. He is very well-grounded in all the branches of archaelology." A bust of the Roman Seneca rests above the door to his Great Studio, and stoicism and humanism were guiding philosophies for Rubens. In a cartouche in the portico, Rubens had inscribed in the stone a line from the Roman poet Juvenal: "Leave it to the gods to give what is fit and useful for us; man is dearer to them than to himself."

Although attempts had been made to buy the house for the city of Antwerp as early as 1762, the Rubens house became a museum only in 1946, following a major reconstruction that returned it to its original state. The furniture visitors see today did not, with rare and noted exception, belong to Rubens, but is authentic in recreating the atmosphere of a patrician house in Antwerp of the 17th century. In the house are some ten paintings by Rubens, perhaps the most interesting being one of his few self-portraits (in the dining room). The art gallery in the house was hung with the artist's favorites in a collection that numbered about 300 at the time of his death. The wide-ranging collection included many Flemish primitives, and it is a sad loss that it was scattered after the artist's death. In the collection were 17 paintings by **Adriaen Brouwer**, whose work Rubens obviously much admired. Brouwer, notorious for a dissolute life, is said to have once been released from imprisonment in the Steen due to Rubens' intercession.

Rubens loved his work and worked hard at it. But the estimated 1,500–2,000 paintings in his *oeuvre* could not possibly have been realized without his studio staff of students and collaborators. Often, Rubens would create the design for a painting, leave the intermediate execution of it to his pupils, and then add the finishing flourishes that gave it his touch. Such a division of work was quite common in the times, if one had sufficent commissions to warrant supporting a studio. It was in the Great Studio, where several Rubens' paintings are displayed, that several pupils would have worked on a cluster of canvases and panels. In order to assess or show to guests and clients his largest works, those destined to decorate palaces or church altars and meant to be viewed from a distance, Rubens used the *bel-etage* or first floor that looked into the Great Studio. Rubens also had a private studio where he sketched and had models sit for him. His pupils also had their own studio. In the so-called large bedroom, though not now furnished as a bedroom, Rubens would have seen his son Nicolaas born and his first wife die (probably of the plague); he shared it with his second wife (Helene Fourmont), whom he brought there when she was 16 and he was 53. Rubens himself stayed in this bedroom when he was sick—he suffered from gout—near the end of his life, and it was here he died in May 1640.

Plantin-Moretus House ★★★

Vrijdagmarkt 22; daily 10 a.m.–5 p.m.; ☎ *233.02.94; English guidebook for sale.* In the elegant 16th-century Plantin-Moretus house, nine generations of the same family lived and ran a printing plant and shop between 1555 and 1876. The first three generations were the most forward-looking and contributed substantially to the intellectual environment of Antwerp, Europe, and well beyond. The founding **Plantin**, French-born Christophe (1520–1589), having been apprenticed to a bookbinder, arrived in Antwerp in 1548, during the city's gilded days. He choose Antwerp over all other cities because "no other town in the world could offer me more facilities for carrying on the trade I intend," and further cited the city's accessibility to skilled craftsmen, raw materials, and international buyers and sellers. Also, Antwerp's place in printing was already well established. In the pre-1500 *incunabula* printing period, Antwerp had been an important center, but when the prosperous early 16th-century era arrived, the city initiated a golden age for the art of mechanical printing. Between 1500 and 1540, half of all the works published in the Netherlands were produced on Antwerp presses.

Plantin turned from binding to printing, and one of his first books, published in 1559, was a volume on the funeral ceremonies of Charles V (who died in 1558) that was nearly as magnificent in its execution as the actual funeral had been. Between 1563 and 1567, Plantin's presses turned out the unheard-of average of 50 quality books a year. Probably Plantin's most outstanding undertaking was the *Biblia Polyglotta*, a reliable edition of the Bible in five languages (Latin, Greek, Hebrew, Syriac, and Chaldaic or Aramaean), with appendices on grammar, vocabulary, and culture of remarkable detail. Begun in 1568, the colossal task was finished in 1572; bound in eight big folios, it remains the most important work ever published in Belgium.

In 1572, Christophe Plantin received a monopoly from Philip II for the sale of certain liturgical works in Spain and its colonies (a monopoly which supported what became a rather stagnant printing house from the fourth generation for nearly two full centuries until the agreement finally was terminated). Production slowed but was not devastated by the 1576 *Spanish Fury* in Antwerp, and Plantin, himself a devout Catholic, managed to walk a fine line between religious factions during the Reformation/Counter-Reformation. Although he never denied the king of Spain, Plantin managed to print several anti-Spanish works and retain the favor of Dutch Protestant Willem of Orange, who was based in Antwerp for a while and visited the printing house. When he died in 1589, having published more than 1,500 important works—his first and foremost concern always was the *content* of the books—of humanists, classical authors, and scientific dissertation in 34 years, Christophe Plantin was buried in the high choir of Antwerp's cathedral.

Plantin bequeathed the printing house and shop to his favorite son-in-law, **Jan Moretus**, who had entered the workshop at the age of 14. Jan's son **Balthasar** (1574–1641), who headed the printing concern from 1610 to 1641, was a man of exceptional intelligence and knowledge, the greatest of the Moretuses. During Antwerp's blossoming in the baroque era, Balthasar, an intimate of Rubens, encouraged and fostered the work of scholars and artists. (He induced Rubens to design and illustrate frontispieces for many volumes.) The books published under Balthasar were the firm's most splendid.

The Plantin-Moretus house, which became a museum in 1877, more or less reached its present form under building changes begun by Plantin and continued by Balthasar Moretus, who designed the appealing inner courtyard. Behind the characteristic 18th-century Louis XV-style facade is hidden one of Belgium's finest civic Renaissance constructions. Many rooms have their original character and, with period furniture, offer a clear picture of a rich Antwerp patrician house from the 16th-18th centuries.

What makes the Plantin-Moretus museum unique is that its working role is emphasized under the same roof: many of the original furnishings of the printing plant, the foundry and fonts, the composers' and correctors' rooms, and shop are in evidence. The house's three richly filled libraries contain about 30,000 volumes, including copies of all the publications by Plantin and the Moretuses and choice works by foreign typographers, including 150 *incunabula* among which is a two-volume Bible (c. 1401) of the Czech miniature school that belonged to King Wenceslas of Bohemia, and a priceless copy of the 36-line Gutenberg Bible, the only one in Belgium. Old sheet music, printed with square notes, is also on display. Antique furniture, art (about 150 paintings and family portraits by Flemish masters, including 18 by Rubens), some 650 drawings, a wall map of Flanders by Mercator, tapestries, walls covered with gilt leather from Mechelen, and tall tiled fireplaces round out the charm of the building. Throughout the darkwood-decorated house are large *Liège* ("Belgium") crystal chandeliers, their pendants cut as carefully as diamonds so as to reflect as much light as possible.

Koninklijk Museum voor Schone Kunsten
(Royal Fine Arts Museum) *Leopole de Waelplaats; daily 10 a.m.–5 p.m., closed Mondays; ☎ 238.78.09; English language catalogues.* Trade brought riches to Antwerp; riches brought art; and the Museum of Fine Arts eventually reaped much of the reward. It houses an exceptional collection of works by the essentially 15th-century **Flemish "Primitives"**: Jan van Eyck, Rogier van der Weyden, Hans Memling, Dirk Bouts, and Gerard David. From the Antwerp School, founded by Quinten Metsys (1466–1530) and the Bruegel family, to the baroque age, of which Pieter Paul Rubens was the towering talent, Belgian masters are well covered. Antwerp's Fine Arts Museum has the world's finest collection of Rubens (17 paintings), and many works by his contemporaries Anthony van Dyck and Jacob Jordaens. Not only the artists of southern but also of northern Netherlands (Holland) are well represented: Hals, Rembrandt, Ter Borch.

Antwerp's nationally owned Museum of Fine Arts celebrated a centennial of residence in its neo-Gothic/neoclassic home in 1990, but the nucleus of the collection had its origins with the Antwerp **Guild of St. Luke** to which city artists belonged between 1454 and 1773. When guilds were disbanded, the paintings that St. Luke's had displayed in the *kunstkamer* (art room or gallery) of its guild house were turned over to Antwerp's *Academy of Fine Arts*, which established a museum. During the French occupations of the city in 1794 and 1796, many paintings—a total of 70, including 30 well-known works by Rubens, according to an official contemporary report—were confiscated from churches, monasteries, and public buildings, and sent to Paris. After the Battle of Waterloo in 1815, 40 were returned, of which 26 went to the museum.

During the period of the United Netherlands (1815–1830), Dutch King Willem donated several paintings to the academy, including its first work by a living artist (*The Death of Rubens* by Matthijs van Bree, who was director of the Fine Arts Academy). Willem also granted the museum a substantial subsidy for the purchase of contemporary art from the salons of Amsterdam, Brussels, Antwerp, and Ghent (though the 1830 Belgian revolution naturally nullified the grant, and it was not until 1873 that the museum began buying contemporary works). The museum's limited collection was boosted in 1840 by a bequest of 141 works from Florent van Ertborn, a former Antwerp burgomaster, who had, with flawless taste, built an exceptional collection of 15th-century paintings at a time when Flemish "primitives" were not appreciated. In 1859, the museum received another gift, 41 works consisting primarily of 17th-century Flemish and Dutch paintings. Together, these donations assured the museum's reputation. Today the collection consists of more than 3,200 paintings, 3,600 drawings, and 400 sculptures.

In the Department of Old Art, displayed on the upper story, the museum owns some 1,200 paintings that give a survey of Flemish art from c. 1360 until the end of the 18th century, as well as covering most aspects of Dutch, Italian, German, and French art. On the ground floor is displayed a fraction of the fine arts' considerable 19th- and 20th-century collection, principally Belgian, beginning with the *romantic movement*, whose leading exponent was **Gustaf Wappers** (1803–1874). **Henri de Braekeleer** (1840–1888), represented in the fine arts by 33 paintings and 45 drawings, is considered by many to be Belgium's first significant 19th-century artistic figure. *Realism* came into being in Belgium between 1850 and 1860, and the museum is particularly well-represented in realistic landscapes. Antwerp-born sculptor **Jef Lambeaux** (1852–1908), exhibited on the streets of Antwerp as well as in the museum, shows the 19th-century move to *naturalism*. Of course, no discussion of modern Belgian art can neglect *surrealism*. Here you find 35 paintings and 606 drawings by **James Ensor** (1860–1949), the reclusive Ostender who held society up to ridicule with his "mask people." Also shown are works by **René Magritte** (1898–1967), who influenced 20th-century art internationally, and **Paul Delvaux** (b. 1897). The museum has an excellent shop.

Museum Mayer van den Bergh   ★

Lange Gasthuisstraat 19; daily 10 a.m.-5p.m., closed Mondays except Easter Monday, White Monday, and Monday after 2nd Sunday in August; ☎ *232.42.37.* It's been called a connoisseur's collection and, in the medieval, late Gothic, and Renaissance art included, it shows the refined taste of its assembler **Fritz Mayer van den Bergh** (1858-1901), who devoted his life, cut short by an accident, to it. His mother, who had encouraged her son's passion for art, subsequently had built a 16th-century style house with a late Gothic/Renaissance facade in which to show her son's substantial accumulated treasure. Van den Bergh was one of the first collectors to be interested in **Pieter Bruegel the Elder** (1858-1569); in 1897 at an auction in Cologne he was able to buy for a trifle what many today consider the centerpiece of his museum. Bruegel's *Dulle Griet* (Mad Meg) fascinates visitors with its strangeness, and its having been created under the influence of Hieronymus Bosch is obvious. Among many notables in the museum are a copy of his father's *Census at Bethlehem* by Pieter Bruegel the Younger; a *Calvary* triptych by **Quinten Metsys**; a breviary that is a masterpiece of Southern Netherlands miniature art; and *John Reclining on Jesus' Bosom*, a life-size sculpture of gilt and polychromed walnut by Master Heinrich of Constance (c. 1300) an art form that's relatively rare in the Netherlands because wood was particularly vulnerable to destruction during the *Iconoclast* in the Reformation. Fine furniture and chimneypieces are found in rooms throughout the museum, and some windows have 15th- and 16th-century stained glass panel inserts.

Provincial Diamond Museum/Diamantmusem
Lange Herentalsestraat 31; daily from 10 a.m.–5 p.m.; ☎ *324.02.07; good guidebook in English.* A gem on Antwerp's list of attractions is the Provincial Diamond Museum where visitors can see the whole sparkling history of the stones that have engaged the attention of cutters, polishers, brokers, and buyers in Antwerp for five centuries. Once a symbol of virtue and virility, diamonds today represent value. They are a compact treasure: one ounce of high-quality diamonds is equal to 400 pounds of pure gold. With four of the world's twenty diamond bourses, Antwerp can be considered the capital for the world's diamond dealings: at least 60 percent of all diamonds traded worldwide pass through Antwerp, and the diamond business by itself represents 7 percent of Belgium's GNP. The diamond museum, opened in 1988, offers an introductory 20-minute video (English version) on Antwerp's historic association with diamonds, and can arrange for you to see a diamond-grinding demonstration. (For more information, see "Diamonds" in "Decorative Arts and Traditional Crafts" under "The Belgian Cultural Legacy.")

Zoo/Dierentuin
Koningin Astridplein 26; daily 8:30 a.m.–5 p.m., 6:30 p.m. in summer; ☎ *231.16.40.* For those who enjoy zoos, Antwerp offers one of the best in Europe (7,000 animals, 900 species, few cages, several special exhibits such as the *nocturama, dolphinarium, aquarium, reptile house* with tropical thunderstorm, and a self-service restaurant) at a surprising location: downtown, directly behind Centraal Station. In 1993, the zoo celebrated its 150th anniversary.

NORTH OF MEIR

Rockox House
Keizerstraat 12; daily 10 a.m.–5 p.m., closed Mondays; ☎ *231.47.10; English guidebook.* Also holding up a mirror to Antwerp's gilded age is the Rockox house, an opulent, splendidly restored, and period-furnished early 17th-century house owned by a former burgomaster and friend of Rubens. The Rockox house was purchased in 1970 by *Kredietbank*—banks in Antwerp make a point of supporting museums—which created a non-profit foundation for it. Nicolaas Rockox (1560–1640) was a member of Antwerp's Civic Guard, seven times alderman, nine times mayor of Antwerp, and a humanist who also was a benefactor and patron of Rubens, with whom he shared a belief in the *Counter-Reformation* and a great knowledge of classical antiquity. Among Rockox's commissions to Rubens was the 1612 *Descent from the Cross* triptych for the chapel in the cathedral of the Arquebusiers' Guild (of which he was captain); *Christ on the Cross* (now in Antwerp's Fine Arts Museum), and *Christ and St. Thomas*, with portraits of himself and his wife on the side panels. *The Adoration of the Magi*, commis-

sioned from Rubens as soon as the artist had returned from eight years in Italy for the Chamber of State in the Antwerp Stadhuis, is now in the **Prado Museum** in Madrid.

In 1603, when Rockox became burgomaster for the first time, he bought this and an adjacent property, combining the two into a fine Flemish Renaissance-style patrician dwelling. The house and its original contents were sold at auction in 1715 (in accordance with Rockox's will, which distributed the proceeds to benefit the poor), but contemporary documents have made it possible to recreate an appropriate degree of wealth in the Rockox interior. Among the many paintings, one of the most moving is Rubens' *The Virgin in Adoration Before the Sleeping Christ Child*, in which the Virgin has the features of Rubens' first wife Isabella Brant, and the Infant Jesus those of his second son Nicolaas. Teniers the Younger, Jordaens, Van Dyck, Jan "Velvet" Brueghel, and Pieter Brueghel the Younger (whose *Proverbs* is a copy of his father's fascinating original) are all shown amid the marvelous pieces of furniture and decorative art that make the house seem so "lived in." The very special atmosphere of the inner courtyard will make you want to linger even longer.

Note: Normally it's only shown to groups, but inquire in any case about seeing the excellent audiovisual presentation (in English) *Nicolaas Rockox and His Time*, which beautifully communicates a feeling for Antwerp, its art, and its architecture during the period 1560–1640.

Sint Jacobskerk (St. James Church)   ★★
Lange Nieuwstraat 73; April 1–Oct. 31; 2–5 p.m., no visitors Sundays and during services; ☎ *232.10.32; brochure with church layout.* Begun in 1491, though not entirely completed until 1656, St. James thus shows a late Gothic/Brabant style with some Renaissance influence. After the cathedral, St. James' is the most important church in Antwerp, and surpasses it in rich baroque adornment. St. James was Rubens' parish church and his second marriage took place there in 1630. In Rubens' day, all Antwerp's leading families had their burial vaults and private chapels there. Visitors may seek out Rubens' own chapel and tomb (he died in 1640), which is situated in the ambulatory directly behind the high altar. The centerpiece of the chapel is the painting, *Our Lady Surrounded by the Saints*, executed by Rubens in 1634 specifically for his sepulchral monument, and considered one of his finest works. It is generally accepted that in the painting the figure of St. George is a self-portrait; Mary has the features of Rubens' first wife; the infant Jesus those of his son; Mary Magdalene his second wife's face; and St. Jerome the features of his father.

Although St. James has known damaging times, in the Calvinist *Iconoclast*, the French Revolution, both world wars, and from arson in 1967, many of its treasures have been saved, and extensive exterior and interior restoration has been completed. Carved-wood confessionals by Artus Quellin the Elder, a majestic marble altar topped with trumpeting angels by Artus Quellin the Younger, and paintings by Jacob Jordaens are among the artistic treasures in the church. There are two organs: the 1727 instrument was once played by nine-year-old Mozart; the 1884 organ, set in a handsome carved 1723 organ-loft, was rebuilt into a concert-organ in 1956.

Hendrik Conscienceplein ★★

This charming Antwerp square is made more so by its location in front of the elaborate Rubens-designed Carrolus Borromeo church facade. Dedicated to the writer who helped raise Flemish consciousness in the 19th century—particularly with his book, *The Lion in Flanders*, see "Belgian Bibliography"—Hendrik Conscienceplein thus is the appropriate site of Antwerp's public library, which is housed in the 17th-century buildings of the former college of the Jesuits who built the church. The square draws lots of readers, at the tables of cafes that line one side, or on seats beside the statue (by Frans Joris, 1883) of the square's namesake.

Carrolus Borromeo

Hendrik Conscienceplein 12; Mon., Wed., Thurs., Fri. 9:30 a.m.–1 p.m., Sat., 9:30 a.m. -noon, and 3–6 p.m.; ☎ *233.84.33.* The superb baroque west-front ★★facade of the 17th-century church of St. Charles Borromeo is thought to have been designed by Rubens, who also was deeply involved with the interior decor, including 39 ceiling paintings from his workshop. The entire original church with its lavish ornamentation was completed in a mere five years (1615–21) thanks to the Jesuits who had heaps of money to throw at the project. But a fire after the church was struck by lightning in 1718 did widespread damage; all that survived from the original was the tower, the west front, three Rubens altarpieces (taken by the Austrians in 1776 and now in Vienna), the choir (dome drawings by Rubens), and two chapels. One, the Chapel of the Virgin, with a ceiling in the style of Rubens, uses 30 types of rare and colored marble; the paintings directly on the marble are by H. van Balen. The surviving 190-foot/58-meter tower, making the transition as it rises in three tiers from square to round, is regarded as a masterpiece. The fine carved confessional stalls of the 1719 rebuilt church are by van Baurscheit.

Handelbeurs ★

at the end of Twaalfmaandenstraat, off Meir. An 1872 reconstruction in the style of the fire-destroyed 1531 Stock Exchange (which served as a model for many other Western European exchanges), the Handelbeurs is now used as a venue for special exhibits or events. With entrances on all four sides, allowing people to walk through the recently restored skylighted, galleried central hall, thereby short-cutting the outside walk around the exterior of city buildings, the Handelbeurs is a fascinating example of how medieval buildings functioned as public passageways in dense, dead-end alley-constricted centers of old cities. Signs posted at each entrance read: "*honden, fietsen, skateboards verboten*" (dogs, bikes, and skateboards forbidden).

St. Paul's   ★

Sint-Paulusstraat 20; May–Sept. 9, a.m.–noon, 2–5 p.m., closed Sun. and Mon., daily Oct.–April, 9:00 a.m.–noon; ☎ *232.32.67.* Begun in 1517, and finally completed in 1639 after a long break following severe damage in the 1570s by the Calvinists, St. Paul's has Antwerp's last—and, by the time it was finished, well out-of-fashion—Gothic exterior. As a result of the lingering construction, the St. Paul's interior missed an entire subsequent architectural style (Renaissance) and went on to baroque. *Mysteries of the Rosary* is the theme of a remarkable ★★series of 15 paintings that line the left wall of the soaring nave, above a no less amazing ★★row of wood-carved confessional stalls and life-size statues; painters include Rubens, Jordaens, Van Dyck, Teniers the Elder, the carvers Verbruggen the Elder, Artus Quellin Elder and Younger, and van Baurscheit the Elder. Rubens' painting, (c. 1609) *The Dispute on the Subject of the Holy Sacrament*, ornaments an altar in the right forward area of the church.

To the right of the entry of St. Paul's is the **Calvary Garden**, with no less than three dozen full-size white stone figures by various sculptors in the theme of the Jerusalem crusaders. The statues are spread about the small garden plot across which a path leads to a grotto set into the side of the church; within it is a carved figure representing Christ lying in his tomb.

WHERE TO STAY

VERY EXPENSIVE

De Rosier

Rosier 21, 2000; ☎ *225.01.40, FAX 231.41.11.* On an ordinary old street in central Antwerp is a most extraordinary hotel: a remarkable antique-filled, interior designer-owner-decorated mansion that is an oasis where attentive personal service prevails. Modern art and sculpture are integrated into the richly comfortable, tastefully original guest and public rooms that feature marble, crystal chandeliers, tapestries, track-lighting, paintings, and plants. The ten individually decorated guest rooms each have private bath, TV, and telephone. Breakfast (only, extra charge), formal afternoon tea, and drinks are served in the enchanting glass-enclosed, garden-surrounded Summerpatio Room. No restaurant. Cozy bar, elevator. Advance reservations essential.

Antwerp Hilton International

Groenplaats; ☎ *204.12.12, FAX 204. 12.13, reservations in North America* ☎ *800-HILTONS, in the U.K.* ☎ *0800-289303.* Opened in the summer of 1993, on a square in the center of Antwerp beside the cathedral, the five-story Hilton rests behind the restored 1920s neo-baroque facade of the newly created *Grand Bazaar*, a 50 up-market shop complex. The hotel's classical decor is mixed with modern accents. Among the varied 211 rooms are a 25-room executive floor, and nonsmoking rooms. Amenities include a health club with sauna and fitness equipment, and direct access to an indoor car park. *Restaurant Isabella and Elena* (the name of Rubens' wives) serves traditional Flemish dishes prepared in an updated manner; the hotel bar is decorated in a maritime style reflecting Antwerp's 16th-century Golden Age.

Alfa de Keyser ★★★★
De Keyserlei 66, 2018; ☎ *234.01.35, FAX 232.39.70.* Situated across from the Centraal Station at the head of de Keyserlei (that leads to the Meir through the center of the city to the Grote Markt) and near public transport, restaurants, and entertainment, the 117-room, 7-story modern hotel with large marble lobby puts a self-conscious emphasis on appearance (uniformed doorman) and service (24-hour). Rooms are contemporary and comfortable, though not particularly distinguished. Some are renovated, some not; a few are nonsmoking, all have hair dryers and cable TV with CNN. There's a popular bar in the lobby, and the gourmet restaurant **Chagall** is noted for its nouvelle cuisine. Continental breakfast is included, buffet breakfast is extra; security boxes at front desk; parking garages nearby. A sidewalk escalator outside the hotel delivers you to the underground passage to Centraal Station; SABENA's Brussels' airport bus is next door.

EXPENSIVE

Hotel Carlton ★★★★
Quinten Matsijslei 25, 2018; ☎ *231.15.15, FAX 225.30.90.* Located across from the city park, a short walk to de Keyserlei, the attractive, 9-story, glass-fronted Carlton has an appealing marble lobby, off which are a relaxing bar and tasteful restaurant (where continental breakfast, included, is also served). The front desk staff is friendly and helpful. A pleasant mix of international business clients predominates, but leisure travelers also will be happy here (and will have reduced rates on Fri. and Sat. nights). The 95 rooms and suites have bath/shower, minibars, remote control cable TV, hair dryers, in-room safes, and turndown service with Godiva pralines on the pillow. An extension with 30 additional rooms recently opened.

Rubens ★★★★
Oude Beurs 29; ☎ *222.48.48, FAX 225.19.40.* Newly opened in 1993, the 36-room Rubens is situated in a restored townhouse mansion close to Antwerp's *Grote Markt.* Features include a stylish entry and green marble-floored, green plant-decorated reception area, off which is an attractive small lobby bar and lounge/breakfast (included) room. In fine weather breakfast or drinks can be enjoyed in the pinkwashed enclosed courtyard, which has trellises, tables, and a 16th-century brick watchtower in one corner. Rooms are pleasantly decorated, with rheostat controls for pleasing, effective lighting. Baths have green

marble and white tiles; toilets in separate room. Windows (which open) are double glazed to keep out traffic sounds for sleeping.

Alfa Theater   ★★★★

Arenbergstraat 30; ☎ *231.17.20, FAX 233.88.58.* Located, as the name suggests, in Antwerp's conveniently central theater district, 3 blocks from the Meir, 3 blocks from the Rubens house, and a reasonable walk to the Grote Markt, the hotel has a very friendly staff and good range of in-room amenities: shower and bidet, sitting area, pants press, hair dryers, in-room safe and, in many cases, a mini-kitchenette with fridge and hot plate. Included among the 83 guest rooms is a nonsmoking floor (15 rooms), and new and nice executive-style rooms (without kitchenette). There's a modern lobby with leather chairs, restaurant (continental breakfast, included), and bar. Advance booking suggested; parking garages nearby.

MODERATE

Hotel Firean   ★★★

Karel Oomsstraat 6, B-2018; ☎ *237.02.60, FAX 238.11.68.* Though beyond walking distance from any of central Antwerp's attractions (but convenient to tram lines to both the cathedral and Centraal Station), this restored, owner-operated, 12-room, 1921 house is so pleasant that it should be considered. The hospitable homelike house-hotel, with intriguing art deco details and all Belgian furnishings, features original Tiffany windows, antique tapestries, backlighted glass panels, and the additional charm of a flood-lighted rear garden (with bar service for guests). Guest rooms are uniquely furnished in soft colors, with pants press, hair dryer, minibar, toiletries, double-glazed windows (for quiet), cable TV, and extra evening housekeeping of rooms. Breakfast (included) is served indoors or on the garden patio; international morning newspapers in lobby. Room service (light food dishes) until midnight, 24-hour laundry, parking, major credit cards. Reservations well-ahead recommended.

Villa Mozart   ★★★★

Handschoenmarkt 3, 2000; ☎ *231.30.31, FAX 231.56.85.* Opened in 1990, this hotel is Antwerp's first in the Grote Markt vicinity, and is located on the delightful Handschoenmarkt across from the cathedral. (Light sleepers take note of the carillon that strikes the hours all night long.) Behind a restored 5-story period facade, 24 guest rooms and 4 suites are tastefully decorated with cane and bamboo furniture upholstered in rich materials. Amenities include extra wide beds, luxury bath, minibar, AC, room service. The hotel's **Vivaldi** restaurant serves fine French and international cuisine based on fresh seasonal produce; there's indoor or terrace cafe seating. Buffet breakfast included; year-round discounted weekend rates; public parking garages within two blocks.

Arcade

Meistraat 39, 2000; ☎ *231.88.30, FAX 234.29.21.* The 150-room, cheerfully decorated, utilitarian modern hotel is located on the Theaterplein (site of general market Sat., bird market Sun.), not far from the Rubens house. Bedrooms have basic contemporary decor: choice of twin or king (small supplement) beds, direct-dial telephone, radio clock alarm, private showers/toilet, an open clothes rack with a wooden bench beneath for suitcases, 2 chairs, and desk. A self-service breakfast (included) is provided in the lobby bar (no restaurant). Major credit cards; front desk staffed 24 hours; disabled-accessible rooms on all floors; public parking in front of hotel.

INEXPENSIVE

Pension Cammerpoorte

Steenhouwersvest 55; ☎ *226.57.60.* This extremely friendly family-run establishment is simple, clean and offers highly helpful service. Located in two adjoining houses on a typical street near the *Vrijdagmarkt*, it has a total of 15 rooms all with bath; 6 are brand new, with TV and two-burner kitchenette with sink. Three stories, steep stairs; no elevator. In-house telephone for wake-up calls; no in-room telephones. Breakfast (included) room.

WHERE TO EAT

Prices in Antwerp's better restaurants are generally less than in Brussels. Reservations are essential at the best restaurants, and a call to book if you have a specific place in mind is always a good bet except for the most casual eateries. A number of restaurants are closed on Sundays and holidays, and some close for personal holiday periods, particularly in August.

Consistently ranked as one of the Antwerp's most appetizing restaurants is **La Perouse** *(Steenplein; noon–2:30 p.m., 7–9:30 p.m., closed Sun., Mon., holidays, and June through mid–Sept. when it is a Scheldt-cruising restaurant for* **Flandia**; ☎ *232.35.28; expensive).* When it isn't floating, La Perouse sits moored on the Scheldt at the foot of Suikkerui. In its ship-shape polished brass and steel atmosphere, seafood is the specialty, especially *waterzooi de poussin,* a creamy fish stew/soup and traditional Flemish dish that doesn't get any better than it is here. **Sir Anthony Van Dijck** *(Oude Koornmarkt 16; Mon.– Fri. noon–2:30 p.m., two evening seatings, reservations required; closed Sat. & Sun.;* ☎ *231.61.70; moderate),* is located in a beautiful setting of antiques, tapestries, candlelight, polished stone tile floors, dark beams, fireplaces, and ivy-draped enclosed courtyard with the sound of dripping water from a fountain in a former burgomeester's home in the charming 16th-century cobbled alley of antique shops called *Vlaeykensgang.* Recently, the owner of this regular on the rolls of the city's best restaurants got tired of being chic and snobbish and purposely let his two Michelin Star rating slide to concentrate on simpler fine cuisine and a more authentic Antwerp ambience. **Neuze Neuze** *(Wijngaardstraat 19; noon–2:15 p.m., 7–9:30 p.m., closed Sun.;* ☎ *232.57.83; moderate/expensive),* reveals Antwerp's love of juxtaposing the old and new with smart modern decor under ancient beamed ceilings and arches. The cuisine is French with the flair of its four chefs, who provide a two-course menu that's always worth consideration.

De Peerdestal *(Wijngaardstraat 8; noon–2:30 p.m., 6–11 p.m., closed Sun.;* ☎ *231.95.03; inexpensive),* located in a 400-year-old building in a small pedestrian street that runs into the Hendrik Conscienceplein, offers excellent atmosphere along with its tasty traditional dishes. Good choices include *tomate aux crevettes* (tomato stuffed with small North Sea shrimp), *fondue au fromage* (melted cheese croquette), and *moules* (mussels) in myriad ways; also served at red-check-covered, candlelighted tables, beneath old beams and beside brick walls are chicken, steak, fish, soups, and salads. There's a long friendly bar at which to eat in somewhat speedier style, or sit over a drink while reading the *International Herald-Tribune*. **In de Schaduw van de Kathedraal** *(Handschoenmarkt 17;* ☎ *232.40.14; inexpensive),* whose name means "in the shadow of the cathedral," sometimes is in the sun; either way, there's always a wonderful view from the base of the lace-like steeple. In addition to the terrace cafe, inside dining is in a pleasant room amid mirrors and banquettes. Not only the setting but the cuisine is traditional Antwerp, from mussels and eel prepared in several ways to meat and potatoes (frites, of course). A very different typical Antwerp atmosphere is found at **'t Hofke** *(Oude Koornmarkt 16; daily noon–1 a.m.;* ☎ *233.86.06; inexpensive),* a tiny lunchroom-tearoom-bistro tucked into the ancient Vlaeykensgang. At the few tables in the garden—open to the sky—along the alleyway, or the several inside; salads, quiches, and larger meals are served to the sound of classical music and a caged songbird. **De Groote Witte Arend** *(Reyndersstraat 18; daily 11 a.m.–1:30 a.m.; inexpensive),* most suitable for outdoor weather, is found through an old courtyard just doors from the house of artist Jacob Jordaens (1593–1678) at Reyndersstraat 6. Salads, pasta of the day, lasagna, waterzooi, and sandwiches are brought out to the tables and benches in the courtyard that is draped with plants, studded with statuary, and lifted by the strains of classical music. Antwerpians often sit here over a drink on Monday nights in summer to hear the carillon concert from the nearby cathedral.

De Foyer *(Komedieplaats 18; Mon.–Fri. noon to midnight, Sat. and Sun. 11 a.m.–6 p.m.;* ☎ *233.55.17; inexpensive)* is upstairs at the exquisite curve-fronted, just restored Bourla Theater. (A bell rings in the restaurant to announce the start of performances.) Occasional live concerts held in the restaurant's neoclassic room accompany the light fare (quiche, soups, sandwiches) and salad buffet bar. Close by, located in a house just past the pleasant *Botanic Garden,* and one street over from the *Mayer van den Bergh Museum,* is **Botanica** *(Leopoldstraat 24; daily 10 a.m.–11 p.m., Fri. and Sat. 1 a.m.;* ☎ *225.10.04; inexpensive).* The cozy 49-seat interior, from which there are views of the garden, has an eclectic decor with Japanese prints, Venetian glass chandeliers, and track lighting on the art work. There's a daily three-course menu and limited à la carte offerings.

Only a block from the Scheldt, with a great view of the handsome historic Vleeshuis, is **Jan Zonder Vrees** *(Krabbenstraat 2; daily 9 a.m.–2 a.m.;* ☎ *232.90.80; inexpensive/moderate),* located in four, former 400-year-old houses. Offerings at the outside tables, at the bar, or in the fashionably decorated restaurant under brick arches, run from snacks, soup and sandwiches to steak and daily specials.

A well-known delicatessen/restaurant near the Centraal Station is **Panache** *(17 Statiestraat 17; daily noon–1:30 a.m., closed August;* ☎ *232.69.05; inexpensive)*, which will provide you with almost anything edible from picnic makings to a particular dish you've been craving. For take-out fare, stop at the *charcuterie* section in front; for sit-down service, walk through to the large busy dining room with its huge menu. Whenever you're looking for something to eat at late hours, or on Sundays when many restaurants are closed, you'll find plenty of places near Panache, in the movie/entertainment streets around the *Franklin Roosevelt Plaats* such as *Anneessensstraat, Breidelstraat,* and *van Ertbornstraat;* most are inexpensive, and offer ethnic fare that reflects Antwerp's cosmopolitan population.

Whether one drinks a pint of pils or a "bowl" of specialty beer, spending time at an atmospheric pub with one or another of Belgium's hundreds of brands of beer is an Antwerp way of life. The oldest pub in the Low Countries is **Quinten Matsys** *(Oude Koornmarkt 21; closed Thurs.;* ☎ *231.45.41)*, dating from 1565. Also in existence since Antwerp's 16th-century golden age is **Pelgrom** *(Pelgrimstraat 15; daily from 11 a.m.;* ☎ *234.08.09)*, which serves bar snacks and beer in marvelous brick-vaulted, candlelit cellars well beneath its handsome stepped-gabled facade. **Bierland** *(Korte Nieuwstraat 28)* claims it sells 1,250 kinds of beer (some 840 are Belgian), more than anywhere else in Antwerp, and possibly the world. **In Den Engel** *(3 Grote Markt)* supposedly never closes its doors, and some say it hasn't since it opened them in 1579. This most typical cafe in the city is where Antwerpians rendezvous to share stadhuis—the town hall is next to it—gossip or to start an evening's drinking. Many might end the evening at **'t elfde Gebod** *(Torfburg 10; open daily til all hours;* ☎ *232.36.11)*, an ivy-draped cafe beside the cathedral whose name means "the 11th Commandment," which Antwerpians interpret to be "Thou shalt enjoy life."

ENTERTAINMENT AND EVENTS

As the unofficial capital of Flanders, Antwerp is home to several performing arts companies. The **Royal Flemish Opera**, the **Flemish Chamber Opera**, the **Royal Flanders Ballet**, and the **Royal Flemish Conservatory** provide a full program. The works of the **Royal Flemish Theater** head a theater bill that is the most extensive in Belgium, although most productions are in Flemish.

Year-round, hour-long concerts are played on the cathedral's 47-bell carillon at 11:30 p.m. Fridays. The weekly mid-June to mid- Sept. Monday night **carillon concerts** at 8 p.m. are a highlight for Antwerpians and visitors alike. Mid-August Antwerp celebrates summer with a week-long list of events, highlighted with the **Rubens Market** and **Ommegangpageant**. Other annual events include the July **Steen Festival**, the August **Middelheim Jazz Festival**, and the November **Antwerp Diamond Awards**. The multifaceted cultural events of the **Festival van Vlaanderen** (Festival of

Flanders) are held each Sept./Oct. Check with the City Tourist Office about the location for the Sept.–May Fri. 12:30 p.m. hour-long **midday concerts**. **Early music** concerts are held from Oct.–March in the Grand Studio at the *Rubenhuis* and in the *Vleeshuis* (Butchers' Hall Museum).

There are several entertainment centers in Antwerp. The **Grote Markt/ Groenplaats** area is known for its cafe terraces. (Also refer to the end of "Where To Eat".) The so-called **high town** (along *Hoogstraat* or High Street, *Pelgrimstraat, Pieter Potstraat,* and surroundings) has some of the most interesting and cozy of Antwerp's supposedly 2,500 cafes and bars; "brown" pubs, bistros, and jazz clubs can be found in this area. **De Keyserlei** is visited for its boulevard-cafes, taverns, and terraces, and the adjoining neighborhood around Centraal Station has night clubs and cinemas. The **Quartier Latin**, near the City Theater, has artists' cafes and bars.

IN THE AREA

Middelheim Open-Air Museum of Sculpture ★★

Middelheimlaan 61, outside the Kleine Ringweg/Small Ring Road, south of center city in lovely Nachtegalen Park; daily from 10 a.m., closing hours range from 9 p.m. in June and July to 5 p.m. in winter; ☎ *827.15.34.* Art in Antwerp is not limited to Old Masters. At the Middelheim Open Air Museum of Sculpture, founded in 1950, almost every important sculptor from **Rodin** to the present is represented by major works; prominent among the Belgian sculptors is **Rik Wouters** (1882–1916) and **Constantin Meunier** (1831–1905). In the early years of the museum's development, many foreign specialists and sculptors—among them Russian-born **Ossip Zadkine** (1890–1976), whose works are well-represented in the Benelux, and England's **Henry Moore**—served as consultants to the museum. The collection currently consists of more than 300 works, which are exhibited in a natural outdoor park setting, to be enjoyed in the changing seasons and weather. The **Middelheim Biennials** of modern sculpture (held during odd-numbered years) are highly regarded both in Belgium and abroad.

Cogels-Oyslei ★

Berchem District, southeast of city center, bus #16 from de Keyserlei. These two and the surrounding streets of Antwerp's Zurenborg Quarter have been given historic monument neighborhood status for their eclectic styles of turn-of-the-century architecture, the foremost influence being *jugendstil* ("art nouveau"). When the tram lines were extended to this new district, development proceeded as a challenge to the architects of the day to realize their dream concepts; the result is an encyclopaedia of late 19th-century romanticism. Along with the intricate wrought-iron whirls, tiles, glass, and mosaic work details of art nouveau are facades inspired by Arthurian legend, Florentine palazzi, Venetian Gothic, Loire Valley chateaus, and Louis XVI. Many are so amazing you may be tempted to record the street numbers of the most remarkable. (On Osylei, I got as far as noting #42–46, 50–52, 60–62, and 80 before I stopped the exercise.) **Melloney's**

(Oyslei 16; 10 a.m.–8 p.m., closed Wed.; ☎ 230.95.45) is a tea salon that serves pastries, waffles, tea, and drinks in a house with some of the neighborhood's typical detail and decor.

Mechelen

Municipal Tourist Office, Stadhuis, Grote Markt; Mon.–Fri. 8 a.m.–6 p.m., except 5 p.m. Oct. 1–Mar. 31, Sat. & Sun. 9:30 a.m.–5 p.m.; ☎ (015) 21.18.73, FAX (015) 20.02.76. Located midway between Antwerp and Brussels (15 minutes by train from either), Mechelen (pop. 80,000), though overshadowed by both of its bigger neighbors today, once was the capital of the Netherlands. Upon the death of Louis de Male, count of Flanders, who had acquired Mechelen in 1357, it and the rest of Flanders passed to the dukes of Burgundy in 1384. In Mechelen, the period encompassing the 13th and 14th centuries was one of flourishing cloth trade. In 1473, Burgundian **Charles the Bold** made Mechelen the seat of his Grand Council, the sovereign tribunal for the Netherlands. Following Charles' death, his widow **Margaret of York**, sister of England's Edward IV, settled in Mechelan in a palace that today is the *Schouwburg* (municipal theater).

In 1506 Mechelen's apogee of influence came under a second Margaret, of the Austrian Hapsburgs, who was appointed governor of the Netherlands to serve as regent for her nephew, the then six-year-old **Charles V**. From her fine palace (today's Mechelen Law Courts), built in 1507 and considered to be the first building in the Netherlands in the Renaissance style, **Margaret of Austria** oversaw the upbringing and education of Ghent born Charles, and formed a brilliant court attended by scholars and artists. Visiting luminaries included Erasmus, Sir Thomas More, Albrecht Durer, painters Jan Mostaert, Jan Gossaert, and Bernard van Orley, as well as Mechelan architect Rombout Keldermans, whose family members would make major contributions to many landmark buildings in the Netherlands. In his home **Hof van Busleyden** (today Mechelen's municipal museum), humanists Hieronymus van Busleyden, Erasmus, and Thomas More laid the foundations of Louvain (Leuven) University's College of the Three Languages. After Margaret's death in 1530, the Netherlands capital was transferred by Charles V to Brussels. Although its glory faded rapidly, Mechelen was compensated by being made an archbishopric in 1559 and to this day is the ecclesiastical capital of Belgium.

Mechelen mirrors the grandeur of its Burgundian-Hapsburg days in many fine buildings. **St. Rombout's cathedral tower**, a symbol of the city, was begun in 1452 and, under the direction of the local Keldermans's family, reached it present height of 318 feet/97 meters in 1546. It contains two complete 49-bell carillons, which are another symbol of Mechelen. St. Rombout's contains the *Crucifixion* (1627) by **Anthony Van Dyck** (one of the artist's most emotive works) and a fine carved baroque communion bench by Artus Quellin the Younger. The **Stadhuis** (town hall) on the Grote Markt, though not obviously unwhole, is composed of finished and unfinished parts. The oldest (14th-century) section, the **Cloth Hall** (on the right), begun in 1320 and modeled on that in Bruges, was never completed because Mechelen's once-illustrious textile industry declined faster than the work on the building progressed. In 1526, the north wing of the Stadhuis was demolished to make way for a new Keldermans-designed grand council meeting hall, but work ceased in 1534, a casualty of the death of Margaret of Austria and subsequent move of the court to Brussels. Finally, in 1911, using Keldermans' original plans, the town hall was completed.

Besides its architecture, visitors to Mechelen note the carillon school, and concerts on the city's four (with a total of 197 bells) instruments (see under "Music" in "The Belgian Cultural Legacy"). Mechelen's centuries-old tapestry weaving (see section on "Decorative Arts and Traditional Crafts") continues at the **de Wit factory**. De Wit not only works to preserve antique tapestries, it also carries on the craft as a contemporary art form by creating modern masterpieces. One huge work designed and executed at de Wit was a present from Belgium to the United Nations Headquarters in New York. The excellent woodwork for which Mechelen was famous in the baroque era is reflected in the fine furniture for which the city is known today.

BRUGES

One of Brugges' many medieval bridges.

GUIDELINES FOR BRUGES

SIGHTS

Bruges (*Brugge*), having become impressively important in commerce and, consequently, in culture between the 12th and 15th centuries, was then all but forgotten as circumstances combined to turn the tide of its fortune. As a result, Bruges (population 35,000 within the historic double encirclement of **canals**) is delightfully stuck visually and atmospherically back in medieval days; many consider it the *best preserved medieval city in Europe*, though it's far too actively engaged in the present to be considered a "museum town." Bruges is small enough for you to manage all major sights on foot, but so densely packed with enchanting places that you'd never get bored wandering aimlessly. Bruges' **architecture** may be even more outstanding than its **art**, which features *Flemish "primitive" painters* **van der Weyden**, **van Eyck**, **Memling**, **van der Goes**, and **Gerard David**, often displayed in historic settings. There are also a Michelangelo sculpture, and exhibits of the traditional town crafts of lace and tapestry. Sounds spill out over the town during the frequent concerts played on the town carillon, high in Belgium's most beautiful **belfry**, but reassuring silence can be found in the peaceful precincts of the **Begijnhof**. A night walk around the intimate town, turned to magic by the tasteful illumination of monument buildings, ivy-covered brick facades, canals, and humpback bridges, is mesmerizing, and each season has special appeal. The prime season for **night illuminations** is May 1 to September 30, but many buildings now are lit year-round.

GETTING AROUND

Many travelers arrive in Bruges by train; the station, just outside the old city to the south, near the **Minnewater** and **Begijnhof**, is about 1 mi./1.5 km. from the **Markt**, considered the center of Bruges. Close to the Markt is the **Burg**, where the **tourist office** is located. In this town of lace shops, you'll want to lace up walking shoes to enjoy the cobbled streets in comfort. Supplemental ways to see the town begin with half-hour **canal cruises** (there are several central departure piers) with multilingual commentary; the open boats afford wonderful photographic angles, and umbrellas when it's misting. A **rental bike**, though a bit bumpy on the cobbles, is a great way to see the outer edges of Bruges. **Horse-drawn carriages** congregate on the Burg and by the Begijnhof if you want to see the town to the sound of horse hooves clopping on cobblestones. A far more modern means is by **minibus tour** (English commentary on headsets) with **Sightseeing Line** (departure point in the center of the Markt). Taxi ranks are found at the station and on the Markt, and otherwise should be ordered by telephone; starting fare 80 BF, tip included. There's a public bus system (several routes have stops on the Markt), but it's unlikely you'll use it within old Bruges itself.

SHOPPING

As capital of West Flanders province, Bruges is well stocked with department stores, boutiques, gift and art galleries. The visitor-season, canalside, weekend **outdoor antiques market** on the Dijver is

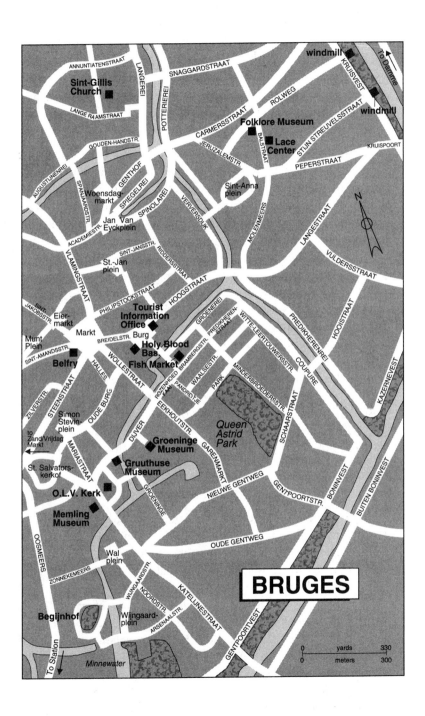

windmill

To Damme

windmill

KRUISVEST

ANNUNTIATENSTRAAT

Sint-Gillis
Church

LANGEREI

SNAGGARDSTRAAT

ROLWEG

LANGE RAAMSTRAAT

POTTERIEREI

CARMERSSTRAAT

STIJN STREUVELSSTRAAT

Folklore Museum

Lace
Center

KRUISPOORT

GOUDEN-HANDSTR.

JERUZALEMSTR.

BALSTRAAT

PEPERSTRAAT

AUGUSTIJNENREI

SPAANSDSTR.

GENTHOF

SPIEGELREI

Sint-Anna
plein

VULDERSSTRAAT

Woensdag-
markt

Jan Van
Eyckplein

ACADEMIESTR.

SPINOLAREI

VEERVERSDIJK

MOLENMEERS

LANGESTRAAT

N

VLAMINGSTRAAT

St.-Jan
plein

SINT-JANSSTR.

RIDDERSSTRAAT

HOOGSTRAAT

HOOISTRAAT

SINT-
JAKOBSSTR.

Eier-
markt

PHILIPSTOCKSTRAAT

Tourist
Information
Office

GROENEREI

PREDIKHEREN-
STRAAT

WITTE-LEERTOUWERSSTR.

PREDIKHERENREI

Markt

Munt
Plein

SINT-AMANDSTR.

Belfry

BREIDELSTR.

Burg

Holy Blood
Bas.

Fish Market

WOLLESTRAAT

HALLES

ROZENHOED

BRAMBERGSTR.

WAALSESTR.

P'ANDRELYE

MINDERBROEDERSSTR.

COUPURE

KAZERNEVEST

STEENSTRAAT

ZILVERSTR.

OUDE BURG

EEKHOUTSTR.

DIJVER

PARK

Queen
Astrid
Park

SCHAARSTRAAT

Simon
Stevin-
plein

to
Zand/Vrijdag
Markt

MARIASTRAAT

Groeninge
Museum

Gruuthuse
Museum

GARENMARKT

NIEUWE GENTWEG

GENTPOORTSTR.

BONINVEST

BUITEN BONINVEST

St. Salvators-
kerkof

O.L.V. Kerk

GROENINGE

Memling
Museum

OUDE GENTWEG

OOSMEERS

Wal
plein

BRUGES

ZONNEKEMEERS

WIJNGAARDSTR.

NOORDSTR.

KATELIJNESTRAAT

Begijnhof

Wijngaard-
plein

ARSENAALSTR.

GENTPOORTVEST

To Station

Minnewater

| 0 | yards | 330 |
| 0 | meters | 300 |

popular. In Breidelstraat, which runs from the Markt to the Burg, and near the Begijnhof, **lace shops** abound.

ENTERTAINMENT AND EVENTS

On the occasion of the 500th anniversary of the death of Flemish "primative" artist Hans Memling, a major exhibition–**Melming and His Time**–is being mounted in Bruges at the *Groeninge* and *Brangwyn* museums, opening August 12 and closing November 14.

The periodically published *Agenda Brugge* (free from the tourist office) gives a multilingual listing of scheduled programs and events. The scope of Bruges' entertainment options run from several *carillon concerts* weekly, and musical events staged on canals and in churches, to elaborately costumed historic pageant processions.

WHERE TO STAY

Bruges, with 100-plus hotels, offers more rooms than any other city in Belgium except Brussels; most are in the historic town, at prices lower in all categories than those in Brussels. Reservations at any time of year are recommended, since Bruges is a highly popular place year-round for weekend getaways for Europeans; particularly heavily booked are the three- and four-day Europe-wide spring holiday weekends at Easter and Whitsun. Bruges is also busy with visitors in July and August, but many come just for the day—a great mistake. Once the bus-borne hordes of day-trippers have left, Bruges generally has space available for overnighters midweek. If you haven't booked ahead, the tourist office offers an accommodations service.

WHERE TO EAT

Bruges also has more restaurants than anywhere in Belgium other than Brussels. Fine food and pleasurable settings are found in all price ranges. The traditional Flemish, fresh seafood, and French *haute cuisine* choices will satisfy most palettes. If you want something a little lighter, you're in the right place: the English word "snack" was derived from the Dutch/Flemish *snakken* ("to yearn for"), and Bruges has plenty of informal eateries that serve both indoors and outside. Bruges is chock full of **chocolate shops**, one of which, **Sukerbuyc** (*Katelijnestraat 5;* ☎ *33.08.87*), offers not only 65 kinds of handmade chocolates including *pralines* (filled chocolates), but from May-December makes *marzipan* in many fancy and unexpected forms. The delicate sweet biscuits called *dentelles de Brugge* are an edible version of local lace.

ARRIVING

Train is the choice of many travelers to Bruges; the direct twice-hourly service from Brussels takes just over an hour. If you arrive by **ferry** from England at Ostend, the first stop on the **boat train** for Brussels (or beyond) is Bruges. Historic Bruges, which has lots of winding one-way streets, was not made for cars. Should you drive, plan to park and forget it until you leave. However, when "disposing" of the car, be sure to do so correctly so you won't be towed; there's an underground garage at **'t Zand**, inside the old city via **Koning Albertlaan** from the station, which is close to major roads, or park on Bruges' ring road.

IN THE AREA

Some 4 mi./7 km. from Bruges, along a canal lined with wind-bent poplars on polderland so flat that it takes the fertile farm fields forever to meet the huge cloud-besprinkled sky at the horizon, is Damme. You can travel by boat, bike, foot, or car to Damme, a hamlet noted for its restaurants, but whose few fine buildings are vestiges of the days centuries ago when it served as Bruges' outer port on the ill-fated Zwin and had a population of 60,000.

TRAVEL TIPS

Bruges is one of Europe's most exceptional destinations—even in the Middle Ages, everyone who could came to see it. Bruges is only a little over an hour from Brussels by train, easy to do on an individual or commercial motorcoach day trip. But just because that's the way the vast majority of travelers see Bruges doesn't mean that you should. And that truism, evident during the day, becomes inescapable in the evening when, no matter what the season, you have the city largely to yourself. It's when the crowds have gone that Bruges will bewitch you with its medieval mystique. After dark, the reflections in its canals will capture you in a reflective mood, and almost anywhere it's safe to slow from a stride to a stroll, you'll want to stop and stare.

BRUGES IN CONTEXT

In 1896, English writer Arnold Bennett noted in his *Journal*: "The difference between Bruges and other cities is that in the latter you look around for the picturesque, while in Bruges, assailed on every side by the picturesque, you look curiously for the unpicturesque, and don't find it easily." The foresight of Bruges' city fathers in the century since must be lauded; by 1904, they had established a *Commission of Urban Beauty* and imposed strictures to preserve Bruges'

Middle Age aspect (even in the Middle Ages, Bruges was considered one of Europe's most beautiful cities). Although in the 20th century commercialism has reached its tentacles into many of the most remote corners tourists can travel to, Bennett's words about Bruges remain remarkably true.

Bruges is not undiscovered as a place of touristic charm. In the late 19th century, the town awoke from a nearly four-century Sleeping Beauty scenario during which relative poverty had preserved its unique architectural heritage. In the century since, Bruges has grown in popularity to the point where it has more pleasure visitors than any other place in Belgium. Paid holidays for workers (a result of the Industrial Revolution) and improved public transportation (particularly the train) in the 19th century woke Bruges (and other areas, see "Ostend" under "The Belgian Coast") to its tourism possibilities. Turn-of-the-century revitalization came, as the government made plans for the long ago silted-up city to have a port again by developing **Zeebrugge** (meaning "Bruges-on-the-sea") and constructing a cross-country canal from the town.

Bruges often is categorized as the "Venice of the North," the canals for which each is noted inviting inevitable comparison. *Bruggelingen* (residents of Bruges) quite reasonably respond that it would make just as much sense to call Venice the *"Bruges of the South."* In fact, the cities have much more in common than watery ways and byways. At their respective apexes of power, Bruges with an earlier start, but their successful 13th to early 15th centuries overlapping, both independent, wealthy city-states exerted far-reaching commercial and artistic influences. Bruges traded wool, fine cloth, lace, and tapestries to Italy in exchange for commissioned paintings. Venetians maintained important consular and trade offices in Bruges, and also commissioned paintings from the Flemish "primitive" masters. Eventually, both cities suffered change from circumstances beyond their control.

To speak again of canals—in the 1970s, when Bruges' inner city waterways had become offensive-smelling due to 20th-century industrial waste, a pipeline was constructed to bring fresh lake water into the dredged and cleaned canals, and the waste water from industry (all of which operates beyond the borders of historic Bruges) was diverted away. Today, the bad odor in Bruges' canals is gone, a situation that can't be said of Venice.

The history of Bruges began in the 9th century, when **Boudewijn** (also known as **Baldwin Iron Arm**) boldly eloped with the daughter of French King Charles the Bald. Though less than pleased, in order to provide a united family front against invading Vikings, Charles gifted his impetuous new son-in-law with the misty lands in the extreme north of Gaul (modern Flanders). To withstand the frequent Viking invasions, Boudewijn built a solid fort on the site of today's **Burg**. Soon a village arose around it, taking its name from the *brug* (bridge) he built over the Reie river. From these beginnings in Bruges, Boudewijn went on to become founder of the powerful dynasty of the counts of Flanders. (See also "Ghent in Context.") At about the time of Boudewijn, Bruges' future was for the short term, favorably influenced by a great North Sea inundation of the coast that greatly deepened an arm of water, the **Zwin**, that reached inland to the Reie.

By the 10th century, Norsemen were no longer a nuisance, and Bruges was becoming a significant business center. Old annals record the first annual trade fair—it would become the most important in Flanders—in 958, for which merchants arrived in vessels in Bruges' harbor, located where the **Minnewater** is today. During the 11th century, Bruges laid the foundations for its future commercial greatness, fortifying itself physically, and in 1089 becoming the administrative capital of the county of Flanders. Churches, hospitals, and monasteries began to be built.

Bruges established important economic relations with Germany, England, France, the Baltic, Russia, and the East, and by the 12th century, had become one of Europe's most prosperous market towns. The cloth trade was becoming highly important—also in the fellow Flemish cities of Ypres and Ghent—and the import and storage of English wool was making a fortune for Fleming nobility and merchants.

On March 2, 1127, Count of Flanders Charles the Good, was assassinated in the Burg's **St. Donatian church** (built in the 9th century, consecrated as a cathedral in 1559, and demolished by post-Revolution, antireligious French fanatics in 1799). A heated dispute over Charles' successor arose, and Bruges' wealthy shopkeepers took advantage of the situation to claim the right to participate in governing the flourishing city. From that time, the *meliores civium* ("the best citizens") in addition to the nobility, could participate, but the manual workers, weavers, and other crafts people were still excluded from the power process.

While Bruges continued to burgeon in business, by late in the 12th century, the **Zwin**, which tidal forces had earlier favored by deepening, began to be **threatened with silt**, and it was dredged between 1175 and 1200. In 1180, Count of Flanders Philip of Alsace granted town rights to the nearby (4 mi/7 km) fishing village of **Damme** on the Zwin. Damme, its harbor created by embanking the Reie in Bruges and damming it (hence its name) where it joined the Zwin, henceforth served as the port for Bruges. The **Spielgelrei**, today dead-ended at Jan van Eyckplein, once brought the waters of the Reie from Damme right to Bruges' Markt; there, barges loaded with wool from ships too large to sail inland beyond Damme unloaded it into the Cloth Hall.

An indication of the size of the new port in Damme (see "In the Area") comes from the fact that, in 1213, Philip II of France used it for his fleet (said to number some 1,000 vessels) while he pillaged the town during his war against Count Ferdinand of Flanders. However, Ferdinand's English allies burned most of Philip's fleet as it lay in Damme harbor (thereby creating a new need to dredge). Damme recovered, growing in a few years from virtual nonexistence to a population of 10,000, and gaining its own maritime law (*Zeerecht van Damme*) and valuable staple rights on wine and herring.

The early 13th century saw many foreign merchants making themselves at home in Bruges. Nobles built mansions and merchants built town houses. To proclaim its fame, fortune, and freedom, Bruges constructed an exceptionally fine **belfry**. (The first edition of the edifice was built in the early 13th century, destroyed by fire in 1280, and reconstructed in 1282–1296.) Bruges founded the **Flemish Hanseatic League of London**, through which it practically monopolized trade with England, and whose wool was vital for the Flemish cloth workers. Bruges also obtained a *kontor* from the *Teutonic Hanseatic League* and was a member of the *Hanseatic League of the Seventeen Cities*, associations which protected members' commercial links. The protection the Bruges-Hansa tie implied led many countries to set up substantial trade missions in the city. Bruges became the transit warehouse for Hansa members from the Baltic to Italy and overflowed with imports: carpets from the East, furs from Russia, velvet from Italy, metals from Poland, exotic fruits from Egypt, and spices from Arabia. The Italian cities of Venice, Florence, Genoa, and Pisa built trade houses in Bruges, which was mentioned by Italian poet **Dante Alighieri** (1265–1321) in *The Divine Comedy's Inferno*.

The growing opulence of Bruges' merchants, who monopolized all trade, contrasted sharply with the poverty of the tens of thousands of exploited workers in the city's 52 guilds. In 1280, the "blue nails" (as textile workers were known due to their dye-stained nails) led a revolt against the more privileged citizens. During this period, Count of Flanders Guy de Dampierre, who had been instrumental in developing Bruges' trade fairs, and sought to maintain Flanders' autonomy from the French crown, met strong resistance from Philip the Fair. Eventually, Philip found an excuse to imprison the rebellious count in Paris, and annexed Flanders. Burgundian **Philip the Fair** came in triumph from France in 1301 to visit Bruges, then Europe's most important commercial city. Most Bruggelingen turned out to see Philip, many so luxuriously turned out that his queen, Joanne of Navarre, is said to have reacted to the sumptuous display of dress and jewels by pronouncing, "I thought that I alone was queen, but I see hundreds around me here."

Under the Burgundians, the unequally favored citizens of Bruges soon squared off into camps: the patricians, who preferred French dominion (*Leliaerts*); against the discontented common people (*Klauwaerts*), who took their name "lion's paw" from the Lion of Flanders, the count's emblem. Klauwaert **Pieter de Coninck**, a weaver, became leader of their rebellion. Philip's appointee as governor of Flanders, his uncle Jacques de Chantillon, treated the guildsmen of Bruges with such oppressive intolerance that the citizens, under Pieter de Coninck and **Jan Breydel**, revolted against Bruges' French garrison within a year. At dawn on May 18, 1302, as the bells rang for matins (the incident became known as the **Bruges Matins**), they attacked some 2,000 French soldiers and patricians who had collaborated with the French. None of these could, when it was demanded of them, properly pronounce the gutteral sounds of the Flemish words *schilt ende vriendt* (shield and friend). All were slaughtered on the spot.

Six weeks later, the two Bruges guild leaders (remembered in a statue on the Markt) led Flemish burghers against French nobility, achieving victory at the *Battle of the Golden Spurs* at Kortrijk. (See "An Historical Perspective" under "Belgium.") This battle broke the control of trade by the rich merchants and patricians, and put more power in the hands of the guilds.

In 1369, the last count of Flanders, Louis de Malle, gave his only daughter's hand in marriage to duke of Burgundy, **Philip the Bold**, and the couple made Bruges their favorite residence in the Netherlands. In 1376, work began on a Stadhuis (town hall) worthy of Bruges (today, the oldest in Belgium and one of the most splendid). Philip fostered the Flemish school of painting, giving commissions to many members of the *Guild of St. Luke*. Burgundian Bruges was the meeting place of Europe's North and South, where intellectual ideas intermingled amid the easy exchange of material goods. These, unloaded on the quays at Damme, where the seagoing ships anchored, and transferred to barges, made a continuous procession up the canalized Reie to Bruges. Some 150 ships entered the Bruges/ Damme ports in a single day, and the population, which included the consuls from 20 nations and city-states, reached 150,000. But even as Bruges was at its best, Damme, too, was becoming afflicted by sand, the insidious silting preventing the deepest-draft ships from sailing to it up the Zwin, from the North Sea.

In 1429, Isabella of Portugal, whose portrait was painted by Jan van Eyck, sailed into Damme to become the bride of **Philip the Good**. The week-long wedding celebrations were the talk of the west. That same year in Bruges, Philip founded the famed *Order of the Golden Fleece*, both to highlight the splendor and stature of his House of Burgundy and in recognition of the skill of Flemish wool weavers. The Order's insignia, a limp lamb's fleece worn on a substantial gold chain around the neck of its knights—as seen in period portraits such as that of "Anthony of Burgundy" by **Rogier van der Weyden** in Brussels' **Museum of Ancient Art**—took its name from the ancient Greek myth of Jason and his Argonauts' search for the Golden Fleece. Membership in the medieval order of chivalry (limited to 24) was a great honor. Members were chosen by Philip and subsequent rulers, who would congregate the knights for consultation at chapter meetings. It was an honor, too, to be the venue for such a meeting: the carved choir stalls in Bruges' St. Saviour's Cathedral were commissioned in 1430 for the occasion of the founding of the Order, which returned there in 1478 for the Thirteenth Chapter meeting. In 1464, Philip named Bruges the meeting place for the first *States General of the Netherlands*.

Bruges' cultural high point came with the long reign of Philip the Good (1419–1467). Flemish art flowered and music played an important part in Bruges life, as shown by the numerous instruments that appear in Flemish paintings. Memling painted *The Last Judgment* as a commission for Tomasso Portunari, who was the director of the Medicis' bank at Bruges, and the same connection may have been the route by which **Hugo van der Goes's** *Nativity* found its way to Florence's Uffizzi Gallery.

By the 15th century, Bruges was a central clearing house for all European trade, as well as the warehouse for the Hanseatic League. At Vlamingstraat 35—today a business address not far from the *Markt*—in a 13th-century family mansion **Huis ter Beurze**, the entreprenurial Brugean innkeeper Joris van der Beurze served the merchants and bankers who met, dined, drank, and negotiated business deals there; an assortment of business services that amounted to the world's first currency and commodities exchange. His name *Beurze*, in the forms *bourse* and *beurs*, still is in use for stock exchanges worldwide. For his 15th-century clients, van der Beurze arranged money exchanges, since each of the states and cities that traded in Bruges coined its own currency; he also coordinated weights, since many dominions also maintained their own measurement systems. Eventually, van der Beurze began a form of *letters of credit* which, given the weight of the all-metal money in those days, was not only safer from robbery but much easier to manage. On the former site of Huis ter Buerze is a modern bank where you can conduct your financial business.

By Philip's death in 1467, Bruges fortunes had begun to decline, though the pomp and circumstance of civic life under the dukes of Burgundy concealed its fading glory. In 1468, Damme hosted the wedding, and Bruges the month-long celebrations after, for **Charles the Bold** and the English princess **Margaret of York**, sister of English King Edward IV. By then, silting on the Zwin made even Damme unreachable by water, and arriving from England, Margaret could sail only as far as Sluis in Holland, where the port for Damme and Bruges had been moved. Nevertheless, the wedding was a grandiose occasion; the knights of the Golden Fleece gathering for a tournament which they called the **Pageant of the Golden Tree** (recreated every five years in Bruges, next in 1996). But two, too-short Burgundian reigns (Charles the Bold died in battle at Nancy in 1477, and his daughter and heir, Mary of Burgundy, only five years later from a fall incurred while falconing on horseback—both have grand mausoleums in Bruges' Onze Lieve Vrouwekerk) led to the transfer of Flemish power from the French Burgundians to the Austrian Hapsburgs through Mary's husband **Archduke Maximilian**.

Hapsburg rule was not a success for Bruges. In 1488, for a period of 11 weeks, Bruggelingen held Maximilian prisoner at the **Craenenburg** (corner of *Markt* and *Sint-Amandsstraat*). The extreme, and ultimately unwise, action was in response to what they considered unjustified infringements upon their freedom (the garrisoning of German soldiers, etc). Having thrown Maximilian in jail to stress how strongly they felt, the citizens also summarily tried and condemned to death the archduke's local right-hand counsellor, **Pieter Lanchals**, whose execution Maximilian was made to witness. A popular local story is that Maximilian, finally released from jail on the basis of promises (later largely unkept), ordered Bruggelingen to forever keep swans on their canals in remembrance of Lanchals, whose name is derived from *lange hals* meaning "long neck" and whose coat of arms bore a swan. Lanchals is buried in a chapel in Onze Lieve Vrouwekerk. Though swans (with a B for Bruges and the year of birth marked on their beaks) remain plentiful to this day, the Maximilian incident proved to be Bruges' swan song. The uprising against him had caused political instability, a serious detriment to trade; many foreign merchants, and Maximilian himself made a permanent move to Antwerp.

The Zwin, continuing to sink under sand, most certainly was a deciding factor in the death blow to Bruges, but there were others. Bruges, among other places in Flanders, had practiced overly restrictive commercial policies in the cloth industry, its merchants and guild members refusing to handle any cloth made by competitive weavers (particularly those in England). As the English industry grew and the country kept more of its own wool, the lack of the raw material led to ruin throughout the Flemish cloth industry. Many out of work Flemish weavers left for England to find new jobs.

Maximilian's grandson, Charles V, made a triumphant entry into Bruges in 1515, the year he became ruler of the Netherlands at the age of 15. But any hopes Bruggelingen had that Charles could change their downhill course ended that year when he selected Brussels as his principal residence. When Bruges perceived the full threat to her very existence, it was too late. Native son **Lancelot Blondeel** (1496–1561), primarily a painter, but also a Renaissance man with an interest in the sciences was called in by municipal officers to plan a canal to give Bruges renewed access to the sea. Blondeel threw himself into the task and eventually proposed a massive project. But such was the extent of work required that it was not implemented.

Religious struggles of the second half of the 16th century completed the process of ruin for Bruges as a commercial center. But, after Iconoclasts had pillaged, killed priests, and disfigured sacred statues, with the coming of the *Counter-Reformation* in Flanders, Bruges became a safe haven for Roman Catholic nuns and priests, many of whose institutions survive today. Wealthy burghers built *godshuizen* (almshouses) for the increasingly impoverished city's poor. Business improved somewhat in the 17th century, and a number of houses date from that period. But, basically, Bruges became a backwater.

Finally, in 1811, **Napoleon Bonaparte** employed Spanish prisoners-of-war to dig a canal between Bruges and the Scheldt—for his own purposes. He wanted to connect Bruges, via Damme, with Breskens in Holland on the Westerscheldt estuary so that his ships could sail from Antwerp to Dunkirk without having to use the North Sea, thereby avoiding the English coast—and the English Navy. But Napoleon's canal plan was interrupted by other events in 1814 and 1815. And the Industrial Revolution continued to bypass Bruges.

Between 1895–1907 the Belgian government under Leopold II built—very much along the lines of Lancelot Blondeel's 16th-century proposal—the **Boudewijn Kanaal** (230 ft/70 m wide, 26 ft/8 m deep, and 6.5 mi/10 km long) to a place on the coast that was named **Zeebrugge**. Subsequent development of the port provided a fishing harbor, an inner harbor, and an outer harbor with 245 acres of water sheltered by a crescent-shaped *mole* or jetty (with *promenade*) that reaches more than 1.5 mi/2.5 km into the North Sea. The once-open mouth of the Zwin is today but a saltwater marsh nature reserve. (See "Het Zoute" under "The Belgian Coast")

Five centuries after its fall from greater glory, though the Zeebrugge port is important for regional business, tourism has placed Bruges back on the map. But Bruges is again playing a part in the history of Europe, through its *College of Europe*, founded in 1949. Today the multilingual international students of the prestigious postgraduate institution (located on the Dijver), well-grounded in cultural and scientific studies of contemporary Europe, are much in demand and serving in positions of importance as the integration process towards a single European marketplace continues.

GUIDEPOSTS

Telephone Code 050

Tourist Information (Dienst voor Toerisme) • Burg 11, ☎ *44.86.86*, FAX *44.86.00*. Mon.–Fri., April-Sept. 9:30 a.m.–6:30 p.m.; Sat., Sun., holidays 10 a.m.-noon and 2-6:30 p.m.; Oct.–Mar., Mon.–Fri. 9:30 a.m.–5 p.m., Sat. 9:30 a.m.–noon, 2-5 p.m., closed Sun., holidays; hotel booking assistance. Guided city walking tours daily July–Aug. 3 p.m.; meeting point: tourist office.

Rail Station • office open Mon.–Fri. 7 a.m.–7 p.m., Sat. and Sun. 9:30 a.m.–5:30 p.m., ☎ *38.23.82*.

Bus • daily 6 a.m.–9 p.m. ☎ *35.31.43*.

Taxis • Taxi ranks at Station and Markt; to book ☎ *33.44.44* and *38.46.60*.

Post Office • Markt 5, ☎ *33.14.11*.

Police • Hauwerstraat 7, ☎ *44.88.44*.

Emergency • ☎ *100*; weekend doctors on duty (Fri. 8 p.m.–Mon. 8 a.m.) ☎ *81.38.99.*

Rental Bikes • Railway station: ☎ *38.58.71*; 't Koffieboontje, Hallestraat 4 (by Belfry), ☎ *33.80.27*; bicycle tour brochure in English available.

Canal Cruises • Five departure points, several on Dijver and Rozenhoed-kaai; Mar.–Nov. 10 a.m.–6 p.m., Dec., Feb. weekends, holidays, closed Jan.; duration 1/2 hour.

Horse-drawn Cab Tours • Mar.–Nov. on Burg, 10 a.m.–8 p.m. **Sightseeing Line**, bus stop in center of Markt, schedule, reser. ☎ *31.13.55.*

Cruises to Damme • Departure point: Noorweegse Kaai 31, Dampoort (Bruges City bus 4); April 1–Sept. 30, departures on the hour 9 a.m.–6 p.m. Info from Damme Tourist Office, ☎ *(050) 35.33.19.*

WHAT TO SEE AND DO

What you most want to do in Bruges is look at the delightful details of this lovely little city in Gothic garb: the texture of century-smoothed cobblestones, the mellow colors of aged building bricks, lacy wrought-iron lanterns, lace curtains at the windows, and flower boxes strung along the canals. Shadings in the changeable sky and reflected creations in canal waters produce natural "special effects" that will leave you looking wonderingly (and wishing, perhaps, for the skill to capture them on film). As rewarding as the insides of Bruges' museums are—the tourist office sells combination tickets to four major museums (BF 350), a savings for visitors who intend to see them all—it may be that by stopping on bridges to gaze down a canal, you'll discover an image of Bruges that lingers in your mind. So *don't*, however little time you have in this atmospheric city, spend it all indoors—*whatever* the weather.

Markt ★

This has been the commercial heart of Bruges for more than a millenium (when the merchants moved the short distance from the town's fortified Burg to set up a permanent main market square). It's unusual for a Markt in the Benelux not to be home to the stadhuis/town hall; Bruges' Markt used to be, but the building burned, and an all important Cloth Hall was built on the site (where the ornate 19th-century West Flanders Provincial House now stands). A new Stadhuis was built on the **Burg**. (See "Burg".) The dominating monument on the Markt is the belfry. Around the square are the gabled facades of guildhouses and former dwellings of dukes and foreign dignitaries, many of which at street-level now support terrace cafes that burst with imbibers in pleasant weather. In the center of the Markt is a statue (1887) of **Pieter De Coninck** and **Jan Breydel**, leaders in the *Bruges Matins* and 1302 *Battle of the Golden Spurs*. To understand the full impact of the activity on the Markt during Bruges' bustling 13th and 14th centuries, keep in mind that the **Reie**, the waterway that connected Bruges to Damme and the sea, came right up to the east side of the Markt, to and under the Cloth Hall for all-weather unloading.

Belfry ★★

Entrance in courtyard of Halle; visits to tower mean climbing 366 mostly stone steps, no elevator; April–Sept., daily 9:30 a.m.–5 p.m.; Oct.–Mar., 9:30 a.m.–12:30 p.m., and 1:30–5 p.m.; English-language guide and printed booklet about tower. The Bruges belfry (265 ft/88 m) is acknowledged to be Belgium's most beautiful. "Thrice consumed and thrice rebuilt," (noted no less a poet than Longfellow [1807–1882] in *The Belfry of Bruges*), its present post-fires square base, which rises from the roof of the Halle (market hall), dates from 1296. Used as a storage depot and market, the front dates from 1248, the sides from 1363–1365, and the back, 1561–1566. The graceful octagonal top of the belfry was added in 1487. The ★★ view from its top, well worth the effort of those up to the climb, inspired Longfellow, who climbed it one winter morning and, gazing down, imagined "pageants splendid that adorned those days of old" and "knights who bore the Golden Fleece, Lombard and Venetian merchants, with deep laden argosies" traversing the Markt. At the 55th step is the former treasure chamber, normally on view only through a wrought-iron railing dating from 1300. A typical early example of this Flemish art form, the railing has six locks. In chests in wall niches were stored the town's precious *Charter of Liberty* and *Great Seal*, both destroyed in the belfry's fire of 1280. (The written evidence of rights awarded to citizens was important; since the count of Flanders at the time was annoyed by the amount of freedom the Bruggelingen had gained, it has always been suspected that he was responsible for the fire.) At the belfry's 333rd step you come to the automatic mechanism for the tower clock. At the 352nd is the chamber with the carillon keyboard, above which, behind the uppermost arched openings, are Bruges' 47 mighty bronze carillon bells.

The carillon is attended to artistically and maintained mechanically by the present holder of the full-time paid position of *stadbeiaardier/* town carillonneur, the amiable **Aimé Lombaert**, whose talents have taken him on carillon-playing tours in the U.S., Canada, and Europe. Perhaps surprisingly, standing by the bells when the carillon is being played won't drive you mad or make you deaf, but you actually hear the music better from below. From above, however, there's a splendid view across Bruges and the Flemish countryside. Blind visitors to Bruges can get an appreciation of the building from the belfry "in braille" in front of the Halle; the "hands on" model of the belfry of which Bruggelingen are so proud also is described in braille.

Burg ★★

This, the most handsome square in Bruges, is the site of the city's founding, where Boudewijn, first count of Flanders, put up a fortified building in the 9th century. It should be any traveler's first stop, too, for the well-supplied and helpful tourist information office is located here. On the site of the present Holiday Inn Crown Plaza once sat the 9th-century St. Donatian church, broken down brick by brick by religion-hating French Revolutionary zealots in 1799. A smaller version of the statue of Jan van Eyck that stands on the nearby Jan van Eyckplein was placed here to commemorate the fact that the artist had been buried in St. Donatian. Remnants of the foundations of the church were discovered in 1955, and have been preserved in a cellar "museum" in the hotel. Several important stops face the square.

Stadhuis ★★

April–Sept., daily 9:30 a.m.–5 p.m., rest of year, closes 12:30–2 p.m.
Bruges' Late Gothic-style Stadhuis was begun in 1376, making it the oldest in Belgium and one of the finest. The ornate ★★facade, which took 45 years to finish, is today once again studded with statues; most of its 48 niches only recently refilled with copies of the figures of counts and countesses of Flanders that were removed and ruined by the French in their devastation of the city in 1799. The entrance hall is decorated with colorful guild banners and historic paintings. Also on display are fine antique maps of Bruges, which show that the inner city has so little changed in 400 years that you can still tour from a copy. Be sure to head upstairs to the spacious ★★Gothic Hall, with its superb wooden rib-arched and vaulted, vividly painted ceiling (1385–1402), an altogether worthy setting for the first council of the *States General of the Netherlands*, seated here by Burgundian Philip the Good in 1464. Town authorities met here for centuries, but now the space is reserved for civil wedding ceremonies and official receptions. The circular vault keys in the ceiling show scenes from the New Testament and ones depicting the 12 months and 4 natural elements. Restoration of the room at the turn of the century resulted in the addition of romantic wall paintings by the Flemish artists **Albert and Juliaan de Vriendt** of events in the history of Bruges. Among these are the triumphal return of Bruges warriors from the Battle of the Golden Spurs in 1302, the founding of the Order of the Golden Fleece by Philip the Good in 1429, Bruges renewing its privileges in the Hanseatic League, and the opening of the new Zwin canal in 1404.

Brugse Vrije/The Liberty of Bruges

Daily year-round 10 a.m.–noon, 1:30–5 p.m. Its seat established on the Burg in a palace built between 1520 and 1525, the Liberty of Bruges was a feudal territorial subdivision of Flanders, with its own administrative, judicial, and financial authority which, in the course of the 14th century, became the fourth most important member of Flanders, after Ghent, Bruges, and Ypres. The Liberty of Bruges existed until 1795 when it was abolished by the French. Its Aldernmen's room is visited for the magnificent 1528 ★★Renaissance chimneypiece, designed by Brugean artist **Lanceloot Blondeel** (1498–1561), that honors Charles V. Charles, portrayed as the worldly prince and Emperor of the Holy Roman Empire, stands in the center, carved in wood with a glowing patina, surrounded by black marble with white alabaster friezes. On either side of Charles are the paired statues of his grandparents, paternal (Emperor Maximilian of Austria and Mary of Burgundy) and maternal (Ferdinand of Aragon and Isabella of Castille); his parents, Philip the Fair and Johanna the Mad, are represented only on medallions, barely visible behind him. On the walls hang copies of two paintings on the theme of justice (originals in the Groeninge Museum) that were commissioned for the Aldermen's room: *The Last Judgement* (1551) by **Pieter Pourbus**, and the horrifying *Judgement of Cambyses* (1498) by **Gerard David**.

Basilique du Saint-Sang/Basilica of the Holy Blood

Daily April–Sept. 9:30 a.m.-noon, 2–6 p.m., Oct.–Mar. daily 10 a.m.–noon, 2–4 p.m., except closed Wed. p.m. The **Holy Blood relic**, which the basilica was built to house and honor, is a phial said to contain a mixture of blood and water washed from Christ's side as he hung on the cross. The traditional accounting for the relic's arrival in Bruges is that because the count of Flanders, Dierick of Alsace, had executed his duties in the Second Crusade in an exemplary manner, he was given the relic. However, historians have now determined that the Holy Blood didn't arrive in Bruges until later at the beginning of the 13th century, via Constantinople. In any case, the **Holy Blood relic** is on view in the *Upper Chapel* every Fri. 8:30–11:45 a.m., 3–4 p.m., and daily for two weeks in the Ascension period from 8:30–11:45 a.m., 3:00–4:00 p.m. (See also "Procession of the Holy Blood" under "Entertainment and Events.") The dimly lit, thick-walled, semicircular vaulted lower chapel is worth a look for being one of the purest examples of Romanesque construction in Flanders.

Off the Burg, down **Blinde Ezelstraat**, identifiable by its arcade to 15th-century former Palace of Justice, and over a 14th-century bridge is the **Vismarkt**, an open beamed, neoclassical, columned market building dating from 1826; a busy scene on mornings (except Sun. and Mon.). Among the buildings surrounding the nearby charming cobbled ★★**Huidevettersplein** (Tanners' Square) are the tanners' guild house (1630) and next to it a facade with bas-reliefs representing the different processes of treating leather. Leaving the square on the far side, you will be on one of Bruges' most beautiful canals, ★★**Rozenhoedkaai**, with picturesque sights in every direction and just down from the **Dijver**, Bruges' *museum row*.

Groeninge Museum

Dijver 12; April–Sept. daily 9:30 a.m.–5 p.m., Oct.–Mar. 9:30 a.m.–12:30 p.m. and 2-5 p.m., closed Tues.; booklet with English translations of the captions by the museum's works of art. Even though they broke new artistic ground as a group, the leading Flemish "primitive" painters can be appreciated for their individual qualities: **Jan van Eyck** (1390–1441) for realism; **Rogier van der Weyden** (1399–1464) for passionate emotion; **Hans Memling** (1435–1494) for delicacy and purity; and Hugo van der Goes (1440–1482) for striking dramatism; a trait duplicated by his student **Gerard David** (1460–1523), the last great master of the *Bruges School*. Its primitive paintings of the Bruges School are the museum's greatest treasure, although the pleasantly human-scale Groeninge collection shows the whole evolution of Flemish art, from the surrealism of **Hieronymous Bosch** (1450–1516) to that of **James Ensor** (1860–1949).

Among the more outstanding paintings are van Eyck's *Madonna with St. Donatian and St. George* with its superb portrait of the donor **Canon van der Paele**, and *Portrait of Margarete van Eyck*, the artist's wife painted in his most realistic mode; Memling's Triptych with donors Willem Moreel, burgomaster of Bruges and his wife; van der Goes' *Death of a Virgin*; David's *Triptych* including the *Baptism of Christ*; and *Last Judgment* by the intensely individual master Hieronymous Bosch, whose contemporaries could make nothing of his spirit and technique, although a century later Breugel seemed able to. The horrifying painting *The Judgment of Cambyses* (1498) by **Gerard David** of a man being skinned alive uses the story from Herodotus of the skin of a corrupt judge being stripped from him and used to make a cushion for the chair on which his son would sit as successor. This painting is said to have been commissioned by the magistrates of Bruges in atonement for the town's execution of Maximilian's adviser *Pieter Lanchals* (see "Bruges in Context") to hang (as a copy does today) in the **Brugse Vrije**, Alderman's room of the court of justice.

At the Groeninge, you'll see many works attributed with the word "*naar*" (meaning "after" or "in the school of"), some of which may be copies (usually contemporary and often excellent—recall Pieter Bruegel the Younger's many copies of his father's works, some of the originals of which no longer exist). The number of works noted "naar" also is an indication, in a world without other methods of artistic reproduction—no art posters—of the popularity of the work in its day. The number of anonymous works ("*anoniem*") is a sign of the substantial artistic activity in Bruges during the 14th-16th-century period, during which the painter's names of some unsigned works were lost.

Gruuthuse Museum

Dijver 17; April–Sept. daily 9:30 a.m.–5 p.m., Oct.–March closed between 12:30–2 p.m. and Tues.; numbered room plan. This was the luxurious mansion of the **Heren van Gruuthuse** (Lords of Gruuthouse), whose fortune came from their right to impose a tax on the import of "gruut," a mixture of dried plants and flowers used by brewers to flavor beer. **Louis de Gruuthuse** (whose representation is above the door) was a counsellor to Philip the Good and Charles the Bold. Decorative art lovers will rarely have had such a wonderful place to wander around, with room after numbered room (19 in all) of tapestries, porcelain, paintings, brass, musical instruments, furniture, and lace. All these are displayed in a fine 15th-century noble family's architecturally homogeneous ivy-covered mansion that alone is worth the walk inside. Among the built-in treasures are chimneypieces, tiled hearths, carved ceilings and moldings, and curious corners such as the one found through Room 16. It's a small windowed ★★oratory built into the wall of Onze Lieve Vrouwekerk (see below) directly above the choir of the church. While the Gruut family obviously used the room as a means of "attending" mass without leaving home (a different variation of a private chapel), we spectators get a strange feeling looking down on the tourists in the church. Also worth seeking out are the 16th-century Flemish kitchen (Room 3), and Rooms 18–20, in the height of the house, which have an excellent exhibit of ★★antique Flemish lace, which includes a lace altar cover that belonged to Charles V. After examining the lace, visit the outside balcony for views, dominated by the tower of Onze Lieve Vrouw, of the ★★attractive garden, canal, and St. Bonifacebrug behind the house. (The garden extends to the *Groeninge Museum* and displays a recent sculpture, *The Four Horsemen of the Apocalypse* by **Rik Poot**.) One of the many oddities in the multifaceted Gruuthuse collection is an 18th-century guillotine, for some reason left in Bruges by the French after they were defeated in the *Battle of Waterloo*. In 1989, on the occasion of the 200th anniversary of the French Revolution, this guillotine was loaned to the Bicentennial Committee in Paris because it was unable to find a real one in France since, after the revolution, they had all been ordered destroyed.

Onze Lieve Vrouwekerk/Church of Our Lady ★

April–Sept., Mon.–Sat. 9:30 a.m.–noon, 12:45–5 p.m.; Oct.–Mar., 9:30 a.m.–12:30 p.m., and 2–5 p.m., closed Wed. p.m., year-round closed Sun. and holidays mornings, open 2:30-4:30 p.m. The Church of Our Lady is predominantly 13th-century Scheldt Gothic. Its 400-foot/122-meter belfry is one of the tallest brick structures in Europe. What draws many here is the ★★ *Madonna and Child* by **Michelangelo** (1475–1564). One of the few works by the master to have left Italy during his lifetime, the Bruges Madonna was one of 15 statues Michelangelo was commissioned to sculpt for the Piccolomini altar in the Duomo of Siena. For various reasons, only four statues of the series were completed, including this is one. The Brugean merchant Jan van Moeskroen is generally credited with bringing the statue to Bruges in 1506 and donating it to this, his own parish church. (He is buried beneath the altar by the statue.) The chubby Christ child and his mother, favorite subjects of Michelangelo, are made of glowing white Carrara marble and sit in a black marble niche. The half-turned pose of the child demonstrates the sculptor at his best and most typical. Though twice stolen (by the French in 1794 and the Nazis in 1944), both times the piece was recovered in good condition.

The untimely death of Mary of Burgundy, wife of Maximilian of Austria, at age 25 from a fall while horseback riding, meant the end of Burgundian rule for Bruges and all Flanders; the Hapsburgs of Austria taking over through her widower Maximilian. Mary was buried here in Bruges' most important church, where her father Charles the Bold also lay. Their life-size recumbent effigies atop *mausoleums* are among the art treasures executed here by Brussels goldsmith **Pieter de Beckere** in 1495-1502. Over the altar which the mausoleums face is the large 16th-century *Crucifixion* triptych by **Barend van Orley**. Other paintings in the church are by **Anthony van Dyck, Gerard David, Pieter Pourbus**. In the north ambulatory you can see the Gothic 1474 oratory of the Gruuthuse (referred to before). The ornate north portal (1465), one of the oldest preserved parts of Our Lady, known as **paradise porch**, has been restored and is used as a baptismal chapel. *Weekend church services Sat. 5 and 7 p.m., Sun. 9 and 11 a.m., 6:30 p.m.*

Memling Museum/Sint-Jan Hospitaal

Mariastraat 38; April–Sept., daily, 9:30 a.m.–5 p.m., Oct.–Mar. 9:30 a.m.–12:30 p.m., 2–5 p.m., closed Wed. p.m. Across the street from the Church of Our Lady is Sint-Jans Hospital, founded in 1118, one of the oldest hospitals in Europe, and the longest operating at one site when it was relocated outside the town in 1965. The beautiful, spacious old hospital wards' brick buildings, largely from the 13th and 14th centuries, welcomed pilgrims, orphans, soldiers, and the sick over the centuries; on display are many early medical instruments, fascinating pieces of early furniture such as an 18th-century "carrying chair" with handles, a pedestrian ambulance. You'll also be rewarded for time spent in the apothecary and with the paintings. The hospital's 19th-century wards have just been restored to serve as a special art exhibition and meeting space in a handsome historic setting. On site is the restaurant/tea room **de Promenade** (☎ *34.56.76*), which has canalside terrace seating.

Set apart, in the former chapel of the hospital, are the ★★★ six sole but exceptional works of German-born, but Bruges-developed Flemish primitive artist **Hans Memling** (c. 1435–1494) that make up his museum. One of the six, the *Ursala Shrine*, actually is itself a series of six magnificent paintings, set in an intricate small Gothic church-shaped reliquary. More like the miniatures in *The Book of Hours*, they depict scenes from Ursala's martyred life. The large triptych of the *Mystical Marriage of Saint Catherine*, its wings extended fully for front and back views, is freestanding in the center of the chapel with chairs for visitors who want to take advantage of the unique opportunity to be able to concentrate on so few wonderful works at one time. *The Lamentation over Christ Triptych* was commissioned by St. Jan's hospital brother Adrian Reyns. After the multipanel pieces, it's a relief to study the single image in the *Portrait of a Woman Sibylla Sambetha*, thought to be the daughter of Moreel, one of Memling's patrons. It is fascinating for its delicacy and mere whisper of lace for the headpiece.

When you exit, turn right on **Mariastraat** and walk the short distance to the canal for a view of a wonderful exterior view of St. Jan's (this location has great photographic potential from cruise boats). If you continue straight on, you'll shortly see Wijngaardstraat on the right leading to the Beginhof.

Begijnhof/Beguinage ★★★

Wijngaardstraat, to Minnewater bridge and entrance gate, is one of Bruges' most memorable spots. **Winston Churchill** was so captivated by the sight of the Begijnhof with spring daffodils in bloom that he recorded it in a watercolor (reprinted on postcards for sale in town). Since the last Begijn died here in 1930 (the first came in 1245), the Begijnhof has been in the loving care of Benedictine nuns, whom you may see strolling in traditional black-robed, flowing white head-clothed, 15th-century-style vestments. They are quietly impressive figures as they walk across the paths to the white-washed buildings of their lovely private world. Part of the Begijnhof's charm is its peacefulness, and though hundreds, perhaps thousands, of tourists may be milling around just beyond the gate on a sunny weekend day in summer, within its precincts the request for quiet usually is respected. The central lawn is dotted with tall trees and parted here and there by paths, all open to the elements; the light and sky seem always to make a fresh, frequently dramatic impression. The ★ **Begijnhof church**, a triple-nave 13th-century Gothic structure (though in rebuilding after a 1584 fire, it took on more baroque lines), has multiple services most days: 6:15 a.m., 7:15 a.m.; noon, 5 p.m.; five services on Sun., one on Sat. at 5 p.m. (Some have chanting and/or organ music; confirm times.)

Beguine's House ★

Daily April–June 11 a.m.–noon, 1:45–5:30 p.m.; July and Aug. 10 a.m.–noon, 1:45–6 p.m.; Sept.–Mar. 10:30 a.m.-noon, 1:45–5 p.m. The house, located to the immediate left as you enter the Begijnhof via the bridge and gate off the Wijngaardplein, is a reconstruction of a 17th-century beguinal residence. The furnishings (among which is a fine oak Renaissance cupboard) and household effects provide a picture of the daily life of the Beguines. The typical Flemish kitchen has Dutch tiles (c. 1500) around the hearth and a biblical-scene, tile tableau over the fireplace. Just beyond the Begijnhof is the *Minnewater* (Lake of Love), Bruges' former commercial dock, now turned poetic corner.

Sint Salvator Cathedral ★

Sint Salvators Kerkhof; April–Sept. Mon.-Sat. 10 a.m.–noon, 2–5 p.m., Sun. and holidays, 3–5 p.m.; Oct.–Mar., Mon.– Sat., 2–5 p.m. closed Sun. and holidays. This, the oldest parish church in Bruges, is essentially 13th-century Gothic, though the base of the West tower is c. 1200 with brickwork among the oldest in Belgium, and the nave from the 14th century, having been rebuilt after a fire. It became Bruges' cathedral in 1834, with the restoration of the bishopric of Bruges, which had been abolished by Napoleon in 1802. The French, in fact, had demolished Bruges' previous cathedral, St. Donatian, in 1799; of the surviving art treasures, many were given to its successor. Sint Salvator is notable for its priceless 18th-century Gobelin and series of six *tapestries* from Brussels. The baroque bronze, wood, and marble rood screen features the *Creator* by **A. Quellin** (1682). Above the choir stalls, commissioned in 1430 on the occasion of the founding of the **Order of the Golden Fleece** in Bruges, are the escutcheons of the Knights of the Order, who met here for the 13th Chapter in 1478. The **cathedral museum** *(April 1–Sept. 30, Mon.-Sat., 10 a.m.–noon, 2–5 p.m., Sun. and holidays, 2–5 p.m.; Oct. 1–Mar. 31, Mon.-Sat., 2–5 p.m.; closed Wed. year-round, Sun. in winter)* was added as an annex in 1912. Of particular note among the paintings, carvings, and metalwork in the seven rooms is the triptych *Martyrdom of St. Hippolytus* by **Dirk Bouts** and **Hugo van der Goes**. *Cathedral services on the weekend are Sat. 4 and 6 p.m., Sun. 11:30 a.m. and 6 p.m.*

Lace Museum/Kantcentrum ★

Peperstraat 3, by Jeruzalem Church; year- round Mon.–Fri, 10 a.m.–noon, 2–6 p.m., Sat. 2–5 p.m., closed Sun., holidays. Lace making is a tradition in Bruges. (See "Lace" section of "Decorative Arts and Traditional Crafts" at front of book.) The fashion of trimming garments with lace (originally as collar protectors) meant that gold and silver threads were sometimes used in lace making for the wealthy. The use of lace in fashion began in the 15th century and reached its height under the hands of Bruges women in the 17th century. On display is bobbin lace made as long ago as the 17th century. A copy of **Vermeer's** *Kantwerkster* (Lacemaker) from that period is on the wall, as well as copies of other 16th- and 17th-century Flemish and Dutch paintings that show fine lace fashion details. Visitors see many lace patterns; the most complicated of which required 250 bobbins. Fully as interesting as the antique pieces is the modern lace in creative new patterns. The museum is located in the tastefully restored 15th-century almshouses of the Jeruzalem Church, still privately owned by the Adornes family. Since the lace museum here has less extensive displays than those at the **Gruuthuse Museum**, perhaps the major reason for seeking out the center is to observe the women learning and working at bobbin lace making on their lap cushions. The interesting, interactive experience is available afternoons only. The center has a small shop with lace making supplies and small framed pieces for sale.

Folklore Museum/Museum voor Volkskunde ★

Rolweg 40; April–Sept., daily, 9:30 a.m.–5 p.m.; Oct.–Mar., 9:30 a.m.–12:30 p.m., 2–5 p.m., closed Tues. p.m.; descriptive details in Dutch only. Local folklore museums are popular in Belgium. But, among the many, Bruges' ranks as one of the best. The attractive museum is in a row of cottage-like buildings, surrounding a garden and set up as a series of old shops: a Flemish version of a general store; pipe, hat, and bootmakers shops; a chocolatier with marvelous old chocolate and cookie molds; and a schoolroom. An authentic old cafe (**De Zwarte Kat/The Black Cat**) serves drinks during open hours.

Not far from the Lace and Folk museums are three windmills perched picturesquely on Bruges' grassy ramparts (with walking/cycling paths) where, in the 13th and 14th centuries, medieval fortifications encircled the city. The 1770 ★ **Sint-Janshuysmolen** (*Rolweg; May 1–Sept. 30, 10 a.m.–noon, 2–5:30 p.m., closed rest of year*), a so-called stilt-windmill, is in working order and in summer, when there's sufficient wind, the vanes turn at full speed. Also standing beside the canal—which nearly encloses the old central city—is the **Kruispoort** (1402), a fortified gate built in unusual white sand/lime bricks. Nearby, you can pick up the canal-side path to Damme.

SHOPPING

Though a small piece of light-weight lace commands a heavy price (handmade, a four-inch square is a full day's production), it's big business in Bruges. Many shop windows are filled with lace for sale, and the product is pretty enough to counter the commercialism. If you're a potential buyer, you'll want to know where you can get what you're paying for, especially if you decide to splurge on handmade lace, as opposed to the Hong Kong machine-made variety sold in many shops. Pieces range from postcard-size scenes to bridal veils to huge tablecloths, and some shops also sell antique lace (about the only way today to get a piece of Bruges' famed Fairy Stitch). Look for shops posting the yellow **Quality Control** shield; they sell government-tested and inspected lace, thereby offering consumer protection and knowledgeable advice. Among Bruges' **Quality Control** shops are **Bobbin Lace Palace** (*Breidelstraat 20;* ☎ *33.08.93*), **Duchesse** (*Breidelstraat 4*), **Melissa** (*Katelijnestraat 38;* ☎ *33.45.32*), and **Het Zwanenspel** (*Jozef Suveestraat 29;* ☎ *34.04.17*). Family-operated **Rococo** (*Wollestraat 9*) is the largest lace shop in Bruges, in a two-story 1892 building with a beautiful *art nouveau/jugendstil* interior. Most of these shops are open seven days a week in the tourist season, accept major credit cards, and advise on tax-free export purchases; at one or more you may be able to see a demonstration of lace making (otherwise, visit the **Lace Museum/Kantcentrum**). Note: Brugean Quality is *not* the same quality-control government organization.

In a different tradition, visit **Classics Kunstatelier** (*Oude Burgstraat 32*), in a 15th-century building near Simon Stevinplein, which has a huge display (up to 250 pieces) of Flemish and Brugean tapestries, wall hangings, and other decorative art. Bruges **carillon recordings** are for sale at the information desk at the base of the belfry.

WHERE TO STAY

All hotels listed are located within canal-enclosed historic Bruges. The tourist office has a list of bed-and-breakfast establishments and can make recommendations. Although restaurants are not a rule in Bruges hotels, those in several are among the finest dining establishments in the city; for simplicity's sake, I have included details with the hotel listing.

EXPENSIVE

Holiday Inn Crowne Plaza

Burg 10; ☎ *34.58.34, in U.S. and Canada* ☎ *800-465-4329, FAX 31.23.93.* This recently opened 96-room hotel, located on Bruges' most architecturally outstanding square, has an essentially modern brick facade of controversial, but carefully-overseen design meant to match neighboring buildings in scale and materials. All guest rooms have TV, telephone, individually controlled a/c, double-glazing on windows, minibar, hair dryer, trouser press; some nonsmoking rooms are available. There's a restaurant, coffee shop with outside terrace, lobby bar, and 16-hour room service. Some space in the cellar has been set aside to show the foundations of the 9th-century St. Donatian church that once existed on the site before it was destroyed by the French in the later 1700s.

De Tuilerieen

Dijver 7; ☎ *34.36.91, FAX 34.04.00.* Located on the canaled Dijver, this luxurious hotel was created several years ago in an elegant town-house whose dignity has been preserved but updated. The black and white marble-floored entry hall and stately chandeliered lobby with delicious plasterwork detail prepare one for the comfort found in the 25 country-home-style guest rooms, all with bath, TV, telephone, and minibar. Under a glass shell behind the hotel are a swimming pool, Jacuzzi, sauna, solarium. Breakfast buffet included; bar; parking.

De Orangerie

Karthuizerinnenstraat 10; ☎ *34.16.49, FAX 33.30.16.* Situated in a 1680s former monastery and mansion, de Orangerie is filled with fine old details such as plasterwork, stained glass windows, stone floors, but, most of all, it's garden-like, from the rattan furniture, greenery-covered trellises, and skylighted green-and-white painted halls. The lovely public rooms with a surprising mix of old Flemish furniture and good copies of contemporary paintings by Belgian artist Paul Delvaux, face onto a canal. Only guests can enjoy the hotel's canalside terrace cafe. All 19 comfortable guest rooms have TV, telephone, bath, mini-bar, hair dryer; some have windows that open over the canal, while others face the interior garden courtyard. Breakfast (only) included; bar; elevator; major credit cards.

MODERATE

Oud Huis Amsterdam

Spiegelrei 3; ☎ *34.18.10, FAX 33.88.91.* These two restored 16th-century former "gentlemen's houses" with full canal frontage offer an owner-overseen oasis just a short walk from the Markt. Each of the 22 antique and old print-decorated guest rooms is furnished individually, all have remote-control TV (placed pleasantly out of view in wardrobe cupboards), telephone, modern bath (some with whirlpool), hand-held shower; there's turn-down service with a praline on your pillow.

Breakfast only (included) is served overlooking Spiegelrei canal, drinks in the warm wood-panelled bar with fireplace and Cordoba-leather covered walls. There's a terrace with tables in the quiet back courtyard, and a garden (which back bedrooms overlook) with a surprising sculpture. Friendly, superior service from reception, including free horse-drawn carriage ride from April-Sept. from/to dinner at the family's excellent **'t Bourgoensche Cruyce restaurant**. Elevator; limited on-street parking.

Pandhotel ★★★★

Pandreitje 16; ☎ *34.06.66, FAX 34.05.56.* This owner-run 18th-century mansion-hotel in the plane-tree shaded Pandreitje at the end of which is Bruges' most famous belfry/canal view, has an intimate, tasteful interior with plenty of personal touches in the service. The classic decor in the entry/reception hall features crystal chandeliers, marble, oriental rugs, oil paintings, plants, and lots of architectural detail. The 24 uniquely decorated rooms have TV, telephone, clock-radio, minibar, bath, and hair dryer; six are specially designed luxury rooms. The comfortable lounge has newspapers, drink service during the day; a buffet (included) is served in the garden-like breakfast drawing-room. Elevator.

Die Swaene ★★★★

Steenhouwersdijk 1; ☎ *34.27.98, FAX 33.66.74.* There's a homelike atmosphere to this fastidiously operated family hotel, created from three adjoining 15–17th-century houses on a particularly picturesque stretch of canal. The hotel is so central that by day cruise boats and horse-drawn carriages pass the front door, but by night its quaint corner of old Bruges is as quiet as you could want. There's a garden for pre-dinner drinks and a tapestry-hung lounge upstairs for after-dinner coffee. Hallways are filled with an eclectic collection of paintings and statues, and the cozy front lobby has English-language newspapers. The 24 guest rooms are comfortably and individually furnished, most with antiques; many face the canal; all have bath/shower, TV, telephone, minibar. Buffet breakfast included; elevator; major credit cards. The in-house **Die Swaene restaurant** (*closed Wed., Thurs. night; expensive*, menus *moderate*) sets a table fit for its superb service and celebrated continental cuisine. Specialties include fresh fish, its in-house foie gras, and homemade sorbet, served between courses, served on Belle Époque china, with soft classical music and candle-light.

Duc de Bourgogne ★★★

Huidenvettersplein 12; ☎ *33.20.38, FAX 34.40.37.* Long revered for its fine food, the guest rooms at the Duc de Bourgogne shouldn't be ignored, especially since they share the same unsurpassed canalside setting in the center of Bruges for which the restaurant is noted. Of the 10 bedrooms in the 1648 building, 6 have water views; all are different in shape, size, and price. Guest-room decor, like the restaurant's, is dark wood and traditional; all rooms have bath with fixed shower head, telephone, TV; breakfast is included. No elevator; major credit cards accepted. The **Duc de Bourgogne restaurant** (*closed Sun. evening, Mon.; expensive*, menu *moderate*) has a lengthy listing of classic choices. Its large-windowed Rubenesque-decorated formal dining room overlooks one of Bruges' loveliest converging of canals, a setting that's illuminated at night, with the belfry in view. Both the hotel and restaurant are closed for the months of Jan. and July.

Biskajer

Biskajerplein 4; ☎ *34.15.06, FAX 34.39.11.* This quiet, modern-but-snug hotel is located on the lovely old Jan van Eyckplein which has a statue of the artist at the end of the Spiegelrei canal. Centrally located, just beyond city congestion, the 17 rooms in the three-story hotel are spacious and contemporary, with TV, telephone, radio, bath/shower. Buffet breakfast included. The hotel's restaurant (**Biskaje**; *Jan van Eyckplein 13; daily 9 a.m.–11 p.m.* ☎ *33.01.40; inexpensive*), whose kitchen is open all day, specializes in spareribs and fish Biskaje; there's a pleasant beam-ceiling interior and outside cafe with pleasant views.

Ter Brughe

Oost Gistelhof 2; ☎ *34.03.24.* This 20-double-room hotel is a 500-year-old restored protected monument building, once a patrician mansion and canalside warehouse. A friendly staff, which makes it more a house than a hotel, welcomes guests to the traditionally decorated lobby that features large paintings of the history of Bruges. All the modern furnished rooms have tile bath, TV, telephone, mini-fridge; some on the top floor have ceiling beams. The handsome vaulted brick cellar where breakfast only (included) is served has huge water-level warehouse doors that swing open to greet the swans that await their breakfast. No elevator; bar; major credit cards.

Egmond

Minnewater 15; ☎ *34.14.45.* A bit basic and old-fashioned, this family-run hotel, in a 300-year-old former manor house in a quiet park setting a short distance from the bustle of the shops by the Begijnhof, offers details such as antique reproduction furniture and tiled fireplaces in some of the 9 rooms (all of which have views on the park, TV, telephone, bath). The (included) breakfast room also looks onto the park, a section of the grassy former ramparts that ring Bruges. Next door in the park is **Kasteel Minnewater**, a terrace cafe/restaurant that overlooks the Lake of Love. Free parking; major credit cards; no elevator, but most rooms are on the ground floor.

Academie

Wijngaardstraat 7; ☎ *33.22.66, FAX 33.21.66.* Located near Bruges' peaceful Begijnhof, this imaginative modern hotel, created from an old brick-walled maltery, comes with high-tech details such as a personal hotel card that turns on the electricity in your room. Public rooms, restaurant, and bar, are situated around a central glass-domed courtyard. The 34 good-size rooms have basic, contemporary decor, with desk, small table and chairs, TV, telephone, shower. There's a tavern in the old vaulted cellar. Breakfast and parking included.

INEXPENSIVE

Adornes
St.-Annarei 26; ☎ *34.13.36, FAX 34.20.85.* With a three-canal-junction location in a residential area of old Bruges, away from but within walking distance of the Markt, this 20-room hotel is situated in three restored 17th-century gabled houses. The big-windowed, small lobby is decorated comfortably with leather couches and an antique tapestry on the wall. Rooms (some on the small side; higher-priced ones on the top floor are larger and have exposed ceiling beams) have basic modern furniture, TV, telephone, clock-radio, desk, and small but cozy bathrooms with bath/hand-held shower, hair dryer. A buffet breakfast only (included) is served in a cozy dining room. Elevator.

Bourgoensch Hof
Wollestraat 39; ☎ *33.16.45, FAX 34.63.78.* Picturesquely situated canalside—7 of the 11 rooms face the water—on a small quiet courtyard not far from the Markt, the hotel's location may be its major amenity. While reception service is only civil, the traditionally decorated, canal-facing breakfast room is delightful. Lounge and bedrooms are a bit old-fashioned, with stuffed furniture. No TV in inexpensive category rooms (others are higher priced, with TV). In the cellar of the hotel at canal-level (and with a few outside terrace tables) is **Bistro 't Traptje** *(7 p.m.–midnight;* ☎ *33.89.18; inexpensive)*, with cozy old wooden decor, brick walls, black and white tile floor, serving a small but varied menu of regional specialties.

Boteniek
Waalsestraat 23; ☎ *34.14.24, FAX 34.59.39.* Opened in 1992 in a tastefully restored 18th-century townhouse, this 9-room hotel on a quiet side street is a few minutes' walk from the center of Bruges. All rooms—doubles, twins, one family with kitchenette—furnished differently; top room has view of town towers lighted at night. All rooms have stall showers, TV, radio, telephone. Breakfast (buffet, included) room with bar facilities, small attractive lounge. Elevator.

WHERE TO EAT

In a country celebrated for its food, Bruges is second only to Brussels for pride of palate. Reservations are recommended for Bruges's better restaurants, a category that certainly includes **Vasquez** *(Zilverstraat 38; daily lunch, dinner, closed Wed. and Thurs. lunch;* ☎ *34.08.45; expensive)*, whose adventurously classical gastronomic cuisine (not nouvelle, but unusual pairings and seasoning of traditional fresh local foods) is served in the elegant surroundings of a 15th-century emmissary of Isabella of Portugal. **DeVos** *(Zilverstraat 41; closed Tues. evening, Wed.;* ☎ *33.55.66; moderate)*, a small

13th-century house originally used by traveling monks now with an art nouveau decor including a stunning 20-foot stained glass ceiling, and garden terrace, offers finely prepared regional specialties that should be lingered over. Located in the delightful, sun-filtered, leafy square just back from the Rozenhoedkaai is **Den Braamberg** *(Pandreitje 11; lunch and dinner, closed Sun. night, Thurs.;* ☎ *33.73.70; moderate),* which serves fish and lamb specialties.

    Restaurant 't Bourgoensche Cruyce *(open lunch and dinner, closed Tues., April–Sept., closed Sun. and Mon. lunch Oct.–Mar.;* ☎ *33.79.26; expensive, menu moderate)* has a small ground floor canal-view dining room, with a few tables on a canalside courtyard terrace. It features gastronomic versions of regional specialties, with fresh in-season fare. Reserve as far ahead as possible. In a discussion of some of Bruges' best restaurants (which includes those mentioned under the **Die Swaene** and **Duc de Bourgogne** hotel listings), one must mention **De Snippe** *(Nieuwe Gentweg 53; closed Sun., Mon. lunch;* ☎ *33.70.70; expensive)* even though it is located outside the old city. Here, *haute cuisine*—caviar mousse, scallops with truffles, wild duck—is offered in an 18th-century townhouse. (It also has 5 rooms; *moderate,* 4 jr. suites; *expensive.)*

    Since **De Visscherie** *(Vismarkt 8; closed Tues.;* ☎ *33.02.12; moderate)* faces the fish market, you could hardly expect it to specialize in anything else, and it does fish well with a wide choice of fresh fare. Equally central, in a casual setting just off the Burg, **Breydel-De Coninck** *(Breidelstraat 24; open noon–9 p.m., closed Tues. and Wed.;* ☎ *33.97.46; inexpensive)* is the place in Bruges for mussels, served in enormous enameled pots until you "say when."

    With its charming olde world interior, and canalside view similar to the expensive **Duc de Bourgogne** next door, **'t Dreveken**, also known as **'t Huidevettershuis**, *(Huidenvettersplein 10–11; kitchen open noon–9:30 p.m., closed Tues.;* ☎ *33.95.06; moderate)* is a great choice for regional specialties. With a less historic atmosphere, but certainly in the center of things is **Den Gouden Cop** *(Steenstraat 1; inexpensive),* one of about a dozen brasseries/terrace cafes that line two sides of the **Markt**. It and most of the others offer a continuous service of soups, sandwiches, and snacks to a full meal during the day and evening. There are both outside and glassed-in dining with a view of town activity. **Restaurant Belfort** *(32 Markt; inexpensive)* is another pleasant, convenient cafe with varied dishes that include such typical local fare as asparagus soup and Dutch herring.

    Tea rooms, a name *Bruggelingen* employ, serve lighter dishes such as pancakes, snacks, and pastry, especially in the afternoon, though many also serve more substantial fare for lunch and dinner. In one of the most picturesque corners of Bruges, where the Groenerei crosses other canals, you can sit on the bricked terrace at **Uilenspiegel** *(Langestraat 2; inexpensive)* and sample a wide range of tasty snacks with a drink. At **Belle Époque** *(Zuidzandstraat 43; daily from noon through dinner;* ☎ *33.18.72; inexpensive to moderate)* there's a cozy yet chic feel to the *art nouveau* decor that accompanies the friendly service and imaginative menu (paté maison, croque monsieur, salads, waterzooi, scampi). **Bistrot De Serre** *(Simon Stevinplein 15; kitchen open daily 11 a.m.–9:15 p.m., closed Tues. year-round, Sun. Sept.– June;* ☎ *34.22.31; inexpensive)* is tucked into a garden behind an attractive square halfway between the Begijnhof and the Markt. Dine indoors or at a marble-top table in the small garden on tasty casual fare—omelettes, salads, toast Hawaii (open-face toasted cheese and pineapple sandwich), soups—or rest from nearby shopping over a beer, wine, or coffee and a dessert crepe. Not far away is **'t Keteltje** *(Oude Burg 20; daily 11 a.m.–11 p.m., closed Thurs.;* ☎ *33.29.79; inexpensive)*, where Belgian waffles and pancakes (25 varieties of sweet and savory) are a specialty.

If you're looking for a place for a drink with a view, you can't do better than **'t Klein Venetie** *(Braambergstraat 1; 10:30 a.m.–2 a.m., closed Tues. from 5:30 p.m., Wed.;* ☎ *34.01.75; inexpensive)*, which offers one of the most pleasant views in Europe, across a confluence of canals and along a converging line of gables, to the belfry. For those who want to become better acquainted with Belgium beer, the helpful bar attendants at tiny **De Garre** *(tucked away at the end of the alley located between 12 and 14 Breidelstraat; 11 a.m.–1 a.m., last call accompanied by the playing of Bolero; closed Wed.)* can certainly begin your education. Courses in beer bartending are taught by the friendly owner of **'t Brugs Beertje** *(Kemelstraat 5; 4 p.m.–1 a.m.; closed Wed.)*, which serves the largest selection of beer in Bruges, more than 300 kinds. Under such conditions, the bartenders obviously have to be prepared to help you choose your Belgian brew.

ENTERTAINMENT AND EVENTS

Bruges offers one of the most extensive programs of ★★**carillon concerts** in the world. Thanks to the talent, energy, and enthusiasm of *stadsbeiaardier* (town carillonneur) **Aimé Lombaert**, more people get to hear a carillon here than perhaps anywhere else in the world. From mid-June through Sept., hour-long concerts are played at 9 p.m. on Mon., Wed., and Sat.; from Oct. 1–mid-June, afternoon concerts are played at 2:15 p.m. on Wed. and Sat. Sundays concerts are played at 2:15 p.m. year-round. For Bruggelingen, high points of the year are the 11 p.m. concerts played by Lombaert on Christmas Eve and New Year's Eve. The annual ★★**Festival of Flanders** (July 30–Aug. 13, 1994) brings some of the continent's best classical music to Bruges in nightly competitions. Booking is strongly recommended because of local popularity. In August 1995 Bruges will stage a ★★★**Festival on the Canals** on six different nights. Historic scenes and periods are recreated in costume, music, by over 500 performers in several squares, all illuminated, continuously from 9 p.m.–midnight. It's a spectacular show for spectators, but be forewarned of crowds.

The ★★★**Procession of the Holy Blood** (on May 12 in 1994), held annually on Ascension Day, is the veneration of what is believed to be a drop or two of Christ's blood mixed with water washed from his crucified body, a relic brought to Bruges in the mid-13th century. The blood is in a rock-crystal phial which rests in a silver reliquary, presented to Bruges in 1611 by archdukes of the Spanish Netherlands Isabella and Albert. After religious services in the morning in the **Basilica of the Holy Blood** and a leisurely lunch break, celebrants carry the relic through the streets, accompanied by a costumed cast of thousands. The centuries-old tradition arose from the annual gathering of feudal lords and burghers 'round the relic to offer oaths of loyalty, and gradually evolved into a procession with the magistrates and guilds of the city in full dress for the affair. The present religious-historical affair through the decorated streets of ancient Bruges includes tableaux (groups which perform episodes from the Bible), floats, and authentically dressed groups recalling old city guilds, foreign merchants from Bruges' 14th-century golden age, the entry into Bruges of the "count of Flanders" and his richly dressed retinue of courtesans, with cortege of choirs, banners, and musical instruments. Reserved grandstand tickets on procession route available from tourist office from Feb. 1.

IN THE AREA

Damme

Tourist information, Huis De Grote Sterre, Jacob van Maerlantstraat 3; Mon.-Fri. 9 a.m.-noon, 2-5 p.m., Sat. and Sun. 2-6 p.m.; ☎ (050) 35.33.19; pop. 1,000. From its founding, Damme's history has been inextricably linked with Bruges, both the flourishing and the fall. Damme's picturesque **Marktplein** shows typical Flemish gables, and a statue of 13th-century poet Jacob van Maerlant who was born here and would have witnessed his city's great growth. The elegant **Stadhuis** *(July 1-Sept. 15 daily 10 a.m.-noon, 4-6 p.m.)* whose elegant 15th-century Gothic facade is studded with statues of counts of Flanders; on the right are the figures of the duke of Burgundy, Charles the Bold, and English princess Margaret of York, who were married in 1468 in Damme (at St. John House, Kerkstraat 4). The original tower clock of the Stadhuis dates from 1459. Several spacious, impressive rooms usually are open inside.

WHERE TO EAT

Die Drie Zilveren Kannen *(Markt 9, Damme; ☎ 35.56.77; moderate)* offers fine Flemish dishes in a decor to match; it's wise to reserve. **Ter Kloeffe Bretoens Pannekoekhuis** *(Hoogstraat 1; closed Mon. evenings, Tues.; ☎ (050) 35.41.24; inexpensive)*, a less formal, typical old beamed and tiled, choice, serves savory and sweet Brittany crepes.

GHENT

Castle of the Counts (Gravensteen)

GUIDELINES FOR GHENT

SIGHTS

A first, and lasting, impression of Ghent (*Gent* in Flemish, *Gand* in French) is of marvelous medieval structures, whose sturdy stone facades reflect well in canal waters. Considering those monuments are mostly in shades of gray, city street scenes are surprisingly vibrant. Prime sights are central, particularly the towers of **St. Bavo's Cathedral** (which contains the famed van Eyck brothers' *The Adoration of the Mystique Lamb*), the **Belfry**, and **St. Nicolaas church**—the three

225

almost aligned in the famous view of them from **St. Michiel's Bridge**. The bridge spans Ghent's former harbor, from the **Graslei**, with its magnificent row of early 13th- to 16th-century buildings, to the **Korenlei**, from which it's a short scenic walk to the **Castle of the Counts** (c.1180).

GETTING AROUND

If you arrive by train at **St. Pieter's Station**, take Tram 1 (1.5 mi/2.5 km) to **Korenmarkt**, in the center of historic Ghent (population 150,000). **Tourist Information** is in the close-by **Stadhuis**/town hall crypt. The bus, tram, trolley system (map available) covers the city well, but since Ghent's major sights are compactly located and its streets and squares warrant walking-speed appreciation, you're unlikely to make much use of it once you're in the center. **Sightseeing Line** offers a minibus tour (commentary in English on headset); horse-drawn carriages are available in season. Canal cruises, while affording some attractive perspectives, are limited in their course; much of the route must be retraced since many canals no longer connect with each other since early 20th-century filling in of some sections.

SHOPPING

As the capital of East Flanders province, Ghent has long been the main market town for a large area. Major commercial streets include **Veldstraat**, which has department and larger stores, **Volderstraat** with smaller and smarter shops, and the surrounding Kouter, Nederkouter, Zonnestraat, and Brabantdam, which all attract their share of business. Ghent has many markets: **Groentenmarkt** (food and general wares) *Mon.–Sat. a.m.*, with artists' works Sun. a.m.; **Vrijdagmarkt** (new wares) *Fri. 7 a.m.–1 p.m., Sat. 1 p.m.–6 p.m.*; **Kouter** (flowers) *daily 7 a.m.–1 p.m.*; and **St. Michielsplein** (food) *Sun. mornings.*

ENTERTAINMENT AND EVENTS

From May–Sept. all historic buildings and monuments are illuminated nightly from sunset to midnight; for the rest of year, they are illuminated each Friday and Saturday night. From late June to the end of August, **carillon concerts** are played Saturdays 9–10 p.m. on the **Belfry's** 53-bell (some *Hemony*-cast) instrument by town carillonneur Jos D'Hollander. In July and August, St. Bavo's offers **organ concerts** Thursdays at 8 p.m. Concerts are Ghent's main events in the annual Sept.–Oct. **Festival of Flanders**; St. Bavo's, the Stadhuis, and old abbeys provide memorable settings. (Schedule is available from the middle of May, ☎ *25.77.80.*) Although staged only once every five years (next in 1995), *Floralia* is an internationally attended flower show that celebrates the beauty of the blooms that annually produce good business for Ghent. Northwest of the city, *begonias* (Belgium's national flower), *azaleas,* and *roses* are cultivated in colorful fields around **Lochristi** (6 mi/9 km), the heart of the flower district where at the end of every August there's a **Begonia Festival**.

WHERE TO STAY

With the opening in the last few years of new properties in the center, Ghent now has a reasonable selection of hotels handy for tourists. However, major trade fairs and exhibitions held several times yearly at the *Palace of the Floralia/Congressgebouw* can fill them with business travelers.

WHERE TO EAT

Ghent restaurants tend toward traditional rather than trendy. You won't have trouble finding historic settings in which to sup and sip.

ARRIVING

St. Pieter's Station has twice hourly service to/from Brussels and Bruges, with Ghent more or less midway between them. There's hourly service to Antwerp and to the northeast. Boat trains meeting North Sea ferries from England at either Ostend or Zeebrugge pass through Ghent on the way to Brussels. Ghent is served by regional/international motorways (the E17 and E40), and is more or less equidistant (35 mi/60 km) from Antwerp, Brussels, Ostend, Tournai, and Lille (France).

TRAVEL TIPS

Not that you wouldn't begin your visit at the tourist office anyway, but in Ghent it's particularly helpful because several city sights (the cathedral, Stadhuis, and Cloth Hall with its multimedia *The Ghent Experience*) offer tours/screenings in English at set times, which are worth knowing when planning your touring.

GHENT IN CONTEXT

Many travelers will be more interested in Ghent's prosperous past than in its prosperous present, particularly the *appearance* of that past. The 12th century is conjured up in the sight of the moated **Castle of the Counts/Gravensteen**, which passes into the realm of fairy tales when floodlit at night. A castle probably was first built on the site by **Boudewijn (Baldwin, the Iron Arm)**, who visited Ghent from Bruges about 867. (Settlement in the area began in the 7th century with two abbeys, *St. Bavo* and *St. Pieter*, the later buildings of both surviving today.) Boudewijn's castle at the confluence of the *Lieve* and *Lys* rivers was originally built for defense against raids by Norsemen, who continued on up the *Scheldt* to Ghent after dropping in on Antwerp. But enlargements to this seat of the *Counts of Flanders* (of whom Boudewijn was the first) in the 11th and 12th centuries increasingly were made with an eye on managing the independently minded people in Ghent's cloth industry, which came to prominence during the 12th century. The basic structure of the castle we see today was completed about 1180.

Ghent's river port was a necessity from the start of its cloth industry, due to the need to import wool from England. The **Graslei**, on the right bank of the Lys, and **Korenlei** on the left, formed the central harbor; the oldest building on the Graslei, the **Staple House** (*Spijker*), dates from c. 1200. Early in the 13th century Ghent supplemented its natural inland waterways with canals, one being dug to Bruges, from which, by way of the Zwin, there was access to the North Sea.

In the 13th century, with the cloth business flourishing, Ghent experienced continued expansion—at the end of the 13th century Ghent had a larger population than Paris—but also increased political unrest, a situation that would continue to shape the city's history. Difficulties arose between the increasingly ambitious town citizen textile workers and Ghent's rich patricians (who generally remained loyal to their suzerain, the French king). Although the Counts of Flanders had granted a charter to Ghent in 1180 and added citizens' rights, such as election of town magistrates, heretofore appointed, in 1212, the economic success generated by the burghers led to their demanding even greater independence. In 1302, a contingent of Ghent workers led by **Jan Borluut** joined other Flemish workers (mostly weavers, particularly from Bruges) in the **Battle of the Golden Spurs** (see "An Historical Perspective" under "Belgium"), a confrontation with French nobility which the workers won.

In 1338, when the count of Flanders at the beginning of the Anglo-French **Hundred Years War** sided with France (thereby threatening Ghent's cloth trade, which depended heavily upon English wool), **Jacob van Artevelde** (1287–1345), a patrician who supported the merchants, took over the leadership of Ghent to protect business and made an independent alliance with English **King Edward III**. (Edward at the beginning of the Hundred Years War had declared *himself* king of France, a position van Artevelde supported.)

In the course of the alliance, Edward visited Ghent, and his third son, **John of Gaunt** (a form of *Ghent*), was born there to Queen Philippa (of Hainaut, in Wallonia) in St. Bavo's Abbey in 1340. Both Ghent merchants and England's wool growers prospered under the arrangement, but guildsmen, unsure of van Artevelde's ambitions, murdered him in 1345.

The Hundred Years War continued with various players, including pro-French **Count of Flanders Louis De Malle** and van Artevelde's son Philip, who lost his life when the French won the battle at Westrozebeke. Upon De Malle's death in 1384, because his daughter and only heir had married **Philip of Burgundy** (in Ghent's St. Bavo's Abbey), Ghent became part of the duchy of Burgundy, and Flanders as a separate county ceased to exist.

From the middle of the 14th century, the cloth industry in Ghent—and elsewhere in Flanders—began to decline, mainly due to competition from the English, who themselves had begun making cloth from their wool. But the excellent reputation of the luxurious Ghent/Flemish cloth, which was exported throughout Europe and as far afield as North Africa and the Middle East, remained a standard: **Geoffrey Chaucer** (c.1340–1400) in his *Canterbury Tales* spoke of the skill of the wife of Bath as surpassing that of the weavers of "Ipres and Gaunt" (Ypres and Ghent). And, a century later, **Jan van Eyck**, using the new oil paint medium, finally could show well enough the texture of the brilliantly colored heavy cloth in art works such as *The Ghent Altarpiece*, so that we can appreciate the quality of the famed Flemish product.

Throughout its history Ghent has been a "fighting" town, constantly striving for both town and civilian rights. As a result, construction on buildings often was interrupted by unrest. Thus, though the city center is a veritable textbook of architectural styles from the 12th to the 20th century, several important structures begun centuries ago were completed only relatively recently. The **Cloth Hall**, started early in the 15th century, was not completed in its original design until the beginning of the 20th. In the case of the **Stadhuis**, construction, begun in the late 15th century, stretched into the 18th with exterior statues added in the 19th; the result is one Renaissance facade, one late-Gothic, and assorted-era outside ornamentation.

Under the Burgundians, who took over rule near the end of the 14th century, Ghent workers didn't alter their fighting ways. In 1453, after a five-year revolt, a humiliating loss of privileges was imposed upon them by **Philip the Good**. In 1477, however, *Gentenaars* rebounded by holding Philip's granddaughter, **Mary of Burgundy**, captive until she signed the *Great Privilege* which conferred many rights back to the people. But Mary was killed in an accident soon after, and back came her widower, **Maximilian of Austria**, who, as the first of the region's Hapsburg line of rulers, subdued Ghent again. The Netherlands-born humanist **Erasmus** (c. 1466–1536) covered both positive and negative points about Gentenaars in his words: "I do not think that one could find in the whole of Christendom a town which could compare with Ghent as for its political organization or the nature of its people."

Because of their particularly impassioned positions on civil rights, Ghent citizens, even more than those in other medieval towns, treasured their **Belfry** (1321–1380) historically, the town's most important building since it served as a safe-deposit box for its charter and rights, as well as a bell tower from which to ring warnings of danger or celebration. In Ghent's belfry hung a huge bell, around whose rim appeared the words: "My name is Roeland. When I clap there is fire. When I toll there is a storm in Flanders." Roeland itself became a player in the stormy year of 1540. By then, **Emperor Charles V**, Maximilian's grandson who was born in Ghent in 1500, had become tired of his birth town's belligerence. Angered at the disorder and defiance of the Gentenaars, Charles ordered the great 12,000-pound/6,000 kg. *Roeland* removed from the belfry, an act of great symbolic significance. Then he dismantled the entire early defensive works of the city. (The 1491 medieval tower *Rabot* is all that survives.) As a result, though he was the most famous person ever born in Ghent, Charles V was disliked there for much of his lifetime.

Although by the end of the 14th century, the cloth industry had been ruined in Flanders by English competition, Ghent shipping got a new source of revenue after 1500—partly as a result of the increasing prominence of Antwerp, with whom Ghent shared the Scheldt river—from the export of grain from France. Boatmen (whose guildhalls stand on the Graslei and Korenlei) replaced cloth makers as Ghent's most important workers. The addition of the 16th-century **Corn Merchant's House** and the **Free Boatmen's Guild Hall** (1500–1531) on the Graslei reflected the new times; the forwarding and carrying trade in grain enabled Ghent to weather the loss of the cloth industry (while the Flemish cloth towns of Ypres and Bruges were not able to do so). By 1547, Ghent had cut a new canal (18.5 mi/30 km) directly north to **Terneuzen** (now in Holland), on the *Westerscheldt*, the wide Scheldt estuary that leads into the North

Sea. All was well until Ghent's port was effectively closed by Dutch demands for sole control of the Scheldt estuary in the 1648 agreement with the Spanish that settled the *Eighty Years War*. Following the fate of Antwerp, whose port also was closed, Ghent remained in decline thereafter until 1795, when the French under **Napoleon Bonaparte**, then in control of the Netherlands north and south, reopened the Scheldt.

In 1814, during the six months of negotiations that preceded the signing of the **Treaty of Ghent** (see "Stadhuis" under "What To See and Do") that ended the American-English War of 1812, U.S. participant **John Quincy Adams** lived in the city. It is said that Ghent was chosen as the site of the negotiations because of the luxury of its amenities. That luxury could be one reason why, the next year, **Louis XVIII** moved to Ghent in refuge during the *Hundred Days* (March 15–June 28, 1815) from Napoleon's return to France following his escape from Elba until his final abdication after defeat in the **Battle of Waterloo**.

Under the **United Kingdom of the Netherlands**, which put Belgium and Holland together as a single country in the European realignment that followed Waterloo, Ghent fully regained the use of its port, and expanded her sea trade. With the encouragement of Dutch King Willem I, Ghent's Terneuzen canal was expanded in 1827 to handle seagoing vessels, an important development in the city's maritime history. Because of trade with Dutch overseas colonies, Ghent remained faithful to the *House of Orange* during the **Belgian Revolution** of 1830, though it lost the business after Belgium achieved independence that year.

Although its impressive 12th-century textile trade had become history during the 14th century, in the early 19th century Ghent entrepreneurs, freed from the framework of guilds—Napoleon had disbanded them—turned again to textiles. The leaders of the thriving cotton mill business became known as "cotton barons." They were enamored of an aristocratic life style: buying titles, marrying into old families, beginning art collections, and building sumptuous town mansions. Fine French-style facades from the era still line **Jan Breydelstraat**, **Koningstraat**, **Kouter**, and **Veldstraat**.

An interesting tale of industrial espionage plays a prominent part in Ghent's second textile success story. **Lieven Bauwens** (1769–1822), a tanner's son and later burgomaster, single-handedly revolutionized the cotton industry in Ghent. In the year 1789, while living in Manchester, England, Bauwens managed to "come by" a copy of the plan for the **spinning jenny** power loom, which, together with parts for an entire machine, he smuggled out of England hidden in sacks of coffee. He also enticed two technicians to join him in Ghent. (The spinning jenny, consisting of a number of spindles turned by a common wheel, worked by hand—the first machine on which a number of threads could be spun at once—was invented (c. 1767) by **James Hargreaves**, a Lancashire, England, weaver.)

Back in Ghent, Bauwens immediately set up a factory featuring his new acquisition. Such was the spinning jenny's impact that in the single subsequent decade, Ghent employees in the cotton-spinning industry jumped from next-to-none to 10,000, many to be housed in makeshift workers' camps. In England, Lieven Bauwens was sentenced to death in absentia and buried in effigy. In Ghent, he's honored with a statue on a square named for him (near St. Bavo cathedral). Belgian historians gave some slight recompense to England by dubbing Ghent the "Manchester of the Continent." A sample of the smuggled spinning jenny is on exhibit at the **Castle of the Counts**, an appropriate location since the venerable structure was enlisted for duty as a cotton factory in the 19th century.

Ghent boomed in the industrial revolution, its population trebling between 1801 and 1900 (from 55,000 to 160,000). As the number of factories increased, so did the overcrowded conditions of the workers. Historic buildings, as well as workers, were sacrificed to the system. So was the Scheldt river, parts of which were covered, its main course diverted out of the center of Ghent. With the city sublimated to industry, its mass of workers pulled from the surrounding countryside and herded into squalid living conditions in back streets, it's little wonder that the socialist movement in Flanders began and became centered in Ghent. With the workers' movement related to the **Flemish Movement**, it was an achievement when, in 1930, the *University of Ghent*—which Willem, king of the United Netherlands had ordered established in 1817—finally became a Flemish-speaking institution.

After 1960, Ghent's economic future focused beyond textiles on the chemical and steel industries, and particularly its port. In 1968 a new lock at Terneuzen made it possible for vessels as large as 60,000 tons to use the canal, and Ghent's tonnage has increased ten fold in the intervening years. The port is to be further expanded so that by the turn of the century ships of 125,000 tons will be able to discharge goods at its inland terminals. Ghent, Belgium's second port, has a different focus from the international outlook of its first, with Antwerp concentrating on incoming vessels that discharge cargoes to be channelled to the European hinterland by barge, road, and rail. Ghent's port provides 50,000 jobs (directly and indirectly) for the greater city population of 250,000.

While patently respecting their past, Gentenaars know that the city and its citizens have always been at their best when industry is doing well, which it is today. But never again, as in the 19th century, will Ghent neglect its historic gables at the expense of business. The medieval **Castle of the Counts** will never again have to house industry within its walls: the **Dienst Monumentenzorg en Stadsarcheologie** (city department for the care of buildings) will see to that.

GUIDEPOSTS

Telephone Code 091

Tourist Information • Crypt of Stadhuis (Town Hall; April–Oct., daily 9:30 a.m.–6:30 p.m.; Nov.-Mar., daily, 9:30 a.m.–4:30 p.m.; ☎ *24.15.55.*

Trains • Main station **St. Pieter's** in SW of city, 1.5 mi./2.5 km from center.

Bus/Tram Info • ☎ *30.41.95.*

Minibus Tours • Sightseeing Line minibus tours, departure from Belfry; schedule, reservations from Bruges office: ☎ *(050) 31.13.55.*

Canal Cruises Bootjes van Gent • open boats, Korenlei, ☎ *23.17.23*; **Benelux**, open and covered boats, Graslei, ☎ *21.84.51*; Easter to end Oct.

Post Office • Main office: Korenmarkt.

WHAT TO SEE AND DO

Ghent's major sights are covered more or less in order of their significance. Conveniently, the most important also are the most centrally located. From the end of April through Oct., and Fri. and Sat. the rest of the year, Ghent's historic buildings are illuminated nightly from 8 p.m. (or dark, which can be as late as 10 p.m. in June, July, and Aug., 9 p.m. in May, Sept.). This makes it difficult to see the ★★★ impressively floodlit **Castle of the Counts**, Graslei, etc. unless you overnight in the city.

St. Bavo's Cathedral ★★
St. Baafs Plein; April 1–Sept. 30, Mon.-Sat., 9:30 a.m.–noon, 2–6 p.m., Sun. 1–6 p.m.; Oct. 1–Mar. 31, Mon.– Sat., 10:30 a.m.–noon, 2:30–4 p.m., Sun., 2–5 p.m.; admission fee of BF30 *includes crypt.* Relatively ordinary on the outside, St. Bavo's is anything but inside, with its admirable proportions and rich ornamentation. The Ghent-born future **Emperor Charles V** was christened here on March 7, 1500. Claiming first attention for most visitors to St. Bavo's, whose choir dates from the 13th century, nave and transepts from the 15th, is the world-famous medieval masterpiece by **Jan** and **Hubert van Eyck**,

★ ★ ★ *The Adoration of the Mystical Lamb* (1432), a 24-panel polyptych also referred to as *The Ghent Altarpiece*. Recently, it has been restored and relocated within the church (a controversial move, many preferring the naturally lit Donors' Chapel where the altarpiece had been displayed for most of its more than five and a half centuries to the artificial lighting at the new position). An improvement for viewers is that now, unlike in the past, they can walk at their own pace completely around the work, whose side panels are now extended out flat. Perhaps the profit from some of *your* travelers' checks helped American Express pay the bill for cleaning the 24 panels (12 paintings each on the front and back), and framing them under protective glass.

Famed in part because it represents a breakthrough in northern European painting style and technique (see Art under "The Belgian Cultural Legacy") with its Flemish "primitive" realism, and very early use of oil mixed with pigments (which greatly heightened the color and texture possible), the *Altarpiece* generally is thought to have been designed by Hubert, the elder van Eyck brother, in 1420. Hubert died in 1426 before he could contribute much to the execution of the altar retable. His brother Jan, considered the superior painter, completed the 24 panels by 1432. The wealthy childless donors of the work, Joos Vijd and his wife Elizabeth Borluut, appear in rich red robes on a panel beneath the *Annunciation*. Jan van Eyck was honored in his lifetime for this and other paintings, being made both court painter and a member of the *Order of the Golden Fleece* by Duke of Burgundy Philip the Good.

The Adoration of the Mystical Lamb is a compilation of Christian, cultural, social, and physical science beliefs about the world at the time of its creation, and it was conceived to assist the faithful by depicting graphically the hidden meaning of the Holy Mass. The center panel shows the slaughtered lamb, on the altar, dripping blood into a cup; the panel above shows Christ enthroned. Other panels show people from all walks of life in the world forming a community of praise and thanksgiving. The van Eycks created over 300 distinct individual faces on the 24 panels, and more than 200 species of flowers, trees, and shrubs are readily identifiable due to their realistic detail. Panels showing music being made recall the centuries-old sentiment that "singing is twice praying, playing is thrice praying."

If an intriguing past adds to a painting's allure, it's little wonder *The Mystical Lamb* is renowned. The 15th-century work had a first brush with destruction in the 1500s, when ultraconservative Calvinists came to St. Bavo's during the **Reformation's** *Iconoclasm* with the mutilation of art works and "graven images" on their mind; the altarpiece survived by being hidden high in the cathedral tower. During the Counter-Reformation, art collector Philip II wanted to acquire the painting for his collection, but in the end it was spared shipment to Spain. Hapsburg Holy Roman Emperor Joseph II, while ruler of the Austrian

Netherlands (1765–1790), carried his modesty to the ridiculous degree of ordering the side-panel nude figures of *Adam* and *Eve* replaced with ones in which the parties were clothed in animal skins. (Adam and Eve were "unclothed" again after his death, and Joseph II's versions now hang near the west entrance.) In 1795, French forces shipped all 24 panels to Paris; fortunately, after the 1815 defeat of Napoleon at Waterloo, they were returned to St. Bavo's. The cathedral itself, having made copies, sold the original side panels in 1816 to pay for church restoration. A British antique dealer acquired them, subsequently selling several to **Kaiser Willem I**, who spliced the double-sided panels so they could be displayed along a wall in **Berlin's Imperial Museum**. The nude Adam and Eve panels eventually were purchased in 1861 by **Brussels' Museum of Ancient Art**, which later returned them to St. Bavo's as part of a multinational plan to reconstruct the masterpiece under its home roof. The 1919 *Treaty of Versailles* at the end of World War I ordered the panels that remained in Germany returned to Ghent, and in 1920 the whole work was once again set up in the cathedral.

Perhaps the strangest episode in the legend of the *Lamb* began the night of April 10, 1934, when the *Righteous Judges* and *John the Baptist* panels disappeared. Eventually, a ransom note for BF 1 million arrived, and *John* was recovered from a luggage locker in Brussels' Gare du Nord. But, to this day, the original *Judges* is missing, the only reference to it since being an inaudible whisper from a man on his death bed to his priest. A once wealthy Ghent burgher and former canon at St. Bavo's admitted stealing the panels for ransom, but the priest could not make out the words of his final confession about the fate of the *Judges*. In 1941, the panel was replaced by a copy made by artist **Jef Vanderveken**, who was so good at his job that, not wanting the copy to be mistaken for the original he included the features of the then Belgian king, Leopold III, in the piece.

After Belgium was occupied in 1940 in World War II, Nazi officer **Gehring** came to Ghent specifically to see *The Adoration of the Mystical Lamb*. He showed so much interest in the altarpiece that, after his visit, the bishop hid and then smuggled it out of Belgium to the town of Pau in unoccupied France. However, when the Nazis reached that region of France in 1942, they took possession and shipped it to a castle in German Bavaria. Near the end of the war, Hitler ordered it and other religious art works taken to a salt mine near Salzburg, Austria, on the pretense of protecting them from the approaching "atheistic" Russians who "would have blown them up." American Army soldiers in Austria at the end of the war stumbled across the stolen art. *The Mystic Lamb*, after restoration in Brussels, was joyously welcomed back to St. Bavo's which proclaimed the occasion a feast day.

St. Bavo's has other important pieces, among which are four pillar-shaped *copper candlesticks* (at the tomb of Bishop Allamont, d. 1673)

that bear the arms of England's Henry VIII, by whose order and for
whose tomb at St. George's Chapel at Windsor they originally were
created in 1530. They came into the hands of Oliver Cromwell, who
sold them to a Bishop Triest, who presented them to St. Bavo's. In the
Rubens' Chapel is Pieter Paul's monumental *Conversion of St. Bavo* (the
saint's face is said to be a self-portrait of the artist), commissioned
directly by the cathedral in 1624. The striking mid-nave white-mar-
ble-entwined-with-dark-oak *pulpit* (**Laurent Delvaux**, 1741–1745) is a
sculptural testament to Old Man Time, who is being awakened by a
trumpet-tooting angel. The *Triptych of the Calvary* (1464) by **Justus
van Gent**, in the 12th-century Romanesque crypt, is considered one of
the church's finest treasures. St. Bavo's organ sports a sumptuous
1653 baroque-style case. Outside, in a small square behind the cathedral, is a bronze sculpture honoring the brothers van Eyck, shown
seated on a bench, their heads wreathed in laurel.

Gravensteen/Castle of the Counts

*Sint-Veerleplein; daily April 1–Sept. 30, 9 a.m.–5:15 p.m., from Oct.
1–Mar. 31 same hours but closed Mon.;* ☎ *25.93.06; important elements
identified in English.* This magnificent, almost unrivaled example of a
feudal fortress of the counts of Flanders with its massive medieval
shape rising from the reflective waters of its moat, was built about
1180 by **Philip of Alsace** and follows the style of crusaders' fortified
castles in Syria. The counts' need for a castle was less for the protection of the town and more for control over demanding citizen-work-
ers in Ghent's rapidly expanding cloth industry. Gravensteen was, in
fact, stormed by such individuals in 1302 during the period of the *Battle of the Golden Spurs*, and again in 1338 by weavers led by Jacob van
Artevelde. In 1349, after occupation by 14 of his fellows, the count of
Flanders abandoned the undoubtedly dark and dreary Gravensteen for
the airier Gothic **Prinsenhof** (which no longer stands). From that
time, the castle ended its military role, though retaining ceremonial
functions. In subsequent centuries, it served as Mint and High Court
of Justice. Before becoming a cotton-spinning factory from 1797 to
1887, it served as a prison, and its extensive collection of torture
instruments, painful even in appearance, date from its prison days and
are displayed throughout the rooms. Between 1894 and 1913 the
Castle of the Counts was restored, and thereafter opened to the public. Although it's possible to find them closed due to more recent restoration, several rooms in the count's residence tower (*donjon*) usually
are open. They include the vaulted *Audience Chamber* where the
Council of Flanders sat for 300 years. From the *Upper Hall*, winding
stairs lead to the roof, from which there's a fine view across Ghent.
The *Great Hall* was the setting for a huge banquet for the seventh
chapter meeting of the *Order of the Golden Fleece* given by Philip the
Good in 1445. Parts of the 9th-century castle formerly on the site survive and can be seen in the cellars of the keep. When leaving the
Gravensteen, go beyond its moat to the corner of Gewad and Burg-

straat (across the street from **Hotel Gravensteen**) to see the 1559 Renaissance facade of the ★**House of the Crowned Heads**, which has portraits of all the Counts of Flanders from Boudewijn to Philip II.

Graslei   ★★★

The Graslei is the site of the old port of Ghent (today, the departure point for cruises of the city's remaining canals). Easily identifiable midway (No. 15) along the row of impressive quayside buildings is **Spijker** or **Koornstapelhuis** (public grain warehouse), the oldest (c. 1200), also the plainest, in Romanesque style, where grain was held as customs duty payment in kind. Also a standout is the 1682 tiny **Tolhuisje** (little customs house). On **Korenlei**, opposite and from which there is a fine view of the Graslei with its buildings reflected in the water the most elegant facade is No. 9, the former 16th-century brewery **De Zwaene** (the swan), on which medallions show swans swimming away from each other.

Vleeshuis/Meat Hall   ★

Groetenmarkt. Built in 1406–1410, and restored in 1912, this long attractive structure of local sandstone included an indoor market for the sale of meat, butchers' guildhall and chapel, and small houses against the south facade where the poor could collect the bowels of slaughtered animals. Lying opposite on the *Lys River* is the **Vishal/Fish Hall** *(Sint-Veerleplein 5)*, reconstructed after an 1872 fire. The monumental baroque entrance gate has a sculpture of *Neptune* and allegorical figures representing the rivers *Lys* and *Scheldt*. Past the Vishal and **Gravensteen** is the lovely ★★**Lievekaai**, a once-busy quay on the large turning-basin of the 13th-century canal—whose waters surround the Gravensteen—that connected Ghent to the sea; today, its waters are a quiet romantic spot, lined with step-gabled houses and weeping willows.

Belfroi/Belfry   ★

Sint-Baafsplein; daily mid-March to mid-Nov. 10 a.m.–noon, 2–5:30 p.m.; elevator. Begun in 1313, Ghent's medieval municipal tower, city symbol of power and autonomy, was finished in 1380 and topped off with a dragon-shaped weathercock. One of the purposes of a belfry was to safeguard town privileges or charters: Ghent's were secured in the *Secret* room under triple lock and key in a solid oak chest. The belfry was named for the bells hung there, which city watchmen would sound in alarm. In 1315, **Roeland** was cast as Ghent's stormbell; weighing 12,000 pounds; it is said to have taken seven strong men to swing Roeland to make it ring. Charles V, displeased with Ghent citizens' rebelliousness, had Roeland removed from the belfry in 1540, though eventually it again took up its position in the tower. In 1659, town fathers melted Roeland down; the vast amount of metal thus produced enabled the famed Hemony brothers to cast a complete 37-bell carillon. (Those bells cast from the original Roeland still form the heart of Ghent's now-expanded carillon, considered one of the best in Belgium.) The largest of the bells cast in 1659, Roeland's heir, rang the hour for Ghent's belfry clock in its G-pitch. Today, it is exhibited on **Emile Braunplein** at the foot of the belfry, having cracked in 1914 when the tower bells were being switched to electric power. The third **Roeland** to hang high in the tower was cast in 1984.

Adjoining the belfry is the ★**Lakenhal/Cloth Hall**, where a 30-minute multimedia show, *The Ghent Experience*, is given (English language showings have been at 10:50 a.m. and 3:20 p.m., but confirm times at tourist information next door). The artistic slide-show triptych, presented in a plush-seat theater, reveals the city's pleasing present face while at the same time offering an historical perspective. The **Cloth Hall**, itself a symbol of Ghent's substantial success in the earliest days of Europe's textile industry was begun in 1425, though with fortunes changed, not completed until this century. Once serving as a place of assembly for wool and cloth merchants, the restored Gothic ★**underground hall**, divided into three aisles by 20 pillars, today is a restaurant. (See "Where to Eat, Raadskelder.")

Stadhuis/Town Hall   ★

On the corner of Botermarkt and Hoogpoort; guided visits in English Mon. to Fri. 4 p.m., meet at tourist information, Stadhuis crypt. The Stadhuis facade shows several architectural styles: flamboyant Gothic (by **Waghemakere** and **R. Keldermans**) fronts the Hoogpoort, a sober Renaissance style employed during the Calvinist period faces Botermarkt, with baroque and empire style elements finally finishing the whole in the 17th and 18th centuries. The spread-out construction, from 1321 to 1750, resulted in part from city politics and policies. The interior, viewed only on guided tours, is best noted for the ★★**Pacificatiezaal**, the room in which the *Pacification of Ghent*—meant to restore order after the Reformation outrages between the Catholics and Protestants—was signed on December 8, 1576. The event is noted by a wall plaque; another announces that here for six months in 1814 meetings took place between England and the United States (represented by **John Quincy Adams**) to arrive at the terms for the *Treaty of Ghent* to end the **War of 1812**. A second name for the great wood-beamed, stained glass windowed room is the **Tribunal Hall**, since the **Court of Justice** sat here. The immense floor of 2,401 polished light-and-dark-toned stones is laid out in a **maze**. One of the punishments meted out by the court was "humiliation," which meant that in front of the 13 aldermen and other representatives, the guilty person had to make his way on his knees from one end of the room to the other, and retracing his route if he wound up at a "dead-end" in the maze. (The shortest successful route is 500 meters/0.3 mile.) In the **Hall of Honors** hangs an impressive portrait of Vienna's Maria Theresa in a gown made all of lace. The dress, made by orphan girls of Ghent, was a present to the Hapsburg empress, who in turn presented Ghent with this painting of herself wearing the impressive attire. The

Troonzaal or throne room, a Gothic hall in which the Ghent city council now meets, is hung with huge historic paintings.

Sint Niklaaskerk

The third of Ghent's acclaimed trio of towers (the others being the Belfry and St. Bavo's) is atop **St. Niklaas Church** (Korenmarkt), next to the Belfry. The church, built beginning in the 13th century, is Belgium's best example of the Scheldt Gothic style. Since 1960 it has been undergoing extensive exterior restoration, and you may still find it closed to the public.

St. Niklaas is steps from one end of ★★**St. Michiel's Bridge**, whose fixed version, though dating only from 1909, is Ghent's most monumental bridge with a fine lantern and sculpture of St. Michiel midway. On the far side of the bridge, which crosses the old harbor from the Graslei to the Korenlei, is the sober Brabantine Gothic **St. Michiel's Church**. Its tower cannot be included in Ghent's skyline since it never was finished. The church, begun in 1440, the era from which it gets its spacious late-Gothic style, was officially completed in 1648. Among many paintings inside, the most noted is Anthony Van Dyck's *Crucifixion*.

Vrijdagmarkt

This square still hosts the Friday market as its name suggests, but from medieval times it also has been the center of political life in the city, serving as the setting for forums and foment for the tradesmen whose former guild houses front it. The dramatic bronze figure (1863) in the center is **Jacob van Artevelde**, who became a martyr in civilian confrontations in 1345. The turreted **Toreken** (1460) at the southeast corner was the Tanners Guild Hall, today a municipal building. A bell in the tower used to be rung to announce the opening of the market. Standing out among older facades is the monumental **Ons Huis, Socialistische Werkersvereneigingen** (Our House, Socialist Workers Unions), built c. 1900 in the art nouveau style.

Just off *Vrijdagmarkt* is **Mad Meg/Dulle Griet** (on *Groot Kanonplein*). This 16-foot/5-meter, 15th-century cannon of wrought iron, weighing 35,000 pounds/16,000 kg, used to shoot heavy stone balls with an ear-shattering sound. Today, Meg sits silently beside the peaceful, picturesque ★★**Kraanlei**, whose canal-front houses, dating as far back as the Renaissance and featuring many ornamental details, drop straight into the water. At Kraanlei 63, in 18 beautifully restored 14th-century former almshouses, is the **Museum of Folklore** *(daily April 1–Oct. 31, 9 a.m.–12:30 p.m., 1:30–5:30 p.m.; Nov. 1–Mar. 31, 10 a.m.–noon, 1–5 p.m., closed Mon.; condensed guide in English)*. The series of rooms in the museum show how life was lived by typical Gentenaars, particularly craftspeople, in the 19th century. Worth a look at from the outside even if you don't have time to delve around inside.

Museum voor Schoen Kunsten/Fine Arts Museum ★

Nicolaas de Liemaeckereplein 3; daily, except Mon., 9 a.m.–12:30 p.m., 1:30– 5:30 p.m. Many major Belgian and Dutch artists are represented in this broad-ranging collection whose coverage goes back to the Flemish primitives. Highlights include two works by **Hieronymus Bosch** (1474–1516) of his name saint *St. Hieronymus* and the *Bearing of the Cross*; the *Stigmata of St. Francis of Assisi* by **Rubens**; and *The Village Lawyer* by **Pieter Breugel the Younger**. Also of interest are paintings from the 20th-century *School of St. Martens-Latem* (Latem is a suburb of Ghent), whose members include **Gustave De Smet** and **Jan Brusselsmans**, as well as several works by **James Ensor**.

Another museum which, like the Fine Arts Museum, is outside the old center of Ghent in the region of St. Pieter's Station, the **Bijlokemuseum** *(Godshuizenlaan 2; daily, except Mon., 9 a.m.–12:30 p.m., 1:30–5:30 p.m.)*. One of Ghent's several ancient abbeys, this of the Cistercian sisters, is notable especially for the beautiful brick Gothic facades of the 14th-century dormitory and refectory (with molded brick ornamentation). The interior of the house of the abbess has been reconstructed in authentic Ghent style. Its other name, the **Museum of Antiquities**, is rather a misnomer for its collections of everyday items, weapons, porcelain, and Chinese art. The nearby **Abbey of St. Bavo** *(Gandastraat; daily, except Mon., 9 a.m.–12:30 p.m., 1:30–5:30 p.m.)* is most interesting for the building, a 12th-century Romanesque refectory and lavatory and ancient cloister, though a **lapidary museum** (with precious stones, mosaics, ornamental pavings and ancient architectural ornaments) has been located there since 1882. The abbey was the site selected by Charles V for a citadel to be built to check the rebellious city after an insurrection against him in 1540; he destroyed the abbey church and used the domestic buildings as barracks. The fortress remained in use until the end of the 18th century, after which much of it was dismantled. The abbey oversees the **Museum voor Sierkunst/ Museum of Decorative Arts** *(Jan Breydelstraat 5; same days, hours as St. Bavo)*, which occupies a 1754 former mansion of the De Coninck family, with fine period woodcarving, furniture, and ceramics.

WHERE TO STAY

All the properties included below are located in the center of historic Ghent. Since the *usual* overnight traveler to Ghent is business oriented, inquire about special hotel rates and packages at weekends.

EXPENSIVE

St. Jorishof (Cour Saint-Georges) ★★★

Botermarkt 2, B-9000; ☎ *24.24.24, FAX 24.26.40.* A hostelry from its beginnings in 1228 (making it, some say, Europe's oldest hotel), St. Jorishof today sports a more modern, 16th-century, stepped-gable facade. Used as a guildhall by Ghent's *Crossbows* and by the *States-*

General of Flanders for its meetings in the 15th century, here on Feb. 11, 1477, **Mary of Burgundy** was forced to sign Ghent's *Great Privilege*. On this occasion the Lion of Flanders symbol was carved into the monumental mantlepiece of the balconied **Gothic Hall**, today one of Ghent's most popular restaurants (gastronomic fare, decor of stained glass, dark wood). **Emperor Charles V**, born in Ghent in 1500, was a frequent guest at the hotel later in his life, and **Emperor Napoleon** stayed here in 1805. All 36 rooms, most of which are in a modern annex in the hotel's inner courtyard, have pleasant traditional decor, bath and/or shower and toilet, TV, telephone, automatic wake-up, and most have a minibar. Elevator; parking; major credit cards. Hotel closed last 3 weeks of July, 2 weeks beginning Christmas Day.

Novotel Gent Centrum

Goudenleeuwplein 5; ☎ *24.22.30, FAX 24.32.95.* This modern 117-room chain hotel, located by the Belfry, has been created behind a preserved 14th-century facade. The basic bedrooms have bath, TV, telephone, individually controlled heat. The hotel's public rooms are light and airy, and include a restaurant, garden terrace, and bar that's become a popular local meeting place. There's also a swimming pool, sauna. Parking; wheelchair access; night reception staff.

MODERATE

Hotel Gravensteen

Jan Breydelstraat 35, B-9000; ☎ *25.11.50, FAX 25.18.50.* A friendly welcome awaits at the elegant marble entryway of this well-restored 1865 second empire-style mansion that once belonged to one of Ghent's textile merchants. It's located across from The Castle of the Counts, doors from the Decorative Arts Museum, and a single attractive block from the Graslei. The 17 comfortable, contemporarily furnished rooms all have bath/shower, toilet, TV, telephone, minibar, and individual heat control; buffet breakfast (included) is served in a room facing the back garden. Ask for access to the hotel's top-floor *belvedere* that overlooks the Castle of the Counts, magically illuminated at night. Elevator; parking; major credit cards; year-round weekend rates, discounts during the week—Dec.–Jan. and July–Aug.

Erasmus

Poel 25; ☎ *24.21.95, FAX 33.42.41.* This recent addition to Ghent's central city hotel scene is situated in a restored 1593 townhouse. Each of the 11 rooms is individually antique-decorated. There's a back garden for outside breakfasts in summer, and a breakfast room and bar in the cellar. Two stories; no elevator.

Ibis Gent

Limburgstraat 2, B-9000; ☎ *33.00.00, in U.S. and Canada* ☎ *800-221-4542, FAX 33.10.00.* This recent modern addition to Ghent's old center hotel stock is almost inexpensive and wonderfully situated a half-block from the cathedral, and an equal distance from a small canal. All 120 contemporary rooms come with bathroom, toilet, TV, telephone; a few are wheelchair accessible. In the lobby are a restaurant (continental breakfast included), bar, and flower shop. Parking; major credit cards.

WHERE TO EAT

Waterzooi, a chicken or fish soup/stew with vegetables, is Ghent's foremost specialty, with *Gentse hutsepot,* a meat stew, and *stoverij,* steak and kidney flavored with beer, also readily available. *Rabbit* comes young and older: the first with prunes, the later as jugged hare. *Mokken,* a small round cake made of flour and syrup, is a local treat, as is almond-bread and rye bread with currants. A spicy Ghent tradition is *Tierenteyn,* a locally made (for 200 years) dijon-style mustard, that's sold in a shop on Groetenmarkt.

Jan Breydel *(Jan Breydelstraat 10;* ☎ *25.62.87; moderate),* just steps from the *Castle of the Counts,* offers relaxed garden-greenery elegance, showing good taste and a delicate touch in the decor as well as the cuisine. There's a priority on fresh ingredients, seafood, and regional specialties. At **Graaf van Egmond** *(St. Michielsplein 21; open daily;* ☎ *25.07.27; moderate downstairs, inexpensive upstairs),* if you're lucky and get a table by the window, you'll enjoy a wonderful view of Ghent's famed towers and the *Graslei.* Downstairs in the delightful c. 1200 townhouse with such Flemish dishes as *carbonnade flamande* (beef stew with beer) and, in season, sensational *asparagus à la flamande* are served. The grill upstairs—same view—offers simpler fare. **Het Coornmetershuys** *(Graslei 12; open lunch through evening;* ☎ *23.49.71; moderate; light lunch, inexpensive),* tucked upstairs behind a 14th-century facade on Ghent's gorgeous *Graslei,* serves Flemish specialties as well as other daily choices to the strains of classical music (music selections are also listed in the menu) in a room whose walls are decorated with musical instruments. In addition to full dinners and light lunches, pancakes, snacks, and pastries are served, so it makes a good refreshment stop even for coffee. With the name **Waterzooi** *(Sint-Veerleplein 2; closed Tues. evening, Wed.;* ☎ *25.05.63; inexpensive)* this could be where you decide to try Ghent's celebrated fish (the original ingredient) or chicken (today, a well-established alternative) stew with vegetables; portions will please your palate and your purse. The **Raadskelder** *(Sint-Baafsplein; open daily 9:30 a.m.–1 a.m.;* ☎ *25.43.34; inexpensive)* is the 15th-century, vaulted cellar of the cloth hall that adjoins the belfry; you can sit in church pews and pause over a cup of coffee or four-course tourist menu. It's large and caters to crowds (you could get caught with a busload of tourists), but the fare is fine, and since you're bound to pass it in your sightseeing at least stick your head in and see the setting.

The **Patershol quarter,** located near the Castle of the Counts, as well as being an interesting district that retains a medieval street pattern. and after long neglect now is being restored, is a neighborhood known for its restaurants. Since many of the buildings in the area were small to begin with, so are the restaurants, and thus reservations are in order. **By den Wyzen en den Zot** *(Hertogstraat 8; noon–2:30 p.m., dinner from 6:30 p.m., closed Sun.,*

Mon.; ☎ *23.42.30; moderate)* serves up its fish and meat dishes in three beamed rooms in this 17th-century, gabled, brick, corner house. **Valentijn** *(Rode Koningstraat 1; open noon–2:30 p.m., 7–9:30 p.m., closed Sat. lunch, Sun., Mon.;* ☎ *25.04.29; inexpensive, special seasonal monthly menu moderate)* includes traditional dishes (*waterzooi*, eels in green sauce) among its offerings to guests seated in the attractive brick-walled space. **Amadeus** *(Plotersgracht 8; daily 6 p.m.–midnight, Sun. from noon;* ☎ *33.27.74; inexpensive),* which bills itself as a spare-rib restaurant, is darkish and cozy with lots of beveled glass, wood, and old tiles; tables are covered with red and white oilskin, but the napkins are cloth.

Ghent cafes with character include **Oud Middelhuis** *(Graslei 6),* which gives you a chance to step behind one of the Graslei's famous facades. This is one from the 17th century; some 300 beers (8 on tap) are listed as being available. In the c. 1439 setting of **De Dulle Griet** *(Vrijdagmarkt 50; daily noon–1 a.m.;* ☎ *24.24.55; inexpensive)* only 250 sorts of beer are served, but that includes all of Belgium's Trappist-and Abbey-produced brews, in a genuine pub setting: mugs hanging above the bar, kegs for tables. If you decide to dine (reservations suggested), there's a restaurant upstairs with scenes of old Ghent on the walls, dark beams, and a view onto historic *Vrijdagmarkt.*

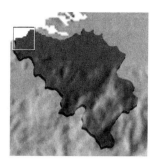

THE BELGIAN COAST

Belgium's 40-mile/65-km. North Sea coast, slanting northeast to southwest from Holland to France, lies entirely within the province of West Flanders. In the 12th and 13th centuries, much of it lay under water at high tide; only in the 14th and 15th centuries did the Belgian coast take its current shape. The wide beaches at low tide (up to 2,000 ft/600 meters in some spots) attest to the flatness of the land, much of which is polder, kept dry by the extensive use of dikes. Perhaps surprisingly, Belgium's seaside towns are sunnier than those inland, even one as nearby as Bruges. Many Belgians take summer holidays on their own beaches, but Germans, French, and the British join them; the Dutch are less likely to because of their own fine sandy shores in Zeeland just up the coast. Despite its limited length, Belgium's North Sea coast has an unbroken string of resorts with piers, promenades, and seaside recreational opportunities; each with a separate character that tends to pull in a different compatible socio-economic crowd. Most summer visitors do not come to the Belgian coast for culture, but overseas travelers may be interested in the area's isolated and interesting artistic attractions. Then again, if you're suffering from a surfeit of fine art, you can find solace by putting sand between your toes during solitary walks on Belgium's firm beaches or soft dunes, knowing all the while that you're never far from a cool drink or fine meal along any of the shop and restaurant-lined seaside promenades.

GUIDELINES FOR THE BELGIAN COAST

SIGHTS

Many area attractions are scenic: sand dunes, broad beaches, nature reserves, sea, all with the hoped-for accompaniment of sun. **De Panne**, whose beach stretches southwest into France to **Dunkirk**, (*Dunkerque*), is renowned for restaurants. Just north at **St. Idesbald** is the home and museum, with the lifelong works of *Belgian surrealist painter*, **Paul Delvaux**. Shrimp are big in **Oostduinkerke-aan-Zee**, where the now-only-for-tourists, horseback fishermen work. *Queen of the Coast* **Ostend** retains something of its grande dame air, still welcoming the passenger and car ferries from England that in the 19th century made it the most British beachhead in Belgium. Ostend fishermen maintain a fleet, fish auction, and market that add color to the hotel and restaurant-lined waterfront. Ostend *symbolist artist* **James Ensor** left a studio in his house and artwork in the local museum. Continuing up the coast, **Da Haan** has an especially broad and safe swimming beach that's sought out by families with children, while **Blankenburge**, once a small fishing village, has become the liveliest location, (especially popular with holiday makers who enjoy dancing and other night life). **Knokke-Heist**, at the northeast end, is by far the most fashionable resort on Belgium's coast, with its *boutiques, galleries,* and *casino*. Gambling is technically against Belgian law, but four casinos flourish on the coast: in addition to Knokke, at Ostend, Blankenburge, and Middelkerke. All have restaurants.

GETTING AROUND

Knokke-Heist, Blankenburge, Zeebrugge, and Ostend are served by **trains** from Brussels through Bruges; otherwise, a **car** is necessary to explore the coast. Modern **coastal trams** are convenient if you have the time; there's half-hourly service in summer from Knokke via Zeebrugge to Ostend, and from Ostend to De Panne (approximately 70 minutes from Ostend to either end of the coast). As at beach resorts everywhere, the coastal road (not always in sight of the sea) can be crowded in summer. **Cycle paths** in dunes and **walking paths** in nature reserves are well signposted.

SHOPPING

Ostend is the main town on the Belgian coast, with the largest selection of stores. Upmarket boutiques and art galleries are found in **Knokke**. Shops in both Ostend and Knokke are open year round, also many on Sundays. Elsewhere one finds the usual resort and souvenir shops in season; they're often open seven days a week and closed completely out of season.

ENTERTAINMENT AND EVENTS

Carrying on tradition for the tourists, the **horseback, shrimp fishermen** appear about low tide in the morning (check exact time locally) at **Oostduinkerke-aan-Zee** in July and August, on sturdy Brabant farm horses. (The tradition, it's said, began as early as the late 1400s when farmers, needing to supplement meager earnings, put their horsepower to work dragging nets through the sea.) At the **Knokke casino**, concerts are performed by internationally known entertainers and musical ensembles, and exhibitions are frequent fare. In summer the **World Press Photo Exhibit** and **art exhibition**, featuring well-known and new talent, make annual appearances. **Ostend's casino** has varied entertainers and entertainment throughout the year.

WHERE TO STAY

The most plentiful choice of better quality hotels is found in Knokke-Heist. Elsewhere along the coast are plenty of three-star properties, a sprinkling of two- and four-star hotels, and a number of *pensions*, many close out of season. In season, especially from late July to early September, when making a reservation be sure to establish whether accommodations are *en pension* (required payment for dinner in the hotel restaurant), and whether there's a minimum-length stay.

WHERE TO EAT

You can choose an eatery with confidence anywhere along the coast. In this resort area for food-loving Belgians, an establishment that didn't deliver much-better-than-decent dishes wouldn't be in business long. Naturally, fresh fish and seafood (especially mussels and the small North Sea "gray" shrimp) are specialties.

ARRIVING

Passenger/car ferries and the speedier hovercraft sail a number of times daily around the clock and year-round between England's channel port of Dover and Belgium's Ostend and Zeebrugge; somewhat less regular service sails to/from Folkestone, Felixstowe, and Hull.

IN THE AREA

Inland from the southwest end of Belgium's coast, from De Panne via Veurne, is **Ypres/Ieper** (pronounced EE'pe), most remembered as the center in World War I of the muddy, bloody Flanders *battle-*

fields where poppies blow. Centuries earlier, Ypres (together with Bruges and Ghent) was famous as one of Flanders' fine cloth-making towns; its magnificent flamboyant Gothic **cloth hall** (rebuilt to the original exterior design after being destroyed in the war) serves as a memorable reminder of the period.

TRAVEL TIPS

Coastal towns are popular with Belgian and European summer holidaymakers, and well-ahead reservations for the better hotel or pension properties in July and August are essential. Tourism information for the whole West Flanders coastal region can be had in Bruges from **Westtoerisme** *(Kasteel Tillegem, 8200 Brugge,* ☎ *(050) 38.02.96)*. Otherwise, visit the tourist centers in individual towns.

ON THE ROAD

By beginning a tour of Belgium's coast at its northern or "upper" end, you'll also be starting with the top socioeconomic stretch of shore. **Knokke-Heist** is signposted on good roads from **Bruges**, the nearest major inland destination (10 mi/16 kms). En route, take in the villages of **Damme** (see "In the Area" under "Bruges") and **Oostkerke** if you want to see the picturesque character of white farmhouses and windmills, tree-lined canals, and big sky in this flat corner of the country.

★ KNOKKE-HEIST

Tourist Information, Zeedijk, Lichttorenplein, Knokke; ☎ *(050) 60.16.16* is part of a five-town community, the cultural and social centerpiece of which is the **casino** *(Zeedijk 509)*. Knokke—pronounced kuhnock-kuh—Heist. Built in 1930 with touches of art deco, the casino is wonderfully decorated with ★★**Rene Magritte's** *Le Domaine Enchante* murals (eight paintings reproduced in enormous enlargements) in the *Salle Magritte* dining room (weekly *gastronomic dinners*). Among the art exhibited elsewhere in the building are paintings by **Paul Delvaux** and a sculpture by **Niki De Saint-Phalle** in the lobby, where hangs a 2,000-light Venetian crystal chandelier, reputed to be the largest in Europe. Just outside is the sculpture *Poet* by **Zadkine**. Though you needn't, if you'd like an occasion to dress to-the-hilt, an evening at Knokke's cosmopolitan casino can provide it. Knokke has 50-plus **art galleries**. (In the latter part of the 19th century, many painters settled here, the best-known being **Felicien Rops** and **Claude Lemonnier**, lending Knokke its aesthetic air.) Branches of many of Brussels' most exclusive clothing and jewelry boutiques appeared too. Somewhere between self-conscious Knokke's fashionable beach-front promenade and its best shopping streets: **Lippenslaan**, **Kunstlaan**, and **Dumortierlaan**, lies **place m'as tu vu?** ("Did You See Me? Square").

WHERE TO STAY

La Reserve   ★★★★★
Elizabethlaan 160, Knokke; ☎ *(050) 61.06.06; first class.* The only five-

star property on the coast, located directly across from the casino; a short walk to the seafront, la Reserve's 110 guest rooms share quarters in a large comfortable complex with the **Thalassa Center** ☎ *(050) 60.06.12,* a health spa offering hot sea-mud baths and other saltwater treatments. The generous-size modern rooms with balconies and minibars have all the amenities associated with a luxury property, including free use of the health spa's fitness center (exercise equipment, sauna, seawater pool), a good restaurant, lounge bar, and tennis.

★ HET ZOUTE

The uppermost of Knokke-Heist's five towns is **Het Zoute**, so exclusive that it borders only ★ ★ *Het Zwin* salt-marsh nature reserve that extends to the Dutch border. (Over the border a *car ferry* at nearby Breskens quickly crosses the **Westerschelde** to **Vlissingen/Flushing** seaport in Holland's *Zeeland).* The Zwin marshes—all that's left of the waterway to the sea that centuries ago was Bruges' route to success—bloom in sea lavender in July and August. (*Reserve open daily Easter–Sept. 9 a.m.–7 p.m., from Oct.–Easter 9 a.m.–5 p.m., closed on Wed.; guided trips on Sun. year- round, also on Thurs. Easter–Sept. at 10 a.m.;* ☎ *(050) 60.70.86;* restaurant *Chalet du Zwin* at entrance.) There, you can climb high dunes for farsighted views of the North Sea, or of flat polderland far across which steeples reveal unseen towns.

Het Zoute actually is called **le Zoute** by the nobility and ultra upwardly mobile who frequent it: the French version of its name is considered far more fashionable, even among Flemings. Le Zoute, an enclave begun at the turn of the century under the design of German urbanist **M. Stubben**, remains a residential region where exterior building style (even the petrol/gas station) is strictly overseen. The winding streets of le Zoute are adorned with dazzling, low-rise, white-walled, red-roofed villas that offer obvious evidence of the taste, as well as the wealth, of the European jet setters who reside within.

★ ★ OSTEND/OOSTENDE

Tourist information at Wapenplein 3; Easter period and late June–midSept., daily, 9 a.m.–1 p.m., 2–8 p.m.; rest of year Mon.–Fri., 8 a.m.-noon, 1:45–5:45 p.m.; Sat. 9 a.m.–noon, 2–5 p.m., closed Sun.; reveal ☎ *(059) 70.11.99; year-round pop. 80,000.* A fishing village from its founding in the 11th century, Ostend was granted approval to build a port in 1445 by Burgundian *Philip the Good.* During a three-year siege (1601-1604) by the Spanish, the dunes east of the town were pierced to flood the hinterland; the gully thereby created was eventually enlarged as a new harbor. The *first passenger ferry* sailed between Ostend and Dover in the English Channel in 1846, and Ostend remains Belgium's most important passenger port with up to 16 daily crossings to/from Dover by ferry, and jet foil in summer, with at least eight in winter. Ostend still is "the most British resort" in Belgium, with many Brits coming over the sea from England for a day of intensive shopping and eating. England's leading position in the **Industrial Revolution** is what first began to bring the British to Ostend in large numbers in the 19th century. Workers in England were among the first "average people" to be given a paid annual holiday, and many took advantage of the Belgian/England ferry crossing to travel to the continent, at least as far as Ostend. (General tourism didn't develop for the Belgians themselves until the 1930s, when the government voted paid annual holidays for workers; thereafter they too headed for their North Sea shore.)

Ostend's greatest glory came with its distinction as a **royal residence**. **Leopold I** first came to Ostend in 1834, and had a *rail line* built from Brussels to Ostend in 1838. The first *casino/kurzaal* opened in 1852. When **Leopold II** made the resort his summer home, and European nobility and other royalty followed him there, Ostend became known as one of the continent's most fashionable places. The turn-of-the-century *Belle Époque* was Ostend's golden age: neoclassical buildings covered with rococo detail decorated the seafront, as did elegantly outfitted ladies parading under parasols along the promenade. The *Wellington Race Course* and thermal baths added more allure. Ostend's climate in winter is milder than in much else of northern Europe so the resort had year-round life, as it does today.

Heavily bombed in World War II and rebuilt by shortsighted developers, Ostend today has few grand facades facing its promenade; but modern buildings, some of controversial height, do face it. Nevertheless, it's still grand to stroll the elevated ★ ★ **Albert I Promenade** that runs the 4 mi/6 km length along Ostend's beaches. The most central is the **Grootstrand** (large beach), which lies between the **Thermae Palace Hotel** (next to the **Palais des Thermes** with its mineral and Turkish baths and other "cures") and **Ostend's Casino**. As well as gaming rooms (one with murals by **Paul Delvaux**), the casino offers top live entertainers, opera, ballet, and concerts in a 1,700-seat hall, and one of the city's best restaurants, **Fortuna** (*Kurzaal; 6:30 p.m.–1 a.m.; moderate; reservations* ☎ *(059) 70.51.11*), set on the upper floor near the action at the tables. The Albert Promenade continues southeast around a bend onto the **Visserskaai**, a favorite with seaside strollers for its atmosphere of fishing ships, fish stalls, and fish restaurants. One highly regarded locally is **Lusitania** (*Visserskaai 35; daily noon-3 p.m., 6–10 p.m.;* ☎ *70.17.65; inexpensive/moderate*), which serves tiny "gray" *North Sea shrimp* at their freshest. Moored in the old harbor is Mercator, a three-masted former training ship of the Belgian merchant fleet, now a museum ☎ *(059) 70.56.54.*

James Ensorhuis   ★
June-Sept., daily, 10–noon, 2–5 p.m., closed Tues. and month of Oct.; from Nov. to May, Sat. and Sun. only, 2–5 p.m. Artist **James Ensor** (1860–1949), the son of an English father and Ostend mother, was born in this house and rarely traveled far from it during his lengthy life. Ensor's art left behind the *impressionist* style he'd grown up with and settled on *symbolism*. He became known for putting masks of the sort used in *carnival* celebrations on the faces of his canvas-bound people, to indicate both the inner worlds of human fears and fantasies, and the falseness and hypocrisy of bourgeois society. For all his reclusiveness, rarely leaving Ostend for a single day, Ensor was an individ-

ual, a socialist, a blasphemer of religious doctrines; his 14-foot *Entry of Christ into Brussels* (1888) is a prime expression of his ideas. The "bad boy" of Ostend was a founder of (and surely must have named) the masked **Ball of the Dead Rat**, which remains one of the social Belgian carnival season's most social affairs. On the ground floor of Ensor's house is the reconstructed shop for shells and souvenirs previously kept by his aunt and uncle; the next floor has memorabilia connected with the artist and his times. The top story contains the studio where Ensor produced virtually all his works; the furniture, and views from the windows are recognizable in many of his paintings.

None of Ensor's original art is on display at his house (though some of his favorite masks are), but his paintings as well as drawings, can be seen at Ostend's **Museum voor Schone Kunsten/Fine Arts Museum** *(Wapenplein; daily 10 a.m.-noon, 2-5 p.m., closed Tues., Jan. 1, May 1, Dec. 25;* ☎ *(059) 80.53.35.* The collection concentrates on Flemish and international paintings of the 19th and 20th centuries. Another eminent Ostend artist, **Leon Spillaert** (1881–1946), also is well represented. The museum is part of the **Feest en Kultuur Paleis** (1958), which also contains the *tourist information office.* The building features a large clock with the signs of the zodiac, and a 49-bell carillon on which concerts are regularly given. (Inquire about schedule.)

WHERE TO STAY

Andromeda ★★★★

Albert I Promenade 60; ☎ *(059) 80.66.11; moderate.* Located right on the sea, next to the casino, this 10-story, modern, balconied building is Ostend's top hotel property, with a marble lobby, 90 comfortably furnished guest rooms, and breakfast included.

ST.-IDESBALD

Not far down the coast you can meet another Belgian artist at the ★★**Paul Delvaux Museum** (*Kabouterweg 42, St.-Idesbald; daily Easter–Sept. 10:30 a.m.–6:30 p.m., closed Mon., except open Mon. in July and Aug; open only weekends, holidays Oct.–Dec. 10:30 a.m.–4:30 p.m., closed Jan. 1 to Easter;* ☎ *(058) 51.29.71.* Paul Delvaux (*born in 1897*), who felt that the light is better by the sea, painted *surrealistic* canvases in this region for more than 40 years before putting up his brushes at about the age of 90. The museum, opened in 1985 and expanded in 1988, displays by far the largest number (perhaps 100) of the artist's works in the world. The earliest painting in the collection (which covers all of Delvaux's artistic periods) is the 1922 *Vue De la Gare du Quartier Leopold* (View of Leopold Quarter's Station), which shows he was already on the track of one of his recurring themes. Growing up in Brussels near that station, Delvaux was always highly interested in trains and has used rail cars and stations in many paintings as a metaphor for life. Are the trains arriving or leaving? Are stations lighted or dark? Are they empty? Cool, distant, white-skinned, nude women, people Delvaux's pictures—sometimes seated in trains, at other times in classical architectural settings where they stand showing as little emotion as a statue. Located in a residential neighborhood, the well-arranged museum also has a small shop with posters and catalogues, and a garden cafe.

DE PANNE

Tourist Information Gemeentehuis, Zeelaan. Situated in a dune "valley" or "pan" on a broad white beach that's a favored summer holiday resort for working and middle-class families with children, De Panne seems an unlikely spot for visitors to discover any close connections with both the world wars that scarred the 20th century. During **World War I**, Belgium's **King Albert I** and **Queen Elizabeth** lived in De Panne, along with the thousands of Allied soldiers stuck in the trenches around nearby **Ypres/Ieper** who clung, at a horrendously high cost, to this small, still-free, slice of land in western Belgium from 1914 to 1918. In De Panne, serving the "capital" of this unconquered corner of Belgium, King Albert and Queen Elizabeth lived for the duration at *Villa Maskens*; the queen tended wounded frontline soldiers in the seafront hotel L'Ocean, which was used as a field hospital.

Inland, 4 mi/6 km from De Panne is ★★**Veurne/Furnes** (*tourist information, Grote Markt 29;* ☎ *(058) 31.21.54* in whose **Gerechtshof** (1613–1618), one of many 16th- and 17th-century Flemish/Spanish-style buildings that rim the town's outstandingly attractive main square, the Belgian military maintained its headquarters during World War I. Just north of De Panne in **Nieuwpoort**, a statue of King Albert commemorates the occasion in October 1914 when, via a network of locks, water-control expert **Hendrik Geeraert** (remembered by a sculpted bust) was able to flood the entire Yser river plain; this act effectively halted the German offensive, and for better or worse, the Belgian and Allied Army was able to entrench itself behind the Yser for the following four years.

A monument on De Panne's **Leopold I Esplanade**—which commemorates where newly independent Belgium's new King Leopold I first set foot on his subjects' soil, in 1831,—marks one of the spots where a retreating British Army in late May 1940 reached the beach. Most of the army also eventually reached Britain, during the subsequently successful evacuation operation, best-known by the name of the nearby French coastal town, **Dunkirk/Dunkerque**. Though many know Dunkirk's place in early World War II history, far fewer know that Belgium's **De Panne**, just 1 mi/2 km from the eastern French border on the North Sea, was just as much involved in the massive rescue operation. After the May 10, 1940 invasion of all three Benelux countries by the Nazis, a 340,000-soldier-strong British and Allied (largely French) Army was landed on the continent, but soon it was overwhelmed. On May 28, Belgium's King Leopold III surrendered near Bruges, which meant that the Allies' northern flank was gone. Faced with the danger of being surrounded and cut off from the sea, and the knowledge that the Allied cause would be seriously, if not fatally, impaired if they were captured, the British Army ordered a retreat to the coast at

Dunkirk, and from there it hoped soldiers could get back to England. The Nazis quickly made Dunkirk harbor unusable to large ships through massive bombardment. A sea evacuation began with soldiers wading out from the beaches to reach the smaller military ships that lay offshore.

A desperate appeal was sounded in England with requests going out to every port, marina, and yacht club to send any boat available to the beaches between Dunkirk and De Panne. Hundreds of craft, tugboats, sailboats, motorboats, and lifeboats, (many with Sunday sailors at the helm), came out of the English Channel and across the North Sea, converging on the French/Belgian border. Though the *Luftwaffe* did its worst, by June 3 the "Mosquito Armada," as it was dubbed, had evacuated 233,000 British and 112,500 other Allied troops—in an operation that British strategists once had hoped would save 50,000. **Winston Churchill** appeared before Parliament on June 4, 1940 to tell the amazing story; elated, he nevertheless warned, "We must be very careful not to assign to this deliverance the attributes of a victory. Wars are not won by evacuations."

IN THE AREA

YPRES/IEPER/WIPERS

Tourist Information Stadhuis, Grote Markt; April 1–Sept. 30, Mon.–Fri. 9:00 a.m.–5:30 p.m., Sat., Sun., holidays 9:30 a.m.–5:30 p.m.; Oct. 1–March 31, Mon.–Sat. 9 a.m.–4:30 p.m., Sun. and holidays 11 a.m.–4:30 p.m.; ☎ (057) 20.26.23; population 35,000. "Hardly a man is now alive who remembers..." wrote Henry Wadsworth Longfellow, more than 80 years after Paul Revere's historic horseback ride on the eve of the beginning battle of the American Revolution. And so it is in Belgium nearly 80 years after World War I. Hardly a man is now alive who actually partook of the mud and the blood of battle around Ypres between 1914 and 1918, but the country, and the countryside itself, can't help remembering. Remembrance of soldiers past comes at any of the 170 military cemeteries that lie thickly around Ypres. It was a place that had the misfortune in October 1914 of being situated between the rivers Lys and Yser; a position that both the Allies and the Germans believed offered a last chance to break out of siege warfare.

As early as 1915, in the 1914–1918 "war to end war" in which he would die, **John McCrea** (1872–1918), an officer with the *Royal Canadian Medical Corps*, wrote in a poem published in *Punch* magazine on December 8:

> *"In Flanders fields the poppies blow*
> *Between the crosses, row on row,*
> *That mark our place; and in the sky*
> *The larks, still bravely singing, fly*
> *Scarce heard amid the guns below.*
>
> *We are the dead. Short days ago*
> *We lived, felt dawn, saw sunset glow,*

Loved and were loved, and now we lie
In Flanders fields."

No countries know better than the Benelux that World War I was not the war to end war. Rather, it deteriorated into "The Great War and the Petty Peace," so-called in *The Outline of History* by H. G. Wells (1866–1946), who also wrote in that 1920 volume: "Human history becomes more and more a race between education and catastrophe."

A scorched tree-stump-strewn landscape, military divisions mired in mud, soldiers in sodden clothes, and four years of a physical and mental health-threatening routine of daily bombardment: this was the truth of trench warfare along the **Ypres Salient**. The water table on this part of Flanders lies only a few feet below ground level even in dry times, and, after rain, the bomb craters and trenches held standing water; survivors said that it always seemed to be raining. Men drowned in mud. **German General Erich Ludendorff** later wrote, "It was no longer life at all. It was mere unspeakable suffering."

The Salient was the name given to the arc-shaped Allied front rounding Ypres; it was an arena of battle that took the maximum toll and returned the minimal result of any in World War I. Once the Salient was established, it became a symbol that the Allies felt they must not lose: the British felt compelled to keep fighting because they'd paid so dearly so far; the French were forbidden by their military doctrine from any action other than fighting to the death; and the Belgians, of course, desperately desired to hold onto the tiny bit of free national territory that remained to them. On three occasions amid the endless months of entrapment in trenches, actual battles broke out; at enormous cost, the Allies managed never to let their line break. During the first battle of Ypres (Oct. 19–Nov. 22, 1914), the Salient position was established. During the second battle (April 22–May 25, 1915), the Germans on the defensive on the Western Front at the time, brought out their new gas weapon, which on meteorological advice was introduced on the Ypres Salient. Still widely known by the name *Ieperiet*, the **chlorine gas** came out of cylinders in a yellowish cloud; those it didn't kill often were impaired for life. The third battle (June 7–Nov. 4) involved valiant Allied marches through quagmires, but to no definitive end.

Located on the Grote Markt at Ypres is the ★★**Cloth Hall**, on the first floor of which is the **Ypres Salient 1914-1918 Remembrance Museum** (*April 1–Nov. 15, 9:30 a.m.-noon, 1:30–5:30 p.m., open to groups by request rest of year;* ☎ *(057) 20.26.26*). Comprehensive and professional—compared with the many smaller, more commercial ventures scattered around the Salient—the museum includes dioramas of the battlefront, a collection of trench signs, trench art, a mock-up of a section of trench, displays showing all aspects of action along the Salient, and a large model of the devastated town of Ypres as it lay after the war. A large collection of photographs taken before, during, and after the war do more than many other exhibits to convey the terror and tedium of the trench warfare. They do little to glamorize the grim events of the four years that left half a million dead.

Ypres' **Cloth Hall**, originally built in 1260–1304, is one of the largest (the facade is 432 feet/132 meters long) and most beautiful civil Gothic buildings in Europe. Its enormous area, used for storing and selling cloth, testifies to the success of the town's trade in the 13th and 14th centuries (when it competed with Bruges and Ghent); the strong square **Belfry**, rising 230 feet/70 meters from the center of the hall, dominates the region. This splendid structure, situated on Ypres' attractive cobbled main square that's garnished with cafes, is itself an example of the mind-boggling expenditure of energy and resources that war demands. By 1918, historic, elegant Ypres had been reduced to *rubble*, a word that describes a level of destruction that most of us have never seen (and which the world did not see again until Dresden in World War II). At the end of World War I, it was said that a man on horseback could see straight across the city of Ypres. Some British proposed leaving post-war Ypres as a relic to the war there, building instead a whole new city for its displaced populace somewhere else. But Ypres rebuilt its Cloth Hall, cathedral, and many other buildings to their original design, stone by stone.

The stones of the reconstructed Cloth Hall at Ypres are monuments to the waste of war, as are the gravestones that fill silent fields in the surrounding countryside. Cemeteries are as much a part of the landscape as any natural feature in this area of Flanders. **Tyne Cot Cemetery**, at **Passendale/Paschendaele**, with 11,908 graves, mainly British, Australians and New Zealanders, and a long wall that bears the names of 34,957 British soldiers who were reported dead or missing after August 15, 1917, is the largest British war cemetery in the world—though it's only one of some 170 here in Flanders. *Vladslo*, a German military cemetery in the Praatbos, contains the gray, flush with the ground, gravestones of 25,638 men. One buried here is Peter Kollwitz, killed at the age of 17 on October 23, 1914. His mother, Berlin artist Kathe Kollwitz-Schmidt, produced a deeply touching two-piece sculpture of mourning parents for the carefully kept cemetery. Stones in many cemeteries in Flanders are marked only with the words: "A Soldier of the Great War."

You can walk Ypres' main street to the ★**Menen Gate** (designed by Sir Reginald Blomfield, 1927) at the end. Covering the huge stone arch are the chiselled names of Britain's 54,896 missing soldiers with no known grave. Every evening since the gate was dedicated (except for the years of World War II), the **Last Post** has been played by two town buglers at 8:00 p.m., while police briefly halt the flow of traffic. The continued playing of the Last Post reinforces what a local man told me, "The War is still close here, still a sort of trauma." And how could it not be? One in three of the shells fired during World War I didn't explode at the time. In the decades since, more than a few unfortunate farmers have plowed up shells in their fields that turned out to be live; even today, one or two people a year die from ammunition fired in 1914–1918.

It's a surrealist switch from war to another event for which Ypres is known, the **Kattestoet/Cat Procession**, whose history may hark back to worries about witchcraft. It is said that long ago, in the belief that black cats held the souls of witches, live black cats were periodically flung from the top of the **Ypres Cloth Hall** tower; since 1870, stuffed cloth cats have been substituted, and a parade and festivities have been added to the occasion on the second Sunday of each May. Another theory about the origin of the cat throwing, which is deeply rooted in Ypres history, is that it began with the early (13th century) days of the Cloth Hall, when woolen cloth ready for sale, was stored in the upper story. In order to keep down the damage from rats in the storehouse, cats were brought in in the fall. In the spring, when the wool cloth had all been sold, the felines—which many people did believe represented evil spirits—were simply tossed out.

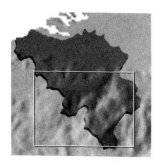

WALLONIA: AN INTRODUCTION

The southern, slightly larger half of Belgium is French-speaking **Wallonia**. Its 5,800 square miles comprise the provinces of **Hainaut**, **Namur**, **Liège**, and **Luxembourg** in their entirety. Wallonia also includes a good chunk of centrally located **Brabant**, Belgium's only province split by the *Language Frontier*. The name Wallonia derives from the *Wala*, romanized early Celtic inhabitants of the northern reaches of Caesar's Gaul, whose development of the French language dates from Roman days. Thus was established the beginnings of Belgium's linguistic/cultural border—to the north of which, in what became Flanders, there arose a Frankish influence, and a Germanic language developed. Today's inhabitants refer to themselves as *les Wallons*, while the Flemish call them *de Walen*.

The preeminence of French in *both* regions that make up present-day Belgium dates from the 14th century, when the **French Burgundians** fought the **counts of Flanders** and won supremacy in language and law. From that time until late in the 20th century in Belgium—and for many centuries, in the courts of most European rulers, including the English—French was *the* language of politics, law, and culture. The status of the French language conferred what amounted to special treatment for Belgium's Walloons over the Flemish. The government of both populations was conducted solely *en français*. In the law courts it was the same, which meant that Flemings frequently were unable even to understand the charges being brought against them. Perhaps most important of all, schools taught classes only in French, which tended to keep the Flemish uneducated and down on their farms. Only as the *Flemish Movement* gathered strength in the late 19th century and into the 20th did Belgium change from an essentially single-language country to a truly bilingual one.

Wallonia takes a back seat to Flanders in terms of the interests of most overseas travelers to Belgium. However, for visitors with time to see more of the country than its unfailingly fine Flemish cities, Wallonia offers a number of choices. The French-speaking community has two historic, artistically and architecturally significant cities: **Tournai**, a Roman-era town and former Frankish capital at the western end of Wallonia, and **Liège**, a once esteemed and influential prince-bishopric, to the east. To a great extent, however, southern Belgium's charms are scenic, clustered in the wooded forests and rushing river gorges of the **Ardennes**.

The *Meuse, Sambre, Ourthe,* and *Semois* river valleys claim picturesque fortress towns: **Namur**, **Dinant**, **Huy**, and **Durbuy**. In the healthy outdoor surroundings, it isn't surprising to find a spa, but Belgium's **spa** was Europe's prototype. Castles (as old as **Bouillon**, one of whose owners mortgaged it to outfit a company for the *First Crusade* in A.D. 1096, and as elegant as the still-occupied **Beloeil**, seat of the princes of Ligne), abbeys (Orval's earliest ruins date from the 12th century), grand gardens (such as the many-fountained ones at **Annevoie**), and gaping natural caves (as at **Han-sur-Lesse**) punctuate a rural driving route with interesting focal points.

Unlike Flanders's World War I sites around Ypres, Wallonia's battlefields shed light on World War II, especially at **Bastogne** near the Luxembourg border. Bastogne was the center of the once-strategic, now primarily scenic, "bulge" of land in the Ardennes that gave name to Hitler's last desperate, doomed and destructive campaign.

Steel and **coal** have given Wallonia prosperity in the past two centuries. Belgium's coalfield band extends into Flanders, but its south central region to the east of Charleroi in Wallonia is the **Pays Noir** (*Black Country*), where conical slag heaps are a lingering aspect of the countryside which, until the 1960s, was one of the world's premier coal mining areas. Coal fired the Walloon economy, and also gave it iron and steel industries. The greatest development of the Belgian coal seams took place in the first half of the 19th century. The **Industrial Revolution** reached Wallonia before it arrived in either northern France or Germany's Ruhr Valley, and well before the rest of continental Europe. Belgium led the way in Europe with its coalpits, iron foundries, and rolling mills (such as the *Cockerill* works at Seraing). The technical advances and economic results achieved in Wallonia affected the development of the industry on the entire continent. Since the region was an entrepreneur in an industry that admittedly produced pits of human misery in the 19th century, sociologists studied the social conditions of Wallonia's mining districts with considerable interest. Many artists were moved to put human faces to the industry, and only recently the sculptor **Zadkine** created a monument to miners for the town of **Wasmes**.

Though he hadn't come to draw and paint its people, an as yet unself-defined Dutchman, **Vincent van Gogh**, arrived in 1878 at the age of 25 at the village of Wasmes in Belgium's **Borinage** district to work as a pastor-on-probation among the miners. Vincent, the son of a Protestant preacher, hadn't done well in two previous attempts (the second in Brussels) at formal training for the clergy. Thus he went unsponsored on a small stipend from his father to Wallonia's grim coal mining region, hoping to succeed there, dispensing care and compassion so that he might have the work assignment made formal. Van Gogh's letters from that period describe the immense heaps of coal at the entrance to the mines, the dunghills and ash heaps that made up the dreary landscape, and the miners: "thin and pale from fever, tired and emaciated, weatherbeaten and prematurely aged; the women as a whole, faded and worn." He went underground to observe miners working in little cubicles "like the partitions in a crypt," and watched too-heavily laden children loading coal on horse-drawn carts. Vincent cared for the casualties of mine cave-ins and explosions, nursed victims of typhus and other diseases, and preached from the Bible.

Van Gogh thought he had found his life's work, and the Brussels missionary society also began to think so. He began to take the words of the New Testament literally: "Sell that thou hast, and give it to the poor." Vincent turned evangelist, moved out of his comfortable rented room into a shack where he slept on the floor, gave away much of his clothing, used his undergarments as bandages for the injured, and let coal dust accumulate on his face to signify his identification with the begrimed miners. Some called him the "Christ of the Coal Mines." But his excessive zeal and hounding of local authorities and mine owners to improve workers' conditions led to Vincent's dismissal.

Shortly thereafter, Vincent "disappeared" in the Borinage for about nine months; he never revealed how he fed and clothed himself during this period of emotional crisis which he later referred to as a "molting time." During this time he made the decision to become an artist. At 27 years of age, beginning with sketches of Belgian coal miners and their surroundings, Van Gogh plunged himself into the art work which would consume him for the remaining ten years of his life.

Vincent's first studio was in the cottage of a Borinage coal miner, in a bedroom he shared with the miner's children. Commencing his self-education in what he described as a "rage of work," with art materials and prints to copy sent from Paris by his brother **Theo**, Van Gogh found his quarters so crowded and dark that he did most of his work outside, until the onset of autumn made that impossible. Finally leaving the Borinage in the fall of 1880, Vincent went to Brussels, where he spent the winter working at drawing until finances forced him to return to Holland. Van Gogh's time in the Borinage was germinal. His work there led Vincent to write five years later (1885) in a letter to Theo: "Painting peasant life is a serious thing and I should reproach myself if I did not try to make pictures which will arouse serious thoughts." Clearly, something of his missionary spirit remained.

In the town of Wasmes, where van Gogh had lived was the *Marcasse mine*, the scene of so many disasters that scarcely a family in that Walloon community was unscathed by contact with it. After the most recent mining disaster, in 1960, tons of concrete were used to seal the shaft of Marcasse, closing what in some ways was a black chapter in Belgium's history. When, by the end of the 1960s, all the mines in Wallonia had been shut down due to the exhaustion of their earthy riches, the move threatened one of the *Black Country's* major monuments.

An industrial architectural triumph is preserved in the restored ruin known as **Grand Hornu**. (*rue Sainte-Louise 82; Mon–Sat. March–Sept. 10 a.m–noon, 2–6 p.m.; Oct.–Feb. 10 a.m.–noon, 2–4 p.m., closed Mon.;* ☎ *(065) 77.07.12 or* ☎ *(065) 38.23.95*). Built between 1820–1832, Hornu was designed by Bruno Renard and Henri de Gorge as a city where work and living space were to complement each other in one complex. This 19th-century urban "utopia" provided miners and their families with housing, schools, library, hospital, and theater, all situated around a great central square. Once the mines were closed, a wrecker's hammer awaited Hornu, since the government couldn't decide upon a future use for the site. But Borinage architect **Henri Guchez**, well-known beyond the borders of Belgium, bought it and has saved Grand Hornu for posterity, not only as a gem of industrial architecture, but a page of Walloon history. Today, restored and a listed industrial archaeological site, the roofless main structure with its arches and columns is a temple to its time.

Wallonia with its last coal mine closed, still remains a leader in steel, an industry centered largely around Liège. Though the steel industry passes through periodic slumps in the international marketplace, in 1991 Belgium's metal/steel companies *Arbed SA and Cockerill Sambre SA* placed 267th and 276th in the U.S. magazine *Forbes's* list of the world's 500 largest non-American corporations. Nevertheless, there has been an overall turn in Belgium's industrial tide in favor of Flanders's preeminent North Sea ports, and the transportation infrastructure of connections through them deep into the continent.

There's a compensation for Walloons. Despite a considerably smaller population and much weaker economy than Flanders, Wallonia can take pleasure in knowing that it pays much less than half of the national tax revenue that equally funds the country's two cultural communities.

TOURNAI

GUIDELINES FOR TOURNAI

SIGHTS

Tournai (*Doornik* in Flemish), with an urban population of 35,000, is dominated by its unique five-towered **cathedral**, a 12th- and 13th-century Romanesque/Gothic masterpiece that's the center-piece for city orientation. Once Roman and by the 5th century the capital for the Franks, Tournai's numerous historic sights are mostly situated in its southwest quarter, near the **Escaut (Scheldt) River**, and crossed by the picturesque 13th-century **pont des Trous** from which there's a superb view of the city and cathedral towers. Tournai has Belgium's oldest **belfry** (c. 1200) and Europe's oldest **burgher houses** (12th century). Victor Horta's *art nouveau* art museum has paintings by Tournai-born, Flemish "primitive" school founding fa-ther **Robert Campin** (*The Master of Flemalle*) and his pupil **Rogier de la Pasture/Rogier van der Weyden**. Other museums show off fine old examples of the city's locally-produced sculpture, tapestries, and porcelain. Skillfully **illuminated**, the cathedral seems to dominate the town center at night even more than during the day.

GETTING AROUND

Tournai's **rail station** is at the northeast edge of the center city. It's more or less a straight line, and a bit over one mile/two kilometers from the train station up rue Royale and across the river to the cathe-dral. If you have luggage or prefer to begin walking in the center from which other important sights (**cathedral/belfry/Grand Place**) are accessible by foot, take a taxi from the station. For a 45-minute overview of the city, the tourist office (across from the belfry) can book you a taxi tour with an English commentary cassette tape that keeps in sync with sites.

SHOPPING

A principal city of the Belgian Walloon province of Hainaut, Tournai is a major shopping center with outlets located principally in the pedestrian precinct around and to the southeast of **place St-Pierre**. Open-air produce and general markets are held Saturdays on the **Grand' Place** and place St-Pierre, 8 a.m.–1 p.m.; at that time there's also a flower market on **place Emile Janson**, which abuts the cathedral. A flea market takes place on place St-Pierre, Sun. 8 a.m.–1 p.m. The **quai du Marché Poisson**, along the river, has assorted antique shops.

ENTERTAINMENT AND EVENTS

Carillon concerts are played at 11:30 a.m. Sats. from June through Aug. in the belfry; there are outside cafes at its base, but because of traffic you might hear the bells better from a bit farther away. Ask at the tourist office about Sunday afternoon **concerts in the cathedral** in July and Aug., and Sunday morning concerts by Conservatory students from Nov.–March. Each second Sunday in June is Tournai's **Day of Four Processions**, which features just that. On the second Sunday in Sept. at 3 p.m. is the historic **Procession of the Plague**, commemorating the deadly epidemic of the year 1090, and during which are displayed some of the cathedral's priceless art treasures.

WHERE TO STAY

Hotels in the old city with good standards of comfort and service are limited. Plan ahead if you anticipate overlapping with Tournai's major annual trade fairs in April/May and Sept/Oct.

WHERE TO EAT

Tournai offers a reasonable selection of in-town restaurants serving appetizing food in appealing settings. Cuisine generally is French-influenced, with an emphasis on fresh Belgium ingredients such as endive, Ardennes ham, rabbit, and asparagus. Local sweets include plum tarts and *faluches* (butter and brown sugar cakes).

ARRIVING

Direct trains from Brussels to Tournai (79 km/48 mi) take about an hour. The city also has direct rail service from Liège and Lille France, (26 km/16 mi). Motorway access is via A 27.

IN THE AREA

Some 16 mi/27 km southeast of Tournai is **Chateau de Beloeil**, the largest of 30-odd, privately-owned castles in Belgium, which has one of Europe's richest legacies. The residence of the *princes de Ligne* since the 14th century, Beloeil has 15th–19th-century furniture, portraits, tapestries, and objets d'art on view to the public. Its park, one of the finest in Belgium, is attributed to **Le Nôtre**, who designed the gardens at Versailles.

TOURNAI IN CONTEXT

Tournai's story spans two thousand years, covering periods as a Roman crossroads, capital of the Frankish empire, and an 11th- and 12th-century bishopric that presided spiritually over a population of more than one million, including all of Flanders. Thereafter, Tournai was more closely tied to France, whose influence and flavor still is felt today in this Walloon city noted for its art and architecture. The history of **Tournai cathedral**, which always has been at the heart of the town both physically and philosophically, in many ways mirrors the history of the city itself.

A rustic Roman settlement, a century before the birth of Christ, **Tornacum** became in the course of Emperor Claudius's organization of Gaul between A.D. 41–54 a post on the road from Boulogne to Cologne. That road, in the Tournai countryside, cut through limestone hills whose quarries would make Tournai wealthy. In A.D. 432, the Romans routed, and Tournai was chosen as a residence by the *Merovingian* kings of the embryonic **Frankish empire**. **Clovis** is believed to have been born in Tournai c. 465, and his father **Childeric** died here in 482. Taking rule that year, Clovis remained in Tournai until near the end of the 5th century when he moved the royal seat to Paris. Before his death in 511, Clovis compensated Tournai by making it an ecclesiastical capital of great authority, encompassing what would become Flanders (including Bruges, Ghent, and Ypres), and a great deal of France. Important civil powers were ceded to the citizens of Tournai—who would later be vassals of the kings of France—which made the town virtually independent as ruled by its bishop. About A.D. 501 Tournai native-son and bishop, **Eleutherus**, built the first church on the site of the present cathedral. Outside that early sacred structure Eleutherus was beaten to death by heretics (c. 532); raised to sainthood, and was named patron saint of Tournai in 1064.

An enlarged cathedral replaced the early one about 850, but it was burned in 881 by Norsemen, who had sailed inland from the North Sea up the river Scheldt. The cathedral was rebuilt with the resources of the bishop, in whom were vested vast powers, including the coining of money, gathering of fines and taxes, the town's judicial and policing authority, the functioning in every way of Tournai's economic, social, intellectual, and political life. A fire in 1060 caused great damage to the cathedral, but it was restored by the time Tournai—and all of Flanders and Brabant—was ravaged by a devasting **plague**.

The sick poured into the cathedral to pray for an end to the pestilence. After several seemingly miraculous cures there, the number of petitioners increased; the statue of the Virgin before which they prayed became known as **Our Lady of the Sick**. On September 14, 1090, Tournai's bishop organized a procession, a sort of demonstration against the plague. To it flocked crowds from Flanders and districts south of the Scheldt, jostling their way through the old city and the cathedral for seven days. (The week-long event immediately became annual, and one of the great pilgrimages of northern European Christendom. The procession itself, often led by a luminary such as the count of Flanders, is observed in Tournai to this day). The popularity of the **Procession of the Plague** led to the construction of the great cathedral we see in Tournai today.

The nave of the new **Romanesque cathedral** was raised by 1171, with the transcept completed by the end of the 12th century. It is considered by many to be the most remarkable Romanesque basilica in Europe. The 11th and 12th centuries were Tournai's golden age. Goldsmith **Nicolas of Verdun** produced what is widely considered to be the city's single most outstanding piece of art. (See "the Shrine of Notre Dame" in the "Cathedral Treasury" under " What To See and Do"). In addition to being excellent goldsmiths, craftsmen in Tournai were also known throughout Europe for their work in wood, ivory, and the city's famous "blue" stone. The blue stone actually is slate-colored, locally quarried limestone (also called "Tournai marble"); well known for its building and carving qualities, it is gray when left rough for exterior work, but when used for ornamental works and polished, it becomes black and shiny. Examples of quality carving can be seen in the cathedral today, but much of the work of its golden age *Tournaisienne*-style sculptors was mutilated during the religious troubles of the 16th century. Also reflecting the heights achieved in 12th century are the **Romanesque burghers' houses**, the oldest (c. 1175) surviving ones in Europe.

During the 11th and 12th centuries, Tournai benefited from the economic expansion of Flanders, since the river Scheldt linked the city with both Ghent and the interior of France. Via the river, Tournai traded Flemish wool, cloth, and its own local stone.

Power struggles arose with the kings of France, who wanted to bring Tournai under their rule in order to gain more direct control in Flanders, and to strengthen their military position by holding Tournai's strategic crossing of the Scheldt River. In 1187, the French got their way, taking over rule of Tournai. With the French firmly established there, French styles and fashion became popular. In 1243, Bishop Walter de Marvis, under the influence of frequent journeys to France, began to find the Romanesque style old-fashioned. He decided upon a makeover of his cathedral in the more *à la mode* Gothic style being fostered in France. The Gothic conversion began with the Choir (modeled after Amiens cathedral), which was completed in 1255. Financial problems prevented re-styling the rest of the cathedral. The nave remains Romanesque, housing Belgium's largest collection of 13th-century mural paintings.

Being under the rule of the French kings, to whom it remained loyal, Tournai supported France against England during the **Hundred Years' War** (1337–1453). The city gave early proof of its stance, withstanding a seige in 1340 by English King Edward III. (He had declared *himself* king of France in 1337, a claim which Ghent and Flemish towns supported because of their dependence upon English wool for their vital cloth trade). Tournai's continued support of France during the succeeding 100 years led **Jeanne D'Arc** (1412–1431), the fervent French maiden who died at the stake, to refer to "the gentle, loyal Franks of Tournai" in 1429.

The Hundred Years' War didn't deter an awakening in art in the Netherlands/Low Countries in the late 14th and early 15th century, and Tournai produced an important pair of painters for the formative Flemish "primitive" style: **Robert Campin** (*"the Master of Flemalle"*) and his pupil, **Rogier van der Weyden**. The city's stone sculptors continued to be active in the 15th century, creating beautiful carved fonts in Tournai "marble" which remain revered art works today in churches as far afield as England and Spain. During the 14th century, services in the cathedral, served by 42 canons, 12 vicars, and some 50 chaplains, were sung continuously throughout the day from *Matin* to *Compline*. From this activity a remarkable school of singing developed. The manuscript still exists for the **Tournai Mass** (c. 1330), the oldest mass for three voices in existence.

Once the Hundred Years' War ended, France and England seemed unable to keep uninvolved. In the 1513 *Treaty of Mechelen*, England's recently crowned (1509) young **King Henry VIII**, still a Roman Catholic at this point, agreed with the Pope and Maximilian to invade France. That year Henry seized Tournai and remained in the city for three weeks, attended services in the cathedral, and awarded **Thomas Wolsey** (later Cardinal Archbishop of York) the city's bishopric. Henry's forces used Tournai as a base, during which time the town was fortified (see "Tour Henry VIII" under "What to See and Do"). With a treaty signed, Wolsey, in order to gain favor with the French, sold Tournai back to them in 1518. A mere three years later, Tournai fell under seige from the army of young **Emperor Charles V**, and thus was wrested from France within a month. It thereafter became a province of the **Spanish Netherlands**.

The religious clashes of the **Reformation** left lasting scars on Tournai's stones. In an attempt to stop the spread of Protestant *Calvinism*, Charles V's Catholic son, Philip II, divided several large bishoprics into smaller ones. As a result, Tournai lost its dominion over Ghent, Bruges, and Ypres (which became independent bishoprics in 1559). The Calvinist rebellion made headway anyway, and on August 24, 1566, extremists among Tournai's local Protestant population forced entry into the cathedral and laid waste to its medieval art treasures. The iconoclastic struggle lasted until September 16, and for the first year in nearly five centuries, Tournai's **Procession of the Plague** did not take place. Philip II contributed further to the devastation by confiscating goods from Protestant churches, burning many of the heretics along the way. When civil order was restored, repair of the cathedral was undertaken. A commission was given to **Cornelis Floris** of Antwerp for a rood-screen to replace the Gothic one destroyed by the religious rioters. An impressive red marble and alabaster arch bridged the cathedral's Romanesque nave and Gothic choir with the Renaissance style.

In 1653, items by unknown artists were unearthed in Tournai by a worker digging in the garden of the Church of St-Brice. His spade having accidentally broken into a tomb, the worker was astonished to find what contemporary reports indicate was a treasure not unlike King Tut's, (located centuries later). What had been uncovered—the inscription inside, *482 Childerici Regis*, left no doubt—was the coffin of 5th-century **Frankish King Childeric**, founder of the Merovingian dynasty and the father of Clovis. His skeleton was wrapped in a robe decorated with hundreds of figures of bees—a symbol for royalty—in gold. In addition, countless coins of gold and silver bearing the image of Childeric, jewelry, and ornate weapons were found. Unfortunately, the items sent out of the country by various foreign rulers do not survive, having been subsequently stolen and/or melted down.

There's a different ending to the discovery in the late 1980s of an even earlier 4th-century tomb near what had been a Roman necropolis in Tournai. The sarcophagus, on view in Tournai's **Museum of History and Archeology**, is adorned with unusually elaborate lateral carvings, which leads experts to believe it belonged to a person of importance. Because of its fragility, archeologists have not opened it for fear of damaging some of the exquisite decoration.

Though trying to throw off the Spanish yoke several times, Tournai remained part of the southern Netherlands until **French King Louis XIV** captured it in 1667. Louis's influence is still felt in the town in domestic and military architecture, the latter in the form of fortifications built by Vauban. Under the *Treaty of Utrecht* (1713), Tournai was made a part of the Austrian Netherlands, remaining so until the 1792-1794 conquest of the Netherlands by post-Revolution anti-cleric French soldiers who wreaked devastation throughout Belgium. In Tournai, they destroyed art both in- and outside the cathedral, with the French government organizing an auction of all contents that could be carried away. The French army even dismantled the cathedral's five famed towers, the symbol of the city, and spoke of demolishing the whole structure. Fortunately, they didn't follow through, and Tournai's subsequent Bishop Francois-Joseph Hirn (1802–1819) committed himself to restoring and re-equipping the cathedral. He successfully recovered Nicolas of Verdun's golden reliquary and that of St. Eleutherus, as well as tapestries and pieces of metal-work that had escaped destruction. Large-scale restoration of Tournai's sacred centerpiece was carried out in the 1840s.

Until 1940, Tournai was one of the best preserved towns in Belgium, with thousands of old houses dating mostly from the 17th and 18th centuries. But, in 1940, Nazi air raids flattened an estimated 60% of the city, including most of the Grand' Place—a model showing the devastation is in the **Musée de Folklore**—but not the city's c. 1200 **belfry**. The cathedral was hit by an incendiary bomb, which turned some art treasures into ashes before prisoners released from the local jail could put out the blaze. Fortunately, the five-towered Tournai landmark escaped serious structural damage.

In a happier ending to the war, Tournai was the first Belgium town to be liberated by British troops (September 1944). Today, the many remaining ancient monuments, and those that have been carefully restored, are plentiful enough by far to give travelers visiting Tournai the look and feel of its distinguished history.

GUIDEPOSTS

Telephone code 069

Tourist Office • Vieux Marché-aux-Poteries 14; ☎ *22.20.45; FAX 21.62.21*; Mon.–Fri. 9 a.m.–7 p.m., Sat. and Sun. 10 a.m.–1 p.m., 3–6 p.m.

River cruises • Landing stage near pont des Trous; May 1–Aug. 31, daily except Mon., one hour duration; departures 11 a.m., 2:30 and 4:15 p.m. (confirm times with Tourist Office).

WHAT TO SEE AND DO

You'll certainly get visual variety in Tournai, in the array of outstanding examples of architecture from the *Romanesque* (12th century), *Gothic* (13–15th century), and *Renaissance* (16–17th century) periods. Sections of city ramparts from the 11th and 13th centuries remain, as centrally located as the **Tower of the Six** in place Reine Astrid, near the **belfry**. Buildings around Tournai's *Grand' Place*, badly damaged by Nazi air raids in 1940, have been reconstructed; colorful banners are flown from its *guildhouse* facades from Easter through September. The **Hôtel de Ville**, originally 1611 ★ **Renaissance Cloth Hall**, (located in the Parc Communal in an 18th-century building that incorporates part of the ancient Saint Martin Abbey), has pride of place on the Grand' Place. All museums and sights in Tournai (except the cathedral, see below) are open daily except Tues., for the same hours year-round (*10 a.m.–noon and 2–5:30 p.m., closed Tuesday, in the month of Sept., and on Jan. 1, Nov. 11, Dec. 25*); most are free.

Cathedral of Notre Dame

Treasury open 10 a.m.–noon, 2–4:30 p.m. daily, the cathedral itself is open earlier. Exhibiting the strength and simplicity of the *Romanesque* style, the vaulted energy and upreaching of the *Gothic*, and a beyond-value *Treasury*, Tournai's cruciform cathedral is considered Belgium's best, and one of Europe's finest. The Romanesque nave of gray Tournai limestone, quarried just outside the town, was completed in 1171. The choir, originally completed in 1200, was rebuilt in the Gothic style by 1255. And to this day, the low Romanesque arches in the large nave (440 feet/132 mt. long, 215 ft/65 mt. wide, 80-110 feet/24-33 mt. high) stand in stark contrast to the soaring Gothic choir beyond, somehow successful aesthetically. Typical of Scaldian architecture are the capitals of the columns carved with flowers, animals, and plants. Alas, the support the columns lend has been slipping; some of the ceiling has fallen in and various columns list to port or starboard. Tournai's burgomaster has formed a committee to oversee the preservation of this amazing example of early Belgian architecture endeavor. The stained glass windows in the apse are copies of ones in

Sainte-Chapelle in Paris; those in the transcept masterpieces are from c. 1500 by Dutch artist **Arnold van der Spits** from Nijmegen. In the **St. Louis Chapel** (1299) are the paintings *Crucifixion* by Jacob Jordaens and *Deliverance of Souls from Purgatory* by Pieter Paul Rubens.

The standout in Tournai Cathedral's well-laden **Treasury** is ★ ★ ★ **Nicolas of Verdun's** *golden reliquary* to the Flemish Notre Dame, which dates from 1205. A second reliquary, by an unknown goldsmith, is the 1247 **Shrine to St. Eleutherus**. A documented ★ ★ **Arras tapestry** from 1402, a gift to the cathedral, shows Tournai's belfry, houses and city walls, and scenes in still-vivid red and blue hues of its history, including the 1090 plague. **Duquesnoy's** fine 17th-century calvary in ivory is quite a contrast to the artist's *Mannequin Pis* statue in Brussels. Also on display is Archbishop of Canterbury **Thomas à Becket's chasuble**, worn when he said mass here in 1170, still in exile from England in the Abbey of Pontigny, France. Only weeks later, after returning to Canterbury, he was murdered in his cathedral. (The chasuble was given to the Bishop of Tournai in 1838 by the last monk at Pontigny). **Charles V's mantle** was worn by the Emperor when he presided at the December 1531 meeting of the Twentieth Chapter of the Order of the Golden Fleece held in the cathedral.

The most outstanding characteristic of the cathedral is its **five towers**, virtually the city's symbol. The massive central tower, wider than the others (though its pyramid-shaped peak is not as high in stone), is topped by a taller cross making it the same height (272 ft./72 mt.) as the four, four-storied square corner towers that surround it. The porch of the Main Portal (west side) displays many beautiful figures carved in relief in Tournai stone. In the center under a canopy is a statue of the Virgin, prayed to as **Our Lady of the Sick** since the cathedral's construction not long after the 1090 plague. A statue near the cathedral on the south side was created by Tournai-born artist **Rogier de la Pasture** (who changed his name from its French form to the Flemish **Rogier van der Weyden** after he moved to Flanders's Brabant and Brussels). Rogier, born c. 1399 to a knife-maker in Tournai, studied under Robert Campin (now believed to be the Master of Flemalle, who was once thought to have been van der Weyden). The Tournai painters' guild register shows that Rogier worked with Campin from 1427–1432. By 1435, he was settled in Brussels, where he worked until he died in 1464. The *Port Mantilus* door on the north side of the cathedral has exceptional 12th-century sculptures. The door is named for the blind man Mantilus whom St. Eleutherus, the cathedral's first bishop, is said to have cured; the incident is alluded to in the nearby sculpture **The Parable of the Blind** (Guillaume Charlier, 1908). Also on the north side of the cathedral is **Janson Square**, from which you have the best view of the cathedral nave and flying buttresses.

Belfry

SE end of the Grand' Place Tournai's belfry is the oldest in northern Europe, c. 1200. Its 236 ft./72 meter height can be mastered on 256 stone steps for a wonderful view of the cathedral, which seems so close you feel you ought to be able to touch it. The belfry carillon (concerts, see "Events") has 43 bells.

Musée des Beaux-Arts

Parc Communal, enclos Saint-Martin. Opened in 1928, its exhibit space enlightened by Victor Horta's art nouveau architectural genius with skylights. The museum has an exceptional collection (left to the city in 1904 by a local business man) that spans the periods from the early Flemish to the present, with an emphasis on Belgian and French artists. Among the Old Masters you'll find **Robert Campin, Rogier van der Weyden, Pieter Breughel the Younger, Jan Breughel**, and **Pieter Paul Rubens**. One of the rooms off the museum's central hall (in which there is a displayed sculpture by **Guillaume Charlier**) is devoted to the huge historical works of Tournai's 19th-century master **Louis Gallait**. One of the most effective and interesting is the *Plague in Tournai*; others of note are *The Abdication of Charles Quint* and the *Last Rites over Counts Egmond and Hoorn*. You certainly won't mind seeing non-Belgian works by **Manet, Monet, Seurat**, and **van Gogh**.

Tapestry Museum

In Hotel de Ville, parc Communal, next to Musee des Beaux Arts. A new addition on the Tournai scene, the Tapestry Museum displays the city's wonderful collection of 15th-century tapestries, which includes many smaller masterpieces. At the museum, you can observe weavers at work, an artistic tradition for which Tournai was renowned for centuries. At the new **Museum of Decorative Arts**, fine examples of another historic Tournai craft, sumptuously colored and decorated porcelain, can be found.

Musée du Folklore ★

Reduit des Sion, alley off Grand' Place; little English documentation, although some exhibits can still be enjoyed. Housed in a typical 1677 house with a double gable and arches on the upper story, the museum illustrates local lifestyles and traditions. Exhibits cover interesting tidbits of city history: items from Belgium's first newspaper, the Tournai-published *Courier de L'Escaut* which began in 1829; a copy of the original city relief plan/model made for Louis XIV in 1707, from which Vauban worked to fortify the city with walls and 68 towers and canalize the Scheldt; and a model of the condition of Tournai's Grand' Place after the 1940 air raids.

Pont des Trous/Bridge of Gaps ★★

Across the Scheldt in the northwest of the old center. Helping Tournai develop astride the Scheldt, this bridge (towers from 1281, the three Gothic-style arches took an additional 25 years) is medieval military architecture at its best. Built to guard the entrance to the city by river, it was defended by a series of portcullises. Restored after World War II, the arches (the "gaps" in the frame) were raised 7 feet/2 meters to facilitate river navigation. From the bridge (cafe on top, eateries inside, see "Restaurants") is a great view of the cathedral's five towers, but if you go back a bridge to the **pont Delwart**, you get a ★★view that includes this very picturesque, restored, ancient, arched, Tournai-stone bridge.

Romanesque Houses   ★

Rue Barre Saint-Brice. On a continuation of rue de Derasse off rue Royale (which follows a straight and pleasant route across the river between the cathedral and the station) are found the strongly-horizontal Romanesque facades that are believed to be western Europe's oldest (1175–1200) burghers' homes. The facades, right up to their gables, are built of the blue-gray Tournai Scheldt valley stone. Also on the same street are Gothic houses, dating from the 14th and 15th centuries.

Continue to the nearby end of rue Barre Saint-Brice to **Eglise Saint Brice**, begun in the 13th century, and most noteworthy for having been built alongside the cemetery where the tomb of **Frankish King Childeric** (father of Clovis), buried in 482, was found in 1653 (plaque on place Clovis 8). From here, it's a short walk southeast across the *rue de Pont* and the river back into the center.

Tour Henri VIII

Place Verte, rue du Rempart. This is all that remains of the citadel—the rest was demolished by Louis XIV—built here under the orders of Henry VIII, who stationed an army of 5,000 in this tower while making war against France from 1513–1515. Squat, cylindrical, 20 ft/6 m thick at the base of its walls, and probably an imitation of the *Tower of London*, the massive keep was built in 1515, two years after Tournai was occupied by the King of England. The two brick-vaulted ceiling halls, one above the other, house displays of weapons and armory and a small World War II resistance museum.

WHERE TO STAY

INEXPENSIVE

Le Parc   ★★★

Place Reine Astrid 7; *21.28.93,* FAX *21.46.82.* Centrally located on an attractive square, steps from the belfry, this 19th-century former villa has 13 tastefully and individually furnished guest rooms, all with bath/toilet, TV/video, telephone, minibar/fridge. Rooms are generous-sized, those on the top floor shaped by the eaves; front rooms have views of cathedral towers. Public rooms in this personable property feature architectural details, an antique-accented decor, and include an attractive bar, winter-garden lounge, and oasis terrace in back. No elevator; parking; breakfast included; major credit cards. The hotel's **le Parc Restaurant** (*daily noon–3 p.m., dinner from 7 p.m.;*

moderate; six-course menu with wines, expensive) is popular locally and concentrates on French cuisine and regional specialties (warm foie gras, sweetbreads, rabbit, duck, fish, rhubarb mousse).

Cathédrale Hotel

Place St-Pierre; ☎ *21.50.77.* This modern hotel, with helpful front desk service, is physically light and bright, but corridor noises carry through the thin walls. If your plans call for a weekend sleep-in, ask for a back room, since the morning markets in the square begin setting up before 7 a.m. All 38 rooms have tile bath/showers, TV with remote control, telephone; some have views of the cathedral that looms just up the street. There's a garden, terrace tables, hotel restaurant (with cathedral view), and lobby bar (open until midnight), all locally popular. Breakfast included; elevator; major credit cards.

WHERE TO EAT

While Tournai may not be on the beaten tourist path, because local residents enjoy dining out, it's wise to inquire at better restaurants about the need for reservations (and which credit cards are accepted). Together with **le Parc** (see under "Accommodations"), **Charles Quint** *(Grand'Place 3; noon–2 p.m., 7–10 p.m., closed Wed. evening, Thurs., 3 weeks late July-mid Aug., a week at Carnival;* ☎ *22.14.41; moderate to expensive)* is considered near the top of Tournai's in-town choices; preparation is classical Belgian cuisine, with a focus on fish. The **Pont des Trous** *(quai Staline; kitchen open from noon for lunch, 6:30 p.m. for dinner, closed Mon.;* ☎ *21.16.16; moderate)* is an atmospheric eatery actually located in Tournai's handsome triple-arched 1304 bridge. À la carte choices in the more formal **Rotisserie** *(11:30 a.m. for lunch, 7:30 p.m. for dinner)* are limited, but the **Taverne** (open from 10 a.m.) offers choices in its casual fare, or simply have a drink on the terrace atop the Scheldt. **Le Pressoir** *(Vieux Marché-aux-Poteries 2; lunch from noon, dinner;* ☎ *22.35.13; moderate)* serves its specialties of foie gras, lobster, and turbot in a 17th-century house with cathedral view; allow enough time for leisurely, even slow service. Across the street from the cathedral is the **Bistro de la Cathédrale** *(Vieux Marché-aux-Poteries 15; daily noon– 2:30 p.m., 7–11 p.m.;* ☎ *21.03.79; inexpensive)*, that can provide informal fare or a more complete meal featuring *Lapin* (rabbit) a la Tournaisienne, *Magret de canard* (duck), or fish. The house specialties at **le Carillon** *(Grand' Place 64; noon–3 p.m., 7–10:30 p.m., closed Sat. noon, Mon., month of Sept.;* ☎ *21.33.79; moderate, plat du jour inexpensive)* are foie gras and fish. Down by the riverside is **O Pere au Quai** *(quai Notre-Dame 18; noon–2:30 p.m., 7–11 p.m., closed Wed., month of Aug.;* ☎ *23.29.22; inexpensive)* serving simply prepared food (grilled fish, meat, salad bar) in a pleasing setting.

IN THE AREA

Beloeil Castle

Rue du Chateau, Beloeil; daily April–Sept., and weekends in Oct. 10 a.m.–6 p.m.; ☎ *(069) 68.94.26, 68.96.55; self-guided visits; printed history of family and chateau in English; parking.* For six centuries Beloeil has been the residence of the 1000-year-old **de Ligne dynasty**. The present Prince de Ligne Antoine is married to Alix of Luxembourg, sister of the Grand Duke of Luxembourg. The distinguished de Lignes have included knights who fought in the crusades. A knight of the *Order of the Golden Fleece*, and Eugene, who, in 1830, was offered the crown of newly-independent Belgium but declined. Fire broke out in Beloeil in 1900, and the chateau had to be rebuilt under Louis, ninth prince of de Ligne. The great marble entrance hall and central staircase create a stately setting, but much of the house, with its valuable and attractive contents (furniture, portraits of family and foreign royalty, master paintings, 17th-century tapestries, silverware, Chinese porcelain, and library with 20,000 leather-bound volumes) is much more intimate. A past president of the *European Historic Houses Association*, Prince Antoine has said of himself, "I am by birth a lifetime caretaker." Among other ongoing maintenance, Beloeil has 240 windows to clean and 6.3 miles/10 km. of hedge to clip. Following the example of many English stately homes, Antoine de Ligne decided to open his chateau to the public to cover the high cost of everyday upkeep.

LIÈGE

GUIDELINES FOR LIÈGE

SIGHTS

At the heart of Liège are the **Prince-Bishops Palace** on place St-Lambert and **Perron** monument on the adjacent *place du Marché*, both attesting to the city's history of independence. Several restored **mansion-museums**, and the **Museum of Walloon Life** in a former convent, shed light on Liège life. The city's selection of churches with Romanesque foundations includes St. Barthelemy's with its famed 12th-century **baptismal font** by **Renier du Huy**. Readers of works by native son **Georges Simenon** will find that the atmosphere of his books, though often set in Paris, is thickly Liège. Adding flavor to Belgium's Walloon bastion is the river **Meuse** (the *Maas* in nearby Holland), which flows through the city, separating the old town from the colorful workers' quarter of **Outremeuse**.

GETTING AROUND

Although Liège is a large city, many of its important sights and museums are located within walking distance of each other, not far from the main **tourist office** (*Feronstree 92*). Staff there can arrange for a guided (English), set-price **city taxi tour**. Taxi ranks are located at *Gare Guillemins, place du Marché, place St-Lambert, place Foch, place de la Cathédrale, place de la Républiqué Française,* and *blvd. d'Avroy.* Liège has a good **bus network**; maps of the system are posted at stops and available at the tourist office. Main terminals are *place Saint-Lambert, place du Theatre, place Cathédrale,* and *place des Guillemins.* There are **boat cruises** on the **Meuse** (schedule at tourist office), though the scenery doesn't justify the full-day river trip to nearby Maastricht in Holland; take a train instead.

SHOPPING

Liège is famed for its Sunday morning (9 a.m.–2 p.m.) market **la Batte**—a Walloon word that means *embankment*—held along the Meuse between *place Cockerill* and *pont Maghin.* The amazing range of foodstuffs, household items, clothing, small animals, and cosmetic merchandise, combined with thousands of browsers and buyers (many from neighboring Holland and Germany), give this flea market something of the flavor of a medieval fair. Shoppers from near and far also come weekdays to Liège, a major regional market town with one of Europe's largest center-city pedestrian precincts. It has some 5,000 retail outlets, from large department stores and fashion boutiques to antiques shops; prime streets include *rue de la Cathédrale, rue St.-Paul, rue de la Regence, blvd. de la Sauveniere, place du Marché, Feronstree, pont d'Avroy,* and across the river, *rue Jean d'Outre-Meuse.* Antiques shops are clustered around *rue St. Thomas, rue des Mineurs,* and *rue du Palais.*

Liège's **Val Saint Lambert** handcut crystal has been produced since 1826 at a factory south of Liège in Seraing *(Crystalworks Val-Saint-Lambert; rue du Val 245;* ☎ *(041) 37.09.60; FAX (041) 37.67.81; , April–Oct. 31 Tues.–Sun. 10 a.m.–5 p.m., closed Mon.; rest of year Sat., Sun., holidays. only, same hours.; exhibition hall and Val Diffusion shop open year-round Tues.–Sun. 10 a.m.–5 p.m., closed Mon.; guided tours; self-service restaurant; accessible by bus from Jemeppe Gare Routiere in Liège).* There are studio demonstrations of glass-blowing, decoration, and engraving. The exhibition hall has a permanent display of antique and contemporary pieces. The *Val Diffusion* shop sells pieces made by trainees and apprentices.

ENTERTAINMENT AND EVENTS

Born in Liège, composer **Cesar Franck** (1822–1890) attended the **Conservatoire** *(rue Forgeur 14;* ☎ *22.03.06),* which still offers concerts of his and other works, as does the **Orchestre Philharmonique** *(rue Forgeur 11;* ☎ *23.67.74).* The active **Opera Royal de Wallonie** *(place de la Republique Francaise;* ☎ *23.59.10)* occasionally pays honor to Liège-born **Andre Ernest Gretry** (1741–1813), a composer particularly noted for his comic operas. For performance schedules of these, midday and Sunday morning concerts and others, inquire at the tourist office. **Jazz** can be heard in rue Roture in Outremeuse at **Le Lions'Envoile** and **Le Cirque Divers**, and at **Les Caves de Porto** in Feronstree in the old town. Music clubs and cafes also are centered in **le Carré** (Old Town), which is bordered by *blvd. Sauveniere, pont d'Avroy, Vinave d'Ile,* and *rue des Dominicaines.* The 4th weekend in June is observed in the **Commune of Saint-Pholien** with morning concerts, open air mass, festive lights and fireworks, and a meeting of the "giants." August 15 is Liège's **Free Republic of Outremeuse's** feast day, celebrated in the streets with spirited traditional events and a fun fair. **September Nights** is an annual Liège music festival. At the end of September, the **Fêtes de Wallonie** is held in the courtyard of the Prince-Bishops Palace.

WHERE TO STAY

Comfortable, convenient hotels in Liège are limited, so plan ahead with reservations when possible. The tourist office will assist.

WHERE TO EAT

Many of Liège's typical dishes are pork specialties (such as *boudin blanc,* a white sausage). City restaurants serve fare from French *haute cuisine* to *potée,* the Walloon word for *stew. Boulets frites* are large firm balls of bread stuffing flavored with meat and doused in gravy. Local street-stand favorites include *bouketes* (thick buckwheat pancakes). The farmstead-studded **Herve** region, to the northeast of Liège, is famous for its odorous cheese; locally, it's served spread on toast and topped with syrup. **Pubs**—Liège's 10,000-strong student population helps support them, and the city's many terrace cafes and taverns—can't legally, but often do, pour *peket,* a powerful local gin.

ARRIVING

Liège is an international rail crossroads, with direct trains from Brussels and Luxembourg City, and many connections. The principal rail station is **Gare des Guillemins** (with taxis), about 1.5 mi./2 kms. from the *place St-Lambert.* The city also is linked to major European cities by motorway, and to regional cities from its **airport**. If you arrive in Liège by **car**, there's a car park beside the main tourist office *(Feronstreet 90),* and others at *place Cathédrale, place du Marché, place Saint-Lambert;* center city driving is hampered around place Saint-Lambert because of traffic overload, coupled with construction.

TRAVEL TIPS

Municipal financial difficulties have interrupted the building of Liège's Metro, leaving an unsightly construction site in front of the **Bishop's Palace** at **place St-Lambert** in the center of the city. The unfortunate fiscal situation also means that museum hours have been reduced because of cutbacks in personnel; confirm the opening hours when you arrive.

LIÈGE IN CONTEXT

Liège (Luik), *la cite ardente*, despite Namur's official position as capital of Belgium's French-speaking Wallonia, acts as if it possesses that status. Certainly Liège, a fiercely independent municipality for far more than a millennium, is an ardent caretaker of the Walloon language. (*Walloon* is an ancient Latin dialect—as French itself was a Latin dialect, originally spoken solely in the *Ile de France* region.) Walloon, the most northern of the Latin languages, didn't gain the same cultural and social status that the French dialect did (by being the language of the Ile de France state which gained wide-ranging political power in the Middle Ages). Instead, Walloon remained an essentially rural tongue; under the status consciousness that came with the affluence of the 19th-century Industrial Revolution, it suffered such a popular decline that it actually was forbidden in schools. Today, though the right to teach Walloon has been restored, its use continues to slide. Liège's support includes Walloon theater, and a language exhibit in the excellent **Museum of Walloon Life** (possibly Belgium's best institute of local culture and folklore).

Liège marks its beginning from the building of a chapel in 558 by St. Monulphus, bishop of Tongeren-Maastricht (two nearby Roman-era towns, considered to be the oldest in Belgium and Holland). A later bishop of Tongeren-Maastricht, St. Lambert, was murdered in Liège (supposedly for having accused nobleman Pepin of Herstal of incest) in 705. His successor **St. Hubert** (see "Saint-Hubert village" in "The Ardennes" section) erected a church in Lambert's honor, which rapidly became a place of pilgrimage, no doubt influencing Hubert's decision to move the see to Liège. The Liège bishopric was established in 721, with a residence for the bishop built next to St.-Lambert's church. First Holy Roman Emperor **Charlemagne** (742–814) is said to have granted Liège its first city privileges (a fact commemorated by an equestrian statue of the Frankish ruler at the north end of the **parc d'Avroy**).

Under **Notger**, who after his coronation as bishop in 980, made sage territorial moves that gained him temporal powers and made him the first to hold the title of *Prince-Bishop of Liège*. The city became the capital of an ecclesiastical/political principality whose rulers would hold power for more than 800 years, until the end of the 18th century, and holding sway over parts of Germany (the Holy Roman Empire) and today's Belgium, Holland, and France, with a total area equivalent to two-thirds of present-day Wallonia. Administrative and judiciary bodies were created and Liège became an intellectual and artistic center. (Among other cultural developments, Liège became famous for its school of song, fostered by the collegiate churches there, and in the 14th century, supplied many of the singers for the Sistene Chapel at the Vatican, which had been re-established in 1376.) Bishop Notger also expanded trade and fortified the city with several sturdy churches being incorporated into the city walls. Under Notger and his successor, the foundations for the churches of **St. Denis**, **St. Martin**, **St. Paul**, **St. Jean**, **St. Jacques**, and **St. Barthelemy** were laid, giving the episcopal town a skyline of steeples. At the end of the 12th century, Bishop Albert de Cuyck recognized the liberties of Liège, and from then on its citizens lived with the until-then-unheard-of concept that "a poor man is king in his castle."

Perhaps inevitably, the powerful, often secular, Prince-Bishops (many "bishops" in name only and enjoying a worldly lifestyle far from Liège) became a dynasty with nephews being elected by the cathedral-chapter in the footsteps of their uncles (even as titular Catholic bishops, the fathers were not supposed to have sons). The authority of the Prince-Bishops often became a source of conflict for the Liègeois, who sought more power for ordinary citizens. Many dissensions in the 13th and 14th centuries ended with concessions made by the Prince-Bishops to the guilds and workers. In the 15th century, the dukes of Burgundy, who had already obtained possession of the rest of what is now Belgium, sought to add the principality of Liège to their sphere.

The independent and unsupportive attitude of the Liègeois finally brought Duke of Burgundy **Charles the Bold** to the boiling point. He and his army marched on the city, arriving at the end of October, 1468. They camped on the heights above the city, near the present Citadel, and prepared to storm the city. On the nights of October 29/30, some 600 daring Liège men, led by **Vincent de Bueren**, made their way up the steep slope to the camp (the 373 steps of the **Montagne de Bueren** commemorate the deed) with the thought of assassinating Charles. But they attacked the wrong tent, were caught, and were killed to the last man. Charles set to the task of leveling Liège, pillaging it first, then setting it afire. The city is said to have burned for seven weeks; across it, only churches and monasteries—Charles being a devout Catholic—were spared (and eight houses as lodging for the religious). Thus, most of Liège's medieval heritage went up in smoke, leaving it with, by Belgium standards, a surprisingly recent Old Town. Before he left to return to Bruges, Charles took with him Liège's symbol of its liberties, the **Perron** (a smaller, and alas portable, form of the Flemish belfries which symbolized civil freedoms), and he annulled the city's rights. Such was this last duke of Burgundy's power that, until his premature death in 1477 at the Battle of Nancy, the Liègeois couldn't even rebuild their homes. Charles's daughter, **Mary of Burgundy**, restored Liège's rights and returned the precious *Perron.*

Under **Prince-Bishop Erard de la Marck** (1505–1538), Liège regained status as a political/religious center, beginning another period of prosperity, and one of relative peace for three centuries. The principality's purposeful policy of neutrality in foreign affairs managed to keep it out of the religious wars of the 16th century. The rebuilding necessitated by the devastation delivered by Charles the Bold continued, first in the old familiar Gothic style but soon succumbing to the newer Italian Renaissance style. The imposing new Prince-Bishops Palace built by Erard de la Marck led the way, and the Italian, and therefore Catholic-sanctioned-style, then spread rapidly during the Counter Reformation; more than 100 churches were built across the principality of Liège in the following century. Also popular was a simpler architectural style which became known as the "Meuse Renaissance." During the 16th century, without the upheaval of the religious wars that embroiled much of northern Europe, the principality of Liège became the first place on the Continent to open and exploit its coal mines (it had done so to some degree since the 12th century), developing the iron ore, coal mining, and munitions industries that continued to serve as a base for its economy in later centuries. (Though remaining politically neutral, Liège felt free to supply arms and ammunition to others, even to those foreign leaders who were fighting wars on its own doorstep.)

In the 17th century, unwise alliances made by the prince-bishopric without the consent of the Liègeois resulted in the principality declaring war on French King Louis XIV. French bombing of Liège in 1691 destroyed the **Hôtel de Ville** and many other buildings and monuments around the place du Marché, including the **Perron**. A new Perron, created in 1697 and mounted firmly on a large fountain, was one of the first of a wave of replacement structures, including the Hôtel de Ville, built in Liège in the 17th and 18th centuries.

Peace and prosperity returned to Liège, but it was accompanied by great social inequalities. On August 18, 1789, a month after the storming of the **Bastille** in Paris (the beginning of the French Revolution), the Liègeois arose in their own revolution. Among the actions taken by Liègeois "patriots" (encouraged by the Revolutionary French Army whose soldiers headed north with their extremist anti-religious fervor) was the tearing down of **Cathédrale St.-Lambert**, to them a symbol of social injustice as strong as the Bastille had been for the French. The participating Liègeois, unlike the French Revolutionary forces that destroyed so many churches in the Benelux, were not against religion, but against the Prince-Bishop and his 60 canons who had grown rich and contemptuous of the privileges of the people. In 1794, Dumouriez captured Liège for revolutionary France and expelled Antoine de Mean, the last Prince-Bishop.

After the Napoleonic era, Liège, no longer an independent principality, became (along with the rest of Belgium) united with Holland. Despite the economic benefits realized by the city under that union (a university in 1817 and the founding of the steel industry at Seraing to the south of the city, as well as expansion of its coal, arms, and glass production), the Liègeois supported the establishment of a free Belgium. Many, under the leadership of Charles Rogier, went to Brussels in the summer of 1830 to support the armed rise against Dutch rule.

With a free Belgian nation finally realized, Liège—one of the earliest cities in Europe to have entered the new Industrial Revolution—continued to move ahead full steam. Installations for modern steel production were built upstream on the Meuse between 1835 and 1850, and docks were expanded downstream. After train tracks were laid to Liège (1842), the mainstream Meuse was straightened in its path through the city, while the side streams were filled in to form fine wide avenues for the flourishing city: rue de la Régence, rue d'Avroy, and boulevard de la Sauveniere, which shows its former river oxbow shape.

Outremeuse, on an island in the Meuse in the center of Liège, long a workers' quarter of the city known for its independent, rebellious working-class character, love of tradition, and devotion to the Liège dialect, had few riches to be content with. Although well established—two ancient crafts had long been localized here, weavers in Saint-Nicolas Outremeuse and tanners in the adjoining commune of Saint-Pholien—much of Outremeuse was little more than a swamp until built up in the 19th century as a workers' residential neighborhood. It was in Outremeuse, at the core of *la cite ardente*, that Liège-born author **Georges Simenon** (1903–1989) was raised. (See also "The Muse" in "The Belgian Cultural Legacy" chapter.) Simenon, perhaps the world's most widely translated 20th-century writer, though he often set his stories in Paris (to which he moved after beginning his career as a reporter for the *Gazette de Liège*) constantly drew on the scenes and experiences of his youth in Liège for the character and characters in his books. In 1973 he wrote: "Most of us owe our experience to our childhood and adolescence. Though I am seventy, I act, think and live like a child from Outremeuse."

Visitors interested in exploring *Simenon's Liège*, which though being restored here and there is not so very different in many ways today from when the writer lived there in the early 20th century, can do so in depth with the help of a guide (arranged through the tourist office), but there are many sites associated with Simenon that you can see on your own (the tourist office pamphlet *Itineraire Simenon* is in French only, but of some use for addresses). The Outremeuse Simenon grew up in, though only just across the Meuse from the old center of Liège, was such a separate world that when those on the "island" needed to cross the **pont des Arches** they changed out of their working clothes (though crossing via the **Passerelle** footbridge they didn't feel the need to do so). Simenon's grandfather, as owner of a hat shop (then at **rue Puits-en-sock 58**), was an important member of Outremeuse's **St.-Nicolas** parish had a pew with his name, and took collections on Sundays. Simenon's mother ran a boarding house on the street that today has been renamed **rue Georges Simenon**. The writer-to-be joined other rebellious youth in the **Impasse de la Houpe** behind **St.-Pholien's** church to drink and do dope. Slightly older, he met other artist friends who considered themselves above the rules and prejudices of the conventional world at **La Cague (The Keg)**. Across the Passerelle foot bridge, he enjoyed the typical **Café Lequet** *(quai dur Meuse 17)*, at one time owned by his aunt and still rich with the atmosphere that Simenon wrote into his books. Simenon was intimately connected with many inhabitants of the nearby narrow **rue du Champion** (running between the *rue de la Cathédrale* and the *quai sur Meuse*), which continues to be a street of prostitute-rented rooms. (Simenon claimed to have "known" some 10,000 women in his life). He frequented Le Carré, in his youth a decent entertainment district with cabarets, though it turned into a dangerous "Little Chicago" from pre-World War II until the 1960s, after which it gradually returned to the pleasant student cafe and up-market bistro neighborhood it is now. Today, Simenon would hardly recognize **rue Roture**, in his day badly run down but now a typical Outremeuse street that is atypical for its restored buildings filled with restaurants and cafes. You may (though many others do not) find it a coincidence that the name *Maigret*—Simenon's famous fictional detective—appears on a memorial at the **Hôtel**

de Ville honoring Liège policemen who died in the First World War. Retaining his ties with Liège, Simenon made a personal gift of a fountain to the university campus.

During World War I, Liège's economic progress, as in the rest of German-occupied Belgium, slowed. Throughout that conflict, workers in Liège's famous small arms factories stood up to the enemy by refusing to produce weapons. Developments after the war included the opening in 1939 of the **Albert Canal**, which connected Liège on the Meuse to Antwerp on the Scheldt and to the North Sea. When the Second World War was over, the importance of the canal doubled. Today the third largest inland port in Europe (after Paris, France and Duisburg, Germany), Liège has port installations on the Meuse upstream and down from the center of the city. The center downstream at Monsin, at the entrance to the Albert Canal, is marked by a monument topped with a 40-foot/12-meter high figure of King Albert.

Many Liègeois feel that more damage was done to the face of their city during "urban planning" than in either world war. With coal still being mined in the 1950s and early 1960s, Liège had the wherewithal to wrap itself in modern trappings. The demolition of grand 19th-century mansions and older, rundown buildings (that no one then had a thought to preserve) has left many an ordinary office high rise in Liège. Today a much greater awareness of Liège's architectural legacy exists, the restored building that houses the tourist office on Feronstree being an example. The coal mines are all closed now, and Liège's future is structured in steel and its excellent mid-continent position in Europe's evolving single-market.

GUIDEPOSTS

Telephone code 041

Tourist Information • Feronstree 92; Mon.–Fri., 9 a.m.–6 p.m. (5 p.m. from Nov. 1–Mar. 31), Sat. 10 a.m.–4 p.m., Sun. and holidays. 10 a.m.–2 p.m.; ☎ *22.24.56*. There's a smaller tourist office at Guillemins station (☎ *21.92.21*).

Bus • 24-hour information: ☎ *67.00.64*.

Trains • Information: ☎ *52.98.50*.

Police • ☎ *101*.

Post Office • Main office: rue de la Regence 51, place du Marche.

Telephone/Telegraph • Rue de l'Universite 32, daily 8 a.m. to 7 p.m.

WHAT TO SEE AND DO

The center of Liège, **place St-Lambert**, currently is an eyesore rather than an elegant open space—due to the presently discontinued construction of a city *Metro* and other road works. Two centuries ago, the square probably looked even worse, after the demolishment by French and local revolutionaries of the site's Cathédrale St.-Lambert, first begun by Bishop Hubert (c. A.D. 705). Liège's ★★**Palais des Princes-Eveques** (Palace of the Prince-Bishops), which faces place St.-Lambert, also has origins dating back to Hubert (later St.-Hubert, patron of hunters), who transferred the see here in 720 and built a modest "bishop's house." The palace it became was destroyed by fire in 1505 and replaced by the one we see today in Renaissance style (except for the classic facade by the Brussels architect Jean-Andre Anneessens built following a 1734 fire). Notable are the two inner courtyards, the first with 60 surrounding columns, the capital of each sculpted with different fantastic faces and figures, inspired by discoveries just then being made in the New World, and by *The Praise of Folly* by **Erasmus** (1466–1536), of whom the builder, Bishop Erard de la Marck, was a devotee. The second courtyard is a particularly peaceful setting. Since the end of the rule of the bishops in 1794, the palace has served as the seat of the Law Courts and, since the birth of the Belgian nation, as home of the provincial government. The ★**Perron** on the adjoining **place du Marché** is the symbol of Liège's communal freedoms, the present one crafted and topped by the *Three Graces* by Liège sculptor **Jean del Cour** in 1697. Attractively surrounded by 17th- and 18th-century buildings, the square hosts a daily flower, fruit, and vegetable market, a function it has performed from the city's earliest days. Although the classical style Hôtel de Ville (town hall) which overlooks place du Marché dates only from the early 18th century (Louis XIV style), town business has been conducted on the site since the 13th century in a house called ★**La Violette**, a term still used locally to refer to the town hall. Inquire in the impressive waiting hall about viewing the richly decorated ceremonial rooms.

Behind and rising above these Liège landmarks is the **Citadel**, located some 400 steps up the so-called **Montagne de Bueren** (built in 1875 and named for Vincent de Bueren, a fierce defender of Liège against Duke of Burgundy Charles the Bold's attack in 1468). Though there's a view of the city from the Citadel, it's no longer as panoramic as advertised, being somewhat blocked by vegetation. An interesting alternative to climbing all 400 stairs is to head from the ★**Hors-Chateau** (a street built in the 11th century outside the city walls, today lined with 17th- and 18th-century houses amid 20th-century structures) to the base of the Montagne de Bueren, and take a left into the **Impasse des Ursulines**. Here is Liège's ★**Museum of Architecture**, a block of 17th-century buildings preserved in *situ* or rebuilt here amid terraced landscaping (the museum is essentially a documentation and cultural center, so the view from the outside is almost as good as going inside). Beyond the museum, further up the Impasse, a door opens in the high wall on the left hand side and leads to a large park reaching up the hillside and to a footpath, ★**Sentier des Coteaux**, which followed to the left offers fine views down the slope, over the old convent buildings housing the Museum of Walloon Life, the Prince-Bishops Palace, and the roofs of the area's 17th- and 18th-century houses. Past the quiet chestnut-shaded yard of the former convent ★**Cour des Minimes**, you come out on *rue du Peri*, which turns downhill into picturesque **rue Pierreuse**, and back to the **Prince-Bishop's Palace** and *place du Marché*.

From *place du Marché*, a relatively short, roughly circular route, on and off the three parallel streets of **Feronstree, Hors-Chateau**, and Meuse riverside **la Batte/quai de Maestricht** (all of which have some interesting 17th- and 18th-century facades) will bring you to most of Liège's major sights. As an aid to those with limited time, they are discussed below in order of relative importance or interest.

Èglise St.-Barthélemy ★

place St-Barthélemy; Mon.–Sat., 10 a.m.–noon, 2–5 p.m., Sun., 2–5 p.m., ☎ *21.89.44.* Although it dates back to the 11th century (the Romanesque narthex is being restored), with many typical local Mosan architectural characteristics and twin Rhenan towers in evidence, St-Barthélemy is visited primarily for its early 12th-century brass ★★★**baptismal font**, one of Belgium's most famed art treasures, attributed to goldsmith **Renier de Huy**. The font was originally ordered by Abbot Hellin at the beginning of the 12th century for **Notre-Dame-aux-Fonts**, the parish church which stood next to **Cathédrale St.-Lambert**. Serving as its baptistry, for centuries it was the only church in Liège where the sacrament of baptism could be celebrated. Like St.-Lambert's, Notre Dame was destroyed during the French period at the end of the 18th century, but the font was hidden and escaped harm (except for the lid, which was lost), to be presented to St.-Barthélemy in 1804. Today it stands in that church to the left of the altar in a glassed-in space that you can enter to examine the art work at close range. The beautiful bronze tub seems to be carried by ten oxen (originally 12, symbolizing the apostles) set in a stone base. Five scenes of baptism, including the main scene in which Christ is being baptized by John the Baptist, are arranged around the tub, the whole design showing the influence of classical, Byzantine, and Mosan art traditions. The small glowing faces of the figures are remarkably expressive. Although it was not operating during my most recent visit, inquire about the 30-minute multilingual audiovisual program that describes the creation of this wonderful work.

Musée de la Vie Wallonne ★★

Museum of Walloon Life; cours des Mineurs 1; Tues.–Sat. 10 a.m.–5 p.m., Sun. and holidays. 10 a.m.–4 p.m., closed Mon.; ☎ *23.60.94; exhibit notes in French only, limited multilingual information given at some points, worth a visit in any case.* This exceptionally well-displayed collection on Wallonia's social and economic history is handsomely housed in the restored Mosan Renaissance brick-and-limestone 17th-century former Minorites convent. It's an appropriate location for such a museum since, during its active days, the convent was a Liègeois gathering spot for guild meetings and other important civic occasions, as explained in the recorded multilingual commentary to which one can listen while seated on a bench on a balcony overlooking the peaceful interior courtyard. From food (a typical Ardennes kitchen and *salle d'alimentation* with cookie molds from Dinant, festive breads, cheese and butter preparation) to local festivals, the important local industries of coal mining and crystal cutting, workers' places (pewtermaker's, pipemaker's, coppersmith's and cooper's), and the geographic and linguistic features of the region, the whole panoply of Wallonia and its traditions from the late-18th to early-20th centuries are presented. Also on hand is an amusing collection of puppets (puppet theater is still active in Liège) including favorite folklore characters and typical Liègeois *Tchantches*. Other popular puppets from the cast of characters in the city's history include Charlemagne, Charles the Bold, and Christ, who hangs on a cross for his part in Passion Plays. The puppets' respective sizes reveals much about them, since "good" characters are always larger. In the basement of the museum (ask at the reception desk), a coal mine gallery has been reconstructed.

Musée Curtius   ★

quai de Maestricht 13; Mon., Thurs., Sat. 2–5 p.m., Wed. and Fri. 10 a.m.–1 p.m., closed Tues., major holidays., 1st and 3rd Sun. each month; ☎ *21.94.04.* Housed in the Mosan Renaissance mansion built on the river bank between 1600 and 1610 by Liège Commissary Jean Curtius, this museum of archeology and decorative arts documents life in the Meuse valley since Roman times. The archeological items displayed in the period interior cover the region's prehistory to early Middle Ages, while the art work is from the medieval period until the end of Liège's *Ancien Regime* (prince-bishopric). Highlights include the *Gospel Book* of Notger, Liège's first prince-bishop (972–1008), beautifully bound and decorated with an ivory sculpture on the cover (to which enamels were added in the 12th century), the *Dom Rupert Virgin*, a masterpiece of 12th-century Mosan sculpture, and two polychrome chimneypieces from 1604. Sharing the building is the **Glass Museum**, with a rich collection of ancient pieces of glass from the Islamic world and Venice, as well as contemporary creations. Belgian glass, which has a prestigious history in Liège through the local **Val-St.-Lambert Crystal Manufacturers** founded in 1826, is particularly well represented.

Musée d'Ansembourg   ★★

Feronstree 114; Tues.–Sun. tours at 1, 2, 3, 4, and 5 p.m.; closed Mon., major holidays.; ☎ *21.94.02.* Another mansion museum (18th century) is devoted to the decorative arts and furniture of Liège's golden age. The sumptuous interior, which remains authentic to its original design of 1738–1741 and includes the Cordoba-leather-lined dining room with remarkable local Regency-style dresser, delft-tiled kitchen hung with copper utensils, and drawing room with tapestries from the

Belgian town of Oudenaarde, can be enjoyed at your own pace. Other rooms are filled with fine plasterwork and painted ceilings, carved wainscoting and panelling, monumental fireplaces and mantel pieces, and fine furniture all executed by Liège craftspeople (Liège was famous for cabinet-making in the 16th–18th centuries).

Musée d'Armes ★

Museum of Arms; quai de Maestricht 8; Mon., Thurs., Sat. 10 a.m.–1 p.m., Wed., Fri. 2–5 p.m., 1st and 3rd Suns. of month 10 a.m.–1 p.m.; closed Tues., major holidays. and first half Feb.; ☎ 21.94.00. Liège has held an important place is the history of firearms manufacturing since the 14th century and still enjoys international fame from its School of Arms Manufacture and the Fabrique Nationale in nearby Herstal. At this museum, which shows the history and evolution of sporting and defense weapons, Liège offers one of the world's foremost collections of firearms. On display are some 12,500 pieces dating from the 14th to the 20th centuries, many exceptional for their beautiful decorative inlaid and engraved work (a hallmark of Liège weapons), others for their rarity (such as the unique 7-barrelled flintlock machine gun, c. 1810, made in the U.S.). All are housed in the neoclassical mansion built in 1814 by Liège architect Barthélemy Digneffe for weapons builder Pierre-Joseph Lemille. Also to be seen is a portrait by **Ingres** of then Major Consul **Napoleon Bonaparte**, who visited Liège in 1803 to sign a decree granting money to reconstruct a city district that had been destroyed in 1794 in French/Austrian conflict.

It is necessary to leave Liège's "museum circuit" to see the most important of the many churches (all Roman Catholic) which, as an episcopal see, the city has long supported. Liège's churches sometimes were spared the devastation wreaked on other city structures, as was the case under Burgundian Charles the Bold's 1468 attack (see "Liège in Context"). The situation was the very opposite for the unfortunate **Cathédrale St.-Lambert**, that historic structure in the center of the city razed by antireligious revolutionaries at the end of the 18th century. Most Liège churches show a mixed architectural heritage due to their great age and subsequent events such as fire, feuds, and fashion. A wonderful example is ★**Eglise St.-Jacques** *(place St-Jacques; Mon.–Fri. 8 a.m.–noon, Sat., Sun. and July and Aug. 8 a.m.–5 p.m.; English booklet).* Built beginning in Romanesque style in the early 11th century (the narthex remains, though the rest of the chancel collapsed on June 30, 1513), the nave and eastern chancel were rebuilt in Flamboyant Gothic, and the porch (in 1558) in Italian Renaissance. During the French Revolution at the end of the 18th century, St.-Jacques managed to escape destruction, and King Leopold I intervened for its restoration in the mid-19th century (another long-term restoration was begun in 1962). From the rear of the nave the view of the lace-like, carved-stone ceiling ★★vaulting is remarkable. The large, impressive white ★statues (most by 17th-century Liège sculptor **Jean del Cour**) hanging on pillars in the nave were carved in lime wood and painted white, since marble was so expensive. Other notable interior details include the

16th-century stained glass windows in the chancel; carved 14th-century stalls dating from the Romanesque church; and beautiful Renaissance-style organ case dated 1600 by Andre Severin of Maastricht, who is buried beneath his creation.

Cathédrale St.-Paul

place Cathédrale. Promoted from church to cathedral in 1801 following the demolishment by revolutionaries of St.-Lambert's, St.-Paul's was founded in 971. Itself demolished in the 13th century, the rebuilding of the present structure spans the centuries from the 14th to the 19th, when stones from dismantled St.-Lambert's were used to complete St.-Paul's with a spire similar to the one toppled from the former cathedral. Restoration in the 19th century left St.-Paul's with little original detail, and the cathedral is visited for its **Tresor/Treasury** *(entry from the south transept or apply at the Sacristan at 2A rue St.-Paul at the side of the church; closed from 12:30-2 p.m., and for the day at 5 p.m.).* The most outstanding articles, saved from the rich collections of St.-Lambert's, are the imposing life-size silver reliquary bust of St.-Lambert containing his skull (1505), a 10th-century icon of the Virgin, and 9th-century book of the Gospels. Best known is the embossed gold reliquary offered to St.-Lambert's by Charles the Bold in 1471 as expiation for having leveled Liège, save for the churches, in 1468. The golden statue, created by his own court jeweler, shows a repentant-faced Charles on his knees in front of a standing St. George; Charles holds a box containing skin from a hand of St.-Lambert.

WHERE TO STAY

EXPENSIVE

Ramada Hotel Liège

blvd de la Sauveniere 100; ☎ *21.77.11, FAX 21.77.01.* With 105 rooms on six floors, the well-located, service-oriented 1960s-built Ramada is Liège's leading hotel. Used most by business travelers, the Ramada, while not elegant, functions well and is comfortable. Its location is more convenient than most hotels in the city, about a three blocks' walk to place St-Lambert, as near to shopping and entertainment. In-room amenities include TV, telephone, minifridge. The hotel's elegant French restaurant, **Rotisserie de la Sauveniere** (moderate), is very well regarded locally. Lobby bar; breakfast extra; parking is available.

INEXPENSIVE

Cygne d'Argent

rue Beekman 49; ☎ *23.70.01.* This 23-room hotel, located in a residential neighborhood just a block outside blvd. Sauveniere, is a longish but possible walk to sights and served by bus routes. Front desk staff is helpful with questions. The front lobby has couches, TV, bar service, and a small restaurant. The standard bedrooms include good mattresses, TV, telephone, private bath with stall showers, hair dryer, and individually controlled heat. Noise from the hall can carry into rooms. A basic continental breakfast is included; additional charge for cooked one. Elevator; major credit cards; short taxi ride to Guillemins station; parking available.

WHERE TO EAT

The height of Liège haute cuisine can be enjoyed at **Au Vieux Liège** *(quai de la Goffe 41; closed Sun., Wed. evening, month of August;* ☎ *23.77.48; res-* *ervations suggested; moderate)*, where the setting also is superb, in a 16th-century national monument townhouse with period furnishings. The menu, served in dining rooms upstairs where formally dressed waiters await in candlelight, features finely prepared fish, but includes other offerings. The best of several eateries situated around the *place du Marché* is **Brasserie As Ouhes** *(place du Marché 21; noon–2:20 p.m., 6 p.m.–midnight, closed Sun., Sat. for lunch, and second half of July;* ☎ *23.32.25; reservations suggested; moderate)*, which offers a broad selection of regional and French fare in an attractive atmosphere.

For *cuisine Liègeoise* head for **Mame Vi Cou** *(rue de la Wache 9; daily 12:30–3 p.m., 7:30–10 p.m.;* ☎ *23.71.81; reservations recommended; menu, moderate, inexpensive)*. Located in a small street beside **Inno** department store, Mame Vi Cou provides an atmosphere of country inn in a city alley, with cozy brick walls and beamed ceiling, a saint's niche on the wall, and live piano music and candlelight, to accompany its reasonably-priced regional dishes. This is the place to sample *boudin blanc* (white sausage), *jambon d'Ardennes* with caramelized onions, vegetable soup, pig's feet, and *pan perdu* as a dessert. **Café Lequet** *(quai sur Meuse 17;* ☎ *22.21.34; inexpensive)* is a typical Liège tavern, with a limited selection of tasty regional fare and daily specials. Once owned by the aunt of author Georges Simenon, it's a great place to mix with the Liègeois he wrote about.

If you're looking for a change of fare, **le Carré**, a pub-/cafe-filled quarter in central Liège, will give you plenty of alternatives. One is **Ristorante i Giardini Pizzeria** *(rue d'Amay 10;* ☎ *22.03.64; inexpensive)*, whose renovated, skylighted garden also offers a change of scenery. **Rue Roture**, across the Passerelle footbridge from old Liège in **Outremeuse**, is that distinctive district's destination for generally inexpensive restaurants. Although the street has been getting a face lift, don't limit your choices just because a facade seems a bit rough or plain: if the menu and atmosphere inside seem inviting, you can be sure the food and service that follow will be too—as the local clientele indicates. **Cirque Divers** *(rue Roture 14;* ☎ *41.02.44)* is a brasserie, restaurant, gallery, and theater.

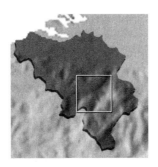

THE MEUSE VALLEY

Dinant's clifftop Citadel.

Upstream and southwest of Liège, the Meuse arches around the western edge of the Ardennes, passing through **Huy**, **Namur**, and **Dinant**, south of which it enters France. Signs of industry and commercial river traffic are few south of Namur, which leaves Dinant favorably situated for the recreational use of the river. Most of the region's other waterways—the **Semois**, **Lesse**, **Sambre**, **Samson**, and **Ourthe**—flow into the **Meuse**, which is Wallonia's water highway of history. From prehistoric days, the Meuse has served as the most convenient means of transportation through the region. It was the route used by Roman legions policing this far northern corner of their Empire, the river road taken by invading Vikings, and a respite river-borne stretch of the long pathway west for medieval central European pilgrims making their way, mostly on foot, from monastery to chapel to Spain's Santiago de Compostela St. James's shrine. The upper valley of the Meuse, which begins south of Namur, has a particular charm, with wooded hillsides, strange rock formations, near-vertical escarpments that plunge to the river, and picturesque villages built in the local blue-gray stone and roofed with local slate.

Today its scenic towns are touted as peaceful sites for tourists, but for many centuries the strategic significance of the Meuse meant that its towns, squeezed onto narrow banks beneath rocky cliffs, were spared few sieges and bombardments. Most Meuse towns are dominated still by their citadels, whose first foundations may have been built more than a thousand years ago.

Although largely vanished as an industry in the upper Meuse valley, the iron ore in its hills, in combination with plentiful timber to feed furnaces, and rushing rivers to power waterwheels, produced a flourishing iron empire in the area early on. Many of today's Mosan titled families can trace their fine castles—some open to the public—and family fortunes back to the forges. The 18th-century gardens that complement the castle at **Annevoie** were funded by ironmaster Charles-Alexis de Montpellier in the 18th century and, at **Jehay Castle**, present resident Count Guy van den Steen carries on the iron tradition as an artist, creating great iron gates and handsome hearthplates for his home.

GUIDELINES FOR THE MEUSE VALLEY

SIGHTS

Anchored by the slate-roofed towns of **Huy** and **Dinant** and the city of **Namur** (the administrative capital of Wallonia), the Meuse Valley is dotted with idyllic villages—such as **Celles**, fortified farms, owner-occupied museum **castles** (some with wonderful gardens), and—above all—**citadels** that crown their towns. Many examples of Mosan-style architecture (a mix of Romanesque and Gothic) are to be seen. The Meuse valley offers the opportunity for white-water kayaking and cruising from one town to another to keep up the region's tradition of river travel. Rock climbers can train on sheer cliffs fronting the Meuse.

GETTING AROUND

You can travel by **train** to Namur and from that major junction to Huy and Dinant, the tracks (and the roads) hugging the river banks in many places. However, the Meuse valley, even with the aid of the

cruise boats that ply between Namur and Dinant and some of the smaller towns in season, cannot be seen in all its scenic beauty without a **car**.

SHOPPING

As a provincial capital, **Namur** is the primary urban center for a wide area; its main shopping street is *rue de l'Ange*. **Dinant** has long produced engraved yellow copper (*Dinanderie*) articles for religious or domestic use. Fashioned since well before the 14th century—by which time some 7,500 of Dinant's population of 50,000 were employed in dinanderie—copperware in Dinant today has experienced a revival as a cottage industry; hand-beaten items can be found in several shops locally. In **Huy**, which has an ancient tradition of metalworking—12th-century goldsmith **Renier de Huy** created Liège's celebrated baptismal font—craftsmen eventually turned to pewter. Many pewter products can be found in shops.

ENTERTAINMENT AND EVENTS

Among the many **Wallonia Festival** activities in Namur in September are the historic *stilt-walkers* (see "Namur" below). Namur and Dinant both have **casinos**, which host many cultural events.

WHERE TO STAY

Hotels in the region are limited in number and inclined to be very small (the exception being the modern **Novotel**, south of Namur in **Wepion**). Country hotels focus on their kitchens as much as and often more than on guest rooms, which can number as few as a half dozen.

WHERE TO EAT

The Meuse Valley offers Belgian countryside tourism at its best, so you can feel certain of reaping rewarding meals. In towns, restaurants at hotels always make good, often the best, choices. In the country, restaurants and hotels usually come coupled and will be your best, maybe only, bet for dining. Their kitchens will feature regional specialties such as the fish dish *Escaveche de la Meuse*, as well as river trout and crayfish, and *flamiche*, a bubbling, warm cheese and butter tart. Dinant is well known for its *couque*, hard pastry and honey cookies baked in molds in many forms, sometimes of considerable size. The *fraises* (strawberries) of Wepion are famous.

ON THE ROAD

From Liège, follow the Meuse upstream (southwest) enroute to Huy and detour north of the river to ★★**Jehay Castle** (*Jahey-Amay; open weekends, only in July, Aug.;* ☎ *(085) 31.17.16; printed guide in English*). A moated Meuse Renaissance castle of the 16th century, Jehay, begun as a fortified manor in the 15th century, achieved its present general form by 1680 when François van den Steen acquired the property, which is still in the family. The outer walls and towers have a unique checkerboard effect created by the use of alternating dark and light square stones. During his long lifetime, present owner **Comte Guy van den Steen** has entirely refurbished the house and filled it with historic furnishings. A respected artist, van den Steen has added to the castle's *objets d'art* with his talents as sculptor and ironwright. Among his works that adorn Jehay are the fine iron entry gate, iron railings, and chimneypieces, the important bronze work *Marsyas Tortured by the Nymphs*, which shows the 3-dimensional relief perspective developed by the artist, a sensitive sculpture of the "floating" figure in *Ophelia's Death*, and other sculpted works in the tradition of Rodin.

Elsewhere in the rooms on display (tours are self-guided, on the ground floor only) are magnificent 17th- and 18th-century European *silver*, fine *tapestries* (16th-century Brussels, and 17th-century Flemish from a cartoon by **Teniers** and **Aubusson**). The large dining room has Renaissance and Gothic furniture, while the small dining room has an 18th-century Liège crystal chandelier, English furniture, a portrait of Nell Gwynn, one of several by Charles II's court painter **Pieter Lely** (1618–1680), and a self-portrait by **"Velvet" Brueghel** (1568–1625). A circular tower room displays collections of *porcelain*—Delft, Limoges, English, and Chinese. The living room and library are handsome and homey rooms that you could live in, which the van den Steens do. Across the moat from the castle are the **gardens**, remodeled in the French style by the current owner, who has also added Italian touches: fountains, urns, and sculpture. In the castle's 12th-century vaulted cellars, the count, also devoted to *archeology*, has assembled an extraordinary private collection of finds from digs across Europe and on the grounds of Jehay, a site that he has proven has been occupied for 30,000 years.

★ HUY

Tourist Office • *quai de Namur 1;* ☎ *(085) 21.29.15; pop. 20,000.*

Huy (pronounced *hwee*), which sits on both banks of the Meuse, is thought to have received the first parish charter in Europe (1066). Its south bank is dominated by the **Citadel**, the site's first fortifications, built in the 11th century. Two of Huy's historic "four wonders" survive: the **Bassinia fountain** on the Grand' Place, and the **Rondia**, a large radiant rose window in the ★**Collegiate Church of Notre-Dame** *(quai de Namur, next to the Tourist Office, inquire about opening hours, due to restoration).* Above the church's former entrance to the canons' cloister are the so-called "Bethelehem" bas-reliefs, with various scenes of the nativity, including a highly unusual reclining Mary recovering from childbirth. Notre-Dame, whose first stone was laid in 1311, also has a carillon with Hemony bells.

Near the church is Huy's ★**old town**, an area of ancient merchant and craftsmen shop-lined streets, centered by the Grand' Place, on which sit the classic brick and bluestone 1766 **Hôtel de Ville** and a cluster of cafes.

The square is anchored with the **Bassinia fountain**, a bronze basin that dates from 1406, to the top of which was later added a tiny town crier. Adjacent is **place Verte**, with its market and 15th-century **Maison Nokin**. Huy's oldest house, the **Maison de la Tour**, an example of Gothic civil architecture from the second half of the 12th century, is at the corner of rue de la Cloche and rue des Freres-Mineurs. The latter street leads to the ★**Municipal Museum** *(the former Frères-Mineurs Monastery, rue Vankeerberghen; April 1–Oct. 20 Mon.–Sat. 2–6 p.m., Sun. and holidays 10 a.m.–noon, and 2–6 p.m.; ☎ (085) 23.03.77)*. The monastery buildings and columned cloister, originally dating from the 13th century, were completely transformed following the secularization of church property by the French throughout Belgium in 1796, but many of the Meuse Renaissance features remain. Collections inside contain artifacts reflecting the history of the town and region. Of interest is the *Huy pewter* (made with tin from Cornish mines in England), which local artisans crafted as early as the 7th century and until the 19th. Some contemporary pieces, made in historical designs, are on display here and on sale in shops in town.

Hôtel de la Cloche *(quai de la Batte on the Meuse; lunch and dinner; inexpensive/moderate)*, a 1406 building that is a marvelous example of the region's medieval architecture, is an atmospheric restaurant on the Meuse bank opposite the citadel (used by the Nazis as a prison for Belgian resisters).

★ NAMUR

Tourist Office • *place Leopold, near the station; Mon. to Fri. 9 a.m.– noon, 2–5 p.m., Sat. and Sun. to 3 p.m.; ☎ (081) 22.28.59; pop. 102,000.*

Namur is the capital of Wallonia (as well as of the province that shares its name), centrally situated on the Meuse, between Belgium's industrial southwest and its scenic southeast Ardennes. Citizens of Namur have a national reputation for being slow, not in the sense of being unintelligent, but in speech and pace of life; the snail is a sort of symbol for their easygoing city.

Namur's outstanding sight is its ★★**Citadel** *(daily April–Sept., 11 a.m.–7 p.m., in Oct. Sat., Sun., holidays; ☎ (081) 22.68.29; car park at top of a winding road, or cable car; illuminated at night year-round; cafeteria; multilingual brochure and plan)*, which has a premier panoramic view of the city. Namur had to pay a price for its superior strategic situation, in sieges over the centuries. During the most famous siege, by the French in 1692, **Louis XIV** looked on while his soldiers eventually captured the city. (Racine, on hand as a war correspondent, did double duty as a writer by producing an ode in honor of the victory.) After the victory Louis let loose his military architect **Vauban**, who modified the citadel to withstand modern fire power. Though the site seems to have been fortified since Celtic times, much of what is seen today dates from the Dutch era of the United Kingdom in the early 19th century; it was used as a military compound until 1975, when it was turned over to the city to be used as a museum. A tourist "train" takes visitors around the pretty hill crest, 16-acre wooded site, pausing at marvelous viewpoints, and stopping at underground galleries, early 19th-century barracks used by the Dutch, and a museum of old tools. A cassette tape (in English and French) is played on the train during the tour, and there's also a 20-minute video that traces the history of the citadel.

The ★**Cathédrale de St-Aubain** *(daily 10 a.m.–6 p.m., closed Mon., holidays, from Nov. 1–Easter 2–5 p.m.)* is one of Belgium's finest baroque churches. In addition to the paintings (a **Jordaens**, possible **Van Dyck**, and several from **Rubens'** studio) is a small black marble cenotaph behind the high altar. It contains the heart of **Don Juan of Austria**, illegimate son of Emperor Charles V and half-brother to Philip II of Spain, who died in Namur in 1578 under mysterious circumstances. In 1577, Don Juan, hero of the **Lepanto** naval battle in which Christians won against the Turks, successfully took Namur by siege, thereafter praising the well-situated citadel by saying, "When Namur falls, Europe falls." In 1578, while camping northeast of Namur at Bourge, Don Juan, aged 31, died. One story suggests that Don Juan was sent a pair of poisoned gloves by a lady jealous of his other amorous adventures. Another tale tells of him dying from wearing a pair of poisoned boots, the plot of his jealous half-brother Philip II.

★**The Convent of the Sisters of Notre-Dame** *(rue Julie-Billiart 17; 10 a.m.–noon, 2–5 p.m., closed Tues.)* holds Namur's most prized treasures, the works of 12th-century master goldsmith **Hugo of Oignies**. Some of the jeweled crosses and reliquaries show Wallonia customs from the artist's era. One reliquary shows a scene of men jousting on *stilts*, a popular pastime that remained so in Namur until relatively recent times. The activity is said to have begun after citizens rebelled against a siege upon their city started by Count Jehay, ruler of the province of Namur. Several citizens tried for an audience at which to discuss the situation, but the count apparently retorted he would receive no supplicants, whether they arrived "by foot, carriage, horse, or boat." Someone devised the idea of sending a delegation on stilts, which so dumbfounded and delighted the count that he agreed to lift the seige.

The **Felicien Rops Museum** *(rue Fumal 12; 10 a.m.–5 p.m., closed Tues.;* ☎ *(081) 22.01.10)* is a complete change—not to everyone's taste, even in the artist's own hometown, and nearly a century after his death (1898). Rops, a painter and illustrator, was admired by many for his explicit and irreverent works, which caused indignation in the 19th century and can still raise an eyebrow. In season, there are **boat trips on the Meuse** *(for information* ☎ *(082) 22.23.15).*

WHERE TO EAT

Le Petit Bedon

rue Armée Grouchy 3; inexpensive/moderate. This restaurant is locally acclaimed in Namur for its meals of the plenty of the region, including *potée Liègeois* (ragout of red cabbage, sausage, potatoes, and pears), cheeses including Namur chevre, and oxtail soup. A number of *inexpensive* restaurants are located along *rue des Brasseurs*, on the city's oldest street, near the Sambre river. There also are cafes, inside and out, in the squares that open up within the network of crooked stone pedestrian streets in the old town.

WHERE TO STAY

Novotel Namur   ★★★★

chaussée de Dinant 1149, Wepion; ☎ *(081) 46.08.11, FAX (081) 46.19.90; moderate.* With 110 rooms, this sprawling modern hotel, 3 mi/5 km south of Namur, is anything but typical of rural Belgium. It's also atypical in its range of amenities, from indoor and outdoor swimming pool, elevators, TV in every room, many in-room refrigerators, and hotel bar. Breakfast extra (BF 375 per person).

★★ANNEVOIE GARDENS

(Chateau d'Annevoie, 5181 Annevoie; gardens open daily April–Oct. 9 a.m.–7 p.m.; castle open daily in July and Aug. 9:30 a.m.–1 p.m., 1:30–6:30 p.m., from mid-April–June and in Sept. weekends and holidays; ☎ *(082) 61.15.55.)* Lying slightly inland west of the Meuse, midway between Namur and Dinant, **Annevoie** is one of the treasures of Belgium for its gardens, in which water is the element that provides the wonder. Landscaped in the mid-18th century by Charles-Alexis Montpellier, whose family seven generations later still remain the caretakers, the gardens incorporate the formal, symmetrical French, the unruly and romantic English, and the classical statuary Italian styles. Annevoie is considered most unusual for its ★★**fountains**. And they are unusual for operating entirely by gravity, with water brought by oak wood pipe from four nearby natural springs. The fountains that splash, spout, and spring from cascades, geysers, reflecting pools, and descending steps, have flowed 365 days each of its nearly 240 years. Silver waters, green trees and plantings, statues, and surprising, secluded corners—not flowers—remain the concept of the older sections of the garden (as at Versailles, with which it is often compared, though Annevoie has more variety of mood). Flowers, which were not in fashion when the garden was constructed, were added in the 1950s to accommodate 20th-century tastes.

Annevoie's ★**chateau**, a manor house enlarged in the 18th century by the founding father of the Montpellier family, is gently curved to match the shape of the valley in which it sits. A highlight is the ★★**white ballroom**, magnificently decorated 200 years ago with rococo bas-reliefs by the Italian Moretti brothers. Though tours of the garden are guided only in May–August, visitors are free to wander independently afterwards. Tours of the chateau are always guided. Near Annevoie's entrance are a **restaurant**, a **cafeteria**, and a **gift shop**. Some summer evenings the gardens are illuminated, and the settings are used for concerts.

★★DINANT

Tourist Office • *rue Grande 37; Mon.–Fri. 8:30 a.m.–5 p.m., and on Sat. & Sun. in July & Aug;* ☎ *(082) 22.28.70, pop. 12,000.*

There's no mistaking Dinant, with the bulbous black steeple of its **Église Notre-Dame** set against the sheer stone face that rises behind it. A surprising appearance on the late 13th-century church, the steeple was built for another building—the Hôtel de Ville—but was later considered too large for it. It's just as well the tower wasn't attached to the church in 1228, when stones from the cliff above fell on the Romanesque church, killing 36 people. Its Gothic successor incorporated the original carved sandstone arch on the north portal and the three carved Romanesque arches in the baptistry.

The shape of Dinant is long and narrow, the main street running a block above and parallel to the right bank of the river. From **place Reine Astrid**, by Église de Notre-Dame and at the base of the 408 steps (and *téléférique*) up to the Citadel, the street is named for **Adolphe Sax** (1814–1894), who was born on this street and invented the saxophone. (Although he had to go to court many times to defend his invention, it finally was patented in 1846.) The extension of the street south of place Reine Astrid is **rue Grande**, on which are located the **Hôtel de Ville** (which was the summer palace of the prince-bishops of Liège) and the **casino**, next to which is the **cultural center** (and tourist office). Rue Grande becomes **rue Leopold**, which runs to the northern edge of Dinant where it passes between a spiny outcrop of stone running down the steep cliff and the single rocky pinnacle (130 ft./60 m.) on the riverbank known as **Rocher Bayard**. Bayard was the name of the magical horse of the legendary Four Sons of Aymon, who waged a lengthy war with Charlemagne, their deeds and valor the stuff of Meuse valley folklore. It was, according to local legend, when the Frankish emperor was in pursuit that Bayard, with the four brothers astride him, is said to have struck a hoof and splintered the rock as he jumped across the Meuse. The truth is that the rock spike was formed when Louis XIV blew up the cut to create a wider path for his soldiers to walk in and seize the town in 1675. A plaque on Rocher Bayard notes that Belgium's **King Albert** climbed the detached needle-shaped stone in 1933. (See also "Freyr.")

No one can ignore Dinant's ★★**Citadel** *(open daily year-round, except closed Fri. in Nov., Dec. Jan., Feb., Christmas, and New Year's, and weekdays in Jan.; 10 a.m.–6:30 p.m. July and Aug., 10 a.m.–4 p.m. rest of year; ☎ (082) 22.21.19; téléférique/cable car from base station near Église Notre-Dame; car park at top).* Dating from 1530, and set 330 feet/100 meters above the Meuse, up 408 steps, pre-9th-century fortifications were destroyed by the Vikings, with replacement defenses built by the bishop of Liège in 1051. Among the history retold in the exhibits at the top is the siege in 1466 by Burgundian **Charles the Bold**, who was often at odds with the powerful prince-bishops of Liège, for whom Dinant was a stronghold and summer residence. During the encounter, Charles reputedly ordered some 800 residents of Dinant, bound in pairs back-to-back, thrown into the Meuse. The Citadel today, as at Namur, is basically Dutch in design; guided tours (only) include the Dutch-era (early 19th century) forge, kitchen, bakery, and prison cells as well as a museum with weapons, historical dioramas, the carriage used by **Madame de Maintenon** (who stayed at Dinant in 1692 while Louis XIV sieged Namur), casements, and the galleries in which

French soldiers held out (unsuccessfully) against the Germans in 1914. A rather effective gimmick near the end of the visit is the "Abri Effondre" (ruined shelter) during which visitors by special effect get the impression that the stone floor is shaking, in a simulation of the force of the devastating bombing unleashed by the Allies on Dinant to unseat the Nazis from the Citadel near the end of World War II. From the terrace of the Citadel are wonderful views; panoramic perspectives of Dinant and the Meuse also are possible from the **Montfort tower**, accessible by chairlift; the amusement park attractions beyond the tower may be of less interest.

WHERE TO EAT

Hostellerie Thermidor *(rue de la Station 3; ☎ (082) 22.31.35; moderate)*, operated by its owner/chef, is one of the best choices for a relaxing lunch or dinner. For more informal fare, **Le Duc de Bourgogne** *(place de Reine Astrid 7; closed Tues.; ☎ (082) 22.22.29; inexpensive)* is well located in the center of Dinant; its daily two-course *menu* that features items such as *omelets, waterzooi, croquettes, fondu,* and *fish soup* is popular with residents. The square on which it sits has several other restaurant/cafes, and, in good weather, terrace tables from which there's a wonderful view straight up to the Citadel and down to the Meuse.

IN THE AREA

Vèves ★★

Celles-Houyet; Easter–Oct. 10 a.m.–noon, 2–6 p.m., guided tours in English available July and Aug.; ☎ (082) 66.63.95; notes on exhibits in French and Dutch only, but detailed printed notes in English on loan from attendant. Vèves looks just the way visitors would wish a castle to, solid yet romantic, with five round towers in a wooded, hilltop setting. The courtyard has a half-timbered 16th-century wall, but most of the castle today dates from the 18th century. Although the **Counts de Liede-kerke Beaufort** who own it live in **Noisy**, a chateau visible on the hill across the valley, Vèves has a pleasantly lived-in look, with fine 18th-century furniture, tapestries, paintings, and portraits. These include a deathbed portrait of Napoleon engraved from an original life drawing by a family member. There also are portraits of England's Charles II and his mistress Barbara Villiers; the child of that liaison, Charlotte Fitz Roy, is a direct ancestor of the current countess of Vèves. The subject of another painting is close to home: the *Siege of Dinant* by Louis XIV. The dining room table is surrounded with 12 rare Louis XV chairs and is set with silver, crystal, and Sèvres; the old kitchen adds to the feeling that someone is going to cook tonight's dinner there.

Celles ★★

This picturesque hamlet in the vicinity of Vèves, 6 mi./10 km. from Dinant, is well worth a stop. The only specific sight in this typical blue-gray stone village (with stone barns, as well as homes) is the partially fortified, Romanesque **Église Saint Hadelin**, an outstanding example of the Mosan style that dates from 1035. Its 13th-century choir stalls are among the oldest in Belgium.

Foy-Notre-Dame

The church (1622–1626) in this village, located between Celles and Dinant, was on a pilgrimage route. It is noted for its coffered ★★oak ceiling, 21 sections of 7 squares, each painted with a scene or a saint from the Gospels; its ornamentation was in reaction to Protestant disdain for all decoration.

Bouvignes   ★

1 mi./2 km. north on the Meuse from Dinant. This medieval town had a running competition with Dinant for centuries. Its 16th-century ★**Maison Espagnole** in the center houses an interesting **Museum of Lights** *(place du Baillage; May–Sept. daily 1–6 p.m., closed Mon.;* ☎ *(082) 22.49.10),* but the building is just as worthy of a visit. There's a far-reaching view over the Meuse above Bouvignes at ruined **Crevecoeur** castle (accessible by car, then some walking). The tale is told that when the French sacked and burned both Dinant and Bouvignes in 1554, three widows of the castle's defenders took over the heroic stance until ammunition ran out, whereupon they leapt, hand-in-hand, to their death.

WHERE TO STAY AND EAT IN THE AREA

Moulin de Lisognes   ★★★★

rue de la Lisonnette, Lisogne; ☎ *(082) 22.63.80, FAX (082) 22.21.47; moderate.* This attractive stone 9-room hotel/restaurant in a former water mill, a short distance northeast of Dinant, offers telephone, minibar, private bath in each of the comfortable rooms; although the prices for all rooms are the same, some have balconies, ceiling beams, the pleasant sound of a rushing stream and garden views out back. There's a terrace with tables, free use of a clay tennis court, and pleasing public rooms. The good restaurant (where breakfast, included, also is served) offers three-course *menus* daily, as well as à la carte choices that feature local specialties.

L'Auberge de Bouvignes   ★★

rue Fetis 112, route de Namur; ☎ *(082) 61.16.00; inexpensive.* This rustic brick inn in a rural location on the banks of the Meuse (2 mi./3 km. north of Dinant) has six guest rooms, several with private bath, but is renowned locally for its kitchen (*à la carte* expensive, *menu–dégustation*–moderate), open for lunch and dinner.

Hostellerie Val Joli   ★★★

rue Saint Hadelin 2, Celles; closed Wed. evenings, Thurs., and Dec. 15–Jan. 15; ☎ *(082) 66.63.63, FAX (082) 66.67.68; inexpensive.* The establishment has seven bedrooms (most with bath and TV), but the real pride of the place is its kitchen, which serves gourmet fare worthy of the Belgians from afar who seek it out. The place is cozily small, so be sure to book ahead (major credit cards accepted).

FREYR

Despite a tragic fall from the sheer sheet of limestone near **Marché-les-Dames** (on the Meuse north of Namur) that killed Belgian climber and beloved soldier-king **Albert** on February 17, 1934, members of the *Royal Belgian Alpine Club* still use the steep rock faces at Freyr, slightly south of Dinant, for practice. Those who make it to the top of the rock wall are rewarded with a far-sweeping view of the Meuse, across to another fine castle—by French architect **Andre Le Nôtre**—featuring extensive formal gardens with orange groves and waterfalls. At **Freyr castle**, French King Louis XIV, in Dinant in 1675 on otherwise unsociable business, is said to have tasted his first cup of coffee.

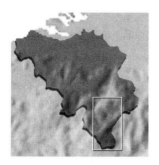

THE ARDENNES

Durbuy

The **Ardennes**—possibly the inspiration for Shakespeare's *Forest of Arden* in *As You Like It*—covers nearly one-third of southeast Belgium. The definition of what strictly is and isn't the Ardennes—many non-Belgians hold the inaccurate idea that everything south and east of the Meuse river is a single undifferentiated area—matters most to those who live there. Visitors consulting a map will note the large green forested stretches that indicate the ruralness of the region. The highest reaches of the **Belgian Ardennes**—the Ardennes extend well into the Grand Duchy of Luxembourg—are farthest east in the German-speaking **Cantons de l'Est**, where fine winter skiing exists. The most visited sections of Belgium's Ardennes are more central, sought out for sport by *hunters*—the wild boar is a virtual symbol of the region, and stags and roe deer also are plentiful—and *fishers*, and by almost everyone for the *gastronomic preparation* of the 75 fresh catch in the region's renowned restaurant retreats.

Rivers run through the Ardennes. The **Ourthe** heads roughly south to north, finishing its course by flowing into the Meuse at Liège. The **Semois** cuts the southern Ardennes laterally, snaking east (its headwaters are near Arlon) to west, where it disappears into France under the name *Semoy*. The **Lesse**, rushing through the mid-Ardennes for centuries, has created limestone caverns so vast that the smallest Ardennes village could be set inside the subterranean space. These rivers and their tributaries have sculpted the scenery on exhibit in the Ardennes.

GUIDELINES FOR THE ARDENNES

SIGHTS

Belgium's forested, river-fed Ardennes region is essentially scenic. The virgin vistas above ground are complemented by an underground landscape of **limestone caves**. (**Han-sur-Lesse's** water-carved caves are an exceptional subterranean sight.) Attractions include **castles** of noble lineage and **monasteries** from the Middle Ages (such as the picturesque ruins of the 9th-century feudal castle—illuminated on summer nights—above **La-Roche**) and small stone-built villages of the Ardennes (like **Redu**, known as the "village du livre" for its many bookshops). **Spa's** natural spring waters and the list of those who have "taken the cure" there since the 16th century have made the town's name synonymous with health resorts since. **Bouillon**, on the viewpoint-stop-studded **Semois** river, is dominated by a castle that its owner *Godfrey* mortgaged to the prince-bishops of Liège for money to raise an army to fight in the **First Crusade** (1096). At **Bastogne**, which put the Ardennes on the map at Christmas of 1944, there's a historical center that brings the Second World War's **Battle of the Bulge** into focus.

GETTING AROUND

A **car** is essential for visiting the Ardennes. Roads are in reasonable-to-better repair, but don't estimate driving time solely on the kilometers to be covered, since switchbacks in and out of river valleys will slow you down—appropriately. The sights described below are highlights of the region, covered roughly north to south, with no suggested route. The *Belgium Tourist Map* (available from tourist offices) designates the particularly attractive stretches of road in green;

you may want to supplement it with a more detailed driving map that shows smaller roads if you plan a real exploration of the Ardennes.

SHOPPING

Other than regional souvenirs along the way, the Ardennes is not the place for serious shopping, its village stores being, by and large, too small to supply much more than basic needs.

ENTERTAINMENT AND EVENTS

Hunting season is celebrated the first Sunday of September with an **International Hunting Day** afternoon pageant at **Saint Hubert**. On Nov. 3rd, at the **Feast of St. Hubert** (the patron saint of hunters), the sound of hunting horns reverberates in the Basilica during the *Huntsmen's Mass* and *Blessing of the Animals*. Torchlight visits to **Bouillon Castle** take place on many evenings in July and August. Bouillon and other hilltop castles, ruins, and citadels in the Ardennes are illuminated at night in July and August, and at holiday periods the rest of the year.

WHERE TO STAY

The most interesting and atmospheric choices in the Ardennes—some of which are renowned—are located in the country or near to but outside of towns, another reason you need a car in the region. Wherever you overnight in the Ardennes, it is expected that you will take dinner there; since most country hotel/restaurants take pride in their kitchen—owners often are chefs—you'll undoubtedly enjoy the experience.

WHERE TO EAT

The Ardennes plays a leading role in Belgium's reputation as a culinary center. Small family-run hotels may be famed for their restaurant fare, and even casual eateries chanced upon are likely to impress visitors with their food standards. *Jambon d'Ardennes* (ham, thinly sliced) is a specialty offered everywhere, as are other high-quality pork products. Goose appears frequently on menus, and goose pâté is a popular starter. *Wild boar* (sometimes marinated), *marcassin* (young wild boar), and *venison* are served during the fall game season, as is *hare ragout. Trout* come fresh from the rivers that rush through the Ardennes, and local *crayfish* may be fried or boiled in hot *bouillon* (named for the region's feudal-age town). Belgian *white* and *blue cattle* produce tasty low-fat beef. If you're not already replete, *tarte au riz* (rice tart) can appropriately end an Ardennes repast.

ARRIVING

Though not themselves part of it, Namur and Liège are the towns that serve as gateways to the Ardennes. Except for the towns of **Spa** (via Liège) and **Bastogne** (via Namur), Ardennes scenery and finest gastronomic fare are virtually unreachable by rail. A **car** is essential for discovering the delights of the region.

TRAVEL TIPS

The Ardennes is highly popular with Belgians and other Europeans for weekends; many country inns and hotels feature all-inclusive *gastronomique weekends*. During the fall game season, inns with a reputation for fine food are even more in demand. To enjoy greater schedule flexibility—though by all means book ahead—try to arrange your countryside travel during the week.

ON THE ROAD

Since much of the rural region's charm comes to light by exploring for favorite viewpoints, villages, and restaurants, the attractions below should be considered only an outline upon which to base your Ardennes adventure.

★SPA

Tourist Office • *Pavillon des Petits Jeux, place Royale 41;* ☎ *(087) 77.25.10, 77.25.19; pop. 10,000.*

In the northern Ardennes, in well-wooded hills 22 mi./35 km. SE of Liège is **Spa**, which served as the archetype for Europe's health resorts that initially grew up around mineral springs whose waters had assorted health-giving minerals and properties. The name *Spa* continues in wide use today, even for establishments (especially in North America) where "the waters" and serious health-care "cures" have been replaced with more

beauty-conscious treatments. Spa's springs were known in Roman days (historian **Pliny the Elder** recorded them as located in northern Gaul at a place called Spa in his *Historia Naturalis*) but rediscovered by local citizens c. 1300. By the 1500s, its waters had made such a name for themselves—for the relief of anemia, gout, rheumatism, and digestive disorders—that people from all over Europe began seeking out Spa. Spa's reputation grew to such an extent that, by the 18th century, people of power and influence summered in Spa whether or not they needed the "cure." The tables at the casino became equally fashionable as a gambling outing, and Spa was dubbed "the cafe of Europe" by no less a personage than **Joseph II**. Russia's **Czar Peter the Great**, who suffered badly from indigestion that produced highly embarrassing burps, came for the cure in 1717, and Spa didn't disappoint him.

Belgian King Leopold II had the neoclassical **Établissement Thermal** (also know simply as the **Therme** or baths) built in the center of Spa from 1868–1875. The attractive building of wrought iron and glass that today houses the tourist office was built in 1860 as the **Pavillon des Petits Jeux**, a games pavilion for rainy days or rendezvous point after concerts in the park. The arrival of the railroad in Spa, which brought the genteel middle class, eventually spelled doom for the resort. It became too egalitarian to serve as an exclusive social preserve. The curative properties of its waters, however, continued to attract people to Spa—as they still do today.

Some of the closing matters of the First World War took place at Spa. In March 1918, it became German General Headquarters (established at the **Hôtel Britannique**, today a school). At Spa, on November 9, **Kaiser Wilhelm**, who had been living at a residence just outside the town, learned of the unauthorized abdication announced in Berlin by his chancellor Prince Max von Baden. Early the next day, the kaiser left Spa by train for Holland. During the Second World War, Spa was taken over by the Nazis. As an important base in occupied Belgium, however, it was physically well treated.

Though no longer a grand resort today, Spa's waters still are big business. Some 350 people, mostly Belgians, undergo nearly 500 treatments daily at the Therme. (See "Établissement Thermal.") Belgian national health care covers the thermal treatments ordered by the many doctors who are scientifically convinced of the health-giving attributes with which the waters are endowed. **Spa Monopole**, which has run the Therme for more than 50 years, also bottles the beneficial waters.

The most accessible place to "take the waters" in Spa is at ★ ★ **Pouhon Pierre-le-Grand** *(place Pierre-le-Grand; daily Easter holidays, April–Oct. 10 a.m.–noon, 2–5:30 p.m.; Jan., Feb., Mar., Nov. and Dec. weekdays 2–5 p.m., weekends and holidays. 10 a.m.–noon, 2–5 p.m., ☎ (087) 77.25.10, 77.25.19)*, named for Spa's most famous patron, Russian Czar Peter the Great. Here, at the fountain that for many years was simply an open spigot in a niche, then put under a colonnaded shelter in 1822, and finally in 1880 encased in a setting of glass and wrought iron in its present octagonal stone building, is the most potent of Spa's *pouhons* (mineral springs, these tasting strongly of iron). The water costs BF 7 per glass, a bargain BF 10 for a liter, though you may not desire that much once you inbibe. In the winter garden section of Pouhon Pierre-le-Grand, decorated with a medal showing the arms of Russia that was a gift from Peter the Great in gratitude for his cure here in 1717, is an immense fresco ★ *The Golden Book*. Finished in 1894 by painter **Antoine Fontaine**, who spent 12 years on it, this monumental work depicts the main characters in Spa's historical pageant as a fashionable health resort. Among them are Pliny the Elder, shown as a Roman statue; philosophers Montaigne and Descartes; composers Meyerbeer, Offenbach, and Gounod; writers Hugo and Dumas; royalty including Cosimo III de Medici and England's King Charles II; Prime Minister Disraeli; and the duke of Wellington (who visited Spa three years after his victory at Waterloo). Occasionally, the artist has employed whimsy in his grouping of the figures, having Pauline Bonaparte, in Spa in 1812, being listened to attentively by Charles II, here in 1654, or Meyerbeer (1859) rubbing shoulders with Czar Peter (1717). The tourist office has a copy on which the nearly 100 figures are identified by number. Outside the building a monument lists distinguished visitors to Spa from the 16th through the 19th centuries, and there's a memorial to the U.S. 1st Army, which liberated Spa on September 10, 1944.

A more formal "taking the cure" occurs at ★ ★ **Établissement Thermal** *(place Royale; Mon.–Fri., 8 a.m.–noon, 1:30–3:30 p.m., Sat., 8 a.m.– noon;* ☎ *(087) 77.25.60)*, which offers a careful medically supervised program of *balneotherapy* (the treatment of diseases by baths and water cures). The Baths, which came into being in 1875 under the encouragement of Leopold II, who wished Spa's facilities aggrandized, are housed in great marble halls and titled *Salon de Repos* (resting room). Private treatment rooms have great copper tubs and pails for the prescribed peat baths. The waters that gush from the bronze sculpted spigot in a marble fountain in the reception lobby are the extremely low-saline waters of the **Reine** spring, with very different qualities—and taste!—from Spa's pouhons. Be sure to step inside to see the fountain and great painted-ceilinged hall, even if just on the excuse of picking up an English brochure at the reception desk.

Therapy practiced at the Therme employs a mix of three natural elements: the low metal-bearing, extremely low sodium-content cold waters of **Spa Reine** (Queen's spring) piped directly to the center; the gaseous carbonaceous waters of the "pouhon" iron-rich waters of the Marie-Henriette and Wellington springs that directly feed the carbonated baths; and peat baths. The nearly salt-free Spa Reine, with the lowest salt content of any mineral water marketed in Belgium, is the basis for all salt-free diets and aids in reducing the body's sodium balance through its effectiveness as a diuretic. Because other thermal treatments often induce sweating, the salt-free replacement of fluid in the body with Spa Reine is encouraged. The naturally carbonated pouhon iron-rich waters, given only upon medical recommendation (a medical examination by a staff doctor is required before treatment) have a sedative and vasodepressive effect on the cardiovascular system. The compression (according to Archimedes's principle) of blood vessels and veins that results from the immersion of the body in copper tubs in body-temperature water eventually increases cardiac flow and decreases cardiac activity; with water temperature regulated and fixed at body temperature, the patient is in thermal equilibrium, which enables the cardiovascular apparatus to function at its lowest level.

Peat baths began with materials from Belgium's **Hautes Fagnes plateau** to the east of Spa. The biological transformation process of that peat bog (the slow rotting of sphagnum, a sort of saturated moss that can grow several feet deep, the first stage of the transformation of vegetable matter into coal) produces an acidic medium. When the finely sieved dried peat is ground and mixed with Spa's carbonated waters, the temperature of the therapeutic mud bath created is 40 C./104 F., and a whole-body mud bath produces muscular relaxation and reduced pain for rheumatic disorders, including gout. Following the peat bath, a washing-off shower is given progressively along the limbs and trunk, followed by a carbonated bath in the same treatment room, for a full relaxation effect. Auxiliary treatments at the Therme include hydrotherapy (various showers and massages at varying temperatures and pressures), mechanotherapy (with exercise machines), and "inhalations." The Thermal Institute has an X-ray and clinical biology laboratory; an independent institute maintains a hydrology laboratory that meticulously tests and regulates the Spa Reine water and all treatments. A medically prescribed cure, a combination program of the above treatments, usually lasts 3 to 4 weeks, but you can make reservations for individual treatments: peat and following carbonated bath about BF 1,000, underwater massage BF 700, or one-day session BF 1,600.

Even if you don't care to indulge in a treatment, you can get an idea of the lifestyle of those who did during Spa's heyday at the **Musée de la Ville d'Eau/Spa Museum** (*avenue Reine Astrid 77; open daily mid-June–mid-Sept. 2:30–5:30 p.m., Sat., Sun., holidays same hrs. April 15–June 14 and Sept. 16–Dec. 31, closed Jan. 1–April 14.;* ☎ *(087) 77.13.06; no English description on exhibits, but the museum will lend you notes in English).* In the villa that was the residence of Belgium's **Queen Marie-Henrietta** (who lived here, apart from her husband Leopold II, for ten years until her death in 1902) is an assortment of articles showing Spa's history as a resort. It also features old posters (postcard-size copies on sale) that advertised Spa's attractions in Britain and across the continent, old bottles once used for its waters, and the local handicrafts created for visitors who came to take the waters (who were called *Bobelins* by the residents of Spa). The items, which date back to early visitors in the 17th century, often relate directly to the matter of "taking the cure." Walking sticks and canes (*bordons*) were popular with those making the steep climbing tour to the **Sauvenière** and **Geronstere** springs outside the town. Gradually, the sticks became embellished, painted, and varnished, and the artisans, accomplished in design, embarked upon other decorated trinkets. These included *orangettes,* small sweetmeat boxes, that held *carminatives* (aniseed, ginger, fennel, and preserved fruits) taken to correct the hardness of Spa's ferruginous pouhon waters on the stomach. Other items were small dials made of ivory, with which Bobelins could keep count of the number of glasses of water they had taken. (Prescribed treatments often meant drinking a dozen or more a day.) Ladies wore the dial at their waist, gentlemen in their buttonhole.

The most successful Spa creations were small decorated toiletry boxes called *jolities,* whose decoration changed with the fashion, the full range of designs on display in the museum. In the 17th century, inlaid mother-of-pearl and tortoise shell were popular. The brilliantly colored ornamentation of the boxes evolved into exquisite miniature works of art. Lacquer ware boxes were so well done that it took an authority to tell them from articles imported from China and Japan. Tastes and techniques kept changing over the centuries, from India ink interpretations to classical mythological motifs, landscapes, and adaptation to any art vogue that came along: Louis XVI, Napoleonic, Romantic. During the 19th century, the idea of soaking the wood for the boxes in the pouhon waters produced a gray background for the decoration. The peak of production for Spa's jolities came in the late 1800s, when the town supported 15 manufacturers. By 1900, when art deco designs were being produced, however, the number had fallen to four. Today, in addition to looking for Spa boxes in shops, you can visit **La Manufacture des Jolities et Bois de Spa** *(rue de Renesse 28; Mon.–Fri. 8:30 a.m.–noon, 1:30–5 p.m., Sat. 2–5 p.m., closed Sun.; guided tours with advance reservations from May 15–Sept. 15;* ☎ *(087) 77.03.40).*

Established in 1577, Spa's ★**Casino** *(rue Royale 4; daily from 3 p.m., closed Dec. 24;* ☎ *(087) 77.20.52)* is the oldest in the world. Though the present impressive center-of-town neoclassical building with gardens that houses the casino dates only from 1921 (rebuilt following a fire), its hall, used for balls and theater, survives from the fine 1763 building built under the orders of Prince-Évêque de Liège. Sharing the gaming room, where blackjack and European and American roulette are played, are a bar and the enjoyable restaurant **La Rotonde** *(moderate).*

Spa Monopole S.A *(rue Auguste Laporte 34, near the station; multilingual bottling plant hour-plus tours and free water-tasting Mon.– Fri. 9:30–11 a.m., 1:30–3 p.m.;* ☎ *(087) 87.73.11; reservations preferred)* features Spa's water. *Spa Reine* (nonsparkling) and *Spa Gazeuse* (carbonated) is bottled locally by Spa Monopole and sold throughout Belgium. Beyond town borders, however, you need to order *Spa* water by name; asking simply for "mineral water" may produce France's *Perrier* for its snob appeal.

Spa Promenades/open sight-seeing trains or baladeuses *(rue Pre Jonas 26; daily June, July, Aug., and in May, Sept., Oct. in good weather;* ☎ *(087) 77.37.51)* offers several itineraries (approximately 45 mins. each) of the town and its surroundings, including Spa's pouhons, other mineral springs in the forest just outside the town. Promenades to these springs under individual foot power is a centuries-old part of the "cure" at Spa. The tourist office has maps of many waymarked walks from the town, but the classic **Tour des Fontaines**/seven springs tour (signposted, reaching an altitude of 1345 feet/410 meters), which can be made by car, takes in the springs on the periphery of Spa (Wellington, Marie-Henriette, Tonnelet, Sauveniere, Groesbeck, Geronstere, and Barisart). The waters of each (classified as ferruginous, carbogaseous, or cold) have varying amounts of iron and are free. The waters flow from small fountains, protected by small shelters or niches; the **Groesbeek** is named after a baron by that name who built the marble niche over that spring in 1651. The **Sauveniere** spring, thought to have been the first discovered, was, by the 14th century, believed to provide a cure for sterility. The sulfureous **Geronstere** was the preferred spring of Peter the Great during the cure for indigestion that he meticulously followed. There's a good tavern and restaurant with terrace at Geronstere *(*☎ *(087) 77.03.72)*; refreshments are also available at Barisart and Tonnelet springs. Inquire at the tourist office about daily guided walks to the springs in July and Aug, and on Fri., Sat., & Sun. out of season.

WHERE TO STAY

Accommodations are surprisingly limited and modest in Spa itself. In town is ★★**L'Auberge** *(place du Monument 3;* ☎ *(087) 77.36.66; inexpensive)* which has 27 rooms with bath and down-home decor and comfort; front rooms overlooking a small square. Breakfast is served in the hotel restaurant, which occupies the ground floor. Some 2 mi./3 km. outside Spa is the much more interesting ★★★★**Manoir de Lebioles** (*in Creppe;* ☎ *(087) 77.10.20; expensive)* an 18th-century turreted castle with terraced gardens, great baronial entrance hall, pretty lounge with period furnishings and open fire for afternoon tea, and six fine guest rooms the size of suites, all with far-reaching views from the windows. The restaurant (expensive, reservations recommended), formal in setting and service, serves haute cuisine. The specialty is the seven-course *Menu Gastronomique,* featuring seasonal fare, but there's a four-course *Menu Traditional* (moderate).

WHERE TO EAT

In Spa, **Le Grand Maur** (*rue Xhrouet 41; closed Mon. and in Feb.;* ☎ *(087) 77.36.16; moderate)* serves classic French and Belgian cuisine in elegant surroundings. Advance booking is suggested. **La Rotonde** (*rue Royale 4;* ☎ *(087) 77.39.29; moderate)* restaurant at Spa's Casino is popular, price-conscious, and tasty in a setting that's good fun.

WHERE TO STAY AND EAT IN THE AREA

Hostellerie Saint-Roch ★★★★

rue du Parc 1, Comblain-la-Tour; ☎ *(041) 69.13.33; moderate.* Located some 30 kms south of Liège, and about the same distance west of Spa, this delightful luxury country inn with gourmet restaurant (moderate) makes for a thoroughly enjoyable visit for any reason, and it's a good point from which to explore many of the sights in the Meuse Valley and northern Ardennes, as well as Liège and Spa. The 12 guest rooms, with a refined country decor, all have private baths. Dining is elegant in taste and service, and drinks are served beforehand by the gracious owner/hosts on a terrace overlooking the Ourthe River and lovely rural scenery. The venison and fish from the Ardennes are succulently supplemented by vegetables from the inn's own garden.

Ferme Libert ★★★

rue du Village 34, Beverce; Malmedy; ☎ *(080) 33.02.47, FAX (080) 33.98.85; inexpensive.* Southeast of Spa is a more rustic experience in a half-timbered, family-style farmhouse, with a sweeping view over the hills of the northern Ardennes, and newly constructed guest rooms in a complementary Tudor-style lodge next door. The restaurant (moderate, some *menus* inexpensive) is the real attraction here, with diners dropping in from far afield for the substantial and satisfying Belgian country cooking.

★★DURBUY

Tourist Information: Corn Market/Spanish House • *rue Halle aux Bles; daily in July and Aug. 10 a.m.–6 p.m., 10 a.m.–noon, and 1–5 p.m. rest of year;* ☎ *(086) 21.24.28; population 321.*

Durbuy (pronounced *door BWEE*) is the quintessential Ardennes *village,* although it has rights granted in 1331 upon which it stakes its claim to be the smallest *town* in the world. Durbuy is more delightful seen without the in-season day-visitor crowds that come by coach and carload but leave at night. Even though Durbuy has some 20 hotel/restaurants, most are 20 rooms or fewer which limits overnight guests (and those out walking in the early morning mountain mists). In a few minutes you can traverse the tiny old town, built mostly of local gray stone, and there are no "must see" sights. That leaves you free to breathe the air, enjoy the rush of the Ourthe river through the village, and maybe take a waymarked walk, which is what the Belgians do to build up an appetite for the much-anticipated meals that are a gastronomic magnet. The **castle** of the Counts of Ursel *(turret 11th century, though mostly 19th reconstruction, open to the public)* hangs high above the banks of the Ourthe; the buildings along Durbuy's two or three streets in the old town (which, with an essentially unaltered ground plan since the 14th century, is vehicle-free—of necessity!—on weekends in July and August) are mostly 16th century. The most unusual structure, housing the tourist office, is the Spanish House, parts of whose timber-framed facade date from the 14th century.

WHERE TO STAY AND EAT

Le Sanglier des Ardennes

rue Comte d'Ursel 99; ☎ *(086) 21.32.62, FAX (086) 21.24.65; hotel moderate, restaurant moderate, except menu gastronomique expensive; hotel closed in Jan., restaurant closed Thurs. as well as in January.* This friendly family-run hotel is comfortable and charming, but the focal point of the establishment is its kitchen. Owner and master chef Maurice and son Frederic, the renowned **Caerdinals**, are known well beyond the borders of Belgium for their inspired classic cuisine, served in the dining room overlooking the rushing Ourthe river, whose soothing sound carries to the rooms at the rear of the hotel. Fish come straight from the river, grilled and flavored with lemon; perhaps roast pigeon will be enhanced with a subtle sauce and sweetbreads with herbs. In season *venison* and *marcassin* are featured. There are 19 rooms at Le Sanglier des Ardennes, all with TV, telephone, and bath, several with exceptional contemporary decor and skylights; back rooms have the sound of the river. (The owners also have three other properties in tiny Durbuy, including the all-suite **Hôtel Caerdinal**, in a corner of the village sheltered by the 14th-century ramparts, which provide a total of 45 rooms.)

The restaurant/hotel does not take its name *Le Sanglier des Ardennes* from the wild beast of which it makes a feast. The "Wild Boar of the Ardennes" was the name given to the historical character **William de la Marck** (1446–1485), a nobleman who was banished from Liège for murdering the secretary of a Prince-Bishop of Liège. (William's family supplied several prince-bishops). Thereafter, he led the life of a robber baron, with strongholds throughout the Ardennes. In 1482, William returned to Liège and captured it, slaying the bishop. He escaped but later, after accepting an invitation to a feast, was captured by the subsequent bishop Jean de Hornes, who sent William off to Maastricht where the saga of *Le Sanglier des Ardennes* (who is referred to by **Sir Walter Scott** in his 1823 novel *Quentin Durward* in which a boar hunt figures prominently) ended with his execution.

WHERE TO STAY AND EAT IN THE AREA

Chateau d'Hassonville ★★★★

5406 Marche-en-Famenne (Aye); ☎ *(084) 31.10.25, FAX (084) 31.60.27; Expensive for park view, Moderate for courtyard-facing rooms.* This turreted 50-room 1687 castle/hotel south of Durbuy, en route for the caves of Han-sur-Lesse surrounded by a forest preserve, was built as a hunting lodge for Louis XIV of France during his belligerent stay in Belgium. Guest rooms are generally spacious, with a mix of antique and contemporary furnishings, all with private bath; resident owners extend gracious and helpful service. Public rooms are charming, and breakfast is served in a winter garden overlooking the lawns outside. There's a restaurant (*closed Mon. evening and Tues.*), so you can settle in for a delicious stay (or gastronomic weekend). Recreation opportunities include wooded walks, use of bicycles, golf putting green, and in-house snooker.

HAN-SUR-LESSE

(From late Feb. Nov. and Christmas holidays. the nearly 2-hr. tours depart several times daily between 10 a.m.–4:30 p.m., daily every 30 mins. 9:30 a.m.–5 p.m. in May and June; and until 6 p.m. July and Aug.; closed Jan. & Feb.; ☎ *(084) 37.72.12; wear flat walking shoes fit for damp surfaces, frequent stairs, and a sweater for the year-round 54°F/12°C temperatures; guides are multilingual, booklet in English.)*

In a region where **world-class caves** are not uncommon, those of ★★ Han-sur-Lesse stand out above others. The small central Ardennes town from which the caves take their name is almost entirely given over to visitors headed underground. In 1771 the first account was made of an excursion to Han's enormous network of caves, carved from limestone by rushing river water and decorated by drippings that have formed stalactites, stalagmite floors, and other crystallizations over 300 million years. As early as 1800, scientists and adventurers came knocking at the doors of local guides seeking a look for themselves. After hours, these same guides gradually explored the caves and expanded their tours. (The most recent rooms you see were discovered in 1962.) The earliest guides led the way with a flickering torch made from rags soaked in kerosene. In the 19th century, oil lamps were employed, but since 1905, electricity has lighted the caves—safely *and* tastefully. The extraordinary caves at Han could have been ruined by touristy technology, but, instead, a marvelous sense of wonderment has been preserved. Stalactites, growing at the rate of 1.5 inches/4 centimeters per century, some hanging several *meters* from the ceiling, help put into perspective the great age of the earth. The tour begins with a steam tram ride from the center of the village (ticket office opposite the church) to the entrance.

The path inside the caves (roughly 1.4 miles/2 km., with a total of about 500 stairs) passes through great galleries, some hung with "draperies" (a kind of stalactite) among other formations, sometimes in sight of the River Lesse (whose circuitous underground course, only recently charted by speleologists, takes water up to 12 hours to travel through the caves), which earlier explorers dubbed the Styx, after the river of the dead in Greek mythology. The largest of Han's caves is called the *Dome*, its ceiling reaching higher than the spire of Brussels's **Hôtel de Ville**. Safely seated in the cavernous *Salle des Armes*, visitors are treated to a short *son-et-lumière* program that highlights various formations to the accompaniment of music, but, while enjoyable, it doesn't outdo the natural grandeur of the setting. More interesting is the experience when the lights are shut off, plunging the huge cave into subterranean darkness, a spot of flickering light appears near the roof and gradually descends, eventually revealing itself to be a torch carried by a runner in imitation of the pre-electric lighting of the caves. Exit is by punt, which glides on the Lesse to the cave mouth, from which it's a short walk back to the center of town, and to cafes and restaurants for refreshments.

In town, the **Museum of the Underground World** *(place Theo Lannoy 3; April 1–Nov. 11 daily from 10 a.m.–6 p.m., except 8 p.m. weekends in May, June, every day in July, Aug.;* ☎ *(084) 37.70.07)* displays the finds from underwater and riverbed research in the caves. These include tools of flint and bone, ornaments of bone and animal teeth, and pottery made by Neolithic Stone Age cave dwellers (2,000 B.C.). Brilliant Bronze Age (1200–700 B.C.) findings include weapons and jewels, brooches, and five plates of a gold necklace. There are also findings from the second *Iron Age* (Gallic Period, the last century B.C.) as well as evidence of the use of the caves during the Middle Ages and during the 16th-century religious wars.

Han-sur-Lesse also has a **safari park** (reduced combination ticket with caves) where animals wander freely and are seen from a motorized safari car. The tour takes about 1.5 hours, same opening times as caves.

SAINT-HUBERT

Tourist Office *(place de l'Abbaye.)*

In the forest of the Ardennes, **Hubert**, son of a noble family, is said to have been converted. On Good Friday in the year 683, his hounds having cornered a stag, Hubert suddenly saw between its antlers a lighted cross and heard a voice reproaching him for hunting on a holy day. Whereupon, he renounced the world and entered the abbey at Stavelot. While in Rome in 705, Hubert learned of the murder in Liège of Lambert, Bishop of Tongeren-Maastricht. Offered the bishopric, he at first refused, considering himself unworthy, but later accepted after having a vision of an angel holding the robes of investiture. Taking office and moving the bishopric to Liège, Hubert eventually became a saint, the *patron of hunters.* His feast day, November 3, is celebrated throughout the Ardennes, though nowhere more colorfully than at the ★ **Mass** attended by the red-jacketed huntsmen in the **Basilica of Saint-Hubert** *(center of town, daily 9:30 a.m.–5 p.m., except* *from Nov. 4–Easter weekends only;* ☎ *(061) 61.23.88).* The church has a baroque facade but exceptional flamboyant Gothic interior with lofty brick vaulting. Of great beauty is the retable with 24 Limoges enamels (1560) based upon **Albrecht Durer's** engravings. The ancient tomb of the saint (who died in 727) is now empty (his relics were buried in the forest during the French invasions and never relocated thereafter). The cenotaph atop it is a gift in 1847 from King Leopold, who loved to hunt.

Those particularly interested in the hunting tradition of the Ardennes can visit ★ **Chateau Lavaux-Sainte-Anne** *(Lavaux-Sainte- Anne, 7 km. west of Han-sur-Lesse; daily, March–Oct., 9 a.m.–6 p.m., except 7 p.m. July and Aug., 5 p.m. Nov.–Feb;* ☎ *(084) 38.83.62; information sheet, some exhibit descriptions in English)*, a moated castle with massive squat round towers (15th and 16th century) that houses a **museum of hunting and nature**. Amid fine oak furniture and chandeliers from Liège, the old kitchen and a well-decorated dining room, are chairs and sconces made of antlers, stuffed and mounted wild boar heads, paintings of pink-jacketed hunters on horseback, and a room with copies of the Stone Age hunting scenes painted on the Lascaux caves in France. The museum's extensive displays of area wildlife do not especially seek to defend hunting, but rather to show the part that hunting plays in biological balance. The castle, grounds with grazing deer, and hills on the horizon provide a pleasing view for diners in the **Restaurant du Chateau de La Vaux Sainte Anne** *(luncheon from noon, dinner from 7:30 p.m., closed Mon., Tues., and Jan.;* ☎ *(084) 38.88.83; moderate, three-course menus inexpensive)*, located in the adjoining 17th-century fortified feudal farm buildings.

★ BOUILLON

Pavillon Du Tourisme *(Porte de France in July & Aug.,* ☎ *(061) 46.62.89; tourist office at castle open all year,* ☎ *(061) 46.62.57; pop. 6,000.)*

Bouillon, the most important town in the Ardennes' scenic Semois valley, is dominated by its castle that crowns a rocky knoll encircled by the Semois. ★ ★ **Bouillon Castle** *(open March, Oct., Nov. 10 a.m.–5 p.m., until 6 p.m. in April, May, June, Sept.; July and Aug. 9:30 a.m.–7 p.m.; Dec. open Wed.–Sun. 10 a.m.–5 p.m., closed Mon. & Tues.; Jan. & Feb. open weekends 10 a.m.–5 p.m., also Feb. weekdays 1–5 p.m.; in summer guided tours in English if requested; in July & Aug. evening tours at 10 p.m. by torchlight daily except Mon., Thurs., and when other special events are scheduled;* ★ ★ *castle illuminated from outside year-round at night;* ☎ *(061) 46.62.57; guide book in English; wear footwear appropriate for uneven and rough stone surfaces)*, whose foundations date from the 11th century, is Belgium's oldest and one of its finest and most interesting feudal remains. It was the property of **Godfrey** (Godefroid) of Bouillon (c. 1060–1100), presented to him, along with the duchy to which it was attached, by a childless uncle. Godfrey de Bouillon, having proved himself a strategist and committed Christian early in life, not surprisingly responded to the call of charismatic Pope Urban II for Knights of Christ to recover the Sacred City of Jerusalem, then held by the Seljuk Turks. The pope set a date when the march to Jerusalem should begin, August 15, 1096. With no heirs of his own, Godfrey made the decision to sell the entirety of his duchy, with castle, to Prince-Bishop of Liège Otbert for funds to raise and support an army for the undertaking. He made an agreement with Otbert for the possibility of buying back his possessions within three years, counting on bringing back riches from the Middle East, but Godfrey was never to return from the *First Crusade.* (Fewer than 50,000 of the original crusaders' army of 600,000 survived.) Having raised further money by selling civic rights to the city of Metz, which was a part of his duchy, Godfrey set off well manned and well supplied. When he eventually reached the Holy Land, he distinguished himself in battle, first at Antioch (where he is said to have cut a Muslim in two at the waist with a strong swipe of his sword), and then at Jerusalem, which was taken by the Christians on July 25, 1099. As a result of his conduct in the First Crusade, Godfrey de Bouillon was offered the title "King of Jerusalem," which he refused on the grounds that he would be unable to wear a golden crown in the city where Christ had worn a crown of thorns. He did accept the title "Protector of the Holy Sepulchre," though he held it for less than a year before dying from poisoned cider in Syria. Godfrey is buried in Jerusalem in a marked grave at the **Church of the Holy Sepulchre**.

Back in Bouillon, his castle remained in the possession of the Prince-Bishops of Liège for six subsequent centuries, until usurped by the de la Marck family, which had running battles over its possession with the de la Tours. Under Louis XIV, the castle and town were taken by the French and fortified by military architect Vauban. Today the castle is the property of the state.

Bouillon castle, which spreads massively along a rocky ridge (the facade is 375 yards/343 meters in length) as we see it today, dates mainly from the 16th and 17th centuries, particularly because of Vauban's many modifications at the end of the 17th century, which were adaptations due to the advent of artillery. Near the entry (admission, tourist information) you can look down upon the moat, which could be filled at will from the castle's excellent wells. There are commanding views of the town from the terrace and of the castle itself from the top of the so-called **Tower of Austria** and the watch turret. At many places, the castle is highly evocative in its unfluffy simple feudal stone strength. There are few furnishings or decorations to speak of. One room, perhaps Godfrey's rock-hewn bedroom, contains a statue of the crusader, armor and some weapons, and an ancient wooden cross flat in the floor, discovered in 1962 and remaining of unknown age and origin. Another room holds Godfrey's Chair, a two-directional lookout, again hewn from bedrock. Rampart walks, semicircular flanking towers, unusual double-storied, three-slitted loopholes, and dungeons all lend authenticity to this fascinating feudal fortress—a great place to visit, but you wouldn't want to live there.

There's parking at the castle and on its grounds. The **Cafe d'Ardenne** *(closed Wed., inexpensive)* has tasty, non-time-consuming snacks and meals.

Ducal Museum and Godfrey of Bouillon Museum

below castle, on road to it; daily April 1 to June 30 10 a.m.–6 p.m., July 1–Aug. 30 9:30 a.m.–7 p.m., Sept. 1–Oct. 31 10 a.m.–5 p.m., Sat. and Sun. in Nov. and Dec. 10 a.m.–5 p.m.; ☎ *(061) 46.68.39; some exhibit notes in English, taped commentary in English played upon request.* Located in an 18th-century building, beneath the castle on the road leading up to it, the museum is divided into two major sections. History and folklore exhibits include a model of Bouillon in 1690, but the section on Godefroid de Bouillon, on the upper floors, is much the more interesting. It focuses largely upon the Crusades, the march through Europe to the Middle East, the weapons such as catapults, crossbows, and battering rams used in the capture of Jerusalem, life-size models of armored knights, Templars' armaments used in their 13th-century fights against the Moslem infidels, and maps of the regions involved in the crusades. A case with small figures shows the dress worn by the various groups of people who went to the crusades. Among the Eastern and ecclesiastical art from the era is a rare 14th-century carved ivory Virgin.

For rental pedal boats and canoes (kayaks, single or two-seater) in Bouillon, see **Les Triton-Semois** *(quai des Saul 2; Easter to end Sept. 9 a.m., last departure 3 p.m.;* ☎ *(061) 46.63.91).* For reservations for a descent of stretches of the Semois by kayak, contact Recreation Center **Moulin de la Falize** *(*☎ *(061) 46.62.00, FAX (061) 46.72.75; March 1–Oct. 31).* In the summer season, **tourist trains** *(*☎ *(061) 46.70.04; weekends mid-Lent to Nov. 11, except daily in July, Aug., from approximately 10 a.m.–5 p.m.; 45 minutes, 5 mi/8 km)* depart regularly from the Pont de Liège and Pont de France in town for rides up to the Castle.

★★TOMBEAU DE GÉANT/GIANT'S TOMB

For a striking sample of the scenery in the Semois valley, turn west about 2 mi./3 km. north of Bouillon, at signs for *Sensenruth* and *Ucimont.* Shortly, just through the hamlet of **Botassart**, you will come upon the rural setting of the beautiful, unspoilt, far-reaching view across to the forested mound of land, almost completely surrounded by an oxbow in the Semois, known locally as the *Tombeau de Géant.* There's a bench or two from which to survey and savor the splendid sight, and a picnic table. Before leaving Botassart, visit the ★village chapel (1625), with its distinctive old Ardennes-style slate-tiled steeple. Note particularly the interesting wooden ceiling, from which the rope connected to the village bell hangs accessibly from the center aisle in case there's a need to ring out an alarm.

WHERE TO STAY AND EAT IN THE AREA

Auberge du Moulin Hideux   ★★★★

rt. de Dohan 1; 6831 Noirefountaine; ☎ *(061) 46.70.15, FAX (061) 46.72.81; expensive.* Its name (the hideous windmill) doesn't seem to fit (though it does sit across from an old water mill) this pretty country inn, situated 2 mi./4 km. north of Bouillon. A fire on the hearth, greenery in the glassed-in bar, and soft leather lounge furniture express the smart but warm welcome extended to guests. The 10 charming bedrooms all have private bath and the same comfortable contemporary coziness found downstairs. The restaurant (à la carte–expensive, *menus*–moderate) is considered one of Belgium's best, with classic French Belgian cuisine featuring, not unexpectedly, wild fresh game from the surrounding forests, saddle of pork, and river fish, with wonderful soups and *mousse de paté* for starters.

Hostellerie Sainte-Cecile

rue Neuve 81; 6819 Sainte-Cecile-sur-Semois; closed Wed. except in July and Aug.; ☎ *(061) 31.31.67, FAX (061) 31.50.04; inexpensive to moderate.* Situated between Bouillon and Orval, this country hotel/restaurant requires that you take dinner; *menus* (a choice of three, all moderate) are varied and enticing. All bedrooms have comfortable furnishings, telephone, and modern bath; those in back overlook a stream, garden, and terrace with tables. There's a TV lounge and bar.

★ABBAYE NORTE-DAME D'ORVAL

If you've followed the Semois valley as far as Florenville, head a bit farther south to the Abbey of Orval *(signposted; daily 9:30 a.m.–6 p.m.;* ☎ *(061) 31.10.60; ground plan in English).* The monastery (the first monks arrived at Orval in 1070) had a resurrection in 1948, when the Cistercian Order was resettled in buildings designed by architect **Henri Vaes**, rising from the foundations of the previous one, laid waste by the French at the end of the 18th century. The new, working buildings cannot be visited by outsiders (except those who have arranged with the Father porter to stay for a contemplative period), but the ★ruins of the monastery built here in the 12th and 13th centuries can be. Among the most evocative of the mellow-colored stones that remain standing are those of the north wall of the transept, with the empty tracery of a one-time rose window. The ancient porch, former refectory, and garden of medicinal plants offer an atmosphere for contemplation. The ruins are in startling contrast to the new church with its gigantic madonna and child, so large you can ponder it from the grounds of the old abbey. A 20-minute audiovisual program (ask to see the English version) not only discusses the history of Orval but describes the lifestyle of a present-day monk. In the shop near the entrance, the Trappist monks, known for their silence with each other, are more than willing to talk to you as you survey the religious souvenirs and give in to the temptation of the ★★Abbey's delicious homemade cheeses, breads, and home-brewed Trappist beer. (Orval produces one of only six authentic Trappist beers in the world, five of which are produced in Belgium, the other in Holland.) Many visitors come to buy bottles of this noblest of beers directly from Orval, but you can't drink it on the premises; for that, there's a cafe across the street.

BASTOGNE

Bastogne to Host 1994 50th Anniversary Memorial Events for the Battle of the Bulge

"The Bulge is the most decisive battle waged on the Western Front during World War II," according to U.S. Army Deputy Chief Historian Charles B. MacDonald, who also calls it "the greatest battle ever fought by the U.S. Army." The 50th anniversary of The Battle of the Bulge, which fanned out from Bastogne to include much of the Ardennes in both Belgium and Luxembourg, will include memorial services and welcoming events for returning veterans throughout the year, beginning April 30.

The Official Memorial Day of the Battle of the Bulge is December 16, 1944, the 50th anniversary of the surprise opening attack on the Allies by the Nazis at Bastogne that began the battle that became one of the bloodiest in World War II. That day's events will include a memorial ceremony in the presence of military and civil authorities, with the participation of veterans of the U.S. Army's 101st Airborne Division, the historical reconstruction of the siege of Bastogne, and a concert of military music.

Tourist Information • *place McAuliffe 24; daily year-round 8:30 a.m.–noon, 1–5:30 p.m., closed Mon.;* ☎ *(062) 21.27.11; pop. 12,000 today, 4,000 in 1944.*

Many people are familiar with the Ardennes because of Bastogne, which held center stage during the **Battle of the Bulge** late in World War II. Since Roman days, the location has been at the intersection of main roads through the Belgian/Luxembourg Ardennes; in 1944 the crossroads became key in the U.S. Army and Allied resistance that made *Bastogne* for **Hitler** comparable to *Waterloo* for Napoleon. In the snowy December of 1944, Bastogne was the gift the Nazis couldn't wrap up for Hitler's Christmas. The ghost of that Christmas past is given substance at the ★★**Bastogne Historical Center** and ★★**Mardasson Monument**.

Today, Bastogne, once again a modest market town, well-endowed with shops that serve the surrounding Ardennes countryside, is mostly recovered from the shattering results of the Nazi surge of Panzer divisions towards the Meuse that stagnated and "bulged" around the town. Three months to the day before he launched the campaign on **December 16, 1944**, Hitler declared, "I have just made a momentous decision. I shall go over to the counterattack out of the Ardennes with *the objective—Antwerp.*"

Hitler's aim was to trap the British and Canadian armies north of Antwerp, forcing them to surrender, and separating them from the U.S. Army, which he believed would then lack the skill and will to continue fighting alone. Though his own leaders seriously questioned the campaign, Hitler pursued it. **Field Marshal von Rundstedt**, who is unfairly credited with developing it, was quoted as saying, "All, absolutely all, conditions for the possible success of such an offensive are lacking." Nevertheless, Hitler issued handwritten orders stating rigidly "No alterations permitted" in the code-named *WACHT AM RHEIN/Watch on the Rhine.* The code later was changed to *HERBSTNEBEL/Autumn Mist,* though *Winter Snow* would have proved more appropriate, for the battles were fought in what proved to be the coldest winter to date in the 20th century. Hitler's push was to be east to west along a 60-mile north/south front between Monschau (Germany) and Echternach (Luxembourg) by Panzer and infantry divisions, which would quickly reach the *Meuse*, cross it south of Liège and Namur, and then turn northwest for Brussels and Antwerp.

What indications of action the Allied intelligence heard didn't seem to warrant interrupting the planning for upcoming Christmas festivities. Most of the forces were already convinced that the Nazis were too weak to mount a broad attack. And the Ardennes, except for the Nazis' easy breakthrough there in September 1940, was thought to be terrain too troublesome for a ground attack, especially in winter. (As a result of that reasoning, *both* sides regarded the eastern Ardennes as a place for tired troops to rest, and untested ones to get their front line bearings.) **Supreme Commander Eisenhower** expressed concern about the lack of Allied coverage in the area, but allowed **General Omar Bradley** to reassure him.

December 16 dawned gray, making Allied air attack impossible; eight Panzer armored divisions rolled forward from their position on the Germany/Luxembourg border to begin their advance to Antwerp. Within a day they were already well behind in their scheduled crossing of the Meuse. They never would make it. One jeep on Dec. 17 brought the Nazis as close as they would come to crossing the Meuse. Moving ahead of their Panzer divisions—in one of seven confiscated American jeeps (the others were all eventually recaptured) that they hoped would help them seize bridges over the Meuse—were four Nazis, disguised in American overcoats. Their jeep was bound for **Dinant**, whose Meuse bridge was under the guard of a *British Royal Tank Regiment*. Reaching the east side of the Dinant bridge, the four American-cloaked Nazis in the American jeep sped through the British guard—who were thus unable to warn the occupants that the west end of the bridge had been set with antitank mines. The jeep occupants were killed instantly, and the British were relieved to find that under the casualties' American overcoats were Nazi uniforms.

One reason their campaign fell behind schedule so soon is that, from the second day, the Nazis were facing a shortage of fuel, having failed to find the stores of hidden Allied petrol that their plan depended upon. And the **U.S. Army** resistance was more resolute than expected, especially in Luxembourg: **German General Von Manteuffel** said later, "The courageous resistance of the 28th at Clervaux and Wiltz made possible the installation of the (Allied) defence of Bastogne." The "closed in" winter weather, though it hampered Allied air strikes, also made cross-country travel far more difficult. The roads, too few and too small for the Panzer divisions, "bulged" from the traffic. Both sides were confused in their movements, particularly when fog settled over the landscape. Only one fact was clear: all roads in the region ran through one of two points, **Bastogne** or **St. Vith**. Once the latter fell on December 21, the focus was all on the former.

In fact, Bastogne had been surrounded by Nazi Panzer infantry since December 20, but their commanders' freedom to act was frozen by the plan Hitler had foisted on them: *Press on to the Meuse, regardless.* Those inflexible orders, from which even Von Manteuffel would not risk straying for fear of Hitler's wrath, saved Bastogne. Von Manteuffel ordered the 2nd Panzer tanks to head for the Meuse, and left only an infantry division to attack Bastogne, which, though it could surround the town, couldn't break into it.

On December 21, there were few U.S. airborne troops holding on in Bastogne, and they were running low on artillery ammunition and supplies. Fearing Allied reinforcements—said to be on the way from *Patton's Third Army* headquartered then in Luxemburg City—Von Rundstedt had to temper the orders to his outnumbered troops: that they take Bastogne but *only* in such a way as to not hinder the Nazi advance to the Meuse.

On December 22, under siege by the surrounding Nazis, the American perimeter was approached at midday by four Nazis carrying a white flag. The only one who could speak English, and that very limited, requested to see the American commander. He was blindfolded and led to **Brigadier General McAuliffe**, to whom he handed a note from Nazi General Von Luttwitz of the Panzer corps. The message demanded the surrender of the American garrison on honorable terms, stating that otherwise the town and all military and civilians in it would be annihilated. Upon reading it, McAuliffe's immediate reaction was *"Aw, Nuts!"* (Many have suggested that he used a stronger term, but, during one of his many postwar visits back to Bastogne, McAuliffe confirmed the response.) Hard-pressed to find the words for a formal refusal, McAuliffe finally followed the suggestion of a staff member, and simply wrote down his first words—now in the annals of Americana. Handed the note by an American lieutenant, the Nazi spokeman found the slang beyond his comprehension and responded, "I do not understand. Is your commander's reply favorable?" To which the lieutenant replied, "It is certainly not affirmative. In plain English it means the same as 'Go to hell'. You understand that, don't you?" The German saluted, was blindfolded, and driven back to his outpost.

December 23 the skies cleared, and huge Allied C47 transport planes dropped in 144 tons of ammunition and medical and other supplies by parachute. Now the Americans could pick off the Nazis, sitting ducks in their dark uniforms against the snow that had begun to fall. Any natural camouflage in the woods was burned away with napalm.

On Christmas Day, just before dawn, Nazis in 18 tanks broke through into Bastogne. But the Americans met them with such firepower that all 18 soon were put out of operation. Thus, even before the first three Sherman tanks of the *4th Armored* finally arrived on December 26, it was clear that the Nazi effort was lost. Nevertheless, that day Von Manteuffel wrote in his journal, "Despite my advice, Hitler remains stubborn about Bastogne."

On December 30, snow fell thicker. On December 31, the Germans attacked Bastogne 17 times, with heavy losses all around. Of the situation in the ebbing hours of 1944, Von Manteuffel would write, "The ultimate defeat of the *Wehrmacht* was only a question of time, for the men and equipment to carry on the war were lacking." Still, the Nazis mounted further attacks on January 3 and 4, the toll of these last encounters in **the Battle of Bastogne** the heaviest of all. Thereafter, action in the Bulge theater moved away from Bastogne to elsewhere in the Ardennes.

In the **Battle of the Bulge** as a whole, between its opening on December 16, 1944, and closing during the final week of January 1945—by which time the Nazis had been forced back to the approximate line they had held when Hitler began his push to Antwerp—casualties, including wounded, missing in action, and those taken prisoner for both sides amounted to well over 150,000, with more than 21,000 dead.

If you're arriving in Bastogne by car, follow signs to **Mardasson**, 1 mi./2 km. north of the center. There, it's best to begin your visit at the ★★**Bastogne Historical Center** *(Colline du Mardasson; daily, late Feb.-April and Oct.-Nov. 10 a.m.–4 p.m., May, June, and Sept. 9:30 a.m.–5 p.m., July and Aug. 9 a.m.–6 p.m.;* ☎ *(061) 21.14.13, FAX (061) 21.73.73; all displays multilingual, gift/ bookshop with English literature)*, which is unique among military museums in that many of the details were authenticated, exhibits created, and commentary scripted with the collaborative help of both **U.S. Army General McAuliffe** and **Nazi General Von Manteuffel**—who worked together here at the center after having fought on opposing sides in the war. The museum has several elements, the first being an illuminated model showing the phases of the Battle of the Bulge around Bastogne, with actual still photographs of the confrontation simultaneously projected onto a circle of screens around the amphitheater. Written and spoken commentary throughout is in English (and other languages). Another of the center's ingredients is its exceptional collection of **authentic uniforms** for both sides (General Baron Von Manteuffel donated the leather greatcoat he wore during the campaign), as well as items brought by returning veterans and those found on the actual battlefield. Several well-done **dioramas** are peopled with wax mannequins of the major players (generals McAuliffe, Von Manteuffel, Patton, Bradley, and Eisenhower) and display battle gear and lighter equipment of the parachute division, vehicles, and weapons. Finally, the cinema shows **film clips** shot by Americans and Germans during the battle days, beginning with Panzer divisions on the move towards Belgium through Wiltz and Clervaux in Luxembourg. We see not only shelling but also the actual taking of prisoners, troops on both sides walking out with their wounded, and scenes showing the snow-camouflage overcoats and tank covers (made for Allied vehicles from bed sheets donated by Belgians). Also on display is a copy of the Christmas message of McAuliffe to his cold, weary soldiers. Of the 200,000 or so annual visitors to the center, approximately 15% are Americans, 50% Dutch, and 20% Belgian. Allow at *least* an hour for a visit and additional time for the Mardasson Monument near it.

A visit to the Historical Center will give you a deeper appreciation for *The Battle of the Bulge*, whose casualties are commemorated at the close-by ★★**Mardasson Monument/American Memorial** *(free access at all times)*, erected in 1950 under the initiative of the Belgo-American Association. The tall, star-shaped memorial, with the names of the U.S. states inlaid around the upper edges and the sides inscribed with the military companies that participated in the battle, also includes, on ten large stone slabs, a detailed account of the battle written by U.S. military historian S.L.M. Marshall. In the crypt beneath the monument, the 76,890 Americans killed, wounded, or missing at Bastogne and other battles in the Bulge theater are remembered with three chapels (Protestant, Catholic, and Jewish) decorated with mosaic murals by **Fernand Léger**. There's a viewing platform atop the monument; at each of the star's five points is a description of the battle action that took place in that compass direction. Today the land is mostly peaceful rolling pasture.

Elsewhere in the town of Bastogne are monuments of the events of the chilling winter of '44/45. A Sherman tank and a bust of McAuliffe are on the square that bears the brigadier general's name. An **area driving route brochure**, available from the tourist office or historical center, enables you to follow the signposted main stages of the campaign in your car. In summer, a tourist train takes visitors to many of the sites. There are several choices for food on **place McAuliffe**, and just off it is Bastogne's leading plain-but-pleasant 27-room hotel/restaurant **Hotel Lebrun** *(rue du Marché 8;* ☎ *(062) 21.54.21, FAX (062) 21.54.23; hotel inexpensive, restaurant moderate, menus inexpensive).*

HOLLAND

Dutch bulbfields in bloom.

AN INTRODUCTION

THE DUTCH LANDSCAPE

The word Holland comes from the Dutch *hol*, meaning "hollow," and the name Nederland means "low land or country." Thus, whether we call the country by the geographically correct *Netherlands* or *Holland* (the name of the historically most populous and prosperous province, now used by many foreigners to mean the country as a whole), by *definition*, it's impossible to discuss the Dutch landscape without the subject of water coming to the surface.

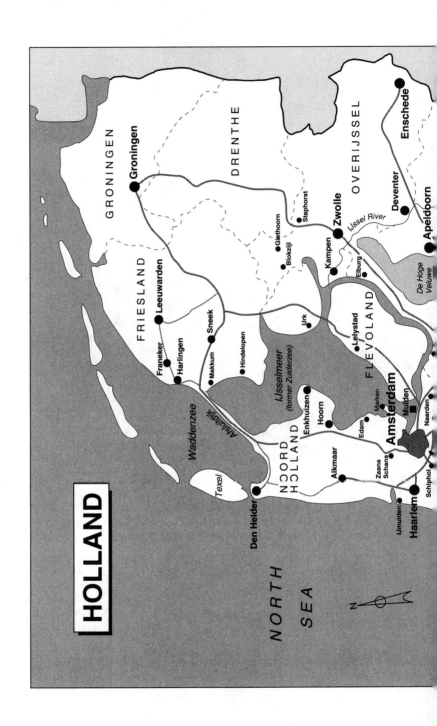

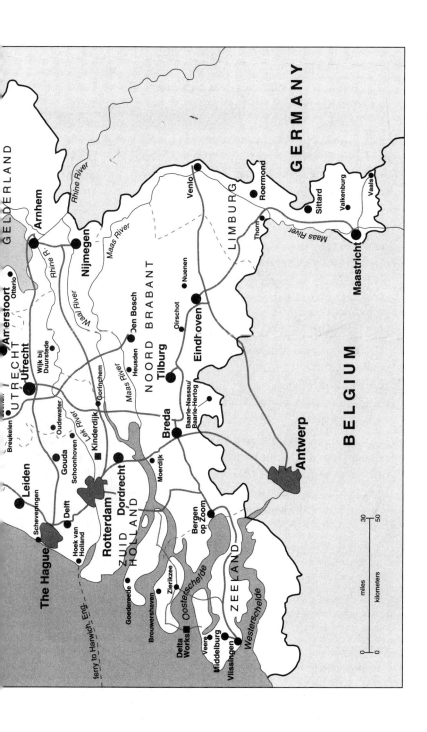

Left on its own, the western half of Holland, an area where 60% of the Dutch population lives, would be below the level of the North Sea and the region's rivers. Much of that area is 15 or more feet below the **NAP** (*Normaal Amsterdams Peil*), the world's reference point for sea level, much as Greenwich Mean Time in London is the planet's time standard. No one, not even the country's fundamentalists Calvinists, considers the saying "God made the world, but the Dutch made Holland" a sacrilege. It's simply fact that if it weren't for Holland's state-of-the-art hydroengineering, the Dutch goal—defined by one man as "to possess land where water wants to be"—couldn't be realized.

Holland occupies the delta formed over millennia at the mouths of Europe's major rivers, the Maas (Meuse) and the Rhine. A line that runs roughly parallel to the North Sea coast divides the Dutch land mass into two more or less equal areas: the *low*, which is at or below sea level in the western, coastal part of the country, and the *high*, in the eastern half of the country. The highland, formed during the Pleistocene Ice Age, consists mostly of sand and gravel. The lowland, clay on which peat has formed, is younger, deposited less than 10,000 years ago. Much of the land was brought downstream by the continental rivers, and some was pushed into ridges by glaciers. The ebb and flow of the marshes and coastal dunes, a more recent element of the formation of Holland, continue uninterrupted today.

A good percentage of Holland today is anything but natural landscape. Rather, it's the result of shaping over centuries through human intervention. In this century alone, more than 550,000 acres of land were recovered from the bottom of the former Zuiderzee (South Sea). But not until the mid-20th century did the balance sheet in Holland's land-reclamation ledger break into the black. Watery as the land already was, by the 13th century the North Sea was breaching the coastal sand dunes. The job was finished by a great storm in the year 1287—which killed 50,000 people in Friesland—when the North Sea reached and flooded a former inland lake, creating the Zuiderzee. That flood, combined with such self-induced inundations as the 1944 Allied bombing of dikes in Zeeland during World War II to flush out the Nazis, gave 40,000 acres back to the sea.

General coastal erosion has cost the Dutch another 1.4 million acres of land in the past millenium. From the year 1000, when Friesland was completely diked—barricaded from the sea by earthen embankments—until World War II, all the land gained by the Dutch with dams, dikes, windmills, and steam engines amounted to a little less than 1.3 million acres. A comparison of these two figures shows that if the Dutch didn't challenge the sea so incessantly, their country wouldn't simply stand still in size: it would shrink—and sink.

The Dutch struggle to contain the sea had begun long before Roman historian **Pliny**, in A.D. 50, described Frisian tribes in the north of the Netherlands as living on ground that "makes one doubt whether the soil belongs to the land or to the sea." He continued: "A miserable people lives there on high hills which they have thrown up with their own hands to a height which they know from experience to be that of the highest tide, and on these spots they have built their huts. They are like seafarers when the water covers the surrounding land, like shipwrecked people when the waves have retreated."

The Frisian mounds (*terpen*) were followed in time by **dikes**, which eroded all too easily on the side facing the sea, especially in storms. Once the durability of dikes had been improved, builders learned to channel the flow of water by the use of dams. Hydrocontrol took a significant step with the discovery that surrounding a parcel of land with dikes and installing a system of sluices permitted the discharge of excess water. Gradually, a network of canals that drained the land in the direction of the North Sea was created. In 1408, the first **windmill** for pumping water was built in Holland. Since the paddle wheel of a single windmill was capable only of raising water about five feet (1.5 meters), it was necessary to use several mills in a series (*molengang*) for greater heights.

Such developments marked the turning point at which the Dutch could become offensive, rather than just defensive, in their efforts to control the relationship between the sea and their land. By about 1600, Jan Adriaanszoon had perfected the method of draining large lakes in order to create **polders** (drained land) of a size to support whole towns. In the process, he acquired the nickname *Leeghwater* ("empty of water"), which he liked so much that he legally adopted it. In a plan to drain the **Haarlemmermeer**, a huge inland lake southeast of Haarlem, Leeghwater, who had successfully drained smaller bodies of water, advocated the use of dikes and 160 windmills. Although the project caught the imagination of the Dutch public, it was deemed too ambitious by Dutch officials of the day.

In 1774, steam power was used for the first time for polder drainage. When the Haarlemmermeer eventually was drained in 1852, three steam pumping stations (one named for Leeghwater) were used. The three stations pumped nonstop for three years from 1849 to 1852, and pumped 800 million cubic meters of water. One of the original steam pumping stations is now a museum. Today, Schiphol Airport is located on land lying 13 feet below sea level that once was at the bottom of the Haarlemmermeer. Having come from the lake bottom, the soil at Schiphol is so richly fertile that farmers cross the runways—with air traffic controllers' permission—to plant the fields between them.

Another Dutch milestone in hydrotechnology was marked in 1932, with the completion of the **Afsluitdijk** (enclosing dike), which sealed off the Zuiderzee from the salt water of the North Sea, and formed the fresh-water IJsselmeer lake. The project had been envisioned as early as 1667 by Hendrik Stevin, a mathematician, but only was realized nearly three centuries later by **Cornelius Lely**, a single-minded engineer who essentially devoted his life to taming the Zuiderzee. (The capital city of the polder province of Flevoland, which has been created from the sea bed, carries his name: Lelystad.) The unfolding of the Zuiderzee Reclamation Act of 1918, which created by stages three large polders, in 1942, 1957, and 1968, is recounted at the **Informatiecentrum Nieuw Land** in Lelystad.

In Zeeland, the southern coastal region of the country, the Dutch have pioneered ways of water control on a grand scale to protect existing land. The **Delta Project**, more than three decades in its realization, was born as a result of a 1953 storm and accompanying tidal surge in Zeeland in which more than 1800 people perished. Most livestock vanished and nearly 500,000 acres were submerged under salt water. The "give and take" with the sea in Zeeland ended in October 1986, when Queen Beatrix threw the switch on a massive storm control system that is a masterpiece of coastal hydroengineering unmatched in the world. In basic terms, the project, through a series of giant fixed dams and sluices, reduced the Dutch coastline (and, therby, its need for smaller, more vulnerable dikes) by 435 miles, making it more defendable.

Water management in the region was of such importance from the earliest days that responsibility for the dikes lay with Holland's counts. Later, when land was individually owned, each man was required to maintain the dikes on his land, and when too old to do so, was obliged to turn his holding over to a younger man who could. Today, Holland has a *Polder Authority*, a *Ministry of Waterworks*, and a *Water Control Board* (one of the country's oldest democratic institutions), functioning full force and having the final words over the country's water control. Of course, they are *only* words. As Amsterdam historian Louis van Gasteren has said: "The sea can never be conquered; the Dutch (just) made a contract with it. We said 'We appreciate you, we respect you, just don't surprise us.' "

THE DUTCH PEOPLE

Beyond doubt, the Dutch character has been shaped by Holland's association with the sea. The Dutch never have had the luxury of being spontaneous: it is their deliberateness that keeps claim on the land captured from the sea. The Dutch sense of responsibility and resourcefulness seems almost to have come in on the tide. And their respectability and religiosity—spiritually, one needed always "to have one's house in order" since one never knew when the next "killer" flood might surge across the low-lying land—could have been blown in on a salty breeze.

The necessity of "constructing" the Dutch land by damming, diking, and draining to wrest it from the sea before building could even begin dictated that individual living space be limited. Since land was so precious, qualities such as orderliness and organization, both in individuals and whole towns, were, and are, a virtue in Holland. Working so hard for the dry ground on which to build them, it's no wonder the Dutch are home lovers.

The relatively small space in which the Dutch must subsist—with a population of 14.9 million, Holland is one of the most densely peopled places in the world—makes respect for personal privacy a must. However, the need to reassure the world (or at least the neighbors) of respectability leads many Dutch to forego privacy by leaving the curtains of front windows undrawn so that all can see how proper— and, perhaps, how prosperous—everything is inside.

In fact, the Dutch character is full of seeming contradictions. The people are both parsimonious and generous, tolerant and strict, cosmopolitan and parochial, pragmatic and sentimental. Though the Dutch, quite correctly, pride themselves on their individualism, the social climate of the country strongly supports a collective style of thinking and conformity to conventional behavior. Few Dutch can wholly avoid being concerned about what their neighbors think. Perhaps the essentially bourgeois approach to life in Holland is summed up in this translation of a Dutch saying: "Act normally, and you're conspicuous enough."

Holland's intimacy with the sea led to a Dutch predilection for shipping, which brought its sailors into contact with cultures around the world. Such exposure to many different ideas and attitudes contributed to making Holland a bastion of tolerance. In conjunction with the open-mindedness that they showed to the many displaced persons who have found solace in their society over the centuries, the Dutch insisted on personal and commercial freedoms in order to be competitive on the seven seas.

Dutch friends have pointed out what *they* consider a national character flaw: always having an opinion on how *other* countries conduct themselves. (For centuries, the Dutch have exhibited a strong sense of mission; their religious zeal at one time was such that one tenth of all the missionaries in the world came from Holland.) Frankly, I find it refreshing that the Dutch *know* and *care* about the rest of the world. And are committed to how well it works.

The Dutch people and their government have shown themselves more than willing to put money where their mouths are, which is a significant stance for a Dutch person, who often is stereotyped as being close-fisted to the point of still having the first *dubbeltje* (10-cent piece) he ever earned. In fact, the Dutch population regularly responds with millions of guilders to relief appeals for natural and man-made disasters. The Dutch government, too, is capable of financial commitment to issues: several years ago, it "fell" over a decision not as to *whether* Holland was going to foot a huge bill for environmental clean-up—largely caused upstream on the Rhine River by other countries' factories—but *how* it was going to finance the enormous project.

Water, which both unites and divides Holland, even delineates its religions, though the lines have blurred in the recent past. While there has been a decline in membership in the Dutch Reformed Church (Calvinist) to less than half its former strength (about 28% of the population in 1989, it stood at 49% in 1900), a rise in the number of people who do not belong to any denomination (32%), and a stable percentage of Roman Catholics (36%), the uniquely Dutch sociopolitical phenomenon of "compartmentalization" still exists. It is the coexistence of separate organizations (political parties, newspapers, schools, social and sports clubs, hospitals, TV stations, old-age homes) whose members all are either Protestant Calvinist or Roman Catholic.

Very roughly, Protestants in Holland are most numerous in a broad band running across the country from the southwest (Zeeland) to the northeast (Groningen). Most Catholics live *below the Moerdijk*—the region south of the great river estuaries near Rotterdam—in the provinces of North Brabant and Limburg, where the sterner aspects of the Protestant work ethic are much less apparent. Although religious compartmentalization is ebbing somewhat in

Holland, nowhere else in Europe—with the exception of Northern Ireland—is such a segmented societal infrastructure in place.

For all the stolid parts of the Dutch character, there's a decidedly sentimental side. The Dutch language is profuse in its use of the diminutive *je* (meaning "little"). It's added to everything from people's names to the most unlikely objects, and also conveys affection. A characteristic Dutch concept is captured in the word *gezellig* (pronounced rather like *HEH' zelick*), which is literally untranslatable, though "cozy" and "congenial" come closest. *Gezellig* might be used to describe the atmosphere of an historic house, a restaurant made romantic by candlelight, or an appealing "brown" cafe.

The Dutch manage to mix an appreciation for the traditional with modern applications. As much as any traveler in Holland, I love the country's cliches: tulips, dikes, windmills, and wooden shoes. But I'm always intrigued at how the Dutch update them. Tulips, no less loved for their beauty, are an enormously important export business; dikes have been developed by the Dutch into state-of-the-art hydrotechnology, and today's sleek wind turbines, though mere shadows of the sturdy windmills from former centuries, capture *and store* the energy of the wind. And just see what the wooden shoe has evolved to: still worn by workers in tulip fields and by farmers throughout Holland for their lightweight, water-resistant features, Dutch *klompen*—which perfectly describes the sound one makes walking in them—were used as the model for astronauts' "moonshoes."

AN HISTORICAL PERSPECTIVE

During the Middle Ages, the area that today is the country named the Netherlands comprised a group of autonomous duchies (*Gelre* and *Brabant*) and counties (*Holland* and *Zeeland*), together with the bishopric of *Utrecht*. Under Emperor **Charles V** (1500–1558), those territories, in combination with what are present-day Belgium and Luxembourg, were known as *the Netherlands*, or Low Countries, and formed part of the great Burgundian-Hapsburg Empire. The Netherlanders had long been accustomed to outside rule and had no quarrel with Charles, who had been born in the Low Countries (in Ghent) and generally allowed them a degree of autonomy. However, when Charles V abdicated in 1556 (amid the spreading **Reformation**), ceding the Netherlands to his son Spanish King **Philip II**, a dictatorial, fanatical Roman Catholic, the stage was being set for the **Eighty Years' War**.

The harsh policies imposed by Philip inflamed Protestants, who also received antipapist preaching from the Calvinists. A wave of religious rebellion swept the Netherlands. The Spanish response to the Iconoclasm of 1566, during which Protestant crowds attacked the contents of Catholic churches, slashed paintings, broke sculptures, and burned all objects connected with the hated priesthood—and in the process destroying a treasure house of medieval art—was brutal. In 1567, Philip II sent the **Duke of Alva** and 10,000 troops to the Low Countries. Years of "*Spanish Fury*" followed, with town after town besieged, their citizens ravaged.

The first step toward establishing an independent Dutch state was taken in 1568, when a number of provinces banded together and rebelled under the leadership of **Prince Willem (the Silent) of Orange** (1533–1584), marking the beginning of the Eighty Years' War. Having survived seiges and other attacks, the **Seven United Provinces of the Northern Netherlands** (one of which was Holland) achieved a *de facto* independence from Spain in 1579, although the official *Peace of Munster* under the *Treaty of Westphalia* wasn't signed until 80 years later in 1648 (when the Southern Netherlands—today's Belgium—also became free of Spanish rule).

Following the Dutch republic's tacit freedom from Spain, the 17th century proved a period of unequaled growth and prosperity in the northern Netherlands. The people of the Seven United Provinces set out to make the most of their considerable commercial skills, modest terrain, and chief natural resource—the sea. Herring provided both food and a major source of income from export, especially after the Dutch discovered the secret of preserving the fish with salt.

Amsterdam became the hub of a far-flung trading and financial empire under the **Dutch East India Company**, which traded with the Far East, and the **Dutch West India Company**, which went to the New World. It was responsible for, among other colonies, the establishment of Nieuw Nederland colony in America in 1623. The colony's settlement of **Nieuw Amsterdam** was later given by the Dutch to the British (who renamed it **New York**) in exchange for **Suriname** (on the northeast coast of South America). Dutch ships from the seven provinces sailed the seven seas, carrying spices, exotic goods, and, most important of all, grain from eastern Europe.

Dutch farmers, thus freed from growing grain themselves, turned to more specialized and profitable pursuits, such as dairy farming and the cultivation of commercial crops such as hemp and tulip bulbs, while employing massive drainage projects that increased the amount of land available for the propagation of such products. An extensive system of canals brought city and country closer together, providing farmers with ready markets and city dwellers with abundant and affordable produce. Economic opportunity and religious and political tolerance drew immigrants, many of them skilled, from Flanders and elsewhere in Europe.

The mix of these ingredients and the energy of the era created a society in Holland that was unique in 17th-century Europe: urban, mercantile, and democratic in spirit, with a strong sense of pride and achievement. Political power lay less with the princes of the *House of Orange* than with the Protestant mercantile elite, who dominated city councils, provincial assemblies, and the national *States General* at The Hague. There was a great flourishing of culture, particularly painting, to celebrate the increased prosperity. The era became known as the **Golden Age**. Eventually, there arose the need for wars—notably with England over sea-trade interests—to protect Dutch fortunes.

Though the tide eventually did turn on its fortune, the Netherlands remained independent—though the forces of French King Louis XIV invaded Holland in the 1670s—until 1795 when it became a vassal state of the French Empire. **Napoleon Bonaparte** put his brother **Louis Napoleon** in charge of the country in 1806. But Louis turned out to be too intent on being a decent ruler to the Dutch, and Bonaparte later deposed him and annexed Holland to France. French occupation came to an end in 1813, and the subsequent *Treaty of Vienna* (1815) established the **Kingdom of the Netherlands**, consisting of Holland, Belgium, and Luxembourg.

The ruler of the new country was Dutch **King Willem I** (son of the last *Stadholder*, Willem V) of Orange, who also held the title Grand Duke of Luxembourg, in a union of hereditary roles that lasted until 1890. However, in the more than 250 years that by then had passed since the southern and northern Netherlands had been one, Holland and Belgium had grown too far apart in outlook to be able to exist as a single country. Following an uprising by its people in 1830, Belgium was awarded independence from Holland in 1839.

The Netherlands Constitution of 1814, which had decreed that the king govern and the ministers report to him, was revised in 1848. The updated Dutch Constitution created a constitutional monarchy with a parliamentary system, wherein ministers were accountable to an elected parliament rather than to the monarch. With the death of King Willem III in 1890, Holland's male succession ended, and Willem's daughter **Wilhelmina** (1880–1962), whose mother, Queen Emma, acted as regent until Wilhelmina reached 18, became the first of what would be three successive Dutch queens. Queen Wilhelmina served Holland from 1890–1948, seeing her country through two world wars.

During the **First World War**, Holland remained neutral, though not without difficulty, since the Allies maintained the neutrality strictly, not wanting any supplies to fall into the hands of Germans by way of Holland. Holland continued to pursue a policy of strict neutrality right up until the outbreak of the **Second World War**. Then, without warning, it was ruthlessly invaded by the Nazis on May 10, 1940, and occupied for what would be a period just five days short of five years. After the Nazis leveled Rotterdam with a bombing blitzkrieg on May 14, Queen Wilhelmina and her ministers, believing that they could better serve the Dutch people from an unoccupied country, fled across the North Sea to England. Crown Princess **Juliana**, whose husband Prince Bernhard, though a German, served as a member of the Dutch forces and aide to his mother-in-law Wilhelmina in England, took up residence with her children in Canada for much of the war. When her third daughter, Margriet, was born there in 1943, the Canadians declared the birth location Dutch soil for the purpose of preserving the baby's royal succession rights.

In the fall of 1944, the southern part of Holland, near Maastricht, was the first region in the country to be freed by the Allies. But due to the disastrous results of the *Market Garden operation* around Arnhem, the northern part of the country remained under Nazi occupation during Holland's long, cold *Hunger Winter* of 1944–45. To the present, *Liberation Day*, May 5, though not a legal holiday, is observed by the Dutch.

Until World War II, Holland was a major colonial power, but after 1945 her colonies began seeking independence. **Indonesia** severed all its constitutional links with the Netherlands in 1949. **Suriname**, after taking over its domestic affairs in 1954, became a fully independent republic in 1975. The **Netherlands Antilles** (Aruba, Curaçao, Bonaire, St. Eustatius, Saba, and St. Maarten) in the Caribbean are equal partners with the Netherlands under a special charter.

On April 30, 1980, **Queen Juliana**—who had been queen since her mother Wilhelmina had abdicated in 1948—with a stroke of a pen in the palace on Dam Square, abdicated in favor of her eldest daughter **Beatrix**, who was installed as queen in a ceremony in Amsterdam's Nieuwe Kerk.

RANDSTAD HOLLAND

Whatever image you have of Holland, its realization is likely to be located in the Randstad. This relatively recently named geopolitical entity includes both the oldest and newest in Dutch urban planning, and encompasses Holland's two most distinctive features: **historic towns**—with their tall, narrow, gabled houses, great churches, quaint canals, and museums laden with treasures from the 17th-century Golden Age—and classic **Dutch countryside** with cows, canals, windmills, tulip fields, and, above the far, low horizon, uninterrupted expanses of sky in which clouds create the mountains missing from the waterlogged, not so *terra firma*.

The **Randstad**, best translated as "city along the rim," is the urbanized region of low-lying western Holland. If you imagine **Amsterdam** at the left tip of the open end of a horseshoe, the rest of the Randstad cities fall roughly around its shape counterclockwise: **Haarlem**, **Leiden**, **The Hague**, **Delft**, **Rotterdam**, and **Gouda**, with **Utrecht** at the right tip. The Randstad is 45 miles north to south, and 40 miles across at its widest point, covering an area roughly the size of Greater London. As urbanized as it is, the Randstad is not a megalopolis or continual conurbation. But it is a chain of highly individual urban entities separated by green spaces. The "green fingers" of the Randstad (and the many "green thumbs" who live there) provide plenty of photogenic Dutch landscape within it.

Though the relative importance of Randstad cities has changed since the 17th century, all retain their historical significance and serve as major centers today. The term Randstad is an informal one, with no official status or administrative authority. Within the Netherlands, the term is used only to refer to the geographic region in general, and is never meant to minimize the historical, functional, and spatial distinctiveness of each of the component cities.

As early as the 16th century, Holland developed an urban consciousness that has marked Dutch culture ever since. By 1514, some 46% of the people in the province of Holland (the combined area of today's separate provinces of North and South Holland) lived in towns. By the 17th century, an estimated 50% of the Dutch population lived in towns, a statistic not reached in England until that country's 19th-century industrial revolution. The fact that the Randstad—with the exception of sand dunes wedged between Haarlem, Leiden, and The Hague and the coast—lies entirely below sea level and necessitated land reclamation to create permanent settlements, doubtless contributed to the early dense development of Dutch towns.

Close living conditions, forced upon the Dutch by their water-bound landscape and the need to congregate in cities in order to be able to defend themselves against invaders of their flat, boggy, barrierless countryside, made early town planning a necessity in Holland. That the Dutch today prefer things well ordered in all aspects of life, including their physical environment, is a natural result of their communal history.

In the 16th century, the towns of Leiden and Haarlem were larger than Amsterdam. A 1514 *Enqueste* (census), showed that Amsterdam had 2532 dwellings, while Haarlem had 2741 houses, Delft 2943, and Leiden 3017. Even at their 16th-century size, Holland's towns were not isolated entities, but a network of larger and smaller urban communities already reflecting the first form of the Randstad. Approximately half of the country's then nearly 300,000 inhabitants lived in towns, while the other half lived close to one. A similar situation holds true today, with 90% of the Dutch population considered urban.

In the 17th century, Amsterdam became Holland's largest city. It remains so, with a population today of about 750,000 in the city proper, one million in the greater metropolitan area. The inland towns of Haarlem and Leiden, and eventually even Delft, which had harbor rights on the River Schie at Delfshaven (today, one of the few remaining historic parts of Rotterdam), lost ground to Amsterdam because of shipping. Once "commerce became king" in 17th-century Holland, Amsterdam, with its connection to the North Sea through the Zuiderzee, and Rotterdam, located near the North Sea mouths of major rivers from the interior of continental Europe, became the most prominent cities due to their preeminent shipping lanes.

From a frame of reference *within* the Randstad, the rest of Holland is apt to be thought of as "the provinces." Nevertheless, while residents of the Randstad have an essentially metropolitan mentality, each thinks of him or herself as being from Leiden, or Delft, or Rotterdam, and identifies with his own town's distinct character. (The differences in character of certain Randstad cities have been described this way: The Dutch make money in Rotterdam, spend it in Amsterdam, and talk about it in The Hague.) As regards new development, an all-important Randstad concept is to keep each major urban center separate from the others by "green" functions, such as agriculture and horticulture (businesses, true, but ones that provide a "green" look), plus natural preserves and recreational areas.

Within the Randstad is located a high percentage of the whole country's infrastructure: significant social-cultural institutions, the national government, commercial centers, six universities, and headquarters for the mass media and railroads. The density of population, economic wealth, and cultural and historical attractions is remarkably different in the Randstad than in the rest of the country, and thus this area is likely to claim much of your Dutch travel time.

AMSTERDAM

GUIDELINES FOR AMSTERDAM
SIGHTS

Amsterdam embodies Holland's **17th-century Golden Age**, when it was the richest, most cosmopolitan city in the world. (It still can compete for most cosmopolitan.) Many of its protected monument buildings (some 7,000) date from that period, as does the distinct fan-shaped pattern of **concentric canals** that provide such a visual sense of place and pleasure. Amsterdam art museums hold numerous masterpieces, many by Dutch artists considered among the world's most revered painters (**Rembrandt** and **van Gogh**, to mention the best known). The broad appeal of this fascinating city comes from clandestine 16th-century Catholic churches to live sex shows, diamond cutters to flower markets, canalside mansion museums to cozy "brown" pub/cafes, and world-renowned performing arts companies to carillon concerts. Amsterdam turns into a veritable fantasyland at night with the tasteful, romantic illumination of canal bridges, gables, and landmark facades.

GETTING AROUND

Amsterdam is a walking city (bring comfortable shoes), not only because of its many inviting corners, but because the *Centrum* (center) is compact. A walk from Centraal Station to the Rijksmuseum (which about covers the city's tourist terrain) would take a purposeful walker 1/2 hour, though it's better to allow time for distractions along the way. The VVV (tourist information) sells a two-cassette-tape package with map for four informative, **self-guided walks** (including *canal houses*, the *Jordaan* district, *old Amsterdam,* and the *Jewish quarter*); you need your own tape player. Amsterdam and its environs have a dense network of **trams**, **buses**, and the **metro**. System maps and economical, multiple-ride tickets are available from the VVV or the GVB (Amsterdam Municipal Transport), both locat-

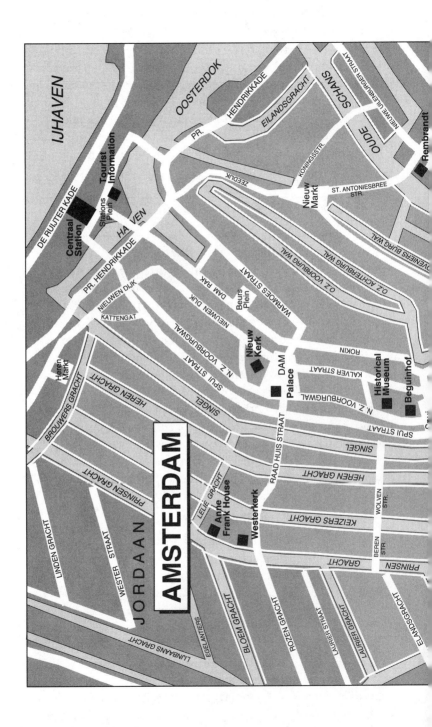

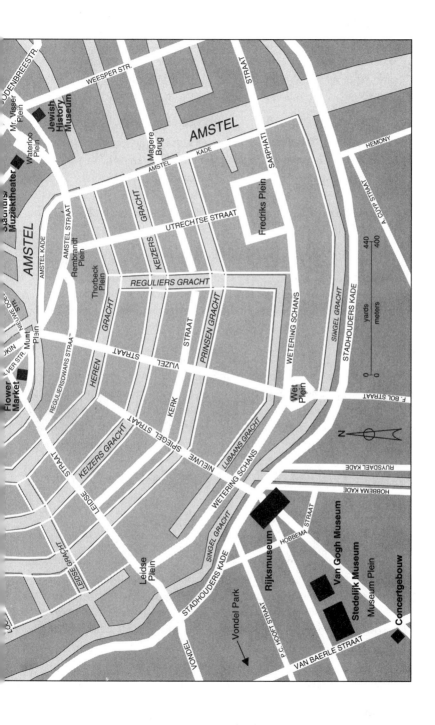

ed opposite Centraal Station. A canal cruise in one of the ubiquitous glass-enclosed boats remains one of the best introductions to the city. **Canal bikes**, with landing stages at several central city locations, provide a pedaling experience on water for up to four. **Water taxis** are expensive but **water buses** and the **museum boat** are more reasonable and provide the same picturesque mode of transportation.

SHOPPING

Since the 17th century, when the sailing ships of the *Dutch East India Company* returned laden with exotic items for sale from the Far East, Amsterdam has been an international marketplace. Amsterdam's diamonds, Delftware, and antiques all attract shoppers' attention, as do the full complement of department stores and fashionable boutiques.

WHERE TO STAY

Accommodations come in a wide range of standards and prices, from luxurious and very expensive to youth hostels. There's good choice in the inexpensive and moderate categories, which always include an ample Dutch breakfast.

WHERE TO EAT

The linguistically adept Dutch claim you "can dine out in any language" in Amsterdam, and you're unlikely to come across a city where the choices of cuisine are more cosmopolitan in character. While the Dutch "kitchen" isn't overly emphasized, its traditional, fresh, well-prepared, and often hearty fare can be sampled in a number of atmospheric settings in the city. Except for the most casual eateries, a call ahead to book is a good bet, and it is essential at better restaurants.

ENTERTAINMENT AND EVENTS

Amsterdam is home to many prestigious residential performing arts companies, which present full schedules from fall through spring. June's mostly Amsterdam-based, month-long, multifaceted **Holland Festival** is an annual cultural highlight. On the **Queen's Birthday** (April 30—a national holiday) Amsterdam becomes a crowded, city-wide, street flea market. The arrival of **Sinterklaas** by boat in mid-November is enjoyed not only by Dutch children but by everyone.

ARRIVING

Those arriving in Holland by air are likely to do so at Amsterdam's **Schiphol Airport**, which is always rated near the top of frequent international travelers' choices for best organized and operated airport in the world. Through **KLM Royal Dutch Airlines**, Holland's national carrier, and other airlines, Schiphol offers flight connections to points around the globe. A full schedule of intra-European flights operates from Amsterdam's Schiphol on KLM, NLM City Hopper, and other major international carriers. Express trains leave Schiphol for central railway stations in Amsterdam, The Hague, Rotterdam, and Utrecht 24 hours a day. KLM Road Transport operates shuttle bus services between Schiphol and major Amsterdam hotels (cost Dfl. 15). The half-hourly service is available between 6:30 a.m. and 5:15 p.m.

Most **international intracity trains** from across the European continent (and from Great Britain, once the **Euro Tunnel** under the *English Channel* is operative) serve Amsterdam, and Holland is a member of both the *Eurail Pass* and *Benelux Tourrail Pass* networks. Within Holland, Amsterdam is a major link on rail lines throughout the country. Various **ferry services** from English ports in the English Channel and on the North Sea arrive at Hoek van Holland, from which boat trains provide direct service to Amsterdam, via Rotterdam. Amsterdam is reached by Europe's principal motorways from Germany and from Belgium.

IN THE AREA

With its excellent rail and bus connections, almost anyplace in Holland can be "in the area" for the independent traveler. A range of half- and whole-day excursions within Holland are bookable at VVVs or through individual local motorcoach tour companies. Many towns located near Amsterdam are described in detail under their own headings, but **Aalsmeer**, **Alkmaar**, and **Zaanse Schans** are covered at the end of this section.

TRAVEL TIPS

Amsterdam's hippie scenes of the '60s and '70s at the Dam Monument are no longer, though "punks" make an appearance. As in any large city, there are street people—though far fewer than in the U.S., thanks to the Dutch social welfare system. Some are homeless and some are on drugs, though hard drug use in Holland has dropped. Since these people congregate in front of Amsterdam's Centraal Station, where they are particularly visible to tourists, one could get a distorted impression of the city as a whole. Violent crime in Amsterdam is rare; once you take precautions against pickpockets—which is an intelligent approach anywhere, including your hometown—you'll find Amsterdam refreshingly easy to enjoy. It's generally safe to stroll at night—always safest where it's well lighted and others are around—and to take public transportation anywhere.

AMSTERDAM IN CONTEXT

While being neither the seat of government nor the residence of the queen, Amsterdam is nevertheless the capital and cultural center of the Netherlands. Amsterdam had its beginning when the few inhabitants along the river *Amstel* (in about the year 1270) built a dam on it that gave the town its name. A harbor, the *Damrak*, was built, and an inner harbor, the *Rokin*, was formed, around which the first trade activities developed. Not many years later (1287), a storm breached the sand dunes to the northwest, creating the *Zuiderzee* (South Sea) and giving Amsterdam easy access to the open sea. A finger of land opposite the mouth of the Amstel protected the port against the westerly winds from the North Sea, and the tidal flow of the Zuiderzee prevented the port from silting up.

As early as 1275, Amsterdam was granted exemption from paying tolls on Dutch waterways, and was thus able to focus on trade as well as fishing. In the 14th and 15th centuries, Amsterdam was the most important port between the *German Hanseatic League* towns (of which it was made a member in 1368) and Bruges, the most important trading town of the time. The favorable situation of Amsterdam led to an increase in trade with the Baltic, and the town became an important stockpiler of grain and other commodities in its many warehouses.

The cargo trade and fishing stimulated industry and attracted many laborers from the countryside. The original town along the banks of the Amstel—today that stretch of the river is the filled-in **Damrak** —expanded on each side, with the **Nieuwendijk** and **Warmoesstraat**, and then the **Oudezijds Voorburgwal** and the **Nieuwezijds Voorburgwal**. In the 15th century, the town had to be enlarged twice with new moats. The 1425 expansion added the **Singel** and the **Kloveniersburgwal**, and the town's first gateways, bastions, and brick fortress.

Amsterdam's buildings, built on soggy soil that is a thick, marshy layer of peat, at first had foundations of light timber rafts that could support a single-story wooden frame dwelling. Because of its water-confined condition, land near the center of Amsterdam was—as it remains today—at a premium. This resulted in the architectural development of narrow, deep, and increasingly tall houses. In the 15th century, bricks increasingly replaced timber as building materials due to fire risk, and in the early 16th century, thatched roofs were replaced with tiles. The resulting increase in the weight of buildings required better foundations. A system was developed in which clusters of wooden piles were driven into the ground through upper layers of mud and peat until they rested on a layer of sand. Foundation piles could go as deep as 60 feet, a fact that elicited a contemporary riddle from Rotterdam's **Erasmus** about "a city whose inhabitants live on the tops of trees like birds."

Because better foundations could also support taller houses, which meant a more intensive use of land, Amsterdam remained the same size physically from 1425 until 1580. Despite the fact that the 16th century was one of the most turbulent in the entire history of the Netherlands, due to the religious and political struggles resulting from the **Reformation**, commerce continued to expand, and Amsterdam saw a steady stream of immigrants coming for work.

It was with the fall of Antwerp to the Spanish in 1585 during the **Eighty Years' War**, however, that prosperity positively exploded in Amsterdam. Within a short period, Amsterdam took over the preeminence of that southern Netherlands trading city. Experienced Antwerp merchants and craftspeople, as well as poor Protestants and rich Portuguese Jews, sought refuge and work in Amsterdam, which gave increased impetus to trade. Amsterdam acquired a larger merchant fleet, and expanded its cargo trade, especially in the Baltic, with grain from Poland and Prussia. The Dutch, through their Amsterdam port, became the "carriers" of Europe, with a fleet that was larger than those of England, Scotland, and France combined.

From 1595 onward, Amsterdam regularly embarked explorers seeking new sea routes, particularly in the East Indies where precious spices and other exotic goods could be obtained. This effort led, in 1602, to the establishment of the **United East India Company**, a limited liability company that obtained a monopoly for the trade in territories east of the Cape of Good Hope in southern Africa. Soon its Dutch ships swarmed over the seven seas, and the company became the most commercially successful organization in the world with trading posts all over the globe.

As a result of these activities, Amsterdam in the early 17th century developed into the main staple market in the world. Buffer stocks of a wide range of commodities were kept in long rows of tall, handsome warehouses that tilted slightly forward, so that bales of goods being raised by hoisting beams wouldn't brush the building. Goods —ranging from weapons to corn and spices to art treasures—could be acquired in Amsterdam. As early as 1578, Prince Willem of Orange foresaw the city's success, predicting: "Amsterdam shall prosper, and shall rise above all other cities."

With Amsterdam the busiest trading town of the 17th century, recruiting inexpensive labor became ever more important to merchants. Between 1570 and 1640, Amsterdam's population increased from 30,000 to 139,000. In 1609, a decision was reached to undertake a considerable expansion of the city, which included the construction of the **concentric pattern of canals** (*Herengracht, Keisersgracht,* and *Prinsengracht*) that continues to give the center city its distinctive shape. Also in 1609, the *Amsterdam Discount Bank* was established, where not only merchants, but princes, towns, and foreign governments opened accounts. Especially after the end of the *Eighty Years' War* in 1648, Amsterdam became *the* leading international center for finance, a position it maintained well into the 18th century.

With abundant commercial wealth, art, especially painting, became an accepted *and* expected form of acquisition. With an active artistic environment free of the restriction of guilds, Amsterdam was a wide-open market for painters. Among the masters most closely associated with the city were **Ferdinand Bol**, **Govert Flinck**, and **Jacob van Ruisdael**. But the grand master in Amsterdam—widely acknowledged as such in his lifetime—was **Rembrandt**. One of Rembrandt's first major commissions came from an Amsterdam merchant family in 1631, the portrait of Nicholas Ruts (now in the Frick Collection, NY). By 1632, Rembrandt had moved permanently from Leiden (where he was born and raised) to Amsterdam, which offered not only a wider artistic scope, but the probability of more profitable portrait commissions. His first commission after the move was a group portrait, *The Anatomy Lesson of Professor Tulp,* for the surgeons' guild; it avoided being merely a series of posed portraits by placing guild members in a dramatic event: a human dissection in progress.

Rembrandt's Amsterdam house (see "What To See and Do") was an easy walk from the new guildhall of the militia companies' building, the Kloveniersdoelen, for which he was commissioned to paint the company of Captain Frans Banning Cocq at the precise moment that he is giving his lieutenant the command for the company to march. The work, Rembrandt's most famous and today the centerpiece of Amsterdam's Rijksmuseum, came to be called *The Night Watch,* although a major restoration in 1975 revealed it to be a daytime scene. Rembrandt never left Holland, claiming that there was enough inspiration in his native land. From Amsterdam, he took long walks out along the river Amstel, finding scenery that suggested paintings, especially, landscape drawings; he made some 250 landscape drawings and etchings in his lifetime, nearly all of them of Amsterdam and its surroundings. Having fallen on unfortunate times, Rembrandt died in Amsterdam in 1669, in relative obscurity. He is buried in the *Westerkerk* (as is his son Titus), though the specific site is unknown.

Amsterdam's prosperity lasted through the 18th century, although its port by then was surpassed in importance by London, Hamburg, and Bremen. **Napoleon Bonaparte's** army occupied Holland from 1795 through 1813. In 1806, he sent his brother Louis Napoleon, despite Louis' disinclination—he even pleaded that the Dutch climate would be hazardous to his health—to rule the conquered country. Living first in The Hague, then Utrecht, Louis Napoleon finally settled most happily in Amsterdam in 1806, and turned what had been the *Stadhuis* (town hall) on the *Dam* since it opened with great pomp and pageantry in 1655 into the *Royal Palace* it remains today. He filled it with a priceless collection of Empire-period furniture, most of which remained when Bonaparte, fed up with his brother's too sympathetic approach to his subjects, recalled Louis to France in 1810. Bonaparte then solved the Dutch "situation" by absorbing the Netherlands into France.

In 1813, the French troops of Napoleon evacuated Holland, leaving it in a state of collapse with Amsterdam's maritime glory all but gone. This stagnation lasted until 1876 when the **Noordzee Kanaal** (North Sea Canal) was cut straight through the dunes roughly along the course of the **River IJ** (pronounced "eye") to give the city a short shipping connection directly to the sea. Other transportation connections also led to Amsterdam's revival. The first railway line, between Amsterdam and Haarlem, was opened in 1839, and soon afterward the line with Utrecht was added. In 1889, the grand **Centraal Station** was built on an artificial island not far from the site of Amsterdam's earliest settlement.

The upturn in the economy helped to remove one of the causes of poverty in Amsterdam, but a new **Poor Law** in 1854 was necessary. The second half of the 19th century saw an increasingly organized welfare policy implemented. Schools were seen as the gateway through which a pauper child might be transformed into a decent, upright member of society, and education soon became the city's largest item of net expense. In the early 20th century, housing, sanitation, and social questions remained concerns that were actively confronted in the city.

World War II hit Amsterdam hard. Of the city's 86,000 Jewish residents (out of 140,000 countrywide) at the beginning of the Nazi occupation, almost all were transported outside the country to camps; fewer than 10,000 returned. The first Nazi roundup and subsequent deportation to Germany of Jews (400 men and boys) in Amsterdam took place in mid-February 1941. On February 24, workers of all religions met in Amsterdam to discuss a protest, with the dock workers in the forefront of the action. A **general work stoppage** (nothing short of treason as far as the Nazis were concerned) began the next morning. Every single factory, workshop, and office emptied; no trains, garbage or mail trucks ran, and Amsterdam fell as silent as a city can. By the afternoon, the strike had spread to a 15-mile radius around Amsterdam. In response, Nazi troops were sent out in Amsterdam to arrest or shoot strikers, and within a few days they succeeded in suppressing the strike. This Amsterdam action was the single instance of broad-based support for the Jews against their oppressors in occupied Europe during the war. When the war was over, Queen Wilhelmina paid a lasting tribute to the Amsterdammers' stand by adding the words "Heroic, Resolute, Merciful" to the Amsterdam city coat of arms. Another lasting tribute to the resistence of the Amsterdammers is on the **Jonas Daniel Meijerplein**, near the site of the Jewish deportations during the war, and across from the **Jewish Historical Museum**: the moving, sculptured figure of *The Dock Worker* by Mari Andriessen (see "What to See and Do").

Although the southern part of the Netherlands had been liberated from the Nazis by then, during the winter of 1944–45, Amsterdam and the rest of northern Holland suffered continued occupation. The period is remembered as the **Hunger Winter**. As well as little food, there was no fuel, electricity, or transport; reportedly highly untasty tulips were dug up, mashed, and made into soup. Some 20,000 died of the cold and hunger in Amsterdam alone. Their bodies piled up at the *Zuiderkerk* (South Church) because it was impossible to bury the dead, with no wood for coffins and none with the strength to dig graves.

The years following the war were spent in a long process of recovery and rebuilding. Numerous urban and industrial projects were undertaken in Amsterdam, with much of the development taking place in the southeast section of the city. The plan for reclamation of land from the IJsselmeer progressed with the *Flevoland* polder province, and with the *Almere* complex of cities becoming brand new "bedroom communities" to Amsterdam. Fortunately, unlike cities such as The Hague and Utrecht, Amsterdam planners avoided the process referred to by the Dutch as *cityworming* (the building of new exclusively commercial complexes or "malls" in the *centrum*), keeping the city center instead to the traditional mixed-function urban concept. After 1960, activity in Amsterdam's harbor—which currently handles about 27 million tons annually, making it Europe's fourth busiest harbor after Rotterdam, Hamburg, and Bremen—increasingly moved west, as a result of which the town and harbor became separated. Present town planning by the Amsterdam City Council is creating offices, museums, hotels, and housing along the river **IJ** (behind the *Centraal Station*) in order to stop further migration of the harbor from the city center.

Since the 16th century, Amsterdam, as well as being a strikingly beautiful and successful commercial center for Holland, has played another important role in Dutch society, one well put into words by William Z. Shetter in his book *The Netherlands in Perspective.* He writes, "Amsterdam is called a *lastige stad*, a term that is difficult to translate, because although *lastig* means something like 'bothersome,' the phrase is used in a way that emphasizes the city's vital role in being on the progressive, and even radical, cutting edge, however uncomfortable that may be."

GUIDEPOSTS

Telephone Code 020

Tourist Info • VVV, Stationplein 10, ☎ *6266444, FAX 6252869*; Mon.–Sat. 9 a.m.–5 p.m.; Easter–Sept. Mon.–Sat. 9 a.m.–11 p.m., Sun. 9 a.m.–9 p.m. (except 11 p.m. July–Aug.); Oct.–Easter Mon.–Sat. 9 a.m.–6 p.m. (Sat. 5 p.m.), Sun. 10 a.m.–1 p.m. and 2–5 p.m. A small VVV office is at Leidsestraat 106: slightly shorter hours.

City Transport • GVB (tram, bus, Metro information): Stationplein: Daily 7 a.m.–10:30 p.m. (except Sat. and Sun. 8 a.m.).

Trains • Central Station Information Office: Mon.–Fri. 8 a.m.–10 p.m., Sat., Sun., holidays 9 a.m.–6 p.m.; ☎ *6202266* (international), ☎ *06-8991121* (national).

Emergency • Medical, central doctors service: ☎ *6642111.* Police: ☎ *6222222*; main police station: Elandsgracht 117, ☎ *5569111.*

Post Office • Postkantoor (main post office): Singel 250-256; ☎ *5563311*; Mon.–Fri. 8:30 a.m.–6 p.m. (Thurs. til 8:30 p.m.), Sat. 9 a.m.–noon.

Telephone/Fax • Telehouse Amsterdam (international calls, telegrams, FAX, money orders): near Dam Square; 24-hrs. daily.

Taxis • Taxicentrale: ☎ *6777777.* It's best not to count on being able to hail a cab. There are taxi ranks at the Centraal Station, Rembrandtsplein, Leidseplein (across from the Concertgebouw at Museumplein), and at major hotels.

Tours • Holland International, Rokin 54; ☎ *5512812.* American Express, Damrak 66; ☎ *5207777* Keytours Holland, Dam 19; ☎ *6247310.*

Books • The American Discount Book Center (specializing in books from the U.S. and U.K.) is at Kalverstraat 185; ☎ *6255537.* The Atheneum Bookstore on the *Spui* has books in English; the Atheneum Newsstand next to it has a large selection of magazines from around the world.

WHAT TO SEE AND DO

It would be impossible to provide information on all there is to see and enjoy in Amsterdam. And many of your lasting impressions won't come from specific attractions, but from activities as offhand as an evening drink at a canalside cafe with a wondrous view of light-outlined bridges. From about mid-March through October, bridges, facades, towers and trees along sections of the city's renowned ring of canals and other historic buildings are illuminated from sunset to 11:30 p.m. (somewhat later at midsummer when, because of Holland's northern latitude, it remains light until nearly 11 p.m.). Many more, though not all, museums now are open Mondays in Amsterdam. Some close January 1, Christmas, and April 30 (Holland's National Day).

The Amsterdam VVV publishes a number of informative, interesting walking-tour brochures in English, including a *Walk Through* series for *Maritime Amsterdam, Jewish Amsterdam,* and the *Jordaan.* The booklet, *Amsterdam in the Footsteps of Vincent van Gogh* (who lived in Amsterdam for more than a year in 1877–8, returned many times thereafter, and made his love for Amsterdam plain in letters to his brother Theo), covers places associated with the artist. There are also brochures on *Sculptures of Amsterdam I and II,* and *"Amsterdam School" Architecture in Amsterdam-South.* Prices are about Dfl. 2.50 apiece.

Knowing the key transportation and entertainment hubs will facilitate familiarity with Amsterdam. **Centraal Station (CS)** is an arrival point for many: all who travel by train and those who fly into Schiphol Airport and take the excellent rail connection into the city. A substantial number of city tram lines originate at the CS. Straight down the **Damrak** from the CS is **Dam Square**, with its *Monument, Royal Palace,* and *Nieuwe Kerk.* The Damrak continues as the **Rokin** to **Muntplein,** with the *Munt Tower* and its carillon (concerts Fri. noon–1 p.m.). Midpoint on the Rokin, where the road narrows, and the Amstel river to here out from the center has been left unfilled, a right turn brings one to the **Spui** and the **Beguinhof**.

With the Rokin at one's back, a *left* turn from the Munt into *Reguliers-breestraat* leads shortly to **Rembrandtsplein,** with its congregation of cafes. Carrying on, one comes to the **Blauwbrug** across the Amstel. To the left is the **Stopera** (the combined new *Stadhuis*, or town hall, and **Muziektheater**, behind which is **Rembrandt's house**).

Straight ahead across the bridge is **Waterlooplein** and the **Jewish Historical Museum**. Turning *right* at the Munt, one can enjoy the block-long **floating flower market** before arriving at *Leidsestraat*. A left turn onto it leads, after crossing the city's three concentric canals (**Herengracht, Keizersgracht**, and **Prisengracht**) to **Leidseplein**, a center of Amsterdam social life, with terrace cafes that are the best place from which to watch the people parade. Just beyond, past the landmark *American Hotel*, is the Singelgracht, over which a left brings one to the **Rijksmuseum** and **Museumplein**.

Rijksmuseum ★★★

Stadhouderskade 42; Tues.–Sat. 10 a.m.–5 p.m., Sun. and holidays 1–5 p.m.; closed Mon.; ☎ *6732121; trams 6, 7, 10.* Built in 1885 by P.J.H. Cuypers, the Rijksmuseum is the cornerstone of Holland's permanent art exhibits, with the largest and finest collection of Dutch paintings in the world. The museum dates from an 1808 decree by then ruler Frenchman Louis Bonaparte, brother of Napoleon, and was first housed at the Dam, in the former Stadhuis, turned into the Royal Palace by Louis. Rembrandt's *Night Watch*, the artist's best-known work, around which the museum was designed, has its own room (Room 224, top floor) with interpretive exhibits located nearby and other rooms of his works, including *The Jewish Bride* and *Self-Portrait as the Apostle Paul.* The top floor is where the masterpieces of Dutch 15th-through 17th-century paintings are, with rooms allocated to multiple works by **Frans Hals** (including *Merry Dinker*), **Jan Steen** (including *Feast of St. Nicholas*), **Vermeer** (*The Milk Maid, Woman Reading a Letter, The Love Letter, The Little Street*), and **Jacob van Ruisdael** (*Windmill at Wijk bij Duurstede* and 1), **Pieter de Hooch** (*Woman with a Child in a Pantry* and *Courtyard behind a House*), and **Nicolaes Maes** (*Old Woman at Prayer*).

Also on the top floor are Flemish works (**Rubens, Van Dyck**), Spanish (including Dutch-born **Anthony Moro, Goya**, and **Murillo**) and Italian (**Fra Angelico, Tiepolo**). In the Applied Arts section, there are three rooms of Delftware. Dutch painting of the 18th and 19th centuries, including Impressionism, The Hague School, and the Amsterdam School are on the ground floor. If you have time to see more, the Rijkmuseum has sections on Dutch history, Asiatic art, sculpture, and applied arts (including Flemish and Dutch tapestries). There are detailed floor plans, brochures and catalogs available in English, a museum shop, and a restaurant.

Rijksmuseum Vincent van Gogh ★★★

Paulus Potterstraat 7; Mon.–Sat. 10 a.m.–5 p.m., Sun. and holidays 1–5 p.m.; ☎ *5705200; trams 2 and 5 from CS.* Opened in 1973 as a permanent home for a Vincent van Gogh (1853–1890) collection of more than 200 paintings, 500 drawings, graphic art, and letters, and some works by his friends and contemporaries, including Gauguin and Toulouse-Lautrec. Van Gogh, who had a troubled, truncated life, and created most of his marvelous works in a mere five years just prior to his death more than a century ago at age 37, today is as popular a painter as any who ever lived. Although he executed many of his most memorable pieces outside Holland, primarily in France, his work is deeply rooted in the Dutch artistic tradition. He dropped the name *van Gogh*, signing only Vincent to the paintings he considered worthy, because he found that outside of Holland no one could pronounce it correctly. Among the best-known paintings at the museum are *The Potato Eaters*, *Vase with Sunflowers*, *The Bedroom/Arles*, and *Crows in the Wheatfields*. (For other van Gogh works in Holland, see the Kroller Muller Museum, Otterlo.)

Stedelijk Museum ★★★

Paulus Potterstraat 13, corner van Baerle Straat; Mon.–Sun. 11 a.m.–5 p.m.; ☎ *5732911; trams 2 and 5 from CS.* Opened at the end of the 19th century, in the 1950s the Stedelijk became one of the first museums in Europe to collect and exhibit contemporary art. Today, it is one of the most influential modern art museums in the world. Chronologically, the collection begins with works of "classic" modern artists, **Manet, Monet, Cezanne, van Gogh, Matisse, Chagall,** and **Picasso**, and advances through the early decades of the 20th century, when new visual "vocabulary" replaced the traditional use of perspective and began letting go of ties to visible reality in favor of the abstract, nonrepresentational art of Dutch-born **Mondriaan** and **Malevich**. Shown through the sweep of the Stedelijk collection, such changes can be seen as logical, even inevitable. Since the early 70s, when the van Gogh Museum was opened next door and most of that artist's work moved to it, the Stedelijk has been devoted exclusively to modern art, and new acquisitions always strive to present the latest developments in visual art. The Stedelijk began collecting photography in 1958 following the museum's highly successful exhibit of *The Family of Man* by Luxembourg-born **Edward Steichen**. (See "Clervaux Castle, Luxembourg, the Family of Man exhibit.") Saturdays at the Stedelijk at 3 p.m. Sept.-June, there are free concerts in the series *Music of Today*; films, videos, lectures, and performance art are frequently offered. Basic floor plan in English; museum shop.

Oude Kerk ★★

Oudekerksplein; April-Oct. Mon.-Sat. 11 a.m.-5 p.m., Sun. 1:30-5 p.m., Nov.-March Mon.-Sat. 1-3 p.m., Sun. 1:30-3 p.m.; tower accessible June 1-Sept. 15 Mon., Thurs. 2-5 p.m., Tues., Wed. 11 a.m.-2 p.m.; ☎ *6249183; year-round concerts Sat. 4-5 p.m. on 47-bell Hemony* ★★ *carillon (restored 1990), one of the finest in Holland; frequent summer evening organ concerts.* The earliest parish church in Amsterdam (c. 1300), the Oude Kerk was built on an artificial mound close to the Amstel. Various rebuildings brought the church to its large present size by the first half of the 16th century and, with the 1578 *Alteration*, the Oude Kerk was transferred from the Catholic to Protestant rite.

Closed temporarily in 1951 because of the imminent danger of its collapse, the Oude Kerk was completely restored between 1955 and 1979. The medieval church has the largest wooden roof (15th century, painted) in the Netherlands. **Dirck Crabeth** is credited with some of the fine 16th- and 17th-century stained glass windows; the **Vater-Muller organ** (the sound is exceptional) dates from 1724-36. Rembrandt's wife **Saskia** was buried beneath the stone that reads: Saskia 19 Juni 1642. Among the interior details, note the antique-decorated **Kerkmeesters Kamer** (vestry room). The Oude Kerk rests in a Linden-tree-shaded cobbled square in the oldest part of Amsterdam, complete with cafes, bicycle and pedestrian traffic, and a few red-light district "shop windows."

Koninklijk Paleis (Royal Palace)
Dam; daily June 15–August, 12:30–5 p.m., call for possible additional times; ☎ *6248698.* When the *Peace of Munster* was signed in 1648, finally officially ending the *Eighty Years' War* with Spain, Amsterdam was the wealthiest city in the world. Laying the foundation stone late the same year for a monumental Stadhuis (today the royal palace on Dam Square) was an appropriate proclamation. Built on 13,000 piles, the massive, free-standing sandstone (all imported and virtually "emptying" two quarries) neoclassical Jacob van Campen building was called by contemporary poet Constantijn Huygens the "**eighth wonder of the world**" (a tired phrase today but one that carried more weight in the 17th century). The Stadhuis was filled with the works of the Golden Age's finest sculptors and artists. Atop the facade, Atlas shoulders the world, as the Dutch then undoubtedly felt they did economically; inside, one flight up, the huge marble Citizens Hall has maps of the two hemispheres inlaid in the floor, so that visitors to the Stadhuis could appreciate how much of the world was Dutch. Many large allegorical sculptures decorate the hall, and frescoes and paintings are inclined to subjects favoring Greek and Roman gods. Nowhere are the moral lessons in the decorative work of the building more evident than in the Bankruptcy Office, where, in addition to reliefs showing rats gnawing at unpaid bills, the decor features the fatal Fall of Icarus. Perhaps **Meindart Hobbema** (1638–1709), one of the last born of the great 17th-century Dutch artists, should have taken note. Hobbema painted many excellent rural landscapes as a young man, but marriage seems to have changed his style. As a result of his wife, who was hired as cook to the burgomaster of Amsterdam, who resided in the Stadhuis and entertained in great style there, Hobbema was able to get the job of wine-measurer for the city. Perhaps life became too easy, for Hobbema didn't paint much after that, and it is said he and his wife died with little to show. The "classical" treatment in the royal palace is even carried to the softly piped-in music. The handsomely furnished former Magistrate Court Room and Burgomaster's Chamber can be visited, as well as rooms where pieces of the valuable Empire furniture collection that Louis Napoleon, installed as king of

Holland in 1808 by his brother Bonaparte, used to decorate the building when he confiscated it as a royal palace. Louis' rule was too sympathetic to Dutch ideas, for which Napoleon removed him from the post, but the famous furniture and the status of the building as a royal palace remain. A good brochure in English is given out, and there is an explanatory video.

Dam Square

In the center of Dam Square, which has been the heart of Amsterdam since its founding c. 1270, is the **Nationaal Monument**, which commemorates all who died from 1940–45. The queen lays a memorial wreath there on May 4th, on the eve of Liberation Day, May 5th.

Nieuwe Kerk   ★

Dam; open conditionally Mon.-Sun. 11 a.m.-5 p.m.; ☎ *6268168; concerts on the 1655 organ in summer.* Since it was begun about the year 1400, the "new" in its name comes only in reference to the century-older Oude Kerk. The deed of foundation was signed in 1408 by Frederick van Blankenheim, Bishop of Utrecht, who thus seems to have approved the division of the growing town of Amsterdam into two parishes: the Old Side, with the Oude Kerk, and the New Side, with the Nieuwe Kerk. The progressive enlargement of the church seems to have been stimulated by the unedifying rivalry between the Old and New parishes. In 1565, when the Oude Kerk acquired its magnificent tower and carillon, the Nieuwe Kerk reacted by laying up a massive foundation for a tower of its own. The project was delayed by the *Eighty Years' War.* Finally, after being badly damaged by fire in 1645 (as a result of which few interior furnishings date from before then), rebuilding plans called for the construction of a tower for the Nieuwe Kerk. But the endiing of the Eighty Years' War caused a burst of building fever for a Stadhuis (town hall, now the royal palace) from 1648-55, and, when not enough funds could be found for that grandiose structure next door to it, the Nieuwe Kerk seems to have lost its last chance for a tower.

In addition to the wonderfully painted classical cases of the two 17th-century organs designed by Jacob van Campen, and the huge carved pulpit, placed mid-church, Calvinist-style, is the monumental black marble tomb of **Admiral de Ruyter** (1607-1676), who died in a naval battle in Sicily while defeating the French fleet, was embalmed, and then sent home to Amsterdam, where thousands attended his funeral at the Nieuwe Kerk in 1677. Though now a "decommissioned" church, all reigning Dutch monarchs since King Wilhem I in 1815 (through Queen Beatrix, 1980) have been inaugurated in the Nieuwe Kerk, a city honor upon which Amsterdam rests its claim of being the country's capital. In the narrow ★ **Gravenstraat** behind the Nieuwe Kerk are a number of tiny old shops. Do peek into #18, de Drie Fleschjes (the three little bottles), a small 17th-century pub.

Amsterdam Historisch Museum ★★

entered via decorative archway at Kalverstraat 92, from St. Luciensteeg 27, or through the Beguinhof (see following item); daily 11 a.m.–5 p.m.; ☎ *5231822.* Whichever route one takes, the Amsterdam Historical Museum, with its extensive complex of buildings and courtyards, is a delightful discovery. Perhaps the pleasant surprise unfolds best from Kalverstraat, coming through the site occupied in 1414 by the sisters of the order of St. Lucy. The cow barn of their convent is now the museum cafe **In de Oude Goliath** (to the right), inside of which is a giant wooden sculpture of Goliath, which was a major attraction in an amusement park in Amsterdam's **Jordaan** district from about 1650 to 1862. To the left, one sees a courtyard wall with lockers for the belongings of boys of the Burgher orphanage, which was established here in 1580 after the convent was taken over by the city under the 1578 Dutch law that confiscated all Catholic church property. The Amsterdam Burgher orphanage occupied the site until 1960, when it moved to new quarters on the edge of town. The building was then extensively restored, and opened as the historical museum in 1975.

To the left of the entrance, which is in a courtyard at the end of the passageway through the orphanage, is one of the most exciting public pedestrian passageways one could ever hope to encounter: the ★★★**Civic Guard Gallery**. The large-scale minimuseum walkway contains a priceless collection of huge civic guard and guild portraits, mounted on the outside brick walls of the handsome old institution, all safely encased under glass. The "museum street" is a stunningly effective and innovative use of space. Inside is a basically chronological treatment of Amsterdam's 700-plus-years history. Borrow a guide written in English at the ticket counter for the general idea behind the exhibits, although many are multimedia or wonderful works of art (old views of Amsterdam, maps, prints) that have been donated to the museum or which came from former city institutions. Some of the Amsterdam themes that are imaginatively covered are city expansions, trade and industry in the 14th and 15th centuries, navigation in the Golden Age, and the history of the Dam as the center of public life since the city was first settled. Retrace your steps to the Civic Guard Gallery and head through it for the Begijnhof.

Begijnhof ★★★

accessible from the Spui or from the Amsterdam Historical Museum's Civic Guard Gallery; daily, use Spui entrance after museum hours. The full diversity of Amsterdam's sights becomes evident when one enters this peaceful, picturesque place, inhabited since 1346 when it was established as a pious community by the Sisters of St. Begga. Unlike those at the neighboring St. Lucy Convent, the Beguines were left in peace after the Alteration of 1578. Most of the houses in the courtyard were privately owned, either by Beguines or outsiders, and the city did not confiscate this private property, especially since many of the Beguines belonged to prominent Amsterdam families. The Beguine church, which had been consecrated in 1419, was another matter, however, and it was taken over by the town. After years of being rented out as a warehouse, the city leased the church to the Presbyterians, Scottish, and English Calvinist Separatists living in Amsterdam who did not want to join the Church of England. (It remains the Scottish/English church today.)

Some of the English pilgrims worshipped here in 1608, moving to Leiden in 1609; some of them sailed from Delfshaven in 1620 (depicted in a stained glass window), boarding the *Mayflower* in England and reaching Plymouth in the New World. The Beguines continued to live and worship, in their garden square, but the mass had to be celebrated in secret, and different houses were used. In 1655, the parish priest bought two houses and converted them into a permanent chapel for the Beguines. (City permission was granted on condition that outwardly nothing would betray the presence of a church.) Today, the Catholic chapel can claim its identity in the Begijnhof. The land in the center of the garden-like Begijnhof was used as a bleaching field until at least the mid-18th century. It is surrounded today by 17th- and 18th-century (restored) house fronts with old gables (neck, clock, and step-style) and old gable stones; some of which have been set in a wall near No. 34. This is the **Houden Huis** (wooden house) with its original wooden exterior, c. 1475; Amsterdam's oldest surviving house.

Anne Frank House

Prinsengracht 263; Mon.–Sat. 9 a.m.–5 p.m., Sun. and most holidays 10 a.m.–5 p.m; in June, July, Aug. open all days until 7 p.m.; ☎ *6264533; trams 13 and 17.* Anne Frank, who would have celebrated her 64th birthday in 1993, died of typhus at the age of 16 in the Bergen-Belsen Nazi concentration camp. Because of a diary she kept during the two years that she, her family, and four others lived in the secret annex upstairs in this 200-year-old canal house, Anne Frank has a face among the millions of Jews who died during the Second World War. Visitors can see the small secret annex in the upper back of the house, where eight people had to endure two years in close confines before their whereabouts were disclosed to the Nazis. Among the touching details are black-and-white magazine pictures of movie stars and young English Princess Elizabeth that Anne had pasted on her bedroom wall. There are two flights of very steep stairs to enter the museum. A video and brochure, in English, set the scene historically, and visitors then go "behind the bookcase" and up to the hidden rooms. Exhibits on the lower floors show photographs of Anne and her family before they fled into hiding and convey details of the Nazi occupation in Amsterdam and life in the concentration camps. The Anne Frank Foundation seeks to prevent discrimination and violations of human rights in the world.

Not long before the group in hiding was betrayed to the Nazis, Anne wrote in her diary: "It's really a wonder that I haven't dropped all of my ideals because they seem so absurd and impossible to carry out. Yet I keep them, because in spite of everything I still believe that people are really good at heart."

NOTE: This is one of the most popular sites in Amsterdam, and waiting lines can be long; plan an early start to avoid them.

Westerkerk   ★

Prinsengracht, corner Raadhuisstraat and Westermarkt; May 15-Sept. 15, Mon.-Sat. 10 a.m.-4 p.m.; tower accessible June-Sept. Tues., Wed., Fri., Sat. 2-5 p.m.; carillon concerts Tues. from noon-1 p.m.; ☎ *6247766; tram 13, 17.* Built between 1620 and 1630 in the Dutch Renaissance style, it is considered to be the masterpiece of architect **Hendrick de Keyser**. The distinctive 265-foot (85 meter) ★★ tower is topped with the Imperial Crown of Maximilian of Austria, a right that Amsterdam received from the Hapsburg Court in 1489. Rembrandt's unmarked grave, and that of his son Titus, are in the Westerkerk. (From 1660 until his death in 1669, the artist lived in modest quarters at Rozengracht 184, nearby.) Standing at the corner of the church is a small modern sculpture of Anne Frank, which often has fresh flowers laid at its feet. Rising high above the statue is the colorfully crowned steeple of the Westerkerk, which, though only doors away from the windows of Anne's Secret Annex, could not be seen by neighbors. But its 47-bell carillon was a comfort to Anne, who wrote in her diary of "the (chiming) clock at the Westertoren which I always find so reassuring."

On the Keizersgracht side of the Westerkerk is Amsterdam's simple triangle-shaped pink granite **Homomonument** (Gay Monument). Nazis required that homosexuals in occupied Holland wear a pink triangle badge.

Jordaan

Across from the Westerkerk on the Prinsengracht is a canal bike dock, and on the far side on the Prinsengracht the distinctive Jordaan neighborhood begins. Noted now for the bohemian, bizarre, and beautiful, and its relaxed and creative character, the Jordaan was developed in the early 17th century, at the same time as the **Grachtengordel** (canal belt), but it was purposefully left unplanned in comparison with the great concentric pattern, and allowed to grow up as a working class, artisan, tradesman, and very early on, immigrant district, with smaller and squatter houses, and narrower streets and canals. Jordaan probably comes from the French "jardin" (garden), since many of its streets have horticultural names. Before long, it deteriorated into an overcrowded slum, a scene of repeated bubonic plague epidemics, and extreme poverty; in the 1890s, with 90,000 inhabitants, it was Europe's most densely populated city quarter. A century later, with 19,000 residents, the Jordaan has been gently gentrified, fortunately not to the point of losing its unique character. Bounded by the Prinsengracht, Rozengracht, Lijnbaansgracht, and the delightful Brouwersgracht, the Jordaan contains some of the city's most characterful cafes, small boutiques and bistros, and hidden *hofjes* (almshouses). The ★ ★ **Brouwersgracht** (brewers' canal) is the point from which construction on the three concentric canals began about 1600.

Willet-Holthuysen Museum   ★ ★

Herengracht 605; Mon.–Sun. 11 a.m.–5 p.m.; ☎ 5231870. Built for the daughter of one of Amsterdam's burgomasters in 1689 and left by the Holthuysen family to the state in 1889, this double-width canal house has furnished rooms reflecting the 18th and 19th centuries and a fine tiled and brass and copper-utensil-adorned 18th-century basement kitchen. One room features a painted ceiling by Jacob de Wit (c. 1740), another an Aubusson wall covering. Two lounges are virtual art galleries. Be sure to reach the top floor, which has a cozy and intimate feel. The back bedroom, overlooking the garden, is set for sewing, a task lighted from the largest window I've ever seen in a house. The floor-to-ceiling windows of the enchanting garden room are on the first floor at the rear. The formal French-style garden behind the house also can be viewed (through iron railings) from Amstelstraat (between Rembrandtsplein and the Blauwbrug).

Museum van Loon   ★ ★

Keizersgracht 672; year-round Mon. 10 a.m.–5 p.m., Sun. 1–5 p.m., closed rest of week; ☎ 6245255. At least the severely limited open hours for this finely furnished late 17th-century canal house come on a day when some of Amsterdam's other museums are closed. One is free to wander around the house at will, with the help of a detailed explanatory booklet (in English). Built in 1671–72, the first tenant of the house was the successful painter **Ferdinand Bol** (once a pupil of Rembrandt). The French influence in the decor of the personable house reflects that style's popularity in the early 1800's because of Napoleon's rule (1795–1813) of the country. The house has been restored to its late 18th-early 19th-century state as much as possible. The garden behind the house also has French flavor in its formal style.

Nederlands Theater Museum

Herengracht 168; Tues.-Sun. and holidays 11 a.m.-5 p.m., closed Mon.; ☎ 6235104. Exhibits primarily concern Dutch theater tradition, and downstairs is a miniature theater from 1781. The real reason for you to visit, however, is the 1638 canal house's exquisite decor detail, particularly wall and ceiling paintings and plaster work in the marble hall and monumental staircase from when it was rebuilt in the Louis XIV-style in the 18th century.

Amsterdam Stadhuis

Amstel 1; Mon.-Fri. 8 a.m.-6 p.m., Sat. 10 a.m.-6 p.m., Sun. and holidays noon-6 p.m.; ☎ 5523458. The ★ **Normaal Amsterdams Peil** (N.A.P.) a.k.a. **Amsterdam Ordnance Datum** (A.O.D.), was established three centuries ago and based on the average high watermark of the Zuiderzee, which was then Amsterdam's connection to the North Sea; it is still the "water table" referral point for all construction in the Netherlands. The A.O.D. bronze knob, mounted in a passage of the Stadhuis, marks ground zero level; the three water columns on view show the high or low tide of the North Sea at the particular moment at IJmuiden, the high or low tide at Vlissingen (in Zeeland, to the south), and the highest level reached during the Zeeland floods in 1953. The Stadhuis shares its setting on the Amstel with the ★ **Muziektheater**, from which there's a splendid view of the evening illumination along the river during intermission and after performances.

Rembrandt House   ★★

Jodenbreestraat 4; Mon.–Sat. 10 a.m.–5 p.m., Sun. and holidays 1–5 p.m.; *6249486.* Holland's most famous artist lived here from 1639–1660, and the house, which dates from 1606, contains a nearly complete record of Rembrandt's etchings. Rembrandt's development in etching, a form for which he is less familiar, can be seen in the works displayed. The museum also shows some paintings by his own teacher, Pieter Lastman, and his pupils.

Jewish Historical Museum   ★★

Jonas Daniel Meijerplein; daily 11 a.m.–5 p.m., closed Yom Kippur; *6269945; tram 9 from CS, Metro to Waterlooplein.* Across from the Portuguese synagogue on the J.D. Meijerplein is the Ashkenazic synagogue complex, four components dating from 1670 to 1752 and now forming the Jewish Historical Museum. The museum, which opened in 1987 and won the 1989 Council of Europe Museum Prize for its imaginative architectural restoration, stands in the former Amsterdam neighborhood Vlooyenburg (built about 1600), into which were moved large numbers of Sephardic Jews from Portugal and Ashkenazic Jews from Germany. A glass-roofed passage connects the four synagogues, added as the Amsterdam Jewish community expanded. One, the Grand (1670), is the oldest public synagogue in western Europe. Exhibits cover the Jewish life cycle and highlight the social history of the Jews in the Netherlands. English brochure, museum shop, Kosher coffee shop. Outside, on the Meijerplein, seek out *de Dokwerker* (*The Dock Worker*), a Mari Andriessen statue, at once powerful and powerless.

Nederlands Scheepvaart Museum (Netherlands Maritime Museum)   ★★

Kattenburgerplein 1; Tues. –Sat. 10 a.m.–5 p.m., Sun. and holidays 1–5 p.m., closed Mon.; ☎ *5232222; bus 22 or 28 from CS.* Located in the 1656 former arsenal of the Admiralty of Amsterdam, the national maritime museum was opened in 1973. The museum aims to present an overall picture of Dutch shipping, past and present, with a focus on overseas trade, naval warfare (and fine, stirring paintings), navigation, and cartography (great globes and maps). There are plenty of models of ships from the Dutch East and West Indies companies' clipper ships, up to the proud passenger liners of the Holland-American Line. Set off in a separate section is the early 18th-century, oar-powered *Royal Barge*, used as recently as 1962 for the occasion of the silver jubilee of Queen (now Princess) Juliana. Museum floor plan in English, exhibit descriptions in Dutch only. Cafe with harbor view; excellent book and gift shop.

Moored next to the museum, among several ships of interest, is the recently completed (it was five years in the construction) full-size replica of the 18th-century merchant ship of the Dutch East India Company *de Amsterdam*, which sank in the English Channel on its maiden voyage in 1749. The interior has been recreated as authentically as possible to give visitors an insight into what life would have been like aboard the vessel.

Museum Amstelkring "Our Lord In The Attic"   ★ ★

Oudezijds Voorburgwal 40: Mon.–Sat. 10 a.m.–5 p.m., Sun. and holidays 1–5 p.m.; ☎ *6246604.* Located in the attics of three contiguous mid-17th-century canal houses in the oldest section of Amsterdam is a full-scale richly decorated Roman Catholic church—in hiding. With the coming of the **Alteration** in 1578, which made Protestantism preeminent and Catholicism technically illegal, the city of Amsterdam, governed by business interests, in general ducked the issue of religion by allowing the practice of the Catholic religion–as long as it wasn't obvious. This led to the rise of the so-called "hidden churches," of which this is the last in Amsterdam. (There were once about 60.) A museum since 1888 and appearing much as it did in 1735, **Our Lord in the Attic** has a poker face exterior and downstairs parlor. There is little to prepare one for the visual shock of the three large adjoining attics at the top of an unprepossessing staircase: a baroque altarpiece (with Jacob de Wit paintings), pews and a balcony, confessional, stowaway pulpit, and separate sacristy, all on a scale substantial enough to have supported a full-time resident priest. One of the many intriguing items in the church is a small silver box in the shape of a coffin. Since Catholics at the time could not be buried in consecrated ground, hallowed earth was kept in the box and scattered, three spoonsful per person, over the bodies of deceased Catholics before their coffins were closed.

Red-Light District

Examples of Amsterdam's traditional tolerance abound around the **Our Lord in the Attic** church, which is located in the center of the city's red-light district, which has been sanctioned in the same area (adjacent to the town's original site on the Dam) since the 14th century. How a city manages its sin may be a good measure of its maturity. In Amsterdam, one senses an unruffled, reasoned approach to prostitution, rather than the overreactive, adolescent attitudes which prevail in many other places that do nothing to improve the situation. Along and in the streets off the quaint, canaled **Oudezijds Voorburgwal**, women sit in small shop-like windows, offering themselves as merchandise. The process may be shockingly direct to some, but it keeps the business of sin behind plate glass, limiting its spillage onto streets and normal city life. Medical checkups and other professional aid and advice for prostitutes are encouraged by officials (and made wide use of), and the *Red Thread* organization works to protect the women's dignity. Thus, in Amsterdam, for all concerned, including tourists, there's a certain safety associated with the practice of "the world's oldest profession."

SHOPPING

As you'd expect with such long-established pragmatic practitioners of trade, prices are set in Holland. No need to think about bargaining (except at flea and antique markets). The VVV sells several excellent shopping/ walking tour brochures for those who want to shop-till-they-drop: *On The Lookout Between Canals, On The Lookout in The Jordaan, On The Lookout for the Chic and Beautiful, On The Lookout for Art and Antiques,* and *On The Lookout for the Amsterdam Open-Air Markets* (pamphlet). Prices shown always include the 17.5% VAT or btw tax. Basic hours are 9 a.m.– 6 p.m. except Saturday when most close at 5 p.m. Virtually all are closed all day Sunday, and many don't open until 1 p.m. Monday. Late-night shopping is Thursday, till 9 p.m.

Amsterdam has been in the diamond trade since 1586, and the *Amsterdam cut* is known for its quality. The **Amsterdam Diamond Center** *(Rokin 1; open daily;* ☎ *6245787)* and several other diamond-cutting houses can be visited for free tours and demonstrations of the "four Cs" qualities of the shining gemstones. Many sell jewelry as well as unmounted stones in their showrooms.

In the European city that has done more to protect its historic architectural heritage than any other, you'd expect to find an active antiques trade. More than 100 antique shops can be found on and just off Amsterdam's short **Nieuwe Spiegelstraat**. As an appropriate backdrop to the *objets d'art* in the shop windows is the Rijksmuseum, which dominates the view at the end of the street. Art and antiques have kept close company in Amsterdam since the opening of the Rijksmuseum in 1885, within a couple years of which the first antique shop had opened on Nieuwe Spiegelstraat. Amsterdam has more than 140 art galleries, most of which specialize in contemporary art, for which the city is considered one of the leading ones in Europe. The galleries are scattered throughout the Centrum.

One of Amsterdam's main shopping areas is the pedestrian **Kalverstraat** (it means "bullock street," and cattle were once driven to market along it), one of the city's earliest streets. Interesting and upscale shops have made the restored former *post office* a success as the **Magna Plaza** enclosed shopping center just behind the royal palace off the Dam. Running parallel to the Rokin, between the Dam (location of the prestigious **de Bijenkorf** store) and the Munt Tower, it has major department stores (**Vroom and Dreesman**) and many boutiques. Just beyond the Munt Tower, which is home to a **de Porceleyne Fles** Delftware shop, on Reguliersbreestraat, is

Hema, for colorful, imaginative housewares and from its small food section the makings of a picnic: fresh bread, cheese, sandwiches, *vin ordinaire.*

The Kalverstraat has Centrum convenience but not quite the cachet of **P.C. Hooftstraat** and **van Baerlestraat** in the museum quarter, which have boutiques carrying fashionable internationally renown names. **Focke and Meltzer** on P.C. Hooftstraat carries the delftware of **de Porceleyne Fles** and other fine china and crystal. The enjoyable Jordaan district has small shops with diverse wares tucked here and there.

You'll probably run across enough typical Dutch souvenirs during your strolls around the city, but a cut-above-the-average and a useful congregation of Dutch artisans and their output can be found in a complex near the Amsterdam Renaissance Hotel. Nearby is **de Klompenboer** (wooden shoe farm) at Nieuwezijds Voorburgwal 20, in case you want to purchase a pair.

Amsterdam's markets include the **flower market** at Singel canal, between Koningsplein and Muntplein *(Mon.–Sat. 9 a.m.–5 p.m.).* The city's largest general goods and produce street market is on **Albert Cuypstraat** *(Mon.–Sat. 9 a.m.–5 p.m.).* The long-standing flea market, not quite what it once was, is at **Waterlooplein** *(Mon.–Sat. 10 a.m.–7 p.m.).* Sundays, go to Nieuwemarkt for open-air antiques *(May-Oct., 10 a.m.–4 p.m.).* The enclosed many-stalled **Antique Market de Looier** is at Elandsgracht 109, *(Sat.– Thurs. 11 a.m.–5 p.m., closed Fri.).* Nearby, at Looiersgracht 38, is **Rommelmarkt** (flea market), same hours. A **stamp market** (*Postzegelmarkt*) lends character to the scene by Nieuwezijds Voorburgwal 280 *(Wed. and Sat. from 1–4 p.m.).* Artists offer diverse works at the Spui and on Thorbeckeplein *(Apr.–Oct., Sun. 11 a.m.–6 p.m.).*

WHERE TO STAY

Some of the most charming hotels, often on canals in Amsterdam—and other Dutch cities—have been made out of one or several attached one-time private houses. These have lots of character and lots of steep stairs since it's often difficult (and always expensive) to install elevators. Staff help with luggage, so *that* needn't be a concern when you consider whether or not to avail yourself of this distinctively Dutch-style accommodation. In the selection of hotels here, both convenience of location and setting have been strongly weighed. Because business travelers are inclined to be absent on weekends, inquire about weekend discount rates, which may be as much as 50% off. Some hotels offer winter rates at substantial savings between Nov. 15 and March 15. At more moderate hotels, always inquire when booking if/ which credit cards are accepted.

VERY EXPENSIVE

De L'Europe

Nieuwe Doelenstraat 2-8, 1012 CP; ☎ *6234836, FAX 6242962.*

Approaching a centennial on its superb site, arguably the best combination of scenery and convenience of any hotel in the city, the Hotel de l'Europe faces the *Amstel River* and *Munt* tower in the confident knowledge that she is an Amsterdam grande dame. The hotel, housed behind a fine six-story Victorian facade, is oldworld, but not old-fashioned; attentive service is a tradition. The excellent reputation of its Excelsior restaurant kitchen is well deserved. There's been recent renovation and redecoration, with dining, afternoon tea, and drinks on a wraparound canal-level terrace, and health club with pool (in surprising classic Roman bath-style) and sauna. You need to ask for a water view; facing the Muziektheater instead of the Munt is quieter. The hotel has 101 rooms; seats in the elegant elevators; bidets in the bath; minibars; in-room safes.

Pulitzer   ★ ★ ★ ★ ★
Prinsengracht 315-331, 1016 GZ; ☎ *5235235, FAX 6276753.* Since being acquired by the Italian Ciga Group, the Pulitzer continues to please guests with its assemblage of historic buildings (19 of them, mostly 17th-century) and its imaginative integration of them into an inviting whole, complete with glass-enclosed connecting corridors and central tree-shaded garden courtyard. Much of the art and furniture is modern, as is the plumbing, but despite those changes, there's a timeless charm to this Pulitzer prize. (In fact, it takes its name from Joseph Pulitzer's grandson, who had a vision for the then-decaying canalside houses and opened the hotel in 1971.) The 195 guest rooms are all unique, with old beams, brick, and, at least until recently, a rather rustic charm. A full range of amenities and services are provided. The canalside coffee shop is highly pleasant, as is the cozy bar. The location puts one in the center of the picturesque and close to much else of interest in Amsterdam.

EXPENSIVE

Grand Hotel Krasnapolsky   ★ ★ ★ ★ ★
Dam 9, 1012 JS; ☎ *5549111, FAX 6383269.* The location couldn't be more in the heart of Amsterdam for this traditionally Dutch hotel, all recently renovated and enlarged by 37 deluxe rooms to 316. Brought back to its 1880 airy elegance is the **Winter Garden** restaurant where breakfast (included) is served. At the marble-topped tables of the **Krasserie** lobby cafe/bar (where a photo of Queen Wilhelmina hangs), which overlooks Dam Square and across to the royal palace, one sits close to the heart of the city, but a bit removed from its bustle. Fitness center; concierge; 24-hour room service; hotel parking garage.

Jan Luyken   ★ ★ ★ ★
Jan Luykenstraat 54, 1071 CS; ☎ *5730730, FAX 6763841.* Located in three former houses on a tree-shaded street, the hotel has a quiet location near the art museums, shopping, Concertgebouw, and beyond the sounds of, but close to the lively Leidseplein. The property's 65-room (all with bath—though I saw some very small tubs—minibars, and in-room safes) size means personal attention from the very pleasant, helpful staff at the front desk. Elevators, though some rooms are a fair distance from them. There's an attractive breakfast (only,

included) room, and a typically Dutch-style cozy lobby bar with small garden terrace where snacks, soup, and toasted sandwiches are served.

Ambassade

Herengracht 335-353, 1016 AZ; ☎ *6262333, FAX 6245321.* Centrally located in seven 17th-century patrician canalside houses, the Ambassade is a delight from one's first step into the elegant, welcoming lobby. Though somewhat less stylish than the public rooms (there's an elegant French-style salon), each of the 47 bedrooms (some 65% of which face the canal, made cheerful with p.m. sun) is distinct and immaculate, and decorated with pretty prints and antiques. Breakfast (included) in an elegant canal-front room; light meals available from the 24-hour room service. Very popular with those who have discovered it, so reserve as far ahead as possible.

American Hotel

Leidsekade 97, 1017 PN; ☎ *6245322, FAX 6253236.* The thoroughly European American hotel has occupied its prominent canaled corner of Amsterdam, just off the Leidseplein, since the 1880s. The 188 comfortable guest rooms are replete with *art deco* details, as is the two-story lobby. Amenities include fitness center (sauna, weight machines), newsstand, room service, and character-filled cafes; terrace, canalside, and the Nightwatch bar. Its most famous feature is the flagrantly art deco **Café Americain** (open 11 a.m.–2 a.m.), a roomy rendezvous favored by the Dutch, and enjoyed by all, for coffee with newspapers, pastry, light and full meals, and after dinner drinks.

MODERATE

Het Canal House

Keizergracht 148, 1015 CX; ☎ *6225182, FAX 6241317.* These two charming mid-17th-century mansions (26 rooms, all with modern tile baths) are filled with an eclectic collection of the long-standing friendly American owner's auction-acquired antiques and Dutch prints. Convenient, prestigious location. Breakfast (only) served in a quite stately garden-view salon. Rooms overlook canal or garden (illuminated at night). Elevator to most rooms, small lobby bar.

Owl Hotel ★★★

Roemer Visscherstraat 1, 1054 EV; ☎ *6189484, FAX 6189441.* A block from the Leidseplein, and just behind the Marriott Hotel, this light, bright, contemporarily decorated 34-room hotel has a quiet location, with a small plant-filled relaxing lounge and bar that open onto a garden. The five-floor, 100-year-old building has an elevator; the generous-sized double rooms all have shower (some bath), TV, telephone; breakfast (only) is included. Very central, near arts museums, trams.

Amsterdam Wiechmann

Prinsengracht 328, 1016 HX; ☎ *6263321.* Located in two restored canal houses, the cheerful, family style hotel has 36 simply decorated rooms, all with telephone, toilet, bath/shower, many have canal views; TV in cozy lobby lounge. There's a wonderful corner breakfast (included) cafe with wide windows overlooking two canals. Three stories, steep narrow stairs, long corridors, no elevators, but help with baggage. No credit cards.

INEXPENSIVE

Washington

Frans van Mierisstraat 10, 1071 RS; ☎ *6796754, FAX 6734435.* The generous-sized rooms (both with and without private modern marble bath facilities) in this recently renovated house-hotel, decorated with antiques and orientals, ornamented with wood wainscoting and other details, are often filled with the sound of musicians, guest performers at the nearby Concertgebouw. On a residential street, close to museums and trams, the hotel features friendly service, breakfast (only); no elevator; guests have own front door key.

Agora Hotel ★★

Singel 462, 1017 AW; ☎ *6272200, FAX 6272202.* Great location on a canal, steps from the flower market, the Spui, and the Beguinhof. You do need to be able to handle steep stairs (help with luggage) to be able to take advantage of the Agora. The small Dutch-style canal- view lobby evolves to a cheerful breakfast (only) room farther back, where coffee and soft drinks are served during the day. The traditionally decorated bedrooms, all different and with private facilities, are inclined to get more interesting architecturally the higher up you go, but it's a hike; ask to be nearer ground level if you prefer. Close to sights, shops, trams.

Rho

Nes 11-23, 1012 KC; ☎ *6207371, FAX 6207826.* It's not lovely to look at from the outside, though the location just steps from the Dam couldn't be much more convenient. Once you step into the lobby of this 1908 former theater (renovated as a hotel in 1989) with its soaring, curved skylit ceiling, you're bound to be intrigued. The 61 rooms are very functional, often generous in size, as are the tile bathrooms (open showers with curtains), and feature telephone and TV. Elevator (four floors), parking available. The intriguing former theater lobby is the breakfast (only) room, light and airy, with potted palms, stained glass, globe lights. Take a drink up to the balcony from the lobby bar to see further signs of the building's past life as a theater.

Seven Bridges

Reguliersgracht 31, 1017 LK; ☎ *6231329.* Located on a lovely canal, close to but beyond the sound of the lively Thorbeck and Rembrandtsplein, this 200-year-old house is clean, bright, and cheerful. Most of the rooms have private shower, all have radio, some TV, no telephones. Room 3 on the garden is especially nice. Breakfast served in rooms.

WHERE TO EAT

The Dutch invariably breakfast at home, so visitors will find few places that serve more than coffee early in the morning except hotels, which begin serving by 7 a.m. A Dutch buffet breakfast (*ontbijt*) will include various breads, sliced cheeses and meats, juices, cereals, milk, perhaps boiled eggs, yogurt, fresh fruit, and coffee or tea. A picturesque little cafe on a tree-shaded square on the Singel canal that does serve breakfast (with eggs) outside in good weather, is the **Cafe-Eethuisje de Roef** (*Stromarkt 4, 8:30 a.m.–9 p.m.;* ☎ *6274515; inexpensive*), at end of Kattengat, just past the Sonesta Hotel. Breakfast is also served at **Greenwoods** (*Singel 103; Mon.–Fri. 9 a.m.–7 p.m., Sat., Sun. 11 a.m.–7 p.m.;* ☎ *6237071; inexpensive*), as well as light lunch and tea in the big-windowed, canalside, cozy, crowded cafe. Remember that dinner is taken relatively early in Holland, and even in the best restaurants many kitchens close by 9:30 p.m. The better the restaurant, the better idea it is to make reservations.

Even if Amsterdam does boast that you "can eat out in any language" there, its Dutch restaurants deserve to come first. **Haesje Claes** (*Spuistraat 275/other entrance N.Z. Voorburgwal 318; open Mon.–Sat. noon-midnight, kitchen closes at 10 p.m., Sun from 5–9:30 p.m.;* ☎ *6249998; inexpensive*) offers the Dfl. 19.75 tourist menu in an appealing dark wood, *gezellig* atmosphere dating from 1520 that makes it a favorite in the neighborhood. Hearty (including Dutch pea soup, *hutspot*) to simple (omelets) choices. Also offering the tourist menu and Dutch flavor and fare is **Oud Holland** (*Nieuwe Zijds Voorburgwal 105; Mon.–Sat. from noon, lunch and dinner;* ☎ *6246848; inexpensive*). **De Roode Leeuw** hotel-restaurant (*Damrak 93; open from noon for lunch and dinner daily;* ☎ *6249683; inexpensive*) offers a Dutch kitchen and a front-row view of the city from its glass-enclosed terrace.

Die Port van Cleve (*Nieuwe Zijds Voorburgwal 178;* ☎ *6240047*), which had been serving meals for nearly a century before it added 100 hotel rooms, offers a choice of two fine Dutch restaurants. **de Poort Restaurant** (*from 11 a.m. daily, lunch and dinner; inexpensive*) is the more relaxed with plants, stained glass, and an old tiled fireplace; a specialty is Dutch *biefstuk* (beef steak) and every one served since 1870 has been numbered: if yours ends in 00, it's free and so's the wine. Across the hall is the **de Blauwe Parade** (*daily, lunch from noon, dinner from 6 p.m.; expensive*), traditional with its solid old oak and leather furniture; it was a tasting room in the mid-1500s for the beer brewery that became *Heineken*, but has become even more notable, since 1886, for its wonderful Delft blue and white *de Porceleyne Fles* wall tile tableaux of children in 17th-century court dress celebrating the gathering of grapes for wine. (The restaurant *does*, appropriately, have a fine wine cellar to accompany the excellent Dutch cuisine.)

The welcome return of one of Amsterdam's longest established traditional Dutch eateries has occurred at the **Holiday Inn Crowne Plaza**, which now houses **Dorrius** (*N.Z. Voor burgwal serves lunch and dinner daily* ☎ *4202224, moderate*), which dates from 1890. Dorrius offers such fabled Dutch fare as IJsselmeer, eel, Zeeland oysters and mussels, Texel lamb, rabbit and Erwtersoep. **Hollands Glorie** *(Kerkstraat 220; daily from 5–10 p.m., closed Mon. Nov.–Mar.;* ☎ *6244764; inexpensive)* is small and pleasantly cluttered with old copper and brass utensils, tiles and antiques, with candles lighted at each table. À la carte choices include mussel cocktail, smoked eel, pork cutlet, and beef steak, and there's a *prix-fixe menu.* **Restaurant Bodega Keyser** *(van Baerlestraat 96; Mon.–Sat., noon–11:30 p.m., closed Sun;* ☎ *6711441; moderate)* opened in 1905 next door to the still-new **Concertgebouw** and has been inseparably associated with concertgoers ever since (so much so that its clocks are set slightly ahead so patrons won't miss the first movement of the program, and its kitchen remains open for postconcert dinners). Keyser's is also convenient for patrons of the neighborhood's fashionable shops and art museums. The typical Dutch decor of the front-of-the-house cafe with its wood furniture, carpets on the table, brass lamps, newspapers, and outside tables when the weather's warmish, is also open for morning coffee. Fresh Dutch seafood, especially *Sole á la Meunieré,* is a specialty served at the clothed and candlelit tables in the rear. Last, but certainly not least in Dutch atmosphere, is **D'Vijff Vlieghan** *(Spuisstraat 294; daily from 5 p.m.;* ☎ *6248369; very expensive),* situated in five 17th-century canal houses. The series of seven dining rooms, each furnished in a different Renaissance-style, creates an intimate whole, upstairs and off passageways, most cozy in candlelight. The traditional Dutch cuisine has recently improved, the result of *nouvelle* nuances.

Even more than traditional Dutch dishes, Indonesian fare seems to be the national food of Holland; most Dutch have a favorite restaurant for it, and the selections are located in various sections of the city. Waiters are usually very helpful in explaining the dishes, and many restaurants have menus translated into English. A perennially popular choice is **Sama Sebo** *(P.C. Hooftstraat 27; daily lunch, dinner;* ☎ *6628146; inexpensive);* very friendly, helpful service, small, authentic, and on everyone's list of one of the best Indonesian restaurants in Amsterdam. **Indonesia** *(Singel 550, at Muntplein; open daily from noon;* ☎ *6232035; inexpensive)* is long established in its upstairs, high-ceilinged, gracious, almost colonial setting, staffed by helpful Indonesians. **Djawa** *(Korte Leidsedwarsstraat 18; open daily from 5 p.m.;* ☎ *6246016; inexpensive)* is another tasty, traditional choice for Indonesian fare, located just off the Leidseplein. In the Jordaan neighborhood is **Speciaal** *(Nieuwe Leliestraat 142;* ☎ *6249706),* which looks far more special and intimate inside than out. This is where many Amsterdammers "in the know" go for Indonesian.

You certainly don't have to go to a seafood restaurant for fish in this sea-minded country, but it's nice to know where the Dutch choose to go. **Licius Visrestaurant** *(Spuisttraat 247, open daily noon–midnight,* ☎ *6241831; moderate/inexpensive menu)* is an unpretentious, very pleasant place that offers six or seven sorts of fresh fish daily, posted on a blackboard, as well as fish soup, salads, and sandwiches until 5 p.m. Fish charts are on the blue and white tiled walls, white cloths are on dark-wood tables. **Le Pecheur** *(Reguliersdwarsstraat 32; Mon.–Fri. lunch and dinner, Sat. and Sun. dinner only, from 5 p.m.;* ☎ *6243121; moderate)* has a trendy, tasteful interior, and a wonderful garden terrace with a view of townhouses for out-door dining.

French/continental cuisine is served at some of the most highly regarded restaurants in Amsterdam. **'T Swarte Schaep** *(The Black Sheep; Korte Leidsedwarsstraat 24; open daily from noon;* ☎ *6223021; expensive),* a calm traditional Dutch backdrop for continental cuisine and singular service, its leather-chair comfort quite removed from the casual liveliness of the Leidseplein cafes it overlooks. Lunch (set menu) and dinner (kitchen open until 11 p.m., late by Dutch standards). **Le Ciel Bleu** *(Hotel Okura, Ferdinand Bolstraat 333; open from 6:30 p.m.;* ☎ *6787111; expensive)* offers fine French cuisine with the most far-reaching view over Amstedam. **Ciel Bleu Bar** *(6 p.m.–1 a.m.)* is a bar atop the Okura, highest view of the night lights. Hotel de l'Europe's exclusive **Excelsior** *(Nieuwe Doelenstraat 208; daily, lunch from 12:30 p.m., dinner from 6 p.m.;* ☎ *6234836; expensive)* serves a menu de la saison, a gourmet alliance menu and, since the opening of the nearby Muziektheater, a theater menu. For post-theater and later, less ex-pensive dining, the Europe's **Le Relais** is a fine choice. **De Silveren Spiegel** *(Kattengat 4; Mon.–Sat. lunch and dinner, closed Sun.;* ☎ *6246589; expensive)* is situated in an enchanting 17th-century house opposite the Ramada Hotel's Koepel Cafe, whose patrons benefit from having a view of the res-taurant. The decor of either dining floor does justice to the fine French food. The appealing old **Restaurant de Bols Taverne** *(Rozengracht 106; Mon.– Sat. noon to midnight;* ☎ *6245752; moderate)* serves a good choice of international dishes, as well as a very broad selection of the liqueurs made by the company from which it takes its name, and other Dutch drinks.

All the world seems interested now, but Amsterdam for many years has had a great following for Japanese food. The city's best Japanese restaurant is **Yamazato** *(Hotel Okura, Ferdinand Bolstraat 333; open daily for lunch, from noon, and dinner, from 6 p.m.;* ☎ *6787111; expensive),* which overlooks a miniature Japanese garden and serves a wide range of traditional Japanese dishes. The Japanese-owned **Okura** emits an Oriental calm that's comple-mented by its somewhat out-of-center canalside locale. The hotel also has the **Sazanka Teppan-Yaki** steak house *(lunch/dinner; expensive)* and a sushi bar.

Cafes seem to sprout on Amsterdam sidewalks whenever the weather comes even close to cooperating. The word "cafe" also indicates a restau-rant of a certain style, so some of the establishments listed below may focus more on food, others on setting (menus are always posted, so you'll know which is which). Its location surprises people, but the **le Klas Grand Cafe Restaurant** *(Spoor/platform 2b; daily 9:30 a.m.–11 p.m., Sun. 10:30 a.m.;* ☎ *6250131; inexpensive),* once the first-class waiting room and now re-stored to past lofty-ceiling splendor, and a dark-wood cafe next door, also serves a more-than-acceptable menu, within sound of the pleasant rumble of the trains. A thoroughly European setting. Sat. 7–10 p.m. live jazz, Sun. brunch with live classical music.

Het Land van Walem (*Keizersgracht 449; daily from mid-morning;* ☎ *6253544; inexpensive*) is an artsy, reading-newspapers sort of coffee-house, and it sprawls along the canal at small tables when the weather warrants. There's a charming courtyard garden sometimes used for dining. The delightful dowager-Dutch **Royal Cafe de Kroon** (*Rembrandtsplein 15; daily 10 a.m.–1 a.m.;* ☎ *6252011; inexpensive*) is up two flights of graceful curving 1898 steps to the huge airy rooms and glassed-in balcony overlooking the tree tops of Rembrandtsplein. For tea, sweets, or more substantial treats, the **Cafe de Jaren** (*Nieuwe Doelenstraat 20; daily 10 a.m.–1 a.m., 2 a.m. Fri., Sat.; inexpensive*), resting between the *de l'Europe* and *Doelen Karena* hotels, has a wonderful view over the Amstel to the Musiektheater, from terrace level and upstairs. Serving soups, salads, sandwiches, and more substantial fare. Located at the edge of the colorful Jordaan neighborhood on one of the loveliest stretches of canal in the city, **de Belhamel** (*Brouwersgracht 60; daily noon-midnight, kitchen open noon–2:30 p.m., dinner 6–10 p.m.;* ☎ *6221095; inexpensive*) serves as a special stop for a drink, with an intriguing intimate two-tier interior with faux marble columns and art nouveau details. Informal menus, daily specials, desserts. Two other cafes worth noting, as much for location as for the edible offerings, although those are certainly worthy, are **Cafe Luxembourg**, facing squarely on the Spui, and **Brasserie de Bock**, with split views of the Spui and the Singel. For food before or after a visit to the Rijksmuseum, or an antique expedition in the shops of the Nieuwe Spiegelstraat, stop at the **Cafe Hans en Grietje** (*Spiegelgracht 27; lunch 11:30 a.m.–5:30 p.m., open til 1 a.m. for light fare;* ☎ *6246782; inexpensive*). The cheerful canalside cafe, which serves *sate*, omelets, *uitsmijters*, and hamburgers, has a wonderful view of the Rijksmuseum.

For platter-size Dutch pancakes, savory or sweet, head for either **The Pancake Bakery** (*Prinsengracht 191; daily noon–9:30 p.m.;* ☎ *6251333*) in the roomy beamed and bricked basement of an old canalside warehouse, or tiny, four-tabled **Upstairs** (*Grimburgwal 2; Tues.-Sun. 9 a.m.–7 p.m., closed Mon.;* ☎ *6265603*) up two steep flights. For tasty, quick *broodjes* (sandwiches), follow in the tracks of Amsterdammers to **Eetsalon van Dobben** (*Korte Reguliersdwarsstraat 5; daily, from 9:30 a.m., 11:30 Sun.;* ☎ *6244200*), near the Rembrandtplein, or one of **Broodje van Kootje's** two locations: Leidseplein 20 and Spui 28, open daily 9:30 a.m. until late.

Although you'll seek them out more for their atmospheric flavor and drinks than for food, most of Amsterdam's famous "**brown cafes**" (or *bruine kroeg*) do serve snacks. The name brown cafe comes from the tobacco-stained walls and ceilings, cozy carpeted tables, and perhaps sawdust on the floor, and the "*gezellig*" ambiance of it all. You'll probably find them to be a cross between an English pub, a French cafe, and an American bar, and although the atmosphere of many may feel like the home of loosely knit family, the ranks are usually open to strangers, and of course everyone will be able to hold an avid conversation in English. Although visitors will find their own favorites, the following are certainly among the most interesting. It is said that a coffin maker around 1600, selling drinks to earn a little extra money, marked the beginnings of **Papeneiland** *(Prinsengracht 2; 11 a.m.–1 a.m.;* ☎ *6241989).* The Prinsengracht is home to several other brown cafes: **de Eland** *(#296; noon–1 a.m.)* and **Van Puffelen** *(#377; 11 a.m.–1 a.m.),* but **Pieper** *(#424; 10:30 a.m.–1 a.m.;* ☎ *6264775)* is one of the most famous. **Frascati** *(Nes 59; 10 a.m.–1 a.m.;* ☎ *6241324),* near Dam Square, is fashionable, and particularly comfortable for women to visit. And **Hoppe** *(Spui 18; 8 a.m.–1 a.m.;* ☎ *6237849)* has a split personality; **Hoppe zit**, the saloon-like seated section of the 1670 establishment, located on the left-hand side, and, on the right, **Hoppe staan**, a standing bar, with sawdust on the floor inside and a rack for drinks outside in season. Also in the Jordaan is **Cafe Nol** *(Westerstraat 109; open 8 p.m.–2 a.m.;* ☎ *6245380),* a splendidly decorated cafe, where, especially on Friday and Saturday nights, amazing scenes occur. Those who like *kitsch* should not miss Cafe Nol.

ENTERTAINMENT AND EVENTS

English-speaking tourists can avail themselves (at the VVV, Dfl. 2.50) of the bimonthly magazine *What's On in Amsterdam* or *Amsterdam This Week,* for daily calendars of entertainment events, as well as listings of museums, galleries, rental car agencies, etc. The **Amsterdams Uit Buro (AUB)** on the Leidseplein and the **VVV's Theaterbespreekbureau,** Stationsplein, open Mon.–Sat. 10 a.m.–4 p.m., will book seats in advance for most concert, opera, ballet, and theater performances (in-person sales only).

Concertgebouw *(van Baerlestraat 98; Box Office* ☎ *6718345; trams 2, 5 from CS).* Recently renovated in honor of its centennial, the Concertgebouw, celebrated worldwide for its acoustics, is home to Amsterdam's renowned **Concertgebouworkest** (Conductor Riccardo Chailly). Concerts by it and visiting companies and performers regularly sell out; contact or visit the box office to see what's available. Chamber music is presented in the Kleine Zaal. From Sept. to June, there are free Wed. lunchtime concerts (12:30–1:15 p.m.); varied programs from full symphony to duets.

Beurs de Berlage *(Damrak 62A;* ☎ *6265257)* is the architecturally intriguing home *(English tours on request at* ☎ *6258908)* of the 140-musician **Netherlands Philharmonic Orchestra.** The Netherlands Chamber Orchestra and other guest artists perform in the new "glass box" Aga Zaal there. **Muziektheater** *(Waterlooplein 22;* ☎ *6255455)* This white-marble-and-glass rounded building at a curve on the Amstel in the heart of the city is Amsterdam's latest cultural landmark. The amazingly intimate, 1600 red-plush-seat Musiektheater is the home for the **Netherlands Opera Company** (Director Pierre Audi) and the **Dutch National Ballet** (both of which create whole new productions each year for the June-long Holland Festival). Some tickets for every performance are reserved for same-day sale at the Musiektheater box office. Schedules for the **Holland Festival,** whose varied cultural programs are focused in Amsterdam, are available in advance from Netherlands Board of Tourism offices.

Year-round at the Amsterdam Renaissance Hotel's **Round Lutheran Kerk Koepelzaal** are 11 a.m. Sunday morning concerts. (Due to extensive repair required following a 1993 fire, confirm location with hotel; ☎ 6212223.) Very popular with the Dutch, they are always well-attended, and a *kopje koffie* (cup of coffee) beforehand is included in the Dfl. 6 price. The great domed 1668 church, long a landmark in the neighborhood, was restored in the 1970s by the *National Monuments Committee* and the *Sonesta Hotel's* owner, who had the imagination to incorporate it into what was then their property. The Renaissance Hotel and the church are connected by underground passage.

During July and August, **organ concerts**—Amsterdam has 42 historic church organs—are given in the following churches: Oude Kerk, Nieuwe Kerk (Dam), Engelse Kerk (Beguinhof), Oude Lutherse Kerk (Spui, part of University of Amsterdam), Westerkerk, and Sint Nicolaaskerk. Consult the VVV or events calendar listings for details.

Amsterdam's new and only casino, **Holland Casino Amsterdam** (which replaced the one formerly in the Hilton Hotel) is located near the **Leidseplein**, at *Max Euweplein 62*. Playing time is daily 1:30 p.m.–2 a.m. Admission is Dfl. 5 (for a day card). Visitors must be at least 18 years of age, suitably dressed (no T-shirts, sport shoes, etc.), and by Dutch law must produce a passport or driver's license. No bags, shopping or otherwise, may be brought into or checked at the casino. Games include *French, American,* and *twin roulette, Black Jack,* and *Punto Banco*. A useful booklet in English, *Rules of the Game,* is available free. The cafe-restaurant and bar on the premises is open from 1 p.m.–3 a.m.

IN THE AREA

Several tour operators—their offices are congregated along the *Damrak,* opposite the *Beurs van Berlage*—offer half- and whole-day motorcoach excursions to various places in the area. Look carefully at the respective brochures or itineraries and ask questions as to how much time you will actually have at the sights you most want to see. It's possible to get to the major places on your own on public transportation, so consider that alternative. **Alkmaar**, an architecturally appealing old town on any occasion, most warrants a visit on Friday mornings (May–Sept.) for its colorful (usually crowded) cheese market activities. On many commercial tours from Amsterdam are the former fishing towns of **Volendam** and **Marken**. I cannot recommend them, *especially* Volendam, since they exist almost exclusively to fulfill tourists' expectations: locals in traditional costumes worn just for you (you can wear one and have your photo taken); wooden shoe factories; and other gimmicky offerings. It's a pretty successful show, but Holland offers far more authenticity of atmosphere elsewhere.

Bloemenveiling Aalsmeer (Aalsmeer Flower Auction)   ★★★
Aalsmeer, Legmeerdijk 313; ☎ *(02977) 32185; open Mon.–Fri. 7:30–11 a.m., closed Sat., Sun., holidays; fee.* Catch a bus to Aalsmeer—ten miles—from near the front of Amsterdam's *Centraal Station*, beginning at 6 a.m.; there's a short bus transfer in Aalsmeer to the flower auction (ask driver for details). Allow 1 to 1-1/2 hours to get there. A return (round trip) bus ticket is the best buy.

Never have tourism and commerce combined more beautifully than at Aalsmeer. The Aalsmeer complex covers 47 acres. (It's so big that many workers "commute" within it on bicycles). A special *visitors' gallery* has been erected, from which visitors can watch the colorful auction spectacle (from 8–9 a.m. the action is the best). There are multilingual information signs and push-button commentary around the route. An explanatory brochure to help you understand the unique Dutch auction process is given out on arrival. Trains of carts with bundles of cut flowers wind through the building on computerized rails, each variety in its own area. The whole process proves it's possible to put a pretty face on business.

Zaanse Schans

Zaanse; site open at all times, special attractions open daily Jan.–Sept. 10a.m.–5p.m., Oct.–Dec. weekends only; ☎ *(075) 214582; no fee.* Located nine miles (15 km.) northwest of Amsterdam near Zaandam, Zaanse Schans (established as a museum village in 1960) is a picturesque and pleasant 17th-century Dutch six-windmill country village on the river Zaan; a truly "living" museum since its houses have inhabitants. Characteristic of the community, which faithfully mirrors the one in Zaan c. 1700, are the tidy green-with-white-trim wooden houses. Among the points of interest to be visited are a cheese farm, a wooden-shoe workshop, an old grocery store, a clock museum, a tin artisan, two windmills, and an antique shop. There are boat excursions on the river. There is a Dutch pancake house, **de Kraai** *(daily 9 a.m.–6 p.m. Feb.–Sept., 10 a.m.–5 p.m. Oct.–Nov., closed Mon. in Nov.),* on the premises, as well as the restaurant **de Hoop op d'Swarte Walvis** *(Mon.–Sat. lunch noon–2:30 p.m., dinner 6–10 p.m., closed Sun.;* ☎ *(075) 165540, FAX (075) 162476; expensive)* with a well-respected kitchen (one Michelin star) and atmospheric antique interior, with terrace dining in good weather. From Amsterdam CS, it's a 15-minute train ride to *Station Koog-Zaandijk* (in the direction of Alkmaar), from which it's about a ten-minute walk to Zaanse Schans. Half-day coach excursions to Zaanse Schans are available from Amsterdam.

If you are traveling by car in the area, some of the lovely waterland villages to include are Westzaan, de Rijp, Wormer, and Jisp. In Zaandam, now quite urbanized, is the Czar Peter cottage, lived in by Peter the Great in 1697 when he came to Holland to learn shipbuilding. He created such a stir in the then small town that he had to remove himself to Amsterdam, where he could remain relatively anonymous as he learned the trade.

Alkmaar Cheese Market

Waagplein (Weigh House Square); Fri. mid-April–mid-Sept. 10 a.m.–noon; approximately 1/2 hour by train from Amsterdam CS, more than 1/2 mile from Alkmaar station to town center. The attractive old town of Alkmaar, which received its charter in 1254, was frequently caught in the crossfire of struggles involving the Dutch provinces of

Holland, Friesland, and Gelder. But Alkmaar is still proud of its citizens' successful stand against the Spanish seige in 1573. The moated and canaled sections of "inner" Alkmaar, within the old grassy green ramparts, retain much of the look they would have had then. While it's probably not the place for an overnight stay, Alkmaar is much more than its cheese market; however, since many of the town's other attractions open to coincide with the market, Friday mornings are the recommended time for a visit.

The cheese market usually attracts large crowds around the Waagplein to watch the colorful carryings-on. Plan to arrive enough in advance to get the good tourist information in English (walking town-tour brochures, background on cheese market tradition and procedure, map) available from the VVV (☎ *072-114284)* located in the **Waaggebouw** (weigh house), which also houses a **cheese museum** *(April 1–Oct. 31, Mon.–Sat. 10 a.m.–4 p.m., Fri. 9 a.m.).* Cheese begins arriving at the market after 7 a.m., and the market manager allocates certain sections of the square to various sellers. The four companies of porters are dressed in white costumes and lacquered straw hats in red, green, blue, or yellow according to their company, and are members of the Cheese-Carriers' Guild, which dates back to the early 17th century, although cheese was being weighed in Alkmaar as early as 1365. The market undoubtedly is continued in its present form largely for tourists, but the business conducted is serious nonetheless. After inspection and weighing, the lots of cheese (primarily the cannon-ball-shaped Edams, here in their natural wax covering, not wrapped in red cellophane for export) are carried off on wide wooden barrows to the buyers' warehouses. Payment is likely to take place over coffee or something stronger in the cafes around the square.

The Waaggebouw dates back to 1341 and served both as a chapel and hostel for needy wayfarers. In 1581, Prince Willem the Silent of Orange restored to the town so-called weighing-rights (in part to reward the town for its brave stand against the Spanish in the 1573 siege); the need for more market space caused the chapel (which probably had been turned over to the town when the Protestant Dutch Reformed Church became the declared religion in 1578) to be rebuilt as the still active weigh house. The 1599 tower has a **carillon** *(concerts on Fri. 11 a.m.–noon during cheese market season, year-round Sat., market day, noon–1 p.m.).* The tower clock has a pair of jousting knights who charge each other on the hour chime. Plan to stay and wander awhile in town after the cheese market: Enjoy the early 16th-century double-stairway Stadhuis, the Vismarkt (fish market), the picturesque old facades along the Oude Gracht, the small narrow streets, canal bridges, and hofjes. The Gothic Grote Kerk (St. Laurens) 1470–1520, which contains the tomb of Count Floris V (died 1296), is noted for its small organ (1511), one of the oldest in regular use, and the 1643 organ designed by Jacob van Campen.

HAARLEM

GUIDELINES FOR HAARLEM

SIGHTS

The Frans Hals Museum and, on Haarlem's gargantuan Grote Markt, **St. Bavokerk** (St. Bavo's church, 1400–1550) with its famed organ, are the city's stellar stops. Throughout the appealing city, fine architecture from the 17th and earlier centuries, both on grand and smaller scales, is in evidence.

GETTING AROUND

Once you get to the **Grote Markt**, the heart of Haarlem, a 15-minute walk from the train station, prime sights are located pretty compactly, the Frans Hals Museum being the farthest point, about a 10-minute walk. Several bus routes from the station stop near the Grote Markt, and there are taxis at the station.

SHOPPING

Old print, antique, and other shops are located around St. Bavo's church along the Oude Groenmarkt, and in the streets that radiate out from the Grote Markt. There also are shops in the Frans Hals Museum and in St. Bavo's church. During the growing season, there's a Saturday flower market on the Oude Groenmarkt.

WHERE TO STAY

Hotels in town are limited, but there's a choice of two comfortable properties with fairly convenient city locations.

WHERE TO EAT

The variety of settings and types of food available will match travelers' taste, time, and pocketbook preferences.

ENTERTAINMENT AND EVENTS

With Keukenhof gardens and the bulb fields nearby, the spring season (Apr. 1–end May) is easily the area's busiest. There are weekly evening concerts on the **St. Bavokerk Christian Muller organ** *mid-May–mid-Oct.*, with an additional afternoon concert a week in July and Aug. Concerts by participants in Haarlem's biennial (1994, 1996, etc.) *International Organ Improvisation Competition* are played nearly daily in July on the St. Bavo's organ. Concerts on the third Sundays of the months of Sept.–May and on occasional candle-light evenings (call for specifics and reservations) are given at the Frans Hals Museum. In early June (check with VVV for date), Haarlem holds its annual **Luilak**, an all-night giant flower and plant sale on the Grote Markt (*4 p.m.–8 a.m.*).

ARRIVING

Haarlem is on the main Amsterdam-Rotterdam rail line, some 15 minutes from Amsterdam by frequent service; its 1908 station is a historic monument. Haarlem has good road and motorway connections.

IN THE AREA

Several intriguing attractions are located close to Haarlem: to the south are the **bulb fields** and **Keukenhof** garden, **Zandvoort,** a favorite North Sea resort, and **Cruquius**, an old steam water pumping station, with a museum that shows how the Haarlemmermeer was drained. To the north, pretty **Spaarndam** village has a statue that illustrates the tale of the boy with his finger plugging a dike. The busy trio of locks at **IJmuiden** sends ships up the *Noordzee Kanaal* to Amsterdam. West of Haarlem are bicycle paths through the dunes at the **National Park de Kennemerduinen** and footpaths (only) in the dunes of **Amsterdamse Waterleiding** reservoir south of Zandvoort.

TRAVEL TIPS

It's not necessary to overnight in Haarlem to attend an evening organ concert at St. Bavo's; evening trains regularly scheduled until nearly midnight provide plenty of time to return to Amsterdam, Rotterdam, or points in between. The Frans Hals Museum, unlike many in Holland, is open Mondays.

HAARLEM IN CONTEXT

By the 10th century, Haarlem had become a township on the Spaarne River, on which the counts of Holland levied tolls. The counts' early fortification here is recalled in the name **Gravenstenenbrug** (counts' fortress bridge) that spans the Spaarne today. By the 13th century, Haarlem had acquired considerable status, as reflected in its coat of arms: a silver sword among four stars, crowned by a cross. The crown and sword had been presented to Haarlem by German Emperor Frederick II as reward for the city's help in occupying Damiata in 1219 during the Second Crusade. The "Damiaatjes," a set of chimes in St. Bavo's belfry, are a further recognition.

In 1245, Count Willem II, from the precincts of his hunting lodge on the 't *Zand* (now the *Grote Markt*), where jousting tournaments were held, presented Haarlem with a city charter. Eventually the site of the lodge, destroyed by city fires in 1347 and 1351, was given to the town, which built a *Stadhuis* (town hall) there by the end of the

14th century. From the 15th through the early 17th century, there were many alterations and additions to the Stadhuis; City Architect Lieven de Key designed the wing along Zijlstraat in 1620-22, and drew up plans for the last major rebuilding (1633), which gave the facade the Italian Renaissance elements it still shows. Haarlem's couples today have their civil marriages in the medieval Knights' Hall (Gravenzaal), which visitors can view when ceremonies aren't on the calendar. Facing the Stadhuis, it's entrance is around the corner on the left. Behind the Stadhuis is a monastery, destroyed by the 14th-century city fires, now somewhat restored. The name *Prinsenhof* there refers to a residence built on the site in 1590 by the Prince of Orange after the monastery's church had been plundered and damaged beyond repair in 1578 during Reformation tumult.

A significant piece of Haarlem's 15th-century history is kept alive by a statue on the Grote Markt near St. Bavo's of **Lourens Coster** (1370–1440), a native with a well-substantiated claim (in 1423) to being at least a co-inventor (with Germany's Gutenberg) of the art of printing with moveable type. Coster is buried in St. Bavo's, the exact location unknown. Holland's first newspapers were published in Haarlem, and more than 570 years after Coster's typesetting here, Haarlem remains a printing center full of book publishers, editors, and newspapers. Also calling Haarlem home is the firm *Enschede*, which prints postage stamps and paper currency, not just for Holland but other governments too. (In case you hadn't noticed, Haarlem artist Frans Hals' portrait appears on the Dutch blue 10-guilder note.)

As with the rest of Holland, 16th-century Haarlem was keenly affected by the northern Netherlands revolt against Spain, known as the Eighty Years' War. In 1572, with a population of 20,000, Haarlem was larger and more important than Amsterdam—not until the 17th century did Amsterdam eclipse Haarlem—and thus served as a symbol of resistance for the Dutch. In December 1572, Haarlem was besieged by Spanish troops, under Frederick of Toledo, son of the dread Duke of Alva. For a while, the Haarlemmers held out, managing to ice skate in and out of town on canals and rivers to acquire supplies. The Spanish were ordered to wear iron cleats to be able to pursue and stop them, but proved unable to. However, spring came, the canals and river melted, and the Spanish gradually gained the upper hand.

The Spanish Navy stationed in the Haarlemmermeer to the north of the town effectively blocked the town's only outside line of supply. Subsequent attempts by Willem the Silent to provide relief, and heroic efforts by the Haarlem women under the leadership of Kenau Simons Hasselaer, proved unsuccessful. In July 1573 the citizens agreed to surrender on condition that a general amnesty be granted if 57 of the town's leaders were handed over. The terms were accepted, but several days later the Spanish wrought wholesale massacre in Haarlem, killing some 1800 of the Holland garrison stationed there, all the Calvinist leaders, and many other Dutch. Several months later, Haarlem's surviving citizens at least had the satisfaction of knowing they had made victory costly for the Spanish: unable to equip their forces adequately after the expenditures at Haarlem, the Spanish, in their subsequent attempt to subdue the nearby town of Alkmaar by siege, failed. This marked the beginning of a downturn in the Spanish domination of Holland.

Haarlem had more to suffer during the drastic decade of the 1570s. While still under Spanish rule in 1576—Haarlem remained occupied by the Spanish for five years following its siege—fire destroyed large parts of the town. Shortly after the Spanish vacated Haarlem in 1578, Dutch Protestant purges in the town succeeded in destroying the treasures in churches and religious houses that had survived the flames. St. Bavo's church, which had escaped the fire, passed into Protestant hands.

But the Reformation also produced positive results for Haarlem. After the Spanish conquest of Antwerp in the southern Netherlands in 1585, many Flemish and Wallonian Protestant refugees fled north. The specialized skills and capital of the many Flemings who settled in Haarlem significantly affected Holland's social, cultural, and economic development, and helped pave the way for Holland's soon-to-appear "Golden Age."

In the 17th century, Haarlem occupied a fairly small, narrow strip of land, bordered on the west by a row of dunes that separated the town from the North Sea, and on the east by the large Haarlemmermeer lake, which was drained in the 19th century. The river Spaarne, which flows through the town south to north, passes through the east side of Haarlem. Boatyards, breweries, and numerous windmills that served as sawmills and in the baking, brewing, tannery, and cloth trades, lined its banks. Due to the generally poor road conditions, transportation then was mainly by water, and the Spaarne formed a vital link between towns in the northern and southern regions of the Holland province. A canal from Haarlem to Amsterdam was dug in 1632, and one to Leiden in 1656. The canals linked up with others, forming an extensive waterway network. The waterways were bordered by bridle paths along which horses towed barges.

Hourly boats between Haarlem and Amsterdam ran on Europe's earliest published transportation schedules.

The clean, fresh water of the Spaarne was partly responsible for the success of two of the city's major early industries. Water sources were important in the production of **beer**, and by 1628 the number of breweries in Haarlem had reached 50. The number would reach 150, though none remain today. The quantity of low-alcohol beer consumed in this period, not only in Haarlem but elsewhere in Holland, was high because the quality of most drinking water was poor.

A second significant industry was **linen**. Haarlem damask graced tables in several European courts, where its sheen, patterns, and whiteness were much admired. The latter quality was the result of lengthy bleaching in the grasslands near Haarlem, where the linen, after many rinsings in the river Spaarne, was spread out to bleach in the clear coastal light. Unfortunately, town linen-makers eventually polluted the river, which ruined the quality of Haarlem beer, causing brewers to begin using the clean, naturally filtered, dune water outside of town.

The same coastal light that so successfully bleached Haarlem's linen attracted artists. In the 17th century, a specialty of the **Haarlem School** was landscapes. But the town's major art figure concentrated on portraits. **Frans Hals**, who had been born in Antwerp about 1580, and whose family came north from Flanders to find freedom from the Spanish, spent the rest of his long life working in Haarlem.

Possibly because so little is known about Frans Hals—*much less* than has actually been written about him—even late 17th-century biographers were highly imaginative in reconstructing his life. Myths that have been perpetuated are exceedingly hard to correct. One glaring inaccuracy is that Hals as an old man lived in the *Oudemannenhuis* (old men's almshouse), whose Governors' group portraits he painted. Hals never lived at the almshouse; the rented house in which he lived at the time of his death (1666) is known to have been in Ridderstraat. In a historical twist, the Oudemannenhuis today is the *Frans Hals Museum*.

Also arriving from Flanders was Ghent-born architect **Lieven de Key** (c. 1560–1627), who by 1593 had been appointed Haarlem's city stonemason and bricklayer. Probably well before he oversaw the construction of the Oudemannenhuis in 1608, he had been elevated to Haarlem's city architect. His **Vleeshal** (Meat Hall), built on the Grote Markt in 1602/03, is one of the outstanding works of the Dutch Renaissance style. Built in brick with gray stone decorative detail, the Vleeshal has a strong horizontal element in its facade design, which keeps it down to earth, in contrast to its Grote Markt neighbor, the gothic **Grote Kerk** (**St. Bavo's**), that reaches for heaven. On the St. Bavo side of the Vleeshal, note the ornamental steer and rams heads sculpted in expensive imported Belgium stone (Holland has no stone quarries) to show what business was conducted within. Today, the restored Vleeshal is a part of the Frans Hals Museum and used for special exhibits and lectures. This is also true for the **Vishal** (1768), which abuts St. Bavo's.

With the arrival of Lieven de Key, southern Netherlands renaissance architecture was introduced to Haarlem. De Key's buildings, and those built under his supervision, show many elements typical of the Flemish style: porches, prominent towers, balconies, balustrades, projecting sandstone cornerstones on facades, gable recesses, and scroll and iron mounting work. These ingredients are found in many buildings on and in the vicinity of the Grote Markt as well as in the Bakensserkerk, the Nieuwekerk, and De Waag (weigh house). The Grote Markt itself is the only such "southern Netherlands-style" square north of Holland's major rivers, thus confirming Haarlem as the most Flemish-appearing city in the northern Netherlands.

Neuwe Gracht was dug in the 17th century to give Haarlem the substantial enlargement of city limits it needed. With an expanding population in the 17th century, Haarlem's churches were no longer capable of caring for the increasing number of needy: the Golden Age meant prosperity for Holland overall, but its benefits didn't necessarily trickle down to all people. Haarlem's prosperous private citizens without children, sensitive to the plight of the poor, often provided material assistance in the form of **hofjes**, modest individual almshouses around a central courtyard. Twenty hofjes existed in the city by the end of the 17th century, and 18 remain to be seen by visitors today.

One of Haarlem's most unusual hofjes is the 18th-century (1768) **Hofje van Oorschot** with the usual family coat of arms over the door of the main building that houses the Governors' Room. Unlike most hofjes that are sheltered from the street behind an enclosing courtyard wall, Oorschot is on view from the street (Kruis Straat) through a tall open iron railing. This was the result of objections from a rich merchant living across the street who didn't want to look out on a bare brick wall. Architectural arrangements were duly made for the hofje and its garden to be open on three sides to the street.

In the 19th and 20th centuries, Haarlem has quietly prospered, growing in population to 150,000, and content in its role as provincial capital of Noord Holland.

GUIDEPOSTS

Telephone Code 023

Tourist Info. • VVV, Stationplein 1; ☎ *319059, FAX 340537.*

Parking • Limited meter parking at the station by the VVV; inquire there about car parks near the sights you plan to visit.

Trains • Schedules and information in the station.

Buses • Local buses 1, 2, and 3 stop at the Grote Markt.

NZH Buses • Bus stops for most routes (including bulb fields, Keukenhof garden, Zandvoort beaches) are in front of train station.

Bike rental • At train station.

Taxis • Available in front of station.

WHAT TO SEE AND DO

If ever a small city brought body and soul together in a single place, Haarlem does so at its **Grote Markt**. Expansive is scarcely a sufficient word for the enormous brick paved main square, around the reaches of which are some of the town's most memorable buildings, including the soaring gothic Grote Kerk (St. Bavo's), which is large enough *not* to be swallowed up by the size of its setting. The Haarlem we enjoy today is a proud product of Holland's 17th-century Golden Age, when only Amsterdam competed with it as an art center.

Frans Hals Museum   ★★★

Groot Heiligland 62; open Mon.–Sat. 11 a.m.–5 p.m., Sun. & holidays 1–5 p.m.; closed Christmas and New Year's; ☎ *319180, fee. The Oudemennenhuis* (old men's house), built in 1608 under the supervision of municipal architect Lieven de Key from the proceeds of a public lottery held in Haarlem in 1606, served as an almshouse for 200 years, and then as an orphanage for another 100, until opening as a museum in 1913 restored to its 17th-century architectural authenticity. Of particular note is the magnificent Renaissance-style corridor, whose squared black and white marble floors, edged with blue and white tiles, seem to recreate one of the delicate Dutch interiors painted by Vermeer of Delft. The reconstruction of the 17th-century garden accentuates the harmony of the whole museum, a fortunate combination of the skill of an architect and the genius of a painter from the same period.

The greater part of the life work of Frans Hals has, alas, been scattered around the world. Nevertheless, particularly in group portraiture, considered one of the crowning accomplishments of the Dutch school of painting, Hals is well represented here. There is a series of five Civic Guard group portraits, most notably the *Banquet of the Officers of the Civic Guard of St. Adrian* (1633), a striking contrast to the group portraits of the *Governors of St. Elizabeth Gasthuis* (1641), and the well-known governors and governesses of the Oudemannenhuis (the museum when it was an almshouse), both painted in 1664, when Hals was older than 80. These important works show the bold, fluent brushstrokes that gave Hals' portraits (Hals captured all segments of Haarlem society from prosperous merchants and military officers to fisherboys and pub crawlers), in particular, such a feeling of the moment. French Impressionists Manet and Monet made special journeys to Haarlem to see these paintings. And Vincent van Gogh, obviously influenced by Hals' remarkable rapid and free brushstroke style, wrote: "What a joy it is to see a Frans Hals, how very different from paintings in which everything is carefully and uniformly smooth."

Hals is the centerpiece of the museum, but many other outstanding Dutch painters and styles (landscapes, seascapes, still lifes, everyday life scenes, and church interiors) are on view. Since Haarlem is so close to the bulb-growing district, in one area of the museum, paintings, drawings, and tiles have been assembled and designated the **tulip route** (with English brochure) to show the enthusiasm (and madness) that the flower has caused. (See "Tulipmania in The Bulb Field Business" chapter.) And there's a *Doll House* (never meant to be used by children) dating from 1750, filled with more than 3000 tiny decorative and artistic treasures.

St. Bavo's or Grote Kerk ★★★

Entrance on Oude Groenmarkt 23; Mon.–Sat. 10 a.m.–4 p.m.;
☎ *324399.* Built between 1390 and 1520 (the date on the face of its tower clock), Haarlem's Gothic Grote Kerk is one of the largest in Holland. Construction of the church was not constant; work often had to be suspended due to lack of funds. Considering the number of individuals who orchestrated the work, St. Bavo's shows a remarkable harmony. A stone lantern tower designed by Keldermans was built in 1506, but had to be pulled down in 1514 because it was judged to be too heavy. In 1518 a new tiered tower was erected, constructed of wood and covered in lead. The most recent major restoration of the church was completed in 1985.

Approaching the entrance (#23) on Oude Groenmarkt (old vegetable market), one sees centuries-old small shuttered shops snuggled into the sides of St. Bavo; with pure Dutch practicality, the shutters open from top to bottom to form a shelf upon which to display wares. The church is entered through a narrow passage beautifully adorned with old blue and white tiles. For centuries after it was built, the church was always open and used by Haarlemmers as a passage from one part of the city to another. Such unhindered entrance was the reason for Dog Whippers (who have a chapel in the church), whose job it was to remove troublesome dogs from the premises. The town brewers also had a chapel.

Among other church aspects of interest are the *Graf van Frans Hals* (the artist's grave), on view through the choir screen, a masterpiece of medieval craftsmanship made in 1517 by Jan Fyerens, a brass founder from Mechelen (Belgium). When candles are mounted in the screen and lit, it resembles the *Burning Bush*. The tomb of the well-known painter of Holland's hulking Protestant church interiors, **Pieter Saenredam**, is elsewhere in the church. Sticking half-way into one church wall is a cannon ball, left as a reminder of the Spanish siege in 1572-73. The carved oak pulpit, always center stage in Dutch Protestant churches, dates from 1679; its brass hand rails are in the shape of snakes slithering down, and meant to represent Satan fleeing from the Gospel.

It's hard to turn away from the 5068-pipe Christian Muller 1748 organ, considered one of the most important instruments in the world, and certainly one of the most beautiful, in its towering (almost 100 ft. high), sculpted case. Handel played the organ on two visits, prior to Mozart's in 1766 at the age of 10; Dr. Albert Schweitzer, a fine organist, has sat at the console, too. When the organ was installed, the huge stained glass window that had decorated the wall had to be bricked over (observable from the exterior, by the Vleeshal). There are guided tours of the church May–Sept. Sat. 11 a.m. and 2 p.m. Free one-hour organ concerts are offered Tues. nights 8:15 p.m. mid- May-mid-Sept., and Thurs. 3 p.m. in July and Aug.

WHERE TO STAY

EXPENSIVE

Carlton Square   ★★★★

Baan 7, 2012 DB; ☎ *319091, FAX 329853, U.S. Sales Office* ☎ *800-223-9815.* Haarlem's newest, largest (97 rooms), and most luxurious hotel is located out of the center, facing a park but within fairly reasonable walking distance of the Grote Markt. The restaurant **Cafe de la Paix** is à la carte, and the **Whiskey Bar** has a British ambiance.

MODERATE

Golden Tulip Lion D'Or   ★★★★

Kruisweg 34, 2011 LC; ☎ *321750, FAX 329543, U.S. sales office* ☎ *800-333-1212.* This long-established hotel is located close to the railway station and across from the bus terminal. (Front rooms will get noise.) Rooms are more or less similar in layout, but make sure you ask for a modernized one with lighter, brighter colors and decor. Lobby lounge has Scandinavian-style modern furniture, perfectly cheerful though not luxurious.

WHERE TO EAT

Sooner or later you'll be on Haarlem's Grote Markt wanting "a little something," and the **Cafe Restaurant Brinkmann** *(Grote Markt; open daily 9 a.m.–midnight, kitchen closes at 11 p.m.; inexpensive)* could hit the spot. A Delft tile tableau, mounted to mark the cafe's 50th anniversary in 1929, decorates the entryway to the art nouveau/continental-style place, with lighted candles at the table even at lunch, stained glass, plants. If you take a window seat, while you partake of something off the varied menu of sandwiches, uitsmijters, pizza or pasta, burgers or steak with salad, quiche, or just coffee and pastry, you can enjoy a great view of the Grote Markt out the grote windows. Just a few doors away is **Cafe Mephisto** *(Grote Markt 29; daily noon–9 p.m., Mon. only noon–3 p.m.; inexpensive)*, a trendy, pleasant place with art nouveau details such as a stained glass ceiling, mirrors, lamps, dark wood, and fresh flowers. Omelettes, uitsmijters, and other tasty light meal fare.

If you're coming from the train, you won't even have to wait for the Grote Markt, since you'll pass several good choices along the route. *Kruisweg* becomes *Kruis Straat* before becoming pedestrianized as *Barteljorisstraat*, which runs into the Grote Markt. **Cafe 1900** *(Barteljorisstraat 10, open Mon.–Sat. 10 a.m.– midnight, Sun. 5 p.m.–midnight;* ☎ *318183; inexpensive)* is a trendy but basic art deco delight, a copy of a Parisian cafe, with dark wood detail, little marble tables and straight wooden cafe chairs, and interesting lighting fixtures. Good choice for informal fare from coffee to uitsmijters. Walk a few doors down to satisfy your sweet tooth at **Tearoom H. Ferd. Knipers** *(Barteljorisstraat 22; open Mon.–Sat. 9 a.m.–5:30 p.m., closed Sun.).* As Haarlem's best pastry shop, it's where Dutch women "of a certain age" share a pick-me-up pause while shopping.

For a proper sit-down meal—for which you'll want to allow time—on the Frans Hals Museum side of the Grote Markt is **Restaurant Peter Cuyper** *(Kleine Houtstraat 70; open Mon.–Sat. noon–3 p.m. and 6–10 p.m., closed Sun., last week Dec., and first 3 weeks Aug.;* ☎ *320885; moderate)*, situated in restored 16th-century townhouse with courtyard (dining outside in decent weather). Lots of Dutch atmosphere with candles, fresh flowers, copper lamps, amid the architectural details and oak furniture. The cuisine is French (preparation a cross between classic and nouvelle), the food Dutch: local salmon, lamb, and chocolate from Haarlem's own factory.

LEIDEN

GUIDELINES FOR LEIDEN

SIGHTS

Leiden has the timeless Dutch beauty that comes with canals, picturesque gables, and a working windmill in the center. **Leiden University** (Holland's oldest, 1575), numerous bookshops, cafes, sites associated with America's **Pilgrim Fathers** who lived here 11 years before sailing for the New World, landmarks from Rembrandt's early life, and interesting museums, give the town broad appeal.

GETTING AROUND

Walking is the best way to see the town, even though its historic center is not as compact as some. Public buses or taxis from the station can supplement your feet. One-hour canal cruises (June, July, Aug. only) pass some of the main sights. The VVV offers guided walking tours of the city Sun. afternoons, June to Sept.

SHOPPING

Leiden serves as the main shopping town for the surrounding region, and has a full range of department and smaller stores. Late-night shopping (*til 9 p.m.*) Thurs.; general market along *Nieuwe Rijn* in the city center Wed. and Sat. 9 a.m.–5 p.m.

WHERE TO STAY

In-town hotels are limited in number, but run from modern first-class accommodations to moderate old canal-fronted townhouses.

WHERE TO EAT

There's a full range of fare, from formal French and cozy candlelit bistros to casual cafes catering to students.

ENTERTAINMENT AND EVENTS

Leiden is a lively student town with "brown" cafes and some music clubs. The VVV prints a monthly events calendar. Oct. 3 is celebrated annually in observance of the end of the *siege of the city* by the Spanish in 1574. A church service on the U.S.'s *Thanksgiving Day* in St. Pieterskerk commemorates the Pilgrim Fathers' 12-year stay in Leiden.

ARRIVING

Leiden lies more or less midway on the main Amsterdam-Rotterdam train line, with Haarlem 15 minutes to the north, The Hague 15 minutes to the south. There are trains every quarter-hour in each direction, and several hourly to/from Schiphol Airport. Leiden is located just off the A 4 motorway. Leiden's canals account for the many one-way and pedestrianized streets, making driving complicated. Your best bet is to arrive by train; if you come by car, park it (legally) and forget it.

IN THE AREA

Leiden lies at the southern boundary of Holland's main **bulb field district**, which normally is in bloom from early April to late May.

The main train line from Leiden north to Haarlem towards Amsterdam (*not* the Schiphol/Amsterdam line) passes through the fields. A bus from Leiden station stops at Keukenhof gardens. Windmill cruises (three hours, mid-June to early Sept.) depart from Leiden and take in the surrounding countryside.

TRAVEL TIPS

Leiden's university students are assertive cyclists who assume the right-of-way, even over pedestrians.

LEIDEN IN CONTEXT

Much of what distinquishes Leiden—the same *Leyden* as it was written in periods past—stems from events that took place in 1574, though the town has a considerably longer history. Traces of Roman settlements have been found near Leiden, but essentially the region remained one of almost inaccessible below-sea-level marsh through much of the first millennium after Christ. One wonders why the Vikings bothered to plunder so persistently. About the year 1000, a stronghold and refuge from high water was built on a small island between two branches of the Rhine River. Around this *Burcht*, which still stands in the center of town, a village grew. By the 11th century, when the Counts of Holland settled there, Leiden's continuance was confirmed.

About 1100, the danger of flooding from the Rhine at Leiden—the name means *place on the waterways*—was diminished by the construction of its first dikes, which also served as city walls. Gradually, craftsmen and brewers augmented the population of farmers and fishermen, and Leiden became the most important market town in the area. In 1266, Count of Holland Floris V awarded Leiden a city charter with extra all-important privileges, including toll-freedom and exemption from certain taxes, which further fostered growth in trade and population.

By the early 14th century, new canals had been dug to encompass the larger town. And Leiden's textile industry, having received a boost from immigrating Flemish weavers, had become famous far afield for the excellent quality of the woolen cloth it produced. In common with much of Europe, Leiden was plagued in the second half of the 14th century by outbreaks of the Black Death, which severely reduced its population. Nevertheless, the city enjoyed relative prosperity until succumbing to a long-lasting economic recession about 1500 that was led by a decline in the cloth trade.

In 1572, Leiden, together with 11 other important cities in the northern Netherlands, joined **Willem (the Silent)**, Prince of Orange, in opposing Spanish rule of the Low Countries. Such support ran the risk of confrontation: In 1573, Spaniards laid siege to Haarlem (successfully), then Alkmaar (unsuccessfully), and the Leijenaars prepared themselves. The town's earliest cornmills lay outside the city, but early in 1573 these were all demolished to keep them from falling to the Spanish. Eight new mills were built on the city walls. Large supplies of food were stored within the town in anticipation of a **siege**, and, late in 1573, Spanish troops did indeed surround Leiden. But the town's preparation paid off, and citizens suffered little deprivation before the Spanish, quite suddenly, withdrew in March 1574. Just as unexpectedly, however—the troops having only temporarily been needed to fight elsewhere—the Spanish reappeared in late May at the city walls. Food stores, so carefully set aside the previous year, had not been replenished, and this time shortages in Leiden occurred alarmingly soon after the onset of the siege.

In what is the most famous Dutch stance during the *Eighty Years' War* with Spain, Leijenaars held their ground courageously. As August advanced to September, food shortages reduced many in the city to eating rats. Willem of Orange had pledged help to Leiden and, though severely ill with a fever at his residence in Delft, he directed defense plans, partly with the communications aid of carrier pigeons from the Leiden home of three brothers at 94 Rapenburg (still known as *Het Duyvenhuis*, the pigeon house). Knowing he had 200 Dutch vessels on the North Sea ready to rout the Spanish, still camped in relative comfort around the walls of Leiden, Willem made what was a drastic decision for a Dutchman: to breach the dikes that had been built over centuries to defend Leiden from the sea. The desperate deed was done: the dikes were cut in 16 places, and the sunken land surrounding Leiden flooded. But the water didn't come in deeply enough to sail the ships—which required a minimum 28-inch draught—over the countryside fields to Leiden. In fact, the wind changed direction, blowing the sea *away* from Leiden.

Within the city, the situation worsened by the day, as *hundreds* of starved-to-death citizens became *thousands*. Edible leaves were stripped from the trees. Horses, then dogs and cats, and finally cows—kept until they were too emaciated to produce milk—were slaughtered and distributed as widely as possible among the population. When such conditions brought the plague, some people finally seemed ready to capitulate, since it had been weeks since the dikes had been severed, and no relief was in sight. It was reported that Leiden's Burgemeester (mayor) Adriaan van der Werf, who preferred death by starvation to dishonorable surrender, offered the restive citizens his own body for food "as far as it will go," thus stunning and/or shaming the citizens into continuing their resistance.

A full two months after the dikes had been damaged, 131 days after Leiden's siege had begun, with at least 6,000 citizens dead, a fierce southwest storm swept Holland on the night of October 2, 1574. The North Sea surged, finally carrying Willem's Dutch naval fleet through the broken dikes to within striking distance of the Spanish. The relief of Leiden finally was realized.

In the morning of October 3, during a search of the abandoned Spanish encampments, one city marksman, Ghijsbert Corneliszoon Schaek, found a huge kettle of *hutspot*, a stew of beef, carrots, potatoes, and onions, which gave survivors of the siege their first fresh food in months. (The reputed iron kettle, often attributed to having been found by an orphan—it makes a more poignant story—is on display at *Leiden's Lakenhal Museum.*) Shortly thereafter, "seabeggars" arrived from south of the city on the Vliet with ships loaded with white bread and herring for the starving citizens. To this day, those are the favored foods during Leiden's annual October 3 city celebrations.

For their brave endurance of the siege, Willem offered the people of Leiden exemption from taxes for a certain period or the establishment of a university. Despite what citizens in heavily-taxed Holland might do today, Leiden residents then took a long-range view and chose the first Dutch university. Its inauguration took place in February 1575, with an elaborate parade and a float procession on the river. Leiden quickly became the most important Protestant university in Europe, attracting the finest minds in Europe, and making Holland a leading center of scientific learning and art.

Deservingly, Leiden experienced better times following the siege. The manufacture of cloth once more became the driving force of the city's economy. Ironically, this was somewhat due to the Roman Catholic Spanish, who still occupied the southern Netherlands (today's Belgium). After they overtook Antwerp in 1585, among the many Protestant Flemish refugees who fled north to Holland were numerous skilled textile workers who settled in Leiden and provided fresh impulse for that industry. Leiden entered the 17th-century Golden Age as one of Holland's most industrialized places, and possibly Europe's largest textile manufacturing town. The impressive 1597 *Stadhuis* on Breestraat (whose facade fortunately survived a 1929 fire) was designed by Lieven de Key to reflect the prosperity of Leiden at this period.

Because Leiden had successfully struggled with Spain for its own spiritual freedom, and because the town had gained a special reputation for welcoming exiles fleeing persecution in other lands, it seems quite natural that English "separatists," seeking to escape the rigid edicts of King James I, wanted to settle there. After months of trying to arrange passage to religiously tolerant Holland, one group of English managed, after several false, near fatal starts, to escape from Boston, England, across the North Sea to Amsterdam. Among that group of "pilgrims" were 18-year-old **William Bradford**, who would later serve as governor of Plymouth Colony (Massachusetts) for many years, and **William Brewster**, who had served in Holland in 1587 with Queen Elizabeth's secretary of state, and would later become the pilgrims' spiritual leader in the New World.

They and others, upon discovering disagreements among the English separatists in Amsterdam, petitioned the liberal Leiden leaders for residence permits for 100. These were granted, "provided such persons behaved themselves," and by May 1, 1609, the pilgrims had moved to Leiden. A measure of Leiden's true support is the lack of attention the city burgemeester paid to English authorities who, learning that Leiden had admitted the "separatists," protested for their return.

Trained for the most part only in farming, the Leiden English exiles in many cases had to accept jobs of physical labor, particularly in the textile industry, which employed most workers in town. Having lost much of their personal property through theft or seizure while trying to get from England to Holland, many had to work long hours at subsistence level just to survive. So hard did they have to work that, despite their strong religious conviction, they were unable to establish their own meeting house until May 1611.

At that time they bought **De Groenpoort** ("the green gate"), which stood on a site that has been occupied since 1683 by the **Jean Pesijnhofje** almshouse, across from the great Pieterskerk (church). The Groenpoort served as the pilgrims' church and as a parsonage for their English religious leader, John Robinson, and his family. Small "cottages" were built around its courtyard as houses for the least well-off members of the English congregation. A plaque near the gate of the Pesijnhofje indicates that here "John Robinson lived, taught, and died—1625." The lovely enclosed garden, surrounded by small houses that today are rented to students and elderly couples, is open to the public.

Unlike many of his pilgrim parish peers, William Brewster was well educated. He was able to tutor in English at Leiden University, and eventually established a small printing press—an evangelical enterprise. The *Pilgrim Press* was located near Pieterskerk on Stincksteeg (Stink Alley, now renamed William Brewster alley), and is indicated today by an explanatory tablet.

Continued poverty and concern about the corruption of their youth, who were growing up without English identity and under the less religiously strict influence of Dutch neighbors, caused growing discontent among the pilgrims. When William Brewster had to flee Holland to escape arrest for one of his Pilgrim Press religious essays —James I's officials had tracked down the typeface—he returned to England under the surname of Williamson. There, he began making arrangements for the pilgrims' passage to the New World. The Separatists in Leiden would probably have read Captain John Smith's enthusiastic *A Description of New England*, published in 1616, and hoped to have better success with "converting" the natives there to their religious outlook than they had had in Holland. Recalled William Bradford later in his *History of Plymouth Plantation*, the young and strong pilgrims who with him left "Leyden, a fair and bewtifull citie," did so "not out of any newfangledness or such like giddy humor—but for sundry weighty and solid reasons."

On the last day of July 1620, 54 of the English group from Leiden—35 of them "saints," those going for religious reasons, the remaining "strangers," those who sought commercial opportunity in the New World—boarded barges by the Vlietbrug (near the present Pilgrim Documentation Center, see "What To See and Do"), and sailed south down the Vliet to Delftshaven (now a picturesque old harbor in a quiet corner of Rotterdam). There, they departed, after prayer, aboard the *Speedwell* for England, where they met up with the good ship *Mayflower*.

John Robinson, the pilgrims' spiritual leader in Leiden, remained behind, since the majority of his parish had not opted for the rigors of the New World. He had hoped to follow eventually, but died in 1625 and was buried in the Pieterskerk. A memorial on the outside wall of the massive old church reads: "… whence at his prompting went forth the Pilgrim Fathers to settle New England." As the pilgrims had foreseen, many of the English who remained in Leiden became assimilated into Dutch society. Robinson's son Isaac was one of the last of the Leiden pilgrims to emigrate to Plymouth (Massachusetts), in 1632.

Dutch influence on the pilgrims who established America's first permanent English colony at Plymouth is hard to pinpoint, but there can be little doubt that some of the Dutch civil laws and precedents the pilgrims had experienced in Leiden were incorporated into the idea of the separation of church and state that, even under the religious-minded pilgrims, was established in America from the start at Plymouth. Some might see a connection between the pilgrims' celebration of a Thanksgiving feast with the Indians, and the annual three days of feasting and prayer in thanksgiving for the relief of Leiden from the Spanish siege. Today, Thanksgiving services are held for both occasions in Leiden's Pieterskerk, on October 3, and on the U.S. Thanksgiving Day in November. The ecumenical service is a meaningful remembrance of the pilgrims' past.

Leiden was one of Holland's thriving centers for painting, and the birthplace of **Lucas van Leyden** (1489?–1533). During Holland's Golden Age, many important painters were born, trained, or continued their artistic lives in Leiden: **Jan van Goyen** (1596–1656); **Rembrandt** (1606–1669); **Willem van der Velde the Elder and the Younger** (1611–1693) and (1633–1707); **Gerrit Dou** (1613–1675); **Jan Steen** (1625/26–1679); **Gabriel Metsu** (1629–1667); and **Frans van Meiris** (1635–1681). Jan Steen, son of a Leiden brewer, and trained as one himself, is known to have owned a tavern in 1672 on the *Lange Brug*. It is reputed—though so much inaccurate biographical data has been perpetuated about Holland's great masters that this story needs to be taken as perhaps just another good tale—that, because Steen was his tavern's own best customer, the tavern that was meant to support him at his art in fact produced bills that had to be paid for in paintings. One biographer wrote, "For a long time his works were to be found only in the hands of dealers in wine." Steen is buried in the Pieterskerk.

Rembrandt is Leiden's greatest son. His father was a fairly prosperous miller, whose surname **Van Rijn** indicates that the family had lived for some generations beside or near the Rhine River, as it did in Rembrandt's day. (His birthplace and residence for most of his 26 years in Leiden, on Weddesteeg near the *Rembrandt Bridge*, is marked by a tablet.) The eighth of nine children, Rembrandt seems to have been the most promising, and was sent to Leiden's Latin School. (In the egalitarian Dutch provinces, it was not unthinkable that a miller's son could aspire to a profession.) The Latin School (built by Lieven de Key in 1599 and used as a school until 1864) is located near the Pieterskerk and, since Rembrandt would have been receiving his schooling in the same period as the pilgrims' sojourn in

Leiden, he might easily have passed one or another of them on the street. The purpose of the Latin School was to prepare young men for Leiden University, then the equal of any in Europe. Although Rembrandt matriculated there, he seems to have left shortly thereafter, having determined to pursue painting.

Rembrandt's first Leiden art instructor is unknown. The second, under whom he served a three-year apprenticeship, was the Leiden painter Jacob van Swanenburgh, who taught Rembrandt the fundamentals, but seems not to have made an important impression upon his pupil; his specialties of architectural scenes and views of hell were two subjects to which Rembrandt never subsequently turned his hand. With Rembrandt showing great talent, his father sent him to Amsterdam for further study under **Pieter Lastman**, then one of the Netherlands' foremost painters of historical scenes. At the age of 18 or 19, Rembrandt returned to Leiden and set himself up as an independent master, developing rapidly as a painter, perfecting his etching technique, and soon surpassing most other Dutch artists.

Leiden was a bustling town during the six or seven years that Rembrandt had his studio there, working closely with artist Jan Lievens (who had also studied under Lastman in Amsterdam). Rembrandt had several students in Leiden, **Gerrit Dou** being the most important. With 50,000 people in 1620 (and 70,000 by 1670), the city of Leiden was then second in size in Holland only to Amsterdam (110,000). Architecturally, Leiden was typically Dutch: narrow houses, with gabled roofs and bright-colored shutters, lined the canals and streets, but if Rembrandt recorded them, no such scenes have survived. Visitors found Leiden conspicuous for its cleanliness, even in well-scrubbed Holland, but, paradoxically, the town also had an abominable stench rising from almost currentless canals that often were clogged with sewage, which perhaps contributed to Leiden's periodic outbreaks of the plague (several deadly epidemic diseases). Some years the death toll was so high that the town's earthen ramparts had to be used as supplemental cemeteries.

In the Leiden of the 1620s, almost all workers, mostly illiterate and underpaid, were associated with the town's textile trade; their living conditions would have fostered Rembrandt's great sense of humanity. He also felt the full influence of the variety of population at Leiden University, where he saw a parade of students and philosophical professors from countries throughout Europe, many from noble families, whose foreign clothes fed his eye for the picturesque, exotic, and sumptuous details in dress that he inserted in his paintings the rest of his life. In 1632, Rembrandt left Leiden for Amsterdam, where he won almost immediate fame and wealth.

Scientifically, due to its university, Leiden attained and maintained a position of prominence in Europe during the Age of Reason, and on into the Enlightenment. The **Museum Boerhaave** pays tribute to **Christian Huygens**, a 17th-century scholar whose most notable achievement was the invention of the pendulum clock, which improved significantly the accuracy of navigation for the all-important Dutch East India Company ships. Also honored is **Antony van Leeuwenhoek**, who invented the first microscope, which is on display.

A century-and-a-half after the pilgrims departed Leiden, another piece of early American history was connected with the town. Under initial encouragement from the province of Friesland, the Dutch were the first to recognize the thirteen colonies' proclamation of freedom from Britain, and to send them much-needed financial aid. (Pragmatic Dutch commercial shipping companies operating out of the Caribbean during the American Revolution actually sold supplies to both sides.) When the war was over, George Washington appointed **John Adams** of Massachusetts (a descendant of *Mayflower* pilgrim John Alden who later became the second president of the U.S.) the first U.S. ambassador to Holland. Adams, his wife, Abigail, and son John Quincy (who would be 6th U.S. president) came to Holland in 1781, at which time John Quincy, then 14, was enrolled at Leiden University. Abigail Adams wrote in a 1786 letter of a visit to the Pieterskerk: "I visited the church at Leyden, in which our forefathers worshipped...I felt a respect upon entering the doors."

By the time of the Adams' appointment to Holland, Leiden's economy was on the wane again, the population reduced to 30,000, the town in physical disrepair. Economic conditions ebbed and flowed during the 19th and 20th centuries, but today, Leiden, population 109,000, appears as lovely as it ever has. Many of the town's fine old buildings, saved from urban-renewal razing because of impoverished periods, have seen recent renovations, and several reconstructions have been completed. Leiden is enjoying a promising present, while preserving its past.

GUIDEPOSTS

Telephone code 071

Tourist Info • VVV, Stationplein 210, 2312 AR, ☎ *146846, FAX 125318;* 1 Apr.–31 Aug., Mon.–Sat. 9 a.m.–8 p.m., Sun. 10 a.m.–4 p.m.; 1 Sept.–31 Mar., Mon.–Fri. 9 a.m.–5:30 p.m., Sat. 10 a.m.–3 p.m., Sun. closed.

Bike rental • Bicycle depot next to railway station, ☎ *131304*; Van der Laan, Merelstraat 13, ☎ *155915*.

Rowboat rental • Jac. Veringa, near Rembrandtbrug, ☎ *149790*.

Canal cruises • Jac. M. Slingerland, Quay Beestenmarkt, ☎ *134938*.

Parking • Carparks indicated on VVV city map; at Stationplein (across from VVV), including Beestenmarkt, Lammermarkt (near De Valk, convenient to De Lakenhal Museum).

Auto. Assn. • ANWB, Stationweg 2, ☎ *146241*.

Train • Information in station hall.

Bus • NZH (local and regional bus services), Stationplein 5, ☎ *134441*.

Emergencies • Police ☎ *144444*; medical ☎ *122222*.

Shopping • Pedestrianized Haarlemmer Straat, Breedstraat, and side streets.

Taxis • Listed in VVV city brochure. Available at train station.

WHAT TO SEE AND DO

Leiden is worthy of a more lingering look than many travelers allow time for. The activities of university students, who live throughout the city, give Leiden a lively evening atmosphere. Leiden is also centrally located, making it a good choice as an overnight alternative, which make it a useful, less expensive base from which to make Dutch day trips. No matter how short your stay, start it at the VVV across from the train station. In addition to a map, which you'll find necessary, it has other excellent English-language booklets on city sights and services, the pilgrims, town history, museums, and several self-guiding walking tour brochures: *A Pilgrimage through Leiden; Leiden, a town of Monuments; Leiden, a true Dutch Heritage*; and *Following in Rembrandt's Footsteps*; each covers many of the town's major landmarks.

Municipal Museum "de Lakenhal"

Oude Singel 32; open Tues.– Sat. 10 a.m.–5 p.m., Sun. and holidays 1–5 p.m., Oct. 3, 10 a.m.–noon; closed Jan. 1, Dec. 25; ☎ *254620*. The handsome *Lakenhal* (Cloth Hall) was built in 1640 to serve as the center of Leiden's wool textile industry and headquarters for the preeminent Cloth Guild. Aspects of the cloth trade are shown in five sculptured plaques on the building's facade; the courtyard was used for the rigorous inspection of the cloth that preserved its high reputation. Turned into Leiden's municipal museum in 1874, the Lakenhal now houses displays in elegant rooms with beamed ceilings, tiled fireplaces, and oak floors. The historic section covers the *Siege of Leiden*, and includes a huge wall tapestry map of the city in the 16th century, and the famed siege *hutspot*. Wonderful period rooms include a delightful 17th-century Dutch-tiled kitchen and the distinguished *Governors' Room* with fine antique furniture. The excellent painting collection has works by famous artists associated with Leiden: Lucas van Leyden, Rembrandt, Jan Steen, Gerrit Dou, and Jan van Goyen's (including his *View of Leyden*, which shows what the town looked like at the time the pilgrims lived here).

St. Pieterskerk   ★★

Pieterskerkhof; ask at the VVV about opening times. This elephantine 15th-century edifice, the sometime house of worship for the English separatist pilgrims, has been restored and now functions as a conference center and setting for Leiden student exams, as well as special church services (particularly on *October 3* in memory of the end of Leiden's siege of 1574, and *Thanksgiving Day* to commemorate the pilgrim connection). The "minimalist" Protestant ★ interior includes many interesting grave slabs that lie flush with the floor. On the exterior is a memorial to John Robinson, religious leader of the pilgrims.

Opposite that memorial is the restored ★ **Jean Pesijnhofje**, an almshouse built in 1683 on the site of the English pilgrims' **De Groene Poort**, still in use as housing for old and student couples. Near the Pieterskerk, on ★ **Pieterskerkchoorsteeg** (Peter's Church Choir Alley) is a plaque over the door to **William Brewster Alley**, where his **Pilgrim Press** operated.

Pilgrim Fathers Document Center   ★★

Vliet 45; open Mon.–Fri. 9 a.m.–noon, 2–4:30 p.m., closed Sat., Sun., holidays, and Oct. 3; ☎ *120191.* The center houses a permanent exhibition of photocopies of personal records documenting details of the pilgrims' lives in Leiden. Marriage and tax records, an edition from Brewster's *Pilgrim Press*, and other items pertaining to Leiden's entire 17th-century English community—with tags designating those who sailed to the New World on the *Mayflower*—can be examined. An informative 20-minute ★★★ film in English can be seen on the pilgrims and the religious times in which they lived.

Windmill Museum De Valk   ★★

Binnenvestgracht; open Tues.–Sat. 10 a.m.–5 p.m., Sun. and holidays 1–5 p.m.; closed Mon., Jan 1, Oct. 3, Dec. 25; ☎ *254639; fee.* I've always found *De Valk* (the falcon) to be one of Leiden's most interesting sights and the best windmill museum in Holland. A tower-style flour mill dating from 1734, *De Valk* is seven stories, beginning with a former miller's living quarters on the ground floor. Everyone can enjoy the miller's rooms, though the exhibits on higher stories, can only be reached via narrow flights of ship-steep stairs. Heading up, one passes the all-wood working mill parts, a self-service slide show (in English) about Leiden and windmills—some 70 of the approximately 900 remaining windmills (9000 once existed in Holland) are located in the greater Leiden region—and exhibits on the historic function and importance of windmills (much of the information is in English), before reaching the reefing stage (5th flight). Here, 45 feet up, on the wide wooden outside platform (from which there's a 360-degree view), is the wheel by which the miller turns the sails (which have a span of 88 feet) into the wind. Wonderfully, the sails at *De Valk* are set to the wind most afternoons from Apr. 1 to Oct. 1.

WHERE TO STAY

The hotels listed are all centrally located. With the exception of the new Golden Tulip property, all are in old townhouses. Guest houses, which may not be in the center of town, can be booked at the VVV.

EXPENSIVE

Golden Tulip Leiden ★★★★

Schipholweg 3, 2316 XB; *221121, FAX 226675,* *1 (800) 333-1212.* This is Leiden's newest, largest (102 beds), most modern, luxorious, center city hotel, situated across from the railway station, on the right (center city) side of the tracks.

MODERATE

De Doelen ★★★

Rapenburg 2, 2311 EV. *120527.* A handsome building on a handsome canal near the university, this nine-room hotel still has the feel of the 15th-century patrician house it was converted from, with features such as old beams, antique tiled fireplaces, dark oak wainscotting, and other old Dutch details in its nooks and crannies. There's no elevator and, needless to say, no two rooms are alike (prices vary somewhat too). A couple of rooms overlook the canal. Some rooms are old-fashioned, decorated in a dark old Dutch style, while others are lighter, more modern, and have less character. The hotel's restaurant is well respected locally and has a walled garden cafe.

WHERE TO EAT

Though limited in number, the restaurants in Leiden will certainly serve your needs. Hotel restaurants and cafes should be kept in mind, since they need to be of a high enough standard to attract a local clientele as well as overnight guests. The "three-course fixed-price menus" and "dish-of-the-day" will represent the best values. If you're looking for a proper restaurant meal, it's always a good idea to call for reservations, since seating capacities can be small and service deliberately unrushed.

A Leiden standard because of its longevity, location, looks, and food is **Oudt Leyden** *(Steenstraat 51-53; restaurant only closed Sun.;* ☎ *133144; restaurant-expensive, pancake house inexpensive/moderate)*; where you get two choices at one address. Long established in a trio of town houses on the main street from the station into the Centrum, the restaurant offers nouvelle-style continental cuisine, with attentive service and handsome atmosphere. The **'t Pannekoekenhuysje** at the left entrance offers the typical Dutch platter-size pancakes and other traditional Dutch specialties.

Sharing space on the same alley just a few doors from the Pieterskerk, where the pilgrims sometimes prayed, are two of Leiden's best bistros, which may put tables out in front when the weather's nice. **De Bisschop** *(Kloksteeg 7;* ☎ *125024; expensive)* offers a pleasant dining space replete with flowers and a prix-fixe menu, among the à la carte dishes. At **La Cloche** *(Kloksteeg 3;* ☎ *123053; expensive)*, fare is apt to be fresh and French in an old house that has been most successfully "smartened" with white rattan and other tasteful details. **La Grand** *(Herengracht 100;* ☎ *140876; closed Mon.; moderate)*, as one of the Neerlands Dis restaurants, is a solid choice for Dutch dishes.

Two *eet-cafes* recommended for informal fare and touching shoulders with students are **De Grote Beer** (*Rembrandtstraat 27*) and **Pardoeza** *(Doezastraat 43)*. According to residents, the town's best Indonesian food can be had at **Surakarta** *(Noordeinde 51;* ☎ *123524; inexpensive)*.

THE HAGUE

GUIDELINES FOR THE HAGUE

SIGHTS

The Hague, the seat of government for Holland and residence of H.M. *Queen Beatrix*—though not the country's capital—has much of appeal for all ages and interests. Several art museums include the exquisite **Mauritshuis** mansion with its masterpieces of 17th century painting, and the **Gemeentemuseum**, with the largest collection of 20th century Dutch artist Mondriaan's works in the world. Other choices range from a museum of instruments of torture, a composite Dutch town constructed at 1:25 scale (**Madurodam**), the **Peace Palace**, and the Parliament's **Ridderzaal**, one of Europe's best preserved pieces of Gothic architecture. In appearance, The Hague differs considerably from a typical Dutch town of canals and narrow gabled houses: being a diplomatic center throughout its history—over 60 nations have embassies or consulates here—led to an expansive, park-like layout. The "downtown" decorum in The Hague is contrasted at its coast, where **Scheveningen's** North Sea resort trappings include **Pier**, **Promenade**, casino, and a nudist beach.

GETTING AROUND

As you'd expect in a city its size (population 450,000), sights in The Hague are spread out, but many are bunched in the **Centrum** (city center), and can be reached on foot from the **Centraal Station (CS)**. The Hague has a fine **tram** and **bus** network, and the CS is close to stops on several routes, including the tram to Delft, less than five miles away. Trams also run from the center of town and from The Hague's **Hollands Spoor (HS)** station to the North Sea-side and Scheveningen. The 1-, 2-, and 3-day local transportation passes, tickets, and maps of the city system are available at the information ("*i*") booth at the CS; the city's main **VVV** tourist office is next door in the Babylon Shopping Complex. Though you may see less orthodox bureaucrats in business suits riding bicycles to work, The Hague's two-wheeler traffic isn't as distracting as in some other Dutch cities; bike rentals are at the HS station and in Scheveningen.

SHOPPING

A cosmopolitan diplomatic capital, The Hague is a sophisticated shopping center. There's a focus on antiques and boutiques, but opportunities run the gamut from market stalls to quality department stores featuring avant-garde goods.

WHERE TO STAY

From the seaside at Scheveningen to the heart of The Hague, choices range from rooms in grand, century-old "establishments" with superb service to small home-like hotels.

WHERE TO EAT

Indonesian food is in plentiful supply, since The Hague is home to the Indonesian community in Holland. But from *hutspot* (stew) to haute cuisine, and from *nieuwe haring* (fresh herring) stands in the courtyard of the Binnenhof Parliament compound to fine seafood in view of the fishing fleet at Scheveningen, you'll find most anything you want in the way of eating in The Hague.

ARRIVING

The Hague is somewhat closer to Rotterdam than Amsterdam on the main rail line between those two cities (a trip which takes slightly over an hour). Trains run in both directions several times hourly, as do trains to/from Schiphol Airport (a half-hour ride). For purposes of visiting The Hague by foot, **Centraal Station (CS)** should be your stop, although there's more frequent service to the **Hollands Spoor (HS)**, from which there are trams and buses to the *Centrum*, about one mile. The Hague can be reached by motorway and other roads.

ENTERTAINMENT AND EVENTS

In addition to the ongoing afterdark illumination of main buildings (Binnenhof, Mauritshuis, etc.), The Hague/Scheveningen have a number of colorful occasions worth noting. The VVV publishes a monthly events booklet (*VVV Info*), and will book tickets (in person only) for performances in The Hague and elsewhere in Holland. The **Nederlands Dans Theater**, a dance company that has acquired an excellent international reputation, and the **Residentie Orkest** *(Den Haag Philharmonic)*, are housed, respectively, in the Dutch Dance Theater and the Dr. Anton Philips Hall, a successful and striking cultural complex on the Spui in the center of the city.

TRAVEL TIPS

The center of The Hague tends to be quiet and relatively unpeopled at night, though it's safe to wander around.

THE HAGUE IN CONTEXT

More than 750 years ago, the Counts of Holland built a first structure on a site where soon would rise the *Binnenhof* (Inner Court), the building that remains the seat of government for the Netherlands' vigorous democracy. The original building, probably a hunting lodge, situated by a pond in the woods lying between coastal dunes and waterlogged land, was begun by Floris IV, Count of Holland from 1222 to 1234. The place is first mentioned in 1242 as *Die Haghe* ("the hedge"), from which comes the city's formal name, *'s-Gravenhage* ("the counts' hedge"); most Dutch shorten it back again to *Den Haag*. Though he never lived there, Floris's son Count Willem II, elected King of the Romans and German Emperor at Aachen in 1247, who was impressed with the German nobility's regal standard of living, began to build a castle more in keeping with his status. Willem's son Floris V, who by then also numbered Zeeland among his territorial possessions, was able to add the **Ridderzaal** (Hall of Knights), an impressive Scheldt-style gothic building, by selling off his inherited rights to the Scottish throne for a handsome fee. The building complex became the *Binnenhof* and was the Count's preferred residence by his death in 1296.

The first Counts of Holland to occupy the Binnenhof with their entire court and families were Albrecht of Bavaria and his son Willem VI, in about 1400. The settlement immediately surrounding the palace was greatly expanded at the time since it had to be largely self-sufficient. Stables, livestock, vegetable gardens (planted on what today is the *Plein*), a saddlery, smithy, bottling room, bakery, and chapel all existed within the Binnenhof. Outside the core settlement was the *Buitenhof* (Outer Court), where craft- and trades-people kept close, in hope of commissions. Today's *Plaats* was a meeting place just outside the court gate (now the Prison Gate or *Gevangenpoort*). The *Vijverberg* was once a playground among the trees, and the *Kneuterdijk* served as tournament grounds. The yet tree-lined *Lange Voorhout*, then an entry into the *Haagse Bos* (Hague Woods), often was brightened with the canopies of tents in which court guests who could not be accommodated at the Binnenhof palace camped. When farms grew up slightly farther afield, The Hague could actually be called a village.

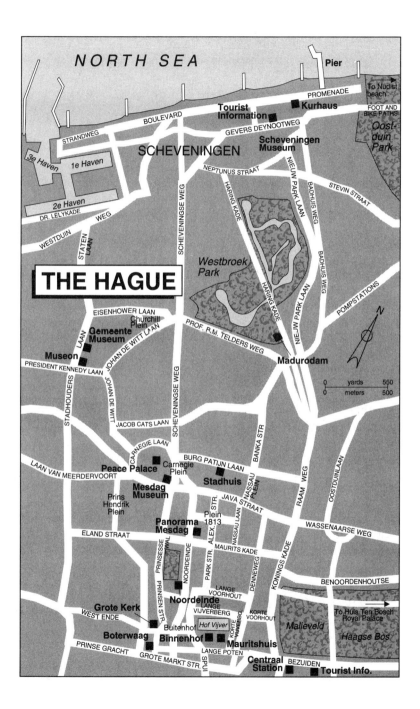

NORTH SEA

Pier

To Nudist
beach

PROMENADE

FOOT AND
BIKE PATHS

Tourist
Information

Kurhaus

BOULEVARD

GEVERS DEYNOOTWEG

Oost-
duin
Park

STRANDWEG

Scheveningen
Museum

SCHEVENINGEN

3e Haven

1e Haven

NEPTUNUS STRAAT

HARING KADE

NIEUW PARK LAAN

BADHUIS WEG

STEVIN STRAAT

2e Haven

DR. LELYKADE

WEG

WESTDUIN

STATEN
LAAN

Westbroek
Park

HARING KADE

BADHUIS WEG

THE HAGUE

POMPSTATIONS

EISENHOWER LAAN

Churchill
Plein

PROF. R.M. TELDERS WEG

NIEUW PARK LAAN

N

Gemeente
Museum

JOHAN DE WITT LAAN

Museon

LAAN

Madurodam

PRESIDENT KENNEDY LAAN

SCHEVENINGSE WEG

yards 550

STADHOUDERS

JOHAN DE WITT

meters 500

JACOB CATS LAAN

SCHEVENINGSE WEG

BANKA STR.

CARNEGIE LAAN

BURG PATIJN LAAN

Peace Palace

Carnegie
Plein

NASSAU PLEIN

RAAM WEG

OOSTDUINLAAN

LAAN VAN MEERDERVOORT

Mesdag
Museum

Stadhuis

Prins
Hendrik
Plein

JAVA STRAAT

WASSENAARSE WEG

Plein
1813

ALEX. STR.

Panorama
Mesdag

ELAND STRAAT

NASSAULAAN

PARK STR.

MAURITS KADE

DENNEWEG

KONINGS KADE

BENOORDENHOUTSE

PRINSESSE WAL

NOORDEINDE

LANGE
VOORHOUT

Grote Kerk

PRINSEN STR.

Noordeinde

WEST ENDE

LANGE
VIJVERBERG

KORTE
VOORHOUT

To Huis Ten Bosch
Royal Palace

Malieveld

Buitenhof

Hof Vijver

KORTE VIJVERBG.

Haagse Bos

Boterwaag

Binnenhof

PRINSE GRACHT

Mauritshuis

LANGE POTEN

GROTE MARKT STR.

SPUI

Centraal
Station

BEZUIDEN

Tourist Info.

Holland and Zeeland, together with the rest of the Netherlands (which then included what today is Belgium), came under the rule of the dukes of Burgundy during the mid-15th century, but day-to-day administration remained with the *Stadholder* (regional ruler), who resided in The Hague. The Burgundian dukes kept court in Brussels, but the peripatetic nature of their business brought them regularly to the Binnenhof. On two occasions Philip the Good held magnificant banquets in the Ridderzaal for the knights of the *Order of the Golden Fleece* (who also attended services in 1456 at the *Grote Kerk* near the Buitenhof).

Early in the 16th century, sovereignty over the Netherlands had passed to Emperor Charles V, who was also the ruler of Spain and Burgundy. By then, The Hague was a prosperous "open" place, with many mansions among its parks. To this day, The Hague looks un-like most other old Dutch towns. This is the result of it never having been a city-wall-enclosed fortified town where space was scarce. (In many Dutch towns taxes on homeowners to pay for the upkeep of the town walls were based on the width of a dwelling, which led to the building of narrow, deep, tall houses.) Without the space con-strictions imposed by city walls, The Hague was set out with wide tree-lined avenues, and mansions amid park settings. Emperor Charles V found The Hague pleasing, and sought to protect its nat-ural beauty. His son Philip II, however, had little love for any part of Holland, and had other things on his mind when he sent his Spanish forces through The Hague.

Its lack of defensive walls came home to haunt The Hague during Holland's *Eighty Years' War* with the Spanish. When the Spanish marched north, the government in the *Binnenhof* under Stadholder **Willem the Silent**, prince of Orange, fled to nearby, somewhat-safer Delft, which was walled. The Hague lay in the pathway to the Dutch cities—Leiden, Haarlem, and Alkmaar—destined for seige by the Spanish, and passing troops, friend or foe, burned and abused it. At one point, Delft burghers proposed burning down what remained of The Hague in order to force the Spanish out of their camping site in the Hague Woods. But Willem defused the idea, suspecting it to be inspired by selfish motives to move the government to Delft.

After Willem's Spanish-inspired assassination in Delft in 1574, the executive of the *States of Holland* resolved to meet only in The Hague. (Their decision was political since The Hague had never had a seat in the assembly of the States because it had never received a town charter, and thus aroused less jealousy than the selection of any *official* town as the seat of government would have.) In 1588, the

States General, which represented all the seven united Dutch provinces, selected The Hague as its headquarters for the same diplomatic reason. Thenceforth, nearly all bodies associated with the government of the Netherlands have located themselves in or around the *Binnenhof*.

As The Hague entered the 17th century, it quickly grew in importance, attracting to its democratic court nobility, merchants, musicians, craftsmen, and architects. The Hague became one of the most important diplomatic posts for foreigners, a prime gathering point for international statesmen. So much so that one contemporary Englishman wrote of it as "the whispering gallery" of Europe by the time the Republic of the United Netherlands had won full recognition when the *Eighty Years' War* was officially ended by the *Peace of Munster* in 1648.

When **Willem II** died in 1650, several Dutch provinces, including powerful Holland, decided not to appoint a new Stadholder. Instead, a role of *Grand Pensionary* was instituted, the holder of that title being the effective leader of the Dutch Republic. **Johan De Witt** served with distinction in the office of Grand Pensionary, and during his leadership the Dutch overseas empire increased substantially. Simultaneously, Johan's brother **Cornelius** distinguished himself as a naval commander against English and French fleets.

Despite this, the brothers' policies became unpopular in 1672. Cornelius De Witt, unjustly accused of plotting against young Willem, Prince of Orange, was imprisoned in the *Gevangenpoort*. In one of Holland's least laudable incidents, political enemies sent a message to Johan under Cornelius' name, asking him to come to the prison. Though friends and his daughter feared a trap and urged him not to go, the loyal Johan felt he had a duty to his brother if he were in need. The message had indeed been false, and now both brothers were under arrest. De Witt disparagers plied the impassioned masses assembled outside the prison with brandy and wine, maneuvering them into a riotous mood. Although legitimate cavalry troops were sent to control the crowd, they were cleverly tricked into leaving, and storming of the prison by an enraged, drunken mob commenced.

Once inside the prison, the rioters found Cornelius lying down, racked with pain from days of torture, unable to stand, and his brother Johan reading to him from the Bible. Both brothers were hauled from the cell, shoved down the prison stairs, and became separated from each other. In the street below, Cornelius was struck on the head and trampled to death. Johan lasted a few minutes longer, before a pike was driven into his face, and he was shot in the neck. It is said that as he fell he managed to clasp his hands in the direction of heaven. Steps from the Gevangenpoort prison (now a museum where the De Witt cell is on view), on the *Plaats*, is a statue of Johan De Witt.

Later in 1672, when France invaded Holland, and threats along its coast came from the combined fleets of the French and English navies, the *States General* once again turned to the *House of Orange* for leadership. They called for **Prince Willem III** (1650–1702), who, in addition to being the Dutch Stadholder, was also to become **King William** of England and Ireland, through marriage to **Mary**, daughter of James II, with whom he became joint English ruler. Naturally, Willem's joint position made The Hague even more of an international meeting center for diplomats and merchants. Even after Willem's death in 1702, splendor continued at the court in The Hague. The pomp and pageantry included mock sea battles on the *Hofvijver* lake by the *Binnenhof*, royal processions through the streets with flaming torches, fireworks displays, and seafront outings at Scheveningen.

During the French rule of the Netherlands from 1795 to 1813, the matter of The Hague not being an official town was rectified by an unexpected supporter. In 1806, Napoleon had his brother **Louis Bonaparte**—who had tried to resist the invitation—come to Holland to act in his place as ruler. Louis arrived at The Hague, which doesn't seem to have suited him. But before he left, first for Utrecht and then Amsterdam, Louis awarded The Hague its first full civic charter.

In 1818, one Jacob Pronk opened a wooden "bathing machine" establishment on the dunes at The Hague's seaside neighbor village of Scheveningen. It consisted of guests "curing" themselves by sitting in sheltered tubs of "seawater with healing power" atop the dunes. Later, Pronk placed two bathing machines right in the surf, with attendants close at hand to help the daring participants. The business was so profitable that it was taken over by Scheveningen village leaders in 1828, and seaside resort activities have been a main business ever since.

Scheveningen's outer and first inner harbor were dug in 1904, and fishing remains a mainstay of the economy. The harbor is home to one of the largest herring fleets in Holland. For the opening of the fishing season in May on *Vlaggetjesdag* (flag day), the fleet is decked out in colorful pennants and more fishermen's wives than usual wear the local costume (long black dress, striped apron, black shawl, and ornamented starched-white headcover). It's still tradition that the first barrel of *nieuwe haring* (fresh, young herring) is delivered with ceremony to the Queen.

The **Peace Palace**, completed in 1913, was an outgrowth of a call for international peace by **Czar Nicholas II of Russia** on August 28, 1898, during a conference that he held in The Hague. In the U.S., **Andrew Carnegie** heeded the call and donated $1.5 million for a building to house various international institutions.

As the seat of government, The Hague had responsibility for, and a resulting influence over, the administration of Dutch colonies, particularly the supremely important **Indonesia**. The island archipelago of Indonesia (today, the fifth largest country in the world based on population) gained its independence in 1949, at which time Indonesian nationals were given the opportunity to move to Holland. The majority who did so settled in The Hague, as did a number of retired Dutch military officers who served in Indonesia, as well as returning executives who had worked in corporations there.

Though its population today has reached 450,000, in certain respects The Hague remains a small town. Nevertheless, its stores and restaurants, and their clientele, reflect the cosmopolitan character of the town that the International Court of Justice calls home. The city also has another instance of "split personality." The Hague favors diplomacy, dignity, and decorum; royal residences and elegant townhouses; well-endowed museums and well-tended lawns. In The Hague, the Dutch prefer to stand on ceremony, and take pride and pleasure in their history and heraldry. Yet, mere minutes from the staid, stately center of the city proper is its seaside escape valve: Scheveningen.

At **Scheveningen** (pronounced *approximately* SCKAY-ven-ing), propriety can be dropped—though some *Hagenaars* don't, as attested to by those who stride the North Sea strand (beach) in business suits and shoes. Scheveningen boasts resort amenities and activities, from wind-screened cafes *on* the sand and sunbathing pits *in* the sand to a gambling casino. From the seafront **Promenade** and **Entertainment Pier** that reaches out over the waves, it's a few minutes' walk north to a naturist (nudist) beach; just to the south is the centuries-old fishing village where fishermen's wives still wear their traditional Dutch costume.

In The Hague, there's larger-than-life pageantry when royal resident **Queen Beatrix** arrives in a golden coach drawn by eight matched horses and uniformed honor guard to open Parliament in September. In another corner of the city, ordinary mortals can play *Gulliver* among the *Lilliputians* in the 1:25 scale miniature Holland at **Madurodam**. But everywhere it's evident that The Hague celebrates rather than suffers its split personality.

GUIDEPOSTS

Telephone Code 070

Tourist Inf. VVV • *In The Hague*: Koningin Julianaplein 30 (in Babylon shopping center, next to CS): open mid-April–mid-Sept. Mon.–Sat. 9 a.m.–9 p.m., Sun. 10 a.m.– 5 p.m.; from mid-Sept.–mid-April, Mon.–Sat. 9 a.m.–6 p.m., Sun. 10 a.m.–5 p.m., closed Jan. 1, Dec. 25 and 26; *In Scheveningen*: Gevers Deynootweg 1134; same hours as above; ☎ *3546200, FAX 3615459.*

Emergencies • Police: ☎ *3104911.* Physician (general info) ☎ *3455300.* Dentist (day, night, weekend) ☎ *3974491.* Pharmacies (evenings and weekends) ☎ *3451000.*

Lost and Found • Police (Mon.–Fri. 9 a.m.–3:30 p.m.: ☎ *3108015.*

Transport Inf. • HMT (public transport) ☎ *06-9292.*

Money • Exchange office at Centraal Station open daily 9 a.m.–9 p.m. (Sun. from 10 a.m.)

Books • American Discount Book Centers (for U.S. and U.K. titles): Spuistraat 72; ☎ *3642742.*

WHAT TO SEE AND DO

Because attractions in The Hague are spread out, they are grouped below by location. Those listed under *The Hague Centrum* are all within roughly a mile of one another. A booklet from the VVV, a self-guided walking tour *Along Seven Centuries of Hague Architecture* (Dfl. 2.50), begins at *Het Plein*, behind the *Binnenhof*, and discusses some 45 sites enroute.

THE HAGUE CENTRUM TO PEACE PALACE

Mauritshuis

Korte Vijverberg 8; Tues.-Sat. 10 a.m.–5 p.m., Sun. 11 a.m.–5 p.m., closed Mon.; ☎ *3654779; fee.* Adjoining the Binnenhof and facing the Hofvijer, a small lake with swans, a fountain jet, flowing flower boxes, and tree-shaded banks, is the recently restored Mauritshuis, acknowledged as one of the finest small museums in the world. Ensconced in a small 17th-century classical mansion, the Mauritshuis imparts a sense of intimacy and welcome, making you feel as if you're visiting an extraordinary private collection. The Mauritshuis owns about 900 works, of which some 350 are exhibited at any one time (head for the upper floor for the Golden Age favorites). The core of the collection, which numbers 10 Jan Steens, three Vermeers (including *View of Delft*) and 14 Rembrandts (including *The Anatomy Lesson*), consists of paintings acquired since the 18th century by the princes of the House of Orange. Some of the paintings were seized by Napoleon in 1795, but returned in 1816, after his defeat at Waterloo in Belgium. In 1822, the paintings were first put on display in the Mauritshuis, where they could be seen on Wednesdays and Saturday mornings by anyone "who was well-dressed and not accompanied by children." There is a fine museum shop and cafe in the basement. An oddity the museum enjoys is the payment of your entry fee when you exit.

Binnenhof   ★★
Information Center, Binnenhof 8a; Mon.–Sat. 10 a.m.-4 p.m., closed Sun, hols.; for booking conducted tours ☎ 3646144; fee. The heart of The Hague is the historic Binnenhof, a complex of portals, courtyards, and palaces built beginning in the 13th century, which is the home of the Dutch Parliament. Tours include 1st and 2nd Chambers when Parliament is not in session, and the ★ ★ **Ridderzaal** (*Hall of the Knights*), a huge, high-ceiling banqueting room, which is one of Europe's medieval architectural treasures. Its decorations include 17th-century Flemish tapestries, a large rose window with the coats of arms of Netherlands, counts and dukes, leaded-glass windows with the coats of arms of the principal Dutch cities, and the flags of the 12 Dutch provinces. Today used as the throne room for the queen's annual *State Opening of Parliament* and state receptions, the Ridderzaal was used by Napoleon as a stable. The ★ *Information Center* has a slide show in English and permanent exhibitions on Holland's government and the Royal Family.

Museum Bredius   ★
Lange Vijverberg 14; Tues.–Sun. noon–5 p.m.; ☎ 3620729. Comprised of the fine private painting collection of **Abraham Bredius**, a former director of the *Mauritshuis Museum*, the recently reopened Bredius Museum is in new quarters, a beautifully restored manor house facing the Mauritshuis across the *Binnenhof's* picturesque *Hofvijver* lake which is lined with large pink-blossomed horse chestnut trees. Bredius collected works by Dutch painters, particularly those of the 17th century; pieces on display include those by Rembrandt, Steen, Van Ostade, and several wonderful ones by Dutch "little masters" Simon Verelst and Hendrik Aerts.

Panorama Mesday   ★★
Zeestraat 65b; Mon.–Sat. 10 a.m.–5 p.m., Sun., hols. from noon; ☎ 3642563; fee. One of the founding figures of The Hague School was H. W. Mesdag. In 1880, he and a group of artist friends painted a protest against authorities who had decided to cart away the sand dunes at Scheveningen to construct a housing project. The result: the

protest made its point, and what is probably the largest canvas in the world—45 feet high, 400 feet in circumference—remains housed in the Panorama Mesdag Museum, specifically designed to display the recently restored painting. At the museum, after progressing through several rooms of smaller works by Mesdag (his subject was almost always Scheveningen: its seascape, fishing fleet, and classic views of women in the local costume waiting on the shore) and his wife (Sina van Houten), visitors pass through a tunnel, and emerge at the top of a flight of stairs in the center of a painted in-the-round scene as seen from atop the dunes at Scheveningen. The details of Dutch fisherfolk life as it was a century ago are marvelous. A taped commentary (multi-lingual, with English) gives some history on panoramas (cycloramas), a popular painting form from the period (though few have survived), appreciated both as a work of art and as a historical document. Panorama Mesday, in which the sense of optical illusion is extraordinary, is made even more realistic since it employs no artificial light; when it's gloomy outside, the beach scene inside is appropriately gray, since the only light that enters the museum comes through a glass dome. Near the exit is the permanent exhibit *The Panorama Phenomenon.*

Peace Palace   ★

Carnegieplein 2; from May–Sept. Mon.–Fri. 10 a.m.–4 p.m., from Oct.–April Mon.–Fri. 10 a.m.–3 p.m.; guided tours at 10, 11, 2, 3; ☎ *3469680; fee; take Trams #7, 8.* Despite its relatively recent appearance on the scene (completed in 1913), the Peace Palace has become a symbol of The Hague. Home of the Permanent Court of International Law (since 1922) and the Academy of International Law (since 1923), the Peace Palace was built with a $1.5 million donation by Scottish-American steel-magnate Andrew Carnegie after the first international conference for the suppression of war was held in The Hague (at Huis ten Bosch) at the insistence of Czar Nicholas II of Russia. As a result of the conference, the Permanent Court of Arbitration was established, and its need for a suitable home reached the ears of Carnegie. The foundation stone was laid in 1907, during a second peace conference in The Hague (held in the Ridderzaal). The Peace Palace is built in the Flemish Renaissance style (by architect Louis Cordonnier of Lille, France, whose design won out over 200 competitors), and the ornate interior is rich in contributions of materials and national craftmanship from dozens of countries. The bronze entrance door is from Belgium, the marble statue *Justice by Peace* from the U.S., the stained-glass windows in the Great Hall from the U.K.

EN ROUTE TO SCHEVENINGEN

Gemeentemuseum   ★ ★

Stadhouderslaan 41; Tues.–Sun. 11 a.m.– 5 p.m., closed Mon.; ☎ *3381111; fee; take Tram #10.* The paintings of a relatively recent Dutch master are highlighted at the Gemeentemuseum (municipal museum), which has the world's largest collection (154) of works by **Piet Mondriaan** (1872–1944). The unique group is particularly strong in Mondriaan's early works, which show his movement from early dark landscapes, through his "blue" period, to the totally abstract primary color blocks and black line-pieces for which he is most known, and was most influential. Dutch painter **Karel Appel**, a member of the COBRA group who has lived in New York for many years, has donated more than 50 drawings to the museum. The building (1935) itself was the swan-song of the grand old man of modern Dutch architecture, **H. P. Berlage**. The **Hall**, with its concrete skeleton visible, is the hub of the museum, whose tiles, lighting (all natural, even in the showcases), colors, and other details all bear the Berlage stamp. The 19th- and 20th-century collections contain paintings and sculpture from many European masters, as well as from The Hague School.

Madurodam   ★★

Haringkade 175; daily 9 a.m.–10:30 p.m. except closes 11 p.m. June–Aug., 9:30 p.m. Sept, 6 p.m. Oct–early Jan., closed early Jan. to March; ☎ *3553900; fee; Trams #1, 9.* The Hague's most whimsical attraction, Madurodam, is located midway between the town's seat of power and the sea. A miniature man-made Holland, at 1/25 scale, Madurodam fills four acres with replicas of 150 of Holland's most famous buildings (including The Hague's Binnenhof), arranged into a tiny working town complete with trains, minimarching bands, a bicycle jam, a small Schiphol airport with KLM craft, and a pint-size port of Rotterdam. The attention to detail at Madurodam delights the child in every adult, and children are enchanted to feel as big as *Gulliver* among the *Lilliputians* at Madurodam.

Note: Madurodam's endearing detail is not as visible under the mini-town's night lights, and the script of its evening **sound and light** show, which I had looked forward to, seemed contrived. I recommend a daylight visit to Madurodam, and a visit to the real *Binnenhof* for its romantic after-dark illumination.

SCHEVENINGEN

If you find the name of this seaside resort hard to pronounce, apparently you're in the company of almost everyone in the world who isn't Dutch. And the Dutch have even put their lives on the line over that fact. During Holland's World War II occupation by the Nazis, in order to determine if the person to whom they were speaking was Dutch or German, members of the Dutch resistance asked the other person to pronounce *Scheveningen*—it's the "sch" sound that makes or breaks it. If the person did so satisfactorily, it was assumed he was Dutch. (A backup tongue-twisting test sometimes used by the Dutch to test the Nazis was the word *Massachusettes*: now that's international for you).

Kurhaus   ★★

Steigenberger Kurhaus Hotel (see also "Where to Stay"), Gevers Dey-

nootplein 30; ☎ *3520052.* The 1885 Kurhaus is as much a Scheveningen monument as it is a five-star hotel. The magnificent and enormous Kurzaal, with its restored frescoed, gilted, and skylighted domed ceiling, and Corinthian columns supporting the balcony, has been the scene of many memorable events in the past century. Many important people, either performing in the concerts that have long been a tradition in the Kurzaal—the Berlin Philharmonic (under the baton of von Karajan), Bruno Walter, Stokowsky, violinist Yehudi Menuhin, Leonard Bernstein (who wielded his baton here in his European debut), singer Marlene Dietrich, Edith Piaf, Jacques Brel, Maurice Chevalier, Vladimir Horowitz, Charles Aznavour, to name a few—or passing through the great hall to meetings or other business— Churchill, Truman, Crawford, Kissinger, Brandt, Hepburn, NATO meeting attendees—have filled more than one leather-bound hotel guestbook. So, whether you're a guest or not, this is the one interior that's a "must see" in Scheveningen.

Promenade/Boulevard   ★

The broad Promenade/Boulevard, which runs for a mile or more parallel to the beach and open North Sea, just above the sandy Strand, is lined with glass-encased, wind-sheltered cafes and coffee houses, souvenir and snack kiosks, and a huge, heated, artificial wave swimming pool/exercise complex.

The Pier   ★

At the Promenade; ☎ *3543677.* The present Pier opened in 1961, rebuilt after the preceding pleasure jetty had been deep-sixed by the Nazis. The Pier reaches out more than 400 yards over the North Sea, offering dining, sun terraces, an amusement arcade, a 45-meter-high **belvedere** (viewing tower), a fishing platform, and shops on its four "islands." There are **fireworks** from the Pier on Friday nights at 11 p.m. in summer. A quiet corner in one of the eateries at its end is a good place from which to watch the sun sink into the North Sea at day's end.

SHOPPING

Most department and clothing stores are located in the *Centrum* (around and off *Spui Straat, Hoog Straat, Grote Markt Straat*), which has a number of pedestrian streets. The **Passage** is an elegant enclosed shopping arcade. Antiques shops line the **Denneweg**, behind the *Hotel Des Indes* on *Lange Voorhout*, and **Noordeinde**, the street named for the palace on it that serves as the Queen's official office. There are some 100 to haunt in The Hague. (Ask at the VVV for the brochure *Antique Walk.*) Antiques, curios, art, books and bric-a-brac also are sold at the **open-air market** on *Lange Voorhout* Thurs. and Sun., mid-May–end Sept., 9 a.m.–9 p.m. From Oct. 1-mid-May, the market is Thurs. only, and moves to the nearby *Plein.* Late-night shopping (9 p.m.) in The Hague is Thurs., with most stores closed Sun. In Scheveningen, especially on and near the beach, opening hours for the plentiful casual shops are longer: seven days a week and, from mid-March–mid-Oct., up until 10 p.m.

WHERE TO STAY

The two deluxe properties described here won't save you much over similar properties in Amsterdam, but both have stellar settings; the character and charm that can come with 100+ years of history; and standards of service on which they pride themselves. If you'll have to be content just to walk through their lobbies, make sure you do. There's no lack of other comfortable corners to book yourself into, keeping in mind that pleasant, less expensive small hotels in Scheveningen—most of them family establishments—in summer are in high demand from Dutch, German, and many other tourists, since this is Holland's premier coastal resort. Make reservations as far ahead as possible, and check about minimum length-of-stay requirements in summer. Especially busy is the second weekend in July, when the **North Sea Jazz Festival** (four days) fills the town with music and fans. The VVV will help with accommodations if you decide on the spot you want to stay overnight. Hotels have been separated under The Hague and Scheveningen.

THE HAGUE

Hotel des Indes (Inter-Continental) ★ ★ ★ ★ ★

Lange Voorhout 54, 2514 EG; ☎ *3632932, FAX 3451721, reservations U.S. and Can.* ☎ *800-327-0200.* Kings, presidents, and statesmen from many countries can attest to the fact that the Hotel des Indes has always held a grand position in The Hague. Built as a lavish town house by a baron, upon his death the family sold it to a local hotelier, and the palatial building was born as the *Hotel des Indes* (a name chosen to combine both French chic and the exoticism of the Dutch East Indies). Many of the baron's original furnishings remain intact in public rooms: massive crystal chandeliers, glittering mirrors, and rich brocade wall coverings. The magnificent central lounge, still the place to take tea, has seen many special guests pass through: Lindbergh, Czar Nicholas II, Eisenhower, Stravinsky, the Dutch spy Mata Hari, and Bing Crosby. The great Russian ballerina Anna Pavlova died here of pneumonia. With only 77 rooms, service can be as attentive as you expect, and the location in this "city of Royal Residence" on the lovely Lange Voorhout is superb. **Le Restaurant**, with its white-glove service, is well-regarded for its classical French flair and fare. The lobby bar is a cosmopolitan meeting place, and the lobby an after theater or symphony rendezvous. Parking available. ***Very Expensive***

Hotel Corona ★ ★ ★ ★

Buitenhof 39-42, 2513 AH; ☎ *3637930, FAX 3615785, reservations U.S.* ☎ *800-221-1074, reservations Can.* ☎ *800-344-4034.* Parliament is just around the corner and, with a handsome terrace cafe in front for those who want to be seen and heard, and widely-spaced tables at the hotel's outstanding restaurant inside for those who don't, the Corona is understandably popular with Dutch politicians. The hotel, with its 26 rooms, all of which were recently renovated in contemporary style with pastel colors, dates from the early 1900s (although the building in the 18th century was a lively coffee house), and its handsome marble and mahogany lobby gracefully reflects its age. Parking available close to hotel.   *Expensive*

Park Hotel Den Haag   ★★★★

Molenstraat 53, 2513 BJ; ☎ *3624371, FAX 3614525.* Built in 1910 as a hotel, the breakfast (included) room overlooks the Noordeinde Palace gardens; some of the 114 guest rooms have balconies with views on to the garden. The Park is conveniently tucked into an antique-and-print-shop-lined street near the center of The Hague. Dignity, not flash, dictates the decor, which has a mix of modern and traditional furniture, and some nice architectural details, including a *Jugenstil* (art nouveau) five-story stairwell in yellow brick. Rooms are spacious, and have large marble baths. There's a lobby bar, but no in-hotel restaurant since there are so many others in the vicinity. The hotel has its own parking garage.   *Moderate*

SCHEVENINGEN

Kurhaus Hotel (Steigenberger)   ★★★★★

Gevers Deynootplein 30, Scheveningen 2586 CK; ☎ *3520052, FAX 3500911, reservations U.S.* ☎ *800-777-5848.* Scheveningen's Grande Dame by the Sea, the Kurhaus went from the very real threat of the wrecker's ball (in the early 1970s) to a glittering celebratory ball in honor of its salvation, complete renovation, and centennial in 1985. The huge **Kurzaal**, with its magnificent painted, skylit ceiling, the dome of which seems to reach halfway to heaven, is headquarters and highlight of the hotel, and the wonderful North Sea views out the enormous windows simply reinforce the sense of being someplace special. And I love the unlikely and light-hearted contrast of the blue sculpture of a mermaid sitting in an easy chair reading a book amid the grandeur. The ambiance of the evening buffet in the Kurzaal is ineffably European: live piano music floats into the lofty space, and you can enjoy an eating experience that can be drawn out to save the setting. (A breakfast buffet in the same superb setting is included for overnight guests). Of the Kurhaus' 241 guest rooms, the best ones face the sea, with French windows opening out onto small wrought-iron balconies. A number of rooms are modest in size, but there's plenty of room to spread out on the property. There's a terrace cafe from which to survey the sea and the Pier, and large wave pool, sauna, and exercise complex.

Off the Kurzaal, under a red awning, is **Casino Scheveningen** *(daily 1:30 p.m.–2 a.m.; minimum age 18; passport identification required)*, which, while perfectly enjoyable if you like casinos, isn't as elegant as the Kurzaal; there are 24 tables for French and American Roulette, Blackjack, and Baccarat for the big spenders. The hotel's **Kandinsky**

Restaurant, in a striking *art deco* room with six original lithographs by the artist, is the hotel's à la carte restaurant, with many of its 60 seats overlooking the sea.   ***Very Expensive***

Bel Park

Belgischeplein 38, 2587 AT; ☎ *3505000, FAX 3523242.* Two rambling turn-of-the-century homes on a green roundabout in a residential neighborhood make this a homey, pleasant choice. It's a 15-minute walk to the Pier, with a tram nearby. Airy, light, and freshly painted, all 14 rooms (and a two-room suite) have shower and toilet, with price varying somewhat with size. No elevator, but wide straight stairs. Free on-street parking.   ***Inexpensive***

Aquarius

Zeekant 107, 2586 JJ; ☎ *3543543, FAX 3543684.* Only a road separates these three connected houses that have been made into a 21-room hotel from the boulevard and beach. Some rooms front sea, several have balconies from which one gets a view of the Pier. Room decor is fairly basic; all rooms have private toilet and curtained shower. There's a breakfast room, pleasant restaurant with three-course menus, and a few tables on the seafront terrace outside. No elevator. Near trams. Parking available.   ***Inexpensive***

Hotel Seinduin

Seinpostduin 15, 2586 EA; ☎ *3551971, FAX 3557891.* Located a block from the boulevard along the beach (near the point from which Mesdag painted the Panorama), a pleasant walk to the Pier. All 18 rooms have shower, toilet, telephone, TV, and mini-bar. Convenient to VVV and trams. Basic but pleasant. On-street parking.   ***Inexpensive***

WHERE TO EAT

Several of the hotels mentioned in the previous section have highly-regarded restaurants, and these should be considered among your dining choices in The Hague. Booking is recommended for the better restaurants. An appetizing aspect of the Dutch colonial inheritance is the large number of *Indonesian restaurants*; this is especially true in The Hague, which has as many as a hundred. **Garoeda** *(Kneuterdijk 18a; open daily; reservations at* ☎ *3465319; inexpensive)* is the one Indonesians themselves, and Hagenaars who have lived there, consider the best, and its location couldn't be much more in the center of things. The dignified atmosphere lends itself to the ceremony of the *rijsttaffel,* but you can dine with fewer dishes if you desire.

De Salon *(Molenstraat 52;* ☎ *3654030; open daily; inexpensive),* which stands out with its distinctive Jugenstil brick exterior, also stands out with Hagenaars for reasonably priced bistro/grill-style meals in the center of town. Located by the picturesque Oude Stadhuis (and in appropriate weather there is a terrace cafe out front from which to view it) is **'t Goude Hooft** *(Groenmarkt 13; open daily;* ☎ *3469713; inexpensive)* which, in addition to the outdoor tables, has its cozy cafe where the three-course Tourist Menu (Dfl. 19.75) is served, and a restaurant upstairs where Dutch specialties are on the menu. Though it serves continental cuisine, **'t Gemeste Schaap** *(Raamstraat 9; closed Thurs.;* ☎ *3639572; moderate)* has a delightful old Dutch interior not far from the Grote Kerk. Whether or not you attend a performance in The Hague's Music and Dance Hall, **Cafe Piccolo Mondo** ("small world") at the Dr. Anton Philipszaal proves intriguing, since it's shaped like an ice cream cone.

Behind the Lange Voorhout is the cozy **Oud Haagsch Pannekoekhuis** *(Maliestraat 10, off Denneweg;* ☎ *3462474; closed Sun. and Mon., inexpensive)*, where you can treat yourself to a plate-size pancake, sweet or savory (my favorite is cheese and chunk ginger) amid a typical old Dutch decor of red-and-white-checked tablecloths and old brass and copper utensils. You can almost count on seeing a Dutch grandmother treating the family. Finish the meal with coffee or a Heineken on the terrace of the pub a few doors down, overlooking a picturesque, unusual canaled corner of The Hague. Even if you're on the hunt for Dutch or English antiques along the Denneweg, you might get the taste for Italian. If so, you won't have far to go to find **Panino Teca** *(Denneweg 41; open daily,* ☎ *3652026; inexpensive)*.

In Scheveningen, local patrons love the **Vispaleis** (fish palace): it's their favorite herring stand at the second inner harbor (Dr. Lelykade). Close at hand is **Ducdalf** *(Dr. Lelykade 5; open daily;* ☎ *3557692; moderate)*, offering a wide variety of seafood (herring, sole, North Sea gray shrimp, Zeeland oysters); it would be hard for it to be fresher, since the fishing fleet and fish auction house are at the next harbor over.

IN VOORBURG

Vreudg and Rust Restaurant-Hotel

Oosteinde 14, 2271 EH, Voorburg; open daily for lunch noon–2:30 p.m., dinner 6:30–10:00 p.m.; restaurant expensive/very expensive, hotel moderate; for reservations ☎ *070-3872081, FAX 070-3877715.* This highly-touted restaurant, within walking distance of the charming old center of Voorburg, a suburb of The Hague, is a 1751 mansion that sits on parkland that runs down to the river Vliet. Refurbished in 1989, the 14 rooms feature such individual details as beamed ceilings, red marble baths with heated marble floors, fine plaster work, and crystal sconces.

IN WASSENAAR

Auberge de Kievet

Stoeplaan 27, Wassenaar-Zuid; open daily lunch noon–3 p.m., dinner 6–10 p.m.; restaurant expensive/very expensive, hotel expensive; for reservations ☎ *(01751) 19232, FAX 10969.* A countrified mansion-inn in a fashionable, wooded suburb of The Hague, Auberge de Kievet is known first for its restaurant, though the 26 guest rooms are no less comfortable for that.

ENTERTAINMENT AND EVENTS

Queen's Birthday *(30th April)* This national holiday is celebrated in the Queen's hometown with a fun fair and street festivities on the Lange Voorhout. Shops are open.

Vlaggetjesdag (Flag Day) *(mid-May at Scheveningen harbor)* The opening of the herring season, with "dressed" fishing fleet ships, food, music, traditional crafts, and boat trips.

Fireworks *(11 p.m. from Scheveningen Pier Fri. evenings July-mid-Aug.; late Aug.)* International Firework Festival with several shows per night (check for dates and time).

North Sea Jazz Festival *(July)* This four-day event at various venues in The Hague is the most prominent jazz festival outside the U.S.

State Opening of Parliament (Prinsjesdag) *(third Tues. in Sept.)* Queen Beatrix, herself a resident of The Hague, arrives at the Binnenhof in a golden coach drawn by eight matched horses, attended by an honor guard, to give the details of the government's plans for the coming year in a speech to the first session of Parliament in the Ridderzaal.

Inquire at the VVV about Friday evening **organ concerts** at various churches in The Hague, and about concerts in the Kurzaal at the Kurhaus in Scheveningen.

DELFT

GUIDELINES FOR DELFT

SIGHTS

Delft's intimate old center is dense with delicate impressions. Along stretches of its tranquil tree-shaded canals, the luminescence seems to have been supplied by the town's 17th-century master painters, and charming street scenes of daily life that served as subjects for those artists can still be seen. Delft's ancient **Grote Markt** (the main market square), one of Holland's most magnificent, is anchored by the **Nieuwe Kerk** (new church, from 1381), and the **Stadhuis**. The **Prinsenhof**, where Willem the Silent (*Father of the Fatherland*) lived, and was slain in 1584, is an atmospheric in-town "palace" museum, just steps from a canalside mansion museum filled with old Dutch tiles. Most visitors head for **De Porceleyne Fles**, the only one of Delft's famous blue and white ware factories to have survived from the 17th century.

GETTING AROUND

Delft is definitely a place to slow your touring pace to a saunter. To be seen and savored as it should, you must walk the compact, canal-laced town. Buses and trams serve the surrounding suburbs, but not the Centrum (old center). Canal boat excursions and tours by horse-drawn tram can supplement, but shouldn't substitute for, your feet in old Delft, especially in and around the **Grote Markt**, and along the **Oude Delft**, **Hippolytusbuurt**, **Voldersgracht**, and **Koornmarkt** canals. For a unique view (and great photographs) of Delft, create your own canal cruise on rented pedal boats and kayaks. If you want to join the bicycle brigades—Delft is a university town with 16,000 students and corresponding number of two-wheelers—rent one at the rail station. That's where taxis are too.

SHOPPING

Delftware, the blue and white porcelain that's virtually synonymous with the town, should rightly top your shopping list, which is just as well since it's hard to avoid it in the shops on and just off the **Grote Markt**. The product's so pretty that the commercialism isn't offensive, though the profusion of choice (and range of quality and price) can cause confusion for the buyer.

WHERE TO STAY

There's an adequate choice of moderately priced, friendly canal-front hotels in the center of old Delft.

WHERE TO EAT

In Delft, you can dine as well as anywhere in Holland. Or catch quicker nourishment around the Markt or along a canal, at one of the many cafes; some offer outside tables when the weather warrants.

ENTERTAINMENT AND EVENTS

The VVV tourist office, located on the Markt, will have the latest listings, but you can count on live carillon concerts on the famed Hemony bells of the Nieuwe Kerk on Tues., Thurs., and Sat., 11 a.m.-noon; in summer, there's also a weekly evening carillon concert (check with VVV for details). Buy a coffee or beer at one of the outside cafes to secure the equivalent of a front-row seat. Inquire, too, at the VVV about the organ concert schedule at the Oude Kerk. Delft's annual *Art and Antique Fair* (ten days in mid-Oct.), held at the Prinsenhof, is considered one of Europe's most prestigious.

ARRIVING

Located between Rotterdam and The Hague, Delft is an inter-city stop on the frequently serviced main Rotterdam-The Hague-Amsterdam rail line. The Delft station, at Van Leeuwenhoeksingel 41, decorated in old blue-and-white tiles, is slightly outside the center, a

10- or 15-minute walk to the Grote Markt. Regional buses and taxis congregate conveniently at the station. Tram #1, which connects Delft with the center of The Hague and Scheveningen (5 miles), has a Delft stop on Phoenixstraat, a 5-10-minute walk to the Markt. If arriving by car, take exit Delft-Noord or Delft Pijnacker off the A13(E19) motorway. Non-metered parking is available on the Phoenixstraat (just outside the old center).

TRAVEL TIPS

Though *not* recommended as the best way to see Delft, if **De Porceleyne Fles** is on your "must see" list and your time very limited, it's wise to get a taxi from the rail station to the factory (a fair walk, none of it within the pretty old center). The factory (at which there is on-street parking if you arrive by car) will call a taxi when you're ready to leave, and you could ask the driver for a quick ride through old Delft before being dropped back at the station.

DELFT IN CONTEXT

Although a small settlement existed previously, the real history of Delft begins with the arrival in 1075 of Duke Godfried van Lotharingen, called Govert the Hunchback, who built a fortress, probably on the site where the Stadhuis is today. He had the first canals of Delft dug, the patterns of which remain essentially the same today. Under the administration of successive Counts of Holland, Delft became a center for the exchange of agricultural goods between the village and surrounding countryside by the early 13th century. In 1226, under Count Willem II, Delft received its first charter, which included the right to hold a weekly market, which it still does (Thurs., on the Grote Markt). The name *Beesten* (animal) *Markt* recalls when pigs were sold there, though today the square's atmosphere, especially in the evening, is more like Paris' *Place du Tertre*. Delft was granted permission in 1389 to excavate the Delfshavense Schie, which provided a direct connection with the Maas River at Rotterdam, an undertaking that contributed substantially to the inland town's prosperity.

As early as the 13th century, beer brewing had developed into an important industry in Delft. By the second half of the 14th century, Delft beer boasted markets not only in Holland, but also in Flanders and Germany. The water in Delft's canals, it seems, was especially well-suited to the preparation of beer and, by the 15th century, Delft had nearly 200 beer breweries.

Another Delft industry of the day, second in success only to brewing, was cloth weaving. It expanded to the manufacture of tapestries (be sure to see the *Tapestry Hall* of the Prinsenhof) and carpets in the 16th century when emigrating Flemish weavers, fleeing difficulties caused by Catholic Spanish rulers there, settled in Delft. Street names are reminders of those days: *Voldersgracht* (Fullers Canal); *Raam* (Frame); and *Versersdijk* (Dyers' Dike).

As well as being distinguished as a center of resistance and headquarters for Dutch leader **Willem (the Silent) of Orange** during the war with the Spanish, Delft was the birthplace of some of the developing nation's proudest figures. Admirals **Piet Hein** (1577–1629) and **Marten Tromp** (1598–1653) achieved national victories that still warm the hearts of Dutch sailors, who both are buried with appropriate monuments in Delft's Oude Kerk. The town's **Hugo de Groot** (*Grotius*) (1583–1645), jurist and statesman who established the principles of international law (see "The Muse" under "The Belgian Cultural Legacy") is singled out by a statue in the center of Delft's Markt. When Holland wrested its territory free from the Spanish in the late 16th- century and began to flourish, Delft was well-positioned to share in the prosperity.

In 1572, during the *Eighty Years' War* engagements with the Spanish on Dutch soil, military leader Willem took up residence at the **Prinsenhof** in Delft (relocating from the Binnenhof in The Hague, which was less protected). Having the p'rince of Orange present within its walls conferred great prestige on Delft. He'd been an inspiring leader when Holland's major towns rose with him to resist the Spanish in the early, most trying years of the Eighty Years' War. While living in Delft, he became generally known affectionately as Father Willem and, more grandly, *Het Vader de het Vaderland* (Father of the Fatherland), the true and trusted leader of the newly Protestant northern Netherlands.

Thus the events of July 10, 1584—a date familiar to all Dutch—at Delft's Prinsenhof were especially tragic. That night, heading to the dining room with his wife Louise de Coligny and guests, Willem passed a man who he had previously received as a Protestant emissary from the French court. In fact, unbeknownst to Willem, the man, **Balthasar Gerard** (or Geraerts) had been to the Prinsenhof Sunday before, lingering in the courtyard. When a guard asked what his business was, Gerard, remaining anonymous, gave the seemingly guileless reply that he had no business there, that what he really wanted was to be in the church opposite (the Waalse Church, still used today), but lacked appropriate stockings and shoes. The guard kindly conveyed Gerard's need to Willem, who had given the guard money for the would-be worshipper. As was later revealed, however,

Gerard did not buy footwear with the prince's money. Instead, he made a long-planned purchase of pistols and bullets, for he was no Protestant emissary from France, but a Catholic fanatic from Burgundy who was out to collect the reward that the Spanish King Philip II had put on Willem's head.

That July evening, Gerard, having obtained entry to the Prinsenhof under false pretenses, waited in hiding. Their dinner done, Willem, leading his party up to his chambers, had only mounted two steps when Gerard stepped out from behind a curtain and fired three bullets, two of which hit Willem, passing through his body, leaving holes in the wall behind him. The beloved 51-year-old leader of the Dutch people, fell, his supposed final words—still learned by all school children—"My God, have pity on me and my poor people." The *teychenen derkoogelen* (marks of the bullets), visible at the bottom of the stairs in the Prinsenhof, have been so enlarged by Dutch visitors touching them that they are now protected behind glass.

Gerard, who had escaped briefly in the ensuing confusion, was soon captured by guards and taken to the prison cell in Delft's *Stadhuis* on the nearby Markt. In the Belfry there—which survived a fire in the Stadhuis in 1618 and was incorporated into the replacement, built in 1620—Gerard was imprisoned while he awaited trial and sentencing in a cell that required him to remain constantly in a prone position. Four days later, on the Grote Markt, Gerard was drawn, quartered, and beheaded, his head later placed on a pike in public.

Holland's 17th-century **Golden Age** glowed in Delft. In 1602, the **Dutch East India Company** established its headquarters there. The owners began to make trading arrangements with China to import that country's popular blue and white ware to Europe. Millions of pieces reached Holland through the Delft-based company between 1602 and 1657. Delft artisans, in trying to imitate the pretty pieces to get in on the profits, developed their own fine product, and the town's fledgling pottery industry took off. By the middle of the 17th-century nearly 30 factories were producing blue and white ware, as well as other patterns, all of which became known simply as **Delftware**. The manufacture of tiles took an enormous upturn, and they can still be seen in old homes, restaurants, and taverns throughout Holland on fireplaces, in kitchens, and to edge walls where they meet the floor. Tiles became so typical in homes that they can be seen in many of Delft artist Vermeer's paintings.

Moving at a parallel with the 17th-century momentum of the pottery industry in Delft was painting. The greatest masters of the **Delft School** were **Jan Vermeer** (1632–1675) and **Pieter de Hoogh** (1629–1684). De Hoogh, a genius at genre, was born in Rotterdam and had moved to Amsterdam by the time of his death, but he called Delft home during the most productive period of his life when he created his memorable and intimate interpretations of domestic life. Genre painter Jan Steen also lived for a while in Delft, though he did not belong to the Delft School; for some years from 1654 onward, he managed the beer brewery *De Slange* on the Oude Delft canal. Several significant local painters, **Anthonie Palamedeszoon** (genre scenes), **Paulus Potter** (famous for his landscapes with animals), **Gerrit van Houckgeest**, **Cornelis van Vliet**, and **Emanuel White**, known for their church interior paintings, served as harbingers for Delft's Golden Age of art.

Most important of all was **Carel Fabritius** (1622–1654), Rembrandt's most accomplished student, and a painter who had a strong influence on Vermeer (although no proof of any formal painter/pupil relationship exists). Already recognized, and considered a painter of enormous potential, Carel Fabritius was killed at the age of 32 in the 1654 calamity, the *Delft Thunderclap*. At half past ten the morning of October 12, a gunpowder magazine (located in the northern part of the old town) containing some 80,000 pounds of powder, left over from the Dutch war with the Spanish, blew up. It killed hundreds of people and completely destroyed or did great damage to at least half the buildings in Delft. The blast buckled the stout walls of the Nieuwe Kerk, which stood diagonally across the street from *Mechelen*, the house on the Delft's Grote Markt (roughly where #62 is today) where Vermeer lived most of his life, and which he used as the setting for and where he created most of his paintings. In the explosion, Carel Fabritius was buried beneath the rubble of his house, along with his family and the man who was sitting for his portrait.

Johannes (Jan) Vermeer is the artist we most closely associate with Delft. It has been suggested that the high finish of Vermeer's enamel-smooth paintings reflects the glaze of Delft porcelain, which would have been an omnipresent influence in the town during his lifetime. In the autumn of 1632, Vermeer, the second child of Reynier Janszoon Vos and his wife Dymphna, was listed in the baptism register of Delft's Nieuwe Kerk. The family home *Mechelen*, on Delft's Grote Markt, was an active establishment: his father kept a tavern there, and designed and sold cloth from there. The year before Jan's birth, his father had been registered by the *Guild of St. Luke* as a Master Art-Dealer. Vermeer was undoubtedly influenced by the paintings his father handled as an art dealer. Many of the works that he bought and sold would have come from nearby Utrecht, a Catholic city whose school of artists were more closely connected to Italy and *Caravaggio,* known for his dramatic use of light. Young Jan would also have seen the works of artists at studios in Delft. Although nothing is known of his art education, it is likely that Vermeer began as an apprentice at about the age of 15,. The register at Delft's Stadhuis notes his marriage on April 5, 1653, to Catharina Bolnes, who came from a prosperous family in Gouda. Jan and his wife lived with his parents at *Mechelen,* remaining there for most of their marriage (which produced 11 children in 20 years). In December 1653, Vermeer was listed as a Master Painter in the local *Guild of St. Luke.*

We know of Vermeer's interest in music from the subjects of his paintings. Living as he did across from the Nieuwe Kerk, the installation in the tower there of a carillon of 36 Hemony Brothers bells —"the latest thing"—in 1663 must have been of interest, perhaps even inspiration, since he would have heard them all day long.

Vermeer was well-respected by his contemporaries: twice he served two-year terms on the board of the Guild of St. Luke. Because the Dutch have always kept meticulous records of financial transactions, it can be deduced that Vermeer lived a frugal life, but his financial condition deteriorated near the end of his life. In 1672, he and his family were forced to rent out *Mechelen* and move to a smaller house (on nearby *Oude Langedijk*). When he died three years later in 1675—and was buried in the Oude Kerk—Vermeer left his wife and eight minor children with almost no money.

Of the several dozen paintings—and little else—his wife Catharina possessed at the time of his death, some 29 were Vermeer's own (only 32 paintings of his entire life's work are known to exist today). Catharina seems to have made great efforts to keep her husband's paintings, but there was no way to make ends meet, and she declared herself bankrupt in April 1676. Designated as receiver for the estate was Delft native Antonie van Leeuwenhoek, a clerk to the Delft bailiff who, on the side, liked to muse over matter under the microscope. Through his improvements on that instrument, Leeuwenhoek is credited with giving the world the first accurate description of red blood corpuscles, and is responsible for the first drawing of bacteria, in 1683. (Although *his* works aren't in as many museums as Vermeer's, some are on view at the *Museum Boerhaave* in Leiden).

Leeuwenhoek seems to have been unsympathetic in his dealings with Vermeer's widow. At the sale of the bankrupt estate, a woman merchant named Jannetje Stevens managed to have 26 paintings by Vermeer seized and held as security against a family debt of 500 guilders "for groceries supplied." Catharina protested, and it was agreed that if she immediately paid 342 guilders, the art works would be returned to her. But there are no records that tell whether Catharina ever saw her husband's paintings again.

In 1696, an Amsterdam auction catalogue listed 21 paintings by Vermeer, with an average asking price of 70 guilders. That catalogue comprises one of the few historical records that critics have for determining genuine Vermeers. The 1696 auction in Amsterdam marked the last time for nearly 200 years that Vermeer's work received any but the most incidental public attention, Vermeer was all but ignored during the 18th and much of the 19th century, and even detailed scholarly volumes about the painters of Holland's remarkable 17th century *Golden Age* of art gave no mention of his work. Attention to Vermeer didn't begin again until 1842, when the French aristocrat **Thore-Burger**, during a visit to Holland, chanced to see *View of Delft*, which hung in a gallery in The Hague. He was so impressed by the painting that he devoted much of the rest of his life to making Vermeer well known.

By the time Vermeer died in Delft in 1675, Amsterdam and Rotterdam, because of the superior size and location of their ports, had progressively taken over the Dutch nation's trade. Although its famous pottery industry continued strong, the rest of Delft slowed down. The number of breweries in the city shrank from 200 to 15. Just before Vermeer's death, Holland as a whole had experienced a complete change in its political fortune. In 1672, Louis XIV of France, who resented the Dutch for their prosperity and coveted their Rhine River ports at the North Sea, sent his armies into the Dutch Republic. In a matter of months, they had swept through most of the country. The French invasion closed the books on the Golden Age, and the country went into a decline that affected every phase of life, including the art market, which completely collapsed. Delft's economy came to a standstill. In the 18th century, even Delftware was in decline, and most of Delft's pottery factories closed. The town became one of retired residents, and a bastion of conservative Calvinism.

A dormant Delft saw the dawn of a new age in the mid-19th century—fostered by the founding of the *Koninklijke Akademie* (Royal Academy), now the **Technical Academy** in 1842, and the linking of the town to the national railway network in 1847. For the sake of expansion, ancient town ramparts were sacrificed, but powerful protests against the further mutilation of the old town—the Oude Delft canal had been threatened with being filled in to make way for a tram track in the center—in large measure prevailed.

Today, as you cruise along prosperous Delft's flower box-decorated canals, or absorb the sights on foot, you see well-preserved historic monuments: the former **East India Company** headquarters (originally three 16th-century houses); the former **St. Barbara Cloister**, founded in 1405, and the 1650 Vleeshal (now both renovated as student clubs); the 1770 **Waag** (Weigh House, used today as a theater); the **Visbanken** (still in use as a fish market, since 1342); and the picturesque **Oostpoort** (the last remaining of Delft's eight 14th-century city gates). Delft's population, which had been 23,000 during the days of Vermeer, but had fallen to 13,000 by the beginning of the 19th century, now numbers 90,000 for greater Delft, with its 16,000 Technical University students making a lively contribution to contemporary life.

GUIDEPOSTS

Telephone Code 015

Tourist info • VVV Markt 85, 2611 GS; ☎ *126100*; open Mon.–Fri. 9 a.m.–6 p.m., Sat. 9 a.m.–5 p.m., Sun. 11 a.m.–3 p.m. (from Oct. 1–March 31 closed Sun.)

Markets • Thursdays, general market on the Markt 8:30 a.m.–5 p.m. (poultry to produce, nuts to knick-knacks); flower market at same time along Hippolytusbuurt canal; flea market along canals in town center Sat. May–Sept., often to the accompaniment of barrel organs and street musicians.

Parking • Metered parking on the Markt (except during Thursday market), near to the VVV, which has map showing other in-town locations. Free parking on Phoenixstraat by windmill, just outside of old town to west.

Canal Cruises • *Rond Vaart Delft*, Koornmarkt; April–Oct..; daily 10:30 a.m.-5:30 p.m.; 45 mins.; ☎ *126385*.

Pedal Boats and Kayak Rental • Rotterdamseweg 148 (near **De Porceleyne Fles**); rentals by the hour; ☎ *571504*.

Horse-drawn Tram • On the Markt; Easter–Sept.; daily except Thursday (market day); ☎ *561828*.

Bike Rental • At the station. Maps of ANWB signposted cycling routes (Delfland and Westland) available at VVV.

Taxis • At the station.

WHAT TO SEE AND DO

Delft is a destination deserving of an overnight stay, even though it's practically in The Hague's backyard. During the day, explore quiet court-yards, quaint interiors, gardens, and gables. Sunlight sifting through an-cient trees highlights fascinating Dutch facades and produces fantastic reflections in the waters (green in summer, dark in winter) of the canals, crossed by humpbacked bridges—all redefined by Delft's special quality of light. After the motorcoach crowds have called it a day, a medieval atmo-sphere moves back to the ★★**Grote Markt**, and seeing the monuments around its expanse illuminated ★★ after dark is a special experience. The Markt, is the showplace of Delft, marked in the center by a statue of native son Hugo de Groot (Grotius), who is most definitely meant to be honored but is unintentionally dwarfed by the scale of the long marketplace (still used as such on Thurs.), has one grouping of Delft's premier attractions, while a cluster of others can be found on the lovely ★★**Oude Delft** canal, only several interesting walking blocks away. On national Dutch holidays, opening hours are different, so check with the Delft VVV.

Prinsenhof   ★★

St. Agathaplein 1 (entrance off Oude Delft); open Tues.–Sat. 10 a.m.–5 p.m., Sun. and holidays 1–5 p.m., closed Mons., during Delft's antique dealers' exhibition in Oct., on Jan.1, and Dec. 2; ☎ *602358.* The Prin-senhof is one of the Dutch nation's most historic buildings, and one of Delft's loveliest, just off the Oude Delft canal in the St. Agathap-lein, an old cobbled courtyard with chestnut trees, a 15th-century chapel, and an ambiance of Burgundian days, when the earliest sec-tions of the building were erected as a cloister. The Prinsenhof has the sad celebrity of being the place where Prince **Willem the Silent**, having lived there from 1572 when he became the leader of the Dutch Prot-estant revolt against the ravages of Spanish Catholic rule in the early days of the *Eighty Years' War*, died from an assassin's bullet in 1584; the event gives the buildings its credentials as the "*Cradle of Dutch Liberty*" (see "Delft in Context"). The fascinating building is a laby-rinth of rooms and corridors of unusual beauty, filled with fresh flow-ers and antique portraits, paintings, and furniture, primarily reflecting Delft's history, particularly in the period of the *Eighty Years' War*. At the reception desk is a detailed English text with the history, layout of building, and description of exhibits, which you can take around with you.

Museum Lambert van Meerten   ★★

Oude Delft 199; hours same as Prinsenhof, except not closed during annual October Antiques Fair; ☎ *602358.* Nearby on the Oude Delft canal is a charming old patrician canal-side mansion, whose owner Lambert van

Meerten set out to make a museum of the decorative arts at the end of the last century. The core of the collection is old Dutch tiles. The tiles, whole walls' worth of individual squares, or grouped together in tableaux (there's a 200-tile representation of a naval victory set in the wall above the stairs that lead from the spacious entry hall), show the full range of artisans' skill and imagination in this traditional Dutch medium from the 16th-18th century. The house has lovely details, heavy oak shutters, leaded window glass, lovely carved wood molding and wainscoting, oak-beamed alcoves, 17th-century Hindeloppen paneling from Friesland, and the so-called Leyden room, whose atmosphere is reminiscent of Vermeer. This is a truly delightful corner of old Delft.

Nieuwe Kerk ★

Markt; Apr. 1–Nov. 1, Mon.–Sat. 9 a.m.–5 p.m., closed Sun., Nov.–March, Mon.-Sat. 11 a.m.–4 p.m.; ☎ 123025. The Niewe Kerk, begun in 1381 and completed in 1496, is designated the "new church" only in comparison with Delft's tilting-towered Oude Kerk, whose origins go back to the year 1240. In the Niewe Kerk crypt are buried all members of the Dutch royal family, the House of Orange. Willem the Silent's mausoleum, designed by Hendrick de Keyser, and years in the making at a staggering cost, shows a white marble recumbent figure, at the foot of which is the effigy of his devoted dog. So the story goes, Willem's dog refused food and water after his master's death, and died within days. Willem's monument is directly above the House of Orange royal burial vaults (not open to the public). The most recent ruler to be put to rest was former Queen Wilhelmina, who died in 1962 and, at her own decree, had an all-white funeral.

For visitors interested in an energetic climb, the 357-foot tower *(April 30–early Sept. Tues.–Sat. 10 a.m.–4:30 p.m., from mid- June–Aug. also on Mons.)* offers a ★panorama of the Dutch countryside from the top that reveals flat green grazing fields speckled with cows, rooftops in The Hague nearby and, beyond, sand dunes and the thin blue line of the North Sea. In the Niewe Kerk tower is a ★Hemony 48-bell carillon, one of the finest in Holland.

SHOPPING

There's a full complement of department and other stores at in-town *In de Veste* pedestrianized shopping center, and in and off the Markt are smaller, more personalized shops, such as the butcher and the baker. But, since this *is* Delft, presumably it's the candlestick maker (of blue and white ware) that you've come to see. Begin with at least a look at the best: De Porceleyne Fles handpainted works. You'll notice the difference in quality of decoration between these pieces and the factory-made ware at the many shops that line the Markt, and also the difference in price.

Royal Delftware Factory De Porceleyne Fles ★★★

Rotterdamseweg 196. Apr.–Oct. Mon.–Sat. 9 a.m.–5 p.m., Sun. and holi-

days. 10 a.m.–4 p.m.; Nov.–March, Mon.–Fri. 9 a.m.–5 p.m., Sat. 10 a.m.–4 p.m., closed Sun.; ☎ *569214, FAX 625635.* De Porceleyne Fles (the porcelain bottle), founded in 1653, schedules potter's wheel and handpainting demonstrations (by one of the firm's 150 artists) frequently during the day, to give you an idea of the personal attention that goes into producing each piece of the factory's ware, distinguished on the bottom by the mark of a jar and initials "JT" to attest to its authenticity. The show rooms are so prettily arrayed that it feels like a museum (and indeed, some of the unique pieces are as expensive as museum objects). Around tiled fireplaces and in a superb display cabinet presented by the Dutch King William III sit blue and white (and other polychrome patterns) jugs and ginger jars, bowls and bud vases, and tiles and teapots.

There are some seconds (25-40% off) on sale at the factory, although the Royal Delft store with the largest selection of seconds in town (also good selection of first quality pieces) is **De Backer vd Hoeck** *(Markt 62, Apr. 1-Oct. 30, open daily 9 a.m.-6 p.m., 123171),* which will mail purchases anywhere. There is also a branch of the shop at *Markt 30 (open year-round)* in the back room of which is a fine collection of colorful tiles; many are seconds, but with careful inspection, you'll find ones that are fine for yourself or as gifts.

Atelier de Candelaer

Kerkstraat 13. Apr. 1–Sept. 30: Mon.–Fri. 9 a.m.–6 p.m., Sat. 9 a.m.–5 p.m., Sun. 10 a.m.–6 p.m.; Oct. 1–Mar. 31 Mon.-Sat. 10 a.m.-5 p.m. ☎ *131848.* In a picturesque corner of Delft just off the Markt behind the Nieuwe Kerk, this two-person studio sells the fine pieces of handmade Delft produced on-site.

WHERE TO STAY

The hotels listed are all very centrally located, only a short walk from the Markt, but on residential streets with canals. Staffs are friendly and very able in English.

MODERATE

Delft Museumhotel   ★★★★

Oude Delft 189, 2611 HD; ☎ *140930, FAX 140935.* This is Delft's most recent hotel, though it's in two contiguous 17th-century houses. The traditional brick, big-windowed, dignified facade shelters a friendly staff and lobby and public rooms that are updated in ambiance. Each of the 28 guest rooms in the hotel proper is different, many with original details. There are 25 additional rooms in a new addition at the back, which are larger and slightly more expensive, that offer views of the gardens. There is a lobby cafe for breakfast (no restaurant) and snacks during the day, and a bar-lounge (that looks out on Delft's Oude Kerk). Prices vary slightly with room view (eight face canal, or garden) or suite, all with modern tiled bath and shower. Nice sense of character, winding corridors.

De Ark ★★★★

Koornmarkt 59-65, 2611 EC; ☎ *157999, FAX 144997.* Housed in three restored canal houses in a lovely residential section of central old Delft are 16 rooms (seven with canal view, others face garden), all different, large, often sunny, neat, though with rather nondescript modern furniture. Never mind. There's plenty of dutch *gezellig* (coziness) about the place, and the friendly front desk is staffed 24 hours. The bricked, beamed dining room with corner fireplace provides a Dutch buffet breakfast, and well-prepared, tasty dinners if you desire. There's parking for a fee, and several one-bedroom suites in the annex across the street (canal).

WHERE TO EAT

You can dine handsomely (and historically) in Delft. But if you prefer a simply savory or sweet snack, you won't have to forgo a scenic setting to do so.

Restaurant De Prinsenkelder, or the Princes' Cellar *(Prinsenhof, entrance Schoolstraat 11; Mon.–Fri. noon–2:30 p.m., and 6–9:30 p.m., dinner only on Sat., closed Sun.;* ☎ *121860; expensive)* is in the attractive brick vaulted basement of the Prinsenhof. Meathooks can still be seen in the ceiling, which shows that while the building served as a cloister and as the home of Willem the Silent, this was the food and wine cellar. The atmosphere for the first class, local Dutch food carefully prepared and presented in the French style (fresh sauteed eel, fillet of tuna with Dutch shrimp, ginger with cream) is historic, romantic, very Dutch, and definitely Delft.

Another touch of old Delft is the **Restaurant "Het Straatje van Vermeer"** *(Molslaan 18; Mon.-Sat. 6-10 p.m.; reservations at* ☎ *126466; expensive)*, which has a cozy ambiance of Dutch decor with antiques, old tiles, and copies of Vermeer paintings on the walls. Reserve for dinner, since the restaurant does serve groups, and you want to be seated in a room with other individual parties. Menus and à la carte choices include a full range of continental and Dutch dishes.

For more informal fare, begin at the Markt. **Monopole** *(Markt 48, daily 9 a.m.–11 p.m.;* ☎ *123059)* is just one of many cafes there, helping to fill the vast space with outdoor tables and chairs when the weather warrants, and providing an excellent vantage point from which to survey the superb setting. You can sit as long as you want over a coffee, juice, or beer, and maybe you'll be thinking you're in heaven if the carillon in the Nieuwe Kerk begins a carillon concert (Tues., Thurs.—market day and quite a different scene—and Sat. at 11 a.m.). Light meals and snacks available from early morning until well into the evening. Across the Markt, about midway along its length, is a **Banketbakkerij** or pastry shop *(corner of J. Gerritstraat, open Mon.–Sat. til 6 p.m.;* ☎ *123388)*, which also sells bread, chocolates, and Holland's *hopjes* (coffee-flavored caramels). Head for the back of the shop, up a few stairs, to the tiny tea room (where you only need buy a cup of coffee). It has four check-clothed tables, a huge old tiled fireplace, walls hung with old wooden cookie molds, all overlooking a little canal.

Nearly next-door neighbors on the lovely Oude Delft canal are two local favorites. **Kleyweg's Stads-Koffyhuis** *(Oude Delft 133, 8 a.m.–7 p.m.;* ☎ *124625; closed Sun.)* for breakfast, lunch, dinner, or coffee, served outside on a barge moored along Delft's oldest, possibly most picturesque, canal if you like. A tasty variety of sandwiches, pancakes, and other light meals is served. The **Stadspannekoeckhuys** *(Oude Delft 113,* ☎ *130193, open daily noon—90 p.m., closed Mon.)* is another good choice for platter-size Dutch pancakes and quick meals. Back at the Prinsenhof Museum is the **Koffiekelder de Nonnerie** *(St. Agathaplein, off Oude Delft, open to 5 p.m.,* ☎ *121860, closed Mon.)*, a cafe in the cellar that serves coffee and lunch, in the garden when the weather's right.

ROTTERDAM

GUIDELINES FOR ROTTERDAM
SIGHTS

Despite a history as lengthy as its neighboring Dutch towns, Rotterdam has an entirely different appearance and personality, largely as a result of the leveling of its center by the German *Luftwaffe* on May 14, 1940. Rotterdam's city skyline, especially at the waterfront, is strikingly contemporary. Sections along its **port**, the largest and busiest in the world, look like a grown-up Erector Set, with cranes locked in their skyward saluting position. Commentary during harbor cruises points out just how state-of-the-art Rotterdam's port is. On land and water, imaginative planning is much in evidence, as you'll discover when visiting the several excellent **museums** and exceptional examples of **modern architecture**. Rotterdam's one preserved historic section has U.S. ties: picturesque **Delfshaven** is the port from which English Separatists who had been living in Leiden departed on a sea pilgrimage aboard the *Mayflower* to the New World where they established Plymouth Colony.

GETTING AROUND

The broad boulevard **Coolsingel**, running north/south through modern Rotterdam's center and continuing to the port as **Schiedamsedijk** from the point where **West Blaak** and **Blaak** make an east/west crossing, provides a basic orientation to the city. Many of the major sights are on or near these streets; too far to reach on foot, there's a good **tram/bus/Metro** network (and helpful system map). A day-pass (Dfl. 8.25) is available from the city transportation booth on Stationplein.

The VVV, which has a city information booth at Centraal Station, runs an hour-long **city tour** from there (daily 1:15 p.m. Apr.–Sept.) on an historic tram; it provides a good look at the city's many faces.

From Easter–Sept. at 1:30 p.m. Mon.–Sat., a comprehensive two-hour city overview **motorcoach tour** that shows off Rotterdam's monuments as well as its modern architecture, and includes a look at the port, parks, and Delfthaven, departs from Coolsingel opposite City Hall, near the VVV office, where tickets (Dfl. 20) are available. At **ArchiCenter Rotterdam**, a special department of, and located at, the VVV, you can get verbal information, maps, and suggested self-guided walk brochures in English about Rotterdam's acclaimed modern architecture. **Spido Havenrondvaarten** (*Willemsplein at waterfront;* ☎ *4135400; tram 5 from CS, Metro: Leuvehaven*) has a selection of frequently scheduled port cruises (1-1/4 and 2-1/4 hours and longer, multilingual commentary). A combination tram/cruise package takes approximately 2-1/2 hours.

SHOPPING

Lijnbaan (opened in 1953), the first center-city pedestrianized shopping precinct in Europe, was a truly revolutionary concept in its era, with more than a mile-long mix of shops, boutiques, and cafes, some under cover; it remains a pleasant shopping area and city passageway, with gardens and sculpture. Major department and clothing stores are found on and around the **Beursplein**, by the bold blue-green *World Trade Center* on Coolsingel. On **Nieuwe Binnenweg** are a number of antique and curio shops; in Delfshaven on Voorhaven is **Adriaan Groenewond Antiques**, considered the best of its kind in the city. Stores are generally closed Mon. until 1 p.m.; late night shopping is Fri. until 9 p.m. Rotterdam's **general market**, also with antiques and curiosities, is Holland's largest: Tues. and Sat. 9 a.m.–5 p.m. on the Mariniersweg and surrounding streets. There's also a book, stamp, and coin market on Grotekerkplein, Tues. and Sat., 9:30 a.m.–4 p.m.

WHERE TO STAY

There's variety enough to meet your personal comfort/cost ratio, from five-star international to cozy neighborhood two-star.

WHERE TO EAT

All aspects of Rotterdam are present in its restaurants. There are architecturally intriguing, contemporary or cozy historic settings for continental or typical Dutch cuisine, and all the flavors of foreign kitchens you'd expect to find in an international port.

ENTERTAINMENT AND EVENTS

Rotterdam's monthly events and exhibitions calendar *Agenda* (in Dutch only) is available from the VVV or hotels, where someone can translate the listings for you. The **Rotterdams Philharmonisch Orkest** (James Conlon, Conductor) resides in **De Doelen**, which opened in 1966 in the center of the city (box office ☎ *4132490*). (In the 1980s, acclaimed English conductor Simon Rattle, City of Birmingham Symphony Orchestra, was principal guest conductor for Rotterdam, a musical company he describes as "exciting.") On Wednesday, October through May, free half-hour **lunch concerts** are presented at De Doelen, beginning at 12:45 p.m. Lunchtime **organ concerts** (12:45–1:15 p.m.) are held in St. Laurenskerk Fridays, with other musical performances in the church on Thursday (except January and February). The annual international **Rotterdam Film Festival** is held in January and February.

ARRIVING

Rotterdam is served at least four times hourly by train on the main Amsterdam-The Hague-Rotterdam line, a branch of which runs to Schiphol Airport. Rotterdam also connects by rail directly to Gouda and Utrecht; all trains use **Centraal Station**. The city's **Zestienhoven Airport** offers various intra-European air connections. Travelers arriving via ferry from England at **Hoek van Holland** can take the boat train directly to Rotterdam (about a half hour) for ongoing destinations. By motorway, Rotterdam is 76 km (47 mi.) south of Amsterdam, 103 km (62 mi.) north of Antwerp in Belgium. Because of the massive size of its port, two tunnels (the *Benelux* and the *Maas*) are part of the complex highway system that serves and encircles Rotterdam.

IN THE AREA

Kinderdijk, in the countryside near Rotterdam, provides windmill fans with 19 in a single scenic setting. The picturesque old port of **Dordrecht**, 20 km (12 mi.) south of Rotterdam, sometimes considered the southernmost city of the Randstad, lies somewhat off today's main tourism track, at the crossroads of Holland's inland waterways. **Spido Cruises** to the waterworks and waterways of the region are available from Rotterdam, as are maps for self-driving routes of the extensive Rotterdam port from the city to the North Sea.

TRAVEL TIPS

Rotterdam is surrounded by an efficient but complex motorway network that is dense with drivers determined to get where they are going as rapidly as possible; it can be confusing for the uninitiated motorist. Arrival in the city by train is recommended. If you do come by car, get specific *place names* to look for on exit ramp signs.

ROTTERDAM IN CONTEXT

Rotterdam, like Rome, wasn't built in a day. But it was laid waste in one. In the very year Rotterdam should have been celebrating its 600th anniversary—festivities commemorating its receiving civic rights in 1340 had been planned—the sudden events of a single day, May 14, 1940, overshadowed the city's entire history. Mere minutes of Nazi air bombardment leveled six centuries of civilization in Rotterdam. It destroyed more than 20,000 homes and historically significant buildings, killed hundreds, and left another 78,000 homeless.

A city's history is reflected in its facades, and you can count on one hand the buildings in the center of Rotterdam that pre-date 1940: the *Stadhuis* (built in 1920 in the Dutch-Renaissance style); the main *Post Office*; the *Schielandhuis* (see "What To See and Do"), and *St. Laurenskerk (Grote Kerk)*. Of all the other historic monuments destroyed, only the cinder-sided St. Laurens church, with its scarred but still-standing tower, a symbol to the city, was cast to play the part of the phoenix in Rotterdam. It was resurrected from the rubble, and reconstructed as it had been to rise again on the city skyline.

For the rest of its rebuilding, in striking contrast to the post-war plans of Europe's other bombed cities, Rotterdam opted for a radical and imaginative concept: creating a whole new contemporary city from the ashes of the old one. **Lewis Mumford**, the American architecture and city-planning critic, wrote in his classic book *The City in History*, "Not every (bombed) city rose to the challenge of its destruction as determinedly and as skillfully as Rotterdam," adding, "The word 'renewal' is a tame one to describe the resurgence of Rotterdam."

Such a fresh start was made possible by the foresight of the Rotterdam city government, which, almost immediately after the 1940 Nazi bombing, expropriated the sites of the bombed buildings, becoming sole proprietor of 415 acres in the heart of Rotterdam. (Former owners received fair compensation for the value of their property as of May 9, 1940, the day before the May 10 Nazi invasion of Holland.) A year after the official end of the war, the provisional city council of Rotterdam approved the so-called "Basic Scheme" for the city, which banned industry from the center, cut by two-thirds the number of residences in what had been a severely overcrowded city center, and built in spaciousness by widening downtown streets and planting plenty of flowers. Of the centralized pedestrian **Lijnbaan**, shopping plaza, first of its kind in the world, Mumford reviewed it as "exemplary in almost every way." (The Lijnbaan may appear pleasant but ordinary to today's visitors, but it should be appreciated for its conceptual contribution to the present worldwide multi-malled landscape.)

Its citizens' reputation for hard work is evident in the half-kidding comment by the Dutch that in Rotterdam "shirts are sold with the sleeves already rolled up." Never was their shirt-sleeve stamina needed more than after the Second World War. Within five weeks of the liberation of Rotterdam, work on reconstruction of the port had begun—the Nazis had blown up half the port's machinery and equipment in 1944. There was no argument from citizens that the port took precedence over other rebuilding, since the prosperity of the city, and indeed much of the country, depended upon shipping.

In his own time, as he remains in the 20th century, **Erasmus** (1466–1536) was Rotterdam's favorite native son, albeit an illegitimate one, since his father was a priest. Fortunately, he didn't let that happenstance hamper his life, obviously believing the words he later wrote: "No one is injured save by himself." Erasmus was one of the first persons since the end of the Roman Empire to earn his living by the pen, and Rotterdammers past and present seem to see their own straightforward selves in many of his words. His *Adages*, sayings adapted from antiquity, are familiar to us all: "as plain as the nose on your face," "call a spade a spade," "caught in his own snare," and "in the country of the blind, the one-eyed man is king."

A brief look back to its beginnings reveals that Rotterdam was first settled in about the year 1000, at a dam on the small river Rotte, where peasants and fishermen gradually became involved with local trade and fishing. A flood in 1164 swept away the wooden huts of the early hamlet, but residents were determined to fight for its survival come hell or high water. In 1299, Rotterdam was officially recognized by its feudal overlord, Wolfert van Borsselen, as an urban entity after citizens in the 19-feet-below-sea-level town had become protected by dikes and adept at driving stilts (wooden piles) into silt for building foundations. The Counts of Holland gave Rotterdam city rights in 1340. Almost completely consumed by fire in 1563, Rotterdam barely left time to rebuild before it joined other Dutch cities in support of Willem I (the Silent) against the Spanish in 1568.

Rotterdam's location on the delta of two significant river systems, the Rhine and the Maas (Meuse), played the leading part in its prominence, but history had a supporting role. At the end of the *Eighty Years' War,* under the provisions of the *Peace of Westphalia* (1648), the **River Scheldt** and **Antwerp's port** in the Southern Netherlands (today's Belgium) were closed. Thereafter sea traffic turned north to Rotterdam (and Amsterdam). Rotterdam, until then just one of the "small towns" of Holland, and its port gradually began to grow.

Another substantial boost for its shipping trade came Rotterdam's way when Holland blockaded the River Scheldt (which had been reopened by Napoleon Bonaparte) from 1830–39, after Belgium seceded from the Kingdom of the Netherlands (established in 1815 by the Congress of Vienna). Much of what had been Antwerp's shipping trade, mostly with the Dutch colonies, again was diverted to Rotterdam. With this incentive, the harbor at Rotterdam developed further but was hindered by silt at the mouth of the Maas, which prevented the entrance of large vessels. This was more than inconvenient as Europe progressed through the *Industrial Revolution* and into an age of steam power. The present-day preeminence of Rotterdam's port is due to the construction of the **Nieuwe Waterweg** (1863–1872), and a subsequent plan of continual dredging. Since 1872, Rotterdam has offered ships a 30 km lock-free entry from the sea to the city.

Beginning in the 20th century, Rotterdam has carried out successive programs of **port development**, water management, and industrialization that have made the city the powerhouse of the Dutch economy. Overcoming the damage done during the Second World War, the port of Rotterdam quickly regained its prewar tonnage. Ironically, Rotterdam's recovery largely grew out of its role as the main furnisher of raw materials by river barge to West Germany during that country's postwar "economic miracle." The process of digging new deep water harbors, the reverse of Holland's more usual land-creating efforts, produced the port/industrial complexes of *Botlek* and *Europort* and put the port at *Pernis* on its way to becoming the largest oil refinery complex on the continent. By 1962, Rotterdam had edged up on and surpassed New York in total tonnage to become the biggest port in the world. Radar facilities were installed to enable ships to enter the port from the North Sea even in zero-visibility fog. Actually 20 miles (37 km) inland from the North Sea, Rotterdam is, more accurately, a series of ports along that length, which is lockless and bridge-free; two major motorway tunnels, the *Benelux* and the *Maas,* pass under the port in the city.

Today Rotterdam services 32,000 sea-going vessels and 180,000 inland waterways barges annually, handling nearly 300 million metric tons of bulk cargo, putting it well ahead of its two nearest international rivals, Kobe, Japan, and New York. In Europe, the port of Rotterdam handles more trade than the ports of Le Havre, Bremen, Hamburg, Antwerp, and Amsterdam combined. More important for its future, Rotterdam is the best-equipped transport, distribution, and trade center in Europe and is linked to the continental hinterland by a sophisticated network of waterways, roads, railway, and pipelines. As the needs of the transport world evolve, Rotterdam is prepared to meet the challenge of offering the best and most efficient harbor service to exporters and importers of raw materials and goods.

Apart from its "no contest" victory in comparative port size, Rotterdam's competition with the city of Amsterdam is keen. There's no casualness in the two cities' confrontation in *voetbal* (pronounced "football,") in America called soccer, when Rotterdam's *Feijenoord* team faces off with Amsterdam's *Ajax*.

Since its original postwar rebuilding, Rotterdam has had a chance to come full circle in city-planning concepts. And again the city is taking the lead by reevaluating some of its earlier groundbreaking urban planning ideals and ideas. **Waterstad** (water city) is the name of the combined new recreational attractions along the riverfront: **Tropicana** with its indoor swimming pool and subtropical environment; open-air museum of inland shipping; Sunday art market; **IMAX** theater; **National Econocenter**, and assorted pubs and restaurants at the attractive **Oude Haven** (old Harbor). That certainly makes Rotterdam the right place for Holland's future National Museum of Architecture. The words "stronger through strife" were added to the city's shield after the war, and Rotterdam's "sleeves-ups" citizens—who now number 575,000 and come from some 125 countries—seem to have proved themselves to be just that.

GUIDEPOSTS

Telephone Code 010

Tourist Info • VVV, Main Office, Coolsingel 67. Open year-round Mon.–Thurs. 9 a.m.–6 p.m., Fri. to 9 p.m., Sat. 9 a.m.–5 p.m., Sun. 10 a.m.–4 p.m. (closed Sun. Oct.–Mar.). Closed Dec. 25, 26, Jan. 1. VVV at Centraal Station (Rotterdam info. only) open daily 9 a.m.–10 p.m. Sun. open 10 a.m.), closed Dec. 25, Jan. 1. ☎ *4136000*; recorded info line ☎ *06-34034065*.

Port Tours • Spido Havenrondvaarten, Willemsplein; ☎ *4135400*. The 1-1/4 hr. harbor tour is offered year-round, varying schedule; additional cruises daily Apr.–Sept.

Emergencies • Police, ambulance: ☎ *06-11*.

Post Office • Coolsingel 42, ☎ *4542221*. Open Mon.–Thurs. 8:30 a.m.–7 p.m. (Fri. 8:30 a.m.–8:30 p.m.).

ANWB • AAA associate organization: Westblaak 210, ☎ *4140000*.

Parking • Public garages (look for "**P**" signs) in center around Centraal Station, Lijnbaan.

Transport • Information on public transportation in Rotterdam and greater region: Stationplein, ☎ *4546890*.

Taxi • Rotterdam Taxi Base: ☎ *4626060*; taxi ranks at Centraal Station, Hilton, on Coolsingel.

WHAT TO SEE AND DO

During its postwar mid-20th-century rebuilding, Rotterdam humanized its contemporary core with plenty of public sculpture, though the most moving piece is a wrenching reminder of WW II: *Devasted City* (by **Ossip Zadkine**, 1952, on *Plein 1940*, behind the Maritime Museum). The human figure, with a gaping hole in its torso that simultaneously symbolizes a "person without a heart" and a "city without a center," its hands raised to the sky, expresses both horror and hope. Far less thought-provoking, but a perennial personal favorite, is the shy yet sturdy *Monsieur Jacques* by **L. O. Wenckebach**, 1959, on Coolsingel (whose "twin" greets visitors at the entrance to the Kroller-Muller Museum in Otterlo). **Rodin's** *L'homme qui marche* meets shoppers at the pedestrianized Korte Lijnbaan. On Grotekerkplein is one of Rotterdam's most beloved sculptures, of native son *Erasmus*, who was born near this square in Oct. 1469. The statue (by **Hendrik de Keyser**, 17th century), which thankfully survived the Nazi bombing and thereafter was safely sequestered for the duration of the war, portrays Erasmus reading a book. **Umberto Mastrianni's** *Kiss* near Centraal Station has been renamed *Goodbye* locally. Many of Rotterdam's museums are free on Wed. (and for children under 16 at all times).

Boymans-van Beuningen Museum   ★★★
Mathenesserlaan 18; Tues.– Sun. 11 a.m.–5 p.m., Sun. and holidays 11 a.m.–5 p.m., closed Mon., Jan. 1, Apr. 30.; ☎ *4419400; Tram 5, Metro: Eendrachtsplein.* As well as offering its works, the Boymans-van Beuningen Museum is the only one in Holland with collections of both fine and applied art from the 14th century to the present.

There are few museums in the world where one can find works by **van Eyck**, **da Vinci**, **van Gogh**, and **Andy Warhol** under one roof. The museum's 250,000-piece collection is well respected worldwide, a well-blended result of private donations (many from local Rotterdam families) and selective acquisitions. One of the showpieces is Pieter **Brue-**

gel the Elder's *The Tower of Babel* (c. 1563), and another is **Rembrandt's** portrait of his son Titus. (Because the Boymans has so many of his drawings, the institution and scholars associated with it have become leading authorities in studies of attributions to Rembrandt.) Among artists represented in the Old Masters department are **Hieronymous Bosch, Rubens, Lucas van Leyden, Jan Steen, Jan van Goyen, Karel Fabritius**, and **Frans Hals**. The print and graphics galleries contain important works by artists from **Durer** to **Dali**; among many renowned representatives in between are **Picasso, Magritte, Max Ernst, Man Ray, Kokoschka**, and **Kandinsky**. There is a large bookstore, and reproductions are available in many forms; the coffee shop has a garden terrace.

The Boymans Museum was an interested party in an intriguing chapter of art history that involved a modern Dutch "master painter." **Hans van Meegeren** wielded his brush so well that he created six "Vermeers," which convinced even experts that they were long-missing works by the 17th-century Dutch master. In 1937, the Boymans paid $286,000 for one of them. During World War II, Nazi German Field Marshall Hermann Goring, an avid art collector, acquired another. When the war was over, Van Meegeren was criminally charged with having cooperated with the Nazis by sending a Vermeer out of Holland to Goring, which forced him to decide which was worse: to be charged as a *forger* or denounced as a *collaborator*. In the country's postwar climate, it seemed far safer to be a forger, so Van Meegeren admitted that Goring's "Vermeer" was a fake. Still, experts on Dutch master artists, studying the works that Van Meegeren said were his, refused to believe that the paintings weren't genuine. Only by actually painting a *new* Old Master *before* the eyes of the court judges was Van Meegeren able to convince the art world that he was a master forger. Finally, he was believed, then convicted and given a year in prison. Van Meegeren died of a heart attack before he was able to serve his sentence.

Delfshaven ★★

Trams 4, 6, Metro: Delfshaven. This picturesque old district (a protected historic area since the late 1960s and largely restored) was incorporated into Rotterdam in 1866, but it was created as a port for **Delft** in the 14th century. Inland Delft, which needed a port to maintain its economic viability, received permission to create a shipping channel along the river *Schie* to the *Maas* in 1389. The port served its purpose until it was sacked in 1488, after which it barely survived. Delfshaven became important again in the 17th century for Delft's **East India Company** ships, but leaders in Delft proper began to be protective of their town and refused to let Delfshaven develop. Dutch naval hero **Piet Hein** was born here (Piet Heynstraat #10) in 1577. (Not surprisingly, a statue of him stands nearby.)

Perhaps Delfshaven's most memorable moment in history came on August 1, 1620 (on the Gregorian calendar), when the so-called **Pilgrim Fathers**, English Separatists who had been living in Leiden, set sail from here aboard the *Speedwell* to England, where they met up with the more seaworthy *Mayflower*. The *Mayflower* eventually reached America, where the pilgrims established Plymouth Colony. The 16th-century **Oude Kerk** *(Aelbrechtskolk 20;* ☎ *4774156)*, where the pilgrims most probably prayed before their departure, is rarely open to individuals (there is a service on Thanksgiving Day), but there's a commemorative plaque by the door. Inside is a stain glass window of the *Speedwell* and a memorial dedicated to the pilgrims. A **Hemony carillon** was placed in the tower of the restored Regency-style church in 1963; inquire at the Rotterdam VVV about summer carillon and organ concerts. Next door to the Oude Kerk is the **Raadhuis** (town hall), dating from 1580 and the days when Delfshaven was independent. In the attractive old **Zakkendragershuisje** (sack carriers house), Voorstraat 13, is a working pewter artisan's shop. At the end of Voorhaven is a working, grain-grinding ★**windmill** that can be visited, including its outside "balcony," from which there's a nice view. Across the Voorhaven footbridge is the **Museum voor Naieve Kunst** (Museum of Naive Art) *(Voorhaven 25; Mon.–Sat. 9:30 a.m.–4:30 p.m., Sun. 1:00–4:30 p.m.;* ☎ *4766611), also an art gallery.*

Delfshaven's ★★**De Dubbelde Palmboom** *(Voorhaven 12; Tues.– Sun. 11 a.m.–5 p.m., Sun. and holidays 1–5 p.m., closed Mon., Jan. 1, Apr. 30;* ☎ *4761533; tram 6 from Coolsingel, Metro: Delfshaven)* is a part of the Rotterdam Historical Museum. Located in a restored (1975) 19th-century warehouse with brick floors and beamed ceilings, the museum has interesting exhibits on living and working in the Rotterdam region in the pre-and post-industrial eras, attractively arranged in rooms on nine levels connected by wooden ramps (and elevators), working their way up into the eaves, where the cafe **De Bonte Hond** is housed. There are cards in English explaining exhibits in each room.

Prins Hendrik Maritime Museum

Leuvehaven 1; Tues.–Sun. 11a.m.–5 p.m., closed Mon., Jan. 1, Apr. 30; ☎ *4132680; Trams 3, 6, 7, Metro: Beurs/Churchillplein.* Meant to provide insight into maritime history as a whole, and the story of shipping in Europe, the Netherlands, and Rotterdam in particular, the Maritime Museum fulfills its mandate by multimedia means: a series of diverting five-minute videos on shipping that bypass the need for language; old paintings and prints; charts showing the comparative sizes of seagoing craft; nautical equipment (there's a highly popular periscope and a complete ship's bridge), and ship models of all sorts. (Kits for even smaller models of ships such as the **Holland America Line's** *Rotterdam* are on sale in the excellent museum shop, which also sells old shipping posters, books in English, etc.) Ramps (good for accessibility) from one floor to another are suggestive of ship gangways and pass windows with fine views of the museum's adjoining water-berthed exhibits: steam tugs, sailing vessels, and the fascinating restored Royal Dutch Navy warship *De Buffel*. *De Buffel* sailed under steam from 1868 to 1896. As shipshape as you'd expect a Dutch crew to keep her, the engine and copper tubing gleam as if new. You'd expect the deluxe quarters of the Commandant and officers, but what were truly progressive for its day was the impressive living standards for the sailors. As for the brig in *De Buffel's* bowels, I've *paid* to sail transatlantic in smaller cabins. Rotterdam's Maritime Museum shows that, as with music, ships and the sea stir emotions that transcend language.

Kijk-Kubus (Public Cube House)   ★

Overblaak 70; Jan.–Feb. Sat. and Sun. 11 a.m.–5 p.m., March–Dec. Tues.-Fri. 10 a.m.–5 p.m., Sat. and Sun. 11 a.m.–5 p.m., Jun.–Sept. also open Mon. 10 a.m.–5 p.m.; ☎ *4142285; Trams 3, 6, 7, Metro: Blaak.* The group of ★★38 **"cube" houses,** of which the Public Cube is one, situated in the central Rotterdam city district of *Blaak*, are collectively called "Het Blaakse Bos" (the Blaak Woods), due to the houses' other nickname, "tree dwellings." Seeing them, I didn't find it surprising that the cube houses had garnered so many descriptive names, since they are so unexpected, so imaginative, in their shape and setting. Designed by architect Piet Blom and built in 1984, the cube houses serve as an upper-level "bridge," linking the waterfront, particularly the picturesque and popular pub-lined ★**Oude Haven**, to the town: Rotterdam's Centraal Library, the general street market's Mariniersweg, and older post-World War II residential areas. As you wander beneath the cube-shaped houses, tipped 'til they're resting on one corner point, you can't help wondering what they're like as living spaces; can the floors *possibly* be level? All is answered in a visit to the intriguing "model" cube. I will say that the windowed top point of the cube made me want to spend a night lying on the floor looking up at the stars.

Euromast & Spacetower   ★

Parkhaven 20; end-March–early-Sept. daily 10 a.m.–7 p.m., Oct.–March daily 10 a.m.–6 p.m., Euromast Spacetower daily 11 a.m.–4 p.m., weekends only in Jan. and Feb., and may be closed at other times due to weather conditions; ☎ *4364811; Tram 6 or 9, Metro Dijkzigt, bus 39.* Today an established silhouette on the city skyline, the Euromast was built in 1960. In 1970 the Spacetower was added, since the 27-story *Erasmus University Medical Faculty* (the large gleaming white, rather ship-like, structure on West Zeedijk), built in the interim, had robbed the Euromast of the 360-degree view that it advertised. At 600 feet (185 meters), the Spacetower's unmarred views over city and port seem secure. The ★★**panoramic view** from the Spacecabin, as it ascends and descends (in a total of five minutes) while slowly revolving, is wonderful in good weather. It has comfortable couch seating aimed outward and, I was told, you can stay seated and go up and down again for the original price of admission. Note that there's an outside flight of stairs (and observation deck) at the Euromast level (340 feet) to reach the Spacecabin. In the Euromast are both formal and informal restaurants, and at the base there's a gift shop.

WHERE TO STAY

EXPENSIVE

Parkhotel ★★★★
Westersingel 70, 3015 LB; ☎ *4363611, FAX 4364212; U.S.* ☎ *800-223-6510, Canada* ☎ *800-424-5500.* Predominantly a business hotel during the week, the Park is located by Museumpark, not far from the Boymans Museum, and within walking distance of transportation, shopping, and most central sights. Of the 154 rooms, 60 are in the new wing, upgraded with air conditioning, minisafes, double-glazed windows, and lightwood decor. Nonsmoking rooms available. An art work passage connects the new and old sections of the hotel, which has a library corner in its fire-placed modern lounge. The well-kept, less expensive (moving them down into the moderate-price category) rooms in the older part of the building have larger bedrooms and baths, luxurious spreads, minibars, hair dryers. Fitness facilities available, free-parking behind hotel; room service 6 a.m.–1 a.m. There's an à la carte restaurant and a casual grill-cafe.

MODERATE

Hotel Inntel ★★★★
Leuvehaven 80, 3011 EA; ☎ *4134139, FAX 4133222.* One of Rotterdam's recent additions on the hotel front comes with harbor and port views, a location from which all city attractions are walkable, or within a quick hop on the tram located across the street. The 150 light, tidy rooms, all with small, modern bathrooms with tubs and wall-mounted showers, remote TV and telephone, feature big windows. Red leather couches, marble, mirrors, stainless steel, recessed lighting, and windows are the ingredients of the cheerful lobby. There's a lobby restaurant, where breakfast (included) also is served; the **Waterway Bar** has snacks 5 p.m.–1 a.m., with a harborview, and skyline lights after dark. The top floor fitness center has a pool with large windows facing harbor; sauna, solarium. No room service. In all, a very pleasant place.

Hotel New York ★★★★
Koninginnenhoofd 1, 3072 AD; ☎ *4390500, FAX 4842701.* Situated midharbor on an island in Rotterdam's busy River Maas, Hotel New York occupies the newly restored early 20th-century art nouveau-style building that served as head office for the **Holland America Line** until its ocean liners discontinued transatlantic service from there to New York City in the early '70s. The remarkable location of the landmark building—its cafe-restaurant looks out mid-river on the world's largest port, across Rotterdam's dramatically modern skyline—makes the present limited access worth overcoming: In decent traffic it's a ten minute taxi ride to the hotel from center city, and a water taxi runs between the hotel and a fairly central city location. (Soon there will be

a new bridge over the Maas connecting downtown with the end of the hotel pier, where a Metro stop is also planned.) The 74 rooms are spacious, with high ceilings; most have river views; windows can be opened. Other amenities include a winter garden, belvedere observation tower, gym, public parking.

INEXPENSIVE

Bienvenue   ★★

Spoorsingel 24, 3033 GL; ☎ *4669394, FAX 4677475.* Located two blocks out the rear door of the Centraal Station, on a residential street fronting a quiet canal, this 1920s house has ten rooms, half with private shower and toilet. The cheerful, family run hotel is basic but very clean and neat; beds have firm mattresses. Front rooms overlook canal and lawns; there's a garden in the back. No elevator; pay telephone at reception. The lobby lounge/reception/breakfast (only) room is one flight up, with window boxes, canal view.

WHERE TO EAT

Located in Het Park, not far from the Euromast, with views of the Nieuwe Maas, **Restaurant Parkheuvel** *(Heuvellaan 21; lunch noon–3 p.m., dinner 6–10 p.m., closed Sun.;* ☎ *4360766; moderate)* also serves nouvelle cuisine that ranks among the best in Holland, complemented by an excellent wine list. **Zochers'** *(Baden Powell Laan 12; open daily for lunch, dinner till 10 p.m.;* ☎ *4364249; inexpensive)* also is located in Het Park, in the former mansion of the restaurant's landscape architect namesake. Varied fare, snacks, exotic drinks, and a Sunday morning brunch buffet with classical music. Outside dining terrace overlooks the formal box gardens.

For dining with a impressive view day or night, there's the Panorama, 320 feet high in the **Euromast** *(Parkhaven 20; daily noon–7 p.m., 5 p.m. in winter;* ☎ *4364811; inexpensive)* for buffet lunches and dinner, or lighter fare. **Silhouet** *(open until 10 p.m., closed Sun., Mon.;* ☎ *4364811; moderate/expensive)* is the à la carte restaurant (also aperitif bar) in the Space-Cabin, serving French-accented continental cuisine. With another wonderful view of Rotterdam's new skyline, at ground-level near *Willemsbrug* (lighted at night) and other port and harbor lights, **La Meuse** *(at Tropicana. Maasboulevard 100; Mon.– Fri. noon–11 p.m., Sat., Sun noon–7 p.m.;* ☎ *4020700; moderate)* has a three-course menu with wine for about Dfl. 50. There's also a meal with a view right in the center of the city, on the 23rd story of the **World Trade Center Restaurant** *(Beursplein 37; Mon.-Fri. noon-9:30 p.m., closed holidays, Sat., Sun.;* ☎ *4054465; moderate).*

At Delfshaven, there are several dining choices. For fish or mussels, head for **Le Harve** *(Havenstraat 9a; daily, lunch, dinner til 10 p.m.;* ☎ *4257172; moderate),* and speak up for a window table. **Eethuis de Parel** (The Pearl) *(Voorhaven 54; Wed.–Sun. 5–11 p.m., kitchen til 9 p.m., closed Mon., Tues.; moderate)* will offer fish but also meat and vegetarian dishes, overlooking the canal from which the Pilgrim Fathers sailed. **Cafe "Oude Sluis"** *(Havenstraat 7; daily;* ☎ *4773068; inexpensive)* has real working class "brown cafe" character and, from the small back terrace or tables on the bridge, a great view of the old harbor.

If you want informal fare in the area of the city that Rotterdammers are most fond of, head for the **Oude Haven**. There, against an eclectic backdrop of the Cube Houses, the Pencil, and the boats in the picturesque harbor, is a neighborhood conglomerate of pubs and restaurants, most of which spill out onto the terraces in good weather. The establishments located around the Oude Haven each have their own character, but **Pardoen** *(Spaansekade 62; daily, kitchen closes at 8 p.m., but open for drinks much later;* *4130910; inexpensive)* is typical in its personableness in service and setting. Uitsmijters, omelets, salads, toasted sandwiches, etc. **Cafe de Unie** *(Mauritsweg 34; daily until 9 p.m.;* ☎ *4117394; inexpensive)* is characterized by post modern minimalist decor and has a De Stijl facade in primary colors. Situated on a canal, with a very large front window, it's a good place for snacks or meals while watching the world go by. Another colorful cafe is **'t Oude Tramhuys** *(Westersingel, at intersection with Nieuwe Binnenweg; inexpensive)*.

IN THE AREA

Kinderdijk ★★

At no other single site in the world will you find as many windmills as in the Dutch town of Kinderdijk (near Alblasserdam), nine miles SE of Rotterdam. In about 1740, 19 mills were built here to drain excess water from the Alblasserwaard polders. Although power-driven pumping engines do the job now, the mills remain well-preserved. The rural Kinderdijk site is always open (no fee) and, though often crowded during the day in season, is an essentially unspoiled setting. From Apr. through Sept., one of the mills is open to visitors daily, except Sun., showing its antique interior with furnishings, and mechanical workings. Every Sat. afternoon in July and Aug., the mills are put into operation. During the second complete week in Sept., the mills are illuminated at night. From May through Oct., there's the possibility of a cruise in the mill region (☎ *01859-12482*).

Rotterdamse Havenroute

The ANWB (Dutch auto club), in conjunction with the Port of Rotterdam publishes a Rotterdam Port Route booklet in English, with detailed information and directions intended to give the automobile-driving traveler the clearest possible picture of the vast installation. Inquire at ANWB or the VVV.

Spido's Delta Works and Seven Waterways Cruise ★

 010-4135400. In July and Aug., Spido runs nine-hour (beginning 10 a.m.) excursions from Rotterdam that take in, by way of water, locations including the Nieuwe Maas, Oude Maas, Haringvliet, Hollands Diep, the Pernis Oil refineries, the sluices near Hellevoetsluis, Willemstad, Dordrecht, and the windmills of Kinderdijk, as well as a visit to the ★★ **Delta Works** in *Zeeland* in Southern Holland.

NORTHERN HOLLAND

The north of the Netherlands includes the provinces of Friesland, Groningen, and Drenthe. The northern provinces are anchored by the cities of Leeuwarden, capital of Friesland, and Groningen, capital of its same-name province.

Friesland has an atmosphere of landed nobility and wealth. Cows (the famous *Frisian black and whites*, bred and exported around the world) have for centuries been so important to the province's economy that a statue of one (named *Us Mem*—"Our Mother") stands near the station in the center of Leeuwarden. The countryside is studded with prosperous farmhouses, distinctive in that the family living quarters and barns often are sheltered under a single huge roof. Black glazed tiles—as distinguished from the more common ones in orange terracotta—were symbols of wealth and used over the home section of the structure.

The Frisians were early settlers of the sea-embattled land in the north, living first on man-made mounds *(terps)* meant to keep them above the high water level. By the year 1000, they had developed an extensive network of dikes. Friesland has always seemed separate from the rest of the Netherlands, its location on the far side of the former **Zuiderzee** (now the enclosed *IJsselmeer*) adding to its sense of remoteness. The road atop the enclosing **Afsluitdijk** (opened in 1932) provided a more accessible driving route to the province and opened Friesland to more outside influence, but even today, few residents of Holland, and fewer visitors, know much about this interesting and attractive area.

In addition to Dutch, Friesland has had its own language (today, a compulsory course in the province's primary schools) and body of literature for centuries; *Frisian* is described as being "a brother to the English language and a cousin to Dutch." The Frisian people have long been friends of the United States. In 1782, while still an independent province, Friesland was the first government to recognize the newly formed United States of America as a country; there's a plaque stating that fact in the historic Provincial House in Leeuwarden. The Frisians also strongly urged the Dutch government to loan the young America some much-needed capital.

Groningen, at the "top" of Holland, has far-stretching fields, rows of poplars permanently bent by the winds off the shallow *Waddenzee*, and horizons marked by "mountains" of clouds. The only town of any size in the province, Groningen was a center of activity by the 11th century and today retains the inner-city waterways that were its moats in earlier eras. The landmark of the attractive historic city center is **Martinikerk**, a lovely church largely 15th-century in appearance, though begun in the 13th. The distinguished **University of Groningen** was founded in 1614.

Mooi **Drenthe** ("lovely Drenthe") is the way this northeastern province, the least well-known of the country's twelve, often is described. With Drenthe's heathland, inland sandbanks, peat fens, and woods, the phrase is apt—and certainly more appealing than Drenthe's other epithet: "the forgotten province." The most intriguing attractions in Drenthe are reminders of its prehistoric (c. 3000 B.C.) inhabitants, great megalithic burial chambers known as *Hunebeds*, many of which survive, especially along the Hondsrug ridge that runs northwest from Emmen.

As interesting as the "far" north of Holland may be, it is the "near" north, with its picturesque old fishing villages around what formerly was the **Zuiderzee** (South Sea, now the IJsselmeer lake) that usually is most rewarding for visitors. Of particular interest are **West Friesland** (the northeast section of today's North Holland province) and, across the Afsluitdijk that closed off the Zuiderzee, the **southwest corner of Friesland**. Most visitors also want to know how the new polder province of **Flevoland**, which exists in a region that until 1932 was under the tidal waters of the Zuiderzee came to be reclaimed from the bottom of that sea.

OLD ZUIDERZEE VILLAGES AND THE NEW POLDER PROVINCE

Following two centuries of topographic turmoil—sinking land, rising seas, and mounting floods—the great storm of 1287 breached the sand dune barrier between the North Sea and what had been an inland lake north of Amsterdam. The flood produced by the storm (which killed 50,000 in Friesland alone) created the **Zuiderzee**, whose tidal shores became the site for the many flourishing fishing villages and seafaring towns that gave the region its identity. Their Zuiderzee connection became the characteristic quality of these quaint, often handsome, seashore communities. So strong was the shaping force of the Zuiderzee on life around its rim that 60 years after the great **Afsluitdijk** (barrier dam) sealed it off from the North Sea once again in 1932, you can still sense the salt in the air of the picturesque old ports, now mostly filled with recreational sail boats instead of commercial sailing ships.

For many visitors to the area, sentimental regret for the passing of the "sailing on the tide" seafaring tradition of the Zuiderzee villages is offset by a fascination with the story of the creation of a whole new province of polderland from what used to be the bottom of the sea. The tale is exceptionally well told—in multiple languages—at the **Informatiecentrum Nieuw Land** located in **Lelystad**, capital of the new Flevoland polder province.

GUIDELINES
SIGHTS

There's a great deal of scenic variety in the region covered in this chapter, from compact waterland villages to prosperous towns that sent forth sea captains around the world in the 17th century. The open-air **Zuiderzee Museum** at Enkhuizen gives an impression of daily life and work in the Zuiderzee region during the period of 1880–1930. The 350-year-old craft of making Dutch tiles and porcelain can be seen in **Makkum**, and Hoorn's **West Fries Museum** is one of the area's most attractive sources of local history. You can also encounter traditional costumes; thatched farmhouses; a village where farmers ferry cattle from one grazing field to another on flat-bottomed boats; castles; and cloudscapes above Friesland's vast and verdant reaches that will make you catch your breath.

GETTING AROUND

Reaching the sights in this section requires a car, although certain places are served by train: Hoorn, Enkhuizen, and Lelystad, more or less conveniently from Amsterdam. Groningen, Leeuwarden, Harlingen, and Kampen can be reached on trains via Utrecht. An historic steam train runs between Medemblik-Hoorn-Enkhuizen from May–Sept. (☎ *02290-16653*). Local and regional buses go to literally every village, but a traveler with limited time will not want to waste it waiting at remote countryside crossroads to make a bus connection. A word of caution about driving on the provincial roads: many are single lane in each direction; the flatness of the polder terrain, combined with the speed at which local drivers go, can fool you about on-coming car distances, so be wary when planning to pass. Also, the smaller the rental car you can manage with, the easier it will be to navigate on tight turns in tiny villages.

SHOPPING

The larger towns on this route (Hoorn, Harlingen, Kampen) have the most varied selection of shops for basic and specialty goods. There's a museum shop with gift items at Enkhuizen's **Zuiderzee**

Museum. **Hindeloopen**, once famed for its painted furniture, has a number of shops with smaller items in its distinctive style. **Makkum** has stores selling its traditional Dutch tiles and porcelain.

ENTERTAINMENT AND EVENTS

Wednesdays from early July to mid-August, there are **folklore markets** in Hoorn. Thursdays (mid-June to mid-August), the West Frisian Folklore markets are held in Schagen. Also on Thursday afternoons in July and August, in both Enkhuizen and at the **Zuiderzee Museum**, large groups from various Zuiderzee villages dress in traditional costume and perform live music. From mid-April-late May, **bulb fields** bloom around West Friesland; those at *Anna Paulowna* are the largest unbroken stretches of flowers in the country. Every 3rd Sunday of the month from Easter to September Naarden celebrates **Civil Guard** days in medieval costume at its Vesting Museum. A small **cheese market** with handicrafts is held in Purmerend on Thurs. in July and Aug. from 11 a.m.–1 p.m. The Dutch are fond of taking guided hikes through the **Waddenzee mud flats** in summer.

WHERE TO STAY

Given the limited quantity and size of hotels in the area, reservations are suggested, and are a must in the summer months when the Dutch and other Europeans come here on holiday. (Even those arriving by private sail boat—which many do—often opt for a hotel with a hot shower.)

WHERE TO EAT

Seafood is bound to come to mind as you circle the former Zuiderzee and see the wealth that fishing brought to its villages and towns. Most hotels have a more-than-reputable restaurant.

TRAVEL TIPS

Keep a stash of *guilders* and *kwartjes* (25-cent pieces) on hand for parking meters, so you can make the most of short stops in towns.

CENTRAL HOLLAND

One of the most noticeable characteristics of the countryside in the central part of Holland is that, east of Utrecht, most of the land lies above sea level. The landscape has large stands of forest primeval that haven't undergone the scourge of centuries of saltwater floods. Thousands of acres of trees adorn Apeldoorn's **Royal Park** and the **National Park De Hoge Veluwe**, both of which fill much of the triangle formed by three of the principal cities in the center of Holland:

Arnhem, **Apeldoorn**, and **Amersfoort**. In addition to old trees, the landscape in this region is lightly rolling, rather than water-surface flat as in the west of the country.

GUIDELINES FOR ARNHEM, APELDOORN, AND AMERSFFORT

SIGHTS

Several of the most interesting and important museums in the country are situated in central Holland, in or near the towns of Arn-hem, Apeldoorn, and Amersfoort. The rich fruit orchards of the **Betuwe** ("good land") and the country's largest national park, **De Hoge Veluwe** ("bad land"), with its drifting sand dunes, heathland (in bloom late August through September), and woods, add another scenic dimension.

GETTING AROUND

The three main cities are served by train. From the rail station in each there are local buses that serve most of the other attractions, towns, and villages covered. However, it must be mentioned that depending upon public transportation, reliable though it is in Holland, will slow you down. A car is certainly recommended if you want to cover more than one of the major sites included here in one day. Taxis, while practical within Arnhem from the station, or for Het Loo from the Apeldoorn station, will be expensive to the **Kroller-Muller Museum** because of its rural location. Bicycle hire is possible at the city train stations, though again here an assessment of time and distance will need to be made. If you take a public bus (from Arnhem station), check with VVV for season and specific times: usu-ally there is a direct bus to the museum July–Sept., year-round public bus to Otterlo or Hoenderloo (3.4 and 4.0 km./approx 2 mi., re-spectively, to Visitor Center) from which bicycle rental and taxis are available. At the **Visitor Center** (*Bezoekerscentrum*) in the center of the national park **De Hoge Veluwe**, one of the famous little fleet of 400 "white bikes" (one speed, no basket or provision for parcels, no time limit) is available to you for free (a service to cut down on car traffic in the national park) on a first-come basis; weekends can be busy, but there's also back-up paid bicycle hire on the premises. The **Kroller-Muller Museum** is an easy and enjoyable bike ride from the park Visitor Center, and there are plenty of paved cycle routes of dif-ferent duration in De Hoge Veluwe.

SHOPPING

These three cities are the main shopping centers in the region. **Het Loo** palace has an excellent gift shop, the museum shop at the **Kroller Muller** has a wide selection of art books, prints, and cards, and there's a gift shop at the Arnhem **Openluchtmuseum**.

ENTERTAINMENT AND EVENTS

Check with VVV about the Amersfoort carillon concerts in the **Onze Lieve Vrouwetoren** and **Belgian Monument** and organ concerts in the **1534 St. Joriskerk**. The cities of Arnhem and Nijmegen commemorate Operation Market-Garden each September. In Spakenburg, traditional costume and crafts fairs take place on the last two Wednesdays in July and the first two in August.

WHERE TO STAY

With the exception of the **Keizerskroon** across from Het Loo in Apeldoorn, country accommodations in the area will prove more interesting than their in-town counterparts.

WHERE TO EAT

Keep in mind that many museums have fine cafes and/or restaurants. There are some excellent country restaurants in the region, located in settings from sophisticated rustic to castles.

ARRIVING

Holland's public transportation and information coordination will impress you anew. At **Arnhem** (pop. 130,000), local and regional buses and the VVV (*Stationplein 45,* ☎ *085-420330*) are located at the train station, as is true in **Amersfoort** (*VVV Stationplein 27,* ☎ *033-635151; pop. 100,000*), and **Apeldoorn** (*VVV Stationplein 6,* ☎ *055-788421; pop. 144,000*).

IN THE AREA

Many visitors come via Arnhem to visit the exceptional **Kroller-Muller Museum** (with its 278 van Goghs and other great 19th-and 20th-century paintings and sculpture) set in the Dutch national Park **De Hoge Veluwe**. **Oosterbeck** has an **Airborne Museum** about the *Market-Garden Operation* of Sept. 1944.

TRAVEL TIPS

Remember that throughout Holland, VVVs in major towns and cities (identified with an "i" sign) can supply you with quite detailed and up-to-date information about museum hours and public transportation in other regions. That way you can plan a day trip ahead of time with the help of your "home base" VVV; having the details about public transportation/opening hours, etc. for your destination beforehand will result in more time to enjoy what you came to see and do.

SOUTHERN HOLLAND

Southern Holland includes the provinces of **Zeeland**, **North Brabant**, and **Limburg**, all lying "below" the great *Rhine, Maas,* and *Waal* rivers, which flow from the interior of the European continent to empty into the North Sea near Rotterdam.

Even Dutch tourism officials use the term "Southern Holland" in their foreign-language literature, since it's a convenient phrase for referring to this less-well-traveled section of the country. However, it's precisely in this region that the resident Dutch want to make the point that their country is **The Netherlands**, *not* Holland—which, technically, is only two provinces, North and South (Holland). Travelers in these southern provinces who use the word "Holland" when speaking of the country may encounter occasional explanations (always given with a smile). When I'm in Zeeland, North Brabant, or Limburg I attempt to be sensitive to the issue by trying to remember—not always successfully—to use the name "Netherlands."

The Dutch provinces in the south of the Netherlands are linked by ties to Belgium, on which they all border. Here, history left the boundaries a bit blurred: not—since the mid-19th century—politically, but psychologically. Rule by the Burgundians and the Spanish lasted longer in the **southern Netherlands** (today's Belgium), and the cross-cultivation across the southern Dutch border—which shifted regularly for centuries—left a greater impact upon the personality of the people there than elsewhere in today's Netherlands. The differences between the Dutch in the north of the country and those in the south may not *leap* out at you, but only the most casual passer-through will not notice the change in mentality and mood between the Holland "north of the rivers" and the Netherlands south of them.

ZEELAND

Well-named, **Zeeland** ("sea land") is as much water as land, and much of what *is* land lies below sea level. The southern section of Zeeland, Zeeuwsch Vlaanderen, is connected to the European continent at Belgium's border but to the rest of its own province only by car ferries across the watery finger of the **Westerschelde**, which points inland to the Belgian port of Antwerp. **Walcheren**, with the provincial capital **Middelburg**, and **Noorde** and **Zuid Beveland**, form Zeeland's largest "island grouping," some linked by modern dikes and dams, and others, once attached to the mainland, now sliced from it by canals but reconnected by bridges. **Zeelandbrug**, Europe's longest bridge at 5,022 meters/3.1 miles, reaches gracefully across the **Oosterschelde**, the mouth of which has been given "the teeth" of the massive 65 concrete pier-*Stormvloedkering* (storm surge barrier), the final complex part of the most impressive hydraulic engineering plan ever undertaken in the world: the **Delta Expo**. Interest in that project has brought a new public to beach-blessed Zeeland, though the remote-seeming province's contact with the greater world still comes mostly in the form of summer holiday makers.

From an early date, Zeeland shared in the trade prominence and prosperity that its access to the sea provided. Historically, the province of Holland (today's North and South Holland combined) also included Zeeland, which had been annexed by Holland in 1323, following long disputes over its territory by the Counts of Holland and Flanders. Basically, Zeeland, Holland, and Flanders shared a similar history for some 500 years up until 1436, at which time Holland itself was annexed into the wide holdings of Duke Philip of Burgundy. Early trade in *wool* and *cloth* with England and Scotland created wealth for the region, a fact attested to by richly adorned public buildings such as the **Middelburg** and **Veere stadhuizen**. It certainly was a boon for Zeeland business when, in 1444, Lord of Veere Wolfert van Borssele married Mary, one of the six daughters of James I of Scotland, a match that led the way to Veere's monopoly in the **Scottish wool trade**, which lasted until the French occupation of Holland of 1795.

Meanwhile, many Zeeland towns were involved in the sieges of the Dutch seven-province struggle against the Spanish. **Vlissingen**, an ancient town of little previous importance, was chosen in 1556 as embarkation port by Spanish King Philip II, who left the Netherlands embittered against his Dutch subjects, accusing Willem the Silent of treachery. When the Spanish attacked in the 1570s, Vlissingen was one of the first towns to revolt against them.

Low-lying Zeeland has a long history of floods. One of the worst was the St. Elizabeth Flood of 1421, which destroyed 72 Zeeland villages and drowned some 10,000 inhabitants. Though fewer human lives (1,835) were lost during the **hurricane of February 1, 1953**, which breached many of Zeeland's dikes, 200,000 livestock died, some 485,000 acres of the country's most fertile farmland were submerged in salt water, and 48,000 homes were damaged, many beyond repair. That catastrophic storm, combined with the degree to which the Dutch had raised the science of hydraulic engineering, resulted in a "never-again" stance that subsequently produced the **Delta Project**. (In February 1990 a hurricane again struck the coast of Holland—the same storm caused death and devastation also in the U.K., Belgium, and inland in Luxembourg,—but, with the Delta Project in place, it was only beaches, not breaches, that required repair from sea damage.)

What must have made the disastrous hurricane of 1953 even more devasting for Zeeland was that it came so soon after the enormous flood damage sustained by the province during World War II's deliberate **bombing** by the RAF in September/October 1944 to unearth the Nazis from their bunkered positions in Walcheren, from which they controlled the Westerschelde entrance to the port of Antwerp. (Following the successful Normandy invasion in June 1944, the Allies had a particular need for Antwerp as a port for landing supplies for the rest of their continental campaign.) Beginning in September, bombs rained down on Walcheren's dikes, the aim being to breach them and literally flood the Nazis out. By the end of October 1944, the RAF had succeeded in causing several serious breaches in the dikes at Westkapelle, Veere, Vlissingen, and Rammekens. Most of Walcheren lay under sea water (where it remained for more than 13 months, during which time most trees, as well as all other vegetation, died). Walcheren was freed by Allied troops (including the *2nd Canadian Division*), landing at **Vlissingen** and **Westkapelle** (*Landing Monument* and other memorials) on November 1, 1944. By the end of 1944, work was begun on repairing the breaches, although it wasn't until February 1946 that the last gap in the dikes of Zeeland closed. And the entire job of reconstruction had not been fully completed when the 1953 hurricane struck.

Today it's possible for travelers as well as residents to put to rest that troubled past, and enjoy Zeeland's peaceful rural setting of dignified farms, remote sand dunes, quaint quiet old towns, a quality of light that's a delight, and long-repaired dikes lined with full-grown rows of fast-growing "replacement" poplars.

GUIDELINES FOR ZEELAND
SIGHTS

Situated in the southwest of the Netherlands, cut by the Eastern and Western Scheldt river arms, Zeeland is made up of areas that originally were islands. That geographical fact created a certain isolation, which, while mitigated today by connecting roads resulting from the Delta Project, produces within the province more vestiges of older customs (such as *traditional costumes*) than are visible in Randstad, Holland. Zeeland's location between Flanders and Holland involved it in important mercantile enterprises in the 15th-17th centuries, a fact reflected in rich and refined buildings such as the stadhuizen in **Middelburg** and the villages of **Veere**. Other historic towns such as **Zierikzee**, **Goes**, **Tholen**, and **Sluis** will make your camera-shutter-finger itchy. **Vlissingen** is a busy long-established port and resort. Today, Zeeland's beaches are busy in summer, and her former sea fishermen have turned their focus to cultivating the famous *Zeeuws oysters* and *mussels*. The ingenious **Delta Works**, the definitive protection for the province against a too-assertive sea, attracts visitors from around the world.

GETTING AROUND

Without question, a **car** is the best way to capture the essence of the area. There's a quite extensive Zeeland provincial **bus** service: tiny Veere can be reached from Middelburg, for instance. Inclusive day **train** trips from major stations to the **Delta Expo** are run by the Netherlands Spoorwegen several times weekly. **Bicycle** rentals are available at Middelburg station (reservations in summer suggested) and many private locations throughout Zeeland. Two-wheelers are common commuting means for Zeelanders, and you're liable to come across Walcheren women in traditioinal dress (cap with lace "blinkers" and golden coils, black shawl, voluminous skirts, and black and white overskirt) pedalling with a full load of parcels.

SHOPPING

The main shopping centers in the region are Middelburg, Vlissingen, Zierikzee, Goes, and Hulst. Some shops close for lunch (*generally 12:30–1:30 p.m.*); most are closed on Sunday, although there's an exception for shops in some towns in Zeeuwsch-Vlaanderen, which keep open to compete with the nearby Belgium shops that open Sundays.

ENTERTAINMENT AND EVENTS

Although *traditional costumes* are seen less and less frequently in Zeeland, they are still worn with some regularity in Walcheren and South-Beveland, the best bet to see them being at the **weekly general markets** (in *Goes* on Tuesday, *Middelburg* and *Zierikzee* on Thursday, *Vlissingen* on Friday), or Sunday mornings en route to a rural church. **Tilting at the Ring**, a traditional "tournament" game with horses (that also amounts to something of a flower festival), is held once in July and once in August (check with the VVV for specific dates).

WHERE TO STAY

One should book well ahead during the peak summer season. Vlissingen has the most hotels, and the most liveliness, no doubt because of its port. Most Zeeland hotels are the small, family run sort. The **Zeeland Provinciale VVV**, upstairs from the Middelburg VVV on the Markt, *(Mon.–Fri. 8:30 a.m.–noon and 1:15–5:00 p.m.;* ☎ *01180-33051)* can help with bed and breakfast-type accommodations (most plentiful, and most heavily booked, in summer).

WHERE TO EAT

There's nothing more appropriate—fresher and more varied—to grace the tables in Zeeland than the "fruits of the sea." Specialties are shellfish: oysters, mussels, North Sea "gray" shrimp, lobsters, winkles. A number of fish are also landed here (sole, turbot, eel). Traditional locally-produced sweets include *bolus* (sweet rolls) and *babelaars* (buttery candies). Do not neglect the restaurants in hotels in Zeeland, since it is through customers' stomachs that those establishments often attract overnight guests.

ARRIVING

Zeeland borders on Belgian Flanders. Daily **car-ferries** run between Sheerness, in Kent, England, and Vlissingen (Flushing) in Zeeland. Locations in Zeeland that can be reached by **train** are limited to Middelburg, Goes, and Vlissingen, *via Roosendaal,* located on the main Brussels–Antwerp–Amsterdam line.

NORTH BRABANT

Brabant was born as a part of the duchy of Lower Lorraine, which was created in the 10th century amid the territorial reshufflings that followed Charlemagne's death. In 1190, Lower Lorraine ruler Duke Henry I took upon himself the new title duke of Brabant. The **Duchy of Brabant** (which included much of what today is the Dutch province of North Brabant and the Belgian provinces of Brabant and Antwerp), lasted from then until 1430, when Duke Anthony died childless, leaving the title to Duke Philip the Good of Burgundy. From that time, Brabant's history merged with the Netherlands.

During the *Eighty Years' War* (1568–1648), Brabant was split in two, the southern section being retained by Spain (and eventually becoming the Belgian provinces of Brabant and Antwerp), while the northern portion was merged with Willem the Silent's Dutch Protestant rebellion. North Brabant became part of the United Provinces under the *Treaty of Munster* (1648), but only as a "land," not a self-governing province. During the occupation of the Netherlands by Napoleon (1795–1814), the two Brabants were reunited. But, with the establishment of the Kingdom of the Netherlands in 1815, Brabant was again separated into its Dutch and Belgian parts, this time North Brabant having full status as a Dutch province.

Historically, the people in North Brabant have been predominantly Roman Catholic (today 85% are so "on paper, not in practice" was the way it was put to me). After the rebellion of the Dutch against Spanish rule in the northern Netherlands, the success of Protestants there led to difficulties for North Brabant's Catholics. They felt that the Protestant leaders of Holland's *States General* in The Hague regarded them as a "colonial" territory, and that the economic well-being of the region was largely neglected.

Traditionally a "poor" province, in that the sand and clay soil from the region's rivers is not fertile enough to support the population economically, North Brabant has come into economic strength in this century largely due to development at **Eindhoven**. There, in 1891, Dr. Anton Philips founded a firm that produced electric light bulbs. As **Philips**, now a world-recognized name in electronic products, grew, Eindhoven became a "company town," such was the firm's influence in attracting talented people and bringing related industry to the region.

GUIDELINES FOR NORTH BRABANT
SIGHTS

Special places of interest are spread out in North Brabant, a roomy province, much of it woodlands, heath, and peat fen, extending west to east along the Belgian border from the Scheldt River to Limburg, and north to the Merwede and Maas river boundary. In **Eindhoven** (*VVV Stationplein 17*, ☎ *040-449231; pop. 192,000*), there's 20th-century art at the respected **Van Abbemuseum**, and a wonderful exhibit of the wonders of technology at Philips' **Evoluon**. Places where the past is palpable are the small fortified river towns of **Willemstad** in the west of the province, *Woudrichem* in the center, and **Grave**, **Ravenstein**, and **Megen** to the east. **Oirschot** (northwest of Eindhoven) has the most attractive and best preserved market square in Brabant (with cobblestones, shady old trees, gas lamps, and the dignified calm of centuries), and the entire town center is a national monument, including the Stadhuis (1463) and Gothic St. Pieterskerk (1465–1500). **Bergen op Zoom**, a historic town in the west of

North Brabant, where the dunes meet the heath, has a Grote Markt that's carefree with cafes in summer, and buildings that reflect its past, including the last 15th-century **Markiezenhof** palace, now a museum.

GETTING AROUND

Since sights of interest to the traveler are scattered, a car is nearly necessary for seeing your selected sites in a reasonable time frame. As everywhere in Holland, there is excellent provincial bus service, but it is time-consuming. Trains serve the major towns: **'s Hertogenbosch (Den Bosch)**; **Breda**; **Eindhoven**; **Bergen op Zoom**. Boat cruises (☎ *566773*) from Den Bosch to **Heusden** (*Tues., Thurs., Sat. 11 a.m. mid-June through Aug.*) and **Woudrichem** (*daily at 10 a.m. mid-June to late Aug.*) leave from the Dommel, near the town's train station.

SHOPPING

Branches of main Dutch stores can be found in the centers of cities and major towns; many will be located on now-pedestrianized streets.

ENTERTAINMENT AND EVENTS

Breda celebrates the pre-Lenten **Carnival** with the most vigor in North Brabant, though Bergen op Zoom and Den Bosch hold their own. In addition to its annual **Art and Antiques Fair**, Breda hosts the colorful **National Tattoo** at the end of each August, and a jazz festival then as well, with performances set mostly in the Grote Kerk. In mid-August, the Grote Kerk is decked out in flowers for *Breda Flora*. Den Bosch has an important annual vocalist competition, and in September Tilburg and Eindhoven have jazz festivals.

WHERE TO STAY

While there are pleasant town and country choices in the two-, three- and, occasionally, four-star categories, five-star luxury in the area is not available (except for a business hotel in Eindhoven). As elsewhere in Holland, the local VVVs are the most up-to-date accommodations authorities.

WHERE TO EAT

Anchovies from Bergen op Zoom can raise a thirst for Brabant-brewed beer. In May and June, asparagus is the traditional treat, and locally-favored sweet specialties include the Den Bosch "Bossche koek" (cake). Both rural bistros and highly regarded restaurants reflect a Burgundian fondness for fine food.

TRAVEL TIPS

When exploring by car in regions near rivers, check your map carefully, and ask questions locally, to make sure of the location of bridge and/or car ferry crossings.

LIMBURG PROVINCE

Limburg Province is an essentially north-south strip of land that stretches roughly 50 kms./30 miles in the southeast corner of the country, along the border that Holland shares with Germany. The Dutch Limburg forms a wedge into Belgium's Limburg province. The two Limburgs once were one, under the early bishoprics of Tongeren, then Maastricht, and finally Liège. Under the *Treaty of Munster* in 1648, the Spanish kept the southern portion of Limburg, but the Dutch United Provinces in the northern Netherlands received Maastricht and all Limburg east of the Maas (Meuse) River. In 1814, the two Limburgs were rejoined under the short-lived Dutch-Belgian United Kingdom of the Netherlands. In 1830, all of Limburg except Maastricht joined in the Belgian uprising against Dutch rule. Thereafter, Limburgers in the north regarded themselves as Belgian until divided again by the 1839 *Treaty of London*, under which the borders of the present Dutch Limburg province were set.

The northern part of Limburg province is made up largely of small industrial towns with rather uninspiring landscape, and travelers will find few sights of sufficient interest to warrant a stop. Exceptions include **Thorn**, cobbled, medieval, and known as the "white village," an epithet derived from its all-painted-white buildings. There's an interesting 13th-century gothic abbey church with baroque interior *(open daily, 9 a.m.–6 p.m., Easter-Oct.)*. Also worthy of a while is the old center of **Sittard**, around whose spacious Markt (parking, terrace cafes, shops) stand a number of 16th-century half-timbered structures. In the town center of **Heerlen** is the **Thermen Museum** *(Tues.–Fri., 10 a.m.–5 p.m., Sat., Sun., holidays 2–5 p.m.;* ☎ *045-764581)* with Roman baths, excavated in the 1970s, imaginatively on view from a bridge above. On display are related exhibits (descriptions in English) and maps of the important Roman roads that led through Heerlen.

Southern Limburg is by far the more physically attractive portion of the province, with wooded rolling hills unlike the landscape anywhere else in Holland. The summer holiday heart of the region is **Valkenburg**, a bustling, family-style place, with countless hotels, casinos, and a new *Thermae 2000* spa complex. But for most travelers, the most attractive, interesting, and historic place in Limburg by far is **Maastricht**. Only 125 miles from Amsterdam, diagonally across the country, Maastricht seems far more distant in terms of the differences in its ambience.

MAASTRICHT

GUIDELINES FOR MAASTRICHT

SIGHTS

Maastricht, with a population of 115,000, has an appealing and compact old center, with narrow cobbled streets, quaint squares, and some 1,450 protected historic monuments, the oldest from Roman days. The mellow yellow stone buildings of local marl in the restored pedestrian **Stokstraat Quarter** are from the 17th and 18th centuries, and many have sculpted gable stones. Maastricht, with its assemblage of churches (Romanesque and Gothic) and cafes, is ringed by rampart walls (built in 1229, 1350, and 1516, respectively), atop which one can encircle much of the town on foot. The river Maas adds interest to the city, which is divided by it, but reconnected by the multi-arched St. Servaas Bridge.

GETTING AROUND

Maastricht's mood is best met on foot; walking allows for poking into picturesque corners, glancing up at gables and gable stones, and making spontaneous stops where and when your senses are engaged. The VVV offers guided 1-1/2 hr. **walking tours** of the city *(at 2 p.m. on holiday weekend days, daily during July and Aug.; Sat. only April–June and Sept.–mid Nov.)*. The VVV also rents a "walkman" cassette taped tour of the city, sells the architecturally detailed book *A Walk Through Maastricht*, and supplies other self-guided walking tour literature. City buses provide coverage of the outskirts, and you can go by river cruise boat to see the St. Pietersburg caves. Taxis and rental bicycles can be had at the station.

SHOPPING

For such a relatively small city, Maastricht has surprisingly sophisticated shops, from boutiques to bakeries. Many of the main department and other stores are located on and just off the pedestrianized Grote Straat, which leads to the Vrijthof (main square). General markets are held on Marktplein in front of the Stadhuis Wednesdays and Fridays. Summer Saturdays from 10 a.m.–4 p.m. there are flea, antique, and art markets on the Markt. Late night shopping (9 p.m.) is on Thursday.

ENTERTAINMENT AND EVENTS

Available free from the VVV is the monthly events calendar *Maastricht Maandagenda*; there's a summary listing in English. Cafes, concerts, and **pub crawls** cover the favored evening activities. Maastrichtenaars enjoy the fact that their city has a church for every *week*, and a pub for every *day* in the year. A number of the pub/cafes have live music, and many remain open until 2 a.m. In summer, weekly evening organ concerts (usually Tuesday) are held at one of several churches. The well-known male choir **Mastreechter Staar** has free open rehearsals (except July and Aug.; details from the VVV). Maastricht is in **Carnival** country, and makes much of pre-lenten festivities; some museums are closed from the Saturday before through *Mardi Gras*. The Burgundian food festival of **Preuvenement** fits in with the city's intense interest in cuisine.

WHERE TO STAY

Maastricht offers a small but solid choice of hotels in the city. Some are family owned and operated; all deliver friendly, personal service. In the surrounding Limburg countryside are several castle/manor house-style hotels with renowned restaurants.

WHERE TO EAT

Without contest, this region is the cuisine capital of The Netherlands. Fresh produce and attention to preparation make it hard to find less than fine food at any eatery, but some restaurants really star on taste tests.

ARRIVING

Tucked into the far southeast corner of the Netherlands—which gives it almost a central continental location—Maastricht is a Dutch destination that can easily be included in an itinerary featuring Belgium, Luxembourg, France, Germany, and/or Switzerland. Maastricht is readily reached by rail, road, and air. There are hourly train arrivals from Amsterdam; an *Intercity* takes about 2.5 hours. Rail connections from The Hague and Rotterdam have a convenient cross-platform change at Eindhoven. Maastricht also is served hourly by trains from Belgium's Bruges, Ghent, Brussels, and Liège, and other European points. Via motorway, Maastricht is 215 kms./125 mi. by road from Amsterdam: it lies roughly halfway between Brussels and Cologne. Maastricht's modern airfield offers, among other service, several flights daily to/from Amsterdam on *NLM Cityhopper* (contact **KLM** for flight information) and to/from London.

IN THE AREA

The only U.S. military cemetery in the Netherlands is nearby at *Margraten*. Old fortified farms, villages with half-timbered buildings, and country castles are scattered in the rolling hills of surrounding southern Limburg.

TRAVEL TIPS

If you don't plan to have a rental car in this rural region of the Netherlands, you needn't worry about missing the province's most important historic and sightseeing highlights, since these are in Maastricht itself. The cruise along the River Maas to Liège, Belgium, (20 kms./12 mi.) is *not* recommended, because the riverside scenery does not justify the length of time the trip takes (several hours one way); if travelling to Liège, take a quick train instead.

MAASTRICHT IN CONTEXT

Masstricht isn't a name that readly rolls off the tongues of tourists, even those fairly familiar with Holland. But it's been in the news a lot lately, primarily because of a treaty signed here at the end of 1991 by the leaders of the 12 **European Community** member countries. The so-called *Maastricht Treaty* provides for monetary union within the EC and for the adoption of a single European currency by 1999. As ratification of the treraty came up in each EC country so again did mention of Maastricht.

Maastricht is the Netherlands' oldest, southernmost (it lies well below Belgium's northern border), and most unexpected city. For starters, the largely Roman Catholic population of Maastricht practices an almost unDutch-like indulgence in the good life, exhibiting a Burgundian *joie de vivre*, and focusing on fine food, drink, and fun. As one resident put it, "We don't have a lazy mentality, but we do love life." That contrasts sharply with the "Black Stocking" attitude towards life endorsed by the dourly conservative, very religious element of the Protestant Dutch Reformed Church in the north of the country, whose numbers undoubtedly would be shocked by the view held *here*: "Catholicism allows you to enjoy yourself."

In Maastricht and surrounding Limburg, features commonly associated with Holland—waterlogged land, windmills, wooden-shoes —make way for other characteristics in the intriguing territory of this tricultured corner of the Netherlands. With **Aachen, Germany** (the ancient city inseparably associated with Charlemagne and the

Holy Roman Empire), and **Liège, Belgium** (the capital of French-speaking Wallonia), each only a dozen miles (20 km.) away, Maastricht merchants have long accepted *marks* and *francs* as freely as *guilders*, providing a foretaste of the European monetary dexterity anticipated under the European Community's "single market" economic initiatives.

Maastricht's "mentality" encompasses the foreign influences of its nearby neighbors. As a guide explained, "In Maastricht we live and let live. Sometimes those who are surrounded only by their own kind become judgmental, but this doesn't happen in Maastricht where so many things mix." Many Maastrichtenaars could be called chauvinists, in that they love their city above all others, but, as one city official said, "People like us who live in places where their history has gone back and forth feel European or international, not overly nationalistic." Another expressed it this way: "We don't feel we're crossing a border when we go to Belgium or Germany, but we do feel we've come home when we get back to Maastricht."

Maastricht was founded by the **Romans** about 50 B.C. Its name derived from the Latin *Mosae Trajectum*, meaning "site where the Maas could be crossed." The settlement, which grew to become a walled *castellum* (fortified district), was located on important roads, the foremost of which ran from the English Channel and North Sea ports to Cologne, and was known as the "Appian Way of the North." Towards the end of the 4th century, after 400 years of occupation during which Maastricht became a center of Christianity, the Romans and their army withdrew to return to Rome, leaving the city vulnerable to attack by Frankish tribes. Their raids were among the first of more than twenty beseigements suffered by Maastricht over succeeding centuries, the most recent being the four-year Nazi occupation during World War II. That ended in September 1944, when the 30th Infantry "Old Hickory" Division of the *U.S. 1st. Army* made Maastricht the first town in war-ravaged Holland to be freed.

From A.D. 380 to 721, Maastricht was a bishop's seat, becoming so when **St. Servaas**, fearing the Frankish tribes, transferred the see from Tongeren (the oldest town in Belgium) to Maastricht. A small chapel was built on the site where he was buried in Maastricht, and several centuries later a cathedral named for him began taking shape there. In 721, **St. Hubert**, Maastricht's last bishop, transferred the see to Liège (which led to an era of great power for the prince-bishops there).

Maastricht came under the influence and favor of Charlemagne's Frankish Empire when the Holy Roman Emperor made his base at nearby Aachen. Having survived the turbulent centuries following the death of Charlemagne (in 814), Maastricht became, in 1204, a joint possession of the dukes of Brabant and the prince-bishops of Liège. With feudal fending required to keep itself intact, Maastricht erected its first protective ramparts in 1229. It wasn't long before the town outgrew them, and a second set of city walls was added about 1350. Sections of each still stand. These were the earliest of many bastions that eventually made Maastricht one of Europe's most strongly fortified cities. With its strategic European location, the armies of the Spanish, French, English, and Germans all too often over the centuries beat a path to the city's sturdy town gates.

In 1576, Maastricht joined with **Willem the Silent's** other Dutch supporters in rebellion against the Spanish. But in 1579, Spanish leader the duke of Parma paid the city back with a four-month seige and ruthless sacking. However, because it had the traditions of both Protestantism (through the House of Orange) and Roman Catholicism (being within the realm of the nearby Bishop of Liège), Maastricht escaped the outbursts of the *Iconoclast* and other religious outbreaks of the Reformation. Eventually, most of the citizens settled on the Catholic faith (about 90 % of the population today).

In 1673, Maastricht fell to the French, in one of the city's most famous beseigements (due to the cast of characters). That year, French king and army commander **Louis XIV** stood on a hilltop watching his forces, which included **D'Artagnan**, (the inspiration for and a captain in Alexandre Dumas' novel *The Three Musketeers*), and 6,000 troops of England's duke of Monmouth, who had pledged to fight with the French against the Dutch United Provinces. During the encounter **Captain John Churchill** (who later became duke of Marlborough, an ancestor of Winston Churchill) was rescued by D'Artagnan, who lost his life in doing so. D'Artagnan is remembered by a statue, supposedly marking the spot at which he fell, in Maastricht's **Waldeckpark**.

In 1795, the once-again occupying French made Maastricht capital of the newly created *Department of the Lower Meuse*. After Napoleon's defeat at Waterloo (1815), Belgium and the Netherlands were ordered to unite under Dutch King William I. But after battling over the union for nine years (1830–1839), the two countries adopted a partition. Perhaps because of the logic of their geographic location, some citizens in Maastricht at the time wanted to join with Belgium, but the Dutch garrison that occupied Maastricht decreed otherwise.

Thus, the ancient province of Limburg was split in two, with Maastricht remaining a part of the Netherlands.

Today it's possible to say that Maastricht has the best of both countries: Dutch-style tidiness and tolerance combined with a Belgian-style appreciation for the fine art of the kitchen and "cafe-society."

GUIDEPOSTS

Telephone code 043

Tourist Info • VVV, Het Dinghuis, Kleine Staat 1; year-round Mon.–Sat. 9 a.m.–6 p.m.; in July and August open until 7 p.m. and also on Sun. 11 a.m.–3 p.m.; Carnival and some holidays 11 a.m.–3 p.m.; ☎ *217878*. Bookings for guided walking tours of city, tours of limited access sites, St. Pietersburg caves, casements, Derlon Museum Cellar, river cruises, day coach trips VVV shop with maps, pamphlets, books, prints, posters, gifts.

Parking • Parking garage beneath Vrijthof in center.

Post Office • Corner of Vrijthof and Statenstraat, Mon.–Fri. 8 a.m.–7 p.m., Thurs. til 8 p.m., Sat. 9 a.m.–noon.

Emergency • Police ☎ *292222*, health ☎ *293333*.

Bike rental • At the Railway Station bicycle stall, 6 am–midnight, 1 am Sat. and Sun. ☎ *211100*. Dfl. 7.50 per day, Dfl. 30 per week; Dfl. 50 deposit and ID required.

Cruises • Stiphout Cruises, Maaspromenade 27; daily Maas River cruises from mid-April-Sept., on the hour 10 a.m.-5 p.m., Sun. 1-5 p.m., 55 mins.; ☎ *254151*.

Taxis • In front of the rail station.

Recreation • The VVV has information on the full range of area recreational opportunities, including fishing (license required), archery, tennis, *jeu de boules* (public courts, sets can be rented), and *Kayak Tours Limburg* for kayak day trips on safe "white-water" on uncanalized stretches of the Maas.

WHAT TO SEE AND DO

The whole of Maastricht city center is a protected area due to its wealth of historic buildings (at least 1,450). New and renovated buildings by law must be adapted to their surroundings. The ★ ★ ★ **old city** is a strolling, cafe-sitting, settling-in at a cozy restaurant paced place. Students at the city's faculties for translation studies, music, and hotel management contribute to the city's atmosphere.

★ ★ **Vrijthof Square**, Maastricht's largest square by far, is generally considered to be the center of town. The expansive space is surrounded by interesting structures, not the least of which are an uninterrupted row of terrace cafes (sidewalk cafes) settled along its east side. Use the VVV brochure *Maastricht Fortifications Walk* as your guide for a walk on the ★★ **city walls**, the Pesthuis being a good place to mount the ramparts. For a good view back to the ramparts, visit **Waldeckpark**, near Tongerseplein. Note that the 17th-century Waldeck Bastion is where Chevalier D'Artagnan, the famous French musketeer, was felled June 25, 1673. **Grote Looiersstraat** (with its French-flavored, tree-shaded center mall where you may see men playing *jeu de boules*) and **Ezel Markt** (with its donkey sculpture and fine view of the pretty 17th-century **Huys op den Jeker**, which straddles that stream) are two delightful corners of the city. Year-round, many historic buildings are floodlit after dark, and from midJune to mid-September and on bank holidays, additional monuments are illuminated, from dusk until the wee hours.

Het Dinghuis   ★★

Kleine Staat 1; same hours as VVV, given above. Today the headquarters of Maastricht's VVV tourist office (ground floor), Het Dinghuis, dating from about 1470, with its beautiful stone gable and a timbered wall on the Jodenstraat side, is the most striking example of Maastricht's many saddleback buildings, with steeply slanting roofs that provided much needed storage space for staples to ensure survival through the sieges that have been so much a part of the city's history.

Onze Lieve Vrouwekerk   ★

(Church of Our Dear Lady) Onze Lieve Vrouweplein; open daily (not during services). Treasure-house (entrance through church) open daily 11 a.m.–5 p.m., Sun. 1–5 p.m. Easter to mid-Sept.; ☎ *251851.* Entry to the church from ★★**Onze Lieve Vrouwe square** is to the left of the formidable ★★**westwerk** (*circa* A.D. 1000), an almost windowless, fortress-like wall, via the **Stella Maris** side chapel (c. 1500). The essence of centuries' worth of incense clings to the candlelit interior, the most notable feature of which is the choir with its richly carved capitals. The church's Treasure includes reliquaries, procession banners, church silver, and other ecclesiastical art and crafts.

St. Pietersberg Caves   ★★

Mount St. Pietersberg; two miles south of Maastricht; guided (only) tours, one hour, several times daily June- mid-Sept., reduced schedule rest of year, must be booked through VVV; ☎ *252121.* Since the St. Pietersberg caves were interesting enough to merit inclusion in Roman historian Pliny's writings in A.D. 50, and have generated interest among most of the city's guests in the two succeeding millennia—the cave walls are a virtual "visitors' book," so we know—you can feel confident about putting them on your list of Maastricht "musts." The limey labyrinth of 45-foot deep galleries cut in marl-limestone (a soft chalky building stone that hardens in the air) has numerous names, the earliest from 1037, carved in its soft walls, among them Sir Walter Scott, Voltaire, princes of the House of Orange, and Napoleon. For a thousand years up until 1875, stonecutters carved huge blocks of limestone here, expanding the caves' already considerable natural size to over 200 miles of some 20,000 subterranean "branches" of dark, silent, and cool caves—a constant year-round temperature of 50°F. Guides delight in telling the story of four 17th-century monks who entered unescorted, having affixed a thread at the cave entrance to find their way out; but the "lifeline" broke and their days ended in a search for a way out of the caves.

For those who could find their way within them, the caves have served as a place of refuge. In the 18th century they harbored Austrian and Italian mercenaries hired to help the Dutch combat the French invaders. In World War II they were readied to shelter up to 50,000 people from Nazi bombing, but were never needed. Deep in the caves, Rembrandt's "The Night Watch" was hidden from the Nazis during the war, rolled up in a specially prepared copper drum. When the war was over and the huge 13 x 16-foot painting was being restored before being rehung in Amsterdam's **Rijksmuseum**, it was discovered that the picture, darkened from the smoke of peat fires in rooms where it had previously hung, actually showed a daytime scene.

Bonnefanten Museum

Dominicanerplein; Tues.–Fri., 10 a.m.–5 p.m.; Sat., Sun. and holidays 11 a.m.–5 p.m.; ☎ *251655.* The collection of Maastricht's main museum, housed in a modern building, includes rich archaeological holdings: The Maas valley has been a time-line of cultures for more than a quarter of a million years, and Maastricht is one of the few European cities that has been inhabited continuously since the Roman period. The Bonnefanten Museum's fine arts collection includes sculpture from the Romanesque and Gothic periods; Italian paintings of the 14th–16th centuries; 16th–18th-century paintings from the southern Netherlands, including several Brueghels, and an expanding contemporary section. Also of interest is the maquette (model) of Maastricht, a modern copy of a 1748 "relief model" of the city (the original is in Paris' *Hotel des Invalides*) that French officers built as a military seige study, with descriptive slide show.

Also shown are fossils found in the area's marl caves: the tableland here was formed 80 million years ago. Elsewhere in Maastricht's, at the ★ **Natural History Museum**, are displays of the particularly wide variety of fossils that were found in the local *St. Pietersberg caves.* **Napoleon** once found there the fossilized head of a massive lizard (known as the "Meuse Lizard"), which experts estimate must have been 20 meters/66 feet long. It was so admirable that he was willing to exchange 500 bottles of fine French wine for it.

Derlon Museum Cellar

Hotel Derlon, Onze Lieve Vrouweplein 6; Sundays 1–5 p.m., or through VVV tours. Since there had been Roman and medieval finds in this oldest part of Maastricht before—in nearby ★ **Op de Thermae square**, the outlines of a Roman bath are indicated on the pavement—prior to excavation (1983) for the most recent hotel on the site, a major archaeological investigation was carried out by the municipality. The astonishing result, the discovery of a 6-meter/20-foot deep virtually undisturbed stratum of the city's history from the first century to the 14th, was in large part preserved through altered building plans; it is on public display as a unique cellar museum beneath the modern Hotel Derlon. On view are a 1st-century cobbled Roman road, a 2nd-century Roman temple square, and a wall that is part of a 4th-century Roman fort (castellum) that once covered Maastricht's entire *Stokstraat quarter.*

St. Servaasbasiliek

Vrijthof; daily 10 a.m.–5 p.m. (4 p.m. winter, 6 p.m. summer). St. Servaas, a massive Romanesque church, reopened in May 1990 following several years of large-scale interior and exterior restoration that produced a magnificent result. The body of this medieval cruciform basilica dates from *circa* 1000, but its soul and name come from St. Servaas (St. Servatius), the first bishop of Maastricht, who moved the bishop's see from Tongeren (in Belgium) to Maastricht in the late 4th century. The **Treasure Chamber** has been part of the basilica since A.D. 827, and its collection of reliquaries is reknown. The showpiece is an arm in silver that contains an arm bone supposedly of the apostle Thomas, a gift from the Crusader Godfrey of Bouillon in 1099.

WHERE TO STAY

EXPENSIVE

Hotel Derlon

Onze Lieve Vrouweplein 66, 6211 HD; ☎ *216770, FAX 251933; reservations in U.S.* ☎ *800-344-1212.* Located on the historic, intimate-yet-lively square that's home to Our Beloved Lady church, a street away from the restored pedestrian Stokstraat, and near the ancient city ramparts, the Derlon couldn't be better or more charmingly situated. Several bedrooms in the modern but tastefully styled, service-oriented 42-room hotel overlook the cafe-cluttered, colorful scene on the square, where patrons gather until the wee hours of warm evenings. It is a special place that rests above Roman ruins that are one of the city's most significant early sites.

INEXPENSIVE

Maison Du Chene

Boschstraat 104, 6211 AZ; ☎ *213523, FAX 250882.* A hotel/restaurant since 1985, with a cozy, especially recommended French brasserie *(daily, noon–2 p.m., 6:30–10 p.m.; moderate)* on the ground floor, this hotel has 21 tidy, modernly outfitted bedrooms in three old townhouses, most with shower/bath. There's a European flavor with friendly service, and it's in an excellent location (just off the Markt with Maastricht's City Hall).

WHERE TO EAT

Residents around Maastricht revel in fine dining, and this strong gastronomic tradition has resulted in the restaurants of southern Limburg province, *en masse*, garnering more recognition than those of any other region of Holland. Local Limburg food favorites include *white asparagus* (fresh in May/early June), fruit flans (*Limgurgse vlaai*), fresh water *trout*, game, and Belgian-style filled chocolate pralines.

For fine dining, **'t Hegske** *(Heggenstraat 3a; 5–11 p.m., closed Tues; for reservations ☎ 251762; moderate)* is a tiny antique-congested restaurant just off centrally located St. Amorsplein. The romantic six-tabled candlelit interior—with another eight under the skylighted enclosed terrace with softly splashing fountain—specializes in fish and meat prepared in the French style.

Lovers of shell fish and seafood also can seek out the chic but relaxed **Restaurant L'Escale** *(Havenstraat 19; 5 p.m.–midnight, closed Sun., Mon., holidays; for reservations ☎ 213364; moderate)*, one of several excellent eateries clustered in the area between the lovely *Onze Lieve Vrouweplein* (on which the restaurant also offers outside terrace dining) and the *Op de Thermen* (site of old Roman baths), both just off handsome Stokstraat. Sharing the same building (and phone and hours) with L'Escale is **Le Vigneron** (*inexpensive*), a cozy darkwood bistro that offers a large selection of wines by the glass and menus of traditional French dishes that include wine. **'t Plenkske** *(Plankstraat 6; noon–10:30 p.m., closed Sun.; for reservations ☎ 218456; expensive)* offers light and bright glassed-in, or outdoor patio, dining overlooking the *Op de Thermen*; regional dishes from Maastricht, Liège, and France fill the bill of fare. **'t Klaoske** *(Plankstraat 20; noon–2:30 p.m., 6–10:30 p.m., closed Sun.; for reservations ☎ 218118; moderate)* has more of an old Dutch look and feel, and the traditional country cuisine makes it a long-standing local favorite; it offers weekday business luncheon specials.

There are plenty of places in Maastricht for lighter, less formal fare. The oldest pub (1673) on the vast Vrijthof is the **In Den Ouden Vogelstruys** *(The Old Ostrich; Vrijthof 15; 9:30 a.m.–2 a.m.; ☎ 214888; inexpensive)*. This traditional cafe bar, with its rustic wooden interior and terrace cafe, has a faithful local following and is a good, yet limited choice for a hearty or light lunch or dinner of Dutch specialties (pate, choucroute garnie, soups, sandwiches of cheese and Ardennes ham). Next door is **Panaché** *(Vrijthof 14; daily 9 a.m.–midnight; ☎ 210516; inexpensive)*, one of the Neeerlands Dis restaurants that promises tasty, traditional dishes (*tournedos-poivre* to pastries). Moving along the row of cafes that anchor the Vrijthof one comes to **Monopole** *(Vrijthof 3; daily 10 a.m.–10 p.m.; ☎ 214090; inexpensive)*, which features light fare and drinks on its terrace.

With more than 365 of them, Maastricht's pubs come in every variety. Many serve food (an excellent value, all *inexpensive*) amid their special and individual ambiance, making them cafes as much as bars. Without doubt the smallest is **De Moriaan** *(Stokstraat 12; 4 p.m.–2 a.m., closed Sun., Mon.; ☎ 211177)* with 3-1/2 tables inside, a terrace on the Op de Thermen out-

side, and good spaghetti. Close by is **In de Karkol** *(Stokstraat 5; noon-2 a.m.,
closed Sun., Mon.;* ☎ *217035).* On the extension of the Stokstraat is in
't Knijpke *(St. Bernardusstraat 13; daily 6 p.m.-midnight;* ☎ *216525),* which
calls itself a cafe cheese-cellar; with the brick vaulted-ceiling room candlelit
and mellow music an accompaniment to the likes of onion soup, mussels,
pate, and escargot, need I add it's atmospheric and friendly. With a stirring
view from its terrace tables of the fortress-like West front of the O.L. Vrouwekerk (memorably illuminated at night) across the square, **Charlemagne**
(O.L. Vrouweplein 24; daily 9 a.m.–11 p.m.; ☎ *219373)* is a popular place.
At the corner of the square is **De Bobbel** *(Wolfstraat 32; 11 a.m.–9 p.m., midnight on weekends, closed Sun;* ☎ *217413).* **Café Sjiek** *(St. Pieterstraat 13;
daily 5 p.m.–2 a.m.;* ☎ *210158)* has a cozy interior of stained glass, wood,
candles, and flowers, and in good weather customers spill out across the
street to a terrace cafe on lawns in view of fragments of ancient city walls
(terrace kitchen hours, noon–9 p.m.). Choices run the gamut from soups and
salad nicoise to crab and steak.

IN THE AREA

Southern Limburg Province

The Netherlands' Limburg Province is popular with the Dutch and
other Europeans for country (especially summer) holidays. Here are
the country's highest hills, commonly called the "Dutch Alps"
(though, to put the topography in perspective, their top elevation of
1000 feet still comes short of New York City's *Empire State Building*).
If you have a car to explore this gently rolling land, you'll find it dotted with fine old (some 17th century) fortified farmsteads *(boerderij)*
built around courtyards and closed to the street side by gates. Villages
such as Epen, Epenheide, and Gulpen have handsome half-timbered
buildings tucked into them. The castles found across the countryside
originally formed a defensive line during the area's turbulent earlier
times, but once their protective elements were no longer politically
important, many were architectually embellished. Sometimes castles
and fortified farms stood side by side. Having a car will enable you to
indulge in some of the countryside restaurants for which South Limburg is renowned. Some are set in castles that also offer guest rooms,
but, frequently the establishments are sought out first and foremost
for their food. Definitely reserve—for meals as much as for rooms.

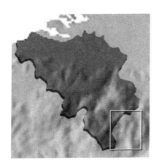

THE GRAND DUCHY
OF LUXEMBOURG

The Bock, Luxembourg City

INTRODUCTION

"*Of all nations on earth, Luxembourg is one of the most stable and prosperous, where nature is preserved and foreigners—whether residents or tourists—are welcomed. In all, one of the world's happiest.*"

.... Former United Nations Secretary-General

Xavier Perez de Cuellar, 1989

The above statement may not quicken the senses, but it's surely reassuring about a country many people know little about. Most are surprised to learn what a wealth of treasure and pleasure awaits in this condensed dose of Europe.

THE LUXEMBOURG LANDSCAPE

The Grand Duchy of Luxembourg, the smallest member state of the European Community, surrounded by Belgium to the north and west, France to the south, and Germany to the east, measures a mere 999 square miles. It is smaller than America's smallest state, Rhode Island, and only 1/16th the size of Switzerland, itself a petite national package. In travel terms, Luxembourg is 50 miles/80 km. north to south, 32 miles/52 km. east to west. You can drive up or down its length in one and a half hours, entirely across it in one.

Geologically, Luxembourg falls into two regions: the hilly slate Ardennes, known as the **Oesling**, in the north and the larger, more populated, fertile river-fed farmland appropriately called **Gutland** (*Good Land*) to the south. The differences in altitude from north to south affect the climate; the high Ardennes have far more rainfall, a cold snowy winter, and a late spring (mid-May), while the south has a milder climate, warmer summer, and longer growing season. More than one third of the Grand Duchy is forest; much of it is preserved by the government or maintained as private hunting reserves—as are the extensive lands owned by Grand Duke Jean.

Geographically, Luxembourg has several distinct regions. Just outside Luxembourg City to the northwest is the **Eisch River Valley**, more memorably known as the *Valley of the Seven Castles*. Most of the famed castles are now picturesque ruins perched above their villages. A short distance directly north, crossing into the Ardennes, is the scenic **Sûre River Valley**. In the forests and towns to the north and south of it, much of Luxembourg's *Battle of the Bulge* action took place in the winter of 1944/45. Midcountry, near the eastern boundary, is the region known as **Little Switzerland**, which is characterized by large, unusual rock formations. Virtually all of Luxembourg's shared eastern border with Germany is created by three rivers, the **Our** in the north, the **Sûre** in the midregion, and the **Moselle** to the south. The Moselle Valley is the vineyard of Luxembourg, and has been since Roman days. The south and southeast sections of the Grand Duchy are the most heavily agricultural.

Luxembourg lies in the heart of industrial Europe, and is itself a highly industrialized nation. Most heavy industry lies in the **terre rouge** in the southwest, where the earth is red from its iron ore con-

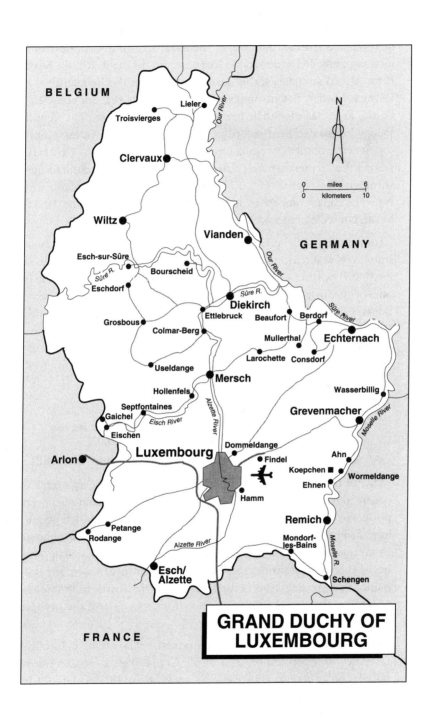

GRAND DUCHY OF
LUXEMBOURG

tent. However, despite its reliance on industry (mostly steel), Luxembourg gives the impression of being full of wide-open, unpopulated spaces. And even in the industrial southwest, development is controlled and green space preserved. In the north, the **Sûre River**, which stretches across Luxembourg from the Belgian to the German border, has no industry on it at all, its reaches conscientiously kept clean for their beauty and recreational use. The Grand Duchy has an excellent record of compliance with European Community environmental regulations, ranking second only to Denmark among the 13 member states. According to the World Resources Institute in Washington, D.C., 21.1% of Luxembourg's total land area is protected, as compared with 8.6% in the United States and 10.6% in the United Kingdom.

Tourism, one of the Grand Duchy's five most important revenue sources, is one reason why Luxembourgers work to keep their land pristine. The offer of rambling and hiking in unspoilt countryside is one of its strongest selling points to European travelers; Luxembourg's network of marked walking paths is the densest in the world. But an even more important factor behind the preservation of the Grand Duchy's naturally scenic landscape is that it is an essential element in the quality of life that Luxembourgers seek for themselves.

THE LUXEMBOURG PEOPLE

"Of all the countries I have visited, the Grand Duchy of Luxembourg is the smallest, but it is the one that has charmed me most and where hospitality has been most simple and cordial."

. . . . **Sir Winston Churchill**

One of the wonders of Luxembourg is that, despite being overrun, occupied, ruled, and even incorporated by many mainland European powers over the centuries—up to and including the 20th—its people have maintained a national character entirely their own. Surrounded by Germany, Belgium, and France, Luxembourg is not a composite of the three, but a distinct social and political entity. Despite an inevitable legacy of linguistic, artistic, and social influences from foreign occupiers, the Grand Duchy's own cultural values have the deepest roots.

Lately, there has been a peaceful, productive, "invasion" of foreigners. They now account for 25% of the Grand Duchy's total resident population. These foreigners—who account for 40% of the jobs in the Grand Duchy's banking industry and include the more than 10,000 individuals who work for one of the European Community institutions based here, plus their families—provide what Luxembourg, with one of the lowest birth rates in the world, does not: a sufficient supply of workers at all skill levels with which to keep its prosperous economy on course.

Luxembourg's commerce is of necessity international. Since its independence in 1839, the country has recognized that it is not large enough to be economically self-supporting. This knowledge creates a cosmopolitan commercial streak in the solid core of traditional family and community values in the Luxembourgers' life. This is illustrated by one humorous self-description: "one Luxembourger, a rose garden; two Luxembourgers, a koffee-klatsch; three Luxembourgers, a band." At heart they are a people who make time for life's basic pleasures.

Amid its international diversity, Luxembourg society retains one element of homogeneity: religion. Some 95% of Luxembourgers are Roman Catholic (down from 99.5% in 1871, 96.9% in 1970). Although they do not hesitate to differentiate themselves as *practicing* or *nonpracticing*, a basic acceptance of the Church and its sacraments is taken for granted. Ever since foreign workers were needed in the country in the last quarter of the 19th century, Luxembourg has drawn mostly Catholic migrants (especially Portuguese, who make up 9% of the current population), thus perserving the singular religious character of the country.

Luxembourgers have managed to fashion a very high standard of living for themselves. According to a recent Larousse-published *Euroscopie* (which contains vast collections of statistics on living and working conditions in the 12 EC countries), Luxembourgers, in both material and nonmaterial ways, are the most satisfied with their lot. In addition to having the highest disposable incomes and longest holidays among their European neighbors, they have the greatest number of houses equipped with central heating, washing machines, dishwashers, and electronic gadgets. (Other surveys show that Luxembourgers are the EC's highest domestic consumers of electricity, but with their many rivers they manage to produce it all themselves.) The Grand Duchy also has the most automobiles and hospital beds. Some 60% of house dwellers own the lodgings they live in. Luxembourg also has the most telephones per capita in Europe, but is small enough to make do with a single code for the whole country.

A complex history has brought Luxembourg to the position that one hears the maxim, "To be a Luxembourger is by necessity to be a European," expressed in one form or another almost every day in conversations with local people. The lingual pluralism that plays an important part in Luxembourgers' social and professional lives, opening them up to other cultures, begins at an early age. German is taught from the age of six, French from the age of seven, and most students learn English.

One of the founding fathers of the European Community concept, **Robert Schuman** (1886–1963), was born and raised in Luxembourg City. The son of a Luxembourg mother and French father—from Lorraine, which, like Luxembourg, has a multicultural historyas a pawn between Germany and France—Robert Schuman lived until the age of 18 in Luxembourg City, in the suburb of **Clausen** in the Alzette Valley. The house in which he grew up, at *rue Jules Wilhelm 4*, is situated just beneath the **Kirchberg Plateau**, where the buildings of the **European Center** rise. In 1990, following restoration, the house opened as the **European Study and Research Centre Robert Schuman**, with the mission of promoting knowledge of the history, and encouraging the further exploration, of European unification.

Raised in Luxembourg, then a student at several German universities, later a French citizen (as a result of the 1919 *Treaty of Versailles* which gave Lorraine back to France) and a member of the French government from 1919 to 1962, Schuman was well prepared and well positioned for his European role. Later in his life, at the pinnacle of his political career, Schuman noted that his early life in Luxembourg had given him "a sense of life I never had to change in the years to follow." He also referred to his formative education in Luxembourg in these words: "there we had the window wide open beyond the political borders, towards East and towards West." Luxembourg is glad to be able to cite Schuman as one of its own; May 9, observed annually as the "birthday" of the European Community, is, in this Catholic country, sometimes referred to as *St. Schuman's Day*.

Luxembourgers have a motto, a line from their national anthem, "*Mir woelle bleiwe wat mir sin*," which translates, "We want to remain what we are." Among the many things Luxembourgers are is a people who have proven they can cope. (Henry Miller once observed: "In Luxembourg there are no neurotic people and no lunatic asylums.") They have avoided the complexes that could come with trying to feel at home in a world in which their homeland is seemingly insignificant. Luxembourgers display a confidence in and an ease with the times that are enviable.

AN HISTORICAL PERSPECTIVE

Luxembourg's geographic position in Europe has been perceived as central and strategic since its settlement by Romans. Throughout most of its history, Luxembourg has been fortified to protect it from foreign armies. Unfortunately, those very fortifications often invited invaders and, later, European power brokers who felt free to arbitrarily cut Luxembourg down in size and install foreign soldiers in its capital.

Given its diminutive dimensions, the name "The Grand Duchy of Luxembourg" could be considered too much of a mouthful. At the peak of its political power in the 14th and 15th centuries, when it provided four rulers who served as Holy Roman Emperors, Luxembourg was much larger physically, but it never has played as important a part on the international stage as it does today. Its petite dimensions allow Luxembourg to help solve sensitive international situations while eliminating any feeling of competition from larger countries

The Luxembourg land spent long centuries in international entanglement before it finally achieved the status of independent state. Foreign occupiers since the Middle Ages left their footprints upon the soil, and more ancient antecedents left artifacts beneath it. Evidence of *Neolithic* man (circa 10,000 B.C.) can be seen in the countryside and in the collections of the Musée de l'État in Luxembourg City. In the millennium before Christ the region was occupied by *Celts*. The most significant of those prehistoric tribes in Luxembourg were the *Treveri* (Trier) and *Mediomatrici* (Metz), both of which followed the faith of their priests, the Druids. Remains of Celtic fortified compounds can be seen on the **Titelberg** and around **Muller-thal** ("Little Switzerland").

Caesar's conquest of Gaul (58–51 B.C.) resulted in the incorporation of the Luxembourg area into the Roman Empire. Three major Roman roads connected it to what is now Germany; the most important led to Trier, an administrative center second in importance only to Rome. There followed in the Luxembourg region a rapid process of Latinization, with increased order and security, as well as flourishing trade and agriculture, in particular, *viniculture* along the Moselle. Gallo-Roman villas with baths, mosaic floors, and murals were built both in towns and in the countryside. (Remnants can be viewed in museums in Luxembourg City and Diekirch.) Despite its domination, the Roman influence did not eradicate the region's Celtic culture. The officially forbidden Druidism remained, but

Christianity also became established in Luxembourg by the 4th century. As Roman power weakened, Luxembourg faced attacks from the Vandals, Visigoths, and Huns. (Their leader **Attila** is recalled in the local town name **Ettelbruck**, meaning "Attila's bridge.") In A.D. 450, the Franks crossed the Rhine, bringing Roman rule of the region to a close. Thereafter the Franks settled large areas of Luxembourg, especially around the Moselle, and established their Germanic language throughout.

In 496, Frankish **King Clovis** converted to Christianity. As a result, the religion spread among the population. All across Europe monastic orders brought enlightenment to the Dark Ages. In Luxembourg, the era was highlighted in 698, when Anglo-Saxon Benedictine **St. Willibrord** founded the **Echternach Abbey**, which became famous for the **Echternach School of Book Illumination**.

The Frankish Empire, of which Luxembourg remained a part, reached its climax under Emperor **Charlemagne**, who sent some one thousand Saxon families to settle the sparsely populated Ardennes during the 9th century. The Frankish empire faced grave territorial divisions under Charlemagne's weak successors. Under the *Treaty of Verdun* (843), Luxembourg became part of Lorraine, which subsequently was divided between France and Germany by the 870 Treaty of Mersen. This marked the beginning of a conflict that would last over a thousand years, as Luxembourg was perpetually bounced between the powers of France and Germany.

On April 12, 963, **the Abbey of St. Maximin in Trier**, which had been established in the same era as Luxembourg's Echternach Abbey, granted to **Sigefroi, count of Ardennes**, a deed to a rocky promontory on which stood the ruins of a Roman fort known as **Castellum Lucilinburhuc** or "Little Castle." (A copy of the deed can be seen in Luxembourg's *National Library*; the original remains in Trier.) At *Lucilinburhuc*—a name that evolved to *Lutzelburg* and eventually to *Luxembourg*—Sigefroi built a fortified castle. The House of Luxembourg thus born at Sigefroi's fortress remained independent as part of the Frankish Empire for nearly five centuries, though its fortunes rose and fell under the combined influences of family landholdings, adeptness at arms, oaths of loyalty, and well-made marriages.

Knights from Luxembourg accompanied Godfrey de Bouillon on the First Crusade, and served in Asia Minor on subsequent ones. They had left their Luxembourg castles (**Bourscheid, Esch-sur-Sûre, Hollenfels**, etc.), whose ruined turrets look so romantic today, though the reality of life within the walls of the feudal fortresses must have been anything but. Some of Luxembourg's absentee landlords fell in battle. Those who returned often were debt ridden, their lands in disarray; some found their castles confiscated by strong arms and swords that had stayed home.

One leader of Luxembourg, **Henry the Blind**, count of Namur, set in motion events that were to improve the region's situation immeasurably. Late in the 12th century, Henry, having no direct heir, was preparing to bequeath his immense possessions to his nephew Baldwin of Hainault when, at the age of 65, love played a hand; he married Agnes of Gelderland, who gave him a daughter. Baldwin showed his displeasure by pillaging Namur and breaking the power of the aged Henry. But Henry's late-in-life daughter, **Ermesinde** (1196–1247), through resourceful marriages and her own far-reaching ideas of leadership and reform, reestablished Luxembourg's prestige and extended its frontiers from the Moselle to the Meuse. After the death of her second husband, Ermesinde herself took over the reins of rule by bringing together feuding noblemen into a kind of council of state and granting burghers (town citizens) rights which loosened the hold of feudal lords over them. In 1244, she granted a charter of freedom to the City of Luxembourg. Realizing that education was the key to the continuation of these reforms, Ermesinde also founded schools, convents, monasteries, and cultural institutions. Her legacy to Luxembourg was a secure, well-administered country with long-lasting social institutions. Her heirs continued the family line that would prove one of the most illustrious of the Middle Ages.

In the 14th century, the House of Luxembourg became one of the dominant forces in Europe. In 1308, Ermesinde's great grandson **Henry VII**, count of Luxembourg, was crowned head of the Holy Roman Empire in Rome. In 1312, **Dante** hailed him as the "Restorer of Justice, Peace, and Liberty." Upon his untimely death in 1313—of malaria in Pisa, where he is buried in the cathedral—Henry's son **John**, who had added Bohemia to the House of Luxembourg by marriage at the age of 14, took over. So popular was John as an ideal of knighthood that he remains Luxembourg's national hero to this day. For the first 30 years of his rule, John set out almost every spring on military campaigns from the North Sea to the Vistula to increase, or keep intact, his landholdings. Despite failing eyesight that gave him the epithet *The Blind*, John answered the appeal of French King Philip VI when England's **Edward II, the Black Prince**, invaded France. All but sightless, he led his army into the

Battle of Crécy (1346), in which he was slain. In tribute, the victorious Edward said of Luxembourg's John the Blind, "The battle was not worth the death of this man." Edward took the three ostrich feathers from John's helmet, and the motto *Ich dien* ("I serve") in tribute to John's loyalty, and adopted them as the crest and motto for the Prince of Wales; they are still in use by England's current Prince Charles.

Charles IV, son of John the Blind, through his own and family marriages and treaties, brought Luxembourg to the size and status his father had sought by the sword. As Holy Roman Emperor, Charles maintained a court at Prague that dazzled all of Europe. When Charles' younger brother **Wenceslas** married **Jeanne, Duchess of Brabant**, thereby acquiring Brabant, Limburg, and much of what is Belgium's Luxembourg province today, he brought the House of Luxembourg to its greatest expanse. Charles honored Wenceslas by making Luxembourg a duchy in 1354. In 1356, Duke Charles and Duchess Jeanne issued one of the most important written municipal charters of merchants' rights, the *Joyeuse Entrée* (Joyous Entry), which was of equivalent significance for Belgium and Luxembourg as the *Magna Carta* was for England. In it, the Duke and Duchess promised that they would impose no restriction on trade, except legal taxes; give subjects the right to revolt if the Duke exceeded his legal powers; and pledged not to declare offensive war "except at the advice, will and consent of our good cities and land."

Nevertheless, **Wenceslas II**, who became Emperor and Duke of Luxembourg in 1383, used his holdings almost exclusively as a source of revenue and troops for armies, and created a series of civil wars between sovereigns that plagued the House of Luxembourg. The last male of the line, Holy Roman Emperor **Sigismund**, who, through marriage, also was the King of Hungary and thus foretold the region's future ties with the Hapsburgs, died in 1437. In 1443, the Duchy of Luxembourg was bought by **Philip the Good of Burgundy** and thereby lost its autonomy and dynasty, becoming a province linked to the Netherlands. Philip established French as Luxembourg's language of government and administration, which it remains today. The Burgundian Netherlands passed to the Hapsburgs in 1477, and among the titles **Charles V** received at his birth in Ghent in 1500 was *Duke of Luxembourg*. From that time, Luxembourg essentially shared the history of the Netherlands.

Staunchly and overwhelmingly Roman Catholic—which it remains today—Luxembourg sided with the Belgians in support of the Catholic Spanish Hapsburg **King Philip II**, rather than with Protestant

Holland during the Reformation and subsequent religious upheavals in the 16th century. Luxembourg, often at stake in the battles waged between the European powers, was annexed in 1684 by France's **Louis XIV**, who held the duchy until 1697 when it was returned to Spain. During the French occupation Louis's military architect **Vauban** fortified the site of Luxembourg City so fully that it became known as the "*Gibraltar of the North.*" In 1714, at the end of the war of the Spanish Succession, Luxembourg, along with Belgium, passed to Austria, and remained a part of the Austrian Netherlands until 1795. From that year until the fall of Napoleon in 1814, Luxembourg, together with both Belgium and Holland, was incorporated into revolutionary France.

In 1815, the European powers, meeting at the *Congress of Vienna* to balance the forces on the continent, dared not leave Luxembourg to itself. They felt its strategic position and fortifications made it too strong to ignore, yet its small size left it vulnerable to takeover from others. They "settled" the situation by raising the status of Luxembourg to *Grand Duchy* and giving it as a personal property to the Dutch king. This made the Dutch *House of Nassau's* **Willem I** and his heirs also the hereditary *Grand Dukes of Luxembourg*, a situation which lasted until 1890. But there was more to the arrangement: the Congress of Vienna also called for the territory of Luxembourg lying east of the Moselle and Our rivers to be joined to **Prussia**, and giving, in compensation to the dismembered Grand Duchy, the greater part of the duchy of Bouillon and part of the former prince-bishopric of Liège (territory that conforms today to Belgium's province of Luxembourg). Although linked by the same sovereign, Luxembourg was designated politically independent of Holland and the United Kingdom of the Netherlands. But Europe's ruling powers meddled further with Luxembourg by deciding that the Grand Duchy must be a part of the *Germanic Confederation*, and that Luxembourg City should be a Confederation fortress with a garrison of *Prussians.*

In 1830, the Grand Duchy—with the exception of Luxembourg City, which, with its Prussian garrison, was not allowed to join and thus remained loyal to Holland—united with Belgium in a revolt against the United Kingdom of the Netherlands. When Belgium achieved independence, the Grand Duchy, again with the exception of Luxembourg City, placed itself under Belgian rule. In 1839, a date of mixed blessings for Luxembourgers—since it marks both its first true independence and the date of its partition—the *Treaty of London* divided the Grand Duchy in two. The larger French-speaking western part went to Belgium, becoming that country's Luxembourg province. The eastern portion remained with the Dutch, whose King Willem I, persuaded by the logistical difficulties entailed in maintaining a fiefdom separated from Holland by a still hostile Belgium, granted Luxembourg a measure of autonomy. Thus, the Grand Duchy assumed her present frontiers and gained a date from which to mark her independence.

In 1842, at Prussia's insistence, Luxembourg joined the German *Zollverein* (customs union). That association, in which Luxembourg remained until the First World War, laid the foundation for the Grand Duchy's development during the Industrial Revolution. German capital, manpower, and markets were the base upon which Luxembourg created its great steel economy in the last quarter of the 19th century. In 1848, **King Willem II** (1792–1849), by far the preferred of the Grand Duchy's Dutch rulers, gave Luxembourg its constitution. Willem II is honored in Luxembourg City with an equestrian statue on **place Guillaume**, named for him. (The statue, cast in 1884 by sculptor Antonin Mercie, was such a good likeness of Willem II that the Dutch themselves ordered a copy 40 years later.) In 1859, with Dutch help, Luxembourg got its first railroad, an event of such surpassing importance to the Grand Duchy that the poem "Feierwon," written to commemorate the occasion, still ranks in importance with the national anthem "Our Homeland." In 1867, upon the dissolution of the Germanic Confederation, the European powers—nations uneasy about the fortress-capital at the fulcrum of Europe—met again in London. They certified Luxembourg's freedom, guaranteed the Grand Duchy's neutrality, set up a program for the dismantling of Luxembourg City's fortresses, and arranged for the withdrawal of the Prussian garrison. Luxembourgers, not noted for excess, are said to have danced in the streets as the Prussians departed. Then they went about the business of reaffirming their constitution. In the century since, the Grand Duchy has progressed from feudal fortress to full-scale modern nation.

In order to maintain its economic independence, Luxembourg was compelled to call in foreign workers from the time of its steel industrial expansion beginning in the 1870s; from that period, a high percentage of foreigners has remained a characteristic of the country. Luxembourg's own work force was particularly small because many residents had emigrated at the end of the 18th and early in the 19th century, when the country had been impoverished and barely able to feed its people. (The people of Luxembourg heritage living in the United States today number more than the Grand Duchy's entire population—about 400,000.)

In 1914, despite its neutrality which had been dictated by the European leaders in 1867, Luxembourg was occupied by Germany on August 2. During the First World War, more than 3,000 Luxembourgers lost their lives fighting for the Allied cause, a substantial sacrifice for so small a nation. At the end of the war in 1918, **Grand Duchess Marie-Adelaide** was accused of alleged pro-German sympathies. From November 1918 to January 1919, Luxembourgers went through a *Grand Crise* (great crisis) that ended with Marie-Adelaide's abdication. Then began a popular process to determine whether Luxembourg should become a republic and elect a president, or place **Charlotte**, sister of Marie-Adelaide, on the throne. In the plebiscite held in the fall of 1919, more than 50% of the people chose Charlotte to be Grand Duchess, and her popularity rose much higher in the course of her 45-year reign, during which she enjoyed undiminished affection.

In 1921, to replace the German *Zollverein* trade union, Luxembourg signed a customs and economic treaty with Belgium (*BLEU, the Belgium-Luxembourg Economic Union*), which pegged their currencies to each other. The internationally outlooking Grand Duchy also joined the *League of Nations*. Despite the worldwide depression, Luxembourg's steel industry grew to the point of being ranked seventh in the world in productivity by the end of the 1930s. In 1939, with rumblings of large-scale war again being heard in Europe, Luxembourg reasserted its neutrality. The Grand Duchy also threw a particularly strenuous centenary celebration of its independence, as a message to Hitler to respect its freedom.

But it was to no avail. On May 10, 1940, Hitler's Nazis occupied not only Luxembourg, but Holland and Belgium as well. However, since Luxembourg City had been home to a Prussian (German) garrison in the 19th century, Hitler used that as an excuse to impose an *"absorption" policy* on the Grand Duchy. Unlike Holland, Belgium, and other countries "occupied" by the Fuhrer's forces, Luxembourg was incorporated into the Third Reich, meaning that its citizens were liable for conscription into the *Wehrmacht*.

In 1941, the Nazis undertook a census in the countries they had occupied in the Second World War. On the printed form under the question "What is your nationality?" was the notation that Luxembourgers, as well as Alsatians, should write "German." On the day before it was due, the Nazis recalled the census in the Grand Duchy, having learned that Luxembourgers were planning wholesale defiance on the nationality issue. This resistance was a precursor to a general strike in 1942, staged in response to the call for military service in the *Wehrmacht*. (Women, too, were conscripted, for labor.) Luxembourgers walked out of their factories, after nailing the country's flags to their masts. Extreme reprisals followed. A number of Luxembourgers managed to escape, thereafter enlisting with British, Canadian, U.S., Free French, and Free Belgian forces to fight Hitler. Many who were inducted into the *Wehrmacht*—under threat that otherwise their families would be deported to Prussia—were sent to fight for the Nazis on the Russian front. Between 1943–1945, many Luxembourgers wound up as "irregular" German troops at the Russian POW camp at Tambow. Luxembourgers at Tambow banded together for support and many survived more than two years of incarceration there.

On September 9, 1944, **Pétange**, near the Belgian border in southwest Luxembourg, became the first town in the Grand Duchy to be liberated by soldiers of the First U.S. Army, Fifth Armored Division. It is impossible for us to fully comprehend what liberation meant to Luxembourgers, except to note that these many years later September 9 is still observed annually in Pétange. And every five years since 1944, a large ceremony has been staged at night with a torchlight parade from Pétange's town hall to its town monument. Erected in 1947, its inscription in French reads "In memory of the first American soldier who fell in the liberation of Luxembourg," followed in Letzebuergesch with "Monument to an Unknown Soldier—We Will Never Forget." However, in 1987 the American soldier was identified, thanks to the Luxembourg group CEBA that researches aspects of the war. At the following five-year observance in 1989, family members of the man who had died in the first armored car to cross the border in 1944 were on hand on September 9 for ceremonies that unveiled a plaque to, and renamed the square for, **Hyman Josephson**, 2nd Lieutenant, U.S. Army.

On September 10, 1944, the U.S. Army pushed through to liberate Luxembourg City. Their progress was made so quickly that, fortunately, the rapidly retreating Nazis did not have time to destroy much of the capital. All of the Grand Duchy was quickly freed by the Allies, mostly American, who were joyously welcomed.

Virtually no one on either side of the war believed the Nazis could —or would—mount another large-scale attack. But Hitler conceived and implemented a counter-offensive that, although the port of Antwerp was its ultimate object, got bogged down and was waged largely in the Luxembourg and Belgian Ardennes. On December 16, with the opening of what became known as the **Battle of the Bulge**, Hitler's soldiers again occupied Luxembourg soil. In the snow and cold of the winter of 1944/45, particularly around **Wiltz** and **Clervaux**, Luxembourg suffered its worst war damage, and the Allies some of their greatest casualties. By the time the last town in Luxembourg was freed for a second time—**Vianden** on February 12, 1945—one-third of Luxembourg's farmland was unusable; 60,000 people were homeless; and half the country's roads, bridges, tunnels, and rail lines had been destroyed. Earlier in the war, many of Luxembourg's steel plants had been burnt out by the Nazis from forced overproduction.

From the late 19th century until the shift away from its industrial base in the latter third of the 20th century, Luxembourg's prosperity rested mainly on steel. The prime company, *Arbed*, at its peak before the widespread steel crisis began in 1975, was Europe's fourth-largest producer, a multinational with 100,000 employees in plants in Europe, America, and Asia. Arbed provided more than steel to Luxembourg's economy since, as was discovered in the 19th century, the waste from the smelting process proved an effective fertilizer for the Grand Duchy's less fertile northern and central farmlands. After the Second World War, Luxembourg put its steel industry back in shape so swiftly that by the mid-1950s, the country had one of the highest GNPs per capita in Europe, but it had learned not to put all its economic aspirations in a single industry. When the steel industry crisis of the 1970s hit, the "Luxembourg Model"—scaling back the number of hours per worker to avoid layoffs—was widely imitated elsewhere. By then, banking had replaced steel as Luxembourg's number one industry.

Post-war economic planning began well before the end came. By September 5, 1944, Antwerp and Brussels had been liberated, and on that day in London, representatives-in-exile of the governments of BElgium, the NEtherlands (Holland), and LUXembourg (which provided the acronym BENELUX) signed a document entitled *Customs Convention*, based roughly on the 1921 BLEU agreement between Belgium and Luxembourg that had proved extremely successful. The intent of the three governments was to form a complete and durable economic union, and restore economic activity by establishing a common tariff of import duties. Not until 1948 did the convention become operational, and not until 1958 was a BENELUX *Treaty of Economic Union* finalized. But, despite rough edges, the treaty survived, primarily because leaders in all three countries never abandoned the conviction that the idea of union was essentially sound. In 1949, Luxembourg became a founding member of the North Atlantic Treaty Organization (NATO), having abandoned its traditional policy of neutrality (it having proved inadequate to guarantee its liberty and independence). The Grand Duchy today has a volunteer army of 450 people.

Even while kinks in the BENELUX treaty were being worked out, Luxembourg was being linked to an expanded European economic union. In 1950 **Jean Monnet**, a far-sighted Frenchman who preferred to remain in the background, proposed a plan to **Robert Schuman**, the Luxembourg-born-and-raised French foreign minister, for the formation of a supranational *European Coal and Steel Community (ECSC)*. Working enthusiastically on the initiative, Schuman suggested that "the pooling of coal and steel production will immediately provide for the establishment of common bases for economic development as a first step in the federation of Europe, and will change the destinies of those regions which have long been devoted to the manufacture of munitions of war, of which they themselves have been the most constant victims." A treaty among the three BENELUX countries, plus Germany, France, and Italy, was signed in 1951, with Luxembourg City established as the seat of High Authority.

The ECSC proved such a success that, in 1955, the foreign ministers of its members solicited suggestions for extended cooperation in economic spheres. The most important message came from the BENELUX, which by then was seeing palpable benefits from its own more complete integration. The BENELUX statement said, "The moment has come to pass into a new state of European integration.... this must be achieved first in the economic field." In 1957, a treaty was signed in Rome between the six ECSC members to form the **European Economic Community** (or *Common Market*). Luxembourg City was designated the headquarters for several of its permanent institutions: the *Secretariat of the European Parliament, the Court of Justice* (which is similar in many ways to the Supreme Court in the United States), the *Court of Auditors*, and, appropriately, the *European Investment Bank*.

Today, with more than 200 banks and a total of close to 1,000 financial institutions that include substantial securities and reinsurance markets, sleek **boulevard Royal** is Luxembourg City's version of *Wall Street*. The Grand Duchy's financial services sector employs about 18,000 people—one in six working Luxembourgers is employed in some facet of the financial business—and accounts for roughly 15% of GNP. Private investments in Luxembourg banks are estimated at well over $160 billion.

The Grand Duchy of Luxembourg had its most recent six-month turn in the rotating presidency of the European Community during the first half of 1991. The country holding the presidency can, among other Community business, put forth ideas of particular interest to it. During its previous presidency in 1985, Luxembourg brought to the signature stage the *Single Europe Act* (referred to as "*1992*"), which was signed onboard the *Marie-Astrid*, the Moselle River cruise ship based at Luxembourg's wine-growing village of **Schentgen**. During its 1991 EC presidency, Luxembourg furthered the implementation of numerous European single-market initiatives.

Among the modern buildings of the **European Center** that rise above Luxembourg City from the **Kirchberg Plateau** is the **European School**. It was the first of its kind when conceived in 1953: an educational system for the children of ECSC-employee families that provided, for students speaking totally different mother tongues, an immersion in varied cultural milieus, and stressed the principle of European unity. Today, teachers originating in all the countries of the EC provide lessons for the school's 3,000 students, who come from all EC nations and many more. Going from nursery school through high school, the school grants a diploma accepted at any university in the EC. Though now copied by nine others in Europe, Luxembourg's school continues to set the pace, helping the children sitting on its school benches to leave their national mentality behind, providing them with an education that seeks to ensure that the European citizen of tomorrow is open-minded.

KEYS TO THE GRAND DUCHY

TOURIST OFFICES

National tourist offices for the Grand Duchy of Luxembourg are located in the U.S.A. at 17 Beekman Place, New York, NY 10022, ☎ *(212) 370-9850*; and in England at 122 Regent St., London W1R 5FE, ☎ *(071)434.28.00*, FAX *(071)734.12.05*. Travel and attraction information within the Grand Duchy are available in Luxembourg City. (See under "Guidelines.")

WEATHER

Luxembourg has a temperate climate, with no extremes. Although the Ardennes shelter the country from some of the wind and rain that are more constant in Holland and Belgium, an umbrella and raincoat still are suggested. The following chart shows the *average* of the daily high and low temperatures (in Fahrenheit) by month for

Luxembourg City, as well as the average number of days each month with no measurable rainfall.

					Average Daily Temperatures in °F In Luxembourg City (Lat. 49 ° 37´—Alt. 1,025´)						
Jan.	Feb.	Mar.	Apr.	May	June	July	Aug.	Sept.	Oct.	Nov.	Dec.
Average Temperature											
35°	38°	42°	49°	55°	61°	64°	64°	60°	50°	43°	38°
Days with No Rain											
16	13	16	14	15	13	15	15	14	14	12	15

NATIONAL HOLIDAYS

New Year's Day; Easter Monday (date varies); Labor Day (May 1); Ascension Day (date varies); Whit Monday (date varies); National Day (June 23); Assumption (date varies); All Saints' Day (Nov. 1); Christmas Day; St. Etienne (Dec. 26). Days that are not national holidays but on which administrative and public offices, schools, and similar institutions are closed are Carnival (including Shrove Tuesday, date varies); Octave (May/June, date varies); Whit Tuesday (date varies); All Souls' Day (Nov. 2); Christmas Eve; New Year's Eve.

LANGUAGE

Luxembourg's official language (since 1984) is **Letzebuergesch**, mostly in oral use. No one else speaks Letzebuergesch: Luxembourgers know that no one learns it unless at his mother's knee. (In fact, the language has been almost entirely an oral tradition over the centuries and only recently was given concrete written form.) Here's a sample to make us appreciate the fact that Luxembourgers have been considerate enough to learn other languages. *Wei geet et lech?* (How are you?), *Kennt Dir mir hellefen?* (Can you help me?) *Vill Gleck!* (Good Luck!).

In practice, Luxembourg is trilingual. Business is conducted in *French* (also the language on street signs). Most newspapers are published in *German* (though ads are in *Letzebuergesch*). Luxembourg City is headquarters for several European Community institutions and many multinational corporations; as in other centers of Europe's Common Market, *English* has long been common ground for communication. English is so widely studied and spoken throughout Luxembourg that you should have no difficulty getting around and meeting people.

CURRENCY

Luxembourg francs—written *FLux*—come in 1, 5, 20, and 50 franc coins, and a 50 centime piece (100 centimes = 1 franc). Bank notes exist in 100, 500, 1,000 and 5,000 values. At press time the U.S. $ was worth approximately 35.14 FLux.

The Luxembourg franc and the Belgian franc, although minted and printed as separate currencies, have the same value and denominations. In Luxembourg, the Belgian franc is accepted everywhere, though the reverse is not the case. When leaving Luxembourg, whether or not you are headed for Belgium, make sure your remaining francs are Belgian, since for currency transactions the Luxembourg franc does not carry the same international recognition as the Belgian franc.

LUXEMBOURG HOTEL PRICE CATEGORIES

Prices are based on double occupancy, with private toilet and shower and/or bath, and include VAT and service; continental breakfast is usually included. All grades of accommodation in Luxembourg are clean.

Very Expensive	FLux 5,000 +
Expensive	4,000–5,000
Moderate	3,000–4,000
Inexpensive	3,000 or less

LUXEMBOURG RESTAURANT PRICE CATEGORIES

Prices are based on a three-course dinner for one, without drinks but *inclusive* of VAT and service.

Very Expensive	FLux 3,000 +
Expensive	2,000–3,000
Moderate	1,000–2,000
Inexpensive	1,000 or less

TOURIST SEASON

Officially, the tourist season in Luxembourg runs from Easter to late October. However, some attractions, even in Luxembourg City, and especially so in more rural areas of the Grand Duchy where the focus is on outdoor tourism, close by mid-September. It's wise to confirm opening hours if your travel plans include specific attractions or museums. There are plenty of reasons (scenery, fine dining, walking, little worry about full hotels) to travel out of season, although keep in mind that a number of small rural hotels close entirely then.

After September, the weather is more inclined to be gray and windy, though Luxembourg can have an "Indian Summer." In the spring allow trees time to grow new leaves if you want to see this *Green Heart of Europe* at its best.

TRAVEL DISTANCES

Luxembourg City is centrally located in Europe, posting the following distances to other major cities and transportation hubs:

City	Miles	Kilometers
Amsterdam	223	360
Brussels	127	205
Frankfurt	160	258
Ostend	206	332
Paris	206	332
Zurich	246	396

TRAINS

While train is an excellent way to get to/from **Luxembourg City**, it is *not* the ideal mode of transportation for touring within the Grand Duchy. The rail network, although serving the major towns of Ettelbruck, Diekirch, Wiltz, and Clervaux, neglects the best scenery and some of the most special countryside towns. While trains do operate in tandem with the national bus system, and thus afford access—eventually—to most places, for travelers with limited time and those desiring to see how exceptionally scenic the Grand Duchy is, they are not recommended. A network ticket is FLux 140 for one day, until 8 a.m. the following day; there's a 50% reduction for those over 65.

DRIVING

If at all possible, explore the remarkably varied and rural regions of the Grand Duchy by car. When working out an itinerary, keep in mind the *scale* of your Luxembourg map. (The tourist office offers a free one of the Grand Duchy that is as detailed a road map as you'll need.) Even allowing for frequent car-stopping scenery and wandering at will in the most interesting towns, you can cover quite a patch of the country on a realistic day's drive. Add an overnight, better two, and you can be a master traveler in this lovely little land.

Although Luxembourg City now faces the same traffic jams at the beginning and end of the business day that have come to plague all European cities, the situation in the countryside of the Grand Duchy is completely different. Never have I driven on such untrammeled roads, almost all of them unbusy byways. Often when both driving and navigating myself, I have opted to collect a rented car at an airport or other location outside a major city, in order to avoid congestion while I'm becoming familiar with unfamiliar traffic patterns. But there's no need for that in Luxembourg. Ten minutes after departing downtown, you'll be completely in the country and nearly to your first destination, no matter in what direction you're heading. You won't need to know route numbers, only the name of the town where you're headed and an interim village or two. As you'll see from the scenic roads that are highlighted on the map in green, there are so many around the country that you'd be unable to avoid them if you tried. I've even found myself spellbound by stretches not specially marked for scenic appeal.

Throughout Luxembourg road signage is extremely well done, with indicators for upcoming villages and towns appearing at every crossroad that requires one. Many of the well-paved roads are two lanes, and you will occasionally come upon a farm vehicle or truck; be cautious about passing because of the *possibility* of oncoming traffic around a road bend. On any road you may hardly see a car from one quarter hour to another, though you must drive prepared at any time to meet an oncoming car traveling speedily. If one approaches from behind, just pull over when it's safe to let it pass, and go on with your leisurely appreciation of the scenery.

Because Luxembourg's *Value-Added Tax* rate (15%) is lower than in many other European countries—an advantage that could eventually disappear as Europe integrates further economically—car-rental rates there are among the least expensive on the continent. Round-trip *Icelandair* transatlantic passengers flying from JFK, New York via Reykjavik, Iceland, to Luxembourg City are entitled to that airline's extremely favorable rental car rates with unlimited mileage (toll-free U.S. inquiries to Icelandair ☎ *(800) 223-5500)*.

THE FLAG

After you've been in Holland, Luxembourg's flag will seem familiar (logically, since until 1890, the hereditary royalty of the Netherlands' *House of Nassau* also were the rulers of Luxembourg). Today, the Grand Duchy's horizontally striped red, white, and blue standard remains the same as Holland's except for a slightly lighter shade of blue, a change made official only in 1981. The historic flag of Luxembourg, an upright red lion on a background of white and blue stripes, is sometimes used within Luxembourg.

THE GRAND DUCAL FAMILY

The Grand Duchy of Luxembourg is a hereditary constitutional monarchy. Although it finally was granted independence by a conference of European nations in 1867, Luxembourg remained under the rule of then **Dutch King Willem III**, who was Grand Duke of Luxembourg in his own right through the **House of Orange-Nassau** (whose ancestral home is a Grand Duchy landmark, **Vianden Castle**—see "Vianden" under "Tour of the Grand Duchy"). In 1890, Willem III died without a male heir, and the Dutch crown passed to his daughter **Wilhelmina**. However, in Luxembourg, since *Salic Law*, making women ineligible to succeed to the throne, applied at the time, there was a discontinuation of dynastic links with the Orange- Nassaus. Rule passed to **Duke Adolphe of Nassau-Weilburg**, who became founder of Luxembourg's Royal House. When Adolphe's son, **Guillaume I**, who had abolished the Salic Law, died in 1912, his eldest daughter **Marie-Adelaide** became Grand Duchess. When Luxembourg was occupied by the Germans in World War I, Marie-Adelaide remained in the country; afterwards, she was faced with charges of alleged pro-German sympathies, which forced her to abdicate. A referendum put to the people in 1919 confirmed the ruling house and called for her sister Charlotte to assume the throne.

Grand Duchess Charlotte, married to **Prince Felix of Bourbon-Parma**, healed Luxembourg's monarchy, becoming a much loved leader. When the Nazis invaded Luxembourg in May 1940, Charlotte escaped the country with her family and ministers and formed a government in exile. Her work—on behalf of Luxembourg and the Allies during the war—in England, Portugal, and Canada (where her son Jean went to university) was a source of pride to her people. On her return to Luxembourg in 1945, Charlotte was greeted by the premier with words of regard from her nation that were often repeated thereafter: "*Madame, we love you.*" (They are inscribed in Letzebuergesch on the sculpture of the former Grand Duchess paid for by public subscription and erected on Luxembourg's **place Clairefontaine** after her death in 1985.) In 1964, after 45 years on the throne, Charlotte abdicated in favor of her son Jean.

Still monarch of Luxembourg today, **Grand Duke Jean**, who was born in 1921 and served as a lieutenant with the *Irish Guards* from 1942 to 1945, married **Princess Josephine-Charlotte** of Belgium, sister of King Albert II. The Ducal Palace in Luxembourg City serves as the royal couple's in-town residence and office; their country castle is north of the capital at Colmar-Berg. Grand Duke Jean, who celebrated the 25th anniversary of his reign in 1989, and Grand Duchess Josephine-Charlotte have five children (and 14 grandchildren). Their eldest son, **H.R.H. Prince Henri**, born in 1955, is heir to the throne. He received his graduate education in France, Switzerland, and England, and holds a masters degree in political science and a Staff College Certificate from the *Royal Military Academy* at Sandhurst, England. The crown prince is highly effective in his job as chairman of the *Board of Economic Development of Luxembourg*. In 1981, he married **Maria Teresa** (now Princess), who was born in Cuba in 1956, her parents moving to New York in 1959 at the time of the revolution. Eventually her family moved to and became citizens of Switzerland, where Maria Teresa met Prince Henri while he was studying at the *University of Geneva*. The popular couple has four children, the eldest a son, **Guillaume**.

LUXEMBOURG CITY

GUIDELINES FOR LUXEMBOURG CITY

SIGHTS

One of the world's most picturesquely situated capitals, Luxembourg City should be enjoyed for its visually engaging setting (with midcity ravine, walled by former fortifications and romantically illuminated at night) as much as for any other specific attractions. From the pedestrian **Promenade de la Corniche** are panoramic vistas that have given it the name "the most beautiful balcony in Europe." The city's *upper town* is set on plateaus above the winding green valley of lower town, the site of several suburbs with cafes, and walking paths with superb views up at the bastions. Centers of activity are in upper town, at the **Place d'Armes** (tourist office), **Marché-aux-Poissons** (the original hub of the ancient city, with the **National Museum** and **Bock casemates**), and **place de la Constitution** (overlooking the *Petrusse Valley*). The **European Center** on Kirchberg Plateau houses the offices of the Luxembourg-based European Community institutions; its modern buildings provide an intriguing contrast to the city's fairy-tale turrets.

GETTING AROUND

Although the city is not large, Luxembourg's layout is complex, set on several levels and cut by two rivers, the *Alzette* and *Petrusse*, with their rock-walled, wooded valleys. Virtually all sights, shopping, and much of the charm are in the old *upper town*, as distinguished from the modern *European Center* on the Kirchberg Plateau across the dramatic **Grand Duchess Charlotte ("Red") Bridge** (1966), and the

19th-century sections of the city, across the arched **pont Adolphe** (1903) in the direction of the *Gare* (station). Since the views from points in the upper and lower city are so much a part of Luxembourg's beauty, sightseeing on foot will prove the most memorable. The upper city is quite compact, with several sections pedestrianized. The tourist office provides an excellent leaflet (*A Walk through the Green Heart of Europe*) that outlines two 3 mi./5 km. walking tours covering the highlights in both the upper and lower city. The elevator (free, operating 6:30 a.m.–2 a.m.) on **place du Saint Espirit** connects the upper town with the lower's **Grund** suburb (cafes and restaurants). Travel by foot can be supplemented as needed by city buses and taxis. Bus terminals and taxi ranks are located at the station, **place Aldringen**, and **place de Paris**; taxis, although tip is included in the fare, are expensive, with surcharges for luggage, travel at night (10%), and on Sundays (25%). For interesting and easy views from the paved pathways through the Petrusse and Alzette valleys, take **Luxembourg Live**, a tourist train *(April 1–Oct. 31, daily departures from 10 a.m.–6 p.m. from the Adolphe Bridge at place de Bruxelles, tickets (220 Flux) from Kiosk Luxembourg Live)*. The 45-minute tours include an English language audio dramatization of the city's turbulent history on headset. Although its audio show is gimmicky, if you're not planning to take independent walks in the center-city valleys, the perspectives of the former fortifications offered during the tour are highly recommended. Because of pedestrian and one-way roads, restricted on-street parking, and the challenge of Luxembourg City's upper and lower city topography, it's preferrable to have a car only when you need one to explore the countryside. **Kemwel** is a reputable, budget-priced, local car rental firm. If you arrive by car, leave it in a center city car park. Two-hour motorcoach tours with a drive past major city sights and a stop at the **U.S. Cemetery at Hamm** are offered by **Voyages H. Sales** *(26 rue du Cure; mornings daily April 1–October 31, several days weekly the rest of the year;* ☎ *46.18.18; bookings also at tourist office, hotels)*. The company also offers diverse day tours in the Grand Duchy on Wednesday, Saturday, and Sunday from spring to Sept. 30.

SHOPPING

Though Luxembourg is not inexpensive, the quality of goods sold is very high, and the range of items for a city its size surprisingly broad, due to the demands of its cosmopolitan population. Choices range from boutiques along the chic pedestrian **Grande Rue**, to fresh produce and general wares at the Wednesday and Saturday morning

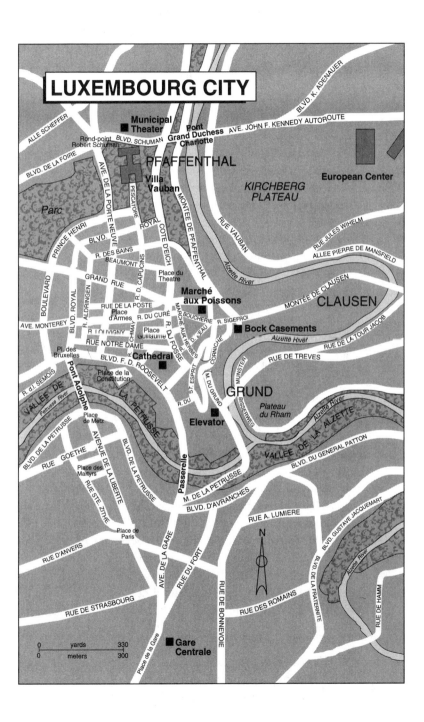

open-air markets held on **place Guillaume** in front of the Hôtel de Ville. Luxembourg's own **Villeroy & Boch** provides desirable souvenirs. **Note**: many shops do not open Mondays until 2 p.m.

ENTERTAINMENT AND EVENTS

In warmer months through September, almost **nightly concerts** on the bandstand entertain *al fresco* diners around **Place d'Armes**. After-dark illumination produces a setting for fairy tales at the former fortifications (year-round in Petrusse Valley). Other city buildings and monuments are floodlighted from late spring through September, and a walk about town to view them is memorable evening entertainment, although the tourist office can provide a listing of concerts and other events. You can also check the "What's On" page in *Luxembourg News Digest*, the country's weekly (Thursday) English-language newspaper. It will give you an idea of the activities of the U.S., British, Canadian, and other English-speaking nationals who live in the Grand Duchy.

WHERE TO STAY

There's adequate choice for pleasant rooms in Luxembourg City. Because of its relatively small size, the location of a hotel makes less difference here than in larger European capitals. Fall start-up sessions for the European Community Council of Ministers and other congresses/conventions make rooms in the better hotels harder to come by in September and October, and again in April and June; plan ahead if you're travelling in those periods.

WHERE TO EAT

French/Belgian preparation and German portions is an apt characterization for Luxembourg cuisine. Foods are generally rich, and many regional specialties are similar to those in the Belgian Ardennes: jambon d'Ardennes, paté, charcuterie, venison, hare, sausage, and river fish: pike, trout, and crawfish. The beginning of the *moules* (mussels) season in September (until April) is on the minds of inland Luxembourgers as much as their Benelux cohorts on the coast. Entirely of local origin are the smoked pork and broad bean dish (*Jud mat gardebo'nen*), *Thuringen sausage*, and a strong local cheese *kachkes* (mysteriously described as "cooked in the making" and served on buttered black bread with mustard). In September, *quetsch* (small plums) tarts are a treat. *Filet Americaine* appears on many a menu, but you won't be asked how you want it cooked; it's *steak tartare*.

ARRIVING

Luxembourg's national passenger airline is **Luxair** (☎ *43.61.61*), with one-class service connecting many major European airports with **Findel Airport**, 3.5 miles/6 km. northeast of Luxembourg City. **Public bus #9** runs between the airport and the train station in Luxembourg City; Luxair also operates a full schedule of buses between the airport and the station, and will accept payment in foreign currency. **Icelandair** has flights to Luxembourg, via Reykjavik, Iceland, from JFK/New York and Baltimore/Washington. **Sabena World Airlines** (*70 Grand Rue;* ☎ *2.12.12*) has service to/from Brussels.

IN THE AREA

The **Luxembourg American Cemetery and Memorial at Hamm** (included on most city coach tours), several miles outside Luxembourg City, is the dignified resting place for 5,067 Americans, including **U.S. Army General George (Blood and Guts) Patton Jr.**, who was headquartered in Luxembourg City during the *Battle of the Bulge*, which produced most of the casualties buried here.

TRAVEL TIPS

Despite their cosmopolitan climate, Luxembourgers maintain a civilized pace of life. Even many professionals hold to the tradition of a two-hour lunch (noon–2 p.m.), which is a standard for most offices, shops, and museums. Many workers go home to have lunch with their families. Even the city's parking meters take a noon–2 p.m. lunch break.

50th ANNIVERSARY OF THE LIBERATION OF LUXEMBOURG

For the occasion of the 50th anniversary of its liberation from occupying Nazi forces by the First U.S. Army, 5th Armored Division, Luxembourg City will stage a major commemoration of the event on September 10, 1994. During Luxembourg City's celebration, residents will be gratefully recalling the speed with which the U.S. Army pushed through to their city, so quickly that the rapidly retreating Nazis did not have time to destroy much of their capital.

LUXEMBOURG CITY IN CONTEXT

Luxembourg City To Be Europe's Cultural Capital In 1995

The European Community has designated Luxembourg City as the European Cultural Capital for 1995. Focusing on worthy cities in community-member countries on a rotating basis, the European Cultural Capital spotlight gives selected destinations a special incentive to shine, such as by encouraging a stepped-up schedule for the restoration of historic buildings. Visitors to Luxembourg City in 1994 will reap early rewards of those efforts: the Grand Ducal Palace, closed for several years for extensive renovations, is slated to be ready in 1994 for its annual summer opening (mid-July to end-August) during the Grand Duke's vacation.

Other projects and special events will be a part of Luxembourg City's 1995 celebration as European Cultural Capital.

Although a small city, its greater population approximately 120,000, Luxembourg is home to a substantial percent of the 377,000 people who live in the Grand Duchy. Atypical of the historic, even romantic, appearance of much of the old capital is **boulevard Royal**, frequently referred to as "Wall Street." But the gleaming glass towers of the modern monetary institutions housed along it do not rise so high that they hide the sky; center city structures cannot surpass in height the *Gella Fra* (gilded woman) atop the **War Memorial** on **Constitution Plaza**. In Luxembourg, buildings are kept in proportion, and business, though prospering, is kept in perspective. Rarely are transactions allowed to encroach on after-work socializing with friends or family over food and drink at one of the cafes on **Place d'Armes** or elsewhere.

Not that business is not held in high regard in Luxembourg City. Luxembourg's annual **Schueberfouer sheep fair**, founded in 1340 by John the Blind, attracted traders of all varieties from all over Europe (on **Grand Rue** a charming sculptured fountain with sheep and musical instruments commemorates the historic fair) and shows an early commitment to commerce. Today some 85% of the country's GNP comes from exports and imports, so there remains a recognition of the country's dependence on foreign trade. Nevertheless, one can hardly argue with Luxembourg's semi-laid-back life-style, since the country has one of the highest standards of living in the world.

From its beginnings, Luxembourg City had a market, **Marché-aux-Poissons** (fish market), situated only a short distance from the castle acquired by Sigefroi in 963. The site may have been one of commercial dealings even earlier, since it was the actual intersection of two important Roman roads: the grand consular road from Paris via Reims and Arlon to Trier, and the one linking Metz via St. Vith and

Liège to Aachen. As early as the 4th century, the clifftop site above the Alzette Valley had an observation tower that formed part of the Roman defense system against the Franks, and it probably was useful during invasions led by the dreaded Hungarian, **Attila**, in the first half of the 5th century. By about 450, the Romans gave up on the region. That early fortress, which had became known as **Castellum Lucilinburhuc**, was probably in ruins when **Sigefroi, count of Ardennes**, acquired it on Palm Sunday in 963, in exchange for the Abbey of St. Maximin in Trier. On a neighboring rock, **the Bock**, Sigefroi set about building a new castle (fortress), using his own workmen and employing the farmers and craftsmen who were already living in the valley on the banks of the Alzette, in what today are the suburbs of **Grund** and **Pfaffenthal**. Around the nearby Marché-aux-Poissons market place, Sigefroi's servants and retainers established their homes, thus making it the true center of the rapidly growing village. Between the market and the Bock, Sigefroi began building a court chapel in 987, naming it for **St. Michel**. Expansion was so rapid that by the year 1050 it was necessary to build a second wall to contain the town (which then reached to the present **rue du Fosse**) and meant the addition of a new market on the site of today's **rue du Marché-aux-Herbes**.

The town continued to prosper, receiving its charter from **Countess Ermesinde** in 1244. A third wall became necessary for the upper town and was begun under **John the Blind** in about 1320, taking most of the century to complete. Between 1387 to 1395, the lower town of **Grund** also was surrounded by fortifications, and **Pfaffenthal** was protected by a wall built across the bottom of the Alzette valley and given three gates. Such security measures were considered essential because of the economic and strategic importance of the mills, tanneries, and, above all, the water supplies in the lower town.

Though Luxembourg was elevated to a duchy (from a county) in 1354, and the House of Luxembourg produced rulers of power and prestige in the 14th and 15th centuries, their additional titles, such as Holy Roman Emperor, meant that its leaders often were absentee landlords. And Luxembourg's fortifications alone couldn't fend off the Burgundians, who, under **Philip the Good**, took the town by force one night in 1443, thus confirming the acquisition of the Duchy of Luxembourg by the **House of Burgundy**. From this time, for five hundred years, the strongly fortified town frequently found itself a pawn in the military policies of foreign powers. The Austrians, Spanish, French, Dutch, Prussians, and Germans all have laid claim to Luxembourg.

The French under **King Louis XIV** did the most to change the face of the city. Having seiged the town in 1683 and claiming it in 1684, Louis set his great military engineer, **Maréchal de Vauban**, to the task of addressing the changes in defensive fortifications required by more modern weaponry. Luxembourg's high walls and massive towers, built in the Middle Ages, could not stand up to the bombardment by the contemporary artillery, and so Vauban transformed the walls into ramparts and added fortifications beneath the ground. Vauban recruited 3,000 laborers and, within the four years from 1684 to 1688, created an impregnable fortress out of the natural advantages of the Luxembourg City setting.

Austrian Hapsburg engineers further strengthened and extended the casemates and forts during their occupation of Luxembourg in the 18th century. By the time they were through, in addition to visible fortified girdles, watchtowers, and bastions, Luxembourg had a virtual underground city in its sandstone rockbed. The **Bock Casemates** alone had a 14 mil./23 km. network of tunnels, and down huge staircases some 120 feet beneath the surface were great galleries to shelter thousands of soldiers as well as their horses, plus barracks, kitchens, bakeries, and slaughterhouses to sustain, and workshops to maintain, the troops.

Again, however, fortifications proved not to be the sole factor for defense. On June 7, 1795, after a seven-month blockade and four-month siege by the *Army of the French Republic*, the fortress city was starved into submission. Reporting the news to the French National Assembly, General Carnot claimed, "This fortress is second only to Gibraltar." After Napoleon's fall in 1814, leaders meeting at the *Congress of Vienna* took over the future course of both the city and the duchy of Luxembourg, though their fates would not, for a while, be the same. Luxembourg City was ordered to accept a Prussian garrison. Dutch **King Willem I** was named hereditary Grand Duke when he was presented with an upgraded Grand Duchy, which he governed as a province in his kingdom. The marking of the boundaries of the Luxembourg City fortress as federal territory took until 1829. (The fortress city, under Prussian insistence, had become a part of the *German Confederation*.) From 1835–1838, Willem undertook extensive repairs and modernization on the fortifications.

Late in the 1850s, the Dutch laid the first railway lines in Luxembourg, and by 1861 the fortress city was connected by train to Trier, and by 1866 to Liège. Ironically, while providing a terrific boost economically, the international rail routes simply enhanced the strategic value of the fortress of Luxembourg, and, as a result, even more extensive work on the fortifications followed. Finally, in 1866, Luxembourg became freed of the need to quarter Prussian troops by the dissolution of the German Confederacy. But it became the object of a complicated conflict between the French Napoleon III and German Bismarck over the use of the famous fortress, leading to a Franco-Prussian crisis that could have degenerated into war. The idea of "neutralizing" Luxembourg, launched by Holland's Prince Henry, took hold with the Dutch King-Grand Duke. In 1867, the **Treaty of London** was signed by Great Britain, Russia, France, Prussia, the Netherlands, Austria, Belgium, Italy, and Luxembourg, guaranteeing perpetual neutrality of the Grand Duchy, and the evacuation and eventual razing of the city's fortress. On September 9, the last Prussian soldier left.

On that day in 1867, before dismantling began, the fortifications of Luxembourg City covered nearly 445 acres/180 hectares, the town itself being only 296 acres/120 hectares in area. The dismantling took 16 years, costing over 1-1/2 million gold-currency francs, a staggering sum for the time. The land freed from fortifications was put to good use—picturesque promenades, fine parks, and new residential and business districts. From 1933, the casemates of the Petrusse, with their monumental staircase and five-story height, were restored, and in 1936 work began on the Bock casemates. In 1938, all the old fortifications were converted to civil defense shelters for thousands.

The Nazis, having incorporated the Grand Duchy into the Third Reich, felt free to change the street signs after they invaded Luxembourg in May 1940. The prominent street that today is *avenue de la Liberté* bore the name *Adolphe Hitler Strasse* from 1940 to 1944. From 1940 until September 10, 1944, the headquarters of the Gestapo was located in a villa at 57 blvd. de la Petrusse. (Today, it's the Ministry of Public Health.) Worse, the Nazis tore down the **War Monument** on place de la Constitution that had been built to honor the dead from the First World War. On September 10, 1944, the Nazis were chased out of Luxembourg City for good by the Allies, primarily by U.S. Army forces. General Omar Bradley immediately set up headquarters for the 12th Army Group at 2 place de Metz, and, across that square, in the turreted State Savings Bank, was General H.S. Vandenberg of the 9th US Air Force. From December 21, 1944 (during the *Battle of the Bulge*) until March 27, 1945, **General**

George Patton established his H.Q. for the 3rd Army in the Pescatore Foundation (today a senior citizens' home). It was in the chapel of the Foundation on December 23rd that Patton delivered the prayer for fair weather for his troops and air forces, that began: *"Sir, this is Patton talking. The last fourteen days have been straight hell. Rain, snow, more rain, more snow—and I'm beginning to wonder what's going on in Your headquarters. Whose side are You on, anyway?"*

Emerging from the war, Luxembourg soon became a center for activities meant to design a Europe that would not again put itself through such armed conflagrations. In 1952, Luxembourg was chosen as headquarters for the High Authority of the supranational **European Coal and Steel Community** (ECSC), brought into existence with the essential support of Robert Schuman, who had been born and educated in the city. The ECSC led directly to the creation of the **European Community** (EC), which also chose Luxembourg as the site for several of its permanent institutions. Luxembourg City's prosperous and peaceful present, its development now under the direction of its own people, is a situation in sharp contrast to its heavily fortified past, perpetuated for centuries by fearful foreigners. Today, disarmed and delightful, Luxembourg is setting an example for the world.

GUIDEPOSTS

Country-wide telephone code 352

City Tourist Office • *Syndicat d'Initiatives et de Tourisme*, place d'Armes ☎ *22.28.09*, FAX *47.48.19*; June 15–Sept. 15 Mon.–Fri. 9 a.m.–7 p.m., Sat. 9 a.m.–1 p.m., 2–7 p.m., Sun. 10 a.m.–noon, 2–6 p.m.; remainder of year Mon.–Fri. 9 a.m.–1 p.m., 2–6 p.m., closed Sat., Sun. Also City and Grand Duchy information offices at Air Terminus at rail station (place de la Gare ☎ *48.11.99*) daily 9 a.m.–noon, 2–6:30 p.m., closed Sun. Dec.– March; and Findel Airport; ☎ *40.08.08*, Mon.–Fri. 10 a.m.–2:30 p.m. and 4–7 p.m., Sat. 10 a.m.–1:45 p.m., Sun. 10 a.m.–2:30 p.m., and 3:30–6:30 p.m.

Auto. Assoc. • *Automobile Club de Luxembourg*, 13 rue de Longwy, Bertrange, open Mon.–Fri. 8:30 a.m.-noon, 1:30–6 p.m.; reciprocal service with other auto clubs, and 24-hour breakdown service, ☎ *45.00.45*.

Emergencies • Medical, police, fire: ☎ *012*.

Post Offices • 25 rue Aldringen, Mon.–Sat. 7 a.m.–8:30 p.m., also FAX services, ☎ *4.76.51*; daily at place de la Gare, 6 a.m.–10 p.m., and Findel Airport daily 7 a.m.–10 p.m. available.

Telephone • 38 place de la Gare; ☎ *4.99.11.*

Trains • Chemins de Fer Luxembourgeois, Gare Centrale, information, reservations: 6 a.m.–8 p.m., ☎ *49.24.24*

Embassies • U.S.A.: 22 blvd. Emmanuel Servais, ☎ *46.01.23*; United Kingdom: 28 blvd. Royal, ☎ *2.98.64.*

WHAT TO SEE AND DO

The city's weathered sandstone walls, great viaducts, plateaus set with steeples and turrets, and river valleys filled with suburban towns and terraced gardens provide scenes of exceptional interest. The views are equally outstanding whether seen from above, along the **Promenade de la Corniche**, or from below, from paths in the green parks in the center of the valley floor, looking up at the solid stone bastions built into the walls. Its setting is what makes Luxembourg delightfully unique, so experience that above all else during your stay. Luxembourg is blessed with many parks, built on the land circling the inner city that became available after the fortifications were dismantled. Other squares, many with statues and monuments, add interest to walks around town. Sights are described below in two groupings, the first radiating out from the **Marché-aux-Poissons**, followed by those near the **place de la Constitution**.

Musée de l'État/National Museum ★★

Marché-aux-Poissons (Fish Market), entrance from rue Wiltheim; Tues.–Fri. 10 a.m.–4:45 p.m., Sat. 2–5:45 p.m., Sun. 10–11:45 a.m. & 2–5:45 p.m., closed Mon. The museum, located in a former governor's house, has an extensive collection of art and artifacts from all periods of Luxembourg's history. The archaeological department has fine prehistoric, Gallo-Roman, and Frankish items, the Gallo-Roman material being outstanding. Something of the history of the city is depicted through maps, weapons, and a bronze model of the fortress before it was dismantled. The art department includes a collection of works by modern Luxembourg artists, in particular **Joseph Kutter** and **Dominique Lang**.

The ★★ **Industrial and Popular Arts** section of the National Museum *(rue Wiltheim; open Tues.–Fri. from 1–5 p.m., Sat. & Sun. 2–6 p.m., closed Mon.;* ☎ *47.93.30; no English documentation but well worth a visit)* is located across the road in two restored 17th- and 18th-century burghers' houses. Worth a visit for themselves, the handsome houses, which retain their original interior design, have high beamed ceilings, old wooden floors, and stone casement windows (out of which are seen wonderful views of the Alzette Valley). The decorations, from the mid-15th to the end of the 18th century, include tapestries, porcelain, paintings, and freestanding and built-in (wall cupboards) furniture. The museum seems to get more wonderful as you wander, especially on the lower floors, which have fully furnished rooms with leather wall coverings, painted panels, and tiled fireplaces. Down in the vaulted cellars, which made me wonder if I had somehow stumbled into the underground network of casemates at the nearby Bock (see below), was an unusual and fascinating display of dozens of 16th-19th-century intricately designed cast-iron fireplace pieces and ornamental stoves.

From the museum, walk a few doors down *rue Wiltheim* to ★ **"Zum Welle Mann"** tavern (*closed Mon.*), a part of the museum. Only light snacks and beverages are served, but the atmosphere and views out the rear windows over the Alzette valley are superb. At the foot of rue Wiltheim are the 11th-century **Trois Towers**, from which you can connect with other roads down to the **Pfaffenthal** suburb.

The National Museum is on the site that became the market and hub of the early town which grew around Sigefroi's castle on the nearby Bock. In this oldest part of the city is Luxembourg's oldest house **Um Bock**, on rue Loge, now a restaurant. Across the road is ★ **St. Michel's Church** (*rue Sigefroi*). Originally founded by Sigefroi as his castle chapel in 987, St. Michel's was extended in the mid-14th century, but was damaged and rebuilt several times until taking its present appearance in 1688. The Renaissance doorway dates from 1689, a gift from Louis XIV, hence the French *fleur de lis*. The facade contains the remains of Roman window vents, while the interior is a typical example of late Gothic vault style.

Bock Casemates   ★★

entrance at Bock/Promenade de la Corniche; March-September, daily 10 a.m.–5 p.m.; self-guided tour; brochure in English; wear flat shoes for several flights of steep narrow stone stairs with handrails, uneven ground. During the dismantling of the fortifications beginning in 1867 (the process took 16 years), most of the city's fortifications were blown up. But it was impossible to destroy the underground casemates without damaging the city above them. The main connections and entrances were closed, but about 11 miles/17 km. remain, on several levels connected by staircases. The garrison of the Bock casemate was 1,200 men, and the main gallery held 50 cannon in loopholes which were enlarged during the dismantling and now afford remarkable views over the city. During this century's wars, the casemates, which have space for 35,000 people, were used as bomb shelters. **Note:** The Bock casemates should be your first choice if you're not planning to visit both of the city's casemate attractions; they give a far better idea of Luxembourg's former underground fortifications and allow you to explore at your own pace.

In 1963, just opposite the Bock, important remains of Sigefroi's ancient 963 **Luxembourg Castle** (*open at all times*) were discovered. They are preserved as the **Monument of the Millennium** of the city. Beyond the castle, on the **Montée de Clausen** road that leads across the Alzette valley and down into the suburb of **Clausen**, is the **"Hollow Tooth,"** a watchtower built by Vauban that got that name from its appearance after being blown up during the dismantlement of Luxembourg's fortifications.

Promenade de la Corniche

Sure-footed, properly shod visitors with stamina for steep stone stairs will find the casemates fascinating from the inside, but if for any reason that excursion isn't possible, a stroll along the pedestrian promenade de la Corniche, which runs downhill from the Bock will give you a good sense of the city's former fortifications and scenic setting. Bridges, here the high arched railway viaduct and the low-lying one across the reflective waters of the Alzette, frame many of Luxembourg's views. From the Corniche you see the 22-story tower (tallest in the Grand Duchy) that indicates the **European Center** on the **Kirchberg Plateau**. It plays a significant part in contemporary Luxembourg life but, unless you have a special interest, there's no real reason for tourists to go there. Walk the Corniche as far as the **place du St-Espirit**, if you want to remain in the upper town, or continue heading steeply down **Montée du Grund** to the bridge at the bottom across the Alzette in the suburb of ★★**Grund** (cafes, restaurants). The free **public elevator** (lift) built into the valley wall will whisk you back up to place du St-Espirit. From there walk to **blvd. Franklin Roosevelt** and past the Cathédrale to place de la Constitution.

Place de la Constitution

is a major orientation point in Luxembourg, which spreads out in odd patterns due to its topography. Crowning the **Bastion Beck**, built to this amazing level above the Petrusse Valley in the course of the fortification of Luxembourg, place de la Constitution is instantly recognizable by the **War Memorial** obelisk. It was erected in 1923 to commemorate Luxembourgers who gave their lives in the First World War. (Although the Grand Duchy had to comply with its **Statute of Unarmed Neutrality**, a number of its citizens volunteered to serve with the Allied armies, particularly the French.) Atop the slim obelisk was placed the ★ golden statue of a woman (a Victory figure), who soon gained the name *Gelle Fra* (gilded woman), which became commonly used for the whole Constitution Square area. Not appreciating the sentiments it instilled in Luxembourgers, the Nazis pulled the monument down on October 21, six months after their invasion of the Grand Duchy in May 1940. Most of the pieces were recovered and hidden by Luxembourgers, but the action came to symbolize Nazi oppression, and, when the war was over, it became important to re-erect the monument. But it could not be completed because the golden statue remained missing. Finally, it was found in the early 1980s, restored, and, on Luxembourg's National Day, June 23, in 1985, the monument was officially reinaugurated in the presence of His Royal Highness Grand Duke Jean.

If you are facing the Petrusse Valley, to the far left of the square is a long stairway that leads down to ★paths beneath the walls of the upper town. Other stairs lead to the ★★ green valley floor itself, where you'll find yourself amid some pretty surprising midcity scenery. Wonderful ★★ floodlighting at night.

Petrusse or Constitution Casemates

place de la Constitution; Easter & Whitsun weekends, July & Aug., approx. 11 a.m.–4 p.m., but hours posted at entrance; guided tours only, 40 mins. The Petrusse casemates date from the first half of the 17th century, the Spanish era of modernization of the fortifications, although the French Vauban and, in the 19th century, the Austrians also implemented their ideas. The Spanish added many bastions, including the formidable **Bastion Beck**, named for the Spanish governor under whose rule it was begun. Its "platform," after the work was finished by Vauban, reached the level of the present place de la Constitution. The casemate tour, which covers lots of stairways, includes a visit to one of the outside terraces that overlooks the Petrusse Valley.

Place Guillaume

is located upstairs opposite the cathedral on rue Notre Dame. It is the setting for the **Hôtel de Ville** *(not open for tours)*, which was built during the 1830s to replace the former one, now the Ducal Palace. *The European Coal and Steel Community Agreement* was signed in the main council hall in 1952. General markets are held in the square on Wenesday and Saturday, their activity then taking center stage instead of the equestrian statue of Dutch King/Grand Duke of Luxembourg **Willem II** (for whom the square is named), which usually dominates. Willem faces down the short rue de la Reine to the Grand Ducal Palace.

Grand Ducal Palace ★★

Corner rue de Marché aux Herbes & rue de la Reine; usually open to the public most days from mid-July to end Aug., during the Grand Duke's vacation. The newly restored palace, whose attractive 1572 facade in Renaissance style has an interesting Spanish-Moorish strapwork decoration—at the time it was built, the Spanish ruled—was originally the town hall, built to replace the previous one on the site, destroyed in 1554 in a gunpowder blast that caused extensive damage in the town. (This site very likely has been the setting for Luxembourg's various town halls since the city received its charter in 1244.) The civil guard met here where, while it served as a town hall, it also housed a prison and the municipal weighing scales. The balustrade, originally in stone, was replaced with one in wrought iron in 1741, when the building was enlarged. From the time Luxembourg was taken by the French in 1795, the palace has served as a building for national government, and, since 1890, it has been the residential palace of the Grand-Ducal family. Various fine buildings that house other government offices are located between the palace and the nearby cathedral.

Place d'Armes

takes its name from the days when it served as a parade ground for the

French stationed in the city in 1685. The place d'Armes today is the social center of the city, the congenial Luxembourgers' favorite **cafe congregating spot**, with a bandstand that keeps a busy schedule in summer. At one end of the square is a statue of **Michel Lentz**, author of the national anthem, with its famous line "We want to remain what we are." At the other, with the **Tourist Office** tucked into offices there, is the 1906 **Cercle** municipal cultural building, whose pediment is decorated with a frieze depicting the granting of the town charter to Luxembourg by Countess Ermesinde in 1244.

Maquette/Model

Rathskeller of the Cercle Theater, entrance on rue de la Cure; daily except Sun. 10 a.m.–12:20 p.m., 2–6 p.m. in July and Aug.; rest of year apply around the corner at City Tourist Office, place d'Armes; 50-min. Audiovisual show and commentary at the Model is presented in English several times daily, at last check at 11 a.m., 3 and 5 p.m., but confirm times at tourist office. The Model, located around the corner from place d'Armes, a copy of that made under French King Louis XIV (the original is in the Hotel des Invalides in Paris), shows the full development of the **Luxembourg City fortress**, as envisioned by Vauban near the end of the 17th century. The **audiovisual presentation** takes you through the high points of the city's history. A careful study of the Model helps you appreciate what nine centuries of evolution as a fortress meant to the layout of Luxembourg in terms of walls, gates, towers, turrets, bastions, and barriers built on the site.

Pescatore Museum

Municipal Park; ave. E. Reuter. Built on municipal parkland on the site of razed Vauban fortifications, the mansion houses a fine art collection that normally is open to the public during July and August. Included are works by **Jan Steen**, **Pieter Breughel the Younger**, **Jan Breughel the Younger**, **Teniers the Younger**, **Dou**, **Canaletto**, and **Courbet**.

Located on an adjoining portion of the Municipal Park, where once Fort Louvigny stood, is Radio-Tele Luxembourg, a powerful component of the Grand Duchy's important telecommunications industry. To the north, at the edge of the Municipal park, is **Rond-Point Robert Schuman**. This founding father of the European Community is honored by a monument located near the modern **Municipal Theater**, the city's main performance center. The focal point of the Schuman Monument are several steel girders, signifying Schuman's role in the establishment of the European Coal and Steel Community, which was a precursor to the Common Market. From the monument, blvd. Robert Schuman leads across the vivid red ★ **Grand Duchess Charlotte Bridge** to the **European Center**, practically passing over the house in which he grew up, which sits in the Alzette valley suburb of Clausen.

SHOPPING

Luxembourg's 15% VAT (Value-Added Tax) is lower than most in Europe. Although that situation could change as a result of Europe's economic union, at present it means savings for shoppers on the high-quality international items for sale on and near the pedestrian **Grand Rue**. (Purchases in a single store of FLux 3,000 or more qualify for a VAT refund; inquire at the time of purchase.) Luxembourg's shops are small and personalized; there are no department stores in the city. Though many of the fine **Villeroy & Boch** (2 rue de Fosse) products are made in factories in Germany, the company maintains its Luxembourg roots (there's a large tableware factory in **Septfontaines** in the Eisch River Valley) that go back to the 18th century. Several of its china patterns are produced in Luxembourg—the 1989 **Mon Jardin** design, **Petite Fleur**, **Naif** (Naive), and Botanic. These lines are somewhat less expensive in the Luxembourg store than they would be elsewhere. A number of private **art galleries** featuring the works of Luxembourgers have opened in the city. If you enjoyed the cast-iron fireback pieces at the Industrial Arts section of the National Museum, look for the miniature items, called "Tak," made in the shape of castles and other subjects by Luxembourg's **Fonderie de Mersch**. There's a flea market on the 2nd and 4th Saturdays each month.

WHERE TO STAY

Most of the hotels in Luxembourg City itself are independent properties, many family run, some multigenerational. Several international chain hotels, particularly popular with business travelers, are located just outside the city. Near Findel Airport is the **Aerogolf-Sheraton**, and in a wooded suburb several kilometers from the city center is the **Inter-Continental**, popular as a quiet conference site. The **Pullman** property (the newly renovated former Holiday Inn) is presently the only hotel at the European Center on Kirchberg plateau. Most hotels included here have their own restaurants, of a more than acceptable standard. The tradition of hotel-restaurants is strong in this region, and you'll rarely go wrong by dining "in house," since a hotel's restaurant also must satisfy discriminating local customers in order to survive outside of the tourist season. All prices are inclusive of taxes and service.

VERY EXPENSIVE

Grand Hotel Cravat   ★★★★

29 blvd. F.D. Roosevelt; ☎ *22.19.75, FAX 22.67.11.* Facing the place de la Constitution, overlooking the Petrusse Valley, the Grand Hotel Cravat sits at the very core of the city's sightseeing, shopping, and business. A fourth-generation family hotel of a superior standard, it offers a traditional European atmosphere and personal Luxembourg service to its international clientele. The renovated rooms on the front facing the Petrusse Valley have the finest hotel room views in the city. The traditional but welcoming marble-floored lobby has a bar that is a popular community convening place, as is the **Taverne**, which serves local informal fare. The 60 guest rooms (most recently renovated) on 6 floors have bath with bidet, hair dryers, makeup mirrors, good lighting, turn-down services, French-slatted shades for complete darkness, TV, and telephone. Continental breakfast, served in the **Cravat** formal restaurant, is included. Although the Cravat family is more than able to serve diplomats, it can still employ cozy touches such as changing the carpets in the elevator to tell you what day of the week it is. Parking lot.

EXPENSIVE

Hotel Central Molitor

28 avenue de la Liberté; ☎ *48.99.11, FAX 48.33.82.* This 1913 3rd-generation refurbished family-run hotel, located midway between the station and place de la Constitution, has a traditional atmosphere in its public rooms, which include a respected restaurant and bar. Behind the stately old facade, the 36 rooms of the 4-story hotel all have modern furniture, private bath, telephone, TV, light and door-lock control panel at bedside, wall safe, and sound-proofed doors and windows, and many have minifridges. Underground parking nearby; multiple bus lines just outside hotel.

MODERATE

Hotel Français

14 place d'Armes; ☎ *47.45.34, FAX 46.42.74.* Situated right in the heart of Luxembourg, on the lively place d'Armes, this 20-room (6 suites), 5-story hotel has attractive hallways decorated with art works and sitting areas. All the modern rooms have TV, telephone, private bath; twins are larger than doubles. Front rooms face the square, where the hotel has a popular terrace cafe and brasserie. Major credit cards; breakfast included; elevator; car parks nearby; guests allowed to drive to hotel (in pedestrian area) to unload luggage.

INEXPENSIVE

Auberge Du Coin

2 blvd. de la Petrusse; ☎ *40.21.01, FAX 40.36.66.* This recently renovated, turn-of-the-century home is located in a quiet residential area near the Petrusse Valley, three blocks from ave. de la Liberté. All 25 rooms have lightwood furniture, private bath, TV and telephone. There's a pleasant lobby and an elegant restaurant and a brasserie where breakfast, included, is served.

WHERE TO EAT

The fact that Luxembourg cuisine can be described as substantial and nourishing doesn't mean it's not refined. French influence is featured at many restaurants, although, with a large number of resident nonnationals, many foreign cuisines are represented, Italian and Chinese being particularly popular. Though Eurocrats on expense accounts cause the best restaurants to be pricey, Luxembourgers' own love of good food encourages value for money in all price ranges. Menu prices generally include both VAT and service charges, though it's still customary locally to tip (about 10%) if service is good. Because it is a diplomatic and international business center, Luxembourg City tends toward the more formal in dress, especially outside the summer tourist season; at the best restaurants, men will be most comfortable in suits, women in appropriate dresses. Menus, always posted, in the larger restaurants generally give an English translation of the French. Except for the most casual places, it's a good idea to inquire about reservations, essential at the top spots.

Considered one of the finest restaurants in the city is **Clairefontaine** *(9 place de Clairefountaine; closed Sat. lunch, Sun., holidays, and three weeks from mid-July;* ☎ *46.22.11, FAX 47.08.21; expensive),* located on the expansive square surrounded by elegant old buildings that now house government departments; its French cuisine was described by one Luxembourger as simply *"extraordinary."* **Saint-Michel** *(32 rue de l'Eau; closed Sat., Sun.;* ☎ *22.32.15, FAX 46.25.93; expensive/very expensive),* also serving classic French cuisine, has an elegant setting and service in Luxembourg's oldest and quaintest quarter. For seasonal and French gourmet fare at a more reasonable price, Luxembourgers have taken themselves to **Speltz** *(8 rue Chimay; closed Sat., Sun.;* ☎ *47.49.50; moderate/expensive)* since it opened in 1989 in a cozy, candlelit 17th-century house.

On at least one night you'll want to dine on the **Place d'Armes** to savor its special local atmosphere. It will be evident that the many Luxembourgers there, who love nothing more than getting together with friends over food and drinks, are among those most enjoying the music coming from the bandstand, the evening air and atmosphere. Cafes rim the square; all have menus posted, so take your pick.

On many local lists the best places for a bottomless bowl of steamed mussels (*moules*) is **Ems** *(30 place de la Gare; daily 11 a.m.–1 a.m.;* ☎ *48.77.99; inexpensive).* Across from the station, it's a friendly brasserie that often gets full, in which case you could find yourself in a great conversation with Luxembourgers sharing your booth. The menu includes a number of regional dishes and local beer and wine. For a complete change of scene and cuisine, but not price, if you've a taste for Italian, a good bet is **Bacchus** *(32 rue du Marché-aux-Herbes; noon–2:30 p.m., 6 p.m.–midnight, closed Mon;* ☎ *47.13.97; inexpensive/moderate).* There's an upmarket atmosphere: peach-colored rattan furniture, lovely Villeroy & Boch pink-marbled ware, and international music piped in for the largely local crowd. The pasta is exceptional (served in starter or main course portions), and there's pizza and calzone.

Fashionable atmospheres are becoming common in the lower town suburb of **Grund**, a delightful excursion via the elevator from place du St. Espirit from the upper town. **Scott's Restaurant** *(4 Bisserweg; noon–2 p.m., 7 p.m.–10:15 p.m., closed Mon.;* ☎ *47.53.52; inexpensive/moderate; reservations taken, ask for table with view of upper city)* was the first eatery to open in the Grund, in 1986, in a restored 1790 building by the Alzette river. Particularly popular with the English, Irish, and Americans living in Luxembourg, the well-presented meals range from fish and meat to salads; decor is fashionable yet fanciful. The pub downstairs is open daily from noon to 1 a.m., serving bar snacks and 25 kinds of beer, inside and on the riverside terrace. Across the way is **Cafe Am/haffchen** *(9 Bisserweg; 5 p.m.–1 a.m. daily, closed Mon.; inexpensive)*, with delightful outdoor garden seating amid lime trees, or indoors in a living room/library setting that's cozy contemporary (the works of Luxembourg artists hang on the walls) and can be crowded. Drinks, sandwiches, and tempting toasties.

The pastries of Luxembourg are renowned. Two shops traditionally compete as the source of the city's best pastries: **Namur** *(rue des Capucins, more than 125 years in business)* and **Oberweis** *(Grand Rue, over 25 years old).* Better try them both. The popularity of cake and coffee is a holdover tradition from the Austrian era here. Luxembourgers' love for coffee is shown by the fact that there is no word in Letzebuergesch for breakfast: the word "coffee" stands in for it. For superior picnic supplies, plus pastries, pay a visit to **Kaempf-Kohler** on *rue du Cure.*

ENTERTAINMENT AND EVENTS

Luxembourg's **Schueberfouer** (late August through early September), a large itinerant fair held on the vast Glacis Square near Rond-Point Robert Schuman, is a direct continuation of the annual trade fair founded in 1340 by **John the Blind**. Luxembourg's **National Day** is June 23, but the festivities begin the night before with fireworks and a torchlight parade through town to the Ducal Palace. In December, the place d'Armes hosts the **Christmas Market**, with its decorated stalls and large central Christmas tree, and food stands selling warm mulled wine. On Easter Monday, Luxembourgers gather on Marché-aux-Poissons for a traditional celebration of **Emais'chen**, often attended by the Grand-Ducal Family, that includes the buying of small whistling porcelain birds, sold only on that day. This Catholic country's main religious ceremony is the **Octave** or Pilgrimage of Our Lady of Luxembourg, the city's patron saint, with processions through the streets, decorated with altars of flowers, between the 3rd and 5th Sundays after Easter. Luxembourgers love music and stage a full and varied program of guest performances in symphony, opera, and ballet by Europe's finest companies at the modernistic **Municipal Theater** (near Rond-Point Robert Schuman); the prime season is fall through spring. Annually in spring, Luxembourg hosts **Printemps Musical**, a festival of international artists catering to all musical tastes. Inquire at the tourist office about possible concerts in the National Library.

IN THE AREA

Luxembourg American Cemetery and Memorial   ★ ★

in suburb of Hamm, 3 mi./5 km. west of Luxembourg City, signposted. At the end of the World War II, 83 temporary U.S. military cemeteries existed in North Africa, the Middle East, Italy, Great Britain, and Western Europe, and a decision was taken after study to consolidate them into 13 permanent U.S. cemeteries in Europe, of which the Luxembourg American Cemetery is one. The people of Luxembourg, in gratitude for the liberation by the *First U.S. Army*, particularly the *Fifth Armored Division*, of their country in September 1944 and again in the Battle of the Bulge in February 1945 by the *U.S. Third Army* commanded by *General George S. Patton Jr.*, purchased this 50 acre/20 hectare site for perpetual use by the American government, the agreement being ratified in 1951.

Most of those buried in the cemetery at Hamm died in the Battle of the Bulge, which opened on December 16, 1944 with a lightning counterattack under **Field Marchal von Rundstedt**, which swept across the northern half of Luxembourg and into Belgium. Northern Luxembourg suffered twice in the Battle of the Bulge, first during the advancing attack by the Nazis, and again during their retreat, forced foot by foot back across the **Siegfried Line** in Germany by the Allies, mostly Americans of the U.S. Third Army. During the heavy fighting in the winter of 1945, the American Burial Service recovered the bodies of victims, burying them in a provisional cemetery at Hamm, which was opened on December 29, 1944. At the end of the war there were 8,411 graves. The cemetery was closed from March 1948 to December 1949, during which time the remains of the dead were either returned to the U.S. or permanently interred in Luxembourg, according to the wishes of the next of kin. When the cemetery opened on December 16, 1949, on the 5th anniversary of the beginning of the battle, 5,076 service people lay buried by name beneath white stone Roman crosses or Stars of David, buried without distinction to rank, race, or religion, an exception being made for the 22 pairs of brothers who are buried side by side. The headstones of the 101 graves of unknown soldiers or airmen read "Here lies in honored glory a comrade in arms known but to God." The grave of General Patton, who wished to be buried with his men, is set slightly aside because of the great numbers of people who visit his grave.

Each of America's war cemeteries in Europe was designed individually by an American architect or firm to complement the specific setting, though all have the common elements of a nondenominational chapel, a permanent inscription of the names of those missing in action, and display of the military campaign in the region where the memorial is located. At Luxembourg, the chapel at the woods-encircled cemetery has inscribed above the Blue Belge (Belgian) marble altar the words: "I give unto them eternal life and they shall never perish." The West Pylon on the cemetery terrace that overlooks the field of markers bears a map that shows the military operations in northwest Europe, from the landing in Normandy until the end of the war; the East Pylon has a map illustrating movements of the Battle of the Bulge.

TOUR OF THE GRAND DUCHY

Luxembourg can claim, with justification, that its historic capital city is also its most picturesque town. This means that visitors whose only time in the Grand Duchy will be spent in Luxembourg City can rest assured that they're seeing sights that are the country's highlights. If you can linger longer, however, you'll be well rewarded for further exploration in the Grand Duchy. As in Luxembourg City, the picturesque and the spectacular combine in the countryside. Though small in scale, the Grand Duchy offers sights and scenery that are remarkable for their variety.

GUIDELINES FOR THE TOUR OF THE GRAND DUCHY

SIGHTS

Specific attractions include **Celtic earth forts** at Aleburg near Larochette; **Roman mosaics** and a **Battle of the Bulge** museum in Diekirch; Luxembourg-born photographer Edward Steichen's just-restored **The Family of Man** exhibit in Clervaux Castle, which also houses a collection of **models of the finest castles** in the Grand Duchy; the attractive historic Abbey town of **Echternach**; and **Vianden Castle**, Luxembourg's finest and best restored feudal fortification (the ancestral home of the House of Orange-Nassau, a heritage shared by the Dutch Royal Family and the Grand-Ducal family). Even without these, the Grand Duchy is memorable for its splendid scenery, which varies from **lush vineyards** that run down sunny slopes to the Moselle, to fantastic **rock formations** in "Little Switzerland," to river-carved valleys and **high plateaus** with far-reaching vistas of fertile farming fields.

GETTING AROUND

Car is by far the best way to get the full impact of the Grand Duchy's appeal. Second best is to take one of the several sightseeing **day motorcoach tours** offered by **Voyages H. Sales** *(26 rue du Cure; April 1 to Sept. 30, every Sat., Sun., or Wed., depending upon the itinerary; departures from Luxembourg City, station and place de la Constitution; information and reservations ☎ 50.10.50).* Among the places visited in different tours are Vianden, Echternach, Clervaux, Little Switzerland, Larochette, and the Moselle Valley, each tour giving a fairly good cross section of Duchy scenery. Luxembourg's **train/bus transportation network** covers the country, but with too time-consuming connections for most visitors. Those who want to give it a try should purchase a bargain one-day *Network Ticket* (FLux

140, valid until 8 a.m. the following day), good for all trains and buses in the Grand Duchy and on municipal buses in Luxembourg City; 50% reduction for those over 65. **Bicycles**, if you can take the hilly terrain, can be rented in Luxembourg City, Diekirch, and Vianden (details at local tourist offices).

SHOPPING

For serious shopping, even Luxembourgers go to the capital, the only city in the Grand Duchy. For basic items and souvenirs, the towns with the largest selection of shops are Diekirch, Wiltz, and Echternach.

ENTERTAINMENT AND EVENTS

The summer season is filled with special concerts and activities, staged for and enjoyed both by tourists and Luxembourgers during July and August. Among the annual events is **Echternach's Dancing Procession** (Whitsun Tuesday at 9 a.m.), and in June, Echternach hosts the **International Music Festival**. **Remembrance Day** (1st weekend in July) is held annually in Ettelbruck in honor of U.S. Army General **George S. Patton**, commander in Luxembourg during the Battle of the Bulge. **Grevenmacher** on the Moselle River holds the largest **Wine and Grape Festival** with procession (2nd weekend each September) of the several celebrations of the gathering of the grapes from the vineyards.

WHERE TO STAY

While hotel choices are limited in number in the Grand Duchy (a greater selection exists in the tourism centers of Vianden and Echternach), very pleasant properties are scattered throughout the countryside. All are spotless, run with pleasant personal attention, almost invariably have restaurants, and offer value-for-FLux. In July and August (the high summer tourist season in the countryside), although many Europeans come on camping holidays, reservations at hotels should be made as far ahead as possible. In June and September you should be able to "drop in" and find rooms available, but later than that you may begin to run into hotels in the tourist areas that have closed for the season. Local tourist offices can provide help with accommodations, and are the best source if you are seeking bed-and-breakfast or pension-style accommodations.

WHERE TO EAT

As has been pointed out before, country hotels, whether rural or in towns, are always a solid choice for a meal.

TRAVEL TIPS—THE FAMILY OF MAN EXHIBITION
(TO REOPEN IN SUMMER 1994)

For the first time since its original, attendance-breaking showing at New York's **Museum of Modern Art** in 1955, the complete 503-image photographic exhibition, **The Family Of Man**, conceived by Luxembourg-born photographer **Edward Steichen**, will be on permanent public view, beginning in the summer of 1994, in renovated space at the Grand Duchy's castle at Clervaux. In 1966 Steichen himself arranged for a near-complete version of images from the exhibition to be donated to the Luxembourg government, but restrictions of space had severely hampered its display since. Now, with exhibition space expanded to accommodate all the restored large, mounted images, Clervaux finally can do itself proud by this outstanding collection.

Remember, when driving on the remarkably traffic-free roads in the Grand Duchy, you must keep in mind the *possibility* of vehicles coming at a good clip around every corner—not always easy to do when, with the possible exception of July and August, you'll often have the roads largely to yourself for miles on end.

THE ROUTE

Because the country's so small, it's possible to take a spontaneous sort of trip in Luxembourg, if that's the type of travel you prefer—keeping in mind the importance of finding a bed for the night in the busy tourist months of July and August. Below is a description of some of the most worthwhile places and sites to consider seeing in the course of your Grand Duchy tour. The route begins with **Clervaux** in the north, then drops southeast to **Vianden**. If you intend to see but one country town in the Grand Duchy, this should be the one. South of Vianden is **Diekirch**, to the southeast of which are **Mullerthal/Little Switzerland** and **Echternach**. South from there the road follows along the **Moselle River**, which forms Luxembourg's border with Germany, past vineyards from which it's a short dash back to Luxembourg City.

ON THE ROAD
★CLERVAUX

Tourist office • *Castle, April 1–June 30, Mon.–Sat. 2–5 p.m.; July–Sept., Mon.–Sat. 10 a.m.–noon & 2–6 p.m; also on Sun. in July & Aug., in Oct.10 a.m.–noon, and 1:30–5:30 p.m.; ☎ 9.20.72; pop. 1,000.*

The first sight as you approach Clervaux is of the neo-Romanesque (1910) **Benedictine Abbey of St. Maurice**, whose extensive red roof rises in pleasing contrast above the green forest that surrounds it. But once you've wound your way over curving Ardennes roads into the steep town, it's ★ **Clervaux Castle**, rising on a rocky spur, that takes your attention. Its origins go back to the 12th century, but since that time the stolid feudal fortress has undergone numerous additions and alterations, particularly while serving as the seat of the powerful counts who were overlords of extended territories. In 1762, then-owner **Count Adrian-John-Baptist of Lannoy** had the splendid **Loreto Chapel** built in the park of the castle; the castle and chapel were spared destruction by the French Revolutionary Army in the 1790s because the people of Clervaux declared them to be the property of a "Citizen Lannoy." Following inheritance quarrels in the 19th century, the legal victor in 1887 had the administrative buildings in the first courtyard demolished, using the stones to build a luxurious villa (today the **Hotel Parc**, see "Where To Stay") in the adjacent park. Clervaux experienced devastating destruction during the *Battle of the Bulge*, including the castle which, defended by the soldiers of the 110th Regiment of the 28th Infantry Division, fell in flames when the town was taken on December 17, 1944 by the 2nd German Armored Division. Clervaux finally was retaken by the 26th U.S. Infantry on January 26, 1945. Clervaux without its castle was unthinkable, so shortly after the Second World War ended, restoration was begun. Today, the castle is the heart not only of the town's history, but of its present life. The town hall (*Mairie*) and the tourist office are located within its walls. The castle also houses several exhibits.

From the summer of 1994, **Clervaux Castle** (*open daily, in June, 1–5 p.m.; July–Sept. 15, 10 a.m.–5 p.m.; rest of year Sun. & holidays. 1–5 p.m.; closed Jan.& Feb.*) will display the complete set of photographic images (503, assembled from 68 countries) from the original attendance-breaking ★ ★ ★ **The Family of Man** show conceived by Luxembourg-born **Edward Steichen** (1879–1973) when he was director of photography of New York's *Museum of Modern Art* (MOMA). Working on the exhibit for which his vision was to show a time span that included birth, the world at work, family life, friendship, leisure, disease, war, and death, Steichen, at the age of 73, scanned some 2 million photographs and then a short list of 10,000, eventually narrowing the number to 503. It ranged from the works of the world's most famous photographers (though Steichen modestly selected only two of his own images) to simple family snapshots. The Family of Man opened at MOMA in New York in 1955, eventually travelled to 69 countries, and was viewed by over 9 million people. Having kept close ties with Luxembourg all his life, even though he had left the country as a two-year-old, in 1966 Steichen arranged for the most complete version of The Family of Man, minus only a dozen images from the original, to be donated to the Luxembourg government. Steichen himself came to Luxembourg in 1966 to help settle the question of where such a large show could be permanently displayed, since many of the pictures are mounted on large boards. The castle at Clervaux was settled upon. But for many years since, only a limited number of the pictures was displayed; the others, in storage, became moldy and yellow. Fortunately, provisions were made in time for them all to be fully restored and displayed. The problem of space, which is why some of the images were in storage in the first place, has been addressed by the renovation of space within Clervaux Castle.

Elsewhere in Clervaux Castle is an extremely interesting permanent display of *models* of the Grand Duchy's most important ★**castles** (notes on the history of each castle in English). Since so many of the castles are now in ruins, the models furnish us with a better idea of the originals and how the fortifications were placed on each site. The largest of the more than a dozen models is for Vianden Castle, and, in this one case, is a model of the whole town.

Across the courtyard, still in Clervaux Castle, is a museum of memorabilia from the **Battle of the Bulge**.

On Maria Theresa Square in the pedestrianized center of Clervaux stands the **Monument to the GI 1944–45**, a statue of a typical soldier to honor the sacrifice of the common GI for the liberation of Luxembourg. Don't miss the charming other memorial, "*To our Liberators*," a modern frieze mounted on the wall of the bank building facing the standing monument that depicts a heartwarming scene of citizens greeting the GI.

WHERE TO STAY AND EAT IN CLERVAUX

Hotel du Parc   ★★★
  2 rue du Parc; ☎ *9.10.68; inexpensive.* This 110-year-old elegant mansion, surrounded by century-old trees, sits on a rise across from and at eye level with Clervaux Castle, some of whose stones went into its construction. The 8 attractive guest rooms all have private bath, telephone, and radio. The public rooms have an old-world charm, with plaster work, wood paneling, and monumental fireplaces (with fires laid when the weather warrants) in the dining room and lounge. The kitchen is well regarded, and the place is particularly popular on weekends. Parking; sauna and solarium in cellar.

★★★VIANDEN

Tourist office • *Victor Hugo House, Grand Rue; open daily, in March and Oct., 10 a.m.–5 p.m.; April–Sept., 10 a.m.–6 p.m.; Nov.–Feb,. 10 a.m.–4 p.m.;* ☎ *8.42.57, FAX 84.90.81; inquire about special summer concerts, events; pop. 1,600.*

For many, Vianden is the favorite destination in the Grand Duchy. A medieval town, spreading down a single steep stone street from its craggy heights with fine views to the river **Our** at the bottom, Vianden is defined mostly by its **castle**, which dominates the entire area. A **chair lift** *(rue du Sanatorium; daily Easter–Sept., 11 a.m.–6 p.m., both earlier and later hours in July and Aug.;*☎ *8.43.23)* provides a silent sweep up and over trees to a height (1,444 feet/440 meters) from which one actually looks *down* at Vianden Castle. At the top there's a terrace cafe, *of course*, from which to enjoy the surpassing view of the river, town, and grandeur of the forests and grassy plateaus.

Vianden Castle   ★ ★ ★

daily in Apri, 10 a.m.–5 p.m.; May 1–Aug. 31, 9 a.m.–7 p.m.; in Sept., 9 a.m.–6 p.m.; in Oct., 10 a.m.–4:30 p.m.; Nov,. Mon.–Fri. 11 a.m.–4 p.m., Sat. & Sun. 10 a.m.–4:30 p.m.; Dec. 1–Mar. 31; Sat., Sun., holidays only 10 a.m.–noon, 1–4 p.m.; English brochure and floor plan for self-guided tour; majestically illuminated at night April 1–Sept. 30. The Grand Duchy's most historic, best restored, and most frequently photographed castle, Vianden is the ancestral home of *Orange-Nassau, Holland's Royal House*, which has ties to Luxembourg's Grand Ducal family through another Nassau branch. One of the largest feudal fortresses in the area, and certainly the one in the best shape today, the spectacularly situated castle was begun in the 12th century and enlarged in the 13th century, Vianden's peak of power, so that its ★ ★ **Count's Hall** could accommodate 500 knights-at-arms. By late in the 13th century, the counts of the *House of Vianden* controlled lands that included 211 villages, hamlets, and mills, and produced **Count Henry II**, who became bishop of Utrecht. That was Vianden's apex. Its nadir came after then-owner King Willem I of Holland/Grand Duke of Luxembourg put the castle up for public auction in 1820. The buyer sold the castle's roof and other parts as building materials, and in 1827 once-proud Vianden was declared a ruin. Ownership eventually evolved back to the Nassaus and the Grand Ducal family, and, in 1978, Grand Duke Jean ceded the castle, then but a shell of its former self, to the state. Since then, Vianden Castle has been painstakingly restored, the process only recently completed. You'll have a great sense of discovery exploring the castle. The "upper" chapel, 13th century, is a jewel, elegant and light, modelled after Charlemagne's palace chapels at Aachen and Nijmegan. It was used by the lords and ladies of Vianden's court, while the "lower" chapel was for the lower classes and servants, who could hear but not see the services in which the upper classes participated. The main section of the castle, built about 1210, has two huge halls. The Count's Hall, lined with wardrobes and wall cabinets, and hung with a 16th-century Flemish tapestry *The Trojan War* and 17th-century tapestries from Amiens and Brussels, is now sometimes the site of **concerts**. The *Banqueting Hall*, where recorded classical music plays faintly, is also finely furnished and has portraits, a 17th-century Aubusson tapestry *The Wedding at Cana*, and an impressive fireplace. Elsewhere in the castle is an Orange-Nassau genealogy painted on the wall. The counts of Vianden and counts of Nassau first merged in the 14th century, and **René de Chalon**, who died in 1544, was the first count of the Orange-Nassau dynasty. In the same way the castle is a magnificent ★ ★ ★ sight from terraces in the town, so are the ★ ★ ★ views of the town magnificent from the castle terraces.

Other attractions in Vianden include the **Victor Hugo House**, which shares quarters and opening hours with the ground floor tourist office *(exhibit material in French only)*. French author Victor Hugo lived here in 1871, having been to Vianden before (in 1862, 1863, and 1865). During those visits he produced a series of drawings of the Grand Duchy's castles, and later he published a book of sketches entitled *Les Ardennes*. The house, in which he stayed only from June 6–August 22, 1871, contains photocopies of some of Hugo's drawings, letters, photographs, and other memorabilia. Across the street from the house is a ★ bust of Hugo by **Rodin**, mounted on the corner of the bridge over the Our. The cafe outside the simple **Hotel Victor Hugo** provides great views to accompany a drink.

The Museum of Rustic Arts

98 Grand rue; Easter–Sept., daily 10 a.m.– noon, and 2–6 p.m., closed Mon. except in July, Aug. and holidays; ☎ *8.45.91; no English documentation.* The museum is a former bourgmestre's house with several ground floor rooms of fine furnishings. Almost across the street from the museum is the ancient twin-naved **Trinitarian church**, built in the Gothic style in 1248 and one of the oldest religious buildings in Luxembourg. The restored cloister behind it holds the tombstones of the Counts of Vianden.

WHERE TO STAY AND EAT IN VIANDEN

Hotel Heintz

55 Grand Rue; ☎ *8.41.55, 8.45.59; inexpensive; closed mid-Nov. until Easter.* The Heintz is famous for its hospitable air and congenial family atmosphere that instill a feeling of being well cared for. Guests to Luxembourg from afar invariably find their way here: **Beatrice Patton**, widow of General George; **Margaret Truman**; and **Perla Mesta**, former U.S. Ambassador to Luxembourg, the "Hostess with the Mostest." But the Heintz isn't grand, it's simply gracious. The 30 guest rooms (8 with balconies and view of hills behind hotel) have basic traditional furnishings, all with private bathroom, telephone. The hallways and public rooms in the centuries-old building are appropriately and delightfully decorated in antiques, oil paintings, and orientals, with wonderful wooden chests and clocks. The restaurant is renowned, every detail overseen by owner **Magda Hansen** herself, the fourth generation to provide personalized attention to guests of the homey Heintz. Elevator; parking; private gardens.

DIEKIRCH

Tourist office • *Esplanade; Mon.–Fri. 9 a.m.–noon, 2–5 p.m., from July 1–Aug. 15 until 6 p.m. and also on Sat. & Sun. 10 a.m.–noon, & 2–4 p.m.;* ☎ *80.30.23, FAX 80.27.86; pop. 5,600.*

Diekirch Historical/Battle of the Bulge Museum

10 Bamertal; daily Easter–Oct., 10 a.m.–noon, 2–6 p.m.; ☎ *80.89.08; guided tours on request; multilingual brochure, exhibit notes.* In large part, the museum commemorates aspects of the Battle of the Bulge around Diekirch in the winter of 1944-45 (although the scope of the museum may be enlarged). The details offered here about what "*absorption*" into the Third Reich, as opposed to "merely" being occupied, meant to the lives of Luxembourgers, make us appreciate their uniquely difficult experience during World War II. Particularly poignant are the exhibits relating to the compulsory conscription of young Luxembourg men into the *Wehrmacht* from August 1942. This act was considered one of the worst of the Nazis war crimes, because it sent Luxembourgers to the German Front (mostly to Russia) to wage armed war against the Allied Forces they supported, those Allies not realizing they were firing on Luxembourgers forced to wear Nazi uniforms. From 1941, all Luxembourg young men and women were obliged to provide the Nazis with labor in war industry factories and to live apart in work camps.

The Diekirch Museum is not political. Its purpose is to show what happened. The exhibits explain facts such as that by the time of the *Battle of the Bulge*, most of the German soldiers who were doing the fighting were not Nazi ideologists but merely 16- or 17-year-olds simply following Hitler's orders. German and American soldiers who once fought each other have since met here. The museum, which opened in 1984, was conceived by a young Luxembourg man who had not been not born when the war ended. **Roland Gaul**, who today is the public relations staff person for the U.S. Embassy in Luxembourg City, explains he "just grew up with the **Battle of the Bulge**" and, as he and his friends out "playing cowboys and Indians" in the woods would find German helmets or pistols, his interest in a museum developed. The effort to open the museum and run it came from volunteer efforts. Among the highly interesting exhibits is a model of the Russian prison camp at **Tambow** that claimed so many Luxembourgers. There are dioramas of the "*white jungle warfare*" in the snow for which Luxembourg women stitched white clothing together to form camouflage for the U.S. soldiers, to examples of the "propaganda pamphlets" used as psychological warfare from both sides. One such piece, written by the Germans in correct American slang that was meant to affect American morale by making them homesick at Christmas, was dropped over the lines in the Ardennes.

Municipal Museum ★

place Guillaume; Easter–Oct., 10 a.m.–12, 2–6 p.m., closed Tues. Highlights of the local relics from Roman culture on display are two large 4th-century mosaics, which give an idea of the decorative detail to be found in the villas of the occupiers of the region in that era. One well-preserved mosaic with a central figure of a lion surrounded by bright geometrical figures was found in 1926 when excavation works were proceeding on Diekirch's Esplanade. The other was found in 1950 when a town street was being widened. In it, a stylized flower motif surrounds an intriguing ★ head of a Medusa, which shows a different face when viewed from opposite ends of the mosaic floor.

★★ LITTLE SWITZERLAND

Set in the valley of the **Ernz Noire** river, this area of fantastically shaped sandstone rocks and outcrops set in wooded glens and ravines, sometimes is in sight of the road, though often it offers its sights only to those who "walk in" a bit further. The proximity of impressive viewing can be gauged by the number of cars at the several parking sites provided along the road that leads through **Mullerthal** *(pop. 45, altitude 820 ft./250 meters)*. That village, more or less at its center, has given its name to the region, which is full of serious hikers and recreational ramblers in the summer and early fall. The region got its unlikely name "Little Switzerland" (*not* used by Luxembourgers) from the Dutch (who, presumably, were responding overenthusiastically to the area's altitude; they call the only slightly higher spots in Holland's SE Limburg Province the "Dutch Alps"). Under the Dutch King/Grand Duke **Willem II**, Holland first became connected to Luxembourg by **rail**. The exclamations over the scenery around Mullerthal by Dutch soldiers who had served in Luxembourg brought many Dutch here on holiday, particularly once the train could bring them to nearby Diekirch in comfort. Their name for Mullerthal stuck, as did their interest in the area, the Dutch still being the main holiday makers here. The authentic character of the restored village of **Christnach** and the popular tourist center of **Consdorf** are two of the entry points into the Mullerthal. The village of **Waldbillig** (pop. 275), set on a green plateau surrounded by deep forest, was the birthplace in 1827 of **Michel Rodange**, Luxembourg's most famous poet.

★ ECHTERNACH

Tourist office • *Porte St. Willibrord at Basilica; Mon.–Fri., 9 a.m.– noon, 2–5 p.m., in July and Aug., also on Sat. & Sun.;* ☎ *7.22.30; pop. 4,000.*

Echternach, known as having the most attractive main square in Luxembourg, is also one of Europe's earliest centers of Christianity. **Willibrord**, an Anglo-Saxon missionary from Northumberland, founded a Benedictine Abbey here in 698, which makes Echternach the oldest settlement in the country. Some Roman remains and medieval ramparts add to its historic interest and atmosphere. Echternach's religious, spiritual, and artistic achievements reached their height with the **Echternach School of Book Illumination** in the 10th and 11th centuries. The Kells style (from the *Book of Kells* in Ireland) influenced the monks at Echternach, and it is thought possible that some of the Kells artist-monks may even have come to St. Willibrord's Abbey, since it became one of the best equipped ateliers in Europe for illuminating manuscripts. (There is a museum of illuminations in the abbey.) Although the **Basilica of St. Willibrord**, built around 800, over Willibrord's original abbey, today dates only from after the Second World War, the crypt, c. 800, remains intact. (The *Ardennes offensive* did more damage than centuries of pillaging.) It houses the tomb of St. Willibrord. Echternach's lovely ★ ★ **main square** lacks symmetry, but that is part of its charm. A noticeable part of the irregularity of shape is caused by the ★ ★ **Denzelt** (the old courtrooms), one reason the Gothic building attracts so much attention. Many of the facades around the square have been restored, which makes it a more pleasant pastime than ever to sit at one of its cafes. The town is known for its unique **Dancing Procession** *(Whitsun Tuesday)*, which takes place on the square, attracting thousands of pilgrims.

Dating from the 13th century, the procession may commemorate a perceived healing of epilepsy by St. Willibrord.

WHERE TO STAY AND EAT IN ECHTERNACH

Hotel Bel-Air   ★★★★

1 Route de Berdorf; ☎ *72.93.83, FAX 72.86.94; moderate.* Located less than a mile/1 km. from the center of Echternach, this modern hotel sits in its own park, offering views from its terraces and glass-walled dining rooms of the Sure Valley. The 33 guest rooms in this well-serviced hotel all have private baths, TV, telephones. Tennis; gourmet restaurant; wooded walks begin just steps from the door.

★MOSELLE VALLEY

Leaving Echternach on a scenic route roughly south, in the direction of Trier, you arrive at the Moselle River, with its attractive tree-shaded and path-lined embankments. It's a lovely ride along the river (and *on* the river, too, if you'd like to cruise on the *Princess Marie-Astrid* boat). The colors of the scenery change with the stage of the grapes growing in the vineyards that cover the banks on both the Luxembourg and German sides of the Moselle. As well as being pretty, the vineyards are important business; Luxembourg's Minister of Agriculture also carries the title of Minister of Viniculture.

As you approach **Wormeldange** (from the north), look for signs to **Koeppchen** and follow them up into the vineyards, your destination as you drive through them being the **St. Donat Chapel.** There is a bench from which to survey the ★★**magnificent panorama** that lies before you. Just beyond Wormeldange is ★**Ehnen,** a delightful village of medieval character, with narrow stone streets and the only round church in the Grand Duchy.

BELGIAN
BIBLIOGRAPHY

Europe, a Tapestry of Nations by Flora Lewis, Simon and Schuster, 1987. Series of essays on Europe and European countries by a long-time observer of Europe for *The New York Times.* Includes chapters on *The Low Countries: The Bourgeois Monarchies* and *Belgium: Divided by Language.*

The Sorrow of Belgium by Hugo Claus, originally published in 1983; U.S. English edition by Pantheon. When published (in Dutch), the novel became an overnight best seller in Flanders and Holland, since it covered a subject of bitter debate, that of collaboration with the occupying Nazi enemy during World War II. The book recalls the period 1939-1947.

The Continuing Battle: Memoirs of a European (1936-1966) by Paul-Henri Spaak published by Little, Brown & Co. 1971. Several times Prime Minister of Belgium between 1938 and 1957, and also foreign minister, president of the United Nations General Assembly, and secretary-general of NATO in 1957, Spaak, as a statesman, had a unique perspective on Europe. This volume follows the development of Spaak's two ideals, the Atlantic Alliance and European unity, through the crises and coalitions of the Benelux Plan, the European Coal and Steel Commission, EEC (Common Market), and the Cold War.

A New Guide to the Battlefields of Northern France and the Low Countries by Michael Glover, Michael Joseph Ltd., 1987. In-depth coverage of Belgian battles: *Waterloo* (1815), *Ypres* (1914 to 1917), and the Bastogne/Ardennes campaigns of *The Battle of the Bulge* (1944-45). (See also under appropriate destination in text.)

519

Pedigree, by Georges Simenon, Hamish Hamilton, London, 1962. A novel about a Belgian youth, Roger Mamelin, up to the age of 16. Simenon, while not wishing the book to be called autobiographical, acknowledges it comes "very close to reality." Simenon was born and grew up in Liège, Belgium. (See also under "Liège, What To See and Do", and "Belgian Authors" under "The Muse" in "The Belgium Cultural Legacy" chapter.)

The Life and Times of Hercule Poirot, by Anne Hart, G. P. Putnam's Sons, 1990. The famed detective created by Agatha Christie was Belgian, and many of the "biographical" details about Poirot in this book, reconstructed from the texts of his adventures, shed light on Belgium. (See also "The Muse.")

BELGIAN LEXICON

While you may never need to know Flemish/Dutch or French in order to communicate in Belgium, it may be *nice* to know some basic words.

English	Flemish-Dutch	French
Numbers		
zero	nul	zéro
one	een	un, une
two	twee	deux
three	drie	trois
four	vier	quatre
five	vijf	cinq
six	zes	six
seven	zeven	sept
eight	acht	huit
nine	negen	neuf
ten	tien	dix
eleven	elf	onze
twelve	twaalf	douze
thirteen	dertien	treize
fourteen	veertien	quatorze
fifteen	vijftien	quinze
sixteen	zestien	seize
seventeen	zeventien	dix-sept
eighteen	achttien	dix-huit
nineteen	negentien	dix-neuf
twenty	twintig	vingt
twenty-one	een en twintig	vingt et un
fifty	vijftig	cinquante
one hundred	honderd	cent
two hundred	tweehonderd	deux cent
one thousand	duizend	mille
1st	eerste	premier (ière)
2nd	tweede	deuxième
3rd	derde	troisième

English	Flemish-Dutch	French
Days	**Dagen**	**Jours**
Monday	Maandag	Lundi
Tuesday	Dinsdag	Mardi
Wednesday	Woensdag	Mercredi
Thursday	Donderdag	Jeudi
Friday	Vrijdag	Vendredi
Saturday	Zaterdag	Samedi
Sunday	Zondag	Dimanche
	General	
Please	Alstublieft	S'il vous plaît
Thank you, very much	Dank U, zeer	Merci, beaucoup
Good morning	Dag	Bonjour
Good evening	Gouden avond	Bonsoir
Good night	Goede nacht	Bonne nuit
Good-bye	Tot ziens	Au revoir
Mr./sir	Mijnheer	Monsieur
Mrs./Ms.	Mevrouw	Madame
Gentlemen	Heren	Messieurs
Ladies	Dames	Mesdames
W.C.	De toilet	La toilette
Excuse me	Pardon	Excusez-moi
Yes, no	Ja, neen	Oui, non
How much?	Hoeveel?	Combien?
Price	Prijs	Prix
Expensive, cheap	Duur, goedkoop	Cher, bon marché
Old, new	Oud, nieuw	Vieux, nouveau
Where is?	Waar is?	Où est?
To the left	Links	À gauche
To the right	Rechts	À droite
Entrance, exit	Ingang, uitgang	Entrée, sortie
Doctor	Dokter	Médecin
Hospital	Ziekenhuis	Hôpital
Post office	Postkantoor	Bureau de poste
Stamp	Postzegel	Timbre
Airmail	Luchtpost	Par avion
Police station	Politiebureau	Poste de police
No smoking	Verboden te roken	Défense de fumer

English	Flemish-Dutch	French
Admission free	Vrije toegang	Entrée libre
Open, closed	Geopen, gesloten	Ouvert, fermé

Travel Terms

Travel bureau	Reisbureau	Bureau de voyage
The railway station	Het station	La gare
Return ticket	Retour	Billet aller-retour
One-way ticket	Enkele reis	Billet aller
Fare	Prijs van het reiskaartje	Prix du billet
First class	Eerste klas	Première classe
Second class	Tweede klas	Seconde classe
Fast train	Sneltrein	Train rapide
Local train	Stoptrein	Train omnibus
Dining car	Restaurantiewagen	Wagon-restaurant
Weekdays only	Alleen op werkdagen	En semaine seulement
Bus/tram stop	Bushalte	Arrêt l'autobus
Room with bath, shower	Kamer met bad, douche	Chamber avec salle de bain, douche
Gasoline, petrol	Benzine	Essence
Oil	Olie	Huile
Parking place	Parkeerplaats	Stationnement, parking
Key	Sleutel	La clef

Belgian Bill of Fare

table d'hôte	menu	prix-fixe
bill of fare, menu	kaart	carte
wine list	wijnkaart	carte des vins
bill	de rekening	l'addition
Is the tip included?	Service inclusief?	Service compris?
fried	gebakken	frites
smoked	gerookt	fumé
rare	bleu (almost raw)	saignant (safely rare)
medium	half gaar	à point
well-done	goed gaar	bien cuit
soup	soep	soupe
bread, white/brown	brood, witte/bruin	pain, blanc/bis
roll	broodje	petit pain
egg	ei	oeuf
cheese	kaas	fromage
whipped cream	slagroom	crème fouettée

English	Flemish-Dutch	French
Meat/ Fish	**Vlees/ Vis**	**Viande/ Poisson**
pork	varkens	porc
sausage	bloedworst	boudin
roast beef	rosbief	rosbif
chicken	kip	poulet
hare	haas	lièvre
rabbit	konijn	lapin
venison	ree	chevreuil
salmon	zalm	saumon
trout	forel	truite
pike	snoek	brochet
sole	tong	sole
monkfish	lotte	lotte
herring	haring	hareng
eel	paling	anguille
lobster	kreeft	homard
oysters	oesters	huîtres
shrimp	garnalen	crevettes
mussels	mosselen	moules
snails	slakken	escargots
Vegetables/ Fruit	**Groeten/ Vruchten**	**Légumes/ Fruit**
asparagus	asperges	asperges
beans	bonen	fèves
string beans	snijbonen	haricots verts
chicory	witloof	chicons
cauliflower	bloemkool	choux-fleur
Brussels sprouts	Brusselse spruitjes	choux de Bruxelles
cabbage	kool	chou
mushrooms	champignons	champignons
onions	uien	oignons
peas	erwten	petit pois
potatoes	aardapplen	pommes de terre
rice	rijs	riz
salad	sla, salade	salade
apple	appel	pomme
cherries	kersen	cerises

English	Flemish-Dutch	French
lemon	citroen	citron
orange	sinaasappel	orange
pineapple	ananas	ananas
strawberries	aardbeien	fraises
pear	peer	poire
peach	perzik	pêche

Seasonings

sugar	suiker	sucre
salt	zout	sel
pepper	peper	poivre
mustard	mosterd	moutarde
vinegar	azijn	vinaigre
oil	olie	huile
honey	honig	miel

Beverages / Dranken / Boissons

a bottle of	een fles	une bouteille de
a glass of, cup of	een glas, kop	un verre, tasse de
coffee, tea	koffie, thee	café, thé
milk	melk	lait
juice	sap	jus
mineral water	mineraalwater	eau minéral
beer	bier	bière
wine (red, white)	wijn (rode, witte)	vin (rouge, blanc)

HOTEL QUICK-REFERENCE TABLES

New national hotel standards have been instituted in Belgium. The cost of bringing small hotels at the lower end of the hotel scale up to snuff has resulted in a rise in prices at many properties in the inexpensive and moderate categories. Prices given below—for a room for two with private bath, *inclusive* of service and VAT—are in local currencies: Belgian and Luxembourg francs (on a par) in those countries, Dutch guilders for Holland. In cases when hotels post a range of rates for double rooms, the lowest price has been given (note that rooms at that rate may be limited in number). The prices quoted were as accurate as possible at press time, but they may increase during the year-long life of this guide. Always inquire about lower weekend and out-of-season rates when making reservations and, again, when checking in.

BELGIUM		
Hotel	Phone	Price (in francs)
Brussels		

(Telephone Code 02)

Hotel	Phone	Price (in francs)
Amigo	547.47.47	6,750
Arcade Saint-Catherine	513.76.20	3,900
Archimede	231.09.09	5,800
Arlequin	514.16.15	2,950
Atlas	502.60.06	3,500
Chambord	513.41.19	3,600
Conrad Brussels	542.42.42	11,500
Dixseptieme	502.57.44	5,400
Hilton International	504.11.11	10,000
Ibis Brussels Center	514.40.40	4,200
Jolly Hotel du Grand Sablon	512.88.00	11,500
La Madeleine	513.29.73	2,600
Le Dome	218.06.80	7,200
Manos	537.96.82	3,500
Metropole	217.23.00	9,000
New Hotel Siru	217.75.80	3,900
Opera	219.43.43	2,000
Pullman Astoria	217.62.90	7,700

BELGIUM		
Hotel	**Phone**	**Price (in francs)**
Royal Windsor	511.42.15	13,000
SAS Royal	219.28.28	11,000
Sheraton Hotel & Towers	224.31.11	11,600
Sofitel Brussels	514.22.00	6,900
Vendome	218.00.70	3,500
Welcome	219.95.46	2,500

Antwerp
(Telephone Code 03)

Alfa De Keyser	234.01.35	8,000
Alfa Theater	231.17.20	5,800
Antwerp Hilton	204.12.12	9,000
Arcade	231.88.30	3,350
Carlton	231.15.15	6,400
De Rosier	225.01.40	8,500
Firean	237.02.60	4,100
Pension Cammerpoorte	231.28.36	2,000
Rubens	222.48.48	5,000
Villa Mozart	231.30.31	4,500

Bruges
(Telephone Code 050)

Academie	33.22.66	3,500
Adornes	34.13.36	2,550
Biskajer	34.15.06	3,200
Botaniek	34.14.24	2,200
Bourgoensch Hof	33.16.45	2,600
Die Swaene	34.27.98	4,050
Duc de Bourgogne	33.20.38	3,500
Egmond	34.14.45	3,000
Holiday Inn Crowne Plaza	34.58.34	6,000
Orangerie	34.16.49	6,000
Oud Huis Amsterdam	34.18.10	4,500
Pandhotel	34.06.66	3,600
Ter Brughe	34.03.24	3,200
Tuilerieen	34.36.91	7,000

Ghent
(Telephone Code 091)

Erasmus	24.21.95	3,600
Gravensteen	25.11.50	4,800
Ibis	33.00.00	3,600
Novotel Gent Centrum	24.22.30	5,800
St. Jorishof	24.24.24	5,500

BELGIUM		
Hotel	**Phone**	**Price (in francs)**

Belgium Coast

Knokke (Telephone Code 050)

| La Reserve | 61.06.06 | 6,000 |

Ostend (Telephone Code 059)

| Hotel Andromeda | 58.66.11 | 5,500 |

Tournai

(Telephone Code 069)

| Cathédrale Hotel | 21.50.77 | 3,100 |
| Parc | 21.28.93 | 2,600 |

Liège

(Telephone Code 041)

| Cygne d'Argent | 23.70.01 | 2,300 |
| Ramada Hotel Liège | 22.49.10 | 5,200 |

The Meuse Valley

Bouvignes (Telephone Code 082)

| L'Auberge de Bouvigne | 61.16.00 | 2,300 |

Celles (Telephone Code 082)

| Hostellerie Le Val Joli | 66.63.63 | 2,000 |

Lisogne (Telephone Code 082)

| Moulin de Lisogne | 22.63.80 | 3,200 |

Ardennes

Spa (Telephone Code 087)

| L'Auberge | 77.36.66 | 2,300 |
| Manoir-de-Lebioles | 77.04.20 | 7,500 |

Beverce (Telephone Code 080)

| Ferme Libert | 33.02.47 | 2,200 |

Comblain-la-Tour (Telephone Code 041)

| Hostellerie Saint-Roch | 69.13.33 | 3,700 |

Durbuy (Telephone Code 086)

| Le Sanglier des Ardennes | 21.32.62 | 3,800 |

Marché-en-Famenne/Aye (Telephone Code 084)

| Chateau d'Hassonville | 31.10.25 | 4,000 |

Noirefontaine (Telephone Code 061)

| Le Moulin Hideux | 46.70.15 | 5,500 |

Sainte-Cecile-sur-Semois (Telephone Code 061)

| Hostellerie Saint-Cecile | 31.31.67 | 2,500 |

HOLLAND

Hotel	Phone	Price (in guilders)

Randstad Holland

Amsterdam (Telephone Code 020)

Hotel	Phone	Price
Agora	6272200	105
Ambassade	6262333	265
American	6245322	425
Amstel	6226060	700
Amsterdam Wiechmann	6263321	150
Borgmann	6735252	185
Canal House	6225182	195
Doelen Karena	6220722	345
De l'Europe	6234836	495
Golden Tulip Barbizon Palace	5564564	480
Jan Luyken	5730730	290
Owl	6189484	165
Pulitzer	5235235	455
Rho	6207371	125
Seven Bridges	6231329	110
Vondel	6120120	170
Washington	6797453	110

Haarlem (Telephone Code 023)

Hotel	Phone	Price
Carlton Square	319091	260
Golden Tulip Lion D'Or	321750	210

Leiden (Telephone Code 071)

Hotel	Phone	Price
De Doelen	120527	155
Golden Tulip Leiden	221121	250
Mayflower	142641	175

The Hague/Scheveningen (Telephone Code 070)

Hotel	Phone	Price
Aquarius	3543543	115
Bel Park	3505000	110
Corona	3637930	310
Des Indes	3632932	595
ParkHotel	3624371	215
Seinduin	3551971	130
Steigenberger Kurhaus	3520052	480

Voorburg (Telephone Code 070)

Hotel	Phone	Price
Vreudg & Rust	3872081	225

Wassenaar (Telephone Code 01751)

Hotel	Phone	Price
Auberge de Kievet	19232	295

HOLLAND		
Hotel	**Phone**	**Price (in guilders)**

Delft (Telephone Code 015)

De Ark	157999	175
Leeuwenbrug	147741	155
MuseumHotel	140930	205

Rotterdam (Telephone Code 010)

Atlanta	4110420	270
Inntel	4134139	250
Hotel New York	4862066	150
Parkhotel	4363611	270

Northern Holland

Edam (Telephone Code 02993)

De Fortuna	71671	70

Enkhuizen (Telephone Code 02280)

Die Port Van Cleve	12510	135

Leeuwarden (Telephone Code 058)

Oranje	126241	220

Blokzijl (Telephone Code 05272)

Kaatje Bij de Sluis	1833	250

Central Holland

Apeldoorn (Telephone Code 055)

De Keizerskroon	217744	295

Zeeland

Veere (Telephone Code 01181)

De Campveerse Toren	1291	130

North Brabant

Heusden (Telephone Code 04162)

In Den Verdwaalde Koogel	1933	145

Limburg

Maastricht (Telephone Code 043)

Du Chene	213523	110
Derlon	216770	340

Wittem (Telephone Code 04450)

Kasteel Wittem	1208	225

Kerkade (Telephone Code 045)

Kasteel Erenstein	461333	175

LUXEMBOURG		
Hotel	**Phone**	**Price (in FLux)**

(Telephone code for country 352)

Luxembourg City

Auberge du Coin	40.21.01	2,800
Central Molitor	48.99.11	4,200
Français	47.45.34	3,900
Grand Hotel Cravat	22.19.75	5,600

The Grand Duchy

Clervaux

Du Parc	9.10.68	2,100

Vianden

Hotel Heintz	8.41.55	1,900

Echternach

Bel-Air	72.93.83	3,500

INDEX

Victor Hugo House, 514–515

W

Wallonia region, 82, 257–291
 Grand Hornu, 260–261
 Liège, 277–291
 Pays Noir, 258–259
 socio-politics, 257
 Tournai, 263–275
Warner, Sally Slade, 63
Wasmes, 259
Water, 10, 334
Waterloo, 96, 113, 145–149, 169, 231
Weather, 11–15
Wepion, 295
Where to Eat, see restaurants under specific locations
Where to Stay, see accommodations under specific locations
Windmills, 331, 437, 441
Wine, 77, 509
World War I, 66, 71, 155, 158, 252, 258
 Holland, 338
World War II, 47, 65, 98–99, 156, 159, 258, 306, 321–324, 330, 350, 459, 463
 Battle of the Bulge, 515–516
 bomb damage, 158–159, 450
 Holland, 330, 338, 350
 Luxembourg, 481–482, 497–498, 507–508, 515–516
Writers, 69–71

Y

Ypres, 253–256
 Cloth Hall, 254–255
 World War I, 253

Z

Zeeland province, 332, 448–452
 accommodations, 452
 entertainment and events, 451
 guidelines, 450–452
 history, 449–450
 restaurants, 452
 shopping, 451
 sightseeing, 450–451

transportation, 451, 452
Zuiderzee, Holland, 332, 442, 443–445

Introducing the 1994 Fielding Travel Guides— fresh, fascinating and fun!

An incisive new attitude and an exciting new look! All-new design and format. In-depth reviews. Fielding delivers travel information the way frequent travelers demand it—written with sparkle, style and humor. Candid insights, sage advice, insider tips. No fluff, no filler, only fresh information that makes the journey more fun, more fascinating, more Fielding. Start planning your next great adventure today!

Australia 1994	**$16.95**
Belgium 1994	**$16.95**
Bermuda/Bahamas 1994	**$16.95**
Brazil 1994	**$16.95**
Britain 1994	**$16.95**
Budget Europe 1994	**$16.95**
Caribbean 1994	**$16.95**
Europe 1994	**$16.95**
Far East 1994	**$16.95**
France 1994	**$16.95**
The Great Sights of Europe 1994	**$16.95**
Hawaii 1994	**$16.95**
Holland 1994	**$16.95**
Italy 1994	**$16.95**
Mexico 1994	**$16.95**
New Zealand 1994	**$16.95**
Scandinavia 1994	**$16.95**
Spain & Portugal 1994	**$16.95**
Switzerland & the Alpine Region 1994	**$16.95**
Worldwide Cruises 1994	**$16.95**
Shopping Europe	**$12.95**

To place an order: call toll-free
1-800-FW-2-GUIDE
add $2.00 shipping & handling, allow 2-6 weeks.

FIELDING'S
TRAVEL
SECRETS

For Travel Insiders Only!

FIELDING'S TRAVEL SECRETS is the insider's travel guide, available only to travel professionals and a very limited number of Fielding Travel Guide readers. Created by Fielding's experienced staff of writers and released in six bi-monthly installments per year, the insider's report is packed with timely travel information, trends, news, tips and reviews. Enroll now and you will also receive a variety of significant discounts and special preview information.

Due to the sensitive nature of the information contained in these reports, subscriptions available to non-travel industry individuals are limited to the first 10,000 subscribers. The annual price for all six installments is $60. This offer also comes with an unconditional money-back guarantee if you are not fully satisfied.

To Reserve Your Subscription
1-800-FW-2-GUIDE

Favorite People, Places & Experiences

ADDRESS:	NOTES:

Name

Address

Telephone

Name

Address

Telephone

Name

Address

Telephone

Name

Address

Telephone

Name

Address

Telephone

Name

Address

Telephone

Name

Address

Telephone

Favorite People, Places & Experiences

ADDRESS:	NOTES:

Name

Address

Telephone

Name

Address

Telephone

Name

Address

Ielephone

Name

Address

Telephone

Name

Address

Telephone

Name

Address

Telephone

Name

Address

Telephone

Favorite People, Places & Experiences

ADDRESS:	NOTES:

Name

Address

Telephone

Name

Address

Telephone

Name

Address

Telephone

Name

Address

Telephone

Name

Address

Telephone

Name

Address

Telephone

Name

Address

Telephone

Favorite People, Places & Experiences

ADDRESS:	NOTES:

Name

Address

Telephone

Name

Address

Telephone

Name

Address

Telephone

Name

Address

Telephone

Name

Address

Telephone

Name

Address

Telephone

Name

Address

Telephone

Favorite People, Places & Experiences

ADDRESS:	NOTES:

Name

Address

Telephone

Name

Address

Telephone

Name

Address

Telephone

Name

Address

Telephone

Name

Address

Telephone

Name

Address

Telephone

Name

Address

Telephone

Favorite People, Places & Experiences

ADDRESS:	NOTES:

Name

Address

Telephone

Name

Address

Telephone

Name

Address

Telcphone

Name

Address

Telephone

Name

Address

Telephone

Name

Address

Telephone

Name

Address

Telephone

Favorite People, Places & Experiences

ADDRESS:	NOTES:

Name

Address

Telephone

Name

Address

Telephone

Name

Address

Telephone

Name

Address

Telephone

Name

Address

Telephone

Name

Address

Telephone

Name

Address

Telephone

Favorite People, Places & Experiences

ADDRESS:	NOTES:

Name

Address

Telephone

Name

Address

Telephone

Name

Address

Telephone

Name

Address

Telephone

Name

Address

Telephone

Name

Address

Telephone

Name

Address

Telephone

Favorite People, Places & Experiences

ADDRESS:	NOTES:

Name

Address

Telephone

Name

Address

Telephone

Name

Address

Telephone

Name

Address

Telephone

Name

Address

Telephone

Name

Address

Telephone

Name

Address

Telephone

Favorite People, Places & Experiences

ADDRESS:	NOTES:

Name

Address

Telephone

Name

Address

Telephone

Name

Address

Telephone

Name

Address

Telephone

Name

Address

Telephone

Name

Address

Telephone

Name

Address

Telephone

Favorite People, Places & Experiences

ADDRESS:	NOTES:

Name

Address

Telephone

Name

Address

Telephone

Name

Address

Telephone

Name

Address

Telephone

Name

Address

Telephone

Name

Address

Telephone

Name

Address

Telephone

Favorite People, Places & Experiences

ADDRESS:	NOTES:

Name

Address

Telephone

Name

Address

Telephone

Name

Address

Telephone

Name

Address

Telephone

Name

Address

Telephone

Name

Address

Telephone

Name

Address

Telephone

Favorite People, Places & Experiences

ADDRESS:	NOTES:

Name

Address

Telephone

Name

Address

Telephone

Name

Address

Telephone

Name

Address

Telephone

Name

Address

Telephone

Name

Address

Telephone

Name

Address

Telephone